Under the General Editorship of Jesse W. Markham

Princeton University · *Houghton Mifflin Adviser in Economics*

Economic
Issues and
Policies :

Edited by **ARTHUR L. GREY, JR.,** *University of Washington*

HOUGHTON MIFFLIN COMPANY · BOSTON

Readings in Introductory Economics

Second Edition

and **JOHN E. ELLIOTT,** *University of Southern California*

New York · Atlanta · Geneva, Ill. · Dallas · Palo Alto

● Editor's Introduction

One scarcely need emphasize in these days of the college population "explosion" and its attendant strain on library facilities, especially the reserve desk, the vital need for excellent collections of readings. The Grey-Elliott first edition of *Economic Issues and Policies* has for three years proven its excellence as being one of the leading supplementary texts in introductory economics courses, and even the more specialized courses in economics.

Economic change fosters change in the literature of economics. In the process, new articles written on the issues of the times attain a high order of relevancy; and older treatments of the same issue, while still of great interest to the profession, often are superseded by newer interpretations based on more complete information. Professors Grey and Elliott have been fully aware of these forces in compiling their revised edition. Two-thirds of their selections are new to this edition. The new selections are designed in part to achieve greater balance than the previous edition, but primarily to recognize the growing concern in economics with such issues as the consequences of disarmament, automation and the "research revolution," the war on poverty, new international balance of payments problems, the development of newly created underdeveloped nations, and changes in Communist economies. The result is a balanced treatment of issues with which economists are concerned in the 1960's. It will be welcomed enthusiastically by teachers and students alike who wish to explore such issues in greater breadth and depth than is possible in the confines of even the best introductory textbooks.

JESSE W. MARKHAM

Princeton University

• Preface to the First Edition

This book is a collection of readings on contemporary economic issues and policies. Its purpose is to provide, in readily accessible form, supplementary materials that are significant to the introductory course in economics, but are not, of necessity, fully developed in the standard textbooks. It is our belief that a book of readings, in order to complement rather than compete with the text, should consistently pursue its own objective, namely, to illustrate, amplify, and enrich generally the understanding of the principles of economic reasoning by striving to show how they apply to the central issues of economic policy in the world today.

Preface writers often demonstrate a disconcerting tendency to become defensive; their statements disintegrate into lengthy explanations of why particular selections were chosen, and anthologist degenerates into apologist. Suffice it to say here that these readings on economic issues of current public interest have been selected with the following criteria foremost in mind: 1) analytical insight; 2) communicability; 3) current, yet continuing, relevance; and 4) provocativeness.

The book is organized into five major parts. The first is introductory and methodological. The other four are each in turn subdivided to focus on more specific areas and issues. The organization is similar in sequence and in the space devoted to each topic to that generally encountered in basic textbooks. This allocation is only approximate, however, since individual textbooks vary in their emphasis on specific topics, and the need for supplementary discussion is not always proportionate to the length of the textbook presentation.

Although few, if any, books of readings for the introductory economics course provide both Part *and* selection editorial introductions, we have done so in order to relate each selection to the Part. We also felt that the inclusion of both Part and selection introductions would serve to place the article in perspective for the student and would help an instructor assess more quickly and accurately how a given selection might best serve his individual classroom requirements.

While controversy abounds in virtually every selection, we have tried to avoid the temptation of lining up "pros" and "cons" on each issue with the implication that truth and wisdom lie somewhere in between. Although the writers represented are acknowledged, even distinguished, scholars or authorities on their subjects, articles have been selected primarily on the basis of their merit and suitability for the student and facility of expression. The selection of meaningful and provocative articles, but not unduly esoteric or technical, has been an exacting responsibility.

Most selections have been edited and many have been abridged to increase their relevance, to focus more sharply upon the issues at hand, and to improve communicability for instructional use. We have also omitted ellipsis marks to free the reader from this distraction. In all instances, however, the original, unabridged source is indicated.

Earlier versions of portions of this book have been extensively "student-tested" in mimeographed form at a large private university, a small liberal arts college, and two state colleges. Although it is realized that a book of readings cannot suit every individual taste, our collective experience over several years of teaching, augmented by that of our colleagues who have generously offered suggestions, encourages us to feel that the time and effort involved has resulted in a publication closely attuned to the realities of the classroom.

Our gratitude is extended to our colleagues and to students at the University of Southern California, Occidental College, Los Angeles State College, and California State Polytechnic College; to Professor Carl Kaysen of Harvard University, editorial adviser in economics for Houghton Mifflin Company; to Professors Douglas F. Dowd of Cornell University, Jesse W. Markham of Princeton University, and Charles M. Tiebout of the University of California at Los Angeles for their constructive criticism; and to the editorial staff of Houghton Mifflin Company, particularly Mr. Hugh E. Joyce, Jr., and Mrs. Ann H. Lamb for their invaluable general helpfulness and many constructive suggestions. We would like especially to thank our wives for their patience and timely help and our six children for being such delightful impediments to the completion of this book.

ARTHUR L. GREY, JR.
JOHN E. ELLIOTT

University of Southern California

• Preface to the Second Edition

The objectives, organization, and criteria for selection of materials included are substantially the same as in the first edition. But the specific contents have necessarily been greatly altered to (1) reflect the changing emphases of professional and public discussion of economic matters and (2) utilize the increased output of competent materials appropriate to the purposes of this book.

We have persisted in our effort to assemble a balanced book, representing the wide spectrum of topics over which general economics endeavors to range. At the same time, this has meant redressing the balance in several directions. New material has been added to reflect such issues as the consequences of disarmament, poverty, automation, and unemployment. Over 25 per cent of the book is devoted to World Economic Problems with new coverage in the specific areas of the balance of payments, changes in the Communist economies, and the diversity of problems of and approaches to the development of economically less advantaged countries.

Among other changes are those in Part I which include a selection providing an overview of the economy and another which offers a perspective of the part economic ideas have played in American political development. These and all other selections appear in what the editors suppose to be a logical order, but we are conscious of the ingenuity of the teaching process and assume that many will find a different sequence of assignments more to their preference.

Altogether, the book is somewhat longer and two-thirds of the selections are new to this edition. Still, by no means every nuance of contemporary economic discussion is represented and it is quite possible that some will look in vain for coverage on subjects which they may believe should contribute to the substance of the first course in economics. Our most difficult task has been to decide what not to include and our path has been strewn with temptations. We hope the results marshal useful resources to sustain the campaigns of the instructor and the economics textbook in behalf of economic enlightenment.

Acknowledgment is due to those who have given us their counsel in this project: Professors M. O. Clement and Richard L. Pfister of Dartmouth College, H. Peter Gray of Wayne State University, and Walter Adams of Michigan State University. Hugh Joyce has extended his usual qualities of encouragement, good judgment, and efficient response to numerous demands which we have made upon him.

Arthur L. Grey, Jr.
University of Washington

JOHN E. ELLIOTT
University of Southern California

● Contents

xi

PART THREE

Business Enterprise, Competition and Monopoly,
and Public Policy

A. The Business Environment

B. Competition and Monopoly

C. Public Policy Toward Business

PART FOUR

Other Sectors of the Economy

A. Agriculture

B. Labor

C. The Consumer

D. Distribution of Income

E. Poverty and Living Standards

Contents   xv

PART FIVE

World Economic Problems

A. FOREIGN TRADE AND AID

B. ECONOMIC GROWTH AND DEVELOPMENT

C. COMPARATIVE ECONOMIC SYSTEMS

ECONOMIC ISSUES AND POLICIES

1. *What is economics?*

2. *Why is economics a controversial subject?*

3. *How are economic ideas related to the setting in which they develop?*

4. *What have been the most important recent developments in the U.S. economy?*

WHAT IS ECONOMICS? Perhaps you conceive of economics as having to do with explaining the operations of the stock market, or why taxes are high and the national debt is so big, or why steel production fluctuates and farm production is too large, or the reasons why people in some countries are so poor, or why strikes occur and job opportunities change. Economics is concerned with all these questions, and more.

Like knowledge generally, economics is an abstract subject, devised by man. In common with other abstract subjects, economics generalizes about a certain body of phenomena in an attempt to formulate propositions, or "laws," which bring order, as well as cause and effect, from a chaotic disarray of isolated facts.

This is the method of economic reasoning, as it is of all science. We have indicated already that the substance of economics is concerned with a great variety of questions. Can we generalize about these? One respected economist has said that "Economics is what economists do." Perhaps he agrees with yet another economist who says it is "unprofitable to draw hard-and-fast lines among the individual sciences." With a trace of the same reluctance, the distinguished English economist, Dennis H. Robertson, does discuss the nature of the substance of economics and says

2

he detects its essence in the term "material welfare." (See Selection 1.)

The purpose of this book of readings is to increase your capacity to reason about questions of public interest having an economic content, to find the meaning which events, statistics, and ideas about economic matters have in relation to one another. Scan the Tables of Contents of this and your other economics books to see the range of topics which the writers of these texts present as the subject matter of economics.

Henry David Thoreau said, "My chief virtue is to want but little." This made Thoreau a remarkable fellow because the wants of most people are, practically speaking, unlimited. On the other hand, the means by which to satisfy these wants is limited. This disparity between what people would like to have and what it is possible to produce is the basic fact upon which the science of economics is founded. (See Selection 2.)

Economic analysis studies the behavior of people in obtaining income and in spending it. These actions take place within an established framework of law, tradition, and institutions. Economists also direct some of their attention to the institutions themselves. Economic policymaking, as distinguished from economic analysis, involves the formulation of lines of action for meeting specific problems and usually requires at least some subtle changes in the present way of doing things. Sometimes policy may propose a return to a former way, but more often it entails the contriving of something that is new. The essence of economic analysis is the interpretation of relationships, for which the economist employs his professional skills. Analysis and policy are related to each other by value judgments. Neither approbation nor criticism of the prevailing economic system is possible without some philosophy or conception of what is good or bad, desirable or undesirable. The ancient Greeks had disputations about the nature of truth, beauty, and virtue; the modern economist (and citizen) must face the unsettling reality that the debate still rages.

Although values and technical matters of fact are intertwined in the discussion of every public economic issue, economists are able, within limits, to subject economic problems, of concern to them and to the public, to methods of scientific inquiry. Part of every question inevitably

3

remains a matter of opinion, of personal preference, but the analysis of its factual part, the searching for factors of cause and effect, is the main business of the economist.

Analysis is necessary in order to formulate intelligent opinions. Analysis by itself, however, is insufficient to answer all questions, because we are still confronted by the need to make judgments in the light of values and personal philosophies. Still, a fuller understanding of the facts often destroys the bases of some opinions, and, at the same time, new facts and insights usually generate new questions.

The well-informed person appreciates the fact that the answers to most questions are rarely confined to only two diametrically opposed extremes as is stressed in Selection 3 by Professor Samuelson.

The informed person understands that the range of choice often includes many possibilities and that the best answers frequently are to be secured by subtle combinations of these. In economics, as discussed by Professor Boulding in Selection 4, this is perhaps where the elusive element of "skill," the artistry of virtuosity of the economist, lies: in his ability to raise new possibilities by skillful recombination of the essential elements involved.

Thus Adam Smith (1723–1790) did not "invent" something new when he emphasized the value of specialization, when he advocated foreign trade, when he praised competition, or even when he argued that the greatest total good will result from each man doing that which is in his own self-interest. But, in combination, these separate elements proved tremendously powerful in shaping public attitudes. A century later when Jevons, Marshall, and the group of economists known as "the Austrian School" propounded the basis for the modern theory of how prices are established in a free market, the building blocks of their explanation were not new. What they did was to reorganize them and raise economics to new heights of understanding. Similarly, although the theory of John Maynard Keynes (who is hailed for his brilliance in significantly expanding our understanding of the causes of prosperity and depression) was new, its major components would have been familiar to his predecessors.

Now or at a later point in your study of this book, you may care to read the article entitled "The Development of Economic Ideas" (Selection 5). This selection will give you a further look at both the substance and the method of economics by noting the main problems which have traditionally occupied economists and the means by which they enlarged our understanding of these problems.

Our own national history is intimately involved with economic issues and economic policies. To the person conversant with our political history, slogans and phrases of oratory from Presidential campaigns come readily to mind such as "You shall not crucify mankind upon a cross of gold" (Bryan, 1896), or "Let's keep the full dinner pail" (McKinley,

1900), or "Prosperity is just around the corner" (Hoover, 1932). The extent to which economic ideals have captivated political thought and action and imputed to it a characteristic American form is discussed in Selection 6.

Selection 7 deals with *events*, in contrast to the *ideas* which have held sway over men's perceptions of the economic world about them. The circumstances of the recent past which it describes are useful particularly because of the insight they can impart about the future. This selection is a point of departure for many of the more detailed discussions which occupy the remainder of this book.

A. SCOPE AND METHOD

• 1

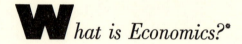

What is Economics?*

SIR DENNIS H. ROBERTSON
Late, Cambridge University, England

The following is taken from a first day's lecture in a beginning class in economics at Cambridge University in England. What is said applies with equal validity in the United States. A long line of distinguished economists at Cambridge, some of whom are mentioned here by Sir Dennis, have profoundly influenced the development of economics throughout the world.

Defining the Word

English economists, unlike Continental ones, have never set much store by matters of definition and terminology; and no doubt it is true, in this matter as in others, that the nature of the pudding is best discovered by eating it. Nevertheless it is quite a good thing even for those of us who

* Taken and adapted from *Lectures on Economic Principles* (London: Staples Press, Ltd., 1957) Vol. I, pp. 16–19, 30. Reproduced with permission.

have made some progress with the meal to lay down our spoons from time to time and take stock of where we have got to.

The first thing to notice is that about three-quarters of a century ago our subject quietly changed its name. I am an anachronism — I am called professor of Political Economy. This older term can perhaps best be defined by literal translation as State Housekeeping; the old Political Economy could be thought of as being primarily a body of maxims for statesmen. The newer term 'economics' brings out two things: (1) the termination -*ics* indicates that our study is or aspires to be a science, like physics, dynamics, and so forth; (2) the dropping of the word "political" emphasizes that our ultimate concern is with individual human beings, not with "States." But while economics thus is or aims at being a branch of objective study, when one considers the wonders of modern physics or the glories of ancient Greek or modern English literature, one is driven to the conclusion that as an intellectual pastime economics is rather a drab and second-rate affair. If it is worth pursuing — and it certainly *is* — it is mainly worth pursuing not for its own sake, but with a practical object.

Reasons for Studying Economics

What is that object? Not personal enrichment — some famous economists have died rich, but most have not — and are not likely to. On the other hand the acquisition of a mental training, and of a body of knowledge, which will be of use in a business career is a common motive for undertaking the study of economics, and an entirely legitimate one, provided that not too much is expected. It can't be too clearly understood that, in this university at least, the course in economics in no sense purports to be a training in business method or administration; provided that *is* understood, the prospective business man can fairly hope to get from it two things — a useful equipment of facts about the real world, and a technique of thinking which, whether or not he can often apply it directly to his problems, should enable him to approach them from a broader point of view and to see more clearly his own relation to the whole set-up of which he will form a part.

But not all students of economics are aiming at a business career. And for the rest — and perhaps for the prospective business man too — the main practical object in undertaking the study of economics is surely the formation of *judgments* which one can bring to bear according to one's opportunities — as employer, as civil servant, as minister of religion, or just as ordinary citizen and voter — on proposals for the promotion of human welfare, proposals which may involve political action.

Scope of the Subject

Well, after that little piece of sermonising about the nature of our sub-ject, can we proceed to define its scope? It is difficult, I think, to improve on Marshall's famous definition as "the study of mankind in the ordinary business of life." It is not precise — no useful definition can be; but it brings out two things — that we are concerned with man, and that we are concerned with him in only some of his many aspects. Perhaps, how-ever, we can learn more by taking another definition, given by Marshall's contemporary Cannan. Economics, says Cannan, is the "study of the things having to do with man's material welfare." In what does this, the material welfare of man, consist?

Not, we don't need telling, in money alone. Nor in material objects alone; our landlady when she sweeps our room, the professional pianist when he plays to us, contribute to our material welfare. The latter must be conceived as a flow of enjoyment or satisfaction derived from the good things of life. But not as consisting in all the possible kinds of satisfaction. Ruskin, enraged at what he regarded as the narrow conception of wealth prevalent among the economists of a hundred years ago, cried out in pro-test: "There is no wealth but life." But that protest goes too far, and to act on it would make our study unmanageable. We must limit ourselves to the more material and less spiritual parts or aspects of welfare. This is admittedly a hazy boundary-line. But vague as the line is, we need have no doubt that it is worthwhile having a separate science of economics to deal with the more material parts of welfare; for to quote an older econo-mist still, Adam Smith, "the subdivision of employment in philosophy, as well as in every other business, improves dexterity and saves time."

Total Welfare and Economic Welfare

Material welfare, then, is not the same as total welfare; and sometimes the pursuit of the one may conflict with the pursuit of the other. Never-theless, we can reasonably plan our studies on the working hypothesis laid down by my predecessor in this chair, Pigou: "when we have ascertained the effect of any cause on economic welfare, we may, unless of course there is special evidence to the contrary, regard this effect as *probably* equivalent in direction, though not in magnitude, to the effect on total welfare." And in pursuing our studies so planned we can pay heed to a piece of advice given by my "grandparent" in this chair, Alfred Marshall: "The less we trouble ourselves with scholastic enquiries as to whether a certain consideration comes within the scope of economics the better. If the matter is important, let us take account of it as far as we can. If it is one on which the general machinery of economic analysis and reasoning cannot get any grip, then let us leave it aside in our purely economic studies, remembering always that some sort of account of it must be taken by our ethical instincts and our common sense, when they as ultimate arbiters come to apply to practical issues the knowledge obtained and arranged by economics and other sciences."

In sum: Economics is the study of mankind in the ordinary business of life, or of the more material part of human welfare. It is a study worth pursuing partly for its intrinsic interest, but mainly because it may help us to form reasoned judgments on matters of public policy and act on them so far as our opportunities offer. Whatever exact definition of the subject we adopt, we shall be concerned not merely with money, not merely even with material objects of wealth, but with human enjoyments and satisfactions, and also with the toil and trouble which go to their making.

• 2

Scarcity: The Basic Fact of Economics*

BEN W. LEWIS
Oberlin College

The preceding selection defined economics as concerned with the "material part of human welfare." Where does that lead us? If wishes were horses, beggars might ride. But they aren't and welfare becomes a matter of human choice, of deciding which use of available resources, of all those that are possible, is the more desirable.

The Economic Problem

"The Economic Problem" is simply: What disposition shall society make of its limited human and natural resources in light of the unlimited needs and desires which these resources can be used to satisfy? This is the most important concept in economics.

"The Economic Problem" is what use shall be made of our resources? And I offer "use" to you as a dynamic concept which confronts us with choices bearing on fullness and growth as well as with choices of kind — with questions of "how much" and "how quickly" as well as with questions of "what?"

"The Economic Problem" emerges from two basic, interrelated conditions — (1) man's unlimited desires for goods in the aggregate and (2)

* Taken and adapted from "Economic Understanding: Why and What," *American Economic Review, Papers and Proceedings*, May 1957, pp. 664–68. Reproduced with permission.

the limited human and natural resources available to society for the production of goods in the aggregate.

Mankind has unlimited desires for goods in the aggregate. Each one of us wants at least a minimum of material goods and services to satisfy his basic needs — such things, for example, as food, shelter, household furnishings, clothing, medical services, and so forth. But each of us desires much more than this basic minimum of essentials. Each would like more, and more varieties, of all of these things and many things in addition. The fact is that if each of us did not have to restrain himself by some notion of what he could afford, his individual desires or wants would run on endlessly. In the aggregate, such limitless desires, multiplied in volume by the number of individuals who inhabit the world, go far beyond anything that society can ever dream of actually satisfying from its limited resources.

Society's human and natural resources available for the production of goods in the aggregate are limited. The goods and services with which we satisfy our desires do not grow in limitless quantities upon limitless trees; they do not appear out of nowhere when we rub a magic lamp or utter a "secret word." Goods must be produced (even those few that do "grow on trees" have to be picked — or picked up — and prepared for use). Production requires the use of human resources (labor) and natural resources (land, water, ores, minerals, fuels, etc.), together with techniques and methods for organizing and combining and processing these resources. And we know that, basically, these resources are scarce relative to human needs and desires. Despite our marvelous advances in technology and despite the fact that our standard of material living has on the average risen markedly over the centuries, we can never produce such an abundance of goods that everyone in the world can have all he wants of everything, with lots left over.

"Surplus" and Scarcity

Let there be no confusion on this point. Occasionally in our society we are confronted by so-called "surpluses" of particular products (the "butter surplus," the "potato surplus," for example, or the "surplus of used-automobiles"). These represent supplies of particular goods in excess of the amounts which buyers with purchasing power at a particular time and place are willing to buy at prevailing prices. In an economic sense they represent particular overproduction in relation to effective demand for particular goods — misproduction or malproduction, or a use or allocation of society's resources of which society, by its market calculus, indicates it does not approve. In the world as we know it, "too many" potatoes means "too few" of other things; it can never mean "too much of everything." And even in the case of a particular surplus at a particular time and place, it does not necessarily follow that human desires for the particular good are not going unsatisfied somewhere else in society at the very same time. Breakdowns in society's institutional arrangements for bringing goods and desires together are not to be interpreted as evidence of society's power to produce without limit. By the same token, we must not be misled by terms and phrases which suggest contradictions where none exist. Specifically, there is no contradiction between an "economy of scarcity" and an "economy of plenty," where "scarcity" is understood as a condition of economizing and "plenty" is understood as its goal.

It behooves us, thus, to take care in the use we make of our resources — to be concerned about their use, to manage them, to "economize" them. The reason we bother to manage or economize our resources is simply that, since they are limited in supply relative to the uses to which we would like to put them — that is, since in an economic sense they are "scarce" — it makes a difference to us how they are used. The degree and manner and direction of their use and the disposition of the product resulting from their use have, of sheer necessity, been a primary, basic concern of all societies through the ages. This is what the study of "economizing," or economics as a social science, is about. It is *all* that economics is about.

Presumably any society will want its scarce resources to be "fully" employed (particularly its labor resources), and so used that their power to produce is great and expanding, and that the "right" goods are produced in the "right" amounts and, in each case, by using the "best" combinations of resources. Any society will be concerned, too, that the goods which are produced from its scarce resources are divided fairly among its members.

Alternatives

But the use of such terms as fully, right, best, fairly, etc. in defining the disposition to be made of resources suggests that alternative uses are possible and that society is faced with the never-ending problem of making millions of continuous and simultaneous decisions in the management or economizing of its resources. Surely we want our resources to be used fully and in the right and best way, but how full is fully? Exactly which ways are right and best and fair? We must remember, too, that society's answers to some of the questions may condition and set limits on its answers to other questions: a decision to promote technological advance *may* make employment less stable, a decision to divide the aggregate product more evenly among everyone *may* have an adverse effect upon the total amount produced, and public policies designed to bring about full employment *may* also promote productive inefficiency and aggravated inequities as an undesired consequence. Nonetheless, answers must be provided by society to "The Economic Problem" faced by men who want to live in harmony and well-being in a world where not everyone can have all he wants of the goods and services that make up his material living and where, hence, the use made of our limited, valuable economic resources is a matter of concern to every living person.

Thus it is that all societies of men who make their living together must inevitably establish and maintain (or acquiesce in) an economic system or economy — a set of man-made arrangements to provide answers to the all-important economic questions which make up the over-all economic problem: How fully shall our limited resources be used? How shall our resources be organized and combined? Who shall produce how much of what? To whom and in what amounts shall the resulting product be divided among the members of society?

The Economic System

It is the job of the economic system (any economic system) to make the decisions and turn out the answers that society wants, whatever they may be, to these questions; and economics as a discipline is a study of "The Economic Problem" in all its parts, and of the institutional arrangements which men have devised to grind out the necessary answers to the questions which it poses.

The data and materials, the concepts and the "principles" with which the study of economics is concerned and the problems to which it attends all stem from and bear on this central problem: How do we and how might we dispose of the resources upon which the level and quality of our material life depend? This is "The Economic Problem." All other economic problems and issues — for example, the farm problem, the labor-management problem, the problem of taxation, the inflation problem, the problem of full employment, the antitrust problem — are simply partial manifestations of it in particular quarters and under particular conditions and can be dealt with effectively only in conscious relation to the central problem — the *core* of economics.

A person who possesses economic understanding will relate his consideration of public economic issues, easily and purposively, to the central core — to the starting point, to home base. He will have a sense of the interrelationship of economic phenomena and problems — the "oneness" of the economy — the tie-in between each sector of the economy and the whole and between the economy and himself.

• 3

The Dangers of Simple Answers
to Complex Questions*

PAUL A. SAMUELSON
Massachusetts Institute of Technology

*The proverbial "man-on-the-street" wants answers to economic
questions that are simple and brief. In the following comment,
Professor Paul A. Samuelson, an economist who incidentally does
have a facility for making difficult things sound simple, rather
than the other way around, warns us that even the "bright boys"
in economics must admit that they don't have all the answers and
that the answers that they do have are not always simple.*

There is much talk about taxes. When I flick on the dial of my radio in
the morning, I hear a Congressman quoted on how our high level of taxes
is ruining the Nation or a Senator's tape-recorded alarm over the unfair
burden the poor man has to carry because the administration has been
favoring big business. My morning paper at breakfast brings me the view
of its editor that the United States has been pursuing unsound fiscal

* From "The New Look in Tax and Fiscal Policy," *Federal Tax Policy for Economic Growth and Stability,* Papers submitted by panelists appearing before the Subcommittee on Tax Policy, Joint Committee on the Economic Report, 84th Congress, 1st session (Washington, D.C.: United States Government Printing Office, 1955), pp. 229–230.

policy for the last 25 years. Scratch the barber who cuts my hair and you find a philosopher ready to prescribe for the Nation's monetary ills.

This is as it should be. We expect sweeping statements in a democracy. We hope that out of the conflict of extreme views there will somehow emerge a desirable compromise. Yet such sweeping statements have almost no validity from a scientific, or even from a leisurely common-sense point of view: spend as little as a year going over the factual experience of American history and of other economies, devote as little as a month to calm analysis of probable cause and effect, or even spend a weekend in a good economics library — and what will you find? Will you find that there breathes anywhere in the world an expert so wise that he can tell you which of a dozen major directions of policy is unquestionably the best? You will not. Campaign oratory aside, the more assuredly a man asserts the direction along which salvation is alone to be found, the more patently he advertises himself as an incompetent or a charlatan.

The plain truth is this, and it is known to anyone who has looked into the matter: the science of economics does not provide simple answers to complex social problems. It does not validate the view of the man who thinks the world is going to hell, nor the view of his fellow idiot that ours is the best of all possible systems.

I do not wish to be misunderstood. When I assert that economic science cannot give unequivocal answers to the big questions of policy, I do not for a moment imply that economists are useless citizens. Quite the contrary. They would indeed be useless if any sensible man could quickly infer for himself simple answers to the big policy questions. No need then to feed economists while they make learned studies of the obvious. It is precisely because public policy in the tax and expenditure area, for example, is so complex that we find it absolutely indispensable to invest thousands of man-years of scholarly time in scholarly economic research in these areas.

Make no mistake about it. The arguments that we all hear every day of our lives on the burning partisan issues have in every case been shaped by economists — by economists in universities, in business, in Government, and by that rarest of all birds, the shrewd self-made economist. What economists do not know about fiscal policy turns out, on simple examination, not to be known by anyone.

• *4*

The Skills of the Economist*

KENNETH E. BOULDING
University of Michigan

Economics, it has been said, is what economists do. According to Professor Kenneth E. Boulding, what economists have been doing is developing techniques or "skills" to simplify our comprehension of the world by systematically selecting or abstracting certain aspects of that world for specialized study. The essence of this study, he argues, has to do with such concepts as commodities, scarcity, exchange, and equilibrium.

My principal objective in this essay is to examine some of the contributions which economics, as a distinct discipline, makes to the culture of our day. It is appropriate to begin by asking what economics is — which is really to ask what economists are. One recalls the famous remark attributed to Professor Jacob Viner that economics *is* what economists *do.* I therefore approach the contribution of economics by way of the skill of the economist, for if economists have anything to contribute to the culture of our time, it is through the employment of those special skills which have been developed in the study of economics.

*Taken and adapted from *The Skills of the Economist* (Cleveland: Howard Allen, Inc., 1958) pp. 1, 3–4, 8–11, 14, 19–23, 30–31. Reproduced with permission of Howard Allen, Inc., and Clarke, Irwin & Company, Ltd., publisher of *The Skills of the Economist* in Canada.

What is an Economist?

Before we examine the skill of the economist we should ask, "Who *are* the economists?" This is an embarrassing question. There are no recognized tests by which economists can be distinguished from those who may claim but who do not deserve the name. We have no professional qualifying examination as do the lawyers, the doctors, the accountants, and in some places, I understand, the beauticians. I know of no one who has been prevented from joining the American Economic Association or any other economic association for reasons of professional incompetence. We have no priesthood guarding the sacred fire handed down from Adam Smith. We do not even follow the practice of so many professions in improving their economic status by raising barriers to entrance. We may understand monopoly but we certainly do not practice it. Indeed, we are one of the few professions which deliberately, it would seem, attempts to undermine its economic status by actually encouraging students to enter it and by refusing to impose any professional standards.

We are popularly supposed to be divided by schools and racked by dissent, speaking with no common voice and being therefore quite unworthy of the name of science. Nevertheless, my experience with noneconomists convinces me there is something, however humble, which can properly be called skill among those who recognize themselves as economists.

In anthropological language there is in the world a tribe, or a subculture, of economists, whose members recognize each other no matter where they live, whether in the United States, in Europe, in Australia, in India, or in South America. It is true of course that within this tribe there exist sub-sub-cultures — the Keynesians and the Institutionalists, the Neo-Manchesterians and the Economic Planners. This is not surprising. Within every tribe there are family quarrels and within any culture there are noticeable divergences. The homogeneity of a tribe or a culture must be judged by the nature of the internal quarrels, not their existence or even their intensity. Indeed, family quarrels are frequently the most intense of all conflicts because of the very closeness of the parties involved. And the quarrels of the economists *are* family quarrels.

What follows is an attempt to describe what an economist does. One can say that the skill of the economist is that which is acquired in studying economic systems and in working with them just as the skill of the carpenter is acquired by "studying" and working with wood. We are thus thrust back somewhat upon the subject matter, since we must ask what an economic system is. Indeed, perhaps we should go farther and ask what a *system* is.

The Economic System

All skill relates to a "system" of some sort, that is, to be a coherent set of quantities, properties, and relationships, abstracted for the purpose of exercising the skill itself, from the immense complexity of the real world around us. It is important to realize that the exercise of *any* skill depends on the ability to create an abstract system of some kind out of the totality of the world around us.

The skill of the economist depends on his ability to abstract a system from the complex social and physical world around him. The basis of the economist's system is the notion of a commodity. The economist sees the world not as men and things, but as commodities, and it is precisely in this abstraction that his peculiar skill resides. A commodity is anything *scarce*, that is, in order to get more of it a quantity of some other commodity must be relinquished.

Scarcity is most obviously manifested in the institution of exchange where one commodity is given up and another acquired by one party and the first commodity is acquired and the second given up by the other party. Exchange, however, is not the only manifestation of scarcity. There are economic systems, like that of Robinson Crusoe, in which there is no exchange in the literal sense of the word.

Nevertheless, there is scarcity in the sense that Crusoe's resources of time and energy are limited. Thus, if Crusoe wishes to build a house, he must do without things he might have acquired, or might have enjoyed, with the time spent in building the house. In this sense his house might be *worth* so many fish, or so many coconuts, or so many hours of dreaming in the sun which he had to give up in order to build it. From his point of view this alternative cost is a form of exchange, almost as if he had bought the house from someone else with fish or coconuts.

Similarly it is not difficult to see that all production is essentially a form of transformation of commodities akin to exchange. The miller exchanges flour for wheat by grinding it. The milkman exchanges milk-in-the-dairy for another commodity, milk-in-the-house, by transporting it from the dairy to the doorstep. It is not too much to claim that the phenomenon of exchange is at the heart of the economist's abstraction and the ability to recognize and analyze exchange constitutes the core of his skill.

An economic system, then, is a system of commodities which are exchanged (i.e., re-shuffled by their owners), produced (transformed from other commodities) and consumed (destroyed). If this process is to be continuous there must be a constant stream of some original commodity or commodities (factors of production) which then undergo the process of transformation, exchange, and eventual consumption.

Simplification of the System

Such a system is immensely complex, and, if it is to be analyzed, various analytical devices and tricks must be used to reduce the intolerably complex mass even of this abstract system to manageable dimensions. One of the most important skills of the economist, therefore, is that of *simplification*. Two important methods of simplification have been developed by economists. One is the method of partial equilibrium analysis (or microeconomics), generally associated with the name of Alfred Marshall and the other is the method of aggregation (or macro-economics), associated with the name of John Maynard Keynes.

In spite of the dynamic nature of the general system the most powerful tool which has been employed to date is still the idea of an *equilibrium* position of the various variables. This notion is an absolutely indispensable part of the toolbag of the economist and one which he can often contribute usefully to other sciences. When an economic quantity is in equilibrium, no one who has the power to change it has the will and no one who has the will has the power.

The Relevance of Economics

Perhaps the best way to test the skill of the economist is to put him in the position of Economic Adviser to the Philosopher King (or President!). If he has any skill at all it will soon be revealed. One needs, of course, a proper humility. There are a great many questions on which the economic adviser cannot presume to give advice, even fundamental questions regarding the most desirable structure of the economic system, or relatively trivial questions about a tariff on buttons. Also there are a great many economic questions which are bound up with matters of peace and war, with the retention of power and the satisfaction of political obligations, with social justice and the racial or cultural stratifications of society, in which the economist has no special competence.

When, however, it comes to the question of what to do about a depression or an inflation, whether price control can be applied without rationing, what sort of public finance leads to inflation, and even on some of the more obvious conditions of economic development, the economist has something to say by virtue of his peculiar skills even if only to give a sense of direction. And if one compares the kind of answers and understanding which the economist is able to give to the question, for instance, of how we avoid or get out of a depression, with the kind of professional answers that the political scientist might give when asked what policies decrease the possibility of war, or the answers a sociologist might give to the question of what policies promote happy families or good race relations, the economist may at least be pardoned a touch of the disagreeable pride that comes from odious comparison.

• 5

The Development of Economic Ideas*

CHARLES HESSION
Brooklyn College

*The history of the great ideas in economics is a record of observ-
ant men's efforts to understand the nature of this one aspect of
their environment. For this reason, to relate these ideas to the
circumstances in which they were propounded helps us to see
something of how the method of economic reasoning is applied.*

The Classical Theory of Economic Progress

Adam Smith's Vision of the Economy

At the time Adam Smith wrote, the Industrial Revolution had not yet
transformed economic life, but markets were widening, new opportunities
were opening up for the small merchant capitalists, if they could but
escape from the restrictions of mercantilism. Adam Smith was really the

* Abridged from *The Dynamics of the American Economy* by Charles H. Hession,
S. M. Miller, and Curwen Stoddart, pp. 23–44, by permission of Alfred A. Knopf,
Inc. Copyright 1956 by Charles H. Hession, S. M. Miller, and Curwen Stoddart.

spokesman for these small, enterprising merchants and in his *Inquiry into the Nature and Causes of the Wealth of Nations* (1776) he made out a classic case against the increasingly archaic restraints of the old system.

In place of the planned economy of mercantilism Smith advocated what he called the "obvious and simple system of natural liberty." Mercantilism is the name given to the varied group of ideas and practices dominant between 1500 and 1750 by which the national state sought to secure its unity and power by control over economic activity. Freedom in combining the factors of production in the manner which made for the largest profit was the secret of production and of the wealth of nations, according to him.

And how will the wealth of the nation be increased but by improving the skill, dexterity, and judgment with which labor is applied? He goes on to show how the division of labor depends upon exchange and contends that the free exchange of goods will make for the greatest production. Why is this? Because it is "the uniform, constant, and uninterrupted effort of every man to better his own condition." Each individual is a better judge of how to spend his own time and labor than any statesman or mercantilist bureaucrat could be. And since the wealth of a nation is simply the sum total of the income of the individuals who compose it, then it follows that the economic good of the nation will be best promoted by allowing each person to seek his own interest. Self-interest, Adam Smith thought, was already at work. He says, "It is not from the benevolence of the butcher, the brewer, or the baker, that we expect our dinner, but from their regard to their own interest." What was needed was to give self-interest greater scope and freedom of action. Government should practice a policy of freedom, of *laissez faire,* as the French economists expressed it.

But what would prevent the profit-seeker from abusing this freedom by exploiting the consumer and the worker? Smith says, by way of an answer, that the individual who directs industry in order to produce the largest value "intends only his own gain, and he is in this, as in many other cases, led by an invisible hand to promote an end which was no part of his intention."

Smith implies by this last statement that there is a harmony of interest between the individual who seeks profit and the community. This was a view which the medieval philosopher or the mercantilist by no means accepted as self-evident. But Adam Smith sees individuals seeking their own self-interest and in so doing creating a competition in which each will check the other and their activities will be harnessed for the social good. Competition is, therefore a very definite essential of the system of free enterprise, or *laissez faire,* which we associate with Smith's brand of classical economics.

In so far as the conditions which Adam Smith assumed were realized, the competitive price mechanism would automatically adjust the economy and make for justice, prosperity, and progress. Market prices in the long run would tend to equal cost of production. If because of changes in raw materials, technology, or demand the market price should be above or below the cost of production, forces would tend to operate to restore the natural balance. Capital and labor would flow out of industries in which prices were low relative to cost and flow into those in which profits were relatively high either because of increased demand or reduced supply. Thus the income of capitalists and laborers of equal ability would tend to be equalized and justice or equity assured.

But this marvelous economic mechanism had still another virtue: it had a dynamic of its own. Motivated by self-interest, capitalists would be led to accumulate wealth, and this accumulation would in turn make possible increased facilities for production and a greater division of labor. Such capital accumulation would also raise wages as entrepreneurs bid for workers to man their new factories. Smith argued that the increased wages, instead of reducing profits permanently, would enable workers to raise their children with fewer infant mortalities. Thus the labor supply would increase and the competition would proceed and society would rise to even higher levels of prosperity.

It would be erroneous, however, to convey the impression that Adam Smith was a doctrinaire believer in *laissez faire.* He made some notable exceptions to the general rule, for example, that it was the duty of the state, apart from providing defense and dispensing justice, to erect and maintain "certain public works and certain public institutions, which it can never be for the interest of any individual, or small number of individuals to erect and maintain. . . ." including the provision of popular education — and this at a time when such advocacy represented an "advanced view." Furthermore, it is important to note that his presumption in favor of *laissez faire* did not extend to joint stock companies, the predecessors of the modern corporation. Of the former he had a very low opinion. His was truly a philosophy of individual enterprise.

The Malthusian Specter

When Napoleon was finally defeated at Waterloo in 1815, industrial capitalism had already made remarkable advances in Great Britain. Factories had become numerous, the population had grown enormously, and England, instead of being a community of harmonizing individuals, was the battleground of hostile classes.

In this new age the optimism and faith in man's reason which had characterized the Enlightenment of the eighteenth century, gave way to pessimism and the recognition of the factors which made man's future not so bright. The process of growing disillusionment is illustrated in the reaction of a young minister, the Rev. Thomas Malthus (1766–1834).

In his *Essay on Population* (1798), Malthus sought to show that the fly in the ointment was "the passion between the sexes," which created a constant threat of overpopulation. Simply put, his thesis was that population always tends to outrun the means of subsistence, the first growing at a dizzy geometric ratio while the latter limps along only at an arithmetic pace. The only alternative which Malthus saw to the inevitable decimation of the redundant population by vice and misery (plagues, wars, and famines) was moral restraint — the postponement of marriage. So the poverty of the poor was explained as the result of an inexorable law of nature or of their own lack of prudence and foresight. This was a very comforting doctrine, indeed, for the upper classes who could show that the plight of the poor was of their own making. It justified the repeal of the Poor Law and the observance of a policy of nonintervention by government in economic affairs.

The Economics of David Ricardo

David Ricardo (1772–1823) exercised an even greater influence than Malthus on the mind and thought of that economic-minded age. His vision of economics was rather different from that of Adam Smith; to him the great problem was not production, but distribution. To determine the laws which regulate distribution, is the principal problem in Political Economy.

Distribution was the principal economic problem in Ricardo's mind because of the bitter political conflict which existed in 1815 between the landlords and the manufacturing class over the question of the Corn Laws. After 1776 England had ceased to be an exporter of grain; with the growth of its population it had been forced to import. Parliament had passed a corn law in 1804 which protected the English landlords from this foreign competition. The consequence was that during the following years the price of wheat soared. Ricardo's discussion of distribution was the direct outgrowth of the Parliamentary debate on this subject of the Corn Laws. He dealt with it in a pamphlet in 1815 and then more fully in his *Principles of Political Economy and Taxation*, published in 1817.

Employing a rigorous, theoretical method, and basing himself firmly on Malthus' principle of population, Ricardo developed a theory of economic growth and of distribution which was far less optimistic than Smith's. He saw the landlord class gaining an unearned monopoly rent and a larger share of the national income as the pressure of population forced the cultivation of inferior lands. The working class could not look forward to more than a subsistence wage because if paid more than that, families would become larger, and the increased supply of labor would force wages down again. In the long run, because of higher food prices and therefore higher wages and costs of production, the profits of the capitalists would decline. The only way to avoid this dismal outcome was to establish free trade and competition. The political triumph which the business class finally won with the repeal of the Corn Laws in 1846 and the establishment of free trade was in no small part due to the persuasive logic of this sharp-minded economist. For his part in accomplishing this major political change, Ricardo is rightfully considered the architect of the British industrial economy of the nineteenth century.

John Stuart Mill

The classical economics is generally considered to have culminated in the work of John Stuart Mill (1806–1873). This genius, philosopher, logician, and economist mirrored in his work the uncertain state of the subject when he published his *Principles* in 1848. Mill's work is largely a restatement of the main doctrines of Ricardo and Malthus with due regard to the criticisms which had been made of them during the intervening years. The changed focus of interest in Mill's time and his own humanitarian concern are reflected in the attention which he devoted in his volume to the condition of the working class. Mill entertained socialistic ideas as he grew older, but the remedies he set forth for society's ills were those of a utilitarian. He never deserted the ideal of competition and was very cautious in urging departures from the principle of *laissez faire*.

The Socialist and Humanist Criticism of Industrial Capitalism

Capitalism was not without its critics in the early nineteenth century. There were Utopian reformers such as the Frenchmen, Charles Fourier and St. Simon, who preached association and cooperation and the Englishman Robert Owen, who first set an example as an ideal employer and later established communistic communities, such as that of New Harmony in Indiana. But the greatest challenge to classical economics and the most sweeping and comprehensive criticism of early nineteenth-century capitalism came from the pen of Karl Marx (1818–1883). This German-Jew, a political refugee from his native land, virtually immured himself in the British Museum and in collaboration with Frederick Engels, heir to a British fortune, wrote a work on political economy, *Das Kapital*, which was destined to have a vast influence on world history. Contemptuously rejecting the reform schemes of previous and contemporary socialists as Utopian, Marx developed an elaborate historical, sociological, and economic analysis of capitalism which, he claimed, was alone entitled to be called "scientific."

Marx defined the task of his analysis as different from that of the orthodox economists. They had speculated about the long-run growth of economic society, but he made the demonstration of the inevitable collapse of capitalism his main problem. The "ultimate aim of this work," Marx wrote in his preface, was "to lay bare the laws of motion of modern society," in order to predict its fate.

Marx found the motive power of social change not in ideas, but in the material conditions of economic life, and especially in the class conflict which reflects the different material conditions of life of the several classes.

The middle class, Marx contended, obsessed with the motive of profit-making and the accumulation of capital (saving), was transforming society, raising it to new levels of productive capacity. But the economic relations of capitalistic society strangled and repressed the productive powers which its development had fostered.

Drawing upon the theories of the classical economists, Marx sought to demonstrate that capitalism was doomed because of its inherent contradictions. Its concentration on profits and capital accumulation would inevitably produce crises (economic depressions) of increasing severity, industry would become more concentrated in the hands of the few, and the deteriorating condition of the masses would eventually lead to its violent, revolutionary downfall. Out of its ruins would emerge a socialist commonwealth, the creation of the victorious proletariat.

British capitalism in the early nineteenth century was subject to critical onslaughts from many of her own men of letters and humanists as well as from the Marxian left. Carlyle and Coleridge spoke disparagingly about the "dismal science" and Ruskin, averring that "there is no wealth but life," sought to show the errors in the philosophy of self-interest.

The Decline of *Laissez Faire*

Even before the institutions of market capitalism had been fully adopted in England a reaction had set in. A countermovement against the harsh rule of *laissez faire* began in 1802 with the passage of the Factory Act of that year. Actually, however, the early statutes regulating the hours and employment of women and minors in factories and mines did not mean much until proper measures of enforcement were provided, as was the case with the Factory Act of 1883. Gradually the protests of the literary men and the criticisms of the landed gentry in Parliament led to the enactment of a number of laws which curbed the worst of the abuses. The agitation reached a high point with the adoption of the Ten-Hour Law of 1847 and the Chartists' demands for respect for the dignity of the worker as a human being. Society, in seeming self-defense against the evils of an unregulated system of industrial capitalism, was protecting its human substance from destruction.

In the latter part of the nineteenth century and the early part of the twentieth Britain went on to adopt social insurance for laborers: workmen's compensation in 1897, unemployment insurance in 1911. The dire predictions of Marx about the progressive deterioration of the working class did not come true. As a matter of fact, their economic and social status seems to have improved as Britain entered the latter decades of the Victorian era. One basic reason for this improvement was that now at last the savings and the capital formation which had been made in the early part of the century with such hardship, especially for the workers, were "paying off"; they were making possible a greater output of consumer goods and services and a higher standard of living for all.

The Optimism of Alfred Marshall

The hope and optimism which characterized these relatively peaceful years in Britain's history stand out in the work of Alfred Marshall (1842–1924), a Cambridge professor, whose *Principles of Economics*, published in 1890, epitomized the state of Victorian economy and economics. Marshall studied the equilibria of supply and demand with mathematical methods and with the aid of static theoretical models which had been suggested by classical mechanics. His analysis tended to stress the efficiency with which a competitive system of industry allocated economic resources rather than focusing on the long-run problems of economic growth such as had been the principal interest of the classical economists.

While Marshall pictured the economy as a self-balancing system, he was one of the first of the orthodox economists to recognize that an unregulated, competitive economy did not produce a Utopia. Indeed he actually urged government subsidies for certain mass-production industries which operate at decreasing cost as output is raised; in this way, he contended, the community's total utility or satisfaction would be increased. On the whole, however, his optimism led him to advocate only mild forms of government intervention. He looked to good will among men and the development of more "economic chivalry" and understanding to promote progress rather than to government action.

Welfare Economics

In the twentieth century Marshall's successor at Cambridge, A. C. Pigou, in his *Wealth and Welfare* (1912), analyzed how economic welfare could be increased by stabilizing employment and by increasing the size of the national dividend (the national income) as well as by achieving a more equal distribution. He called attention to certain social costs of private enterprise, such as steam and air pollution, unemployment, etc., which at the time he wrote were not taken into account in the narrow pecuniary accounting of the individual enterprises responsible for them.

Two years later John A. Hobson (1858–1940), a journalist-economist, published an original study entitled *Work and Wealth* which took its inspiration from Ruskin's philosophy of economic life. Hobson did not try to isolate *economic* welfare from general well-being, as had Pigou, but argued that welfare is an organic whole, not an arithmetic sum of marginal units of satisfaction. His treatment of the effect of the character of work on the worker and the elements of disutility in much modern consumption was noteworthy, but the underlying psychology of his work was of an impressionistic nature. The academic economists were not impressed, regarding Hobson's analysis as non-scientific.

Trends in Modern Economic Development and Thought

As the industrial economies of Great Britain, the United States, and other nations of the Western world have reached an advanced stage of development in the twentieth century, there has been a progressive movement away from *laissez faire* toward managed or controlled systems. The growth in the size and concentrated economic power of business enterprises, the dislocations caused by two world wars and major economic depressions, the spread of economic nationalism, all these political and economic changes have contributed very much to the trend away from the ideal of a self-regulating, competitive economy.

Institutional Economics

In the latter decades of the nineteenth century, and with seeming increased tempo in the twentieth, business has been undergoing an "organizational revolution" which has transformed it almost beyond recognition from the small, competitive firms of Alfred Marshall's day. This revolutionary change in the nature of the American economy seemed crystal clear to one economist who was writing in the midst of it all. That was Thorstein Veblen (1857–1929), an irreverent, iconoclastic Middle Westerner, who made what some regard as the most original contribution to American economic thought.

Rather than isolating and abstracting economic behavior from its cultural context, Veblen insisted that economic phenomena are not "neatly isolable" from the culture as a whole. Economics must be an evolutionary science; it must study economic and social life from a genetic, developmental point of view. This approach has since been termed "institutional economics."

As Veblen saw it, the main areas of economic life requiring study were not the operations of small, competitive enterprise but of the corporate colossi which had grown up in his lifetime. Big business, reflecting the culturally acquired interest of Americans in acquisitive money making, subordinated the industry of the engineers and the workmen, specialists in the technical arts of making goods, to its financial demands. Coercion, or the exercise of economic power, rather than competition is a main theme of Veblen's type of institutional economics.

Veblen inspired a number of American economists who turned their attention from theoretical speculation to what they regarded as indispensable empirical study of such institutions as private property, corporations, trade unions, and such practical problems as the "business cycle" and monetary affairs.

The Theory of Monopolistic Competition

The Great Depression of the thirties contributed greatly to the destruction of faith in the policy of competitive *laissez faire*. During its devastating course, individuals, corporations, and even governments went bankrupt while waiting for so-called "natural" forces to return the economy to tolerable levels of production and employment. This practically traumatic experience in the life of the nation and of the world made it almost a "watershed" in the development of economic thought. New ideas emerged in the realm of thought and practice which have influenced economic theory and public policy in a most profound way to this day.

One of these intellectual developments which had been in the making for some time was a new theory of prices, paradoxically dubbed the theory of monopolistic competition. The older Marshallian theory of price had revolved around two cases, pure competition (the general case) and pure monopoly (the special, rare case). With the growing concentration of enterprise and the increased use of salesmanship and advertising, the assumptions of the theoretical model of pure competition seemed to be far removed from the real world. And, on the other hand, though economic concentration had grown, there were not many cases of pure, single-firm monopolies. The realities of price making seemed to fall between the two conventional categories of theory. Now two economists, Professor Edward H. Chamberlin and Mrs. Joan Robinson of Cambridge, Massachusetts, and England, respectively, published analyses in 1933 which dealt with price behavior intermediate between the two polar cases of pure competition and pure monopoly.

The new theories were a major blow to complacency concerning the outcome of a *laissez-faire* philosophy in a highly organized, industrial world. Indeed, these theories suggested that where sellers are few and advertising is used to create "brand monopolies" prices will be high relative to what they would be under pure competition, and production will be more restricted. Furthermore, much waste in the form of excess plant capacity and useless advertising may be encouraged. The business world was now seen in a very different light from that of the theory of pure competition.

Keynesian Economics

An even more important revolution in economic thinking occurred in 1936 with the publication by the brilliant British economist, John Maynard Keynes (1883–1946), of *The General Theory of Employment, Interest and Money*. In this volume, Keynes showed the inadequacy of the older theory of saving and investment and in so doing expounded a new view of the causes and "cure" of business depressions. In the Keynesian view the advanced capitalistic nations were suffering from a sort of arteriosclerotic process in which the price system was unable, unaided, to bring about economic equilibrium at a level of full employment. The saving habits of the people of these economies, are pictured as resulting in a constant tendency to excess. This "oversaving" relative to current investment opportunities causes a general deficiency of aggregate demand (mass purchasing power) with resulting depression and widespread unemployment. Keynes argued the need for government intervention to achieve full employment and to close the gap between full employment saving and investment. He advocated such fiscal measures as public-works construction or other forms of "public investment" and taxation of large incomes as a means of maintaining equality between savings and investment.

Keynes' work was a *tour de force*. In it he forged valuable concepts, invented novel terms, and cast an altogether new light on the dynamics of modern capitalism. The book was widely debated and discussed by economists, won many adherents, and stimulated a great amount of theoretical and empirical analysis. Keynes' admirers spoke of his inaugurating a "new economics." But perhaps the most significant aspect of his work was that it represented a devastating blow at *laissez-faire* policies of government. Prosperity and economic stability were now seen to be attainable only through foresight and economic planning and management, not as a result of the unguided activities of profit-making enterprise.

Economic Ideas in American History*

ARTHUR M. SCHLESINGER, JR.
Harvard University

What are the sources of American economic philosophy? The writer, a distinguished historian knowledgeable in the inner workings of politics and the White House, offers the opinion that the temper of American political action in matters economic is today more as it was in 1790 in the founding days of the Republic than as it was in 1880. Foreign "isms," notably the ideas of Karl Marx, have had little influence on the mainstream of either thought or action, and now, as in the beginning of our history, domestic perceptions of economic reality are the most influential.

Early Years: Jefferson and Hamilton

The Wealth of Nations and the Declaration of Independence were both phenomena of the year 1776 — a coincidence that has led some to suppose that the stars of *laissez faire* and of the American republic rose in unison and shone forth jointly on the world.

It was not so simple as this. The characteristic economic philosophy of Western Europe in the late eighteenth century was still mercantilism. Most Americans who thought at all about economic matters were raised in the mercantilist tradition.

Mercantilism was essentially the means by which predominantly agri-

* From *American Economic History* by S. E. Harris, Editor. Copyright © 1961. McGraw-Hill Book Company. Used by permission.

cultural countries in the seventeenth and eighteenth centuries set to work to change themselves into modern industrial states. In time, though, the new economic classes helped into prosperity by mercantilism began to find mercantilist constraints irksome and, in consequence, mercantilist economics fallacious. The rising protest against mercantilism was given its most comprehensive and trenchant statement by Adam Smith. Still, as Adam Smith wrote, many people, while impressed by the aspirations of the *laissez-faire* economy, were yet unwilling to surrender cherished mercantilist objectives, especially those concerned with the development of national power.

This was essentially the state of mind of Alexander Hamilton, who dominated economic policy in the United States in the first years of the republic. Hamilton's dream was to transform sleepy rural America into a great industrial nation, and he saw in the national government the great instrument to attain this goal. Yet he recoiled from notions of minute governmental supervision of the economy. He had deep faith in the dynamics of individual acquisition, if tempered by a measure of public control. His countrymen had, as he wrote, "a certain fermentation of mind, a certain activity of speculation and enterprise which, if properly directed, may be made subservient to useful purposes but which, if left entirely to itself, may be attended with pernicious effects." The essence of Hamilton's policy was to transfer capital to those most likely to make use of it to increase the national productive power; in a series of notable reports, he spelled out the tactics of this policy. The task of government, as he saw it, was thus to guide economic activity while at the same time inciting individual energy.

In the traditional antithesis, Hamilton stood against Jefferson. Certainly Jefferson was, in a general way, the champion of the agricultural way of life against the impending financial and industrial revolution. Jefferson was far too astute a statesman to become a doctrinaire defender of the agrarian economy. To the end, however, he remained deeply suspicious of banking and stockjobbing; and, if the role of activist government was nothing more than to upset the natural order of things in which the producer (*i.e.*, farmer) enjoyed the fruits of his own labor, then, Jefferson concluded, that government was best which governed least.

So, at the start of the republic, because men like Hamilton regarded government initiative as necessary to induce capital formation and industrial development, the economic philosophy of the business community tended to be interventionist. On the other hand, because men like Jefferson could conceive of no government action other than that which transferred wealth from the actual producers, "the plundered ploughman and beggared yeomanry," to the businessmen, the economic philosophy of the opponents of business rule was that of the negative state. The history of economic policy in the next century was the history of the gradual exchange of these positions.

The Age of Jackson

The age of Jackson marked the first stage in this process of exchange. The United States was now entering the period of take-off. This meant that there was a measure of self-generating economic activity, and, in this situation, the relationship of the government and the private entrepreneur began to undergo significant changes. Thus, as private capital formation began to supply a larger share of capital needs, government was no longer playing so indispensable a role as the provider of capital.

The change in the corporation itself was symptomatic. As the number of corporations multiplied, the link between each specific corporation and the state became more tenuous. In consequence, a distinction began to arise between public and private corporation, in which the profit-making corporation began to lose its original character as a public instrumentality and became increasingly exempt from public regulation (an exemption rapidly transformed into immunity by judicial action). The agitation of the Jackson period for general laws of incorporation was a recognition of the extent to which the state had lost control over the corporative process.

Without at first being aware of it, the business community was growing away from the Hamiltonian conception of publicly guided private enterprise. Then the politics of the Jackson period shocked businessmen into a conscious change of their attitude toward the state. The business community of the 1830s was angered not only by Jackson's aggressive conception of the presidential power but even more by the use to which he put this conception in disciplining and ultimately dispossessing the great contemporary symbol of American capitalism, the Second United States Bank. In the states too, Jacksonians displayed an irritating penchant for economic regulation and administrative experiment. If Jackson's own economic ideas were naive and obsolescent, the political philosophy behind them was not. He was contending in effect that in a free society the democratic state had to be more powerful than any private concentration of wealth within that society. Jackson now demonstrated that strong government could easily turn into the regulator, if not the foe, of business. The issue of the interventionist state could no longer be avoided.

The politics of the Jackson period was in consequence a traumatic experience for businessmen. The result was to make business reconsider the whole mercantilist assumption that strong government was a good thing. In the new economic context, businessmen no longer felt the old economic need for governmental activism. Under the glittering eye of Jackson, they began to discern a new charm in the Jeffersonian proposition that that government was best which governed least. Their perception was still confused by the fact that they wanted government action in specified realms, especially in internal improvements, tariff protection, and the acceptance of bank paper money as legal tender; they were not quite ready for a full-blown *laissez-faire* declaration. But mercantilism was beginning to be left behind.

Hamiltonianism survived in the shape of Henry Clay's American system, while the Jacksonians remained *laissez faire* in theory, interventionist in fact. In this season of intellectual transition, nearly everyone professed an indiscriminate mixture of economic ideas. The American economist who perhaps came nearest to giving these ideas some shape and order was Henry Charles Carey.

Carey's effort was to reconcile Hamilton and Adam Smith — to provide enough scope for government action to vindicate at least tariff protection (and perhaps a measure of social legislation) but not enough to hamper capitalist accumulation. He constantly insisted on "the necessity for the exercise of the social body, of that same coordinating and regulating power, we see to be so constantly exercised in the physical man." He was savagely critical of contemporary British economists, especially Ricardo, and sought to relieve Adam Smith from responsibility for the wage-fund theory and other hard-hearted doctrines.

> Adam Smith did *not* believe in the abdication, by the governments, of the power of so co-ordinating the movements of the individual members of a society, as to enable all to become more productive. His successors do — the result exhibiting itself in the fact, that "markets have become fields of battle," strewed with the corpses of slaves and paupers.

Against the economics of despair Carey seemed to assert an optimistic economics, centered about man rather than production and dedicated to the thesis that applied intelligence could outwit iron laws.

But in detail Carey was much closer to *laissez faire* than he would concede. The point of national leadership, as he saw it, was to remove obstacles to "association and combination," in other words, to set free the corporation, which he saw as the providential agency of economic change. The corporation itself became the operative center of his economics: Anything which strengthened the corporation, from the high tariff to limited liability, was good; anything which weakened it, from trade unions to factory legislation, was bad. Having thus expelled the international version of *laissez faire*, which served the purposes of the British economy, Carey devised a national version which fitted what he conceived to be the needs of his own land. The old Hamiltonianism was reduced to a few phrases and a single issue — the high tariff. By thus identifying protection with free enterprise, Carey assisted the process which won the tariff immunity from the general *laissez-faire* upsurge after the Civil War. He himself was the key figure in the transformation of the economics of the business community from Hamilton to Herbert Spencer.

Post Civil War Transformation

The Civil War completed this transformation. It provided new stimulus to American industrial development and eliminated the main political forces opposing business control of the economy: the slave-holding aristocracy of the South, the foundation of whose power was destroyed, and the Jackson–Van Buren "radical democracy" of the North, whose energies, diverted for a generation to the crusade against the slave power, could not now reorganize to cope with the new power of business. The result was to enable the business community, entering an epoch of tremendous economic growth, to command the most potent resources of politics and ideology in making sure that this growth took place on its own terms.

Those terms were "sound" money, the protective tariff, and, above all, a ban on all forms of unsolicited government intervention, from regulation to taxation. This meant a repudiation of Hamiltonian notions about the economic leadership of the state, even in the diluted form espoused by Henry Charles Carey. Instead, the corporation and the entrepreneur came to the forefront as the sacrosanct agencies of economic activity; the ideological problem was now to move beyond Carey in making America intellectually safe for private economic enterprise. In this venture, American economists drew on elements in their own tradition; they drew even more particularly on the great European exponents of *laissez faire*, especially on Herbert Spencer.

The political economy of Spencer represented a fusion of a simplistic version of the economics of laissez-faire with a simplistic version of the new evolutionary philosophy derived from Darwin. Both Ricardian economics and Darwinian biology seemed to conclude with the doctrine that the survival of the fittest through free competition was the necessary condition to the progress of the race. Applied to public policy, this doctrine appeared to mean that government must avoid, above all else, doing anything to derail the evolutionary (or competitive) process.

At a time of undisputed business supremacy, the Spencerian doctrine seemed a miraculous interpretation of American experience. "Light came as in a flood," Andrew Carnegie wrote after reading Spencer. His works sold widely. His viewpoint permeated the colleges and the press. It cast a spell on the American judiciary, which proceeded to enshrine Spencer's conceptions of what was legitimate in economic and political action and what was not, thereby denying to the post-Civil War generations forms of government intervention which had been considered beyond constitutional challenge in the first seventy-five years of the republic. The infatuation of the Supreme Court with Spencer became so spectacular that in 1905 Justice Oliver Wendell Holmes in a notable dissent reminded his brethren (in vain), "The Fourteenth Amendment does not embody Mr. Herbert Spencer's Social Statics."

By the nineties, the confrontation between *laissez faire* and the interventionist state was growing acute. At first the argument turned ostensibly on free silver versus the gold standard, but what was more deeply involved was the question whether monetary policy was a public or a private function — whether, indeed, the national government was entitled to control the national economy. It was the Jacksonian question all over again, and the speed-up in the merger movement at the end of the nineties, creating a new tableau of the trusts versus the government, gave the question a new form and greater urgency. But, as the Progressive period showed, events were settling the matter. From this point on, *laissez-faire* economics were on the defensive. Intervention by the state, which the electorate was coming to deem necessary for a multitude of practical reasons, soon began to develop a substantial rationale of its own.

Marxism

A comprehensive critique of capitalist economics had long since developed in Europe, of course, in the shape of Marxist socialism. Marx followed American developments and exchanged letters with American friends. From the seventies on, there were Socialist parties in American politics. Yet the result of the socialist agitation was surprisingly meager. If some American theorists (notably Daniel De Leon, who was praised by Lenin) had impact on Marxist doctrine, no American Marxist had much influence on American economic thought.

There are obvious reasons for the limited impact of Marxism — above all the continuing social mobility of American life and the consequent absence, except for fleeting moments, of any deep or embittered sense of class consciousness. Marxist categories practically never (except in the depths of depression) seemed to interpret the actualities of American experience. Beyond this, the American style and temper seemed inherently hostile to Marxist determinism. Thus the prediction of increasing proletarian misery was central to the Marxist account of capitalism. But this prediction had little application to the United States, at first because of the abundance of natural wealth, and later, when this became less available, because of the pragmatic use of government as a means of directing social evolution.

Marx had supposed that the state, as the faithful servant of capitalist power, was incapable of acting independently — and certainly incapable of acting against the wishes — of the business community. But a central point of the American experience was to demonstrate that this was not so. In distress, Americans always turned to government, and the resort to the interventionist state enabled the American nation to move toward promoting the redistribution of wealth and controlling the business cycle — the two things which most confounded Marx's prophecy. In effect, American politics, aided by American resources, frustrated Marxist economics, and the result was to render Marxism irrelevant to American development.

Homegrown Critique of Laissez Faire

The effective criticism of *laissez faire*, in consequence, took place from within the capitalist order. To some in the early thirties the invocation of the affirmative state seemed to violate the American way of life. But it actually violated only the precepts of Herbert Spencer, and it had, in fact, deeper antecedents than Spencer in the American tradition.

The thirties were a welter of experiment. As in the eighteenth century technology outran science — so that science made its theoretical breakthroughs by explaining what practical men had already achieved — so in the early part of the twentieth century, under the stress of the Great Depression, economics lagged behind politics, and economists made their mark by explaining what politicians were already doing. Franklin D. Roosevelt's New Deal enlisted economists of various schools united only by a zest for experiment.

One basic difference divided the New Deal economists. Those in the institutionalist tradition demanded structural changes in the economy; in particular they proposed a revision of traditional modes of decision over resources allocation, production, and price.

The opposing group was less concerned about the structure of the capitalist engine than about its fuel. Their reliance was on the modern ingenuities of fiscal policy. Some of them were disciples of the Englishmen J. A. Hobson and, above all, John Maynard Keynes. Whatever their inspiration, they counted far more on government action to increase spending in the economy than on government action to reconstruct the pattern of economic decision. Statistical inventions, especially in the field of national-income measurement, happily now appeared to make Keynesian manipulation of economic aggregates administratively practicable.

Conclusions

As late as the 1950s the *laissez-faire* faith of the post-Civil War period still had nominal devotees. An influential Secretary of the Treasury, George Humphrey, said that, in case of depression, he would favor a reduction of public spending; he would cut taxes only if prosperity yielded surpluses in the budget. The national government in this period proudly divested itself of a significant measure of control over monetary policy. The President of the United States seemed more concerned with diminishing than with exercising public control over the economy.

Yet, to many observers, this seemed a form of fair-weather piety. The American people, it was evident, had crossed the great divide. If anything were to go seriously wrong with the economy, the demand for public action would surely be irresistible. Spencer was dead beyond recall. In affirming the inability of unassisted "free private enterprise" to achieve the national economic goals, the United States was not abandoning its traditions in order to pursue foreign "isms"; it was, in fact, returning to the earliest traditions of the republic. The conceptions of the role of government, of the proper mix between public and private enterprise, of the need for a national economic policy — all these were more alike in 1790 and 1960 than any were like the conceptions of 1880.

The "mixed economy" of the mid-twentieth century represented an advance not only beyond classical *laissez faire* but beyond classical socialism. The advocates of both these classical creeds had agreed in rejecting the notion of a half-way house between them. The economy, they said, could be entirely private, or it could be entirely public, but one could never, never mix freedom and control.

The great battle of the 1930s was to dispel this ideological superstition; it was the battle of American pragmatism against all forms of economic dogmatism, of the right and of the left. Whether conservatives or radicals, the dogmatists saw themselves as hard-headed realists. But they were really unconscious Platonists, confusing abstract models with practical reality and thereby committing the "fallacy of misplaced concreteness." Capitalism was, by definition, one thing, socialism another, and so doctrinaire capitalists agreed with doctrinaire socialists that no compromise between the two was possible. But economics properly should deal, not with essence, but with existence; in fact, the very sort of mixed economy whose viability the dogmatists of the thirties denied turned out to be the salvation of the free system.

The American record thus shows the potency of ideas in economic development. It also shows the danger when ideas harden into all-encompassing, rigid systems. Americans have characteristically regarded ideas as efficient tools, not as sacred truths. Throughout American history ideas have served as a means of releasing economic initiative and then as a means of chastening economic arrogance; as a means of stimulating private energy and then as a means of reasserting public responsibility. One set of ideas helped to launch American economic growth. Another assisted in the great phase of private accumulation. When the passion for private accumulation threatened the values of democracy, another set of ideas prepared for public supervision and regulation. When private enterprise proved inadequate to maintain national growth, further ideas accustomed the nation to a new national commitment for economic development. What mattered was the philosophical flexibility, the intellectual resilience, of the people — the capacity to face new problems relatively unencumbered by the cults and clichés of the past. One must say "relatively": America, in face of every new crisis, has had to fight its way out of the "conventional wisdom" which would otherwise condemn it to repeating the same old mistakes. Yet in the end reality has generally triumphed over dogma. The ability to change one's mind turns out to be the secret of American economic growth, without which resources, population, climate, and the other favoring factors would have been of no avail. If the American experience bequeaths anything to nations facing today even more formidable problems of economic self-development, it is that nothing counts more than a faith in thought combined with an instinct for empirical reality — and an understanding that reality is forever changing.

• 7

Amerca at Mid-Century: A Panoply
of Recent Economic Developments*

HAROLD G. VATTER
Carleton College

What is the American economy like today? What are its characteristics, its accomplishments, its problems? What were the major developments of the U.S. economy during the 1950's?

The Abundant Economy

It became clear to all the world that the United States economy after mid-century was capable of producing enough to provide every man, woman, and child with a minimum-comfort level of living. A rough index of this potential is revealed by the fact that per capita consumption in 1960 was $1,824. Although this is an average, it nevertheless indicates the capacity of the economy at that time to provide all Americans with necessities and some comforts. Moreover, the $329 billion of consumer expenditures still left an enormous margin of output above consumption, for gross national product (GNP) was $504 billion.

The remarkable capacity of the United States economy in 1960 represents the crossing of a great divide in the history of humanity, especially significant in view of the fact that a number of other industrially ad-

* Reprinted from *The U.S. Economy in the 1950's* by Harold G. Vatter. By permission of W. W. Norton & Company, Inc. Copyright © 1963 by Harold G. Vatter.

vanced countries possessed similar capabilities. The full significance for all mankind lies in the possibility that poverty can be eliminated within the foreseeable future. "The poor are always with us" became a dated proposition in the 1950's.

Of course per capita statistics on consumption are little more than brute indexes. They do not reveal levels of living; neither do they reveal the distribution of the national income. There was much discussion during the 1950's of the low income stratum in the population, of especially disadvantaged groups, and of the so-called depressed areas. With the onset of the 1960's structural unemployment (due to failure of the economy to attain an adequate rate of growth) was added to the growing list of welfare problems.

During the 1950's and at present, great theoretical activity has been centered upon the question whether the rate of growth of aggregate demand can keep pace, at remunerative prices, with the projected potential for sustained growth of total capacity. Such a query is really addressed to a society which is groping for a way to deal with abundant capacity.

Mass Unemployment Eliminated

The central economic goal of the 1930's was the achievement of full employment. The goal was not attained, and unemployment ranged from about 15 per cent to 25 per cent of the civilian labor force between 1931 and 1940. The 1950's escaped such mass unemployment ratios. Average unemployment for the decade was 4.6 per cent of the civilian labor force. Despite various deficiencies in the concept and measurement of unemployment statistics, it seems reasonable to generalize that the postwar decade had at least temporarily solved the major problem that the 1930's had been unable to solve.

The elimination of mass unemployment by no means left the economy free of any unemployment problem. The lowest unemployment level was recorded during the Korean War of 1950–1953. In other years the minimum unemployment approached 3 million, which was in excess of 4 per cent of the civilian labor force and an even higher per cent of the nonfarm labor force. Furthermore, as the decade waned the ratios crept upward. Consequently the period was distinguished only by the absence of large-scale unemployment.

A Decade of Large Government Budgets

The 1950's proved to be the first decade without great depression or global war in which large public budgets were a prominent economic condition. The ratio of all government purchases to gross private product in real terms (1954 prices) was about .15 in 1950. By 1955 it had risen to .20 (it had been about .11 in 1929 and .17 in 1939), around which figure it hovered each year through 1960.

Retardation of the Incipient Welfare State

A breakdown of the public budgets according to the level of government and the type of expenditure reveals that the historically high ratios of public expenditures to United States national product in the 1950's were overwhelmingly attributable to military expenditures of the Federal government. Transfer payments (such as old age and survivors insurance (OASI) benefits, unemployment insurance benefits, and veterans' benefits), considered a hallmark of the so-called welfare state as it has emerged in the United States, have, since the 1920's, risen absolutely and relatively to GNP. However, the 1950's failed to reveal any noteworthy rise in the importance of Federal transfer payments as compared to the New Deal days. They accounted for about 4 per cent of GNP in 1939 and 4.4 per cent in 1960. If one adds Federal civilian expenditures to these, then the total of such Federal expenditures plus transfers equaled 7.4 per cent of GNP in 1939 but only 6.0 per cent in 1960. The momentum toward a welfare state gained during the great depression decade was largely, although not entirely, dissipated during the 1950's.

The relative importance of all state and local expenditures edged upward slightly during the 1950's, a decade which began with such expenditures accounting for 7.0 per cent of GNP (identical with 1929) and ended with 9.4 per cent. The upward drift was not erratic, but steady and clear.

A Decade of Moderate Economic Growth

There has been much concern in the 1960's regarding the rate of growth of total output. Most persons accept the goal of a high rate of economic growth. Indeed, by the mid-1950's many had already substituted the achievement of higher growth rates for mass unemployment as the central problem confronting the economy. Aside from the matter of national pride, together with various domestic economic reasons for rapid growth, the competition with the Soviet Union and the clamor of less developed countries for more aid seemed to call for improved performance in this regard.

Real GNP in 1954 prices exhibited an average annual increment of 2.9 per cent over the period 1950–59. This performance was notably below the 4.7 per cent annual increment for 1921–29 and the 3.72 per cent per year for the period 1879–1919. The 1950's seemed to extend a secular, *i.e.*, long-run downward drift in the growth rate of total output.

The 1950's revealed substantial average annual rates of expansion during the first half and weak expansion rates during the second half. The former phase was of course dominated by the Korean War. Real GNP increased at an average annual rate of 4.7 per cent from 1950 to 1955, but the rate from 1955 to 1959 was only 2.25 per cent. Of the two periods, the latter seems unfortunately the more significant for analytical purposes since no hot war was present.

If the annual growth rates of GNP in the first half of the decade are extrapolated and viewed as the potential growth rate applicable to the last half of the decade, the data reveal a substantial and continuous gap between potential and actual GNP from the beginning of 1956 through 1961. Furthermore, each recovery period subsequent to 1953 saw a higher proportion of the civilian labor force unemployed than before.

The Population Burst

As a unit the 1950's exhibited a reversal of the long-run decline in the rate of population growth since the Civil War. The reversal began with the onset of World War II and was overwhelmingly due to a rise in the birth rate that was caused chiefly by the gains in employment, income, and general economic security associated with war conditions.

The 1950's were distinguished by high absolute rates of population growth exceeding even those of the 1940's, but this trend reached a peak in 1956, after which the rates began to be retarded. It would be sensible to postulate that the rate of economic growth in the late 1950's was insufficient to stimulate population growth rates as high as those obtaining in the early 1950's. The highly sensitive marriage rate per 1,000 of population declined fairly steadily throughout the decade, from 11.1 in 1950 to 8.5 in 1959.

Accelerated Technological Advance

The 1950's were a period of rapid technological progress. But technological progress in a general sense was hardly unique to the 1950's. It was the rate of the advance and the character of the technological innovations that set the 1950's apart from earlier decades.

Aside from the lengthy list of new-product technology and certain new organizational techniques, the major innovations in process technology can be subsumed under three types:

1. An upsurge in the established trend toward substitution of the mechanical direction of operations for direct human supervision.

2. The incorporation into mechanical control, feeder, and handling equipment of the feedback principle — automation.

3. Integration of processes, consisting of two general types. One in-

volved the extension of established continuous-flow production methods to encompass and link together more operations, accelerating the rate of flow of the whole.

The other process was the combination into a simultaneous action of a number of operations formerly accomplished sequentially. Since sequential operation, either discrete or continuous, was developed historically through specialization, this new form of integration of operations represents a reversal of a long-established trend and is one of the great new technological changes of our time. Examples: a machine for drilling the holes in an automobile crankshaft in one operation that was formerly performed by twenty-nine different machines; also, the fabrication of a complete printed circuit board in one operation instead of by separate hand-wiring in sections. The board itself was "unitized," that is produced as a single complex item without separable components.

Inauguration of an Inflationary Era?

As a unit the 1950's were a decade of rising prices. In the case of consumer goods and services, the upward trend of prices is even clearer, for that index lacks the downward sag in the early 1950's which appears in the wholesale index. In March of 1961, consumer prices stood at 127.5 per cent of 1947–49.

With farm products and processed foods omitted, the index for all other commodities traced out the same pattern of price climb after 1955 as it did for consumer prices, for it rose from 117.0 in 1955 to 128.0 in early 1961. Indeed, this index edged slightly upward even during the slump of 1953–54, so that a continuous upward movement is visible as far back as 1953 — an eight-year period containing three recessions. It is this pattern which elicited so much discussion during the 1950's about the possibility of chronic inflation.

Persistence of Moderate Instability

Although the 1950's escaped severe unemployment, they did not avoid some fluctuation in output, employment, income, prices, and a number of other important components in the economic system. Statistics of aggregates traditionally sensitive to the business cycle, such as private investment, corporate profits before taxes, unemployment, and industrial production, generally showed unstable patterns in the three recessions already mentioned as well as in the recession of 1948–49. It gradually became clear that the system was still subject to endogenous forces which continued to generate fluctuations in the private sphere. In addition the Federal budget, and at one point total exports, were sharply destabilizing forces. The business cycle, although modified, was still present in the economy.

New Sensitivity to the Rest of the World

Three major external forces in the 1950's significantly raised the sensitivity of the United States to events in the world economy: Soviet-bloc rivalry, increased intervention by less developed countries into international relations, and the rise of powerful competition from Western Europe and Japan.

The "Soviet effect" (by which is meant a direct and often short-sighted countermove in the United States to some initiating Soviet move) penetrated almost every aspect of American economic life — the United States military budget, subsidies to higher education, professional salaries, R & D outlays, tariff policy, foreign aid, and numerous others. In the sphere of United States foreign policy in particular, Soviet-bloc rivalry dominated the magnitude and direction of the government's foreign aid program, totaling almost $73 billion between mid-1945 and the end of 1959.

The less developed countries exerted an important external influence, which increased as the decade unfolded, on the American economy and American foreign economic policy during the 1950's. It was clear, for example, by the end of the 1950's that something closely approximating agricultural price parity in principle would have to be established in the foreseeable future in order to protect the terms of trade of the less developed countries, whose exports consist principally of raw materials. And generally, the emerging nations came to articulate ever more cogently their demands for some form of planned international subsidies from the rich nations. United States sensitivity to those demands was strikingly acknowledged in annual appropriations for foreign aid that in 1960 exceeded $4 billion per year. Toward the end of the decade the United States showed some restiveness at bearing the international burden of aid virtually alone.

The decade was also outstanding for the improvement in the international competitive position of Western Europe and Japan in the commodity markets as these areas recovered, partly with United States aid, from the economic impairment of World War II.

Internal factors were also at work in the 1950's to change America's role in the world economy and increase its dependence on events in the rest of the world.

From the domestic perspective, the fact that imports followed the level of economic activity as a dog's tail follows the dog attests to the constant functional attachment of the two. But the vital aspect was the specter of domestic exhaustion of natural resources as they were drawn upon at fantastic rates to feed the more affluent consumer strata and the insatiable demands of the defense program.

The increased reliance of the domestic economy on the rest of the world because of internal factors was further represented in (1) the restoration of private capital outflows to proportions resembling the high rates of the 1920's and (2) enormous gifts to foreigners.

A final notable feature of the 1950's was the much-discussed gold drain during the latter part of the decade. The United States gold stock, which had risen almost steadily from 1929 to an all-time high of $24.4 billion in 1949, dropped to a plateau at around $22–$23 billion between 1950 and 1957, then fell sharply to somewhat less than $18 billion in December, 1960. Associated with the drain after 1957 was a growing deficit in the balance of international payments.

Suburbanization and Urban Sprawl

The industrialization of the United States brought with it the relative decline of agriculture, the rise of the industrial metropolis, and the spread of urban civilization. These trends which were uniquely geared to the expansion of manufacturing, transportation, and public utilities, matured by about 1925. Thereafter, certain new forces began to cause substantial changes in the character of American cities. Superimposed on the older, typical industrial-city framework, these changes reached a high point of development in the 1950's, bringing with them a constellation of economic and other problems that had reached disturbing proportions by the beginning of the 1960's problems of the "exploding metropolis."

The adjective "exploding" was applied in the 1950's to two developments in the life of the American metropolis. One was the continuation, albeit at a reduced rate, of the long-run tendency of the population of metropolitan areas to grow faster than the total population.

The second component of explosive character in the urbanization process was the greater growth of the metropolitan areas surrounding the central or core city.

The role of this vast population growth in old and new suburbs and old suburban cities in stimulating economic expansion throughout the whole economy has not been fully appreciated. This growth accounted for enormous outlays for public services; social overhead capital such as power facilities, highways, streets, sewage plants, water systems, schools, etc.; housing; transportation equipment; motor fuel; new investment in private industrial and commercial plant and equipment; and a host of private service, maintenance, and repair activities. Small wonder that city government expenditures jumped 73 per cent between 1952 and 1959 while GNP rose 40 per cent!

Depressed Areas

The growing economic problems of metropolitan communities were functionally linked with another development which attracted much attention in the late 1950's and early 1960's as the overall rate of growth in the economy slowed. This was the problem of the so-called "depressed areas."

Twenty major industrial communities and ninety other areas were classified as suffering from substantial and persistent unemployment in May, 1961, many of them with a long-standing unemployment problem. These areas could have been relieved of their problem largely through outward labor mobility and/or the establishment of new activities, processes that would have been facilitated by rapid expansion in the overall economy. The latter would have reduced the problem to one of particular pockets of stagnation or decay, rather than a general one of an inadequate rate of total growth.

A Rich Mixture of New and Old

It is clear from this introductory review that the 1950's had produced a rich constellation of distinguishing features — historically relative affluence, the liquidation of mass unemployment, large government budgets reflecting chiefly the chronic cold war, a plateau in the rise of the welfare state, slowed economic growth, the population spurt, accelerated technological advance, persistent inflation, moderate cyclical instability, a new receptivity to the outside world, the urban explosion, the distressed area, and the inauguration of the space age.

1. *What are the goals of economic policy?*

2. *Are depressions now out of date?*

3. *What are the economic consequences of automation?*

4. *Can we have full employment without inflation?*

5. *How can monetary and fiscal policies be used to help stabilize the economy?*

Economic Growth and Instability

IF YOU WERE TO PICK UP THE BRUSH of the historian and attempt to paint in a few quick strokes the broad sweep of economic development in the United States (or, indeed, in any other modern society organized around the institutions of capitalistic methods of production and private enterprise), what would the results on your canvas look like? What would you consider to be the most important or dominant features of American economic development in the last 150 to 200 years?

If you are anything like most other college students enrolled in an introductory course in economics, two thoughts will probably be foremost in your mind: one, the idea that the economy has gone "up"; two, that it has gone "up and down." If, indeed, you have been thinking in these directions, you are quite close to the target. An examination of the broad sweep of economic history in the United States does reveal two major facts or features: first, a sustained, long-run upward movement in income or output per capita (total output divided by population); second, short-run oscillations or fluctuations — sometimes longer and more severe, sometimes shorter and milder — around the long-run growth trend. To put the matter briefly: our economy has been characterized by economic growth, but that growth has been unstable.

The readings in Part Two raise and attempt to provide some answers to two types of questions in relation to these issues: (1) What are the major characteristics, causes, and effects of economic growth and instability? (2) What has, can, might, or should be done about these issues? The former is a problem for economic *analysis,* the latter for economic *policy.*

Macroeconomics

The analysis of economic growth and instability draws heavily upon *macro*economics, that is, that part of economics which is concerned with a study of the economy as a whole rather than with particular sectors or parts of economic activity. If you thought economics was concerned with the big, overall issues of national life such as inflation and deflation, prosperity and depression, you will find your anticipations corroborated when you read the following selections.

These readings (as is true in the book as a whole) were selected with the idea of focusing attention upon continuing, yet current, issues. In the 1930's, depression and deflation were the order of the day. Since 1939, the American economy has experienced neither a major depression nor a major deflation (although the "business cycle" is far from dead as is shown by Alvin H. Hansen in Selection 15). Interest has understand-ably shifted to the problems of a prosperous economy, and the question arises: Can we have high rates of expansion in output, reasonably full employment, and yet avoid inflation? All of the readings in Section A are concerned with one or more aspects of this general issue. Note that one of the selections (by Richard Musgrave) is a statement before the Congressional Joint Economic Committee. This pinpoints two important facts: first, the importance of this issue for national and public life, and, second, the growing concern of government with these big economic issues.

Role of Government

Prior to the 1930's, American governments did not play a significant or major role in counteracting the swings of economic cycles, or, indeed, in influencing the overall level of economic activity. The depression of the 'thirties and world war in the 'forties changed all this. Government now plays a large and important role in the aggregate economy, and it is generally agreed that this role should be played in such a way as to promote high levels of employment, price, stability, and economic growth. This shift in the economic philosophy of government in the United States is illustrated by the policy declaration of the Employment Act of 1946 which states the responsibilities of the federal government in maintaining and promoting "maximum employment, production and purchasing power."

Monetary and Fiscal Policy

The major governmental measures used in the postwar attempts to promote stable economic growth have been monetary and fiscal policies. Monetary policy is concerned with the volume, availability, cost, and types of money and credit. Fiscal policy involves government's powers to tax, spend, and borrow, and the effects of these activities on the economy. Monetary and fiscal policies have the advantage for an essentially private enterprise economy of affecting the volume or level of money income, and employment, while leaving decisions about particular prices, wages, and outputs to individuals and business firms.

Most of the selections in Section B deal with the nature, consequences, advantages, and disadvantages of monetary and fiscal measures as means of promoting full employment-price stability-economic growth. The concluding selection explores the economic consequences which might occur if "peace were to break out" and how government policy might deal with such a promising yet challenging contingency.

A. CONCEPTS, PROBLEMS, AND ISSUES

• 8

Reconciling the Major Objectives*

RICHARD A. MUSGRAVE
Johns Hopkins University

In an ideal, but unreal universe, our national objectives would coalesce in perfect harmony. In our imperfect, but very real, world, the underlying goals toward the attainment of which our policies are directed are often in conflict. The following selection summarizes the possibilities and problems involved in simultaneously pursuing high employment, stable prices, and economic growth, which is something like riding three horses at once.

The objectives of employment, price level stability and growth are all desirables, but they are relative objectives, which can be accomplished in varying degrees, and since conflicts may arise among them, little is gained by listing them without some understanding regarding the degrees of urgency involved.

* Taken and adapted from *Employment, Growth, and Price Levels,* Hearings before the Joint Economic Committee, 86th Congress, 1st Session (Washington, D.C.: United States Government Printing Office, 1959), Part 9A, pp. 2758–2762.

Employment

It is my view that high and, if reasonably defined, full employment is a basic requirement of a satisfactory social system. Unemployment relief, no matter how ample, is not a substitute for employment, which provides the major link of integration between individual and society. For this reason, or, if you wish, value judgment, I am most hesitant to pay the price of involuntary unemployment in order to achieve the other objectives.

On balance, I do not believe that there is a serious conflict between high employment and growth. To be sure, the two objectives may clash in certain situations. Shifts between jobs, needed to accommodate technical progress, will be more rapid if unemployment is higher, and the danger of unemployment may, under some conditions, be a spur to greater work effort. However, greater labor mobility may be achieved by other means than unemployment, and the long-run effects of job insecurity on incentives may well be detrimental rather than helpful.

The more basic point is that growth is furthered by the intensive use of all of our resources, and that only in a buoyant economy will there be sufficient incentive for private enterprise to undertake the aggressive policy of expansion which, in the absence of extensive Government investment, is needed for rapid growth. These seem to me the more important factors so that, in all, growth and high employment are complementary, not rival, objectives.

The same cannot be said for the goals of high employment and upward stability in the price level. Some causes of inflation, such as a generally excessive level of demand, clearly do not call for unemployment as a solution. Hence there is no conflict. Potentially, the most serious conflict arises where the basic inflationary force stems from excessive wage demands, and where these demands are a function of a guaranteed policy of high employment. The argument is that such demands would not be forthcoming in the absence of a full-employment policy, either because union leaders would wish to avoid unemployment, or because employers would be unwilling to grant the requested increases if the necessary market was not assured. Perhaps such would be the case, but I fear that the amount of unemployment required to secure the necessary discipline might be substantial, and there is a good reason to expect that its major incidence would be among the innocent, including firms as well as unions, rather than the guilty. If such a situation exists, the solution lies in some degree of public control over wage and price policy in the basic industries, and not in the wastes and hardships of unemployment.

Where inflation is the reflection of adjustments in relative prices occurring in an economy with downward rigidity in wages and prices, there is again some conflict, but the degree of conflict is much less serious. A substantial degree of unemployment may be required to remedy a relatively minor tendency to price rise, since a moderate degree of general unemployment does not assure that the lubricant of unemployment will be available in just the right places. The resulting degree of inflation is likely to be slight, and less damaging than the remedy of substantial unemployment. Appropriate policies here require selective controls over demand, designed to smooth the course of structural adjustments.

Thus, my general emphasis on high employment, as a matter of social value, is strengthened by skepticism regarding the efficacy of modest unemployment as a means of stabilizing the price level. At the same time, it is obvious that high employment, as a policy objective, must allow for the fact that job changes are unavoidable in a dynamic economy, and that it takes time to transfer between jobs. If everyone changes his job once a year, and if a week is required for transfer, about 2 per cent of the labor force will be unemployed on this count. Given adequate market organization, and a sustained level of high employment, 2 or 3 per cent should suffice for what is required for this purpose.

The case for high employment has suffered since the enactment of the Employment Act by the ambiguities which arise from the term "full employment." Opponents of a full employment policy delight in pointing to the difficulties of defining "full employment," and proponents have been forced to retreat into the vague nebula of "high employment." Public discussion might be aided, and full employment be restored to its rightful place of No. 1 policy objective, if the current measure of unemployment, that is, ratio of total unemployed to labor force, was replaced by a more reasonable concept, making allowance for the type and duration of unemployment and for other essentially qualitative aspects of the unemployment problem. We now have general public acceptance of the BLS[1] index of cost of living as a measure of price level stability, and it serves its purpose. A counterpart is needed with regard to an index by which current performance relative to the target of full employment may be measured.

Stability of Price Level

My emphasis upon full employment, as just defined, as a primary policy objective must not be taken to mean that I am impervious to the dangers of inflation. This goes without saying for the disaster type of inflation, such as may be found in the wake of war finance, especially of defeated nations. The more relevant point is that even a modest rate of price increase, if continued sufficiently long, may result in serious inequities to various groups in the economy.

While the much-quoted case of schoolteachers has lost some of its

[1] Bureau of Labor Statistics.

force and other groups, such as OASI recipients, are similarly securing price-level adjustments, there remains the case of the private saver who has placed his assets in fixed obligations. Even if we assume that his earnings and hence his savings rise with the price level, an annual rate of inflation of, say 3 per cent, may shrink by 40 per cent the real value of savings accumulated over his working life. This assumes savings of 10 per cent of income, compound interest at 4 per cent, and a 30-year span. If the inflation rate is 2 per cent and interest is 3 per cent, the loss is 27 per cent.

This is not to be taken lightly. It forces the small saver to invest in equity capital, thereby assuming a degree of risk which is unreasonable from his economic position. A well-organized society should not impose such compulsion to take risk; it should offer an opportunity for a riskless form in which to preserve one's assets, riskless with regard to changes in price-level as well as possible default.

If appropriate policies, monetary and fiscal, are pursued to avoid general excess demand, and if the generation of autonomous cost-push is checked at the source, we shall still be left with some upward bias in the price level. In an economy in which money wages are generally rigid in the downward direction, this remains to be expected. As to the existence of this downward rigidity, no one will deny it, and I believe that little can be done about it. However, and this is a point usually forgotten in the current discussion, I do not believe that this downward rigidity is altogether a bad thing. A pretty good case can be made for arguing that the relative mildness of the postwar recessions was due, in significant degree, to the existence of this downward rigidity which, by its very nature, helped to prevent the development of a downward spiral, based on anticipation of falling prices and shrinking purchasing power.

A visitor from Mars, sitting in on recent arguments about the inflation problem, might well be led to believe that we have just emerged from a holocaust of runaway inflation. This, of course, is far from the truth. The fact of the matter is that the average annual price rise from 1948 to 1958, as measured by the BLS index of wholesale prices, was about 2 per cent, which is considerably below the rate, nearly 3 per cent, of average advance in the BLS index during the golden years of 1895 to 1910. According to a new series by C. D. Long and A. Rees, the average rise in wholesale prices from 1895 to 1910 was 1.9 per cent, or about the same as for 1948–58.

Also, the fact of the matter is that the cost of living remained about constant from 1948 to 1950, from 1952 to 1956, and again since 1958. Thus since 1948, significant price advances occurred only in connection with the Korean war and in 1956–57. The experience of 1956 to 1957 is disturbing, and all comparisons have their weakness, but in all, this is hardly the story of an alarming record.

The main change in the longer-run picture is that we have learned, we hope, to maintain employment, and hence will be relieved of periods of severe depression, in which prices have declined traditionally. On balance, this should be a considerable improvement, not a worsening, of our position.

Growth

I now turn to growth, our final and most difficult policy objective. If we did not have to worry about international problems, I would clearly rank growth third in my list of policy objectives. And this for two reasons. Other things being equal, everyone will agree, as a matter of course, that an increase in growth is a net gain. However, this is a truism only. In reality, other things are not likely to be equal, and forced growth is likely to be a costly affair.

Unless generated entirely by an increased rate of innovation, more rapid growth will require a higher level of capital formation, and hence a lower level of current consumption. For this and other reasons, social welfare policies may have to be curtailed, the tax structure may have to be made less progressive, investment may have to be subsidized, and so forth. The extent to which these things will have to be done will depend upon the rate of growth which we wish to attain, but I think that we would be mistaken to assume the objectives of social welfare and growth to be coincidental.

Normal growth, such as has been customary in the past, is necessary to provide a healthy social climate and to help overcome the remnants of poverty in our country, but forced growth will add little, and may even endanger these objectives. Also, a forced rate of growth will complicate the task of maintaining stability of price level. Rapid growth generates, and to some degree requires, excess demand. The inverse proposition, that rapid growth is needed to meet wage demands in a noninflationary fashion, is unconvincing. It assumes that such demands are independent of productivity gains, an assumption which seems quite unrealistic.

For these reasons, my enthusiasm for a policy of forced growth is limited. I am in favor of technical progress, to be sure, especially if the costs thereof are borne equitably; but beyond this, I am unwilling to accept substantial sacrifices in the form of inflation or extensive controls in order to raise the rate of growth above a level of, say, 3 per cent, such as has been customary in the past. This much for growth in the absence of international considerations.

In reality, we do not live in isolation, and these international considerations are all important. Here much depends on the urgency of the international situation. If it were necessary, as a matter of national survival, to raise the level of GNP, a vast increase of 25 per cent or more could be accomplished in a rather short period, and this even without the substantial initial unemployment which characterized the prewar position. By increasing working hours and labor force, by allocating strategic resources to essential uses, and by taking other measures typical of a war economy, an increase in output could be accomplished within a year's span, raising GNP to a level which, in the normal course of events, it might take a decade to accomplish. Evidently the cost would be high and the sense of urgency is not that great. Yet we can hardly argue that the growth objective should be just that which can be achieved without doing anything inconvenient, and, in particular, without requiring any sort of direct controls. The requirements of the international situation will hardly happen to coincide with this convenient target. Some inbetween solution is needed.

The proper target, it seems to me, cannot be stated simply in terms of an overall rate of growth in GNP. I see no important international objective which is served by increasing the supply of luxury services to the American consumer. Rather, we have to focus on the contribution of growth to our capacity for defense, and to our ability to help underdeveloped countries to improve their standard of living. Therefore, my concern for rapid growth is primarily a concern for the kind of growth which helps to further these objectives. This shifts the problem from one of overall growth to one of structure of growth.

With regard to defense, such unpleasant matters as relocation of industry to maintain capacity under attack, as well as provision of shelters for the civilian population, should be given high priority. These are both projects of such magnitude as may absorb a good part of the incremental growth which we can achieve. Our persistent refusal to face these needs seems beyond rational understanding. Also, the different degrees of convertibility of civilian into defense production in various areas of growth cannot be overlooked and our disastrous lag in rocketry requires drastic action.

With regard to economic aid, I am quite aware that redistribution of our output among the vast populations of the underdeveloped countries would not go far in solving the problem, and that more harm than good might be done by destroying the original sources of wealth. But I am also unable to escape the thought that our concern for social justice cannot stop within the boundaries of our own country, if decent international society is to develop.

Hence, the case for substantial and sustained economic aid seems to me imperative, and if it is to be met, it will have considerable bearing on the structure of growth at home. Certainly the existence of poverty in vast areas of the world renders invalid the proposition that this is the age of opulence, where production has ceased to be of economic concern.

• 9

Sector Accounts in National
Income Accounting*

John E. Elliott
University of Southern California
and
United States Department of Commerce

Students of economics have become familiar with various ways of measuring the aggregate performance of the national economy, from gross national product or GNP (the money or market value of currently produced final products and services) to disposable personal income (derived from GNP through a process of deductions and additions). This selection presents national income data organized around five major "sector accounts" and shows for each the sources and disposition of income.

As can be seen in the accompanying table, sector accounting data is organized around five major divisions or sectors of the national economy: (1) National income and product account; (2) personal income and outlay account; (3) government receipts and expenditures account; (4) foreign transactions account; (5) gross saving and investment account. (Strictly speaking, accounts (1) and (5) are summary accounts rather

* Taken from "Sector Accounts in National Income Accounting," article written for this book. Table 1 taken and adapted from "Summary Data, 1962," *Survey of Current Business*, July, 1963 (Washington, D.C.: U.S. Government Printing Office, 1963), p. 16.

Table 1.   Sector Account Data, 1962

I. National Income and Product Account, 1962
(billions of dollars)

1 Compensation of employees	322.9	11 Personal consumption	
Wages and salaries (II-4)	297.1	expenditures (II-2)	355.4
Employer contributions for		12 Gross private domestic	
social insurance (III-9)	13.7	investment (V-1)	78.8
Other labor income (II-5)	12.1	13 Net exports of goods and	
2 Proprietors' income (II-6)	49.8	services	3.8
3 Rental income (II-7)	12.0	Exports (IV-1)	28.9
4 Corporate profits	46.8	Imports (IV-2)	25.1
Tax liability (III-7)	22.2	14 Government purchases of goods	
Dividends (II-8)	16.6	and services (III-1)	117.0
Undistributed corporate			
profits (V-4)	8.1		
5 Net interest (II-9)	22.0		
NATIONAL INCOME	453.7		
6 Business transfer payments			
(II-10)	2.3		
7 Indirect business tax (III-8)	53.0		
8 Subsidies less current surplus			
of government enter-			
prises (III-4)	—1.7		
9 Capital consumption allowances			
(V-5)	49.4		
10 Statistical discrepancy (V-7)	—1.8		
GROSS NATIONAL		GROSS NATIONAL	
PRODUCT	554.9	PRODUCT	554.9

II. Personal Income and Outlay Account, 1962
(billions of dollars)

1 Personal taxes (III-6)	57.7	4 Wages and salaries (I-1)	297.1
2 Personal consumption		Manufacturing	94.2
expenditures (I-11)	355.4	Other private	147.4
Durable goods	48.2	Government	55.6
Nondurable goods	161.4	5 Other labor income (I-1)	12.1
Services	145.7	6 Proprietors' income (I-2)	49.8
3 Personal saving (V-3)	29.1	Business and professional	36.5
		Farm	13.3
		7 Rental income of persons (I-3)	12.0
		8 Dividends (I-4)	16.0
		9 Personal interest income	30.6
		Net interest (I-5)	22.0
		Net interest paid by	
		government (III-3)	8.0
		10 Transfer payments	34.8
		Business (I-6)	2.3
		Government (III-2)	32.5
		11 Less: Personal contributions for	
		social insurance (III-9)	10.2
PERSONAL OUTLAY			
AND SAVING	442.1	PERSONAL INCOME	442.1

III. Government Receipts and Expenditures Account, 1962
(billions of dollars)

1 Purchases of goods and services (I-14)	117.0		6 Personal tax and nontax receipts (II-1)	57.7
Federal	62.4		Federal	49.0
National defense (less sales)	52.5		State and local	8.7
Other	10.0		7 Corporate profits tax accruals (I-11)	22.2
State and local	54.6		8 Indirect business accruals (I-7)	53.0
2 Transfer payments	34.1		9 Contributions for social insurance	23.9
To persons (II-10)	32.5		Employer (I-1)	13.7
Foreign (IV-3)	1.6		Personal (II-11)	10.2
3 Net interest paid (II-9)	8.0			
4 Subsidies less current surplus of government enterprises (I-8)	1.7			
5 Surplus or deficit (—) on income and product account (V-6)	—3.9			
GOVERNMENT EXPENDITURES AND SURPLUS	156.8		GOVERNMENT RECEIPTS	156.8

IV. Foreign Transactions Account, 1962
(billions of dollars)

1 Exports of goods and services (I-13)	28.9		2 Imports of goods and services (I-13)	25.1
			3 Transfer payments from U.S. Government (III-2)	1.6
			4 Net foreign investment (V-2)	2.2
RECEIPTS FROM ABROAD	28.9		PAYMENTS TO ABROAD	28.9

V. Gross Saving and Investment Account, 1962
(billions of dollars)

1 Gross private domestic investment (I-12)	78.8		3 Personal saving (II-3)	29.1
New construction	44.4		4 Undistributed corporate profits (I-4)	8.1
Producers' durable equipment	28.8		5 Capital consumption allowances (I-9)	49.4
Change in business inventories	5.5		6 Government surplus or deficit (—) on income and product account (III-5)	—3.9
2 Net foreign investment (IV-4)	2.2		7 Statistical discrepancy (I-10)	—1.8
GROSS INVESTMENT	81.0		GROSS SAVING AND STATISTICAL DISCREPANCY	81.0

than sector accounts.) For each sector, the *sources* and the *disposition* of income is identified.

The sector accounting data constitutes a double-entry bookkeeping system, since all expenditures are made in one of the sectors and all income must come from one of the sectors and since each item appears in both of these categories. Three examples: Personal consumption expenditures are one way of disposing of personal income (II_2) and at the same time are one source of the gross national product (I_{11}). Undistributed corporate profits are both a mode of disposing of the gross national product (I_4) and a source of business saving (V_4). Government transfer payments are one way of disposing of government receipts (III_2) and are also a source of personal income (II_{10}). Can you discover others?

National Income and Product Account

The first sector account is probably the most familiar to students of economics. It shows the sources and the disposition of the GNP. The employment of resources results in the production of output and creation of income. Output is measured by the flow of money or market expenditures upon or purchases of currently produced products and services, organized around the four traditional headings of personal consumption expenditures; gross private domestic investment; net exports; government purchases of products and services. The claims against the GNP are basically of two types: first, the income claims of resource owners (wages, proprietors' incomes, rents, corporate profits, interest) for current contributions to production, which together constitute net national income at factor cost; second, the non-income claims (principally, indirect business taxes and capital consumption allowances), that is, claims which do not represent payments to resource-owners for current contributions to production.

Personal Income and Outlay Account

Personal income measures the income actually received by persons or households (including non-profit institutions) and differs from net national product at factor cost in two basic ways: first, it subtracts income earned for some current productive contribution but not received by resource owners (*e.g.*, corporate profits taxes, undistributed corporate profits, contributions for social insurance); second, it adds income received by persons but not earned for some current contribution to production. Thus, personal income consists basically of that portion of net national income that is received by persons ($II_{4.8}$ + net interest) and net income received for which no current productive contribution has been made (interest from government, business and government transfer payments minus personal contributions for social insurance).

Government Receipts and Expenditures Account

The government sector account is largely self-explanatory. The sources of government receipts from the national product or income are listed on the right-hand side and the disposition of these receipts to national product or income are shown on the left. This data is to be distinguished from both cash and administration receipts and expenditures as defined in the cash and administrative budgets of the federal government (cf. Selection 19). Similarly, the surplus or deficit (in 1962, a deficit of $3.9 billion) on the product and income account should not be confused with either the administrative or cash surplus or deficit of the federal government, partly because the items included are not the same and partly because sector III includes state and local as well as federal government activities. Note also that although government transfer payments and interest are forms of government expenditures or ways of disposing of government receipts, they are not purchases of currently produced products and services and are thus not found in sector I — although they do constitute contributions to personal income, as already noted, and shown in sector II.

Foreign Transactions Account

The foreign transactions account shows the relation between the product and income data of the United States and the rest of the world. Exports of products and services, shown on the left-hand side, constitute receipts by the United States for the sale of domestic output to foreign countries. The items on the right-hand side represent that portion of current domestic money income that is not spent on domestic output but is rather spent upon the purchase of imports, is transferred by government through taxation to foreign countries, or is invested abroad. (Note that net foreign investment is not the same as net exports because that latter figure includes government transfers to foreign countries.) The foreign transactions account should not be confused with the balance of payments (cf. Selection 58), which includes also purely financial transactions with foreign countries.

Gross Saving and Investment Account

This last account summarizes the forms of investment and the sources of saving. At present, national income accounting terminology ascribes the process of investment to businesses (except for residential construction) and to the foreign sector. "Investment" by households (for example, education, consumer durable goods) and governments (for example, education, dams) are not presently distinguished in the national income accounts from consumption expenditures and government purchases in general. The major sources of saving are three: personal; business (undistributed corporate profits and capital consumption allowances); and government (the excess of government receipts over government expenditures).*

National Income Identities

The sector accounts provide valuable and instructive illustrations of the various national income *identities.* An identity is a relation of equality between variables which is true by definition. Our national income accounting system, including the sector accounts, incorporate certain fundamental accounting identities.

Identities are generally of two major types. First, a variable may be measured in two or more different ways. Thus, the totals for each will be equal by definition since they refer to different ways of measuring the same thing. For example, the total figures (although not necessarily individual components) in the two columns for account I are the same, since GNP in the sense of expenditures upon output is equal by definition to the national income and non-income claims against output. Similarly, personal income is equal by definition to the uses to which personal income may be put.

A second type of accounting identity is to define a total as equal to the sum of its parts. For example, gross national expenditures is composed of personal consumption (C), gross private domestic investment (I), government purchases (G), and exports minus imports (X − M). Thus GNE ≡ C + I + G + X − M. (The ≡ refers to an identity in contrast to = which typically represents a true equality or equilibrium between planned or desired magnitudes of economic variables, as, for example, between planned saving and planned investment.)

Sometimes, the specification of the identity includes a residual item. In the personal income sector, for example, personal saving is defined as that portion of personal income which is not spent on consumption and/or is not taxed away by government. Thus, letting PY stand for personal income and C, S, and T for consumption, personal saving, and personal taxes, respectively, it follows that PY ≡ C + S + T.

* Statistical discrepancy, incidentally, does not mean that the government or the national income accountants in the Department of Commerce have mislaid or misappropriated $1.8 billion in 1962. It merely represents an error in statistical compilation which is unavoidable in a double-entry bookkeeping system when data is drawn from different sources. Actually, a statistical error of $1.8 billion out of a total GNP of $554.9 billion is quite low.

A third kind of identity, derivative from the first two, is found in sector V. Our first kind of identity tells us that gross national expenditures are equal to gross national income. Our second type tells us that GNE $= C + I + X - M$ and that GNY is composed of consumption plus saving plus taxes (minus transfers which may be treated as a sort of "negative tax"). Since GNE equals GNY by definition and since C equals C, it follows that $I + G + IF$ (net foreign investment) $\equiv S + T_n$ (taxes net of transfers). Rearranging this information in a more convenient form, we have $I + IF \equiv S + (T_n - G)$. Note that if the government sector has incurred a surplus $(T_n > G)$, the private sector must have incurred a deficit $[(I + IF) >)S]$, while if government has incurred a deficit $(G > T_n)$, the private sector must have incurred a surplus $[S > (I + IF)]$! The explanation, of course, is that while one sector of the economy may incur a "deficit" or "surplus," the system as a whole can incur neither, since the total sources of income (including investment) are in balance with the total disposition of income (including saving) *by definition.*

• 10

Inflation in Perspective*

GEORGE L. BACH
Carnegie Institute of Technology

The usual conception of inflation, at least until lately, has been that of the "demand-pull" variety, which occurs when excessively rising demand "pulls" up prices. More recently, the "cost-push" variety of inflation, where costs and prices are "pushed" up by the market power of sellers, has been subjected to extended discussion. The following selection compares these two types of inflation and appraises possible measures of public policy to cope with them.

Definitions

By inflation I shall mean a rise in the price level or, what is the same thing, a fall in the purchasing power of the monetary unit. To measure changes in the price level, I shall generally use the well-known United States Bureau of Labor Statistics Index of Consumer Prices or Index of Wholesale Prices. But for most of what I say the precise index used is not of crucial importance, so long as it is a broadly based one and represents many prices in the economy.

We could analyze inflation with any one of several definitions. The critically important thing is that the definition be clear and operational

* Taken and adapted from "Inflation in Perspective," *Harvard Business Review,* January–February, 1958, pp. 99–110. Reproduced with permission.

64

— a definition under which inflation can be recognized and measured unambiguously. It is on this score that definitions emphasizing the "cause" of rising prices fall short; with them we can never tell for sure what has caused a rise in prices and hence can never know whether we are looking at inflation or at some different phenomenon that is only associated with it.

Under the proposed definition, rising prices are inflation whether they rise rapidly or slowly (a small rise in prices is a little inflation, and a big rise a large inflation), and whether there is full employment or not. The likelihood of rising prices is, of course, greater after full employment has been reached, but history shows us that prices may rise substantially before resources are fully employed. And there is some reason to suppose this phenomenon of rising prices together with some unemployment may become increasingly common.

The New Version

In the new inflation, it is argued, powerful labor unions push wages upward faster than productivity increases. Then the leading firms in oligopolistic industries (where one or a few firms dominate the field and substantially establish prices, as in the automobile industry) raise their prices at least enough to cover the increase in costs, and often more. When total demand is strong, this wage-price spiral may rise rapidly. Even when the aggregate demand is relatively weak, some economists argue, union wages and administered prices will continue their upward push. Appreciable unemployment is no sure check to this "sellers' inflation."

The new inflation, according to this view, does not necessarily depend upon excess total monetary demand for its existence. Though wages and prices in highly competitive sectors of the economy may not rise rapidly or at all, unionized wages and administered prices — both widespread in our economy — mean persistent secular inflation.

By contrast, the traditional view of inflation is that prices in the aggregate rise when there is too much money chasing too few goods — that is, when there is excess total demand for goods and services offered for sale at prevailing prices. This is "demand-pull" inflation. Such a view looks on markets as competitive to a substantial degree. Prices rise when demand runs ahead of supply and only then to any significant degree. Where individual firms or unions set wages or prices, they cannot get far out of line with what the demand side of the market will bear. If they do, surplus labor and surplus goods will exert a heavy drag on further price advances or even bring price reductions. Persistent long-run inflation will occur only if for some reason excess total demand prevails. And the traditional view suggests that excess demand can prevail for long only if the money supply (demand deposits and currency) increases more rapidly than total output of goods and services.

How Different and How Far?

In extreme cases the new and the old inflations may be quite different. If inflation is generated by a large increase in the money supply (say by huge government expenditures financed by bank borrowing), it is clear that we have traditional excess-demand inflation. Whether the wage-price structure is highly competitive or not, both wages and prices will be bid up rapidly as the new money is spent.

In most cases, however, the difference between the new and the old is plainly one of degree. The economy has never been perfectly competitive with prices and wages responding only to impersonal market forces of supply and demand. Both wages and prices have long been administered to varying degrees in different markets. And with nearly all administered wages and prices there is a margin, large or small, within which the price is set mainly according to the judgment of the price setter. If competitive pressures are strong, this discretionary margin is small; but if the seller has a substantial monopoly position, it may be quite large.

But no seller, no matter how administered his prices, can long escape the test of the market. He can raise his wage or price; but if his price moves far beyond customers' willingness or ability to buy, he will lose sales. If many prices are moving up at the same time, widespread sales losses may occur as prices across the board begin to outrun consumer incomes.

The important thing is that a cost-push, administered-price inflation cannot continue long unless there is growing total demand in the economy. Costs may "push" upward on prices, but, unless total demand is growing, the resultant price increases will not go very far. Thus there is a limit — the cold hand of lack of demand — which every seller must ultimately face unless the demand side of the market is rising too.

If the new and the old inflations are different only in degree, what of the argument that a long-run inflationary drift is inevitable because of the union wage push and the administered-price structure of our economy? The answer is: it is inevitable only if excess demand is provided to support the inflation. Organized labor is much stronger now than over past decades; moreover, there are many administrative price setters. But this is clearly not enough to guarantee long-run inflation. Indeed, we may have intermittent periods of some deflation.

The past decade has seen several circumstances especially conducive to inflation (shortage of labor, strong postwar demand, and high postwar liquidity), and these may well vanish in the near future. But, to argue that because these special forces vanish the likelihood of long-range inflation also vanishes, seems to me to miss the main point: whether there will be excess demand.

There will be persistent excess total demand if governmental policy, as made by the Federal Reserve Board, Congress, and the executive branch in budget making, assures the excess total demand — whether in response to excessive wage-price policies or to more traditional pressures like defense spending needs. If the policy of the Federal Reserve Board and of the rest of the government denies excess total demand, then there will not be any substantial amount of long-range inflation.

This brings us squarely to the issue of governmental monetary-fiscal policy in assessing the likelihood of long-range inflation.

Creep or Gallop?

The real danger of creeping inflation is that it will pick up steam and grow beyond a creep. While there is little evidence that creeping inflation is disastrous, there is overwhelming evidence that a hyperinflation is. Just where the costs of inflation mount to major proportions is hard to specify. It is clear, though, that the more rapid the rise in prices is, the more inequitable and disruptive shifts in income and wealth may become, and also the greater the danger that productive activity may be shifted into unproductive lines to "beat the inflation."

Is the danger that creeping inflation will turn into galloping inflation a real one for the United States if we do not check it in the creeping stage? I believe that real hyperinflation is extremely unlikely. On the other hand, I am concerned that the creep may become a little faster during the next five years, even though it may possibly be interrupted by a business recession.

My prediction is that excess income claims of labor, business, and agriculture will persist — and probably mount. Our democratic government, essentially committed to maintaining high-level employment, will find it extremely difficult not to provide the additional purchasing power needed to support employment at higher cost and price levels as wages and prices of strong income groups are pushed up. This it can do either through deficit financing or by providing additional bank reserves to finance private loans.

Once people understand this process and trust government underwriting of high-level employment, there is logically no limit to the rate of inflation which might develop. But, as a practical matter, the inflation is not likely to be a rapid one (outside of war periods) because income groups are not yet confident enough of government policy to put aside caution in their income claims, because widespread competition slows price increases, and because public fear of inflation is strong enough to restrain private and public action that conspicuously produces rapid price increases.

This is the long-run peacetime inflation danger. It arises from the fact that we are a society of powerful economic and political groups, and that as such we place top priority on the maintenance of a high level of employment and are willing to use federal monetary and fiscal policies to achieve this. Without these two interacting factors of powerful excess income claims and governmental high-employment policy, there is little reason to expect persistent secular inflation in America — in the absence of war.

Accordingly, a fundamental approach to limit inflation must either blunt the excess income claims or prevent the provision of additional purchasing power through the banking system.

Coping with Inflation

The first approach does not seem promising. President Eisenhower repeatedly exhorted labor and management to moderate their wage and price claims, but with little success. A few economists have suggested drastic action to break up the monopolistic powers of large unions and large corporations, but action sufficiently strong to eliminate the problem this way seems unrealistic on the modern scene. Others have suggested countervailing power — making businesses and other groups even stronger to resist the pressures of the unions. But it will still be tempting for management to give in to the unions and merely pass the cost along in the form of higher prices, which is by all odds the easier solution when two powerful giants meet.

A more sophisticated suggestion is that we improve the inducements to businesses to hold down costs, perhaps by lowering the corporation income tax rate and thereby reducing the extent to which the government itself indirectly bears the cost of any wage increase granted. Some have suggested imposition of direct governmental controls over wages and prices. Still other writers have emphasized that the ultimate solution must lie in an increased sense of responsibility on the part both of unions and of management in moderating their claims for higher wages and prices.

Each of these ideas has merit. But none of them provides a very reliable basis for giving up a search for effective inflation hedges.

In the last analysis, almost everyone comes back to federal monetary-fiscal policy — if the job is to be done. Monetary-fiscal policy has a harder time in an economy of administered prices and wages since its impact may be slower and less predictable in any short period. The credit squeeze of tight money falls unequally on different firms and different industries; in general, the least credit-worthy (often the smaller, highly competitive firms) feel the pinch of monetary restriction first. Slower though the check may be, however, shortage of total monetary demand is one sure way of checking inflation.

But if it is extremely difficult in times of moderate inflation to generate large federal surpluses to fight inflation, and if a really tight money policy can work only by generating unemployment, is this approach a *realistic* solution? My answer is that monetary policy against inflation is workable if it has the support of the public — and only if it does!

By limiting the supply of money the Federal Reserve Board can check inflation. Without more money, total expenditures will not long continue to grow.

No seller, no matter how powerful, will continue to raise prices if the consumer cannot continue to buy at the higher prices; and, with a fixed money supply, consumers can continue to buy at higher prices only if they spend the existing money supply faster — only if there is an increase for V in the old textbook equation $MV = PT$ (where M represents money, V, the velocity of turnover of money, P, the price, T, the number of units sold). It is true that V may increase to a moderate extent. History shows, though, that no *major* inflation will occur without an increase in the money supply. While a federal policy that holds the money supply constant may not work precisely and completely, it will certainly shut off any substantial inflationary sweep within a moderate amount of time. Perhaps selective controls, like consumer credit, can help to pinpoint monetary restraint where inflationary rises are strongest, but they can do only a small part of the job.

The real issue, thus, is whether the Federal Reserve Board (and the federal government) will stand firm and refuse to increase the money supply when the pressure for higher prices and wages necessitates more total spending power to prevent falling sales and unemployment.

Tight money that checks inflation may cause unemployment, and the Federal Reserve authorities do not want that particular result. Economists have argued vigorously about just how much unemployment would be required to hold down inflationary wage demands if tight money pressure were applied. Argument of this sort is helpful in exposing the issues, but it seems to me quite illusory to suppose that we can answer this question accurately now.

Critics of tight money argue that only large-scale unemployment can be counted on to check inflationary wage and price policies. This seems overly pessimistic to me. Our post-World War II experience has provided encouraging evidence, as has that of other countries. Whatever the weight of these arguments, the crucial point is that, to avoid inflation in an economy of major power groups, the government must convince the public and the major economic groups within the public, by temporary unemployment or otherwise, that we *will* act to check inflation, even at the cost of some temporary unemployment and unsold goods.

If we do not convince them, we will have inflation and probably as much unemployment too in the long run. For, however fast a government pumps in money, the wage and price demands of the powerful groups can readily be raised more rapidly. Thus, we face the same temporary unemployment issue whether we draw the line against power-group inflation at the creeping or at some more advanced stage.

The basic issue is not, then, whether we shall have inflation with full employment, or stable prices with unemployment. It is likelier to be whether we shall have stable prices or inflation, with some temporary unemployment in either case. Viewed in this way, the case for creeping inflation becomes a good deal less appealing than some have made it seem.

Where shall we take our stand against ever-rising income claims? A stable price level policy is not necessarily better than others, such as a slowly rising price level policy, but it seems to me to present by all odds the strongest rallying point for public support. It is the most equitable position, given the general presumption in our habits and economic mores that the value of the monetary unit is roughly stable. We can all agree that high-level employment is our first objective, but we must still face the fact that inflation is not necessarily, or even probably, the road to maintaining high-level employment.

Conclusion

Can we hope to avoid inflation completely through a stern monetary-fiscal policy over the years immediately ahead? Probably not. But we can certainly hold it to a slow creep if we are willing to keep a tight enough monetary rein.

My guess is that at best there will be some "give" in the monetary checks imposed, especially if important prices push upward just when other short-run weaknesses appear in the economy, which will undoubtedly be true from time to time. A quasi-independent Federal Reserve Board can stand against inflation to a considerable extent (with some buffer provided by its special position), but only so long as the public does not fear unemployment more than rising prices. And even the Federal Reserve Board has no desire to be the scapegoat for the next recession.

But the basic solution depends on the public's own willingness to see limits imposed on its income claims, probably through a persistently dragging and superficially unpopular monetary policy.

11

U*nemployment and the Gap between Actual and Potential GNP**

PRESIDENT'S COUNCIL OF ECONOMIC ADVISERS

Major depressions and mass unemployment in the United States economy are fading into dim recollections. Yet unemployment, even during periods of postwar cyclical expansion, has kept the actual level of our GNP significantly below its full employment potential every year since 1955, say the President's economic advisers.

Although expansion brought rising levels of economic welfare to most Americans during the past 3 years, it was marred by continuing excessive unemployment. The 16-per cent increase in demand from the first quarter of 1961 to the fourth quarter of 1963 brought about a 4-per cent increase in civilian employment; but even so, in the last quarter of the year 5.6 per cent of the civilian labor force was unemployed. Moreover, lack of job opportunities kept many potential workers out of the labor force, while others held jobs well below their capabilities.

In the first year of recovery substantial progress was made in cutting unemployment. The over-all seasonally adjusted rate dropped from 6.7

* Taken and adapted from *Economic Report of the President together with The Annual Report of the Council of Economic Advisers,* January 1964 (Washington, D.C.: U.S. Government Printing Office, 1964), pp. 36–38.

per cent in 1961 to 5.6 per cent in 1962. Reductions were largest among those workers most affected by the 1960–61 recession; the unemployment rate fell 1.5 percentage points for nonwhites, 2.1 points for semiskilled and unskilled workers, and 1.9 points for manufacturing workers. However, during 1963, no further progress was made. The monthly unemployment rate varied within narrow limits about an average of 5.7 per cent.

Excessive unemployment is the most obvious symptom and one of the worst consequences of a level of demand that falls short of the Nation's potential output. During 1963 the Council of Economic Advisers carefully re-examined its measure of potential GNP. This concept defines "potential" as the output that would be produced if unemployment were at the interim-target level of 4 per cent. For the period to date, the earlier conclusion still holds: the level of constant-dollar GNP needed to maintain the unemployment rate at 4 per cent has been growing at an average rate of about 3½ per cent a year since mid-1955, when the unemployment rate was close to 4 per cent.

As Chart 1 shows, the cumulative effect of actual output growth at a rate less than 3½ percent after mid-1955 had produced a gap of $50 billion (1963 prices) between actual and potential output by the first quarter of 1961. The rapid recovery in the first year of expansion lowered this gap to $30 billion by the first quarter of 1962, but since that time expansion in output has just about kept pace with the growth in potential. As a

Chart 1

GROSS NATIONAL PRODUCT, ACTUAL AND POTENTIAL

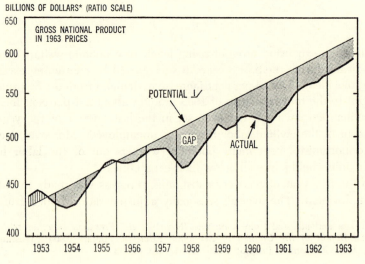

consequence, unemployment has failed to decline to a tolerable level, and a gap close to $30 billion between actual and potential output remained in the fourth quarter of 1963.

Merely avoiding recession or even maintaining a rate of expansion comparable to that of 1962–63 will not close the gap or eliminate excessive unemployment. Only a significant acceleration of expansion can enable the Nation to make full use of its growing labor force and productive potential.

12

Productivity: Definitions and Trends*

Solomon Fabricant

National Bureau of Economic Research and New York University

The concept of productivity — the ratio of output to input — is a useful instrument of economic analysis. It is a tool which can be defined and applied with precision. So utilized, it tells us where we have been and, inferentially, where we are going in matters of economic performance.

Productivity touches us all, as employees, employers or consumers. Facts on productivity are among the fundamental facts of economic and political life. When the Russians stare into the future and imagine Soviet production surpassing that of the United States, when an American President asks that wages and prices be kept "in line," when automation is welcomed by some for its promise or feared by others for its threat, a better understanding of productivity can help us resolve such issues successfully. It is important to know just what productivity is and how fast it is growing; and although researches in this field have by no means provided all the answers, enough is known about productivity to make the knowledge of significant value to all affected by it.

In the broadest possible terms, we can say that productivity is a measure of our power to produce the goods and services we need and want. When we get more units of output from the same resources as employed

* Reprinted from CHALLENGE, The Magazine of Economic Affairs, a publication of the Institute of Economic Affairs, New York University.

in the past, we can say that productivity has increased. Or, when the same output is obtained through the employment of fewer resources, we can again say that productivity has increased. Obviously, attempts to establish how much our power to produce is increasing or decreasing must take into account the relationship between what goes *into* production and what comes *out*.

Why, then, should there be any question about the meaning of productivity? Why, for example, when labor and management meet to discuss wages, do they get into arguments over the meaning as well as the measurement of productivity (among other things!)? Or, when productivity growth in this country is compared with productivity growth abroad — in Russia or in the Common Market countries — are different answers possible?

These differences arise because some people have in mind output in relation to manpower resources alone when they talk about productivity. Other people have in mind output in relation to all resources, including capital as well as labor.

Three Productivity Concepts

In other words, sometimes the question is: How many more units of output — more than before — are we getting from an hour of work done? At other times, the question is: How many more units of output are we getting now from a unit of labor and capital combined? And there are still other variations in the definition of the resources that go into production. It is not strange, therefore, to find variations in the figures cited for productivity change.

There are, in fact, three main concepts of productivity which may be — and are — used. It is important that we carefully delineate these three concepts and understand what each actually spells out for us; for without this understanding we could be like the three blind men who went away with three different impressions of what an elephant is.

In the first concept, output is compared with the simple sum of all the man-hours of labor employed in production. Very often we find this concept expressed as output per man-hour. This seems simple enough, but its meaning is not at all simple, as we shall see.

In the second concept of productivity, output is compared with the "weighted" sum of man-hours employed. This represents a refinement of the first concept, for the word "weighted" means that a highly paid man-hour of work counts for proportionately more than a lower wage man-hour. In this way, some account is taken of differences in skill, education, length of experience and other factors determining the quality of labor. Thus, also, some account is taken of the intangible capital invested to improve the quality of labor.

In the third concept of productivity, output is compared with all the resources employed in production, each appropriately weighted. These include not only manpower, and the intangible capital invested in manpower, but also plant, equipment and other forms of tangible capital without which today's production process would be quite impossible.

Each of the concepts contributes to a better understanding of our power to produce. But they are not interchangeable. They tell us different things about the power to produce. The concepts must therefore be sharply distinguished, and this requires that they be tagged with different labels.

When we compare output with man-hours, it would be correct to call the relationship "labor productivity." But if people are not careful, such a comparison will occasionally be read to mean that labor is wholly responsible for productivity and for increases in it, which is not the case. To avoid misunderstandings of this type, and to help distinguish among the three concepts, it is better to use more explicit labels, even at the cost of some clumsiness. We can speak of:

(1) Output per man-hour, meaning the ratio of output to unweighted man-hours;

(2) Output per unit of labor, meaning the ratio of output to weighted man-hours;

(3) Output per unit of labor and capital, meaning the ratio of output to both weighted man-hours and tangible capital.

It is interesting that as we go from concept No. 1 to concept No. 3, we pass through increasing degrees of sophistication in our measurements. Output per man-hour is simpler to calculate than output per unit of labor, and the latter is simpler to calculate than output per unit of labor and capital. It is even more interesting that as we go from No. 1 to No. 3, we pass through *decreasing* degrees of complexity in the content or meaning of the concepts. The meaning of output per man-hour — what it tells us — is more, not less, complex than the meaning of output per unit of labor. And the meaning of output per unit of labor is more, not less, complex than the meaning of output per unit of labor and capital. To demonstrate this, let us look at the three concepts again, but this time in reverse order.

Change in output per unit of labor and capital combined (concept No. 3) tells us whether efficiency in the conversion into output of labor and capital — total resources — is rising or falling. Rises or falls in efficiency result from changes in technology, economic organization, management skills and the host of other determinants of efficiency. These changes in efficiency in the use of resources cannot be determined by comparing change in output with change in labor alone, or capital alone. For example, output per unit of plant and equipment may fall, yet total efficiency will rise if savings from labor's services per unit of product exceed the increase in the services of capital per unit of product. Similarly, a rise in output per man-hour will overstate the increase in efficiency, if some of the savings in man-hours result from investment in capital — that is, from substitution of labor by capital.

Change in output per unit of labor (concept No. 2) reflects the combined effect of change in *two* things. One is change in efficiency in the sense just mentioned, as measured by output per unit of total input — labor and capital combined. The other is change in intangible capital, in the form of labor quality, per man-hour.

Change in output per man-hour (concept No. 1) reflects the combined effect of change in *three* things: in efficiency, in labor quality per man-hour and in tangible capital per man-hour. Output per man-hour will rise if efficiency rises, even if tangible and intangible capital per man-hour remains unchanged. Output per man hour will also rise if tangible or intangible capital per man-hour rises, even if efficiency remains unchanged. Consequently, output per man-hour will reflect the net balance among the three changes possible (each given its proper weight).

In the normal course of economic development, output per man-hour rises because all three—efficiency, labor quality and capital per man-hour — go up. Output per man-hour, therefore, usually shows a greater rise than output per unit of labor or output per unit of labor and capital combined. And output per unit of labor usually shows a greater rise than output per unit of labor and capital.

Trends in Productivity

We may now turn to the figures to see what the trend of productivity has been in the United States. *The* trend, as we have learned, is really a *set* of trends in productivity, defined in a variety of meaningful ways. Each is worth looking at, for each presents some significant aspect of our country's economic growth.

What does the record show on the long-term rate of increase in national productivity? Over the past three-quarters of a century — the period which has been examined most closely and for which presently available statistics are most adequate — the rate of increase in productivity has been as follows:

Output in relation to total resources, including not only man-hours of work, but also the work done by capital invested in education and training and that done by tangible capital — our index of output per unit of labor and capital (concept No. 3) — grew 1.5 to 1.7 per cent per annum.[1]

These figures tell us that efficiency in the use of the country's labor and

---

[1] The lower figure relates to the entire economy, which is what we want, but it includes a rather rough and, therefore uncertain estimate for government. The higher figure is more reliable, but it is for the private economy only, which is a very large part but not the whole of the national economy.

tangible and intangible capital resources has been greatly improved over the years.

Comparing output not with total resources but simply with labor input, in which allowance is made for increase both in man-hours and in quality of labor per man-hour — our output per unit of labor (concept No. 2) — yields a measure of productivity that grew at the rate of 1.8 to two per cent per annum. That is, output per unit of labor has risen, first, because of the greatly improved efficiency in the use of the country's labor and tangible and intangible capital resources — a rise in efficiency which, we have just seen, was at the average annual rate of 1.5 to 1.7 per cent. Output per unit of labor has risen, second, because of heavy investment in business and farm plant and equipment, in public improvements and in other tangible capital goods, which caused the volume of tangible capital per unit of labor to increase substantially. The rise in efficiency, plus the rise in tangible capital, each properly weighted, gives the annual rise of 1.8 to two per cent in output per unit of labor.

Output in relation to man-hours of labor, lumped together without regard to grade or quality — our index of output per man-hour (concept No. 1) — grew at an average rate of 2.2 to 2.4 per cent per annum. That is, output per man-hour has risen, first, because of increase in economic efficiency; second, because of investment in tangible capital; and third, because of investment in education and training and other improvements in the quality of our labor supply. The figures for the last item are very rough and probably understate the rate of improvement. But accepting them as they are, the annual rise in efficiency, plus the annual rise in tangible capital per unit of labor, plus the annual rise in average labor quality, each with appropriate weights, gives the annual rise of 2.2 to 2.4 per cent in output per man-hour. It is important to understand that the rise in this most widely used measure of productivity reflects all three developments — improved efficiency, investment in tangible capital and investment in labor quality.

A figure of 2.2 to 2.4 per cent may seem small, but it is not. Such an annual rate means an increase of about 25 per cent in a decade, and a doubling in 30 years. Few countries have long-term records that look as good as this. Indeed, many countries would be very happy to have their *current* level of output per man-hour equal to what we *add* in an average decade. Over the larger part of the globe output per man-hour is less than 25 per cent of the U.S. level.

Uneven Progress

The long-term rates we have been looking at are averages which balance out any year-to-year fluctuations there may be in the rate of productivity increase. In fact, productivity did grow at an uneven rate.

The rate of growth of productivity has undergone a number of shifts, of which one of the most interesting is the distinct change in trend that appeared sometime after World War I. Productivity has increased, on the average, more rapidly after World War I than before. This change in trend is visible not only in the indexes for the private domestic economy, but it can be found also in the figures for the whole economy, including government. All available statistics make it clear that the rate of growth in productivity witnessed by the present generation has been substantially higher than the rate experienced in the quarter-century before World War I.

There have been cyclical fluctuations in productivity also — that is, both before and after World War I, productivity fluctuated with the state of business. Year-to-year rises in productivity have been greater than the long-term rate when business was generally expanding and less (often falling) when business was generally contracting.

Beyond the cyclical fluctuations, there are other changes that show up when one looks at the year-to-year statistics. These include occasional spurts and slowdowns in productivity growth that extend over a period of years.

AVERAGE RATES OF INCREASE IN PRODUCTIVITY, 1889-1960
PRIVATE DOMESTIC ECONOMY

	AVERAGE ANNUAL PERCENTAGE RATE OF CHANGE		
	1889-1960	1889-1919	1919-1960
OUTPUT PER MAN-HOUR	2.4	2.0	2.6
OUTPUT PER UNIT OF LABOR	2.0	1.6	2.3
OUTPUT PER UNIT OF LABOR & CAPITAL	1.7	1.3	2.1

SOURCE: *National Bureau of Economic Research, Inc.*

Of particular interest is the trend over the 15-year period since World War II. Output per man-hour rose after the war at an average rate that was distinctly high, though not unprecedentedly so, for a period of 15 years. The postwar rate of increase, over three per cent per year, was much higher than the rate over the full 75-year period, and significantly higher than the rate over the period between 1919 and 1960. Unusually rapid increase in tangible capital per man-hour helps to explain this spurt in output per man-hour.

But while it has been rapid by our historical standards, the postwar rate of increase in output per man-hour seems to have been substantially exceeded by corresponding rates in some Western European countries, in Russia and in Japan. Their high rates probably reflect recovery from the disastrously low levels of the war and immediate postwar periods, and high rates of investment in plant and equipment — higher even than in this country. But there are undoubtedly other factors, also, which economists still must ferret out.

Year-to-year changes in productivity were appreciably influenced not only in business cycles but also by random factors. Some of these irregular changes reflect the inadequacies of the figures themselves. Productivity change is measured by the ratio of two indexes, output and input, each subject to error; and even slight errors in these will sometimes combine to produce considerable error in the ratio, just as they will sometimes cancel out one another. We cannot be sure whether the change between any particular pair of years is the result simply of statistical error. On the other hand, that the errors are not overwhelming is suggested by the fairly systematic business cycle behavior that we have noticed. We know, also, that some of the irregularities reflect not statistical error, but the impact of weather, strikes and the other real random factors to which life is subject.

Because the rate of increase in productivity has been far from uniform, the user of productivity figures must know the period to which they relate. Rates of productivity increase derived from one period will differ, sometimes considerably, from those derived from a longer, or shorter, or altogether different period. The same caution may be noted with regard to extrapolations of past trends into the future. These, the record suggests, will always be rather risky.

Thus far the rate of growth in the entire economy's productivity is the prime fact with which we have been concerned. The facts on productivity in individual industries also deserve attention, however, because they help us to understand the process by which national productivity has been raised.

A General Phenomenon

These additional facts show that rise in productivity has been a general industrial phenomenon. Although there was great variation among them in the average rate of rise, every one of the individual industries included in the chart experienced an upward trend in output per man-hour, and this was just as universally true of output per unit of labor and capital. (Information on output per unit of labor is lacking for individual industries.)

Productivity statistics relate to a limited number of industries, largely from the commodity-producing sectors of the economy. Lack of statistics prevents giving similar information for the service industries, construction, trade and government, and even some individual manufacturing, mining and utility industries. However, it is very likely that productivity has generally increased also in these.

What we know of technological developments and the other immediate causes of productivity change in the service industries, for example, supports the impression of a general rise. We know, too, that the factors that make for increasing efficiency in the use of resources are felt everywhere in the economy. Virtually all industries use mechanical power and have reaped some advantages from broadened national markets. No industry has been free of the drives that improve efficiency. Further, connections between industries provide channels along which new, improved or lower cost materials, fuel, power, services and equipment, as well as ideas, flow to improve efficiency.

This leads us to an important conclusion about the sources of an industry's productivity gain. It is true that what happens in an industry is influenced by the diligence, enterprise and ability of its workers, management and investors. But it is also true that what happens in an industry is influenced also by the quality and quantity of what the industry obtains from other industries, domestic and foreign.

Before we leave the indexes for individual industries, another comment is desirable. These indexes are often less reliable than the indexes for the economy at large. It should be recalled, also, that for many individual industries productivity indexes are entirely lacking, a lack that makes itself felt when policies are proposed that require such individual indexes.

Finally, a word of caution is needed even about the national indexes. These, like all estimates, are surrounded by margins of error. There is reason to believe that, for general historical and analytical purposes, the indexes are not too wide of the mark. But this is not to say that they are also good enough to be used in directing the course of wages and prices, as some people have proposed.

The main facts we have learned may be summarized as follows:

1. National efficiency, as measured by output per unit of labor and capital, has increased over the past three-quarters of a century at an average annual rate of 1.5 to 1.7 per cent.

2. Output per man-hour has grown 2.2 to 2.4 per cent per year — even more rapidly than output per unit of labor and capital combined. This is so because output per man-hour reflects not only the increase in efficiency but, in addition, the increase in tangible and intangible capital per man-hour, which also has been substantial.

3. Rise in productivity has been experienced by virtually every industry, but the rate of rise has varied greatly among industries.

4. The trend of national productivity, whether measured by output per unit of labor and capital, output per unit of labor or output per man-hour,

has been significantly steeper since World War I than in prior decades.

5. During the 15-year period after World War II, output per man-hour has risen at an exceptionally high average annual rate, mainly because tangible capital per man-hour also has risen more rapidly than in most earlier periods.

How these facts on productivity change are related to the changes that have occurred in wages and in the prices of individual commodities, and the bearing of these facts on how wages and prices should change — these questions belong in other chapters of the story of productivity in the United States.

• *13*

The Triple Revolution*

THE AD HOC COMMITTEE ON THE TRIPLE REVOLUTION
Center for the Study of Democratic Institutions

In the following policy statement, an Ad Hoc Committee of the Center for the Study of Democratic Institutions considers the implications of "cybernation" — that alleged revolutionary "combination of the computer and the automated self-regulating machine" — and makes the provocative recommendation that we sever the link between income and jobs by a governmental guarantee of "adequate income" to all "as a matter of right." For a more orthodox view, consult Selection 14.

1. *The Cybernation Revolution:* A new era of production has begun. Its principles of organization are as different from those of the industrial era as those of the industrial era were different from the agricultural. The cybernation revolution has been brought about by the combination of the computer and the automated self-regulating machine. This results in a system of almost unlimited productive capacity which requires progressively less human labor. Cybernation is already reorganizing the economic and social system to meet its own needs.

2. *The Weaponry Revolution:* New forms of weaponry have been developed which cannot win wars but which can obliterate civilization. We are recognizing only now that the great weapons have eliminated

* Taken and adapted from "The Triple Revolution," (Washington, D.C.: The Ad Hoc Committee on the Triple Revolution, March 1964), pp. 1–22.

war as a method for resolving international conflicts. The ever-present threat of total destruction is tempered by the knowledge of the final futility of war. The need of a "warless world" is generally recognized, though achieving it will be a long and frustrating process.

3. *The Human Rights Revolution:* A universal demand for full human rights is now clearly evident. It continues to be demonstrated in the civil rights movement within the United States. But this is only the local manifestation of a world-wide movement toward the establishment of social and political regimes in which every individual will feel valued and none will feel rejected on account of his race.

We are particularly concerned in this statement with the first of these revolutionary phenomena. This is not because we underestimate the significance of the other two. On the contrary, we affirm that it is the simultaneous occurrence and interaction of all three developments which make evident the necessity for radical alterations in attitude and policy.

Interaction of the Three Revolutions

The Negro claims, as a matter of simple justice, his full share in America's economic and social life. He sees adequate employment opportunities as a chief means of attaining this goal: the March on Washington demanded freedom *and* jobs. The Negro's claim to a job is not being met. Negroes are the hardest-hit of the many groups being exiled from the economy by cybernation. Negro unemployment rates cannot be expected to drop substantially. Promises of jobs are a cruel and dangerous hoax on hundreds of thousands of Negroes and whites alike who are especially vulnerable to cybernation because of age or inadequate education.

The demand of the civil rights movement cannot be fulfilled within the present context of society. The Negro is trying to enter a social community and a tradition of work-and-income which are in the process of vanishing even for the hitherto privileged white worker. Jobs are disappearing under the impact of highly efficient, progressively less costly machines.

The United States operates on the thesis, set out in the Employment Act of 1946, that every person will be able to obtain a job if he wishes to do so and that this job will provide him with resources adequate to live and maintain a family decently. Thus job-holding is the general mechanism through which economic resources are distributed. Those without work have access only to a minimal income, hardly sufficient to provide the necessities of life, and enabling those receiving it to function as only "minimum consumers." As a result, the goods and services which are needed by these crippled consumers, and which they would buy if they could, are not produced. This in turn deprives other workers of jobs, thus reducing their incomes and consumption.

Present excessive levels of unemployment would be multiplied several times if military and space expenditures did not continue to absorb 10% of the Gross National Product (*i.e.*, the total goods and services produced). Some 6–8 million people are employed as a direct result of purchases for space and military activities. At least an equal number hold their jobs as an indirect result of military or space expenditures. In recent years, the military and space budgets have absorbed a rising proportion of national production and formed a strong support for the economy.

However, these expenditures are coming in for more and more criticism, at least partially in recognition of the fact that nuclear weapons have eliminated war as an acceptable method for resolving international conflicts.

The Nature of the Cybernation Revolution

Cybernation is manifesting the characteristics of a revolution in production. These include the development of radically different techniques and the subsequent appearance of novel principles of the organization of production; a basic reordering of man's relationship to his environment; and a dramatic increase in total available and potential energy.

The fundamental problem posed by the cybernation revolution in the United States is that it invalidates the general mechanism so far employed to undergird people's rights as consumers. Up to this time economic resources have been distributed on the basis of contributions to production, with machines and men competing for employment on somewhat equal terms. In the developing cybernated system, potentially unlimited output can be achieved by systems of machines which will require little cooperation from human beings. As machines take over production from men, they absorb an increasing proportion of resources while the men who are displaced become dependent on minimal and unrelated government measures — unemployment insurance, social security, welfare payments. These measures are less and less able to disguise a historic paradox: that a growing proportion of the population is subsisting on minimal incomes, often below the poverty line, at a time when sufficient productive potential is available to supply the needs of everyone in the United States.

The industrial system does not possess any adequate mechanisms to permit these potentials to become realities. The industrial system was designed to produce an ever-increasing quantity of goods as efficiently as possible, and it was assumed that the distribution of the power to purchase these goods would occur almost automatically. The continuance of the income-through-jobs link as the only major mechanism for distributing effective demand — for granting the right to consume — now acts as the main brake on the almost unlimited capacity of a cybernated productive system.

An adequate distribution of the potential abundance of goods and services will be achieved only when it is understood that the major economic problem is not how to increase production but how to distribute the abundance that is the great potential of cybernation. There is an urgent need for a fundamental change in the mechanisms employed to insure consumer rights.

The Cybernation Revolution — Facts and Figures

No responsible observer would attempt to describe the exact pace or the full sweep of a phenomenon that is developing with the speed of cybernation. Some aspects of this revolution, however, are already clear: (1) the rate of productivity increase has risen with the onset of cybernation; (2) an industrial economic system postulated on scarcity has been unable to distribute the abundant goods and services produced by a cybernated system or potential in it; (3) surplus capacity and unemployment have thus co-existed at excessive levels over the last six years; (4) the underlying cause of excessive unemployment is the fact that the capability of machines is rising more rapidly than the capacity of many human beings to keep pace; (5) a permanent impoverished and jobless class is established in the midst of potential abundance.

Evidence for these statements follows:

1. The increased efficiency for machine systems is shown in the more rapid increase in productivity per man hour since 1960, a year that marks the first visible upsurge of the cybernation revolution. In 1961, 1962 and 1963, productivity per man-hour rose at an average pace above 3.5% — a rate well above both the historical average and the post-war rate.

Companies are finding cybernation more and more attractive. Even at the present early stage of cybernation, costs have already been lowered to a point where the price of a durable machine may be as little as one-third of the current annual wage-cost of the worker it replaces. A more rapid rise in the rate of productivity increase per man-hour can be expected from now on.

2. In recent years it has proved impossible to increase demand fast enough to bring about the full use of either men or plant capacities. The task of developing sufficient additional demand promises to become more difficult each year. A $30 billion annual increase in Gross National Product is now required to prevent unemployment rates from rising. An

additional $40–60 billion increase would be required to bring unemployment rates down to an acceptable level.

3. The official rate of unemployment has remained at or above 5.5% during the Sixties. The unemployment rate for teenagers has been rising steadily and now stands around 15%. The unemployment rate for Negro teenagers stands at about 30%. The unemployment rate for teenagers in minority ghettoes sometimes exceeds 50%. Unemployment rates for Negroes are regularly more than twice those for whites, whatever their occupation, educational level, age or sex. The unemployment position for other racial minorities is similarly unfavorable. Unemployment rates in depressed areas often exceed 50%.

These official figures seriously underestimate the true extent of unemployment. The statistics take no notice of under employment or featherbedding. Besides the 5.5% of the labor force who are officially designated as unemployed, nearly 4% of the labor force sought full-time work in 1962 but could find only part-time jobs. In addition, methods of calculating unemployment rates — a person is counted as unemployed only if he has actively sought a job recently — ignore the fact that many men and women who would like to find jobs have not looked for them because they know there are no employment opportunities. Underestimates for this reason are pervasive among groups whose unemployment rates are high — the young, the old, and racial minorities. Many people in the depressed agricultural, mining and industrial areas, who by official definition hold jobs but who are actually grossly underemployed, would move if there were prospects of finding work elsewhere. It is reasonable to estimate that over 8 million people are not working who would like to have jobs today as compared with the 4 million shown in the official statistics.

Even more serious is the fact that the number of people who have voluntarily removed themselves from the labor force is not constant but increases continuously. These people have decided to stop looking for employment and seem to have accepted the fact that they will never hold jobs again. This decision is largely irreversible, in economic and also in social and psychological terms. The older worker calls himself "retired"; he cannot accept work without affecting his social security status. The worker in his prime years is forced onto relief: in most states the requirements for becoming a relief recipient bring about such fundamental alterations in an individual's situation that a reversal of the process is always difficult and often totally infeasible. Teenagers, especially "drop-outs" and Negroes, are coming to realize that there is no place for them in the labor force but at the same time they are given no realistic alternative. These people and their dependents make up a large part of the "poverty" sector of the American population.

4. An efficiently functioning industrial system is assumed to provide

the great majority of new jobs through the expansion of the private enterprise sector. But well over half of the new jobs created during the period 1957–1962 were in the public sector — predominantly in teaching. Job creation in the private sector has now almost entirely ceased except in services; of the 4,300,000 jobs created in this period, only about 200,000 were provided by private industry through its own efforts. Many authorities anticipate that the application of cybernation to certain service industries, which is only just beginning, will be particularly effective. If this is the case, no significant job creation will take place in the private sector in coming years. Cybernation raises the level of the skills of the machine. Secretary of Labor Wirtz has recently stated that the machines being produced today have, on the average, skills equivalent to a high school diploma. If a human being is to compete with such machines, therefore, he must at least possess a high school diploma. The Department of Labor estimates, however, that on the basis of present trends as many as 30% of all students will be high school drop-outs in this decade.

5. A permanently depressed class is developing in the United States. Some 38,000,000 Americans, almost one-fifth of the nation, still live in poverty. The percentage of total income received by the poorest 20% of the population was 4.9% in 1944 and 4.7% in 1963.

Proposal for Action

We believe that the industrial productive system is no longer viable. We assert that the only way to turn technological change to the benefit of the individual and the service of the general welfare is to accept the process and to utilize it rationally and humanely. The new science of political economy will be built on the encouragement and planned expansion of cybernation.

As a first step, it is essential to recognize that the traditional link between jobs and incomes is being broken. The economy of abundance can sustain all citizens in comfort and economic security whether or not they engage in what is commonly reckoned as work. Wealth produced by machines rather than by men is still wealth. We urge, therefore, that society, through its appropriate legal and governmental institutions, undertake an unqualified commitment to provide every individual and every family with an adequate income as a matter of right.

The unqualified right to an income would take the place of the patchwork of welfare measures — from unemployment insurance to relief — designed to ensure that no citizen or resident of the United States actually starves. We believe that many creative activities and interests commonly thought of as non-economic will absorb the time and the commitment of many of those no longer needed to produce goods and services. Principal among these are activities such as teaching and learning that relate people to people rather than people to things. Education has never been primarily conducted for profit in our society; it represents the first and most obvious activity inviting the expansion of the public sector to meet the needs of this period of transition.

The Transition

We recognize that the drastic alterations in circumstances and in our way of life ushered in by cybernation and the economy of abundance will not be completed overnight.

We must develop programs for a transition designed to give hope to the dispossessed and those cast out by the economic system, and to provide a basis for the rallying of people to bring about those changes in political and social institutions which are essential to the age of technology. The program here suggested is not intended to be inclusive but rather to indicate its necessary scope. We propose:

(1) A massive program to build up our educational system, designed especially with the needs of the chronically undereducated in mind. (2) Massive public works. The need is to develop and put into effect programs of public works to construct dams, reservoirs, ports, water and air pollution facilities, community recreation facilities. (3) A massive program of low-cost housing, to be built both publicly and privately, and aimed at a rate of 700,000–1,000,000 units a year. (4) Development and financing of rapid transit systems, urban and interurban; and other programs to cope with the spreading problems of the great metropolitan centers. (5) A public power system built on the abundance of coal in distressed areas, designed for low-cost power to heavy industrial and residential sections. (6) Rehabilitation of obsolete military bases for community or educational use. (7) A major revision of our tax structure aimed at redistributing income as well as apportioning the costs of the transition period equitably. To this end an expansion of the use of excess profits tax would be important. Subsidies and tax credit plans are required to ease the human suffering involved in the transition of many industries from manpower to machinepower. (8) The use of the licensing power of government to regulate the speed and direction of cybernation to minimize hardship; and the use of minimum wage power as well as taxing powers to provide the incentives for moving as rapidly as possible toward the goals indicated by this paper.

14

Automation: *Economic Revolution or Variation on an Old Theme?**

ROBERT LEKACHMAN
Barnard College

Does automation constitute a revolutionary break with the past, a novel development creating unprecedented problems and requiring radically new solutions? Or, is it merely a variation on the old theme of the substitution of machinery for manual labor? Historical examples can be selected to illustrate the latter hypothesis. Yet, a strong case can also be made for the hypothesis that recent technological innovations are in some ways significantly different from those of the past and have caused exceptionally difficult problems of adjustment. What is your opinion on these issues after having read this and the preceding selection?

New or Old? Historical Examples

Is the United States being transformed by an unprecedented technological revolution? Is automation making old skills and traditional aptitudes obsolete? Is education lagging far behind new economic necessities? Is the prevailing division of labor between men and machines outmoded by the human capabilities of computers and control devices?

* Reprinted from CHALLENGE, The Magazine of Economic Affairs, a publication of the Institute of Economic Affairs, New York University.

It is extraordinarily difficult to answer questions of this sort. A large segment of the new technology appears qualitatively different from that of the past. And yet, we may be witnessing only a further evolution in the historical substitution of machines for manual labor. Rapid technical change first made its appearance in England during the second half of the 18th century. In the succeeding century, the factory system spread to the United States, France and Germany.

Three historical examples will suffice to show that in the last two centuries workers often had to adjust their lives and marketable skills to new realities of technological progress. Consider, first, England in 1810. Weavers were smashing textile machines, burning factories and assaulting managers in a desperate attempt to prevent the extinction of their trade. In 1810 about 100,000 men, women and children operated power looms in textile mills. But there were still 200,000 highly skilled and well-paid hand loom weavers outside of the factory system. By 1840 the ratio was reversed: 262,000 workers attended power looms while 123,000 hand loom weavers eked out an increasingly meager livelihood. By 1860 factories employed 427,000 workers while the ranks of the hand loom weavers had shrunk to 10,000. Thus in one man's lifetime a traditional skill had all but vanished.

Half a century later, in the United States, Ottmar Mergenthaler's linotype machine rendered obsolete the skills of men who set type by hand. Mergenthaler's linotypes came into use in the middle 1890s. Within 10 years the new machines — which set type anywhere from three and a half to 10 times as rapidly as a skilled hand compositor — were adopted in printing shops all over the nation.

The typesetters, however, were more fortunate than the hand loom weavers. The powerful International Typographical Union was able to secure some control over the implementation of the process. In this way, the typesetters were given the opportunity of learning to operate the new machines at union wage rates. Moreover, the enormous expansion of printing which the linotype encouraged actually enlarged total employment.

Finally, the case of the A. O. Smith Co. shows that even the automated factory is not a complete novelty. In the early 1920s the company drastically altered the manufacture of automobile frames. So dramatic was the change that by 1930 Smith was able to dispense with 99 per cent of its work force and at the same time increase its output.

Productivity and Employment

In short, the industrialization of Western nations during the last two centuries has been fueled by numerous technological improvements which have affected the pattern of employment. Broadly speaking, each year it is possible to equal the previous year's output with fewer workers. Or, when aggregate demand expands, it is possible to increase gross output with the same labor force.

Solomon Fabricant, Director of Research at the National Bureau of Economic Research, has estimated that in the U.S. between 1889 and 1953 output per man-hour increased at an average annual rate of 2.3 per cent. This may not seem a large increase, but it enabled the American economy to produce in 1961 as many goods as in 1960 with *1.5 million fewer workers.* Whether the workers who are displaced find other jobs depends upon the buoyancy of demand, the adaptability of workers and employers, and the policies of the industries where technical change occurs.

In recent years the pace of productivity improvement has not been startling enough to constitute a break with the past. Although between 1940 and 1955 the rate of increase in terms of per-man output did exceed the historical trend, the rate of change since then has been much less rapid. In fact, the most startling improvements in efficiency have come on the farm rather than in the factory or the office. If we take output per man-hour in the years 1957–59 as equaling 100, then agricultural output in 1947 was only 50.2. By 1962 it had soared to 121.8. Thus it is not surprising that the Department of Labor currently projects a 17 per cent decline in the number of farmers and farm workers between 1960 and 1970.

The record of improvement in manufacturing is much less striking. Starting from the same 1957–59 base of 100, manufacturing output per man-hour was 74.8 in 1947 and 114.9 in 1962.

Automation seems to be a natural extension of the historical economic progress of an industrial society. If the workers displaced by machines were fortunate or enterprising, they learned new skills or took jobs which required no special training. In printing and automobile manufacturing, as elsewhere, technical innovation, while eliminating some jobs, permitted over-all expansion, and workers found other jobs in the same industries.

Sometimes the prosperity of the economy was such that the victims of specific technical changes were easily absorbed. The drastic reduction in the workweek and the increased power of trade unions also helped to cushion the hardships of individual adjustment. In our own century the dire fate of the hand loom weavers has not been repeated.

New Problems

The technological changes of today are in some ways similar to and in other ways different from those of the past. As Ben B. Seligman, Director of Education and Research, Retail Clerks International Assn., pointed out, the combination of computers and machines in factories can convert manufacturing into a series of automated processes requiring no human intervention.

Standards can be uniform. Computers can correct errors. Consequently, chemicals, steel, drugs and television sets can be produced almost anywhere with a limited employment of labor and extremely little executive supervision. It may or may not be accurate to say that the processes themselves constitute a revolutionary departure from existing manufacturing procedures. But it is clear that the innovations will have both a qualitative and a quantitative impact on the labor force.

For instance, the role of junior and middle management may be diminished because their decisions can better be made by properly programed computers. At the same time it may become necessary to expand the ranks of top management to control larger and more complex organizations.

Professors of economics like to explain to their classes that the limited capacity of even the most efficient executives to coordinate the affairs of a giant enterprise constitutes one of the major disadvantages of size. No human being can absorb unlimited amounts of information, organize it, weigh the important variables and then make the proper decisions quickly. Smaller, more flexible organizations will move more rapidly, perceive and grasp market opportunities faster, and shift more speedily to more profitable activities.

Computers may well increase the "efficient" size of an organization. Electronic machines that can absorb, organize and analyze huge masses of data in a short span of time promise to enhance tremendously the executive's command over his business environment.

Technological innovation is partly responsible for the vast reshuffling of skills which is now under way. It is evident that unskilled and semiskilled workers will find it increasingly difficult to secure employment in the coming years. The Department of Labor predicts that in the 1960s there will be no net increase in the demand for unskilled workers. Job opportunities for semiskilled employees may expand 18 per cent by 1970, compared to a 41 per cent rise in demand for professional and technical workers. In the future an increasingly large percentage of workers may well be doing interesting work which requires judgment, knowledge, training and skill.

It is no less certain, however, that the comparatively moderate technical innovations of recent years have caused exceptional social and educational difficulties and that an acceleration of the rate of change will enlarge the problems. Those most affected by technical change are not skilled workers in unionized industries. Rather, the victims are untrained 17- or 18-year-old youths who are seeking employment for the first time.

They have no seniority and their chances of finding unskilled jobs are diminishing. The unemployment rate among young people is twice the national average.

Unskilled work has been the traditional refuge of minority groups. Negroes and Puerto Ricans whose opportunities have been circumscribed by prejudice and a lack of education suffer most when opportunities for unskilled workers diminish significantly. Unemployment among young Negroes probably exceeds 20 per cent, and no foreseeable development is likely to diminish this dangerously high level of idleness.

It is precisely at this point that historical analogies are dangerous. In 19th-century England a vast shift from domestic industry to manufacturing in factories enhanced Britain's position in the world. Yet unemployment was not absent during this period. Depression in the post-Napoleonic years and in the 1840s brought many workers to the brink of starvation.

But the long-run trend was upward. The English economy grew, and displaced workers usually found new niches. At the very worst, skilled workers could find unskilled factory work. Most hand-loom weavers could find employment operating the hated power looms.

In 20th-century America readjustment is more complex. To begin with, young people entering the labor force must possess greater skills than ever before. Skilled workers who are thrown out of work find it harder to obtain employment requiring less experience for the simple reason that such jobs are fewer. The problem is intensified by our still unresolved dilemma. Our own vast shift from a production-oriented economy to a service-oriented economy is occurring during a period of very slow economic growth.

Intensive advertising (itself one of the less pleasant concomitants of wealth) intimates that Americans must be coaxed, frightened or bulldozed into spending much of their income. Eager consumers are not waiting to snatch up factory products.

Promise and Policy

Technology, whether or not we call it automation, is a promise as well as a problem. At last every American's dream of abundance can be realized by the proper utilization of known technology. But it is precisely because America is closer to abundance than ever before that the next steps are so difficult.

The needs of a humane social order are obvious. It requires numerous teachers, nurses, recreational leaders, social workers, psychiatrists, doctors and an extraordinarily wide selection of supporting workers like nurses' aides, laboratory technicians, teaching assistants and youth workers.

Our educational system is ill-adapted to train the vast numbers of specialists our society urgently needs. Nor are our national attitudes yet sufficiently altered to set a proper value on those who pursue such occupations. Yet a beginning, though it may be inadequate, has been made at several levels. Junior and community colleges are offering training for some of the service occupations which are most valuable to a society that has practically reached the limit of mass consumption. Private companies like Kaiser and Armour have been experimenting with job retraining.

The future course of our society depends to a considerable extent on federal action which is still in an experimental stage. The 87th Congress authorized various retraining programs in the Trade Expansion Act, the Area Redevelopment Act and the Manpower Retraining Act. This year the President has proposed a program of selective assistance to education, a youth opportunities bill, a domestic peace corps and a comprehensive health program.

The latter program includes provisions for the expansion of the supply of doctors and nurses, for more effective use of existing medical manpower, the improvement and modernization of existing health facilities, more comprehensive care for older patients and the protection of people from contaminated food, air and water as well as from hazardous drugs and cosmetics.

A really successful attempt to deal with the consequence of technological change seems to depend on vastly improved schools which would provide students with the knowledge and skills our time requires.

The pace of technological change during the last generation does not warrant either excessive optimism nor gloomy pessimism. Productivity gains have not transcended normal historical limits. True, computers and factory control devices have contributed to the nagging problems of unemployment. Certainly automation has caused localized crises. Yet unemployment itself seems to derive from multiple causes, among them the shift from manufacturing to the service industries, minority problems of discrimination and unequal educational opportunities, an oppressive tax system, the expansion of the labor force and the termination of our postwar boom.

Machines capable of learning from their environment have been constructed. They are able to add to their memories and refine their judgments entirely without human intervention. They may eliminate large numbers of manual workers and many individuals in the lower echelons of management. They offer the promise of a full human life which makes full use of man's intellect, generosity and esthetic sensibilities rather than of his muscles and patience.

In the absence of collective prudence, technology can carry with it the threat of massive unemployment and the frustration of the young, and may impede the natural aspirations of groups which have not yet been accorded the full privileges of citizenship. Now, as in the past, machines are impartial. Partiality is a human characteristic.

15

Four Postwar Cycles in the United States*

ALVIN H. HANSEN
Emeritus, Harvard University

The postwar American economy has not experienced a major
*business cycle, associated with large-scale swings in fixed plant
and equipment investment so characteristic of the period from
the Civil War to World War II. Yet, cyclical fluctuations in output, income, and employment, although tempered in length and
severity, are "still with us," attests Alvin H. Hansen, in the following selection. And with them, since 1957, has come a new
problem of "semistagnation," that is, "anemic" recoveries from
cyclical recessions which have failed to push the actual level of
output to its full potential or to reduce unemployment to an
acceptable level.*

The Cycle New and Old

Following the First World War, several leading economists voiced the
belief that the business cycle had vanished for good. And after the
Second World War some expressed the view that continued and sustained
prosperity was here to stay. But now, however, experience has demon-

* Reprinted from *The Postwar American Economy: Performances and Problems* by
Alvin H. Hansen. By permission of W. W. Norton & Company, Inc. Copyright ©
1964 by W. W. Norton & Company, Inc.

strated beyond doubt that the cycle of production, income, and employment is still with us.

The cycle is indeed in some ways a new kind of phenomenon. The
basic interactions are the same, yet something new has obviously been
built into the economic structure. The "rocking chair" doesn't rock in
quite the old familiar way.

Some things are much the same. For one thing, investment in inventory
stocks continues to play a very important role. Fluctuations in investment in fixed capital (new construction and producers' equipment) have
toned down. In consequence, we have had no truly *major* cycle in the
postwar period. But a new actor in the cycle drama, or at least one that
has by now assumed a leading role, is the federal budget.

War and Postwar Developments

The European war boosted United States exports, and soon the nation
itself became involved. Before the Second World War was over, nearly
half our productive resources had been drawn into the struggle. Unemployment vanished. The country came out of the war rich in monetary
assets and monetary savings and desperately short of consumers' durables, houses, business plant and equipment. This laid the groundwork
for a vast postwar prosperity which continued (with two short interruptions) until 1957. In the meantime, the Korean war added still more
fuel to the burst of prosperity.

After 1957, progress continued, but at a slower pace. The whole fifteen-
year period 1948–63, however, shows a degree of stability and growth
rarely, if ever, matched at any time in our history. The standard of living
rose steadily. Per capita consumer expenditures, after correcting for price
changes, increased 30 per cent from 1948 to 1963, or 2 per cent a year.
The "social dividend" (private consumption plus government civilian outlays) increased every year, including the recession years. Compared to
the turbulent history of the nineteenth century and the disastrous nine-
teen-thirties, the period 1948–63 must be regarded as one of high stability
and growth. But gradually, high-level prosperity was slipping. The unemployment rate was rising. Recoveries were becoming short-lived. The
cycle was running down.

A broad general picture of economic fluctuations and trends in the last
fifteen years can be obtained from data on gross national product in real
terms. This discloses fluctuations with peaks in 1948, 1953, 1957, 1960 and
troughs in 1949, 1954, 1958, and 1961. A careful inspection will reveal a
sharp upward trend from 1948 to 1956, and a marked slowing down in
this rate of growth from 1956 to 1963. This matter will be discussed in
some detail.

Troughs, Peaks, and Time Spans in Four Cycles

The peaks and troughs of each of the four cycles are as follows:

	Pre-recession Peaks	Troughs	Recovery Peaks
First cycle	November, 1948	October, 1949	July, 1953
Second cycle	July, 1953	August, 1954	July, 1957
Third cycle	July, 1957	April, 1958	May, 1960
Fourth cycle	May, 1960	February, 1961	?

Each cycle is labeled by its recession trough. Thus the first cycle is referred to as the 1949 cycle; the second, as the 1954 cycle; the third, as the 1958 cycle; and the fourth, as the 1961 cycle.

From the table, the time span of each cycle, from its pre-recession peak to the subsequent recovery peak can readily be calculated. The 1949 cycle, from peak to peak, ran for 4 years and 8 months; the 1954 cycle ran exactly 4 years; the 1958 cycle 2 years and 10 months (an abnormally short cycle), whereas the 1961 cycle bids fair to run a more normal length.

The time span of the recession phase was approximately similar for all the four cycles — 11 months, 13 months, 9 months, and 9 months, respectively. The expansion phase, however, varied greatly. The 1949 recovery ran for 45 months; the 1954 recovery, 35 months; the 1958 recovery, only 25 months; and the 1961 recovery, it is hoped, will run a more normal period. Indeed, perhaps for the first time, a strong effort is being made, months in advance, to forestall a recession altogether. Many, perhaps most, professional economists believe that this could be achieved. But Congress is reluctant to act before the recession has actually occurred. Some Congressmen have said they would favor a tax cut *after* a recession is clearly already upon us, but not in advance of a downturn.

Each cycle is characterized by circumstances peculiar to itself. The 1949 cycle was prolonged and buoyed up by the Korean war, and its termination in 1953 was closely associated with the cessation of hostilities. The 1954 cycle, in the recovery phase, was swayed by a burst of business investment and consumer acquisitions of durables (cars, household electrical appliances, and furniture). In part these outlays represented advances in technology; in part, catching up on accumulated shortages. The 1958 cycle was peculiar in that it had two jagged peaks caused by abnormal inventory developments incident to a strike by steelworkers in 1959. The recovery phase of this cycle, moreover, was cut short by a sharp curtailment in federal budget expenditures from $80.3 billion to $76.5 billion. Finally, the incomplete character of the 1958 recovery may have contributed to the mildness of the downturn that followed, beginning in May, 1960.

Relative Severity of the Four Recessions

Among the various criteria of severity, employment and production indexes probably give the clearest answer. We have two over-all measures of production: (a) the index of industrial production and (b) the GNP in real terms (*i.e.*, at constant prices). Both point to the 1958 recession as the most severe. The GNP in real terms declined by $22.1 billion; the index of industrial production fell by 14 per cent. The unemployment rate rose from 3.6 per cent of the labor force to 7.5 per cent (seasonally corrected).

Why was the 1958 recession so severe? The preceding investment spurt was clearly overdone. Investment in producers' plant and equipment rose by 40 per cent from a level which was already high. Consumers' durables jumped nearly 25 per cent in one year, automobiles 37 per cent. These rates were not maintainable. Offsets to the subsequent decline were nowhere in evidence. Accumulated shortages, emerging from the two wars and from delayed technological advances, had, for the most part, been filled. The time was ripe for a pretty sharp drop ($9.6 billion) in producers' investment in plant and equipment.

In the 1954 recession, the GNP in real terms fell by $13.7 billion. The index of industrial production fell 10 per cent, and unemployment rose from an average of 2.9 per cent for 1953 to a quarterly high of 6 per cent in 1954.

The 1949 recession was on balance not very different. The industrial production index fell by 9 per cent and the GNP in real terms by $7 billion. Unemployment rose from a 1948 yearly average of 3.8 to a quarterly high of 7 per cent in 1949.

Both the 1949 and the 1954 recessions were followed by long and buoyant recoveries. The 1949 recovery was, of course, fed by the Korean war; the 1954 recovery, by a burst of private investment.

In contrast, both the 1958 and the 1961 recoveries enjoyed nothing that could remotely be called a boom. The recoveries were incomplete and fell far short of reaching full employment. Whereas the first two cycles registered, at their pre-recession peaks, unemployment rates around 3.5 per cent (or less in the best quarters), the last two cycles displayed unemployment rates of around 5 to 5.5 per cent at their pre-recession peaks.

In one important respect, the last two cycles were very different. Although the 1958 decline was the most severe of all four cycles, the 1961 decline was the mildest. The index of industrial production in the 1961 cycle fell by only 6 per cent, and the GNP declined by only 2 per cent.

Unemployment, however, increased by 2.1 percentage points. But although the decline was mild in terms of product, the 1961 cycle started the downswing from a low performance peak. The unemployment rate at the pre-recession peak was nearly 5 per cent and the GNP in real terms was running some $30 billion or more below our historically determined potential growth trend.

Both the 1958 and the 1961 recoveries turned out to be anemic — equally unable to reduce unemployment to an acceptable level. The unemployment rate for the entire peak year 1960 was 5.6 per cent, and again 5.6 per cent for 1963.

Under favorable employment opportunities, the labor force tends currently to grow at the rate of 1.3 per cent per year, and the potential increase in productivity per worker is estimated by the Council of Economic Advisers as 2.7 per cent per year. This would put our potential rate of growth at 4 per cent per annum. Indeed a line on a ratio chart drawn through the GNP (in real terms) for 1948 and 1956 (both years of good employment, but not overemployment, rates) discloses a 4 per cent (compounded) growth rate. On this basis, the GNP record in the last two cycles has run some $50 billion below the full-employment level. Thus although the 1961 recession was mild, as measured from the pre-recession peak, the bottom of the recession was low, as measured from the potential growth trend.

Expansion vs. Semistagnation

The weakness of the last two recoveries becomes painfully evident when we compare the last six years (1957–63) with the preceding eight years (1948–56). Table 1 presents the data on output; Table 2 on employment, income, and profits. It is evident that the growth rates in terms of output were far stronger in the period 1948–56 than in the period 1957–63.

Table 1. Percentage Increases in Output

Period	GNP (in constant dollars)	Industrial Production Index	Durable Goods Output (in constant dollars)	Industrial Production Index of Durable Manufactures
1948–56	38.0	46.0	50.0	55.0
Increase per year	4.7	5.7	6.2	6.9
1956–62	18.0	6.0	9.0	13.0
Increase per year	3.0	1.0	1.5	2.2

These tables show how dynamic the period 1948 to 1956 was, and how stagnant the period from 1957 to 1963. Cyclical comparisons alone fail to bring out this important point. In the period of the last two cycles, employment, income, and output had dropped substantially below the economy's potential. The gap between actual performances and the potential growth trend was widening.

Table 2.   Increases in Employment and Income
(Percentage Increases)

Period	Total Employment	Personal Disposable Income (in constant dollars)	Corporate Profits before Taxes	Unemployment Rate (average per period)
1948–56	9.5	37.0	36.0	4.3
Per Year	1.2	4.6	4.5	
1956–62	3.5	18.0	14.0	5.6
Per Year	0.6	3.0	2.3	

• 16

Progress *Toward Economic Stability**

ARTHUR F. BURNS
Columbia University

*Writing in the mid-nineteenth century, Karl Marx predicted an
increasing severity of cyclical fluctuations in economic activity
which would doom the capitalist system to ultimate destruction.
Not at all, declares Arthur F. Burns, one of the most famous
twentieth-century experts on business cycles, as he reviews the
developments of recent times which have smoothed out many of
the former undulations on the economic landscape.*

It is a fact of the highest importance, I think, that although our economy continues to be swayed by the business cycle, its impact on the lives
and fortunes of individuals has been substantially reduced in our generation. More than twenty-five years have elapsed since we last experienced
a financial panic or a deep depression of production and employment.
Over twenty years have elapsed since we last had a severe business
recession. Between the end of the second world war and the present, we
have experienced four recessions, but each was a relatively mild setback.
Since 1937 we have had five recessions, the longest of which lasted only
13 months. There is no parallel for such a sequence of mild — or such a
sequence of brief — contractions, at least during the past hundred years
in our own country.

* Taken and adapted from *American Economic Review*, March 1960, pp. 1–19.
Reproduced with permission.

103

The structure of an economy inevitably leaves its stamp on the character of its fluctuations. In our generation the structure of the American economy has changed profoundly, partly as a result of deliberate economic policies, partly as a result of unplanned developments. In considering problems of the future, we can proceed more surely by recognizing the changes in economic organization which already appear to have done much to blunt the impact of business cycles.

Divergence Between Personal Income and Production

The increasing complexity of modern life, a larger concept of the proper function of government, and the mounting requirements of national defense have resulted in sharp increases of governmental spending. Fifty years ago the combined expenditure of federal, state, and local governments was about 7 per cent of the dollar volume of the nation's total output. Governmental expenditures rose to 10 per cent of total output in 1929 and to 26 per cent in 1957. This huge expansion of governmental enterprise naturally led to increases in tax rates and to an energetic search for new sources of revenue. In time, taxes came to be imposed on estates, gifts, employment, sales, and — most important of all — on the incomes of both corporations and individuals.

This dominance of the income tax in current governmental finance, together with the recent shift of tax collection toward a pay-as-you-go basis, has measurably enlarged the government's participation in the shifting fortunes of the private economy. In recent years, governmental revenues have become very sensitive to fluctuations of business conditions. When corporate profits decline by, say, a billion dollars, the federal government will collect under existing law about a half billion less from corporations. When individual incomes decline by a billion, the federal government may be expected to collect about $150 million less from individuals. State income taxes accentuate these effects. In short, when a recession occurs, our current tax system requires the government to reduce rather promptly and substantially the amount of money that it withdraws from the private economy for its own use. The result is that the income from production which corporations and individuals have at their disposal declines much less than does the national income.

Moreover, the operations of government are now so organized that the flow of personal income from production is bolstered during a recession by increased payments of unemployment insurance benefits.

Other parts of the vast system of social security that we have devised since the 1930's have also served to support the flow of personal income at times when business activity is declining. Payments made to retired workers kept increasing during each recession of the postwar period. The reason is partly that workers handicapped by old age or physical disability experience greater difficulty at such times in keeping their jobs or finding new ones and therefore apply for pensions in somewhat larger numbers. But the most important reason for the steady increase of old-age pensions is the maturing of the social security system.

As a result of these several major developments in our national life, the movement of aggregate personal income is no longer closely linked to the movement of aggregate production. In earlier times personal incomes would have responded decisively to a decline in production. Now the government absorbs a substantial part of the drop in the dollar volume of production by putting up with a sharp decline of its revenues despite the need to raise expenditures. Corporations absorb another part of the decline by maintaining dividends while their undistributed profits slumped. In the end, the aggregate of personal incomes, after taxes, declined less than 1 per cent and the decline was over before the recession ended.

Although the details have varied from one case to the next, a marked divergence between the movements of personal income and production has occurred in each of the postwar recessions. Indeed, during 1953–54 the total income at the disposal of individuals defied the recession by continuing to increase. This unique achievement was due to the tax reduction that became effective soon after the onset of recession as well as to the structural changes that have reduced the dependence of personal income on the short-run movements of production.

Employment

When we turn from personal income to employment, we find that the imprint of the business cycle is still strong. During each recession since 1948, unemployment reached a level which, while decidedly low in comparison with the experience of the 'thirties, was sufficient to cause serious concern. But although the fluctuations of employment have continued to synchronize closely with the movements of production, the relation between the two has been changing in ways which favor greater stability of employment in the future.

As the industrialization of our economy proceeded during the nineteenth century, an increasing part of the population became exposed to the hazards of the business cycle. Manufacturing, mining, construction, freight transportation — these are the strategic industries of a developing economy and they are also the industries in which both production and jobs have been notoriously unstable.

Clearly, the broad effect of economic evolution until about 1920 was to increase the concentration of jobs in the cyclically volatile industries, and this was a major force tending to intensify declines of employment during business contractions. Since then, the continued progress of technology, the very factor which originally was mainly responsible for the concentration in the cyclical industries, has served to arrest this tendency. Advances of technology have come so swiftly that an increasing part of the nation's labor could turn to the "service" industries and the professions. The proportion of employees attached to the cyclically volatile industries has not risen since 1919. Or to express this entire development in another way, the proportion of workers having rather steady jobs, either because they work for themselves or because they are employed in industries that are relatively free from the influence of business cycles, kept declining from the beginning of our industrial revolution until about 1920, and since then has moved slightly but irregularly upward. Thus, the changing structure of industry, which previously had exercised a powerful destabilizing influence on employment and output, particularly the former, has ceased to do so.

Consumption

Turning next to consumer spending, we must try once again to see recent developments in historical perspective. The fact that stands out is that the impact of business cycles on consumption has recently diminished, while the effects of consumption on the business cycle have become more decisive.

In the classical business cycle, as we came to know it in this country, once business investment began declining appreciably, a reduction of consumer spending soon followed. Whatever the cause or causes of the decline in investment, it made its influence felt over an increasing area of the economy. For a while consumer spending was maintained at a peak level or even kept rising. But since businessmen were now buying on a smaller scale from one another, more and more workers lost their jobs or their overtime pay, financial embarrassments and business failures became more frequent, and uncertainty about the business outlook spread to parts of the economy in which sales and profits were still flourishing. If some consumers reacted to these developments by curtailing their spending in the interest of caution, others did so as a matter of necessity. Before long, these curtailments proved sufficient to bring on some decline in the aggregate spending of consumers. The impulses for reducing business investments therefore quickened and the entire round of events was repeated, with both investment and consumption declining in a cumulative process.

Driven by hard necessity, business firms moved with energy to reduce costs and increase efficiency. Consumers whose incomes were declining often saved less or dissaved in order not to disrupt their customary living standards. Hence, even if sales and prices were still falling, profit margins improved here and there. In the meantime, bank credit became more readily available, costs of building and terms of borrowing became more favorable, the bond market revived. When recovery finally came, it was likely to be led by a reduced rate of disinvestment in inventories or by a new rush to make investments in fixed capital. At this stage of the business cycle, consumer spending was at its very lowest level, if not still declining.

Many of these features of earlier business cycles have carried over to the present. However, the behavior of consumers in the postwar recessions has departed from the traditional pattern in two respects. In the first place, consumers maintained their spending at a high level even after business activity had been declining for some months, so that the tendency of recessions to cumulate was severely checked. During the recession of 1945 consumer spending actually kept increasing. In each of the later recessions it fell somewhat; but the decline at no time exceeded one per cent and lasted only a quarter or two. In the second place, instead of lagging at the recovery stage of the business cycle, as it had in earlier times, consumer spending turned upward before production or employment resumed its expansion. This shift in cyclical behavior appears clearly in department store sales, which have been recorded on a substantially uniform basis for several decades and are widely accepted as a tolerably good indicator of consumer spending. In the recoveries of 1921, 1924, 1927, and 1938, these sales lagged by intervals ranging from two to four months. In 1933 their upturn came at the same time as in production and employment. It thus appears that, during the 1920's and 1930's, consumer spending in no instance led the economy out of a slump. In the postwar period, on the other hand, department store sales have led successive recoveries by intervals stretching from two to five months. We may therefore conclude with considerable assurance that consumer spending has played a more dynamic role in recent times. Not only have consumers managed their spending during recessions so that the cumulative process of deflation has been curbed, but consumer spending has emerged as one of the active factors in arresting recession and hastening recovery.

This new role of the consumer in the business cycle reflects some of the developments of the postwar period that we considered earlier, particularly the greatly enhanced stability in the flow of personal income, the steady expansion in the number of income recipients, and the relative increase in the number of steady jobs. It reflects also the improvements of financial organization and other structural changes which have strengthened the confidence of people, whether acting as consumers or investors, in their own and the nation's economic future. Whatever may have been true of the past, it can no longer be held that consumers are passive creatures who lack the power or the habit of initiating changes in economic activities. There is no harm in thinking of consumer spending as being largely "determined" by past and current incomes, provided we also recognize that the level of current incomes is itself shaped to a significant degree by the willingness of people to work hard to earn what they need to live as they feel they should.

Control of the Business Cycle

In concentrating, as I have thus far, on the changes of economic organization which have lately served to reduce the impact of business cycles on the lives of individuals, I have provisionally taken the cyclical movement of production for granted. Of course, if the fluctuations of production had been larger, the impact on people would have been greater. On the other hand, the stabilized tendency of personal income and consumption has itself been a major reason why recent recessions of production have been brief and of only moderate intensity. Many other factors have contributed to this development. Among them are the deliberate efforts made in our generation to control the business cycle, of which I have as yet said little.

More basic than the financial innovations or any other specific measures of policy has been the change in economic and political attitudes which took root during the 'thirties. The economic theory that depressions promote industrial efficiency and economic progress lost adherents as evidence accumulated of the wreckage caused by unemployment and business failures. The political belief that it was best to leave business storms to blow themselves out lost its grip on men's minds as the depression stretched out. In increasing numbers citizens in all walks of life came around to the view that mass unemployment was intolerable under modern conditions and that the federal government has a continuing responsibility to foster competitive enterprise, to prevent or moderate general economic declines, and to promote a high and rising level of employment and production. This new philosophy of intervention was articulated by the Congress in the Employment Act of 1946, which solemnly expressed what had by then become a national consensus.

In recent times, therefore, the business cycle has no longer run a free course and this fact has figured prominently in the plans of businessmen as well as consumers.

The specific measures adopted by the government in dealing with the recessions of the postwar period have varied from one case to the next. In all of them, monetary, fiscal, and housekeeping policies played some part, with agricultural price-support programs assuming special prominence in one recession, tax reductions in another, and increases of public expenditure in still another. Taking a long view, the most nearly consistent part of contracyclical policy has been in the monetary sphere. Since the early 1920's, when the Federal Reserve authorities first learned how to influence credit conditions through open-market operations, long-term interest rates have tended to move down as soon as the cyclical peak of economic activity was reached, in contrast to the long lags that were characteristic of earlier times. Since 1948 the decline of long-term interest rates in the early stages of a recession has also become more rapid. This change in the cyclical behavior of capital markets reflects the increased vigor and effectiveness of recent monetary policies. Inasmuch as optimism, as a rule, is still widespread during the initial stages of an economic decline, a substantial easing of credit, provided it comes early enough, can appreciably hasten economic recovery. This influence is exerted only in part through lower interest rates. Of greater consequence is the fact that credit becomes more readily available, that the money supply is increased or kept from falling, that the liquidity of financial assets is improved, and that financial markets are generally stimulated. The effects of easier credit are apt to be felt most promptly by smaller businesses and the home-building industry, but they tend to work their way through the entire economy. There can be little doubt that the rather prompt easing of credit conditions, which occurred during recent setbacks of production, was of some significance in keeping their duration so short.

Business firms have also been paying closer attention to the business cycle, and not a few of them have even tried to do something about it. These efforts have been expressed in a variety of ways — through the adoption of long-range capital budgets, closer control of inventories, and more energetic selling or some relaxation of credit standards in times of recession. I do not know enough to assess either the extent or the success of some of these business policies. Surely, business investment in fixed capital has remained a highly volatile activity — a fact that is sometimes overlooked by concentrating attention on years instead of months and on actual expenditures instead of new commitments. There is, however, strong evidence that the businessmen of our generation manage inventories better than did their predecessors. The inventory-sales ratio of manufacturing firms has lately averaged about a fourth less than during the 1920's, despite the increased importance of the durable goods sector where inventories are especially heavy. The trend of the inventory-sales ratio has also moved down substantially in the case of distributive firms. This success in economizing on inventories has tended to reduce the fluctuations of inventory investment relative to the scale of business operations and this in turn has helped to moderate the cyclical swings in production. Not only that, but it appears that the cyclical downturns of both inventories and inventory investment have tended to come at an earlier stage of the business cycle in the postwar period than they did previously, so that any imbalance between inventories and sales could be corrected sooner. Since consumer outlays — and often also other expenditures — were well maintained during the recent recessions of production, the rising phase of inventory disinvestment ceased rather early and this naturally favored a fairly prompt recovery of production.

Thus, numerous changes in the structure of our economy have combined to stimulate over-all expansion during the postwar period and to keep within moderate limits the cyclical declines that occurred in production.

Conclusions

I have tried to show how a conjuncture of structural changes in our economy has served to modify the business cycle of our times. Some of these changes were planned while others were unplanned. Some resulted from efforts to control the business cycle while others originated in policies aimed at different ends. Some arose from private and others from public activities. Some are of very recent origin and others of long standing. The net result has been that the intensity of cyclical swings of production has become smaller. The links that previously tied together the cyclical movements of production, employment, personal income, and consumption have become looser. And, as everyone knows, the once familiar parallelism of the short-term movements in the physical volume of total production, on the one hand, and the average level of wholesale or consumer prices, on the other, has become somewhat elusive.

It seems reasonable to expect that the structural changes in our economy, which have recently served to moderate and humanize the business cycle, will continue to do so. The growth of corporations is not likely to be checked, nor is the tendency to pay fairly stable dividends likely to be modified. The scale of governmental activities will remain very extensive, and so it would be even if the communist threat to our national security were somehow banished. Our methods of taxation might change materially, but the income tax will remain a major source of governmental revenue. Governmental expenditures might fluctuate sharply, but they are not likely to decline during a recession merely because governmental revenues are then declining. The social security system is more likely to grow than to remain stationary or contract. Private pension arrangements will multiply and so also may private supplements to unemployment insurance. Our population will continue to grow. The restlessness and eagerness of consumers to live better is likely to remain a dynamic force. Research and development activities will continue to enlarge opportunities for investment. Governmental efforts to promote a high and expanding level of economic activity are not likely to weaken. Private businesses will continue to seek ways to economize on inventories and otherwise minimize the risk of cyclical fluctuations in their operations. Employment in agriculture is already so low that its further decline can no longer offset future gains of the service industries on the scale experienced in the past. The spread of white-collar occupations throughout the range of industry will continue and may even accelerate. For all these reasons, the business cycle is unlikely to be as disturbing or troublesome to our children as it once was to us or our fathers.

• *17*

Automatic Stabilizers Evaluated*

M. O. CLEMENT
Dartmouth College

Economists have long been fascinated with the idea of developing machinery which would keep the economy running smoothly without anyone thinking much about it. In the heyday of classical economics, this machinery was believed to reside exclusively in the workings of the private sector of the economy. In recent years, as the following selection illustrates, economists have given special attention to the fact that we can "build in" to the public sector of the economy policy measures which would "automatically" tend to counteract inflation and depression.

Since World War II there has been a growing conviction that the great economic convulsions of past experience are no longer likely. This persuasion is based in part on recent historical evidence, which is in turn reinforced by changes in the institutional structure of the economy.

* Taken and adapted from "The Concept of Automatic Stabilizers," *Southern Economic Journal*, January, 1959, pp. 303–314. Reproduced with permission.

There is one institutional change that is stressed by many who feel that future cycles in economic activity will not be severe. During the latter stages of the war, economists, on the basis of theoretical arguments, proposed that the fiscal system exerted an automatic countercyclical impact. With no change in tax rates, revenues from the existing tax system would expand and contract in positive relation to changes in national income and probably more than proportionately; federal outlays would exhibit an opposite tendency, although quite likely to a lesser degree. It was also on this favorable operation of the expanded system of automatic stabilizers that hopes for less severe business fluctuations in the future were pinned. Indeed, the refusal to lower tax rates during the 1957–58 recession is, in part, an illustration of government belief in considerable built-in stabilization potential.

The Concept of Automatic Stabilizers

In discussions of the role of automatic stabilizers in counteracting cyclical swings it is usually assumed that the impact of these devices is fiscal in nature. This rather limited interpretation of the scope of automatic stabilization measures runs throughout the literature. A few economists, however, have visualized built-in flexibility as having a broader impact than the term "fiscal" would suggest. Professor Albert Gaylord Hart proposed several criteria by which to judge the automatic stabilization qualities of a particular countercyclical measure. Any device which begins its compensatory effect without waiting for a new policy decision and which also (1) tends to produce budget deficits during slumps and surpluses during upswings, or (2) expands the community's stock of cash in slumps and reduces it in high prosperity, or (3) tends to lower the public's demand for cash balances during slumps and raise it in high prosperity, or (4) any combination of these would, according to Hart, be designated a built-in stabilizer.

While Hart's criteria posit the minimum conditions by which it is possible to determine whether a particular stabilization measure is automatic in its operation, they do not constitute the conditions which a relatively *effective* system of automatic stabilizers must satisfy. In order to have the maximum anticipated favorable economic impact, both direct and indirect, an automatic countercyclical device must not detract from the possible beneficial results. Negation of the beneficial results could be incurred by an adverse impact on expectations. Persons responsible for making economic decisions must be able to anticipate a fairly definite pattern of action from the stabilization policies and from the economic system. In the absence of this "predictability of action" the expectations of decision-makers will vacillate, the stability of the economy's internal response mechanism diminishes, and what may have been an effective stabilization policy becomes less satisfactory, if not damaging.

(1) An automatic stabilization arrangement which possesses predictability of action must fulfill criteria in addition to those already set forth. Decision-makers cannot adopt reasonably stable responses to economic change, influenced as it is by a system of automatic devices, without a relatively extended period of adaptation. Consequently, one of the additional requisites of an automatic countercyclical program is that the devices must have enough permanence to become part of the economic milieu of decision-making units.

The purely fortuitous nature of the present arsenal of automatic stabilizers may have been a blessing. These stabilizers became a part of the economic response mechanism without fanfare and the public unconsciously adjusted its thinking to take them into account. When economists ultimately became cognizant of the existence of a considerable amount of built-in stabilization and made their awareness known, the public's economic adjustment was already an accomplished fact. Had the government overtly instituted a system of automatic stabilization measures for the express purpose of decreasing cyclical instability, expectations would have been grossly revised. By the unplanned and, for the period that mattered, unknown intrusion of automatic countercyclical devices the additional dislocations attendant to the revision of expectations were minimized.

(2) An additional requirement for an effective set of automatic devices is that the objectives and important provisions of the stabilization complex must be clearly defined. The stabilizing effect as such need not be blueprinted; rather the essence of this requirement is procedural. If there is to be predictability of action, automatic stabilizers must preclude the possibility of administrative discretion and recourse to new legislative enactments. To some extent this is not entirely possible. Yet an effort must be made to minimize substantially the area in which discretion can be exercised. Otherwise, human vagaries and frailties would unnecessarily impair the effectiveness of automatic devices. The true merit of the built-in stabilizers is their automatism.

(3) Accepting the dual stabilization goals of a relatively stable general price level and relatively full employment and giving neither preeminence, and also recognizing that neither of these is perfectly attainable under any foreseeable system of countercyclical measures, what is the ideal timing of the compensatory contribution of the automatic stabilizers? Letting the trend-line represent the achievement of the joint stabilization objectives, an ideal countercyclical mechanism would abet cyclical movements toward the trend-line and tend to cancel movements away from it. During prosperity and recession, therefore, the compensatory devices should tend toward a government surplus and a diminution

of liquidity; during depression and recovery periods the opposite should be true. If the countercyclical impact of the built-in devices were instantaneous, then rigidity tying their activation to variables that conform perfectly with the turning points in economic activity would provide the desired compensatory effect during depression and prosperity. It seems likely that, in fact, automatic stabilizers that are linked to cyclically conforming series do approximate the desired compensatory performance. Ideally, therefore, the automatic stabilizers' countercyclical action should be rigidly fixed to conforming variables and, of course, variables which at the same time exhibit a wider amplitude than the cycle itself. Hence, the final requirement of effective built-in stabilizers is that they be closely tied to operational variables that are sensitive to and conform with economic fluctuations.

If these conditions are met — if a stabilization device is relatively permanent, well-defined, and linked to cyclically sensitive and conforming series, *i.e.*, if it possesses predictability of action — and at the same time Hart's amended criteria are fulfilled, a countercyclical measure may be said to be automatic and, chances are, relatively effective.

The Current Battery of Automatic Stabilizers

What are the currently operating federal stabilization devices which qualify as automatic countercyclical compensators?

The three major sources of federal revenue — personal income and corporate income taxes and excise taxes — clearly meet the tests. The current collection features, cyclical volatility of the base, and progressive rates of the personal income tax combine to make it a powerful automatic stabilizer. Excise taxes and the corporate income tax possess countercyclical flexibility because of the volatility of the tax base alone, although in the case of the latter there is rudimentary progression due to favorable treatment extended small corporations. There can be little debate that these taxes satisfy Hart's conditions, nor can it be convincingly denied that they are clearly defined, of a by-product nature, tied to cyclically sensitive and conforming variables, and possess an aspect of permanency.

The techniques by which the above forms of government revenue exert their automatic countercyclical influence are certain enough. Because of the sensitivity of the tax base and, where applicable, due to the progression in the structure of rates, these built-in tax devices permit the retention of a larger share of income than would otherwise be the case in the event of an economic contraction. In the upswing, conversely, these measures tax away a larger share of income.

None of the criteria postulated above make reference to the specific mechanism by which the countercyclical impact must be achieved. All that was proposed was that built-in stabilizers should (1) possess predictability of action, (2) go into effect without the need for fresh policy decisions, and (3) have the proper effect on the government's budget and on the supply of or demand for liquid assets.

Not many government expenditures programs qualify on the basis of these three criteria, but certainly the social security schemes fit. The countercyclical effect of the Old Age and Survivors Insurance program depends upon the variation in aggregate contributions growing out of fluctuations in the "covered" payroll base with the flexibility of benefit disbursements coming from the withdrawal out of or entry into the "covered" labor force of insured persons over the requisite age-level for eligibility. The unemployment insurance program is probably the most direct and automatic of the various built-in devices. The countercyclical effect of both these programs is twofold: a drop in the level of economic activity tends to lower employers' and employees' aggregate contributions and to increase the amount of benefit payments from the trust funds; an increase in economic activity tends to raise the aggregate amount of contributions and to lower the total value of benefit payments.

One other government expenditure program deserves consideration. It has been fashionable to accord the status of built-in stabilizer to the federal farm price-support programs. According to the arguments presented in favor of their inclusion it is immaterial whether support payments are designed to maintain agricultural prices during a deflationary period or to provide parity incomes for producers of certain important products. If the price-support programs are to maintain farm prices, the amount of payments made to producers will increase as deflation progresses. Contrastingly, government support payments during periods of high prices will presumably slacken. Thus, the farm price-support programs, according to this line of reasoning, contain a substantial measure of built-in flexibility.

At one time these arguments may have possessed validity. During the first term of the Eisenhower administration, however, rigid price supports gave way to a flexible farm price-support system in which not only the support levels can be altered, within a range, at the discretion of the executive branch of the government but also the parity prices themselves are calculated on a more flexible basis. This encroachment of flexibility into the price-support system is a telling blow to its automatic stabilization potential. The program is still, in a way, capable of satisfying the criterion of being well-defined. Congress has only given the Administration discretion to alter support levels within specified limits. But in a fundamental sense, the discretion of the executive branch creates a situation in which it is difficult to hold expectations with relative certainty. The devices are no longer as assuredly installed on a relatively permanent basis and, because of the discretionary element, they are no longer closely tied to cyclically sensitive variables. Hence, the farm price-support programs lack predictability of action and, therefore, do not qualify as automatic stabilizers.

In Summary

The prevailing professional assessment is that the existing automatic compensatory arsenal is not very effective. An intuitively compiled weighted average of economic opinion on the efficacy of the existing battery of automatic stabilizers might be the following: the automatic stabilization features of the current fiscal system cannot be relied upon alone to dependably stabilize the economy. They are capable, certainly, of reducing the amplitude of the relatively mild swings in economic activity, they might conceivably provide a floor and a ceiling to these fluctuations, but in no event can they initiate an actual reversal of cumulative movements.

• *18*

*In Defense of Discretionary Monetary Policy**

COMMISSION ON MONEY AND CREDIT

The Commission on Money and Credit, established in 1958 to study the financial and monetary system of the United States and to determine what changes, if any, are needed to better attain our national goals, here defends discretionary monetary policy against its critics. Monetary policy is an effective contributor to cyclical stabilization (and can be made more so), the Commission asserts. And while "the average rate of growth of the money supply should reflect the rate of growth of real output at high employment and stable prices," this principle should be interpreted, as a general rule, subject to modification in the presence of unforeseen shifts in the demand for money and the demand for goods. It should not be viewed as an automatic panacea which can remove the need for discretionary judgment.

Our monetary, credit, and fiscal policies and the instruments and institutions through which they operate must be so designed that they can make an essential contribution in the decades ahead to the improve-

* Taken and adapted from *Money and Credit, Their Influence on Jobs, Prices, and Growth*, The Report of the Commission on Money and Credit (Englewood Cliffs, N.J.: Prentice-Hall, 1961), pp. 1, 46–48, 53–61. Reproduced with permission.

ment of our standards of living through simultaneously achieving low levels of unemployment, an adequate rate of economic growth, and reasonable price stability.

The Commission on Money and Credit was established in 1958 in response to widespread concern as to the adequacy of the nation's monetary and financial structure and its regulation and control. It was directed to study these broad general problems as it saw fit and to make recommendations on what changes, if any, should be made.

Control over conditions governing the quantity of money is inevitable in a modern industrial society. As the nation has adopted more positive economic goals, it has become interested in how and to what extent monetary control can be used flexibly to influence the behavior of expenditures, output, employment, and prices.

Monetary policy is directly concerned with the provision of money, defined to include currency and demand deposits at commercial banks. In the United States, monetary policy is essentially Federal Reserve policy, which operates primarily through the System's exercise of conscious and continuous control over the reserve position of commercial banks. The reserves of commercial banks serve as the basis for expansion or contraction of their loans and investments and the consequent creation or reduction of demand deposits.

Changes in the degree of restraint or ease in monetary policy have an effect on the total flow of expenditures and in turn on output, employment, and prices. Because the link between the initial actions taken by the Federal Reserve to influence bank reserves and these variables is general, pervasive, and indirect, and because no attempt is made by the monetary authority to allocate credit among specific users, this approach to monetary policy is frequently referred to as *general* monetary control.

General Monetary Control

Monetary restraint reduces the availability of credit and increases its interest cost, thus retarding the flow of expenditures, output, employment, and income. Monetary ease makes credit more available and reduces its cost, and thus encourages an expansion in these flows.

The primary and most predictable effect of monetary measures is its impact on the "net reserve" position of member banks. All three instruments of policy, however, have direct impacts on other economic variables as well.

For example, the Federal Reserve may try to restrain economic activity by engaging in open market sales of Treasury bills. These sales influence at least six elements in the economy: net bank reserves are reduced; the money supply falls; the price of government securities tends to decline and yields to rise; the money value of total assets tends to fall; the overall liquidity of financial portfolios is reduced; and the ability and willingness of banks to lend is reduced.

Effects of a Policy of Restraint

A change in monetary policy may take the form of positive actions, such as open market sales, increases in required reserve ratios, or increases in discount rates. But, a shift to a restrictive policy is often passive; it takes the form of failing to increase reserves in the face of a rising demand for credit.

When the commercial banking system loses reserves as a result of open market sales by the Federal Reserve, or is faced with an increasing demand for loans by its customers while total reserves remain constant, some adjustments in bank portfolios must be made. If there are no excess reserves in the system, banks must either borrow additional reserves from the Federal Reserve or must restrict their earning assets either by curbing loans, disposing of security holdings, or both.

Although individual banks may borrow the excess reserves of other banks in the federal funds market, the amount of excess reserves in the system at any time is limited. Borrowing from the Federal Reserve is also limited and may be discouraged further by discount rate increases. Thus, even though earning assets may fail to contract immediately in response to an active restrictive policy, eventually they will if the restrictive pressure continues.

Effects of an Expansionary Policy

A policy of monetary ease to stimulate an expansion of expenditures will operate through the same processes as a restrictive policy but in the reverse direction. Such an expansive policy will tend to increase the net reserve position of member banks, to increase the prices and reduce the yields on Treasury securities, to improve the liquidity of banks and other lending institutions, to enhance the wealth position of all holders of financial assets, and to increase the money supply. At times, however, these changes may not be as effective in stimulating economic activity as the reverse measures can be in restraining it.

As the reserve positions of commercial banks are improved, as interest rates and bond yields fall, and as liquidity positions of all lending institutions improve, both bank and nonbank lenders are decidedly more able and willing to extend additional credit. There is a definite increase in the availability of credit on more liberal terms and at lower costs to the borrower. But, whereas further restrictive actions can definitely restrain the volume of actual lending in boom times, further easing actions may in slumps bring about credit availability which is excessive in relation to the demand for it by spenders.

For credit ease to be effective, the demand for borrowing must be large enough to use the additional supply made available. Under given conditions of prospective product demand and profitability of expanded capacity to produce, any reduction of credit costs should increase the attractiveness of new investment. But during recessions the prospective profitability of added investment may already be so low that the reduced credit costs provide an insufficient stimulus to borrowing and to capital formation.

This is in contrast to the opposite case, when the underlying demand for investment is strong. At such times, a policy of credit ease is very likely to be effective in stimulating increased borrowing and capital expenditures.

Monetary Policy and Cyclical Stabilization

There is fairly general agreement about the nature of the processes through which monetary policy affects economic activity. Some experts contend, however, that monetary policy does not have large enough effects to be useful, and others contend that an active monetary policy works too slowly to be useful. These two contentions will be considered in turn.

Volume Effects

The effectiveness of countercyclical monetary policy must be considered in relation to the objectives it seeks to achieve. The purpose of restraint during prosperity is to exert a moderating effect on total spending so as to prevent unsustainable boom conditions; its purpose is not to extinguish a large proportion of demand. Even a relatively small stimulus to spending can be helpful during a decline in business activity. The changes in the degree of monetary restraint or ease appropriate to the conduct of countercyclical policy do not have to have a controlling impact of any specific type of expenditure, but the pervasive and cumulative combination of a number of small effects does make flexible monetary policy a useful instrument of stabilization policy.

The Commission believes that the restrictive monetary policies in 1955–57 and again in 1959 demonstrate that monetary policy can have a very substantial effect on the level and rate of growth and of demand. In both periods monetary restriction seemed to induce a decline in the annual rate of residential construction of $3 to $4 billion. Business investment was lower than it would have been if credit had been freely available at low rates. If allowance is made for the indirect effects that the restraint on some investment had on consumption and on types of investment not directly affected, monetary restraint seems to have had an important effect on the level and rate of growth of economic activity.

Moreover, during the postwar period, the monetary authorities have not exerted the maximum practicable degree of restraint within their power. If it had been considered desirable, the severity of monetary policy could have been somewhat greater without the danger of exceeding the practicable limit.

Speed of Effects

Some experts have argued that monetary policy works so slowly that its effects become perverse, because the effects of a restrictive policy are not felt until after the start of the ensuing downswing and the effects of monetary expansion until the next boom.

It is true that a policy of monetary restriction has at times been carried on for too long, and that at other times the expansion of bank reserves or reduction in reserve requirements in a recession has created problems in controlling the ensuing upswing. These weaknesses reflect not inherent defects of monetary management but rather the inadequacy of the techniques employed and the criteria used for the timing of the changes in monetary policy. Also, certain actions can be taken which will speed up the effects of monetary policy.

Measures which restrain the growth of commercial bank assets have an impact on both bank and nonbank lending. But the speed of the impact will vary depending on the asset positions of lending institutions and the public, what types of borrowers are seeking credit, and how the maturity composition of the publicly held Treasury debt has changed during the upswing. When banks hold a large amount of relatively short-term securities and have excess reserves, when other lending institutions have comfortable liquidity positions, and when individuals and businesses hold a substantial amount of idle cash and liquid assets, then a policy of monetary restraint will not affect credit extensions for some time. But if bank liquidity is relatively low, at the time the Federal Reserve initiates restraint, and the idle cash holdings and liquid positions of the public are also relatively low, the impact of credit restriction on bank lending will come much sooner. In addition, a more direct and immediate pressure on long rates can be brought to bear by both Treasury and Federal Reserve sales of the long-term securities.

Monetary restraint on the upswing will be more effective if idle cash in the hands of the public is at a minimum, if excess bank liquidity at the start of the upswing is minimal, and if the Federal Reserve and Treasury together work to increase the long-term federal debt in the hands of the public, normally reducing short-term debt at the same time.

The effectiveness of monetary policy on the downswing will be increased if the Treasury and the Federal Reserve take direct action to reduce long-term as well as short-term interest rates. If excessive liquidity positions of banks, other lending institutions, and the public are not allowed to develop, and if the Federal Reserve and the Treasury take direct action to speed the adjustment process of long-term as well as short-term interest rates, the impact of monetary policy should be felt sooner.

The monetary authorities should make full use of the fact that monetary measures can be varied continually in either direction and reversed quickly at their discretion. These properties make it possible to change monetary policy gradually in the restrictive direction before the economy has generated excessive demand, and to ease restrictions gradually before aggregate income has actually declined.

The Commission does not advocate placing sole reliance on monetary policy for stabilization purposes. Because of its reversibility and the possibility of changing policy by small steps, monetary policy can be used in many circumstances when discretionary fiscal policy changes should not be used because the need for so powerful an instrument has not yet become clear. In summary, the Commission believes that monetary policy is a valuable and effective instrument of stabilization policy.

Differential Effects

Another objection to the use of monetary measures for stabilization is that it is discriminatory in its application, with its restrictive effects falling particularly severely on investment in housing and on small business. Large businesses, which depend more on internal sources of financing and which have long-term relations with lending institutions, are held to be far less affected.

The available data which pertain mainly to the 1955–57 experience show that bank lending to large business increased relatively more during the cyclical upswing when money was tight than to small business. However, to a large extent the differences in the rates of growth of lending reflect cyclical differences in *demand* for credit. Industries in which large firms predominate were growing at a faster rate than industries with mainly small firms. In addition, small retail firms normally rely on trade credit more than on bank loans; and large corporations did increase their lending to small corporations and to noncorporate firms faster than their own sales increased.

Bank credit rationing did occur and was not uniform. But the criterion for rationing did not appear to be size of firm. The two criteria which prevailed for loans other than mortgage and consumer installment loans were credit-worthiness and the value to the bank of obtaining or retaining the borrower as a depositor. Banks tightened their credit standards and refused to make loans to marginal borrowers who might have been accommodated in an easy money period. They also shortened maturities on term loans.

But because small banks, all of whose customers are small, were generally less loaned-up than large banks, small businesses with good credit ratings and good bank connections may have often had less difficulty in obtaining loans than some large businesses.

Firms with poor credit ratings and poor banking connections appear relatively more often in the category of small businesses. Firms with low credit ratings may have either inexperienced management or insufficient equity capital, frequently both. To the extent that well-managed firms have weak credit ratings, they often cannot get bank accommodation because they lack sufficient equity capital. The gap in the equity capital could be helped by a more realistic attitude on the part of the owners and by further development of specialized institutions, including small business investment corporations.

It is also claimed that monetary restraint affects adversely the distribution of income among individuals. This income distribution effect, however, is difficult to measure. On the assumption that employment will be the same if any of the following three measures is used, monetary restraint may be considered an alternative to outright inflation or as an alternative to control of demand by fiscal policy.

Clearly those who are net creditors will fare better with monetary restraint than with inflation. They avoid a reduction in the real value of their net assets, and they obtain a higher interest income.

At any level of government expenditures, a given level of demand may be achieved with a restrictive monetary policy and relatively low taxes or with an easier monetary policy and higher taxes. The use of restrictive monetary policy will tend to improve the position of net creditors and worsen the position of net debtors. How tax increases will affect them will depend on the character and composition of the increases. In general the Commission sees no reason to object to the use of monetary policy relative to tax policy on account of its differential impacts among sectors of the economy or size of business, or its direct income distribution effects.

Long-Run Monetary Policy

Countercyclical monetary policy tries to time net injections or withdrawals of bank reserves so that they will best dampen fluctuations in the level of economic activity. Long-run monetary policies on the other hand must provide a monetary climate consonant with an adequate and sustainable rate of growth and over-all price stability. This climate should permit the banking system to expand its loans and investments and concomitantly the supply of money at a rate commensurate with the economy's underlying growth potential. Since the quantity of money needed to permit economic growth will depend on a variety of elements, including changes in the stock of money substitutes, the money supply need not always increase at the same rate as the increase in the economy's growth potential.

Since the end of World War II, the money supply has grown by less than 2 per cent per year. The money supply in real terms has declined since 1947. Some authorities have contended that the failure of the money supply to grow in pace with our productive potential is responsible for retarding the rate of growth of output. It is important to note some special circumstances which have influenced policy governing the growth of the money supply.

The conduct of long-run monetary policy since the end of World War II must be interpreted against the background of depression and war finance. Between 1930 and 1946 the money supply increased much more rapidly than did the gross national product in money terms. Both the absolute supply of money and the ratio of money to GNP were at all-time highs in 1946. Possessing the money and liquid assets to make their pent-up demands effective, consumers and business firms in this country and abroad increased their purchases to unprecedented levels. These demands resulted in inflationary pressures during the early postwar years.

Money incomes rose by over 100 per cent between 1946 and 1951 while money supply rose by only 17 per cent, but there was relatively little increase in longer-term interest rates. Because of the growth in incomes, the relationship between the money supply and the volume of transactions had been restored to more normal levels by the end of 1951. From the end of 1951 to the end of 1959 the money supply continued to rise at a relatively slow rate, about 2½ per cent per year. From 1951 to 1959 the ratio of GNP to the money supply rose from 3 per year to approximately 4. Part of the increase in this ratio would have taken place without a rise in interest rates, but part of it was a by-product of general monetary policy. As has already been shown, a restrictive monetary policy may consist of limiting the growth of the money supply to an amount less than that required to satisfy all demands for credit at the interest rates ruling when the policy decision is made. The resultant shortage of credit led to rising interest rates and induced a reduction in money holdings relative to economic activity. The relatively slow growth of the money supply since 1951 was in considerable measure a reflection and embodiment of the generally restrictive tone of monetary policy.

The average rate of growth of the money supply should reflect the rate of growth of real output at high employment and stable prices. However, the exact rate of growth of money supply will have to depend on the strength of private demand and the character of fiscal policy in that these will affect the demand for money. If private demand and fiscal policy together tend to push up aggregate demand at a high rate, a greater degree of monetary restriction will be necessary to maintain adequate but not excessive levels of demand. Since monetary control is achieved through control of the money supply, the rate of growth of the money supply must reflect our choice of a combination of monetary and fiscal policy as well as the strength of private demand.

The Commission urges that the average rate of growth of the money supply should be consistent with the continued maintenance of high employment at stable prices and adequate economic growth, but it recognizes that it may be appropriate for the money supply to grow more or less rapidly than the output of the economy at high employment.

19

Three Kinds of Federal Budgets and "Fiscal Drag"*

JOINT ECONOMIC COMMITTEE OF THE U.S. CONGRESS

Specialists in public finance have long urged their students to distinguish between the "administrative" and the "cash" budgets of the federal government. More recently, a third budget, of potentially great importance for understanding the effects of federal government fiscal operations upon the national economy, has been added to the first two: the income and product account budget. (See also Selection 9). A variation of this third budget is to estimate what government expenditures and receipts would be if the economy were to operate at full employment. Analysis of this suggests that under certain circumstances federal taxation may provide a "fiscal drag," an automatic government surplus which can have repressive effects upon further expansion if it is not offset by increased private investment.

Significance of the Three Federal Budgets

One of the most useful innovations in the analysis of Government budgets has been the development of the procedures for estimating Federal Government receipts and expenditures so that it is possible to set up a

* Taken and adapted from the *Annual Report of the Joint Economic Committee* on the January 1962 Economic Report of the President (Washington, D.C.: U.S. Government Printing Office, 1962), pp. 33–38.

budget to represent the receipts and expenditures as they would work out if the economy were working continuously throughout the budget period at full employment. For the first time, the concept of the full employment receipts, expenditures, and surplus or deficit has found its way into the President's economic messages to the Congress, particularly into the Economic Report. These developments represent significant progress, for which the administration is to be commended.

This newer method of estimating the impact of Government fiscal operations on the general economy relates, moreover, not to the usual "administrative" or "cash" budgets but to what is now called the income-and-product-accounts budget. This latter is not constructed just to show how much funds need to be appropriated, or the total cash which Federal fiscal operations will take in or pay out. Rather, the income-and-product-accounts budget seeks to measure the direct effect on the economy of all Federal fiscal operations, and at the time when these effects occur, not just when bills are submitted and paid.

Since it is important to make a clear distinction among these three forms of budgets, a brief review may be in order.

Administrative Budget

The administrative budget has been developed in the form most useful to the appropriations committees of Congress. Expenditures are included in this budget because they are made from funds which have been considered by the Congress to be Government owned. Receipts are shown on a net basis, after refunds, to indicate only the amounts that will be available to meet expenditures. Many items, such as the receipts and expenditures of the Post Office Department and other public enterprises, are shown in the administrative budget only as net expenditures. These enterprises generally have the authority to spend against the receipts they collect, and Congress provides Government-owned money solely to meet any net deficits. Many other operations of the Government, such as trust funds and Government-sponsored enterprises, are largely ignored in the administrative budget because virtually no Government funds (technically defined) are required in these operations.

Cash Budget

The cash budget is designed primarily to show the cash flows between the Federal Government and the private economy (including state and local governments). It differs from the administrative budget in two principal ways: (1) The cash budget excludes transactions between agencies of the Government; for example, interest and other payments between the Treasury Department and the social security and other trust funds; and (2) the cash budget includes various transactions between the Federal Government and the private economy which involves the U.S.

Treasury, though the amounts do not technically qualify as "Government-owned funds" and therefore are not reflected in the administrative budget. The principal amounts included in the cash budget, but not in the administrative budget, are the transactions between Federal trust funds and the public. For example, the cash budget includes as receipts all employment taxes which enter social security trust funds and includes as expenditures all payments of social security benefits.

Income-and-Product-Account Budget

The income-and-product-account budget is provided in the national income and product accounts developed by the Commerce Department. Like the cash budget, it includes both the transactions of trust funds and some Government enterprises as well as administrative budget receipts and expenditures. It excludes financial items and exchanges of existing assets (such as the purchase of a site for a new post office, or the sale of a surplus military base) — transactions which affect liquidity in the private economy but have no direct effect on production or national income. It also excludes loans and guarantee programs of the Government (such as by the Department of Agriculture or the Federal housing agencies), which do have an impact on the economy.

While both the cash budget and the administrative budget generally reflect receipts and expenditures in the year when cash changes hands, the income and product budget attempts to show receipts at the time when tax liabilities accrue, and expenditures for purchases of goods and services are shown as of the time the goods and services are produced and delivered.

Changes in the Three Budgets Compared

From these definitions of the differences in the three budgets, let us look at what the differences can mean in dollars. For purposes of illustration, Table 1 compares anticipated receipts and expenditures for the three different budgets for fiscal 1963, giving also the indicated changes from fiscal 1962. In addition, the table also shows estimates of what receipts and expenditures in the national income budget would be at an average rate of unemployment of 4 per cent during each of the 2 fiscal years, instead of the unemployment rates actually prevailing in 1962 and that are expected to prevail in 1963 when this analysis was made. (The actual years and amounts themselves are not so important; our interest is in the comparisons.)

Thus it may be noted that the administrative budget for fiscal 1963 anticipates expenditures of $92.5 billion. This is an increase of $3.4 billion over fiscal 1962, of which $2.6 billion is for defense and space affairs, $0.4 billion for increased interest charges on the Federal debt, and $0.4 billion for all of the other functions of the Government combined.

Table 1. Various Federal Budget Totals for the Fiscal Years 1962 and 1963
(*billions of dollars*)

	1962 estimate	*1963 estimate*	*Change from 1962 to 1963*
Administrative budget:			
Expenditures:			
National defense	51.2	52.7	1.5
International affairs and finance	2.9	3.0	.1
Space research and technology	1.3	2.4	1.1
Subtotal	55.4	58.1	2.7
Interest	9.0	9.4	.4
Other expenditures, net	24.7	25.1	.4
Total budget expenditures	89.1	92.5	3.4
Receipts	82.1	93.0	10.9
Cash budget:			
Expenditures	111.1	114.8	3.7
Receipts	102.6	116.6	14.0
National income budget:			
Expenditures	106.1	111.9	5.8
Receipts	105.6	116.3	10.7
National income budget at 4-per cent unemployment levels:			
Expenditures	105.3	111.6	6.3
Receipts	113.1	120.3	7.2
Gross national product	547.5	592.5	45.0

Whereas the administrative budget for 1962 ran a deficit of $7 billion, the estimated administrative budget for fiscal 1963 is in balance. At the time of this analysis, it was, in fact, expected to run a small surplus of approximately $0.5 billion. The cash budget, on the other hand, anticipates receipts of $116.6 billion in fiscal 1963 and expenditures of $114.8 billion. The cash budget was also in deficit in fiscal 1962. The substantial surplus position ($1.6 billion) expected in 1963 is due largely to (*a*) net increases in payments into the trust accounts because of increased employment, and (*b*) higher unemployment compensation and social security tax rates.

As previously discussed, however, for purposes of judging the influence of the budget on the general economy, we are most interested in the national income budget. Here we may note that whereas this budget was almost in balance in fiscal 1962 ($0.5 billion deficit), for fiscal 1963 it is expected to run a sizable surplus ($4.4 billion). Thus, if the estimates are correct, Federal budget operations in fiscal 1963 will have a somewhat repressive effect on the general economy, even though the administrative budget is in balance.

Finally, coming to the national income budget as it would appear at a 4-per cent rate of unemployment, we may note that for fiscal 1962 the surplus would have been $7.8 billion, whereas in fiscal 1963 it would be $8.7 billion. In addition to the absolute size of this surplus, it is also important to note that receipts will be increasing in fiscal 1963 a great deal more rapidly than expenditures. Elsewhere we point out that other estimates suggest that the 4-per cent unemployment surplus in the national income budget may be substantially higher than the Council has estimated, because of even more rapid increases in receipts than the Council estimates.

Fiscal Drag: Repressive Effect of 1963 Budget

It is now anticipated that GNP will reach an annual rate of about $600 billion (in 1961 prices) by the end of fiscal 1963. If GNP could be increased more rapidly to levels that would reduce unemployment to 4 per cent of the work force throughout the entire fiscal year 1963, what amount of "full employment" budget surplus would occur? Federal expenditures, on an income-and-product-account basis, would apparently amount to about $111 billion, approximately 18.6 percent of the GNP at the 4-per cent unemployment level, according to the projections made by the Council of Economic Advisers.

At the same time, however, if 4-percent unemployment existed throughout fiscal 1963, the Council has estimated that Federal revenues in the national income accounts would amount to approximately $120 billion, about 20 percent of the high employment GNP.

Hence, if the Nation were at a 4-percent unemployment level throughout fiscal 1963, the income-and-product budget would show a surplus of about $9 billion, approximately 1.5 percent of the 4-percent unemployment GNP.

A high employment surplus amounting to 1.5 percent of high employment GNP would, under present noninflationary conditions, raise significantly the proportion of the total flow of incomes through the economy that is set aside for savings, without necessarily insuring a parallel rise in investment. In fact, it seems possible that the additional flow of funds to the Federal Government would — either by adding to the Treasury cash balance or by returning funds to private savers via debt retirement — choke off recovery short of 96-percent employment by reason of holding the total of consumption and investment expenditures below 96-percent employment levels.

Obviously this does not mean that the Federal Government cannot, under any circumstances, run a high employment surplus as large as 1½ percent or more of the GNP. Indeed, under the inflationary conditions of 1947–48 and 1950–51 the Federal Government surplus ran to about 5 percent of the GNP, helping to reduce inflationary pressures. As we have repeatedly pointed out, the Government should set its budget policies so as to produce an excess of revenues over expenditures at high employment and make retirements of the public debt under high employment conditions.

But even a good policy can be carried too far. We are seriously concerned lest our revenue system be capable of generating too large a Federal surplus at high employment, in which case employment high enough to produce any surplus will likely not be achieved.

20

A Balanced View of the Annually Balanced Budget*

ARTHUR F. SMITHIES

Harvard University

That "the annually balanced budget is the path of financial virtue" is a bit of American fiscal folklore. That the promotion of full employment without inflation requires an agile and flexible combination of monetary and fiscal policies without any special concern for budgetary balance per se is an underlying tenet of "functional finance." Somewhere between these two views of fiscal orthodoxy and functional finance (although closer to the latter than the former) is the following critical evaluation.

The Balanced Budget Rule: A Fiscal Dogma?

For over a quarter of a century, economists, or the majority of them, have been protesting against the dogma that the annually balanced budget is the path of financial virtue. I regret to have to report that we have made remarkably little headway at the high political levels. Despite the economists, or perhaps because of them, every President has clung tenaciously to the dogma. President Roosevelt's papers clearly reveal that he regarded budget deficits as an evil that had to be tolerated in order to

* Taken and adapted from "The Balanced Budget," *American Economic Review, Papers and Proceedings*, May 1960, pp. 301–09. Reproduced with permission.

133

achieve a greater good. The published views of President Truman make his views on the subject abundantly clear. The spoken utterances of President Eisenhower leave no doubt about where he stands on the matter. But despite our failure to demolish this pillar of the financial temple, there seems to be general acceptance of the view that deficits, though evil, are inevitable during depressions.

The survival of the balanced budget rule, however, is not entirely a matter of dogma. Individuals and groups with no dogmatic convictions have a strong interest in keeping the dogma alive. The classical objection to government debt was a natural reaction to the consequences of government extravagance during the seventeenth and eighteenth centuries.

The requirement of a balanced budget was and still is the simplest and clearest rule to impose "fiscal discipline" and to hold government functions and expenditure to a minimum. Those who still entertain this desire as an overriding objective may be well advised not to retreat from the general rule until they are reasonably sure that the retreat will not become a rout.

The advocates of unbalanced budgets have not been reassuring from the conservative point of view. The unbalanced budget usually means fiscal freedom, borrowing, and deficits, and not deficits or surpluses as the occasion demands. The New Deal deficits were associated not simply with recovery but with recovery and reform; and when the New Deal was in full flower, the President took pains to insist that recovery was inseparable from reform.

Even an avowedly countercyclical fiscal policy is believed to give rise to an upward trend in expenditures that might not otherwise occur. The expenditures undertaken to counteract a depression are unlikely to be discontinued in the succeeding boom. If the boom is countered at all, the measures taken will be credit restriction or increased taxation; and then further expenditure programs will be taken to offset the next depression.

The discipline of the balanced budget is not necessarily the right degree of discipline. It is generally agreed that in time of war the unwilling taxpayer should not be allowed to hamper the defense of the country. The taxpayer is supposed to come into his own in times of peace. But the present situation is neither peace nor war. Despite amiable conversations among heads of state, a permanent state of military readiness for the indefinite future will be imperative. Organized groups of taxpayers have not shown a clear appreciation of the situation. The President and the leaders of Congress must have some freedom to act even though they cannot pay the bills from current revenue. But if all notions of fiscal discipline and budget balance were removed and no alternative was provided, there can be no doubt that expenditures would increase to a level that was economically undesirable and politically demoralizing. However rich we become, public and private wants are likely to increase more rapidly than the means of satisfying them; and in our complex political system some rules of financial conduct that are simple enough to survive in a political context seem to me to be desirable.

The Balanced Budget and Resource Allocation

Nevertheless, the rule that the budget should be balanced annually is inadequate to secure the proper allocation of resources between the public and the private sectors. The objections to it have been stated time and again. I shall therefore confine myself to a brief summary of those I consider the most important.

First, to attempt to balance the budget on an annual basis is inconsistent with the long-range character of many government programs. Research, development, and procurement for defense purposes inevitably involve activities extending over a number of years. If the programs are well conceived in the first place, waste and inefficiency will result from disrupting them in order to achieve particular budget results.

Another case where the requirement of annual balance is disruptive is the foreign aid program. This program is the favorite target for indignant charges of waste and inefficiency. But there is no surer way to waste and ineffectiveness than to expose our own program to such vicissitudes and uncertainties that the receiving countries are unable to mesh their own activities with it. Everyone who has examined the problem with understanding and sympathy has stressed the need for continuity.

A second objection to the balanced budget rule is that stress on the balanced budget as a criterion tends to give the misleading impression that the government is well managed if the budget is balanced. There is no indication that some over-all rule will secure efficiency down the line. When budget requests are cut to conform to the rule, the programs most likely to suffer are the new ones designed to meet new situations; and those most likely to survive are those that have acquired the support of powerful vested interests inside or outside the government. Not all new activities are necessarily more meritorious than the old.

Government efficiency cannot be achieved by budget ceilings imposed at the behest of hardhearted budget directors and appropriations committees. While some discipline of this kind is probably inevitable, the solution must lie in application of the economics of choice, subject to budget constraints, at every level of government. Public administrators traditionally do not learn economics, and vested interests have a strong interest in avoiding the application of economic principles.

The third objection relates to the effect of the balanced budget on economic fluctuations. Surely it is now agreed by economists that attempts, especially successful ones, to balance the budget every year worsen economic fluctuations. If governments curtail their expenditures when they are short of revenues and expand them when yields rise as a result of economic prosperity, their activities will be cyclical rather than countercyclical.

My final objection is that the balanced budget will not necessarily be the policy needed for achieving desired rates of economic growth. We are not prepared to get the additional resources needed for national security and social welfare by cutting back on consumption. That would mean higher taxes. We must therefore grow in order to obtain more resources. Some eminent authorities maintain that the American economy must grow at 5 per cent a year instead of its traditional 3 per cent. If accelerated growth is required, it seems to me very likely that the total rate of national saving must be increased, and the only practicable way to increase total saving is through the generation of budget surpluses. Budgetary doctrine in this country has hardly begun to contemplate this possibility.

—And General Economic Policy

A more general objection to the balanced budget or any other budgetary rule is that it places unnecessary restrictions on ability to achieve a variety of economic policy objectives.

The point can be illustrated very simply. Let us ignore for the moment pressing issues such as inflation and the balance of payments and assume that the government has only three policy objectives: first, it must spend enough to give effect to foreign and domestic policy objectives; second, it must maintain full employment; and, third, it must ensure that private investment will, in each year, be carried out at the rate required to maintain a given rate of economic growth for the economy as a whole. Thus every year it has three fixed targets: national income or output, private investment, and government expenditures. With present institutional arrangements, convictions, and predilections, it is virtually restricted to three instruments; namely, appropriations, taxation, and general credit expansion or contraction.

If the government has freedom to use these three instruments, it can attain the three objectives. If in addition it must balance the budget or maintain any prescribed relationship between expenditures and revenues, it has set for itself a fourth objective and is consequently one instrument short.

So long as it possesses only the three instruments, some other must give way: growth, full employment, or the government's own programs. As a matter of fact, during the last few years the government has placed even more severe restrictions on itself. It has attempted not only to balance the budget but to balance it at existing levels of taxation. This means that it has denied itself the use of one instrument. The expenditure objective necessarily gives way to this requirement (insofar as the requirement is met), and the government is left with general credit policy to achieve both full employment and a satisfactory rate of growth — a task that it is logically and practically impossible for the harassed monetary authorities to perform. Their difficulties are compounded when in addition they are expected to help correct the balance of payments and to prevent inflation.

If the government is short of instruments, it must acquire new instruments if it is to attain its objectives. Such new instruments could be selective credit controls, selective tax measures, and various kinds of direct controls. It would take me too far afield to discuss these possibilities in detail. Suffice it to say that many of them are pure anathema to those who must vehemently support the balanced budget doctrine. They are likely to be required to pay a high price for the dogma.

—And Economic Stability

We are unlikely to achieve full coherence in the formation of fiscal and budget policy. Some incoherence is likely to remain so long as there is separation of powers between the President and Congress and between the powerful committees of the Congress. Nevertheless, considerable improvement is possible and feasible. To be optimistic about that, one only has to reflect on the extent to which economic thinking has penetrated the government since World War II, largely as an outcome of the Employment Act of 1946 and the institutions set up under it. I therefore consider it worth while to offer some suggestions concerning the directions that improvement might take.

First of all, the President should transmit his budget to Congress as part of a comprehensive economic program. This is not done at the present time. The present Budget Message is notable for its lack of economic analysis. The President's Economic Report, on the other hand, is equally notable for its lack of an analysis of the economic impact of the budget. However much they may consort in private, the Budget Bureau and the Council of Economic Advisers do not embrace in public. The President's program would analyze economic policy as a whole in terms of the variety of objectives to be attained and the instruments to be employed.

With respect to the budget itself, the President would recommend a surplus, balance, or a deficit, depending on economic conditions. If a deficit were proposed, this should be proposed as a positive recommendation, not as a confession of failure to balance the budget combined with a wistful hope that balance will be achieved next year.

This approach could have the same disciplinary value as the balanced budget. If the President were prepared to give the weight of his authority to the need for a surplus or a deficit of a certain amount, that should have the same disciplinary value as balance from the point of view of the Congress and the executive departments.

For this suggestion to be as effective as possible, the Congress would have to co-operate. In particular, the Joint Economic Committee should join with the Appropriations Committee and the Ways and Means Committee in considering the President's program and in formulating Congressional economic and budgetary policy. But such a change in Congressional procedure is unlikely to come about unless the President takes the lead.

Second, the President's economic program should distinguish between long-run economic policy and the policy needed to counteract particular episodes of boom and recession. The long-run policy should contemplate continuity in government operations and continued growth of the economy. Budgetary policy in particular should be designed to conform with the requirements of long-run growth.

Of course long-run policy would be revised from year to year, to take account of changing circumstances and to correct errors in diagnosis. But in the absence of violent changes, say in defense requirements, it seems unlikely that abrupt changes in the relation of government expenditures to revenues would be required. Consequently, some simple budgetary rule that should apply in normal circumstances may be feasible. In times of full employment without inflation, it could be said that the budget should have a surplus or a deficit of some known order of magnitude.

It follows that the basic revenue and expenditure estimates should be made and published with reference to a full employment situation rather than to the situation actually predicted. This is the stabilizing budget approach that has long been advocated by the Committee for Economic Development, but which has made very little headway in official circles.

I suggest, also, that if the government's policy is to keep a stable price level, the expenditure and revenue estimates should be made in stable prices. This procedure provides an automatic check on inflation. It would tend to prevent inflationary increase in revenues from being regarded as a substitute for taxation. It would also put some pressure on the spending agencies in the event of inflation. They should make some contribution by attempting to curtail their activities. But if they consider that impossible, they should demonstrate the fact in requests for supplemental appropriations.

Thirdly, the question of countercyclical policy should be dealt with in a separate chapter of the President's program. This would include a discussion of the effects of recessions or booms on the budget and recommendations concerning the budgetary measures needed as correctives.

In view of what I said above, long-range government procurement programs should be interfered with as little as possible for cyclical policies. Nor should new programs that will last for a number of years be hastily adopted merely for the sake of relieving a single recession. This, however, does not mean that all public works should be continued at the same rate regardless of booms and depressions. Highway construction and many items authorized by the Rivers and Harbors Bill can be adjusted to short-term economic needs.

If the main emphasis were placed on changes in taxation and transfer payments for purposes of short-run stability, the inefficiencies connected with abrupt alterations in expenditure programs could be avoided. Nevertheless, once reduced, taxes are notoriously hard to restore. In fact it is hard to think of any tax increases during the last thirty years that were not undertaken in response to emergency situations. If the existing tax rates are likely to be needed for long-run purposes, it is of questionable wisdom to reduce them for short-run reasons, unless the reduction can be of an explicitly temporary character.

Built-in Flexibility

This leads me, and has led many others, to the conclusion that short-run stability should be achieved as far as possible through "built-in flexibility" of the budget and through monetary measures that can be readily reversed.

Built-in flexibility has increased appreciably as a result of social security, unemployment compensation, and agricultural support on the expenditure side and through the automatic operation of the tax system. But such measures — even in conjunction with vigorous credit measures — are unlikely to meet the requirements of a severe recession. There is need for further automatic measures. Consequently, I venture to repeat a proposal in which I participated some years ago. Under certain specified signs of recession, there should be an automatic reduction in the first bracket of the income tax. The reduction should be restored automatically when recovery has reached a prescribed point. To guard against inappropriate use of the remedy, its application should be subject to veto by the President. Devices such as this could give reasonable assurance that anything but the deepest depression would be corrected and would help materially to avoid the psychological conditions that might produce depressions of the catastrophic kind.

Our proposal was considered in the chancelleries of the world and was unanimously rejected by respectable opinion. But automatic reversible devices are the most effective way to avoid the radical political consequences of a flexible fiscal policy, and thus to allay the fears of those who cling to the balanced budget rule on rational rather than superstitious grounds.

21

Functional Finance[*]

ABBA P. LERNER
Michigan State University

"Functional" furniture is meant to be sat on. This same criterion of functionalism should be applied, suggests Professor Lerner, to the taxing, spending, and borrowing measures of government. These financial activities of government should be judged, he proposes, not by customary notions of fiscal propriety or by their effects upon the government, but in terms of their utility to the economy and general public.

The essential idea of Functional Finance is very simple. It is that the financial activities of the government should be judged not by any traditional canons of fiscal propriety but by considering the effects of each act and deciding whether these effects are desired or not.

The effects that government should consider are primarily the effects on the public, in whose interest the government is supposed to be acting. The effects on the government are always relatively unimportant.

The effects can be considered in their most simple and literal sense. For example, two effects of any tax payment are that the taxpayer has less money and that the government has more money. The first of these effects is important, so that the tax should be imposed if there is a good reason for wanting the taxpayer to have less money. The effect on the

[*] Taken and adapted from "An Integrated Full Employment Policy," *International Postwar Problems* (New York: American Labor Conference on International Affairs, January, 1946), pp. 69–73. Reproduced with permission.

government, namely, that the government will have more money is not important because the government can always get more money quite easily without impoverishing any taxpayer. If the government needs more money for any purpose it can simply create some money, either directly by printing it or indirectly by borrowing it from the banks.

From this it follows that taxes should never be imposed simply because the government needs money. Economic transactions, like purchases or sales of goods, should be taxed only when it is thought desirable to discourage these transactions. Individuals should be taxed only to the extent that it is desired to make the taxpayer poorer. The government should borrow money only if it desires to replace cash in the hands of the public by government IOU's (and should lend money or repay debt if it wishes to bring about the opposite effect). The government should sell goods if it is desirable that the public should have goods instead of cash, and should buy goods if it is desirable that the public should have more cash instead of the goods. For these are the effects of the government action and it is the distinguishing mark of reasonable behavior that action is governed only by a consideration of its effects. Functional Finance is nothing but the systematic application of this principle of rationality to governmental financial activities.

Every governmental financial activity can be reduced to one or more of six basic elements. The six elements form three pairs, one of each pair being the reverse of its partner. The three pairs of elementary financial instruments are:

1. Buying and Selling
2. Subsidizing and Taxing (*i.e.*, giving money to people and taking money from people)
3. Lending and Borrowing

These six elements include everything that the government can do in the economic field. Everything else can be considered as a combination of two or more of the elements. Requisitioning, for example, is equivalent to *Buying* the goods from an individual and then taking the money away from him by *Taxation*.

All this is related to the problem of full employment because the level of employment depends on the rate at which money is being spent on all goods and services together. The greater the total rate of spending, that is, the greater the amount of money spent on all goods and services every day of every week, both by the public and by the government, the greater will be the number of men and women that employers will find it profitable to employ. If the total rate of spending is low, employers will not be able to sell at a profit the output of all the people who want to work, and we will have unemployment. The degree of unemployment will depend on the degree to which the total rate of spending is below that level which would make it profitable to employ all who want to work.

A total rate of spending *above* this ideal level would mean that the public is trying to buy more goods than it is possible to produce even when everybody has a job. When everybody who wants to work is already working, such a great demand for goods cannot increase employment further. It can only raise prices and start an inflation.

Since inflation and unemployment should be prevented if possible, and since these scourges result from too high or too low a total rate of spending, it is impossible to avoid the conclusion that one of the most important duties of the government is to direct its financial policies toward keeping the total rate of spending from going too high or too low.

The three pairs of instruments fit so well into such a conception of the financial duties of the government that it is easy to identify Functional Finance with a policy for keeping the total rate of spending in the economy at the right level for preventing inflations and unemployment.

Buying goods and services directly increases the total rate of spending and is appropriate when the rate of spending is deficient. *Selling* goods (that have been acquired by the government in the past) naturally has the opposite effect, absorbing excessive spending, and is appropriate when the rate of spending is too high. (Government buying includes the undertaking of public works, the acquisition of products for storage, as has been done with cotton and wheat, and the purchase by the government of the products of industry for purposes such as war.)

Subsidies increase the total rate of spending by encouraging the transactions which are subsidized or simply by increasing the amount of money that the receivers of the subsidy can spend. Taxes work in the opposite direction by discouraging the transactions subject to the tax or simply by diminishing the amount of money that the taxpayers have left to spend. Subsidies may in fact be considered as negative taxes.

Lending by government has the effect of making it easier for borrowers to obtain loans which they could then spend either on consumption or more probably on investment in new construction. (Although government lending is rare, the repayment of government debt has exactly the same effects and must be included in government lending.) *Borrowing* by the government has the opposite effects, making it harder for borrowers to obtain loans by diminishing the expenditure out of such loans and so lowering the total rate of spending.[1]

---

[1] If the government borrows from banks holding excess reserves, this effect will not come about. The excess reserves would permit the banks to lend to the government without reducing their loans to other borrowers. The same is true if the government borrows from individuals who have an excess of cash which they would otherwise have kept idle. In all such cases the effects are just as if the government had created new money — bank money or cash money as the case may be.

Sometimes it is said that borrowing from the banks is inflationary (meaning that it tends to increase the total rate of spending). This is not correct. Government borrowing from the banks can never make it easier for others to borrow.

Thus the six fiscal instruments provide the government with six ways of dealing with an excessive total rate of spending and six ways of dealing with a deficiency in the total rate of spending. If spending is excessive the government can cut down on its *Buying* or its *Subsidies* or its *Lending* (an increase in debt repayment counting as an increase in lending), or it can step up its *Selling* or its *Taxes* or its *Borrowing*. In other words it can cut down on the first item in one of the three pairs of elementary governmental financial instruments or step up the second item in one of them. If the total rate of spending is deficient the whole business is simply reversed. The government can then step up the first item in one of the three pairs of instruments or it can cut down on the second element in one of them.

22

The Economic Theory Behind the Tax Cut*

MORGAN GUARANTY BANK AND TRUST COMPANY

Multipliers and accelerators are not merely tools of contemporary economic analysis. They also provide an "intellectual groundwork" for public policy and legislative action. So affirms a large New York bank in the following selection.

As Congress, which prides itself on its practicality, moved toward final consideration and enactment of the "Revenue Act of 1964," the legislators were fashioning a monument to a long line of theorists. For, in a sense, the real authors of the tax-cut bill are such academic economists as John Maurice Clark, R. F. Kahn, John R. Hicks, and — theoretician as well as man of practical affairs — John Maynard Keynes.

Names like these have not been much invoked in support of tax reduction; indeed, reference to some of them would have given the cause more hurt than help. Nevertheless, they — and others involved in the development of modern income-and-employment theory — laid the intellectual groundwork over the past four decades for the action Congress has taken. Without their work, it is hardly likely the nation today would be prepared for a step so unconventional as deliberate reduction of the Federal government's revenues at a time when the budget already is in deficit and the economy is expanding.

Thus passage of tax-cut legislation may seem to validate the spirit if

* Reprinted from the January 1964 issue of *The Morgan Guaranty Survey*, published by Morgan Guaranty Trust Company of New York.

not the letter of the oft-quoted Keynesian overstatement: "The ideas of economists and political philosophers, both when they are right and when they are wrong, are more powerful than is commonly understood. Indeed the world is ruled by little else."

Beneath the Fringe

The reason for looking to the theoretical origins of tax reduction, however, is not merely to nail down the genealogy of an idea. Much more important is a widespread understanding of the intended workings of this form of economic stimulus, its limitations and risks, and the need for auxiliary policies to help it in the task of promoting sound growth.

During the debate of the past year and a half, the case for cutting tax rates has accumulated a considerable fringe of half-truth and oversimplification, tacked on by advocates in their zeal to convert doubters of various kinds. Some of the liberals who have reversed traditional positions to support tax relief, for instance, clearly do so in an assumption that the fiscal boost to the economy will be reinforced by generous monetary stimulus. There are conservatives, on the other hand, who accept prolongation of the budget deficit only on the rigorous condition that it be financed entirely by the issuance of long-term Treasury securities. Both expectations may have to be disappointed if tax reduction is to do its job safely and effectively.

Multiply and Accelerate

The theoretical basis for tax reduction as an economic booster involves two concepts so reasonable that the layman is likely to dismiss them as obvious, yet so susceptible of elaboration that the economist has been able to build them into a specialty of his science. These are the "multiplier" and the "accelerator." Modern theory uses these two concepts to explain fluctuations in output and employment — and to suggest how an economy that is underproducing and underemploying can be prodded to better performance. The multiplier concept relates to consumption, the accelerator to investment.

When an outside force such as the government applies a stimulus to the economy — for example, by reducing taxes — a fairly direct effect on consumption can be expected. Consumers tend, with reasonable regularity, to spend between 92% and 94% of their disposable income. It can be rather confidently expected, therefore, that after a cut in individual income taxes the immediate beneficiaries will spend a substantial part of their new-found funds on goods and services.

Some part of this addition to gross business receipts flows into the hands of a second group of consumers in the form of wages, salaries, interest, dividends, and other kinds of payment. This second group is then likely to step up its own consumption outlays, providing still a third group with the wherewithal to raise its spending. Likewise on to a fourth round, and a fifth, ultimately raising the question: Why doesn't the multiplication process, once initiated with even a relatively modest starter, go on and on until there are no longer any idle resources left in the economy with which to meet the increased consumption demand?

The answer, according to multiplier theory, is that the consumption stream started by the tax cut suffers "leakages" in each round of reaction. Personal saving, drawing funds away from consumption (and, normally, transferring them to some form of investment), is one such leakage. A part of each added surge of gross business receipts flows into corporate retained earnings, another form of leakage. Expenditures on imports give rise to a third, since part of the amount spent leaves the domestic economy. Most important of all in size is the combined drain of Federal, state, and local taxes.

Two for One

Statisticians have expended a great deal of effort trying to calculate the percentage of leakage that typically occurs at each stage of the spending process. Estimates tend to cluster near or just slightly below 50%. This suggests that, for each $1 of tax-cut money initially spent on consumer goods, another 50 cents would be spent at a second stage, 25 cents at a third, 12½ cents at a fourth, and so on. Computing the downward progression yields a total of $2 in expenditures at all stages, with virtually the entire sum accounted for by the end of the first six expenditure rounds.

Since cumulative spending for consumer goods, on this basis, is just double the amount of the initial stimulus, the multiplier is said to have a numerical value of two. With a lower estimate of leakage, the multiplier would be higher. The Council of Economic Advisers has used a multiplier valued at two in its try at judging the direct effect on consumption of the cuts that have been proposed in income taxes. If, as now appears probable, the direct gain to consumers is to be something over $9 billion annually (allowing both for the cuts in individual income tax rates and for somewhat higher dividends likely to result from the cut in corporate tax rates), a multiplier of two would raise consumer spending by more than $18 billion above what it would be in the absence of tax reduction. Since the reduction in tax liabilities would be permanent, to be enjoyed by consumers year after year, the higher level of consumption expenditures — once achieved — could also be expected to be permanent.

Of course, the full impact could not reasonably be expected to occur until well into 1965 at the earliest, since the proposed two-stage tax cut would become fully effective only at the start of that year. Actually, the multiplier probably would take even longer to work itself out fully. Past consumer behavior indicates that considerable time lags sometimes occur before consumption habits are completely adjusted to changes in disposable income. This suggests the likelihood of some rise in the personal savings rate immediately after tax reduction occurs, and consequently a somewhat slow start for the multiplier. It also affords, however, the comforting inference that the promised tax cut has not already been largely discounted by consumers, as is sometimes suggested.

For Investment, A "Flash Point"

While the multiplier is at work in the realm of consumption, a proportionally even greater reaction, according to the theory, takes place in investment. This is attributed to a phenomenon known in the language of economic analysis as "acceleration."

Theoreticians recognize that, so long as substantial excess industrial capacity exists, businessmen will be slow to invest in new plant and equipment. However, as the multiplier process narrows the gap between capacity and output, a dramatic response in investment activity becomes likely. A sort of "flash point" is approached, in other words, at which something like an investment explosion takes place.

This interpretation of investment behavior rests on an assumption, seemingly reasonable, that the typical business firm tries to maintain a fixed relation between its capital equipment and what it regards as the normal demand for its products. Unless it judges demand to be heading for a permanently higher level, the firm is likely to confine new investment to meeting replacement needs. When the firm's managers become convinced, however, that a new and lasting element of demand for their products is emerging, they will step up their investment outlays so as to assure maintenance of the desired capital-output ratio. At this stage, incidentally, some of the income leakage that went on during the multiplier process begins to be recaptured, as firms draw on retained earnings and tap personal savings via capital issues or other borrowings.

The results that this turn of events can produce are evident from a simple hypothetical example. A firm that has been using 100 units of machinery may have been replacing ten units a year (reflecting, say, an average machine life of ten years). If it should decide at some point that a permanent increase of 5% in product demand is coming, it would then need 105 units to carry on its operations. Its total demand for new equipment in the single year in which the reassessment of prospects occurred would jump from the pattern of ten units per year to fifteen per year, an increase of 50%.

When the theoretical "flash point" is reached in any given enterprise, the percentage change in investment demand can thus be far greater than the change in underlying product demand. This difference is what gives the accelerator its name.

Feedback to Consumption

To the extent that the accelerator actually works, it also creates a new stimulus in consumer-goods activity, wholly apart from the primary multiplier. The expansion of capital-goods production generates its own flow of consumer income, which is spent and respent in what can be thought of as a second chain reaction. This, in turn, plays back to the investment area, providing it as well with a second round of support. In fact, once the initial stimulus has begun to work, a theoretical leap-frogging is set up between the multiplier and the accelerator.

It is much more difficult — even in the realm of theory — to put a quantitative value on the combined multiplier-accelerator effect than on the primary consumption multiplier alone. Most economists have avoided predicting how far the interaction might go beyond the $18-billion rise in consumption expenditures indicated by the multiplier of two. A few have ventured to suggest that gross national product may eventually benefit by three and one-half to four times the net initial reduction in over-all tax liabilities. On the total tax cut of $11 billion implied by the bill passed by the House of Representatives, this would point to an ultimate effect on GNP of something like $40 billion. This exceeds by roughly $10 billion the gap which the Council of Economic Advisers currently estimates as existing between potential and actual output.

Thus, on this basis at least, the proposed tax program is tailored generously enough to achieve the goals at which it aims, including a significant whittling down of the unemployment rate. In practice, of course, the one-two punch of the multiplier-accelerator is subject to the influence of all other forces that may be operating in the economy at any given time. At a point when business activity was about to start downhill, it might take a considerable multiplier effect merely to compensate for the basic weakness. If piled atop an already buoyant trend, the amplifying of demand could produce an unhealthy inflationary surge.

Handle with Care

Tax reduction, all this makes clear, is a high-powered tonic to pour into the body economic. Yet there is no certainty that it contains the specific for whatever has been retarding the body's metabolism. Fortunately, the means exist for either moderating or supplementing the effects of tax reduction as they begin to appear. The principal auxiliaries for this purpose are monetary policy and debt-management policy, and it is of crucial importance that they be kept free to move as required.

Like all experiments, tax reduction carries some risk of failure and some risk of oversuccess. Considerable boldness has been required to bring it as close to launching as it now is. Even more boldness, tempered with prudence, may have to be displayed before the experiment is finished.

• *23*

Economic Growth Through Taxation*

JAMES TOBIN
Yale University

The following selection gives some estimates of what needs to happen to consumption, investment, and government spending if we are to accelerate our rate of growth to 5 per cent per year and, also, some policy proposals on how to accomplish this objective. Professor Tobin does not assume that the total volume of consumption will decrease. He does, however, project sharp changes in the marginal propensity to consume (note the percentage shifts from 1959 to 1965 in Table 4) and higher taxes.

The overriding issue of political economy in the 1960's is how to allocate the national output. How much to private consumption? How much for private investment in plant and equipment? For government investment and public services? For national defense? For foreign aid and overseas investment?

Requirements for Accelerated Growth

The importance of accelerating economic growth brings the question of allocation to the fore. Can we as a nation, by political decision and governmental action, increase our rate of growth? Or must the rate of growth

* Taken and adapted from "Growth Through Taxation," *The New Republic*, July 25, 1960, pp. 15–18. Reproduced with permission.

be regarded fatalistically, the result of uncoordinated decisions and habits of millions of consumers, businessmen and governments. The Communists are telling the world that they alone know how to mobilize economic resources for rapid growth. The appeal of free institutions in the under-developed world, and perhaps even their survival in the West, may depend on whether the Communists are right. We cannot, we need not leave the outcome to chance.

How can an increase in the rate of growth of national output be achieved? The answer is straightforward and painful. We must devote more of our current capacity to uses that increase our future capacity, and correspondingly less to other uses. The uses of current capacity that build up future productive capacity are of three major types: (1) *Investment:* replacement and expansion of the country's stock of productive capital — factories, machines, roads, trucks, school buildings, hospitals, power dams, pipelines, etc. (2) *Research,* both in basic science and in industrial application, by government, private industry and non-profit institutions, leading sooner or later to more efficient processes and new products. (3) *Education* of all kinds augmenting the skill of the future labor force. The competing uses of current capacity are: (1) *Unemployment:* failure to employ current capacity to the full, letting potential production be lost through unemployment. (2) *Consumption,* where most of our resources are engaged, providing us with the goods, services, and leisure that constitute the most luxurious standard of living the world has known.

Since 1953 the economy has been operating at an average unemployment level of about 5 per cent of the labor force. A society geared to the objective of growth should keep the average unemployment rate down to 3 per cent. Reduction of unemployment to this level could increase Gross National Product from the current labor force and capital stock by about $20 billion. *But this increase in output will contribute to economic growth only if it is used in substantial part for investment, research and education;* it will make no contribution if it is all consumed.

Two Shifts in Resource Use

To stimulate growth we must somehow engineer two shifts in the composition of actual and potential national output. One is from *private consumption to the public sector* — federal, state and local. Domestic economic growth is, of course, not the only reason for such a shift. Increased defense, increased foreign aid, increased public consumption are possibly equally urgent reasons. The second shift of resources that must be engineered is *from private consumption to private investment.* About three-quarters of Gross National Product is produced with the help of business plant and equipment. Faster growth of output requires a more rapidly expanding and more up-to-date stock of plant and equipment. Every $1 increase of GNP requires in the neighborhood of $1.50 new plant and equipment investment. Thus to raise the rate of growth two percentage points, say from 3 per cent to 5 per cent per annum, the share of plant and equipment investment in current GNP must rise by three percentage points, *e.g.* from 10 per cent to 13 per cent.

Table 1 provides a concrete illustration of the kind of change we need in the relative composition of output if we are serious about increasing our rate of growth. It shows the composition of GNP in the three years with correction for price changes, *i.e.*, in "constant 1959 dollars." Table 2 brings out the essential point more clearly. It shows how the actual increase in GNP between 1953 and 1959 was allocated among major uses, and, in contrast, how we should allocate the growth in output over the next six years if we really want output to grow.

Unemployment, Consumption, Prices

Between 1953 and 1959 potential GNP rose from $365 billion to an estimated $500 billion. Some of the potential increase went to waste in unemployment. Of the realized increase, 69 per cent went into consump-

Table 1.   Composition of Gross National Product in Constant 1959 Dollars

	1953	*1959*	*1965 Target*
	(billions of dollars)		
Potential Gross National Product (3% unemployment)	417	500 (104%)	650
Actual Gross National Product	417 (100%)	479 (100%)	650 (100%)
Private Consumption	254 (61%)	311 (65%)	390 (60%)
Government Purchase of Goods and Services	102 (24%)	98 (20%)	145 (22%)
a. Privately Produced	59 (14%)	53 (11%)	80 (12%)
b. Services of Gov't. Employees	43 (10%)	45 (9%)	65 (10%)
Gross Private Investment	60 (15%)	70 (15%)	115 (17%)
a. Plant & Equipment	44 (11%)	44 (9%)	80 (12%)
b. Increase in Inventories	1 (—)	4 (1%)	8 (1%)
c. Residential Construction	15 (4%)	22 (5%)	27 (4%)
Net Private Foreign Investment	1 (—)	−1 (—)	0 (0%)

Source for actual data 1953 and 1959: *Economic Report of the President, 1960.*

tion, 13 per cent into government activity, and 18 per cent into investment. Unfortunately these calculations *understate* the effective growth of
consumption relative to government and investment. The reason is that
the prices of goods and services needed for government activity and
private investment rose relative to the prices of consumption goods and
services. For example, the services of government employees (teachers, policemen, clerks, etc.) rose in price 34 per cent while consumer prices rose 9 per cent. Although we managed to increase government expenditure for such services by $13 billion, $11 billion of the
increase was simply the higher cost of the volume of services we were
already getting in 1953 and only $2 billion represented a real expansion
of such services. When account is taken of this and other unfavorable
relative price changes, some 92 per cent of the growth in output "in
constant dollars" went to consumption; *government activity actually
diminished;* private investment got 16 per cent of the increase in GNP,
and *none of this increase was for plant and equipment.* (See Table 2.)

Unfortunately we will probably have to continue to do some running
just to stay in the same place. The targets suggested for 1965 in
Table 1 assumes that prices of goods and services for investment and
government will rise relative to consumer prices. If consumption prices
are kept stable from 1959 to 1965, potential 1965 GNP is estimated at
$688 billion. If we resolve to increase to 25 per cent the government share
of that output, and to 18 per cent the investment share, the assumed price

Table 2.   Disposition of Increases in GNP

	Constant 1959 Dollars	
	(billions of dollars)	
	1953 to 1959	1959 to 1965
Potential Gross National Product	83 (133%)	150 (88%)
Actual Gross National Product	62 (100%)	171 (100%)
Private Consumption	57 (92%)	79 (46%)
Government Purchase of Goods and Services	−4 (−7%)	47 (27%)
a. Privately Produced	−6 (−10%)	27 (16%)
b. Services of Government Employees	2 (3%)	20 (11%)
Gross Private Investment	10 (16%)	45 (26%)
a. Plant and Equipment	0 (0%)	36 (21%)
b. Increase in Inventories	3 (5%)	4 (2%)
c. Residential Construction	7 (11%)	5 (3%)
Net Private Foreign Investment	−1 (−2%)	1 (−)

increases in those sectors would nullify part of those increases, leaving us a GNP of $650 billion in constant 1959 dollars, with the composition shown in Table 1. In order to keep from consuming more than 46 per cent of the projected increase in real output we must restrain consumption to 46 per cent of the growth of output. (See Table 2.)

Program for Growth

Policy to accelerate growth must be double-edged. On the one hand, it must stimulate the desired government and private expenditures. On the other hand, it must discourage consumption. Here are some major constituents of a program for growth:

1. Increased expenditure by federal, state, and local governments for education, basic and applied research, urban redevelopment, resource conservation and development, transportation and other public facilities.

2. Stimulus to private investment expenditures by:

(a) Federal Reserve and Treasury policy to create and maintain "easy money" conditions, with credit readily available and interest rates low, especially long-term capital markets.

(b) Improvements of averaging and loss-offset provisions in taxation of corporate income, to increase the degree to which the tax collector shares the risk of investment as well as the reward.

(c) The privilege of deducting from corporate net income for tax purposes a certain percentage of a corporation's outlays for plant and equipment to the extent that these outlays exceed a specified minimum. The specified minimum would be the sum of depreciation and (on the assumption that the tax rate is 52 per cent) 48 per cent of net income before tax. To qualify for the tax concession, a corporation would have to be investing more than its normal gross profits after tax. The concession, and the minimum requirement for eligibility for it, are designed to encourage greater corporate saving, the full investment of internal funds, and, most important, the undertaking of investment financed by outside saving obtained from the capital market. An analogous proposal to encourage non-corporate saving and investment is suggested below.

If these measures were adopted, a reduction in the basic corporate income tax rate, advocated by many as essential to growth, would be neither necessary nor equitable. Indeed the strength of these measures might be greater if the rate were increased.

3. Restriction of consumption by:

(a) Increase in personal income tax at all levels, accompanied by permission to deduct a certain amount of saving from income subject to tax. Like present deductions for charity, medical care, etc., the saving deduction would be claimed at the taxpayer's option, with the burden of proof on him. A schedule of "normal" saving for taxpayers of various incomes and family circumstances would be established, and only saving in excess of a taxpayer's "normal" would be eligible for deduction. A scheme of this kind seems the most feasible equitable way to use the tax instrument to favor saving at the expense of consumption.

(b) Improvements in the social security system — *e.g.* raising retirement benefits and relating their amount, above a common minimum, to cumulated covered earnings — should be introduced on a quasi-contributory basis. Since the payroll tax contributions then precede the benefits, the funds accumulate and can be an important channel of national saving.

(c) Increase in state and local taxes — property or sales or income as the case may be — to keep pace with the share of these governments in the necessary expansion of the public sector.

(d) Limitation, to a reasonable proportion of sales, of the privilege of deducting advertising and promotional expenses from corporate income subject to tax. No observer of the American scene doubts that advertising is excessive. From the economic point of view, it absorbs too large a share of the nation's resources; at the same time it generates synthetic pressure for higher consumption.

Increased Taxation Is the Price of Growth

We must tax ourselves not only to finance the necessary increase in public expenditures but also to finance, indirectly, the expansion of private investment. A federal budget surplus is a method by which we as a nation can expand the volume of saving available for private investment beyond the current saving of individuals and corporations. The surplus must, to be sure, be coupled with measures to stimulate investment, so that the national resolution to save actually leads to capital formation and is not wasted in unemployment and unrequited loss of consumption. It is only superficially paradoxical to combine anti-inflationary fiscal policy with an expansionary monetary policy. The policies outlined above must be combined in the right proportions, so that aggregate demand is high enough to maintain a 3 per cent unemployment rate but not higher. There are several mixtures which can do that job; of them we must choose the one that gives the desired composition of aggregate demand. If the overwhelming problem of democratic capitalism in the '30's and even the '50's was to bring the business cycle under social control, the challenge of the '60's is to bring under public decision the broad allocation of national output. Unless we master it, we shall not fare well in the competition for economic growth and national survival.

• 24

Types of Depression and Programs to Combat Them *

ROBERT A. GORDON
University of California, Berkeley

"Depression" is an important concept in economics. It is a problem of such magnitude that no quick and easy remedy can solve it. Each depression requires a program tailored to its severity and duration.

Three Types of Contraction

Cyclical forces can lead to different sorts of cyclical contractions, which we can conveniently group into three broad types.

First, we have the case of the "pure" minor recession, in which the cyclical response mechanism operates without affecting long-term investment. The downturn comes because of a downward revision of short-period production plans. The stock of investment opportunities remains large, and there is no significant deterioration in the inducements to exploit these opportunities. The necessary adjustments are brought about through moderate price declines, some contraction of short-term debt, and the curtailment of production in order to reduce inventories. Ex-

* Taken and adapted from National Bureau of Economic Research, *Policies to Combat Depression* edited by Herbert Stein (Princeton, N.J.: Princeton University Press, 1956), pp. 10–19. Reproduced with permission.

amples of minor-cycle contractions of this sort are those which occurred in 1923–1924, 1927, 1949, and 1953–1954.

The "pure" minor cycle becomes less pure as changes in production plans lead also to changes in investment plans. This brings us to our next case, which results in sharp but relatively short cyclical contractions. We may call this the "hybrid" case, intermediate between the pure minor and the pure major cycle.

A hybrid contraction may occur for either of two reasons. In the first place, once a downswing begins for any reason, the deterioration in short-term expectations may affect long-term expectations, even though investment opportunities remain large enough to support long-term investment at its previous peak rate. The second possibility is that, at the end of a particularly vigorous boom, a cyclically induced monetary or real capital shortage may temporarily reduce the stock of profitable investment opportunities.

What is important about this hybrid case is that the revival of long-term investment is brought about endogenously through the operation of the cyclical response mechanism: as soon as excess inventories are liquidated, prices stop falling, interest rates and capital goods prices fall to lower levels, etc. Thus while contractions which arise in this way may be quite sharp, they are not likely to last very long. It is more useful to think of the depressions of 1907, 1937–1938, and (with some qualifications) 1921 in these terms, as hybrid contractions, rather than as "major" depressions.

Finally, we have the case of the major cycle proper, in which a high level of investment has been maintained for a long enough time so that long-term investment opportunities become seriously impaired. When a depression develops for this reason, the forces making for revival that gradually emerge from the contraction will not be enough in themselves to restore the stock of investment opportunities. The severity of the depression will depend particularly on how much overbuilding went on during the preceding boom, on the strength of the forces making for further growth which open up new investment opportunities, and on the nature of the financial maladjustments resulting from earlier speculative excesses. To this category of prolonged (and usually severe) major depressions belong the depressions of the 1870's, 1890's, and 1930's and probably also that of 1882–1885.

Stabilization Policy

Let us turn now to a consideration of some of the implications of the preceding analysis for business cycle policy. (1) There is no one kind of program which would be equally effective against all cyclical contractions. (2) An effective stabilization program needs to be flexible, and its details should to some extent be tailor-made to fit the changing character of the cycle. (3) Therefore, an essential requirement is continuing and careful diagnosis of current cyclical developments, both in order to influence the current phase of the cycle (if that is desired) and as preparation for prompt action in the most effective way if future developments should take an unfavorable turn. (4) A further conclusion, derived from the preceding ones, is that an effective stabilization program cannot rely exclusively on automatic stabilizers. Discretionary action, extending beyond the field of merely monetary policy, is necessary in all except relatively pure minor cycles.

Certain minimal techniques are appropriate regardless of the type of instability anticipated. This is particularly true of the so-called automatic stabilizers and of monetary policy. Two essential and familiar features of all cyclical contractions are the multiplier process whereby a decline in spending reduces incomes and therefore leads to still further reductions in spending, and the effect of the increased desire for liquidity on production and investment plans.

The automatic stabilizers — by reducing tax receipts and increasing transfer payments as the national income declines — moderate the cumulative contraction in disposable income and in consumers' expenditures. Undoubtedly, the effectiveness of the present stabilizers could be improved, but any retardation in the decline in disposable income and consumption will have some influence, in a degree depending on the circumstances, in ameliorating the deterioration in profit expectations and in liquidity attitudes and will reduce the decline in production necessary to bring about a given decrease in inventories. Some favorable effects on long-term investment, again in a degree depending on the circumstances, may also be expected.

The principal role of monetary policy, regardless of the type of depression, is to combat the increased desire for liquidity. To the extent that it is successful in doing so, it will hold back the liquidation of inventories and the consequently exaggerated decline in output, ameliorate the decline in commodity and security prices and the resulting further deterioration of expectations, and lend some support to the inducement to exploit existing investment opportunities. It is likely also to have some beneficial effect on consumers' expenditures, particularly for durable goods.

The Minor Recession

Let us now look at our three main types of depression to see what additional measures are best suited to each. A "pure" minor recession, with little or no decline in the sum of private long-term investment and government expenditure, does not, of course, cause a great deal of damage. For such mild and short-lived deflationary episodes, one might argue that no correctives are needed beyond the mechanical working of the automatic stabilizers and a prompt and strong dose of an easy money policy. The stronger the underlying trend toward secular inflation, the stronger the argument against going farther than this if one is confident that only a minor recession is involved.

Since we can never feel perfectly sure of our diagnosis, and particularly if the community is not prepared to tolerate an unemployment rate higher than, say, 5 per cent even for a short period, additional discretionary action might be taken to ameliorate a minor recession and hasten revival. "Formula flexibility" might be introduced into the system of unemployment insurance, so that payment provisions become more liberal as the unemployment rate rises. Expenditures on the lighter types of public works, which could be started quickly and completed within a short period, could be accelerated. It does not seem to me, however, that this sort of minor recession is the time for discretionary tax cuts, to be reversed later, or for an elaborate public works program.

The Hybrid Case

Let us now look at our second and more interesting type of contraction, the "intermediate" or "hybrid" case. I think most discussions of depression policy envisage this sort of recession — *i.e.* a contraction of considerable amplitude, associated with a fairly sharp drop in private long-term (as well as inventory) investment, but with no significant impairment of underlying investment opportunities.

Clearly, the measures suggested above for a minor recession are suitable here also. The more successfully income and consumption can be maintained through the operation of the automatic stabilizers and a discretionary increase in government expenditures, the less serious will be the impairment of inducements to exploit existing investment opportunities. In this type of sharp contraction, also, it is particularly essential that everything possible be done to combat the rapid and cumulative deterioration in attitudes toward liquidity. A vigorous use of the conventional instruments of monetary policy can flood the system with excess reserves, the purpose being not only to reduce interest rates but, more important, to minimize the increase in credit rationing resulting from the re-evaluation of risks by lenders and to satisfy the increased desire for liquidity by business firms. An easy money policy, particularly if promptly initiated, should also help to hold back the decline in security and commodity prices and therefore further bolster business confidence.

Beyond these minimal measures, something can be done directly to stimulate the inducements for exploiting existing investment opportunities and possibly, also, to create new opportunities. Lower interest rates will obviously help. A proposal frequently suggested is some form of tax remission or direct subsidy for private investment undertaken during periods of depressed activity.

In general, it is this "hybrid" type of depression which offers the fullest scope for the conventional instruments of stabilization policy because, by vigorous and prompt action, we can hope to bring about a revival in private spending without undue delay. The more successfully aggregate demand is maintained, the more willing will businessmen be to exploit existing investment opportunities. A combined monetary and fiscal policy can slow down the decline in private spending; fiscal policy working through increased government expenditures and reduced tax receipts can partially offset the decline in private investment; and the specific measures previously mentioned, as well as others, can be used to stimulate private investment.

The Major Depression

The hybrid case shades into the more serious situation of a major depression, in which there is a significant impairment of underlying investment opportunities. Reference to reduced investment opportunities does not necessarily mean secular stagnation in a really long-run sense. The impairment of investment opportunities may be and in the past has been temporary. But, while this situation lasts, measures aimed at maintaining or reviving disposable income and consumption will not be enough to restore private investment to the level needed for full employment. In short, this is the case in which pump priming will have only limited success and the "leverage effects" of expansionary measures will be disappointingly small.

The types of policy already discussed should also be appropriate in a major depression; but, if these restorative efforts seem to have only limited effect and if private investment continues to decline, further steps can be taken. The public works program can be expanded, with particular attention being paid to those types of construction and those geographical areas which have been hardest hit. Efforts can be intensified to stimulate investment by monetary policy and by tax and other investment incentives. In addition, lower interest rates and reduced prices for capital goods will extend the margin of profitable investment opportunities in some directions.

What are some of the ways in which the stock of private investment opportunities might be expanded?

Lower interest rates and prices of capital goods have already been mentioned. Special aid might be given to relatively young industries which perhaps had become temporarily overbuilt but which had considerable growth ahead of them — for example, financial assistance to firms in difficulties and technical help in accelerating the reduction in cost and improvement in product. Tax incentives and other government help could be offered generally to stimulate industrial research and modernization. Public expenditures might be made with a view to expanding particular industries. Thus road and street improvements might stimulate the automobile and house-building industries; construction and improvement of airports would help the aircraft and related industries; government assistance in the exploration for new oil reserves might result in a substantial increment of private investment in the important oil industry; and so on. Undoubtedly there are many other ways of helping private industry to develop new opportunities for expansion of which it is not yet aware.

Particularly difficult problems are created when a major depression is brought on or intensified by the downswing of a building cycle, particularly in residential construction. A serious decline in residential building is likely to mean that there has been a decline in the stock of investment opportunities in one or both of two ways. There may have been overbuilding, so that the current stock of housing is too large, given the size and other characteristics of the population and given also current incomes and prices. Second, and less serious, there may not have been any overbuilding, but the past rate of building may have been larger than that called for by current and expected future increments of demand.

These considerations suggest the general lines along which attempts to revive residential building activity might proceed. Slum clearance and other forms of subsidized demolition can contribute to reducing an excess stock of housing. Special tax and financial inducements can be offered to private builders of housing for low and middle income groups. Special efforts can be made to bring down building costs and to stimulate the maintenance and improvement of existing dwellings. Public works can be undertaken in part with a view to stimulating residential and commercial building — for example, improvement of streets and roads and public transportation systems.

The measures discussed in the preceding pages can do some good, but undoubtedly they cannot *prevent* a major depression. Delays in diagnosis and the inevitable political and economic problems involved in putting any large-scale discretionary program into effect mean that, if a serious impairment of investment opportunities were to occur, steps could not be taken in time to prevent a business contraction of considerable magnitude. But perhaps I am more pessimistic than I should be.

The Fiscal Policy of the Kennedy-Johnson Administration: Goals and Performance*

NEIL H. JACOBY
U.C.L.A.

The following selection brings to mind the Shakespearean adage that "there is many a slip 'twixt cup and lip." It contends that the Kennedy-Johnson fiscal performance has been more conservative than Democratic pronouncements and that the Eisenhower fiscal performance was less conservative than Republican orthodoxy. Thus both administrations in practice have hewn to the center of the fiscal road (although K-J get commendations for placing an increasing emphasis upon growth-oriented tax and expenditure policies). What evidence is provided to support these conclusions and what criteria are suggested to measure fiscal performance?

My assignment is to assess Federal fiscal performance under the Kennedy-Johnson Administration against the announced goals of the Administration.[1]

I propose four objective measures of Federal fiscal performance:

* Taken and adapted from "The Fiscal Policy of the Kennedy-Johnson Administration," *The Journal of Finance, Papers and Proceedings*, May 1964, pp. 353–69. Reproduced with permission.

[1] One may fairly treat the Kennedy-Johnson Administration as an entity, because President Johnson has squarely endorsed and supported the fiscal policies and programs of the late President J. F. Kennedy.

1. The *size* of the Federal budget in relation to the GNP, measured by the ratio of Federal cash payments to GNP, ideally for a cash budget that is in balance under conditions of full employment.

2. The *structure of expenditures* in the budget, broadly classified as between investment-type expenditures which are growth-promoting in their effect upon the private sector, and consumption-type expenditure which are not growth-promoting although they may elevate the current standard of living.

3. The *structure of revenues* in the budget, also broadly dichotomized into taxes on net incomes and estates, on the one hand, and those on payrolls and commodities, on the other hand. The first class of imposts tend to fall most heavily upon savings and investments in the private sector; the latter class bear relatively more heavily upon consumption.

4. The *stabilizing effectiveness* of fiscal policy, measured by the degree to which changes in private demand are offset by changes in governmental expenditure and revenue flows.

The Fiscal Goals of the Administration

We may characterize broadly the announced fiscal goals of the Kennedy-Johnson Administration by three features:

First, espousal of an active Federal government, alert to opportunities for expanding Federal services to the public, and ready to enlarge the role of government in the economy as producer, as purchaser, and as regulator of the private sector.

Second, emphasis upon raising the long-term growth rate of the economy *vis-à-vis* other national economic aims. Public statements of the Administration's spokesmen have been replete with laments over "gaps" and "output deficits" in U.S. economic performance, and call for bold measures to get the economy "moving ahead" more rapidly.

Third, advocacy of a "strong" fiscal policy designed to play a relatively more important role in the attainment of economic goals than was assigned to it by the Eisenhower Administration. Both the academic economists and the executives of the Kennedy-Johnson Administration hold to the Keynesian emphasis upon fiscal policy as the predominant instrument of management of the economy. For this reason, and because of recent balance of payments constraints, they tend to assign monetary policy a less active and continuous part than it played during the 1950's.

If the broad fiscal goals of the Kennedy-Johnson Administration have been correctly characterized, one would expect that, after three years in office, Federal fiscal policy would reveal some distinct changes of direction. One would anticipate the emergence of a significantly higher ratio of Federal cash payments in relation to gross national expenditure. One would confidently look for a market shift in the Federal government's use of its resources toward growth-promoting public investment in human and physical capital, and away from outlays on currently-consumed public services. Likewise, one would expect to find that the Federal government's withdrawals of resources from the private sector of the economy, *via* revenue receipts, would weigh less heavily upon private savings and investment and more heavily upon current consumption expenditures. Finally, one would expect to find definite gains in the counter-cyclical stabilization effects of Federal fiscal action. Have these changes in fact occurred?

In a search for answers to these questions, we may appropriately begin with the fiscal year 1954, because this was the first full year of operation under the Eisenhower Administration and presumably reflected its influence. We shall compare actual fiscal performance in this base year with: (1) President Eisenhower's *proposals* for fiscal year 1962 — the last of his Administration, (2) *actual* performance for fiscal year 1962 — the first full year under the Kennedy Administration, (3) President Kennedy's *estimates* for fiscal year 1963 and his *proposals* for fiscal year 1964, and (4) *probable* performance for fiscal year 1964.

Changes in the Ratio of Federal Cash Outlays to Gross National Expenditure

The best broad measure of change in the economic role of the Federal government is the change between fiscal years in the ratio of Federal cash payments to gross national expenditure. Federal cash payments formed 19.7 per cent of GNE during fiscal year 1954. Eight years later President Eisenhower proposed for fiscal year 1962 a budget in which Federal payments would be 19.0 per cent of GNE. Evidently, eight years of Republican emphasis upon "limited government" and "reliance upon private enterprise" in the nation's economic life had not succeeded in reducing very much the role of the Federal government in total national expenditures.

Actual Federal cash payments during fiscal year 1962 under the Kennedy Administration rose materially to 19.8 per cent of GNE, and President Kennedy's budget for fiscal year 1964 proposed payments of 20.4 per cent. But the Congress is obviously determined to restrain rather than to expand Federal spending, and President Johnson has publicly accepted those restraints. Present indications are that actual cash payments in fiscal year 1964 will be only about $2 billion more than in fiscal year 1963, and will form about 19.7 per cent of an estimated GNE of $601 billion in fiscal year 1964. Thus the prospect is that the *relative* role of Federal payments in gross national expenditure will be identical to that during the 1954 fiscal year of the Eisenhower Administration and will expand by only 0.7 percentage point over the level of payments it *proposed* for 1962.

The record suggests that both the Kennedy-Johnson and Eisenhower Administrations were frustrated in their efforts to attain their professed — but opposite — goals. It reveals the great power of Congress which, by pulling against the Executive branch first in one direction and then in the other, kept both of them chained near the middle of the fiscal road. Virtually no change has occurred during the past decade in the proportion of aggregate demand *financed* by the Federal government. Evidently, aggregate Federal spending in the U.S. economy has been determined primarily by fundamental politico-economic changes, foreign and domestic, and only tangentially by partisan ideologies. The dominant factor has been the tapering off of the great national security buildup of recent years. This will probably cause aggregate Federal purchases of goods and services to grow less rapidly than the economy in the future.

Changes in the Structure of Federal Expenditures and in Resource Allocation Within the Federal Sector

The degree to which Federal expenditure programs have been reoriented to the goal of more rapid economic growth can be measured by observing changes in the proportions of investment-type and consumption-type outlays to total expenditures during the past decade.

The major structural change in aggregate civil and defense Federal budget expenditures over the decade 1954–1963 was a modest increase in the proportion of investment-type outlays — for additions to physical assets and for development of human capital and the stock of knowledge through outlays on research, development, health, and education — and a small decline in the proportion of consumption-type outlays — for aids, subsidies, and services to particular groups and for general purposes. This shift occurred under the Eisenhower Administration, and it proceeded slowly and steadily under the Kennedy-Johnson Administration. Investment-type expenditures rose from 38.2 per cent of total budget expenditures in fiscal year 1954 to 39.3 per cent proposed by President Eisenhower for fiscal year 1962. They are estimated to rise to 40.5 per cent of expenditures in the current fiscal year 1963, and President Kennedy proposed that they should be 40.9 per cent in fiscal year 1964. Thus, if Congress were to act affirmatively on the Administration's fiscal year 1964 budget, the *relative* increase in investment-type spending over the decade would be about 12½ per cent.

Confining our analysis to changes in Federal *civil* expenditures between fiscal year 1954 and proposals for fiscal year 1964, we find not only a doubling of total civil outlays, but also a truly massive shift to investment-type outlays under both the Eisenhower and Kennedy-Johnson Administrations. In round numbers, total civil spending will double from $21.4 billion to $43.7 billion; consumption-type spending will rise by 80 per cent from $17.0 billion to $30.5 billion; and investment-type spending will triple from $4.4 billion to $13.1 billion. Civil investment spending has been growing at a compound annual rate of about 12 per cent; consumption spending at about 6 per cent.

Although the Kennedy-Johnson Administration did not initiate a new trend, its progress toward a growth-promoting structure of Federal civil spending has been impressive. It can be credited for giving increased emphasis to public investment in both human and physical assets. The major investment-type civil programs initiated under Eisenhower were the National Federal-Aid Highway Fund, the National Aviation and Space Agency, and the National Defense Education Fund. In addition to expanding these programs, the Kennedy-Johnson Administration fostered the Area Redevelopment Act of 1961, the Public Works Acceleration Act of 1963, the Manpower Development and Retraining Act of 1962, and the Senior Citizens Housing Act of 1962.

Few will question the desirability of the rising emphasis in Federal spending upon the expansion and improvement of our nation's physical and human resources. However, many will question the wisdom of continuing large subsidies and aids to special groups and sectors of the economy, which not only involve mal-allocations of Federal resources, but also have the effect of impeding the movement of private resources to more productive uses. The present Administration (as well as its predecessor) is vulnerable to the criticism that it has failed to press for reductions of large subsidies to agriculture, ship-building, veterans, and other groups, for which the marginal social utility of Federal expenditures has become minuscule, if not negative.

Changes in the Structure of Federal Revenues and Their Effects Upon Resource Allocation within the Private Sector

The major structural change in the Federal revenue system between fiscal year 1954 and that proposed for fiscal year 1964 has been a rise in the relative importance of payroll and commodity taxation and a decline in the relative reliance upon net income and property taxation. This shift has been of substantial proportions, and it has continued through both the Eisenhower and Kennedy-Johnson Administrations. It has been the product of three sets of forces: first, a continued erosion of the net income tax base by credits, exemptions, and enlargements of depreciation allowances and other deductions from taxable income; secondly, income tax rate reductions enacted by the Congress effective in March 1964; thirdly, a remarkable rise in the rates and bases of payroll taxes for social security purposes. Like the shift in the Federal expenditure structure, this change in the Federal revenue structure is growth-promoting in its effects upon the economy. The Federal burden upon private savings and investment is being gradually lightened, while that upon consumption is rising.

This change has proceeded slowly and almost imperceptibly. In fiscal year 1954, 73 per cent of Federal government receipts from the public derived from taxes on net incomes and estates and 27 per cent from taxes on payrolls and commodities. President Eisenhower's budget proposals for fiscal year 1962 involved a 67 per cent — 33 per cent division of burdens. President Kennedy's budget proposals for fiscal year 1964, after giving effect to his program of income tax reduction and reform, would further reduce the role of income and estate taxation to 64 per cent and raise that of payroll and commodity taxes to 36 per cent of Federal receipts.

The primary criticism to be made of President Kennedy's program of tax reduction is that it concentrates the preponderance of all tax reduction on low-bracket personal incomes, where its ultimate effects in expanding aggregate demand are likely to be modest. The employment-generating effects of tax-rate reduction, per dollar of immediate revenue loss, would be much larger by concentrating on the corporate tax rate. The slow growth of the U.S. economy in recent years has been due primarily to a deficiency of domestic private investment. This can be rectified by improving prospective rates of return by reducing the prospective tax liabilities of investors.

Changes in the Stabilizing Effectiveness of Fiscal Policy

How effectively has the Kennedy-Johnson Administration used fiscal policy in the interests of counter-cyclical stabilization? Certainly, a highly flexible counter-cyclical behavior is desirable, resulting both from automatic changes built into Federal revenue and expenditure programs and also from deliberate changes in those programs, provided that such behavior can be attained without sacrificing other ends of national policy.

There has been some loss in automatic Federal budget flexibility as a result of erosion of the net income tax base, and some gain from the rise in the effective tax rate as incomes have risen. Moreover, expansion of the coverage and scale of benefits of unemployment compensation payments has strengthened the stabilizing effect. Payroll tax revenues, which have been rising in relative importance, are quite sensitive to cyclical changes in employment and average weekly hours of work. All in all, the probabilities are that the power of the automatic stabilizers in the Federal fiscal system has been well maintained during the past decade, although the rise in relative importance of state and local fiscal transactions, which have little, if any, countercyclical effects, may have reduced the stabilizing effectiveness of governmental fiscal action as a whole.

A Federal Administration should be judged primarily upon a basis of its *deliberate* use of fiscal measures for stabilization, and upon its efforts to build stronger automatic devices into the system. On both counts the Kennedy-Johnson Administration has a good record. Upon taking office in January 1961 at the nadir of a short recession, President Kennedy acted vigorously to accelerate Federal public works and procurement programs, and to pay veterans' life insurance dividends and tax refunds. More importantly, he sought to implement recommendations of the Commission on Money and Credit for greater Presidential discretionary fiscal power. He asked Congress for Presidential stand-by authority to make prompt temporary reductions in income tax rates and to accelerate and initiate public capital improvements expenditures, upon a finding that unemployment was excessive and rising.[2] Although a different form of authority would have been more effective, I believe that the principle of Presidential discretionary authority to change Federal tax and spending rates — within carefully defined limits — has great merit, and the Kennedy-Johnson Administration deserves credit for trying — albeit unsuccessfully — to implement it.

This Administration has not yet had occasion to demonstrate the effectiveness of its fiscal policies to curb an inflationary boom, because such an economic condition has not developed. Although one must withhold judgment on the stabilizing effectiveness of its fiscal policy until the full record is in, performance to date augurs well for the future.

Relation of Fiscal Policy to Economic Growth

To what extent has fiscal policy under the Kennedy-Johnson Administration contributed to the growth of the U.S. economy? Manifestly, the annual rise of real output during the period 1961–63 has much exceeded the average of the preceding decade; but nearly all of this rise occurred during a period of cyclical expansion which cannot fairly be compared with the years 1953–1960 which included the recession phases of two business cycles. So many forces, such as monetary actions, determine the growth of output — most of them beyond the scope of Federal fiscal policy — that it is impossible to weigh the influence of fiscal policy *per se*. Nevertheless, Federal fiscal policy during 1961–63 appears to have made a positive contribution to the duration and strength of the cyclical upswing that continued into 1964. Maintenance of a substantial cash deficit contributed to aggregate demand, and changes in the structure of Federal revenues and expenditures were growth promoting in their short-run and long-run influences. It appears clear, however,

[2] See *Economic Report of the President, January 1962*, pp. 17–21.

that a radical overhauling of the Federal income tax structure in the direction of lower, less progressive rates applied to a broader segment of personal income would have a much more powerful influence upon economic growth than any fiscal actions taken during 1961–1963.

Action on Emerging Fiscal Problems of the Nation

How foresighted has the Kennedy-Johnson Administration been in anticipating and putting in motion processes intended to resolve the large fiscal problems of the future? Among the many salient problems one might mention, including reform of the Federal income tax structure, perhaps the largest is the adequate financing of American state and local governments. This is a problem beyond the scope of this paper, but one in the solution of which the Federal government must necessarily take leadership.

A truly phenomenal development of the postwar era has been the rise in the level of state and local expenditures. During the decade 1953–1962 annual Federal expenditures rose about 43 per cent, while state and local expenditures rose by 118 per cent.[3] Federal outlays rose at an average compound rate of about 3½ per cent a year, while state and local outlays grew about 8 per cent a year — two and one-half times the rate of growth of the U.S. economy. These trends reflected rapidly rising demands for the "products" of state and local governments — mainly schools, streets and roads, police, fire, sanitation, recreational and welfare services, and slowly rising demands for the "products" of the Federal government, of which the dominant element has been national security.

These trends will undoubtedly continue during the next decade. Demand for Federal government services will grow less rapidly than the economy. The postwar population "explosion" which the nation has so far felt in its elementary and secondary school system will strike with full force the markets for higher education, housing, and other state and municipal services. Continued urbanization of this expanding population will create appalling problems for our already under-financed and overburdened towns and cities.

The basic problem is a mismatching of the limited revenue-raising powers of state and local governments with their large and rising governmental responsibilities under the present constitutional system. Limited jurisdiction makes states and municipalities inefficient collectors of income taxes. Yet, considerations of equity as well as efficiency put definite limits on the degree to which the burgeoning demand for their services should be financed by higher retail sales and *ad valorem* property taxes.

---

[3] Expenditures are as calculated in the national income accounts which include Federal grants-in-aid in *both* Federal and state and local expenditures. See *Economic Report of the President, January 1, 1963*, p. 241.

Our nation is thus faced with these alternatives: increasing inequities and inefficiencies in state and local finance; rising Federal grants-in-aid to the states; adoption of some formula of Federal revenue-sharing with the states; or a reapportionment of governmental responsibilities among levels of government. What is the right course of action?

In one of his first messages to the Congress in March 1963, President Eisenhower recommended the creation of a Commission on Intergovernmental Relations, which was duly appointed and reported in June 1955. The main thrust of its advice was to leave the present division of governmental functions undisturbed, and to expand Federal grants-in-aid to the states. Subsequently, there has been an enormous growth under both the Eisenhower and Kennedy-Johnson Administrations in the annual amounts of such grants and in the number of their end-uses. Federal grants-in-aid nearly quadrupled from $2.7 billion during fiscal year 1954 to a proposed $10.4 billion in fiscal year 1964.

I suggest that further *ad hoc* actions to meet state and local financing crises in urban transportation and other fields by the instrument of new Federal loans or grants-in-aid are inadvisable. It is time that President Johnson asked Congress for authority to appoint a special Commission of Inquiry into Intergovernmental Finance, charged with the duty of making a searching inquiry into present and impending problems in this area, and recommending long-range solutions. Such a temporary Commission would examine the basic institutional framework of intergovernmental finance. It would not duplicate the valuable coordinating functions now being performed by the permanent Advisory Commission on Intergovernmental Relations, established by the Congress in 1959.[4]

Recapitulation

Federal performance under the Kennedy-Johnson Administration has been much different from the fiscal policy pronouncements of the Democratic Party. Just as fiscal performance under the Eisenhower Administration was decidedly *less* conservative than Republican preachments, so has fiscal performance under the Kennedy Administration been *more* conservative than Democratic orthodoxy. In fact, this Administration's proposal of a massive reduction in Federal taxation, accompanied by an effort to hold the line on expenditures, is an essentially conservative adjustment to the working of a progressive Federal tax system in a growing economy. The orthodox Democratic adjustment would be a further expansion of Federal expenditures!

[4] The Advisory Commission on Intergovernmental Relations is a permanent organ of fiscal coordination, which meets at intervals, and whose members are mainly Federal, state and municipal government officials. Cooperation within the existing institutional framework is obviously necessary; but the framework itself needs restudy and possibly redesign.

The most remarkable characteristic of Federal fiscal performance under the Kennedy-Johnson Administration has been its continuity with that under the Eisenhower Administration. The overall role of Federal cash payments in total spending of the economy has been maintained at an almost constant level of 19.7 per cent during the past decade. There has been a persistent and massive shift toward investment-type Federal expenditures, and toward greater relative reliance upon revenues derived from commodity and payroll taxation instead of from net income and estate taxation. The automatic counter-cyclical stabilizers in the Federal budget have been well maintained; both Administrations have used their executive powers vigorously to smooth the nation's economic progress; and President Kennedy sought — though unsuccessfully — to persuade Congress to increase the President's powers to take stabilizing action. All of these trends are growth-promoting in their effects.

Most economists will, I believe, find these trends satisfactory. But three major criticisms of this Administration's record remain. *First,* it has *not* acted vigorously to curb and reduce some spending programs which on a basis of abundant evidence are not producing much social welfare per dollar. *Secondly,* the emphasis in its tax reduction program on personal instead of corporate tax cuts is inconsistent with its avowed aim of faster economic growth. *Thirdly,* it has not yet put in motion machinery aimed to resolve on a fundamental long-term basis the explosive problems of Federal-State-Local financial relations, which are rising in urgency year by year.

• *26*

*Social Imbalance: Pros and Cons**

CAMPBELL R. MCCONNELL
University of Nebraska

According to an economic "law" propounded by Adolf Wagner, a nineteenth-century German economist, public expenditures tend to become an increasing share of the gross national product. A wryly cynical observation on this general subject is the "law" of British wit, C. Northcote Parkinson, declaring that of course "make-work" tends to expand in a bureaucracy. The following article, reviewing recent controversy on government spending for the general welfare, surmises that whether one feels that expenditures are too big or too small, the only way to be just right is to adopt a "socially optimum" budget.

The primary purposes of this paper are to synthesize, expand modestly, and communicate the views of several leading economists who are convinced that a serious problem of social imbalance exists in our society; to outline several criticisms of, and counterarguments to, the social imbalance thesis; and to analyze various policy recommendations designed to alleviate the social imbalance problem, should it exist now or in the future.

* Taken and adapted from "Social Imbalance: Where Do We Stand?" *Quarterly Review of Business and Economics*, May 1961, pp. 6–23. Reproduced with permission.

The Nature of Social Imbalance

A number of well known economists[1] — particularly Alvin H. Hansen and John Kenneth Galbraith — have argued that the evolution of the United States from a nation of relative poverty to one of relative abundance has created a distortion in the composition of the economy's total output. It is asserted that the increasing affluence of American capitalism has been accompanied by a lack of social balance. That is, an inefficient allocation of resources between private goods and services, on the one hand, and social goods and services, on the other, has arisen. Television sets, automobiles, and a profligacy of gadgetry are produced in abundance, while education, police and fire protection, streets and highways, and a myriad of basic community services are slighted.[2]

Hansen and Galbraith argue that there is substantial evidence which lends credence to the position that social imbalance now exists as a basic economic problem. Simple observation — evidence of the eye — is said to be abundant: overcrowded and ill-equipped schools, a paucity of parks and recreation areas; overcrowded streets and inadequate highways; underpaid and undermanned police forces; and so on. Simple statistical comparisons may also be invoked as evidence. In 1959 United States consumers spent $18.3 billion on recreation as compared with the $17.0 billion which the three levels of government spent on education. Approximately $11 billion was spent on advertising, some $7 billion on tobacco products, and $15 billion on automobile purchases, as opposed

[1] Writing in 1957, Alvin H. Hansen devoted a penetrating chapter of his *The American Economy* (New York: McGraw-Hill, 1957) to the problem of social priorities in a rich society. However, the development and detailed analysis of the concept of social balance awaited John Kenneth Galbraith's *The Affluent Society* (Boston: Houghton, 1958). Galbraith, the poet laureate of the economists, incisively analyzes the causes and implications of social imbalance in this major work. Hansen's *Economic Issues of the 1960s* (New York: McGraw-Hill, 1960), further develops the social imbalance theme. W. W. Rostow has viewed some of the consequences of social imbalance in a wider context in Book 6 of his *The United States in the World Arena* (New York: Harper, 1960). Francis M. Bator deals directly and skillfully with *The Question of Government Spending* (New York: Harper, 1960), analyzing statistically the economic role of government and exploring the major economic and political implications of these data.

[2] EDITOR'S NOTE — Or, as Galbraith has more graphically expressed this complaint: "The family which takes its mauve and cerise, air-conditioned, power-steered, and power-braked automobile out for a tour passes through cities that are badly paved, made hideous by litter, blighted buildings, billboards, and posts for wires that should long since have been put underground. They pass on into a countryside that has been rendered largely invisible by commercial art. They picnic on exquisitely packaged food from a portable icebox by a polluted stream and go on to spend the night at a park which is a menace to public health and morals. Just before dozing off on an air mattress, beneath a nylon tent, amid the stench of decaying refuse, they may reflect vaguely on the curious unevenness of their blessings. Is this, indeed, the American genius?"

to total (public and private) spending of $10.2 billion for research and development.

What of more comprehensive statistical information on the question of social imbalance? Francis M. Bator has explored this general problem, deriving elaborate statistics on the economic role of government.

By contrasting government's nondefense purchases of goods and services with the size of the nondefense GNP over a period of years, we can envision what share of "civilian" GNP has been in the form of social goods and services. His data show that government's nondefense spending as a percentage of nondefense GNP rose from 7.5 per cent in 1929 to 13.4 per cent in 1939, only to decline to 10.3 per cent by 1957.

Bator's per capita data are also revealing. Per capita real nondefense spending by government was approximately the same in 1957 at $234 as in 1939, despite the fact that total real civilian output per head increased from $1,514 to $2,281 in the same period.

Social Imbalance as an Economic Problem

Those who embrace the social imbalance thesis argue that it constitutes a first-rank economic problem because it embodies a misallocation of resources, constitutes a threat to economic stability and full employment, and has critical implications for the economy's rate of economic growth.

The Allocation of Resources

As already noted, social imbalance suggests a misallocation of economic resources and, therefore, a failure of the economic system to maximize the satisfactions of society. More specifically, private goods, because of their very superabundance, are now relatively low priority (low marginal utility) goods; the production of additional private goods is not a matter of very high urgency. In contrast, the very paucity of social goods makes them relatively high priority (high marginal utility) goods; the production of more social goods *is* a matter of relatively high urgency. It is argued, in brief, that given an initial position of social imbalance — too much private and not enough public goods — a reallocation of resources in favor of the latter is a rechannelling of resources away from low toward high marginal utility employments. This obviously accomplishes an increase in the total satisfaction (utility) of society.

Economic Stability

Social imbalance is also a crucial economic problem because of the contribution it might make to economic instability and unemployment. Galbraith has emphasized that a sustained demand for private consumer goods has become highly dependent upon the want-creating activities of the admen and the willingness and ability of consumers to increase their indebtedness. Now, if a point is reached where the myriad of claims and counterclaims of advertisers renders consumers immune to the claims of all, or, if any of the innumerable uncertainties which characterize our economy should interrupt the expansion of consumer credit, then consumption spending would decline and, *ceteris paribus,* unemployment would result. The reduction or amelioration of social imbalance would lessen the possibility of these difficulties arising.

Since public wants are not contrived, they are not subject to a failure of contrivance. Since they are not sold on the installment plan, they are not subject to curtailment by any of the factors which make people unwilling or unable to incur debt. Thus the better the social balance the more immune the economy to fluctuations in private demand.

Economic Growth

The final reason for the great significance of social imbalance as an economic problem may well be the most crucial of all.

The present relationship between private and social goods may be an important determinant of the nation's economic growth potential. This is so because many basic social goods — *e.g.,* education, basic scientific research, and preventive medicine — are important factors contributing to the process of economic growth. Thus a current public-private goods choice which puts heavy emphasis upon such private consumer goods as automobiles, television sets, and air conditioners and therefore slights the aforementioned social goods is necessarily reducing its potential rate of growth in so doing.

Alleged Causes of Social Imbalance

How has this alleged paucity of social goods developed amidst an affluence of private goods?

It would seem that mixed capitalism embodies the mechanisms necessary for obtaining a reasonably good balance between private and public output. Consumers govern the production of private goods by the dollar votes they register in the market place. Through political means — the process of political voting — consumers in effect select the amount of social goods they desire. In brief, in a democracy is not the considered judgment of the majority of the citizenry transformed through dollar and political voting into a choice as to how total output is to be divided among private and social goods? How, then, can social imbalance arise?

Economists who envision a social imbalance in current GNP argue that in practice certain historical, attitudinal, and politico-economic forces cause the production of social goods to fall seriously out of balance with the production of private goods. What are these distorting forces?

Demand for Social Goods: Wagner's Law

The forces underlying the growing demand for social goods and services are well known: hot and cold wars; population growth, industrialization and the subsequent urbanization and socio-economic complexity which it entails; and so forth. Also, of course, as real incomes rise, the demand for both private and social goods can be expected to increase. There are plausible reasons to argue that as real per capita incomes rise, the pattern of consumer wants may alter in favor of relatively more social goods and relatively less private goods. This alleged alteration of wants in the growing economy is labeled Wagner's Law.

The rationale underlying Wagner's Law is relatively simple. After basic wants have been largely fulfilled, the growing wealth of society permits it to turn its attention more and more to the satisfaction of somewhat less urgent but nevertheless important wants. Many of these new wants entail social goods — for example, education, streets and highways, police and fire protection. Economic growth is characterized by increasing industrialization and urbanization. This creates a demand for sanitation and sewage facilities, a water supply, extensive police and fire protection and similar social goods which in a poorer and simpler agrarian society would be provided by each family for itself or simply not provided at all. Similarly, the industrialization and urbanization which characterizes an expanding economy leads to increasing interdependence and greater socio-economic complexity. Government's regulatory role may therefore be expected to expand markedly. All of these considerations may give rise to a tendency for the demand for social goods to increase, not only absolutely, but also relative to the demand for private goods.

Supply of Social Goods

Those who view social imbalance as an acute issue feel there are a number of considerations which prevent the supply of social goods from keeping pace with the growing demand for them.

1. The Mechanisms and Mores of Capitalism

The very nature of the capitalistic ideology and the attitudes of large numbers of Americans concerning the public sector of the economy have both fostered obstacles to an expanding volume of social goods production.

1. The ideology of pure capitalism embraces the concepts of con-

sumer sovereignty, free competitive markets, and a highly restricted economic role for government. This long-obsolete portrayal of capitalism provides that virtually all resources are channeled into the production of private goods and services. Furthermore, as the economy evolves and becomes more affluent, the capitalistic ideology obviously provides both the philosophical basis and the mechanism — consumer sovereignty and the price system — to provide for ever increasing amounts of private goods. No such philosophy or mechanism exists to provide automatically for the additional social goods which a growing and more opulent nation may require.

2. The attitude of much of the business community and large parts of the citizenry envisions private goods to be sacrosanct while public goods are held to be wasteful, of secondary significance, or at best a necessary evil. The closely related notion that "economy in government" is synonymous with minimal public expenditures is also widely and blindly accepted; believers are apparently oblivious of the fact that "economy" is concerned with the employment and efficient allocation of resources.

2. *Political Realities*

Because they are overweighted with the representatives of sparsely populated, rural areas, the federal legislature and many state legislatures are relatively insensitive to the acute social goods needs of the heavily populated metropolitan areas. Similarly, the dire social needs of the Negro are clearly underrepresented in the southern states. At the level of local government, heavy dependence upon property taxes works against the expansion of social goods production.

3. *Character of Social Goods*

The inherent characteristics of public goods, as opposed to private goods, also tend to impede their production.

In the first place, the remoteness and uncertainty of the benefits derived from social goods prejudice the consumer (voter) against their production. In the realm of goods and services, individuals prefer the immediate and certain benefits of autos, television sets, and automatic dishwashers to the remote benefits of public education, municipal libraries, streets and highways, a boost in the budget of the local park department, or the highly uncertain benefits of aid to underdeveloped countries, space research, and a continuing arms race.

There is a second characteristic of social goods or, more precisely, of the public sector, which allegedly impedes the achievement of social balance. In the private sector of the economy each individual consumer exercises a great deal of selectivity in his purchases. He considers the marginal utility of various commodities relative to their prices and, subject to his budget restraint, achieves consumer equilibrium by freely selecting those goods and services which yield the greatest marginal utility per dollar and rejecting those yielding less. However, the individual's economic dealings with government are on a nonselective basis. The consumer cannot select and therefore contribute financially only to those programs in the public sector's budget which he favors, thereby rejecting and withholding tax payments for programs he disfavors. Thus, assuming realistically that the policy mix of the government is so complex that it will not precisely match the social good preferences of any specific consumer, it follows that there will invariably be a number of social goods and services which he is compelled to help finance, but of which he does not approve. The practical conclusion is that each voter feels that the public budget is too high relative to the benefits he derives from it; that is, each taxpayer feels that a cut in government spending is warranted. Government, therefore, is persistently faced with significant pressure to reduce the flow of social goods and services.

4. Tax Obstacles

It is also asserted that a number of tax problems contribute to the problem of social imbalance.

Tax levels. Over a period of time the existing level of taxation tends to become acceptable — to become "proper" — to large numbers of households and businesses for the simple reason that they have had time to adjust to it. As a result, it becomes politically feasible to maintain existing levels of taxation, while at the same time it becomes extremely dangerous politically to raise tax levels. Allegiance to existing tax levels works against the expansion of social goods production.

Allocating tax burdens. Even where voters are in general agreement as to the desirability of having more of particular social goods and are willing to accept a higher tax level to finance them, the problem of allocating the tax cost of these goods may still impede their production. The citizenry might be convinced of the need to hasten the development of domestic natural resources, or to strengthen our national defense posture. But, these projects might be blocked by disagreement as to how the tax cost should be distributed. Inability to reach agreement on the distribution of tax costs may cause the community and the nation to forego sorely needed social goods and services.

5. Advertising and Emulation

Advertising and sales promotion activities, which are an integral part of the production and sale of private goods, are almost entirely absent with respect to social goods. For example, while gigantic advertising campaigns by automobile manufacturers operate to convince consumers of the virtues of being a two-car family, no comparable persuasion extolls to the citizenry the need for more and better roads on which to operate the ever expanding mass of automobiles. The public sector, under persistent pressure to reduce expenditures, is prohibited from the exhortative techniques which characterize the private sector. Anthony Downs has masterfully pinpointed the assymetry of the problem: "Whereas private power corporations advertise both the virtues of their own product and the evils of public power, government utilities cannot even advertise their existence for fear of being accused of wasting public funds." The result is a tendency for private to expand ahead of social goods.

Like advertising, emulation also favors greater production of private goods. Families witness the new gadgetry of their neighbors — a second car, an automatic dishwasher, a food freezer, a backyard swimming pool — and feel compelled to "keep pace" by also acquiring these amenities. Emulative inducements work very weakly, if at all, between towns and between states in stimulating the output of social goods and services.

6. Inflation

The contribution of persistent inflation to the relative shrinkage and deterioration of public goods and services is twofold.

1. Inflation causes product and resource prices to rise in a very uneven and irregular fashion. While the incomes of most profit receivers (stockholders and proprietors) and many wage earners rise rapidly and significantly, the wages and salaries of public employees typically rise belatedly and by considerably less than the general level of prices — inflation tends to reduce the real incomes of many government employees. Thus, as a practical matter, it is particularly difficult for governmental agencies to match the increasingly lucrative salaries offered by private industries which, in the mainstream of inflation, are generally in a good position to raise their prices and revenues in time with or ahead of the general level of prices. In brief, inflation tends to divert human resources from public services to private industry. Through this diversion, inflation discriminates in favor of private goods at the expense of public goods.

2. By creating inflationary pressure a burgeoning private sector tends to create automatically and simultaneously strong political pressures to retrench on government spending as an anti-inflationary technique. Given the previously noted disposition to hold taxes at present levels and the questionable effectiveness of a tight money policy, the obvious and politically least offensive means of ameliorating inflation is to restrain government purchases of social goods and services. Thus it is that, when the rate of production of private goods is very high and inflation occurs, the pressure may be greatest for the output of social goods to be constrained.

Some Counterarguments

There are those who seriously question that social imbalance is a pressing problem; and, even if it were to assume acute dimensions, it is argued that the suggested remedies may be ineffective and very costly.

Does Social Imbalance Really Exist?

Critics of the social imbalance thesis have raised a number of points in questioning whether or not social imbalance actually exists.

1. Any conception of an efficient allocation of resources ultimately rests upon a value judgment as to what the optimum composition of output ought to be. As a result, there is obviously no scientific way of proving (or, by the same token, of disproving) that social imbalance actually exists.

2. Though Wagner's Law may state with some accuracy the nature of the changes in consumer tastes which accompany increasing affluence, it does not logically follow that these wants should be met by relative growth in the public sector.

3. The simple observations and statistics which are cited as evidence of social imbalance may exaggerate the problem. (a) The pointed comparisons of Galbraith and Hansen may be misleading. Note, for example that "expenditures for all kinds of durable consumer goods, including automobiles, run about 14 per cent of personal consumption," and most of this is for essential equipment rather than gadgetry and frills. (b) Because defense spending involves a very basic social good and enmeshes the government deeply into the economy, it is of very questionable legitimacy to accept Bator's comparison of private spending and non-defense public spending in assessing the degree of social imbalance.

4. Though the obstacles which allegedly impede the expansion of social goods production infer the existence of social imbalance, there are important counterbiases which facilitate the growth of social goods output at the expense of private goods. (a) The apparent unrelatedness of taxation and public spending decisions has encouraged the public attitude that government spending is costless, that is, the benefits of social goods and services are relatively free. It can be, and has been, argued that this attitude has encouraged public goods production. (b) Assuming that taxing and public spending decisions are related by the citizenry, some citizens are very willing to vote for expenditures from which they expect to benefit, although they have not contributed. Indeed, our progressive tax structure means that most of the taxpayers who are in the lower income brackets obtain social goods at bargain prices; hence, there is every reason for them as a political majority to be inclined to favor and vote for the expansion of social goods. (c) Fi-

nally, political reality is such that vocal and active minorities constantly press for and achieve increased public expenditures. Wallich therefore concludes: "As between the forces that inhibit and those that advance public expenditures, no one can say for sure where the balance lies."

Public Spending: A Corrective?

Assuming social imbalance actually exists, will the advocated increases in public spending resolve this imbalance? It is argued that this need not be the case. To suggest that more public and less private spending will resolve social imbalance invokes the implicit assumption that the reallocation of resources from private to public uses will necessarily entail less "unwise" private expenditure and more "wise" public spending. Is it not possible that reductions in private spending may come more at the expense of adequate housing, medical care, education, and cultural pursuits rather than at the expense of TV sets, electric can openers, and microscopic radios? Might not a disproportionate share of any increase in public expenditures on, say, education be for gymnasia and stadia as opposed to laboratories and classrooms?

The Costs of Social Balance

Wallich argues that, if social imbalance is really an acute problem, certain very substantial costs may be involved in its resolution — costs which may well be prohibitive.

In the first place, the provision of tax-financed public services "is a very inefficient way of catering to consumer needs." This is so because, in contrast to the market, there is no neat this-for-that adjustment of benefits and costs. This poor adjustment means that the taxpayer is likely to get more or less of some public service than he desires. Furthermore, the "free" character of social goods and services provides no incentive for the taxpayer to economize in their use.

Secondly, Wallich contends that short of a military emergency the balance of interests in our society works against any marked shifts in the composition of public spending. This "balance of interests" effect causes components of the government budget to increase and decrease, not selectively, but rather on an across-the-board basis. Assuming that not all public expenditures are conducive to the elimination of social imbalance, the consequence is that increased spending on "desirable" public programs entails a heavy political surcharge in the form of increased spending on other unrelated and "less desirable" programs. Stated briefly, the over-all cost of those public programs which are essential in rectifying a condition of social imbalance may be inordinately high.

Finally, and of greatest significance, Wallich argues that the expansion of the public sector advocated as a corrective for social imbalance may come at the very high cost of freedom. In drawing a line between the public and the private sectors, it must be recognized that not only economics, but also freedom, is involved. Wallich suggests that, because the expansion of government impinges upon freedom "it would have to be shown that the people could do something only very imperfectly, and the government very substantially better, before the government should step in." The implied economic inefficiency is the price of the extra freedom that stems from greater containment of the growing public sector. This price, it is stated, can well be afforded by an affluent society.

Correctives for Social Imbalance

It is interesting to examine what might be done to remedy social imbalance, if it now exists or arises in the future as a significant economic problem.

Disarmament

Potentially the happiest solution to the problem of social imbalance would be an effective disarmament agreement. A transfer of government expenditures from defense to nondefense categories imposes no direct constraints upon private goods output. In fact, in the absence of the huge backlog of consumer and business demand and the condition of overemployment which facilitated reconversion after World War II, increased spending on public goods might be imperative in sustaining full employment.

Most obviously, the main difficulty with demobilization as a remedy for social imbalance is the fact that its potential pleasantness as a corrective is greatly exceeded by its unlikeliness of occurrence. Even waiving this, there is a further possible problem. Disarmament could generate tremendous public pressures for tax cuts; tax rates which are acceptable during hot or cold wars might prove highly objectionable when peace breaks out.

Growth as a Palliative

It must also be noted that the extent to which the provision of more social goods collides with the production of private goods depends upon the rate of growth achieved by the economy. The correcting of social imbalance in a static economy — that is, an economy whose GNP is unchanging — obviously implies a painful retrenchment in consumer goods production both absolutely and relatively. However, if the economy continues to achieve the 3 to 4 per cent annual growth rate of past full employment years, an annual increment of $14 billion to $19 billion in output will result. A division of this increment which favors social goods can clearly alleviate social imbalance and simultaneously provide for modest increases in total consumption. Moreover, it is of no little significance that such a distribution of the increment might contribute to an acceleration of the growth rate.

Again, this solution is not devoid of problems. Even with a favorable annual growth rate, the correcting of fairly acute social imbalance may require an absolute decline in private consumption. Furthermore, it must be remembered that, although growth and affluence can contribute to the correction of social imbalance, the growth process itself may also intensify certain aspects of the social imbalance problem, for example, urban redevelopment.

Increased Use of Sales Taxes

Galbraith and Hansen have both strongly endorsed the greater use of sales taxation as a means of attacking social imbalance. Because they are shifted to consumers, sales taxes raise the prices of consumer goods. The result is that a given total amount of consumer spending commands less private goods and automatically provides more government revenues to reabsorb the released resources through larger purchases of social goods. As private production expands, public revenues and therefore public goods increase on a pro rata basis. Furthermore, to the degree that sales taxes are hidden in prices and paid in relatively small amounts spread more or less evenly over a period of time, the cost of the social goods financed thereby is neither very explicit nor very immediate to the taxpayer. To the extent that this remoteness or vagueness of tax costs offsets the remoteness of social goods benefits, the cause of social balance may be furthered.

A Socially Optimum Budget

Waiving the many inherent political problems, perhaps the most direct approach to correcting social imbalance is simply for government to set that level of public spending which will achieve at least a rough social balance. This implies that government expenditures will be established largely independently of short-run cyclical fluctuations and that tax rates must then be adjusted to achieve any desired compensatory fiscal effect. This measure, which we shall label a "socially optimum" fiscal policy, differs from both the current notions of a cyclically balanced budget and from functional finance. In particular, the socially optimum policy is freer of the compensatory approach to government spending and taxing which may severely limit the other two budget philosophies in promoting social balance.

Instead of adjusting the public sector to the exuberance or lethargy of the private sector, the two sectors would compete on a more nearly equal footing for the economy's resources under a socially optimum fiscal policy.

Government spending would be aligned with the long-run cause of social balance, not the short-run objective of alleviating cyclical variations in output and employment. This means, of course, that the task of providing short-term stability through fiscal policy would fall primarily upon taxation. Greater tax variations would be required to provide a given anticyclical impact upon the economy.

Would such a budget philosophy weaken the stabilizing potential of fiscal policy and therefore promote social balance at the cost of short-run cyclical instability? At first glance this would appear to be the case; yet there are certain possible offsetting considerations.

1. Gearing government expenditures to the objective of social balance may not greatly weaken the potential or real effectiveness of fiscal policy. In the first place, it must be recognized that the level of federal spending is already very stable.

2. An increase in government spending does not rule out all flexibility in such spending. The purchase of various social goods and services may differ considerably in priority; those of less urgency may well be postponable within limits.

3. It is possible that taxation may be strengthened as a fiscal device and that new stabilizing measures may be introduced. For example, automatic adjustments may be applied to the first income bracket so that tax collections will vary directly with production and employment.

One point is clear: If social imbalance is deemed acute, then there is a serious need for a change in our budget philosophy — to one that gives explicit recognition to the problem. In these circumstances, we can hardly afford not to probe the potentialities of unexplored stabilization techniques. In a rapidly changing world, few successes accrue to the complacent and the hesitant.

• 27

Critique of the Public Debt*

JAMES BUCHANAN
University of Virginia

This selection critically evaluates the "new orthodoxy" in regard to the "burden of the public debt." First, it argues that the real burden of the public debt can be passed on to "future generations," then, that a public debt is essentially similar to a private debt and, finally, that an internal public debt is essentially similar to an external public debt. The highly controversial character both of this issue and of Professor Buchanan's critique can be best appreciated by comparing this with the subsequent selection by Alvin H. Hansen.

The Burden of Public Debt

Viewed in terms of the contrast with taxation, it is clear that the financing of public services through the issue of debt instruments does not impose any real burden on citizens at the time that the public expenditure is undertaken. This is true despite the fact that the resources available for private disposition are fewer than before. Real

* Taken and adapted from "Critique of the Public Debt" by James Buchanan, *The Public Finances* (Homewood, Illinois: Irwin, 1960), pp. 342–347. Reproduced with permission.

resources are, of course, shifted from the private to the public sector by the combined debt issue — government spending operation. But this transfer involves no real sacrifice or burden to individuals because those giving up current purchasing power, those who purchase government bonds, do so in voluntary exchange for debt instruments which embody some obligation on the part of government to make a return income payment in the future.

From this conception, it follows that the real burden of debt must rest with taxpayers during the future periods when the previously issued debt requires servicing and amortization. As contrasted with taxation, which must impose a current real burden on individuals, debt creation provides one way of financing public services without current cost. It provides a means whereby taxpayers in any given period may *shift or postpone* the payment for public services to the shoulders of taxpayers in future periods. "Future generations" may be exploited through the choice of debt issue to finance public services.

This elementary analysis concludes that the real burden of the public debt, and by real burden is meant the sacrifice of individual utility, must be shouldered by those individuals and groups who must pay the taxes necessary to service and to amortize previously issued debt. The logic of this analysis is irrefutable within the limits of the model discussed, and this seems to be the only fully appropriate model for the purpose at hand. Nevertheless, this conclusion has not been widely accepted in recent years. The claim has repeatedly been made to the effect that the burden of debt cannot be postponed or shifted to future generations. Although this argument seems fundamentally fallacious, it now commands such widespread acceptance that careful consideration is indicated. The argument is based on the idea that it is impossible to transfer a real cost to future periods when the resources providing the public services are used up during the initial period of debt issue. The steel, copper, and oil, for instance, that were actually used up in producing war materials in 1944 were used up in 1944, not in some later year. The real cost, the sacrificed alternatives, of these resources could only have been shouldered by those individuals who lived during 1944, who were forced to sacrifice current consumption of such materials during that time. This argument seems initially to be sound until it is recalled that, insofar as genuine debt was used as a means of financing these purchases, private individuals were not "forced" to sacrifice consumption or investment opportunities at all. They gave up purchasing power voluntarily in exchange for the government's promise to pay to them a somewhat larger income in the future. When this point is accepted, debt issue cannot be claimed to impose a real cost on anyone during the period of resource use, despite the reduction in the amount of resources left available for private disposition.

The Transfer Argument

How can the whole group be subjected to a net burden of public debt in periods after that in which resources are actually used up for public purposes? One reason for a continued adherence to an essentially fallacious view is the concentration on the *transfer* aspects of debt service operations. If the government sells a bond to an individual living within its borders, the payment of interest on this bond represents a transfer of purchasing power or income from the taxpayer to the bondholders, and in many cases this person may be one and the same. In the transfer process, the real income of the taxpayer is reduced; the real income of the bondholder is increased. But how can the whole group, taken in the aggregate, be said to shoulder any burden, any net reduction in individual utility as a result of the servicing of previously issued debt? This is the most persuasive part of the widely accepted argument concerning the location of the debt burden, and the effective refutation of this part requires a careful examination of the underlying logical or methodological assumptions.

We must return to the period of debt issue itself and ask the question: What would happen if the public debt were not to be issued? The individual who now purchases the government bond would purchase instead a private security, some other income-earning asset, or he would spend the funds in current consumption. In either case, the discounted value of the alternative purchase would be approximately equal to that of the government bond. There would be only a slight and insignificant differential between the purchase of the government bond and its substitutes. Now let us consider the position of this individual in later periods, assuming that he did not purchase the government bond. The analysis is simpler if we assume that instead of the government bond, the individual purchases a private bond, although this is not a necessary assumption. The private security will provide an interest income approximately equal to what the individual could have earned on the government bond. Therefore, we conclude that, differentially speaking, he is no better off without the government bond, without public debt having been issued, than he would be with the public debt. The existence of the public debt, as such, does not provide the bondholder with any differential benefit or burden.

The situation of the taxpayer in these later periods is wholly different. With the public debt in existence, he is subjected to a coercive levy imposed in order to finance the interest payments on the debt. *This is the real burden of the public debt,* since the taxpayer in this situation is the only person who must suffer a net reduction in utility due to the past expenditure having been undertaken. If the expenditure had not been carried out in previous periods, no debt obligation would have been created by government. The taxpayer, as such, would have been under no charge to service a public debt.

If this analysis is accepted, it is clear that it is erroneous to look upon the payment of interest on an internal or domestic public debt as a "transfer" in any real sense. Bondholders receive the interest as a part of a contract; taxpayers lose purchasing power through the imposition of a compulsory levy. To call these two effects canceling overlooks the fundamental difference between taxation and borrowing as means of financing public expenditure.

If the debt-financed expenditure turns out to be productive, the taxpayer in later periods may, of course, be better off, even with the necessity of paying the interest charge, than he would be without the debt having been issued. But this is irrelevant to the problem of locating the debt burden. The problem is precisely that of locating the individual or group of individuals who does "pay for" the benefits secured from the public outlay, quite independently of whether or not the outlay itself is productive or unproductive. Debt issue tends to shift this burden of payment onto the taxpayer in periods subsequent to the debt issue-expenditure operation. Taxation, by contrast, places the burden on the individuals living during the period when the expenditure is undertaken. This is the basic difference between the two methods of financing public expenditure, and the failure to recognize this point can only lead to confusion.

The Analogy with Private Debt

One of the points that is often made in the modern discussions of the public debt is that it is fallacious to draw any analogy between the debts of governments and the debts of individuals, between public and private debt. The emphasis on this point stems from an acceptance of the argument that has been critically examined previously. In many particular respects, public debt must be different from private debt and any analogy between the two must be used with great care, as is the case with all such analogies. But this does not suggest that the underlying similarity between the individual and the public economy as regards debt issue can be overlooked. In the most essential respects, debt issue for the individual and debt issue for the state are analogous.

In each instance, borrowing (debt issue) constitutes an alternative to the more normally accepted means of raising revenues. Borrowing takes the place of earning additional income for the individual and of "earning" additional revenues through taxation for governments. Borrowing in either case is a means of securing additional current purchasing power without undergoing supplementary current cost. The costs of expenditures currently undertaken are effectively shifted to future time periods. In such future periods, creditors hold a primary claim against the revenue or income of either the individual or the government.

It may, of course, be fully rational for either the individual or the government to borrow instead of raising funds in a more normal way. The desirability of borrowing depends on the expected productivity of the expenditure and time pattern of the expected yield. Here it is noted only that there is no basic difference between the individual and the government economy as regards the essential aspects of debt versus current financing of expenditure.

External and Internal Public Debt

Still another result of accepting what has been labeled here the falla, cious conception of public debt has been the sharp distinction made between an internal and an external or foreign debt. A government borrows internally or domestically when it sells securities to its own citizens. In purchasing the bonds, the individuals voluntarily give up command over current usage of resources in exchange for the government's promise to pay a return in future periods. The government uses this purchasing power to acquire resources and services from the private economy. The citizens of the private economy have a smaller total of real goods and services available for private disposition than before the sale of public debt, but they hold debt instruments in the place of the differential amount of private goods, claims against the government which are at least equal to these private goods in value. No person in this initial period in which the borrowing takes place suffers any loss in utility as a result of the operation. It is important to emphasize that this conclusion holds even if the public expenditures financed are completely wasteful.

Let us now compare this with the process of exernal borrowing. Here the government sells securities to citizens of foreign countries who give up units of their own purchasing power in exchange. The government uses this purchasing power to acquire goods and services abroad, or to exchange with citizens who desire to acquire goods and services abroad. The total amount of resources available for private disposition in the domestic economy is not changed. As with domestic or internal public debt creation, no one suffers any reduction in utility during the period of debt issue and expenditure, and, if the project financed is at all beneficial, some individuals should receive net additions to utility. It must be concluded, therefore, that, at least in the initial period, there is no basic difference between the internal and the external public debt.

Similar results hold if we consider comparable situations in a period subsequent to that in which the government borrows. For an internal or domestic debt, sufficient taxes will have to be levied to finance the interest charges. These payments will be made to bondholders who, in this case, are citizens living in the domestic economy. If, instead, the debt is externally held, the tax payments must be made to foreign citizens. On this level of comparison, the external debt seems clearly to be more burdensome than the internal debt since there is no offsetting receipt of interest by local bondholders. The interest payments represent a net drainage of funds out of the domestic economy.

This is the source of much confusion. If a correct and careful analysis is made, the conclusion that the external debt is more burdensome can be shown to be erroneous. The previous simple comparison overlooks the central fact that the total national income must always be larger in the external debt case. The reason is clear. Resources are not drawn away from the private economy when the debt is originally created; instead, resources are drawn from abroad. Consequently, the private income in any subsequent period must be higher than it would be if internal rather than external debt is issued. The fact that income is higher in a situation with external debt allows for the necessary drainage of interest payments out of the economy. There is no real distinction in the two cases, so long as the comparisons are properly made.

All of this should not suggest that there are not important institutional differences between the external and the internal public debt. The sale of securities to foreigners will introduce many supplementary problems that are not present when securities are sold to citizens. These relate to such factors as possible changes in exchange rates and transfer difficulties. There is no denying that such problems may arise, and, given the fact that the international payments mechanism may work somewhat less smoothly than the domestic payments mechanism, the servicing of an external debt may be more difficult for a government than the servicing of an equally large internal debt. The point made here is only that the differences lie in these institutional arrangements, not in the fact that the two debt forms are intrinsically distinct in some more fundamental way.

28

Defense of the Public Debt*

ALVIN H. HANSEN
Emeritus, Harvard University

*The "new orthodoxy" does not lack for defenders. In this selec-
tion, Alvin H. Hansen, elder statesman among American neo-
Keynesian economists, responds to Professor Buchanan's three
major criticisms of the public debt. In addition, Hansen defends
the public debt in its own right, as a built-in stabilizer (recall
Selection 17) and as a contributor to liquidity.*

Debt in Relation to Income

Let it be noted first of all that everything in the field of economics has
to be viewed in terms of relatives, not in terms of absolutes. It means
nothing to recite, as some do, the fact that the Federal debt in George
Washington's time was inconsequential compared to the current $290
billion. What is far more relevant is the fact that half of Washington's
budget was devoted to interest payments on the public debt. What has
real meaning is not the absolute size of the debt, but rather the ratio of
debt to the Gross National Product. In these terms the *net* public debt
has declined to less than half since 1946, *i.e.*, from 125 per cent of GNP
to only 60 per cent. Our GNP can be expected to rise by some $15 to $20
billion a year even though we achieve no great increases in the rate of

---

* From *Economic Issues of the 1960's* by Alvin H. Hansen. Copyright © 1960.
McGraw-Hill Book Company. Used by permission.

growth. Thus a stationary public debt is in realistic terms a rapidly declining one: that is to say, declining in relation to GNP. And even though the public debt should rise by as much as $20 billion per year for twenty years, it would still be only 75 per cent of the GNP twenty years hence, far below the 1946 ratio. From the standpoint of ratio of debt to GNP there is no problem at all.

It is sometimes noted that the interest payment on the debt is now equal to the entire Federal budget prior to the Second World War. Yet the ratio of interest charges to GNP had fallen from 2.1 per cent in 1947 to 1.7 per cent by 1960. And it may also be noted, by way of historical comparison, that after the Civil War, interest charges were about double the aggregate Federal expenditures for all purposes prior to the war.

The public debt, however, has to be judged on its own merits. Is it a good or a bad thing? Like almost everything else in economic life, it is both. Its size relative to national income is one thing to consider, and on this score I do not think we need worry. At the current ratio to GNP the benefits may well outweigh the disadvantages. What are some of the things we gain by having a fairly large public debt? They are very real, and we would miss them greatly if the debt by some magic suddenly disappeared. Emerson once said: "Be careful what you wish, it might be granted." And so it is in economics. Many of the things we complain about are things we would only learn to appreciate once they were gone.

The Public Debt as Stabilizer

For one thing the public debt is one of our very important built-in stabilizers. This is peculiarly true for the United States by reason of the widespread popular ownership of government securities. This applies not only to the $50 billion of savings bonds so widely held throughout the country, but also to the $50 billion of government securities held in trust for the people by the savings banks, life insurance companies, State and local governments, savings and loan associations, and pension trust funds. Moreover, all depositors in commercial banks enjoy the security provided by nearly $95 billion of United States securities held by commercial banks and by the Federal Reserve banks. Finally $55 billion of government securities are held in trust under the social security program. Out of the total of $290 billion debt, $250 billion is in effect held in trust for pretty much the entire population. A part of this provides a purchasing power upon which to fall back in recession periods. And even though it is not drawn upon, it strengthens consumer confidence. This is one of the reasons why consumer expenditures have not declined, as in former times, in recent recession periods.

With respect to the great importance of a wide distribution in the holdings of the public debt, Abraham Lincoln put the matter in clear perspective. "Held, as it is, for the most part by our own people, it has become a substantial branch of the national, though private, property. For obvious reasons the more nearly this property can be distributed among all the people the better. . . . Men readily perceive that they cannot be much oppressed by a debt which they owe to themselves." The debt could indeed be oppressive if it were held primarily by the very rich and if the tax structure were heavily regressive.

Private Debt and Public Debt

Another point of great importance is the well-known fact that when public debt increases, private debt tends to rise relatively little, or even to fall. It appears to be a fact that the ratio of aggregate debt (public and private) to GNP tends to be highly stable. Thus aggregate debt (public and private) was 183 per cent of GNP in 1929, 189 per cent in 1940, 190 per cent in 1946, and 173 per cent in 1959. Federal debt increased by $28.3 billion from 1929 to 1940 while private debt decreased by $32.6 billion. From 1946 to 1959 the net Federal debt increased by $13.3 billion, while private debt increased by the enormous figure of $374.9 billion.

Now, which represents the greater burden on the economy as a whole — the interest charges on private debt or the taxes paid to cover charges on the public debt? The answer is certainly not obvious. It depends upon a great many factors. But one thing is clear. In a depression the tax liabilities sharply decline, easing the burden in this difficult period. On the other hand, interest charges on private debt remain fixed, depression or no depression. Again it is the built-in stabilizer feature of the public debt that weighs in the balance.

Public Debt and Monetary Liquidity

Consider also the impact of the public debt upon monetary liquidity. It is possible to have too much liquidity, and it is possible to have too little. It is my view, and it is shared by many economists, that in recent years we have had too little liquidity. A nation's liquidity in modern times consists of the money supply plus the outstanding public debt. Demand deposits, currency, and public debt — these together constitute our liquid assets. Now as a nation grows, it needs more liquid assets. It needs not only a larger money supply, but also a growth in the public debt more or less in proportion to the growth in the GNP. The money supply can be based either on private debt or on public debt, but it is in fact based on one or the other. Formerly the money supply was primarily based on private debt. Modern nations, however, have by now had long experience in developing efficient monetary systems built in large part on public debt. In our system today, our "high-powered" money — *i.e.*, the note and deposit liabilities of the Federal Reserve banks — is based largely on United States securities. Moreover some $65 billion of the deposits of the commercial banks are backed on the asset side of the ledger by United States securities. And it is well to remember that the public debt plays a role not only in the creation of the money supply, but in addition it itself constitutes the major part of aggregate liquid assets.

There are good reasons for believing that a country like the United States with a GNP of $600 billion could not function effectively without a high degree of liquidity. As the GNP rises, long-run, restrictive tendencies could well develop by reason of an inadequate volume of liquid assets if in fact the public debt were not permitted to rise at all. And matters would be still worse if we should be foolish enough to undertake a drastic reduction of the public debt.

In Reply to Professor Buchanan

Buchanan argues (against the "new orthodoxy") that the primary real burden of a public debt is shifted to future generations, that public and private debt are fundamentally similar, and that external and internal debt are fundamentally alike.

I cannot help feeling that no inconsiderable part of the disagreement on these issues springs from the fact that the contestants are talking about different things. Were this not the case it is not probable that competent economists could battle over these relatively simple issues over a period of 200 years or so, without coming to definite conclusions. It is always possible to make rigid definitions and assumptions and to rule out of the discussion matters that in fact are highly relevant.

Thus, for example, Buchanan says that public and private debt are basically alike. Yet an unbridgeable difference exists in the fact that the national government has the power (a) to issue money (either directly or through the central bank) and (b) to tax all of its citizens. As a borrower this puts the national government in a class by itself. No private borrower has at his command either of these vast financial resources. This fact alone makes a national debt something very different from a private debt, and on this issue nothing more needs really to be said. But in fact much more can be said. For example, an increase in public debt increases the property holdings of the country — the wealth-effect. Increases in private debt can have no such effect. There are, of course, many similarities between public and private debt. This no one denies, and if one concentrates on these alone one can quite easily tell a considerable story.

Or take the matter of external and internal debt. Here again Buchanan makes some sensible remarks. There are nonetheless important respects in which external and internal debt are fundamentally unlike. True, public investments made from the proceeds of an external debt may well add enough to real income to cover, and more than cover, the interest charges. And (when resources are not already fully employed) the same applies to public investments made from the proceeds of an internal debt. But in the former case, the foreign exchange mechanism will demand payment in real terms (unless further loans are made), while in the latter case, the added output is consumed at home or else exchanged for other goods in foreign trade. Moreover in the case of domestic debt, cyclical adverse balance of payments problems are not intensified as they may well be in the case of external debt. And in the event of depression (or recession) consumer income is sustained by internal interest payments, while at the same time under a progressive tax structure, tax payments decline. Thus the internal debt serves as a built-in stabilizer. No such stabilizing effect can emerge from an external debt.

With respect to the matter of shifting the burden to future generations, the issue basically relates to the impact of the borrowing process and the resulting debt upon the real income of the future generation as a whole. If wartime borrowing achieves a smoother shift of resources to the war effort, if it produces fuller and more efficient use of resources, then the society will emerge from the war stronger and better equipped to go forward. If this is the case (and I believe most economists would subscribe to this view) it follows that the future generation will have benefited from moderate wartime borrowing. There remains the incentive problem and the fact that future tax payers must pay more taxes to offset the inflationary effects of the added money income received by the bondholders. On balance is the future generation better or worse off by reason of the debt? Probably no unequivocal answer can be given to this question, but it is in these terms that the so-called shifting problem must be discussed.

The conventional argument that no shifting occurs simply because the job of producing the war materiel and fighting the battles must be borne by the present generation and can not in the nature of the case be borne by future generations — this argument, while significant and important, does not come to grips with the real issue. All too often, it has been assumed by the "new orthodoxy" that this is all that need be said. On the other hand, Professor Buchanan appears to exclude altogether the matter of real sacrifices — harder work and restricted consumption — and to limit himself too exclusively to financial considerations. It is however the *real* factors that are important: in particular the impact of the borrowing upon the *real* income and *real* assets of future generations.

29

A *ffording Disarmament: An Analysis, A Model, Some Proposals* *

Emile Benoit
Columbia University

The question of disarmament is not primarily an economic one. However, disarmament would have economic consequences, and an understanding of economics could minimize the adverse costs of disarmament and maximize the benefits of such a program. Professor Benoit believes that the potential benefits of disarmament are large but will be realized in substantial degree only to the extent that we demonstrate a capacity for straight-thinking in economics right now.

The time would seem to be ripe for examining in detail the notion that the United States cannot "afford" disarmament. Assuming a politically satisfactory disarmament agreement were ever obtained, what economic perils would in fact await us if we were to lay down the "burden" of armaments, or, conversely, to renounce our alleged economic "dependence" upon war production?

* Reprinted from the COLUMBIA UNIVERSITY FORUM by permission of the publisher Columbia University, Copyright © 1962; and *Disarmament and the Economy* (New York: Harper & Row, 1963), pp. 204–205, 218–220.

The Defense Economy

Whether we call defense spending a "burden" or speak of the "dependence" of an economy on armaments, the main facts are roughly as follows.

The world as a whole spends approximately $115 billion a year on defense programs — almost three times as much as is spent in the United States for automobiles and other consumer durables. Probably over three-fourths of all defense expenditures occur in the United States and the USSR. United States defense expenditures represent about 9 per cent of our national output of goods and services, our gross national product. Probably the arms expenditures of the Soviet Union are, in real terms, a little less than ours, but because their total output, or GNP, is only about half as large, the "burden" on their economy is almost twice as great.

Arms expenditure appears largely as "waste" from the point of view of the civilian economy, although the same can be said of the cost of police departments: there would be more left for more positive uses if we did not feel the need for special provisions to guard our "security." On the other hand, some of the defense budget is spent for food, clothing, housing, and medical services and contributes to consumption, even though our national accounts do not indicate this.

Even more important, a substantial part of defense expenditures in the United States, and in other industrial countries as well, goes to support research and development. In the United States, about half of industrial research and development, and a quarter of pure research, is now financed directly or indirectly by the defense program. While most of this is immediately directed toward arms, the indirect stimulus to the civilian economy is often profound. Most of the important technological masterworks of recent years have originated in defense research; including radar, atomic energy, jet engines, and space exploration. In turn, these have had important effects upon the development of new civilian products and services.

The foregoing is, of course, all very general — what of jobs and specific industries and plants? If we assume a continued build-up of the defense program, we can calculate that about 7⅛ million people may be dependent on defense expenditures in 1965 — over 3 million in the defense industry, and 4 million in the armed forces or as civilian employees of the Defense Department. Further, defense employment is of course heavily concentrated in particular industries. About 95 per cent of the output of aircraft and missiles, 60 per cent of the demand for ship and boat building, and 40 per cent of all employment in radio and communications equipment are dependent on the defense program.

The dependence on defense production is also heavily concentrated in certain *areas* of the country. Thus in Kansas, Washington, New Mexico, California, and Connecticut, 20 to 30 per cent of all manufacturing employment is based on major defense procurement.

A Disarmament Model

Obviously, to project more specific economic consequences of disarmament we must suggest a fairly specific way of going about disarming. If proper means are to be organized to achieve our end, the process of genuine disarmament could not, in my opinion, be accomplished in less than a dozen years; and that estimate is optimistic. For these reasons, our model assumes a 12-year disarmament period, starting in 1965, with rising defense expenditures between 1960 and 1965.

Let us consider a disarmament model in which US defense expenditures are reduced over a 12-year period from $56 billion, estimated for 1965, to $10 billion, estimated for 1977. Two partial offsets may be assumed. First, we project a growth of about $7 billion during this period in the non-military space and atomic energy programs of the government: NASA and AEC. Second, we assume a buildup of the US share in the current costs of the judicial, administrative inspection, police, and deterrent functions of a World Peace Authority, rising to about $7 billion a year. With these assumed offsets, the net reduction in total security expenditures and related programs might be only $32 billion over our 12-year period. Of this total, however, some $15 billion would be likely to occur in the first three years. It is during this initial period of the disarmament program that the maximum impact would probably be felt.

Would a defense cutback of $5 billion a year — involving, be it noted, less than 1 per cent of the total Gross National Product — risk putting the economy into a depression? The answer is "probably not," but it does depend somewhat on the adjustment policies we follow. An initial reduction of $5 billion in spending, if not offset by compensatory programs would likely lead, through its "multiplier" effects, to a decline in aggregate demand of between $10 and $12 billion a year — enough to begin a fairly serious downward spiral. However, it seems unlikely that we would not resort to some compensatory programs. Congressmen and the public are not, after all, rigidly opposed to tax reduction, and presumably there would be some willingness to launch public service programs which have been held back because of the heavy burden of defense expenditures. It is hard to believe we would make the same mistake as was made in 1953–54 when Federal non-defense programs were cut by $2 billion at the very time when defense expenditures were being reduced.

The most serious danger might rather arise from the psychological effects of altered anticipations by businesses and consumers. We have never before *foreseen* a long series of deflationary stimuli stretching over a number of years, and it is hard to know just how discouraging this would prove. If it brought on a severe decline in business investment in new plant and equipment, or a sudden drop in purchases of houses or automobiles or other consumer durables, the effects could be serious. Everything may depend upon the attitude and programs of the Government itself. If the Government were ready to move promptly with adequate offset programs, and could convince business and consumers that there was no need to fear any significant letdown, a depression should be avoidable.

Obstacles to Disarmament Adjustments

Even if the initial impact of our disarmament program is absorbed without a depression — and the chances for this do seem to be good — we can predict some difficulty in obtaining adequate and sufficiently prompt acceptance and implementation of tax cuts, and in launching our expanded and peaceful government expenditure programs to offset the annual deflationary cutbacks in defense spending. If these programs are too little or too late we might still avoid depression, but we might also face a protracted period of slow economic growth and mounting unemployment — with unfortunate effects on domestic morale and on our international position.

The difficulties in getting adequate offsets are of several types. First, there is the aversion of Congress to new or larger Federal spending programs for other purposes than defense. Contrary to the general notion that government expenditures have been rapidly rising, non-defense Federal purchases, now running at about $8 billion a year, are about a third lower, in real terms (*i.e.*, after discounting for price increases) than they were back in 1953. Even if they were now rapidly doubled — and it is hard to see Congress approving even that much expansion — this would offset *only a quarter* of the minimum net cutback in defense expenditures here projected.

Yet if tax cuts were mainly counted upon to stabilize the economy, the amount of such tax cuts would have to be extraordinarily large — so large, in fact, as to imply deficit financing; *i.e.*, taxes would have to be cut *more* than government expenditures. Up to now, at least, the Congress has never been willing to approve the deliberate use of deficit-financed tax cuts as a means of stimulating the economy.

Another difficulty arises from the cumbersome and slow-moving procedures involved in Congressional hearings, authorizations, and appropriations, which would make it difficult to get either new government spending programs or tax cuts decided upon and implemented fast enough to take up the slack left by the annually recurring defense cutbacks. Another problem relates to what I call "the propensity to reduce the national debt out of defense savings." A recent public opinion poll showed a strong sentiment, particularly among college-educated people, in favor of applying government funds saved from defense expenditures to a reduction of the national debt. This idea also has strong Congressional backing. Attempts to carry out such a policy would result in holding up tax cuts or new non-defense government expenditure programs in the attempt to achieve a budget surplus for debt reduction. The net effect, under the conditions likely to prevail, would be seriously deflationary and restrictive.

Maintaining Adequate Overall Demand

The adjustment problem falls into two major segments. First is the problem of maintaining adequate overall demand for the new goods and services into the production of which the defense resources will be re-channelled. This is essentially the domain of fiscal and monetary policies. Second, we have the structural problem of overcoming various obstacles to a prompt and smooth shift of the displaced resources into the new uses.

Adequate and dependable mechanisms exist by which redundant defense resources may be shifted either to other government programs by changes in the pattern of budget expenditures or to private use by tax reductions. In regard to the former, many persons have the general impression that there is nothing of any urgency left to do which could justify or motivate additional expenditure. Actually, there are a variety of high-priority "needs" to which unutilized resources could be shifted. Obvious among them are the continuous strengthening of education and research, particularly of the more advanced sorts and in various scientific fields, the modernization and improvement of industrial equipment, the elimination of the anomalous and unnecessary pools of severe poverty remaining within the country, and the provision of adequate resources for international economic development. Beyond these we have numerous pressing "needs" of a collective sort, especially in urban improvement, public health, commuter transportation, etc.

The estimated additional average annual cost of such high-priority programs[1] during the 1960's is summarized in Table 1. No claim is here made as to the objectivity of this list of "needs" and expenditure programs. It is presented simply as a summary of what well-informed students of current social and economic conditions consider desirable and

---

[1] Most of these programs have been set forth as national objectives in an official United States document sent to the United Nations: *The Economic and Social Consequences of Disarmament; U.S. Reply to the Inquiry of the Secretary-General of the United Nations*, Part II, U.S. Arms Control and Disarmament Agency, March 1962.

appropriate uses of additional resources. The chief purpose of this presentation is to emphasize the immense backlog of valuable uses for the resources that may be released from the defense sector by disarmament.

Moreover, despite much glib talk about the "affluent society," our average consumer incomes are far from princely. A spendable per-capita income of $40 a week might seem very affluent to an African or Indian farmer, but it does not permit excessive self-indulgence in a modern American city. Thus some part of disarmament savings might well be devoted to tax cuts designed to raise U.S. living standards.

The widely-expressed fear that tax cuts would *not* raise the expenditures of the individuals and businesses that receive them has little apparent justification. The percentage of personal disposable income which is spent by consumers is one of the more stable of economic phenomena. Since 1950, the annual rate has varied only between 92 and 94 per cent. We know less about the marginal propensity to consume, but budget studies suggest that at least two dollars out of three will be spent. Cuts in corporate taxes will also raise aggregate demand even though the precise effects are not easy to measure.

In sum, the problem will not be to find important alternate uses for resources released from the defense effort: It will be to achieve a consensus on priorities, and to endow the chosen programs with enough purchasing power to make them effectively able to bid for and absorb the released resources. In any case, it is less important that we agree on the *best* uses of the resources released from the defense program than that we make sure that nothing we have is wasted. The major vehicles for doing this are fiscal-monetary policy.

Structural Problems

But even under the best of conditions, we shall face some vexing problems arising out of the heavy concentration of defense activity in certain industries, occupations and locales.

Today, the heart of the defense production effort is the creation of highly specialized military equipment that bears little resemblance to any civilian production. A good share of defense production is in the hands of highly specialized defense contractors who have little or no experience with civilian production and for whom disarmament would imply, not reconversion, but radical diversification into types of production with which they were quite inexperienced. Unfortunately, most of the attempts of these firms to diversify into civilian lines have so far been financially unsuccessful. Even under conditions of adequate aggregate demand, then, a disarmament program would involve such sharp and major changes in the pattern of work and output that many people, companies, and communities would find it impossible to make the necessary

Table 1. Additional National Expenditures Required During the 1960's
(billions of dollars)

Program	Additional Average Annual Cost	Content of Program
Ending serious poverty in the United States	$6.4–8.8[a]	OASDI benefits to match increased productivity; cash sickness insurance programs extended to all workers, with improved benefits; complete medical care and improvements for beneficiaries under Workmen's Compensation laws; reasonable standard of living for public assistance recipients and increased counseling services; extension of child welfare services
Industrial plant and equipment	16.3	To maintain average ratio of new investment to corporate cash flow achieved during 1951–1957
Health	7.8	Replacement, renovation, and modernization of hospital and clinics; increased rehabilitation facilities; provision of minimum level of community health services, adequate medical care for public assistance recipients; intensified program of air pollution control; medical research as deemed feasible with available personnel and facilities
Education	1.6	Additional investment needed in universities to double number of science and engineering Ph.D.'s
	10.0	Increased capital facilities to match population growth; training additional teachers, increasing salaries
Housing	4.5	Replacement of demolitions, improvements in home ownership, elimination of dilapidated units

Urban water, sewage, and solid-waste disposal	4.5	To correct present unsatisfactory practices and to meet increasing needs
Urban transportation	1.0	Investment for urban transit and suburban railway plant and equipment
Water resource development	7.9	Programs to meet deficiencies, obsolescence, and growth
Natural resources	1.6	Land acquisition and physical improvement to forests, range lands, parks and recreation facilities, fish and wildlife habitats
Research and development	0.9	Expanded basic research facilities in colleges and universities
	0.5	R&D expenditures implied by the $1.6 billion of additional plant and equipment outlays
	?	NASA, civilian AEC, and special R&D programs of national importance
Foreign assistance	2.0	To maintain a 1 per cent ratio of foreign assistance to GNP.
Total	65.0–67.4+	

a This range represents the difference between the amount necessary to raise the weekly income of the lowest-income one-eighth of all house-holds up to $40, and the cost of certain specific programs indicated in the following column.

transitions expeditiously and without severe losses — unless they have outside assistance.

Certain states (more especially particular towns and communities) have an excessive concentration of economic activity dependent on defense work, excessive in relation to other available opportunities. While in theory such difficulties might be met by the relocation of superfluous workers, this is not likely to be a strategy wildly favored by the workers concerned, by the local businesses who depend on their patronage, or by the political representatives of both. With the rapidly rising cost of housing, roads, schools, hospitals, shopping centers and other community facilities relative to the cost of factories; and with the relatively lower cost and increased diversity of transportation and power; and also with the increased rate of obsolescence of plant and equipment — the advantages of moving new industry into areas where a skilled labor force and community facilities already exist begin to outweigh the advantages of moving unemployed workers to other areas where there may be idle industrial facilities.

Need we plan exactly how to shift highly specialized human and material resources from defense to non-defense activities, just where each worker will go, and to what type of production each factory will convert? I think not. In our type of free market-directed economy, many of these shifts will be easily and automatically made through the spontaneous activities of businesses seeking to obtain new markets and workers seeking to obtain new jobs wherever the new opportunities are to be found. It is a serious mistake to underestimate the flexibility of our economy in regrouping its resources to meet new patterns of demand as they arise.

Nevertheless, because of highly specialized developments in American industry connected with the defense program, we are bound to watch for and consider special cases. As we have already seen, the economy has come to include and protect much that comes under the heading of research and development. Particularly is this true in the electronics, nucleonics, and aerospace industries (industries which are, by the way, heavily concentrated in certain geographic areas). It is here that we may encounter unusually stubborn kinks in economic re-structuring.

Among the special programs which might well be embarked upon, and in which these industries could figure with remarkable results, are the following: 1) disarmament inspection technology; 2) a civilian space program going beyond even the present ambitious plans (expansion of such plans is already under active consideration in Washington); 3) the development of atomic energy for power — particularly if, in the meantime, a major breakthrough in atomic fusion processes has occurred; 4) development of other unconventional energy sources; 5) industrial exploitation of our ocean resources (to which our naval research people could undoubtedly contribute a great deal); 6) a renewed attack on major health problems, centering around cell chemistry and possibly including determined efforts to improve the electron microscope (the benefits of which, if achieved, might be astonishing); 7) a new research and development effort aimed at achieving more effective technology for world economic development.

Conclusion

Disarmament relates to the physical survival and political security of the nation, and economic adjustments connected with it are trivial in relation to themes of such magnitude. The real reason for disarmament is not that modern armaments are so expensive but that they are so *dangerous* — that the classic unilateral defense system can no longer provide the basic security that was its only possible justification; a collective security system under enforceable international law would better preserve our physical security and essential freedoms. Within very broad limits, this nation can afford to spend as much or as little on defense as its genuine needs require. To determine the nature and size of our security program by the incidental economic hardships or benefits of arms spending, or of variations in the amount of such spending, would be a bad case of the tail wagging the dog.

• *Part Three*   BUSINESS ENTERPRISE,

1. *What is the price system and how important is it?*

2. *Who "runs" the modern corporation?*

3. *Is the American economy basically competitive?*

4. *How is government policy used for the purpose of maintaining competition?*

EVERY SOCIETY HAS REQUIRED THE DEVELOPMENT of some system of procedures for resolving basic and recurrent economic problems. These problems include the determination of what products and services are going to be produced with man's limited resources, what methods or techniques are to be used in production, how goods are to be distributed among the population, and so on. These allocational and distributional problems are, of course, more apparent in a prosperous country like the United States than in poor countries.

The Modern Corporation and Economic Organization

In the American economy of the 1960's, the sector of society directly responsible for making decisions about these issues is that of the business enterprise, and the dominant form of business enterprise is the large-scale corporation. Although small in terms of numbers, the corporate form of business organization produces most of the output of the country, owns most of the industrial plant and equipment, and employs most of the labor force. One of these corporate behemoths — General Motors — is the largest producer of *both* automobiles *and* refrigerators in the country and makes a contribution to GNP which is roughly the size of the *total* GNP of a nation like Yugoslavia. But the American corporation operates in a social setting, a setting in which it exerts a tremendous influence upon and in turn is influenced by consumers, stockholders, labor unions, and governments. It is this broad social setting of the business environment that is the theme of the three selections in Section A of these readings.

Prices and Markets

Whereas Part Two was concerned with the big, overall issues of *macro*economics, Part Three (and much of Part Four) deals with some of the major problems of *micro*economics. This branch of our subject examines the economy in terms of its individual parts or sectors and of the interrelation and co-ordination of these parts. As a part of the economy, the American business enterprise is essentially an exchanging and producing unit. It purchases from other firms or owners of productive services the resources that it requires for production, combines and transforms these resources in a process of production into products and services that it sells to other firms and/or consumers. This is a complex process involving big and little businesses, rivalry and combination, price and non-price competition. The readings in Section B are concerned with these issues, with analyzing the alternative circumstances of competition and monopoly.

Public Policy Toward Business: Standards and Problems

One of the facts of life in our contemporary American mixed or hybrid economy is that the actions of business enterprises are subject to the scrutiny, control, and regulation of government, as discussed in Section C. This, in itself, is not unique. What is special about government control of business in the United States is the use of government controls as a vehicle for encouraging competition and discouraging monopoly. No other country in the world has developed in such profusion laws and policies to prevent or curb monopoly in business, and in no other country is the goal of competition so firmly imbedded in public and business attitudes. This anti-monopolistic cast of our public policies has not, of course, been applied with precision or with equal vigor and effectiveness at all times. Nor, indeed, has the subject of monopoly in business and its control by government been free from argument.

Part of this controversy has technological overtones. One aspect of this has already been alluded to in reference to the efficient size of business plants. Another is the role of research and what size of enterprise it finds to be a congenial environment in which to flourish. Research and development activities are now an important element in the economy and a new factor to be considered in public policies toward business.

Competition is a hoary doctrine and there are powerful considerations to dissuade us from putting faith in it nowadays. Yet, economists persist in applying and refining the notion of efficiency to see what course of action is desirable, and the laws against monopoly are now more carefully formulated than ever before and their enforcement is energetically sustained. One thing is sure: the pros and cons of monopoly, the various alternatives, and the criteria proposed for public policy toward business provide an abundant opportunity to develop one's capacities for economic reasoning.

• *30*

The Social Significance of the
Modern Corporation*

CARL KAYSEN
Harvard University

President Coolidge once said that "the business of America is business." According to Professor Kaysen, times have changed. He says that the modern corporation is "soulful" which, in the 1920's, probably would have sounded like "monkey business." Still, says Kaysen, ours remains a business culture, with present-day managers revering the time-honored concern with profits, while influencing society at large in ways inconceivable for their predecessors.

Corporate Structure

The characteristic structure of the modern corporation can be sketched as follows. It is large, both in terms of measures of absolute size, such as

* Taken and adapted from "The Social Significance of the Modern Corporation," *American Economic Review, Papers and Proceedings*, May, 1957, pp. 311–319. Reproduced with permission.

total assets, and in relative terms compared to the size of the major markets that it serves. In these markets, the firm is either dominant or one of a small group which jointly dominate the market; in either event, it has considerable market power. It is generally complex in structure: operating a multitude of establishments widely spread geographically; selling a variety of products and operating in a large number of industries; often crossing the boundaries of industrial divisions and engaging in primary production, manufacturing and trade. It is founded on mass production and mass marketing; where its primary activity is manufacturing, it relies on complex technologies which are frequently changing and which cover a wide range of potential applications. The development and promotion of new products and new methods of marketing play an important role in its activities.

Ownership is disappearing. Stockholding is widely dispersed; no single group of persons, in or out of management, has significant control over corporate action resting on stock ownership. Dividends are stabilized in the neighborhood of half average earnings; stockholders in effect become holders of perpetual bonds. With the sublimation of ownership, management has become professionalized. Managers are not owners. Typically, they are internally recruited; the winners in a career of bureaucratic competition within the enterprise which they manage. Directors and officers become less distinct; the board of directors is simply the "committee of the whole" of the executive group.

Corporate Behavior

What are the characteristic features of behavior in the modern corporation? First is the emphasis on "scientific management" — on rationality in the managerial function. Management itself is subject to an intensive division of labor. The tools of academic science increasingly invade areas of decision in which "business judgment" once held sway. Intuition gives way to computation.

Second is the great weight attached to growth and technical progress as measures of achievement. Growth itself is important; the successful firm should be growing at least as fast as total output. Indeed, through the constant addition of new activities, the firm aims at even more. So long as there are substantial sectors of the economy not dominated by the modern corporation, this aim can be achieved. Growth is presented in terms of change rather than mere expansion of existing activities. This means substantial investment in research and development to create new products, and further substantial investment in advertising and promotion to create demand for them. Coupled with the emphasis on growth is an emphasis on long-range planning and a corresponding desire for short-run stability. Short-run price policies are fixed; selling efforts vary to maintain demand. In the longer run, falling costs arising from cost reduction permit lower prices or more output at given prices.

The third characteristic of the behavior of the modern corporation is the wide-ranging scope of responsibility assumed by management. No longer the agent of proprietorship seeking to maximize return on investment, management sees itself as responsible to stockholders, employees, customers, the general public, and, perhaps most important, the firm itself as an institution. To the customers, management owes an improving product, good service, and fair dealing. To the employees, management owes high wages, pensions and insurance systems, medical care programs, stable employment, agreeable working conditions, a human personnel policy. Its responsibilities to the general public are widespread: leadership in local charitable enterprises, provision of support for higher education, and even research in pure science, to name a few. To the firm itself, as an institution, the management owes the primary responsibility of insuring the maintenance and, if possible, the expansion of its long-run position; in other words, sustained and rapid growth.

The Corporation: Responsible or Irresponsible?

From one point of view, this behavior can be termed "responsible": there is no display of greed or graspingness; there is no attempt to push off onto the workers or the community at large part of the social costs of the enterprise. The modern corporation is a soulful corporation.

In trying to appraise the soulful corporation, we can examine it from two different points of view. The first is from the standpoint of market power. It is worth repeating that the possession of a substantial degree of market power is characteristic of the modern corporation and, indeed, a necessary condition for the display of its characteristic behavior. Only the ability to continue to earn a substantial surplus over costs makes possible a variety of expenditures whose benefits are broad, uncertain, and distant; the enterprise closely constrained by the pressures of market competition does not have that ability.

From this point of view, the orientation toward growth and development and especially toward the novel — may be seen simply as a device for maintaining power. As products become established in the market and technologies familiar, the advantages of the leading producer may tend to diminish and competition to grow. In one perspective this is Schumpeterian competition — the process of creative destruction — and clearly desirable. But if the same firm or small group of firms continues in leadership, both because their present power enables them to spend more on product development and promotion than their minor rivals and their past dominance furnishes a great marketing advantage in leading consumer preferences in the direction of their innovations, the competitive character of the process is less clear. Further, what limit is set on the costs of product development and promotion? Clearly, there is no strong market check which ensures that what consumers pay for novelty is in some sense close to its long-run supply price when innovation is in the hands of a dominant firm or a tight group of oligopolistic rivals.

These same phenomena of growth and innovation in the context of the modern corporation present another set of problems. Resources are committed to expansion, to development of new products, to changing consumer tastes. Decisions as to how much to spend in these ways and how to allocate these expenditures are made inside the firm, relatively insulated from the processes of the market. The combination of a high proportion of internal financing with the inherent bias toward expansion and change leads to exemption of these decisions from the capital market tests of profitability; and even the test of profitability, alone, is not an adequate one in the circumstances of noncompetitive markets. So the question of the economic rationality of the criteria governing these decisions is left open. Further, it is far from clear that the tests of the market are appropriate to determine the answers to these questions. Is it clear that there is a meaningful market test of profitability which is appropriate to investment in changing consumer tastes or in developing new products?

The economic aspect of these questions is not necessarily the most important one. Whether or not the investment and development decisions discussed above are rational or efficient in an economic sense, the very fact that the managers of the modern corporation have a wide scope of choice in making them presents a problem. The chief virtue of a competitive market in practice is not necessarily that it leads to economic efficiency but that it constrains private economic power. Ideally, the businessman in the competitive market has only one set of actions open to him; and any others will lead to failure. Practically, all markets leave some scope for policy choice, but the more competitive the market, the narrower the scope. In the evolving giant corporation, managers possess great scope for decision making unconstrained by market forces — nowhere more so than in their decisions with respect to future growth and change. These decisions have wide impacts — on workers, on consumers, on the community at large. Formally speaking, however, management in making these decisions is responsible only to itself. To be sure, there is a wide variety of possible repercussions of their actions which managements take into account in making their choices; decisions are taken in a certain political, economic, social environment, not in a corporate vacuum. But what management takes into account is what management decides to take into account, and however responsible management policy is, in the sense described above, it is responsible only in terms of the goals, values, and knowledge of management. No direct responsibility, made effective by formal and functioning machinery of control, exists.

No matter how responsible managers strive to be, they remain in the fundamental sense irresponsible oligarchs in the context of the modern corporate system.

The Broader Impact of the Corporation

Yet at the same time, the modern corporation changes the substance of economic activity in such a way that the relevance to its activity of the basic notions of economic rationality becomes doubtful. In a world in which tastes are substantially formed and rapidly changed by sellers, concepts of efficiency which rest on satisfying given consumer preferences lose their sharpness. While new products are created, old ones are in effect destroyed, not just displaced by consumer preference for the new. On the cost side, the new plasticity of technology under the efforts of organized applied science again dulls the edge of the notion of a best technique. Seek, and ye shall find. New techniques are to be had for the (costly) asking. The question becomes, what shall we ask for? If products were fixed, this part of the problem might be manageable, taken alone, but the intimate association of new techniques and new products makes this a poor consolation. The broader the scope of research, the greater its quantitative importance, the more the output of anything new is jointly supplied with that of everything new, and the less close is the relation between a particular output and its costs on which the rationale of efficiency rests.

We classically contrast favorably the operation of business with that of a government department aimed at promoting the public welfare. But the soulful corporation becomes less and less distinguishable, except in the matter of formal control and management responsibility, from the socialist enterprise if the latter operates under instructions to serve the public welfare but not to rely on the public treasury.

Even as it transforms the substance of business in such a manner as to rob the business spirit of its former significance, the modern corporation operates to spread business valuations and business ideas widely through the whole society. It does this most obviously through the mass media, the tone of which is set by the themes of sales promotion. But the more subtle effect of membership in the corporate institution is probably more important. Increasingly, membership in the modern corporation becomes the single strongest social force shaping its career members in the whole hierarchy above the production line. For various reasons, this is less true of production workers; but changing technology may diminish the importance of this distinction. The older and more varied types are disappearing, to be replaced by one of two types: the career bureaucrat (managerial) and the career worker.

• *31*

Efficient Business: How Big?*

Joe S. Bain
University of California at Berkeley

How big must a business be to be efficient? Can we have both small-scale enterprise and low costs of production? Or, is large size and/or concentration of industrial output necessary for efficient business? The following selection presents one economist's estimates on this controversial subject.

Ever since the merger movement of the late nineteenth century, American economists have been recurrently interested in the extent to which large size is necessary for business efficiency. In any industry, the minimal scales of plant and of firm which are required for lowest production costs determine the degree of concentration by plants and firms needed for reasonable efficiency in the industry.

In the course of a recent general study of American manufacturing industries, it has been possible to develop some further data on economies of scale. These data have been developed almost entirely from managerial or "engineering" estimates supplied by certain firms in the industries involved.

The twenty manufacturing industries studied were selected to obtain a maximum possible diversity of industry types consistent with the availability of data, but the fact that data have been more frequently devel-

* Taken and adapted from "Economics of Scale, Concentration and Entry," *American Economic Review*, March, 1954, pp. 15–24, 38. Reproduced with permission.

oped for large and for highly concentrated industries than for others has resulted in some systematic differences between the sample and the whole population of manufacturing industries.

The following characteristics of the sample deserve brief note: First, it features large industries, with fifteen of the twenty having value products above a half billion in 1947. Whereas it includes only a little over 4 per cent of the total number (452) of manufacturing industries, it accounts for about 20 per cent of the value of product of all manufacture in 1947. Second, it contains a substantially larger proportion of moderately and highly concentrated manufacturing industries than the total population. Otherwise, the sample is fairly representative. Eight industries are classed as making consumer goods, eight producer goods, and four goods bought by both producers and consumers.

The table revises the engineering estimates of the optimal scales for the twenty industry groups. In each case, the plant size referred to is the minimal physical production capacity of plant required for lowest production costs, this capacity being expressed as a percentage of total national capacity within the industry.

The Percentage of an Industry's Total Capacity Necessary in Each Plant of Most Efficient Size — Sample of 20 Industries

Industry	Percentage of National Industry Capacity Contained in One Plant of Minimal Efficient Scale	Industry	Percentage of National Industry Capacity Contained in One Plant of Minimal Efficient Scale
Flour milling	$\frac{1}{10}$ to $\frac{1}{2}$	Rubber tires and	
Shoes	$\frac{1}{7}$ to $\frac{1}{2}$	tubes	3
Canned fruits and		Rayon	4 to 6
vegetables	$\frac{1}{4}$ to $\frac{1}{2}$	Soap	4 to 6
Cement	$\frac{4}{5}$ to 1	Farm machines, ex-	
Distilled liquors	$1\frac{1}{4}$ to $1\frac{3}{4}$	cepting tractors	4 to 6
Petroleum refining	$1\frac{3}{4}$	Cigarettes	5 to 6
Steel	1 to $2\frac{1}{2}$	Automobiles	5 to 10
Metal containers	$\frac{1}{2}$ to 3	Fountain pens	5 to 10
Meat Packing		Copper	10
fresh	$\frac{1}{50}$ to $\frac{1}{5}$	Tractors	10 to 15
diversified	2 to $2\frac{1}{2}$	Typewriters	10 to 30
Gypsum products	$2\frac{1}{2}$ to 3		

In nine of the twenty industries an optimal plant would account for a quite small fraction of national capacity (under 2½ per cent), whereas in five others the fraction would run above 7½ per cent. In general, the industries with slight economies of scale of plant are engaged in processing of agricultural or mineral materials, whereas greater plant economies are frequently encountered in industries making mechanical devices.

Regarding the importance of economies of large plants, the percentage of a market supplied by one efficient plant in some cases is and in some cases is not sufficient to account for high firm concentration or to impede entry. Where it is, these economies might easily propagate high concentration and serious impediments to entry; the number of cases where it is sufficient increase as we refer to the smaller regional or product submarkets in various industries. A significant corollary of these findings is that the following popular horseback observations are apparently *not true:* that economies of scale of plant are never or almost never important in encouraging oligopoly or impeding entry, and that such economies always or almost always are important in these ways. The picture is not extreme in either direction and not simple.

• *32*

The Research Revolution*

LEONARD S. SILK
McGraw-Hill Book Co., Inc.

There has been an explosion in "know-how" which has laid the basis for continued promotion of rapid economic change. Why and how did it happen? What made "R & D" one of the important growth sectors of the economy?

Technology and Change

The great thing the United States will have going for it in the years ahead will be the swift scientific and technological progress of our time — and a rising tide of investment resulting from American industry's new principle and practice of programmed innovation, creating a multiple flow of planned new products out of research in a new and powerful extension of capitalism's growth process.

How important this force is you can see by looking at the past impact of improving technology on output. Robert Solow of M.I.T. has estimated that, of the total increase in United States output per man-hour from 1909 to 1949, only 12.5 per cent was due to increase in capital equipment, while 87.5 per cent was due to technological progress. In a second study, Solomon Fabricant of the National Bureau of Economic Research has found that, during the period 1871 to 1951, technological advance

* From *The Research Revolution* by Leonard S. Silk. Copyright © 1960. McGraw-Hill Book Company. Used by permission.

217

accounted for 90 per cent of the rise in output per man-hour, as against 10 per cent for capital formation. And Benton F. Massell, in still a third independent study, done at the Cowles Foundation for Research in Economics, likewise has found that, during the period 1919 to 1955, technological change accounted for approximately 90 per cent of the rise in output per man-hour.

In other words, it was not primarily more machinery in back of every worker, but an unknown combination of better machinery and technology, better organization, better management, and greater skills on the part of workers, that sent United States output soaring in the past half century.

The implications of these findings are of outstanding importance for policy makers and economists. They mean that the overwhelming emphasis of any program for growth must come to focus on technological progress — and the factors that promote it or obstruct it.

Like many "new ideas" in economics, this new stress on the role of technology and research represents simply a shift of emphasis, perhaps a somewhat different way of looking at old knowledge — but a way that can be of crucial importance in reconstructing the economics of growth.

In the future, policy makers will have to concern themselves more with "the variables which govern the rate at which innovations are injected into the economic system than with the variables which determine the rate at which additions are made to the capital stock." Such issues as expenditure by business on research and the policies of firms regarding the replacement of obsolescent equipment should come to be regarded as even more important than the rate of net investment.

Up till now, economists have simply assumed that capital, labor, and land (or subcategories of those factors) were the significant inputs, with technology taken as "given," in producing any output. An improvement in technology was simply represented by a shift in the production curve. This crude way of treating changes in production was perhaps satisfactory in the days of Ricardo when the "given" state of technological knowledge was relatively static, but it becomes meaningless, and seriously misleading, nowadays when technological change is swift and perpetual. But, whatever the past justifications, we are certainly in a strange state of analysis when the factors which are explicitly considered account for only 10 per cent of the increase in output per man-hour, and the remainder is attributed to an "outside" force, ". . . which is little understood, and about which we are able to offer little explanation."

To stress the role of technological advance is, of course, not to deny that its impact upon the economy is largely communicated through the investment process. By and large, technological progress does not become "real" until it is embodied in new investment: Knowing how to plough a field faster does nothing until tractors replace horses. To be sure, changes in organization, techniques, and skills requiring little or no capital investment can also be important; and such new knowledge, similarly, means nothing until it is put to work. As one old farmer once told the expert from the university experiment station, "Hell, I ain't farming half as well as I know how already."

Generally speaking, however, an economy which is rapidly increasing its capital stock is also likely to be accelerating the process of technical advance. And that proposition has its converse: The rate of capital investment will be greatest when innovational change comes fastest — because the rate of profit will then also be high.

Rising R&D Curve

To speed up technological progress, the curve of research and development expenditures in the United States keeps rising. In 1928, American industry spent less than $100 million on R&D. By 1953–1954, over-all research spending had jumped to more than $5 billion a year. In 1959, the total was $12 billion.

To be sure, there is some question as to how much of this growth in R&D spending is due to inflation and changing definitions, and how much of it is real. Data in current dollars undoubtedly overstate the increase in real R&D outlays. Nevertheless, even when all the "water" has been squeezed out of the research spending figures, the rise has still been tremendous.

There is, furthermore, the question of whether the increase in the volume of research and development work should not also be adjusted to take account of the increased productivity (that is, the changed quality) of both researchers and research equipment. If, through the use of computers, modern test equipment, and other devices, more highly qualified researchers are able enormously to increase their output, the dimensions of the real research effort — if it can be measured by the number and difficulty of the tasks undertaken and successfully executed — may have increased far more than even the unadjusted current dollar figures on research and development spending imply. It must be borne in mind that research is not a commodity like apples or pretzels that can readily be adjusted for price change; its output is knowledge, the value of which — especially over the long run — is incalculable.

One certainly must try to distinguish the real rise from the phony. But one needs only one's naked eyes, regardless of what the imperfect data show, to reveal how the research revolution has transfigured the American scene.

And the research spending curve, which has done all this, will continue to rise. By 1969, according to a new McGraw-Hill study, the R&D

total will be more than $22 billion. Some observers put the future level of research spending still higher, as high as $35 billion by 1970.

At some point, clearly, R&D spending must taper off — or else, as Guy Suits, vice-president and research director of General Electric, says, ". . . it would eventually constitute the entire economy" — an anomaly that even the most partisan supporters of R&D would view with dismay.

Why the R&D Curve Rises

The most obvious (and doubtless the most fundamental) cause of the rise of research spending lies in the nature of scientific research itself. Research feeds upon itself: Discovery breeds discovery; innovation breeds innovation; and with each new discovery or innovation, the total body of scientific and technological knowledge increases.

Of course, this has always been so. But in our time the process has been accelerating. The thing that seems to be happening in our time is that all the once widely separated avenues of scientific and technological knowledge are converging, like the roads that lead into a city — a city where ideas are then swiftly exchanged, where civilization then swiftly grows.

The "Building Blocks" of Change

Unlike the situation in earlier centuries, vast numbers of elements needed for further scientific and technological progress are now at hand, waiting for scientists and engineers to put them together. Miller B. Spangler has categorized these elements — which he calls "building blocks" — in this way:

1. Process materials — metals (including "new" metals like uranium, titanium, beryllium), alloys, plastics, laminates, fuels, chemicals, fibers, clay, etc. New or improved process materials frequently lead to technological changes in many industries where cost saving is involved.

2. Process equipment — turret lathes, boring mills, planers, milling machines, gear cutters, grinders, welding machines, forges, deep-drawing presses, centrifuges, agitators, ball mills, boilers, condensers, compressors, jet-molding machines, glass-blowing machines, extrusion dies, rolling mills, billeting machines, cyclotrons, etc. New models of these machines are capable of greater speeds and precision than those of only a decade ago. Automatic or semi-automatic operation of these machines has led to large cost reductions. New process equipment may result from new process materials — for instance, metallurgical advances may permit the construction of machinery of greater durability, or permit its operation under greater ranges of temperature and pressure.

3. Tools of measurement and observation — chronometers, compasses,

sextants, telescopes, microscopes, pressure gauges, thermometers, calorimeters, micrometer calipers, protractors, planimeters, levels, plumbs, transits, spring scales, analytical balances, volumeters, ammeters, wattmeters, oscilloscopes, conductivity bridges, thread gages, surfaces gages, sine bars, hydrometers, anemometers, polarimeters, spectrometers, spectroscopes, gravimeters, magnetometers, surface tensiometers, viscosimeters, torquemeters, vibrometers, X rays, polariscopes, Nicol prisms, photometers, Wilson cloud chambers, Geiger counters, seismographs, etc. These have importance in many industrial applications, such as exploration or quality control or automatic operations, but their most significant use is in scientific and industrial research itself. New and better instruments lead to new experiments — and whole series of scientific discoveries and industrial innovations.

4. Calculating devices — adding machines, electronic computers, mathematical tables such as trigonometrical functions, random numbers, Poisson distributions, nomographs, Mollier diagrams, fugacity charts, entropy and enthalpy charts. New calculating devices enormously reduce the costs of research, make it possible to solve problems which formerly were simply too expensive and time-consuming to tackle. The greatest importance of these devices probably is that they astronomically expand the productivity of scientific investigators.

5. Recording devices — photographic equipment, sound-recording equipment, microfilm, memory tapes, geophones, time recorders, temperature recorders, pressure readers, volume-of-production recorders, etc. These impove production control and facilitate automation. Improved handling of statistical and engineering information accelerates research and development.

6. Instruments of communication — telegraph, telephone, radio, television, intercom systems, teletype, radar, photoelectric cells, dictaphones, signaling devices, sirens, limit switches, alarms, moving pictures, etc. These permit the swift interchange of ideas and information from human to human — and from machine to machine. The growth of electronics brings advance in this communications area at a fantastic rate — and removes the cost deterrents to their use in many industrial applications.

7. Inventories of standardized items — wrenches and repair tools, nuts and bolts, chemicals, batteries, condensers, transistors, valves, motors, pumps, fork lifts, etc. These minimize delay in fabrication and repair, and reduce the costs of industrial processes and of research and development work.

8. Reference literature — encyclopedias, dictionaries, bibliographies, indexes, technical books, handbooks, periodicals, trade journals, etc. These stores of information are of enormous importance to the scientist and engineer. Accounts of previous experiments, experiences, and observations are essential if the scientist is to keep abreast of his field, be

alert to opportunities for additional research, and avoid duplication in research.

The Likelihood of Further Change

The enormous expansion of scientific and technical endeavor, utilizing the building blocks of new materials, new tools of measurement and observation, new calculating devices, recording devices, instruments of communication, standardized parts, and catalogued stores of ancient and recent information and ideas, makes it virtually certain that we are still in the *early* phase of our research revolution.

With so many interrelated elements being brought to bear on research problems today, the probability of further technological progress — of continuing scientific break-throughs and economic innovations — is very high, because of the operation of the "law of large numbers." The law of large numbers maintains that the larger a random sample is, the more closely will it resemble the characteristics of the population from which the sample was drawn. This is sometimes called "the law of averages."

While such probability estimates lead to "pessimistic" conclusions about the chances of achieving any particular innovation (meaning an *economic* solution), the law of large numbers leads to "optimistic" conclusions about the chances for *over-all* technological progress.

The Role of Government

The United States government is, by far, the major source of funds for over-all (both fundamental and applied) research and development work. In 1959, the government put up $7.2 billion — or 60 per cent of total R&D outlays.

Most research prognosticators today believe that, although the government's annual R&D expenditures will probably not increase much in the decade ahead, it will probably not decrease much either. The reason lies in the role Federal spending has come to assume in basic research. This is because basic research, especially in some of the newer fields of physical science costs big money. Except for the very largest companies, few individual corporate budgets are big enough to support this highly risky research investment; the probability of success in cases of individual projects is pretty low. But the results of successful gambles may be so tremendously valuable not just to industry but to the nation and its security that the risks of investment in research should be socially borne. For the probability of *some* rich strikes among the total volume of research endeavors, owing to the law of large numbers, is good. This conclusion need not, however, rest only on probability analysis: various wartime research efforts — the development of radar, synthetic rubber, and the atomic bomb, to name just three — demonstrated that almost any scientific problem can be solved if enough high-powered, organized scientific brain power is directed at it. With so many big scientific and technological problems set out before us as a nation — everything from the building of a more secure national defense to deter Communist attack, to exploring space, to solving the resource and urban and transportation problems created by population growth — there is every reason to expect that heavy Federal support of R&D will continue.

Industrial Research, Profits and Growth

It would, however, be a serious mistake to exaggerate the degree to which the continuing rise in all research spending (pure and applied) depends on government support. Of the $9.1 billion in R&D work performed by industry in 1959, industry itself did, after all, provide half the financing. And that $4.5 billion spent by industry on R&D in 1959 was more than twice as much as industry put into research in 1953, more than four times as much as it invested in research in 1946.

Since World War II, the most profitable industries and companies, and the ones with the best growth records, have been those that had an outstanding performance in research and innovation. The importance of the research-profit-growth nexus has been sharply pointed up by a study of fifty big industrial companies by AT&T. This study clearly showed that, as between different industries or between companies within the same industry, the research-minded companies tended to be the most profitable. One cannot, of course, lay out a simple cause-effect (or chronological) sequence leading from research to profit to growth. Some would make profit the initiating factor. Some would put far more emphasis on good management. Some would give more weight to shifts of demand upon particular companies or industries from outside political, demographic, or technological forces. The causes of company profit and growth are obviously highly complex. Nevertheless, some of AT&T's case histories reveal that research can in fact frequently be isolated as the critical cause of a company's profits and growth.

More and more companies have come to regard expenditures for research not as a luxury but as a necessity to meet both domestic and foreign competition; many executives have come to refer to research as the lifeblood of successful business operation.

Real research will go on expanding — thanks to the logic of science, the quest for profits, and the awful responsibilities facing our government.

• 33

The Price System in a Prison Camp*

RICHARD A. RADFORD
International Monetary Fund

The following was written by an observant inmate of a German prison camp for Allied soldiers in World War II. While seemingly far removed from everyday economic life, it actually is noteworthy as a clear and simple demonstration of basic economic principles. We live in a period when we are being continuously urged to live up to our responsibilities, to see "the big picture." The price system is the more intriguing in such circumstances because it operates with great precision almost automatically, asking nothing more of the participants than that they be themselves — buyer or seller.

After allowance has been made for abnormal circumstances, the social institutions, ideas and habits of groups in the outside world are to be found reflected in a Prisoner of War Camp. One aspect of social organi-

* Taken and adapted from "The Economic Organization of a Prison Camp," *Economica*, November, 1945, pp. 189–201. Reproduced with permission.

zation is to be found in economic activity, and this is to be found in any P.O.W. camp. True, a prisoner is not dependent on his exertions for the provision of the necessaries, or even the luxuries of life, but through his economic activity, the exchange of goods and services, his standard of material comfort is considerably enhanced.

Everyone receives a roughly equal share of essentials; it is by trade that individual preferences are given expression and comfort increased. All at some time, and most people regularly, make exchanges of one sort or another. Our essential interest lies in the universality and the spontaneity of this economic life; it came into existence not by conscious imitation but as a response to the immediate needs and circumstances. Any similarity between prison organization and outside organization arises from similar stimuli evoking similar responses.

The Development and Organization of the Market

We reached a transit camp in Italy and received one-quarter of a Red Cross food parcel each a week later. At once exchanges, already established, multiplied in volume. Starting with simple direct barter, such as a non-smoker giving a smoker friend his cigarette issue in exchange for a chocolate ration, more complex exchanges soon became an accepted custom. Stories circulated of a padre who started off round the camp with a tin of cheese and five cigarettes and returned to his bed with a complete parcel in addition to his original cheese and cigarettes; the market was not yet perfect. Within a week or two, as the volume of trade grew, rough scales of exchange values came into existence. Sikhs, who had at first exchanged tinned beef for practically any other foodstuff, began to insist on jam and margarine. It was realized that a tin of jam was worth one-half pound of margarine plus something else; that a cigarette issue was worth several chocolate issues, and a tin of diced carrots was worth practically nothing.

By the end of a month, when we reached our permanent camp, there was a lively trade in all commodities and their relative values were well known, and expressed not in terms of one another, but in terms of cigarettes. The cigarette became the standard of value. In the permanent camp people started by wandering through the bungalows calling their offers — "cheese for seven" (cigarettes) — and the hours after parcel issue were bedlam. The inconvenience of this system soon led to its replacement by an Exchange and Mart notice board in every bungalow, where sales and wants were advertised. When a deal went through, it was crossed off the board. The public and semi-permanent records of transactions led to cigarette prices being well known and thus tending to equality throughout the camp, although there were always opportunities for an astute trader to make a profit from arbitrage. With this development everyone, including non-smokers, was willing to sell for cigarettes, using them to buy at another time and place. Cigarettes became the normal currency, though, of course, barter was never extinguished.

The unity of the market and the prevalence of a single price varied directly with the general level of organization and comfort in the camp. A transit camp was always chaotic. Organization was too slender to include an Exchange and Mart board, and private advertisements were the most that appeared. Consequently a transit camp was not one market but many. The price of a tin of salmon is known to have varied by two cigarettes in 20 between one end of a hut and the other. Despite a high level of organization in Italy, the market was morcellated in this manner at the first transit camp we reached after our removal to Germany. In this camp there were up to 50,000 prisoners of all nationalities. French, Russian, Italian and Jugo-Slavs were free to move about within the camp: British and Americans were confined to their compounds, although a few cigarettes given to a sentry would always procure permission for one or two men to visit other compounds. The people who first visited the highly organized French trading center, with its stalls and known prices, found coffee extract — relatively cheap among the tea-drinking English — commanding a fancy price in biscuits or cigarettes, and some enterprising people made small fortunes that way.

The permanent camps in Germany saw the highest level of commercial organization. In addition to the Exchange and Mart notice boards, a shop was organized as a public utility, controlled by representatives of the Senior British Officer, on a no-profit basis. People left their surplus clothing, toilet requisites and food there until they were sold at a fixed price in cigarettes. Only sales in cigarettes were accepted and there was no higgling. The capital was provided by a loan from the bulk store of Red Cross cigarettes and repaid by a small commission taken on the first transaction. Thus the cigarette attained its fullest currency status, and the market was almost completely unified.

There was an embryo labor market. Even when cigarettes were not scarce, there was usually some unlucky person willing to perform services for them. Laundry advertised at two cigarettes a garment. A good pastel portrait cost thirty. Odd tailoring and other jobs similarly had their prices.

There were also entrepreneurial services. There was a coffee stall owner who sold tea, coffee or cocoa at two cigarettes a cup, buying his raw materials at market prices and hiring labor to gather fuel and to stoke; he actually enjoyed the services of a chartered accountant at one stage. After a period of great prosperity he overreached himself and failed disastrously for several hundred cigarettes. Such large-scale private enterprise was rare but several middlemen or professional traders existed. One man capitalized his knowledge of Urdu by buying meat from the Sikhs and selling butter and jam in return: as his operations became better known more and more people entered this trade, prices in the Indian Wing approximated more nearly to those elsewhere, though to the end a "contact" among the Indians was valuable, as linguistic difficulties prevented the trade from being quite free. Some were specialists in the Indian trade, the food, or even the watch trade. Middlemen traded on their own account or on commission. Price rings and agreements were suspected and the traders certainly cooperated. Nor did they welcome newcomers. Unfortunately the writer knows little of the workings of these people: public opinion was hostile and the professionals were usually of a retiring disposition.

One trader in food and cigarettes, operating in a period of dearth, enjoyed a high reputation. His capital was originally about 50 cigarettes, with which he bought rations on issue days and held them until the price rose just before the next issue. He also picked up a little by arbitrage; several times a day he visited every Exchange or Mart notice board and took advantage of every discrepancy between prices of goods offered and wanted. His knowledge of prices, markets and names of those who had received cigarette parcels was phenomenal. By these means he kept himself smoking steadily — his profits — while his capital remained intact.

Credit entered into many transactions. Naturally prices varied according to the terms of sale. A treacle ration might be advertised for four cigarettes now or five next week. And in the future market "bread now" was a vastly different thing from "bread Thursday." Bread was issued on Thursday and Monday, and by Wednesday and Sunday night it had risen at least one cigarette per ration. One man always saved a ration to sell then at the peak price: his offer of "bread now" stood out on the board among a number of "bread Monday's" fetching one or two less, or not selling at all — and he always smoked on Sunday night.

The Cigarette Currency

Although cigarettes as currency had certain peculiarities, they performed all the functions of a metallic currency as a unit of account, as a measure of value and as a store of value, and shared most of its characteristics.

Cigarettes were also subject to the working of Gresham's Law. Certain brands were more popular than others as smokes, but for currency purposes a cigarette was a cigarette. Consequently buyers used the poorer qualities and the Shop rarely saw the more popular brands: cigarettes such as Churchman's No. 1 were rarely used for trading. At one time cigarettes hand-rolled from pipe tobacco began to circulate. Pipe tobacco was issued in lieu of cigarettes by the Red Cross at a rate of 25 cigarettes to the ounce and this rate was standard in exchanges, but an ounce would produce 30 home-made cigarettes. Naturally, people with machine-made cigarettes broke them down and re-rolled the tobacco, and the real cigarette virtually disappeared from the market. For a time we suffered all the inconveniences of a debased currency.

While the Red Cross issue of 50 or 25 cigarettes per man per week came in regularly, and while there were fair stocks held, the cigarette currency suited its purpose admirably. But when the issue was interrupted, stocks soon ran out, prices fell, trading declined in volume and became increasingly a matter of barter. This deflationary tendency was periodically offset by the sudden injection of new currency. Private cigarette parcels arrived in a trickle throughout the year, but the big numbers came in quarterly when the Red Cross received its allocation of transport. Several hundred thousand cigarettes might arrive in the space of a fortnight. Prices soared, and then began to fall, slowly at first but with increasing rapidity as stocks ran out, until the next big delivery. Most of our economic troubles could be attributed to this fundamental instability.

Price Movements

The general price level was affected by other factors. An influx of new prisoners, proverbially hungry, raised it. Heavy air raids in the vicinity of the camp probably increased the non-monetary demand for cigarettes and accentuated deflation. Good and bad war news certainly had its effect, and the general waves of optimism and pessimism which swept the camp were reflected in prices. Before breakfast one morning a rumor of the arrival of parcels and cigarettes was circulated. Within ten minutes I sold a treacle ration for four cigarettes (hitherto offered in vain for three). By 10 o'clock the rumour was denied, and treacle that day found no more buyers even at two cigarettes.

Changes in the supply of a commodity, in the ration scale or in the make-up of Red Cross parcels, would raise the price of one commodity relative to others. Tins of oatmeal, once a rare and much sought after luxury in the parcels, became a commonplace in 1943, and the price fell. In hot weather the demand for cocoa fell, and that for soap rose. A new recipe would be reflected in the price level: the discovery that raisins and sugar could be turned into an alcohol liquor of remarkable potency reacted permanently on the dried fruit market. The invention of electric immersion heaters run off the power points made tea, a drug on the market in Italy, a certain seller in Germany. Any change in conditions affected both the general price level and the price structure.

Public Opinion

Public opinion on the subject of trading was vocal if confused and changeable. Certain forms of trading were more generally condemned; trade with the Germans was criticized by many. At one time, when there had been several cases of malnutrition reported among the more devoted smokers, no trade in German rations was permitted, as the victims became an additional burden on the depleted food reserves of the Hospital. But while certain activities were condemned as anti-social, trade itself was practised, and its utility appreciated, by almost everyone in the camp.

Taken as a whole, opinion was hostile to the middleman. His function, and his hard work in bringing buyer and seller together, were ignored; profits were not regarded as a reward for labour, but as a result of sharp practice. Despite the fact that his very existence was proof to the contrary, the middleman was held to be redundant in view of the existence of an Official Shop and the Exchange and Mart. Appreciation only came his way when he was willing to advance the price of a sugar ration, or to buy goods spot and carry them against a future sale. In these cases the element of risk was obvious to all, and the convenience of the service was felt to merit some reward. Particularly unpopular was the middleman with an element of monopoly, the man who contacted the ration wagon driver, or the man who utilised his knowledge of Urdu.

There was a strong feeling that everything had its "just price" in cigarettes. While the assessment of the just price, which incidentally varied between camps, was impossible of explanation, this price was nevertheless pretty closely known. It can best be defined as the price usually fetched by an article in good times when cigarettes were plentiful. The "just price" changed slowly; it was unaffected by short-term variations in supply, and while opinion might be resigned to departures from the "just price," a strong feeling of resentment persisted.

Conclusion

The economic organization described was both elaborate and smooth-working in the summer of 1944. Then came the August cuts and deflation. Prices fell, rallied with deliveries of cigarette parcels in September and December, and fell again. In January, 1945, supplies of Red Cross cigarettes ran out; and prices slumped still further; in February the supplies of food parcels were exhausted and the depression became a blizzard. Food, itself scarce, was almost given away in order to meet the non-monetary demand for cigarettes. Laundries ceased to operate, or worked for £'s or Reichmarks: food and cigarettes sold for fancy prices in £'s, hitherto unheard of. The Shop was empty and the Exchange

Mart notices were full of unaccepted offers for cigarettes. Barter increased in volume, becoming a large portion of a smaller value of trade.

By April, 1945, chaos had replaced order in the economic sphere: sales were difficult, prices lacked stability. Economics has been defined as the science of distributing limited means among unlimited and competing ends. On 12 April, with the arrival of elements of the 30th U.S. Infantry Division, the ushering in of an age of plenty demonstrated the hypothesis that with infinite means economic organization and activity would be redundant, as every want could be satisfied without effort.

• *34*

Competition Versus Monopoly*

CLAIR WILCOX
Swarthmore College

*In a strict sense, "pure monopoly" is the end point on a con-
tinuum representing varying degrees of competition. Pure monopoly is the point of no competition just as "pure competition"
is the point of no monopoly. Many market situations (such as
those of monopolistic competition and oligopoly), however, lie
between the two extremes. In some cases, the actual market
situation, although not purely monopolistic, does involve a significant degree of monopoly power, where one or a small number
of firms effectively controls price, output, and product or style
changes. In others, competition may not be pure (that is, it
may necessarily involve a degree of monopoly power), but it may
still be "effective" or "workable." The pros and cons of competition versus monopoly, a matter of endless debate, are summarized here in a systematic manner.*

Terminology

At the one extreme of possible market situations stands perfect competition, a condition which is nonexistent. At the other stands absolute

* Taken and adapted from *Competition and Monopoly in American Industry*,
Monograph No. 21, Temporary National Economic Committee, Investigation of
Concentration of Economic Power, 76th Congress, 3rd Session (Washington, D.C.:
United States Government Printing Office, 1940), pp. 11–18.

monopoly power, a condition which is likewise nonexistent. If the use of the term competition is confined to those situations which fulfill the requirements of perfection and if all those which fall short of this ideal are regarded as monopolistic, then all markets are monopolistic. If, on the other hand, the use of the term monopoly is confined to situations in which monopoly power is absolute and if all others are regarded as competitive, then all markets are competitive. If both terms are defined in their strictest possible sense, then no actual market can be described as either competitive or monopolistic. In none of these cases would it be possible to use the terms competition or monopoly to distinguish among actual market situations, which range all the way from those that approach perfect competition on the one hand to those that approach absolute monopoly power on the other. If they are to be practically useful, the terms must be employed in a looser sense. It is possible to describe as competitive those situations in which the conditions requisite to effective or workable competition appear to obtain and as monopolistic those in which there appears to exist an appreciable degree of monopoly power. It is in this loose sense that the terms are here to be employed.

The Advantages of Competition

Private business, whether it be competitive or monopolistic, seeks to realize a profit. But profit-seeking activity, under the differing conditions of competition and monopoly, employs quite different methods and produces dissimilar results. The probable effects of competition and monopoly, in general, may be briefly outlined.

Resources are limited in supply. The varieties of goods which might be produced with these resources are many. Economy requires that scarce resources be devoted to the production of those goods which consumers demand and that they be allocated among the nation's industries in proportions which correspond to that demand. Competition operates to bring about this result. Failure in business curtails the supply of unwanted goods. Freedom of entry into business enlarges the supply of wanted goods. Land, labor, and capital are withdrawn from one field and added to others in response to the changing direction of consumer demand. The mobility characteristic of competition thus tends to achieve that allocation of resources which economy requires.

Competition serves the consumer. It operates negatively to protect him against extortion. If the quality of the product offered by one producer is low, the quality of that offered by another may be high. If the price charged by one producer is high, that asked by another may be low. The consumer is not at the mercy of the one as long as he has the alternative of buying from the other. Competition operates affirmatively to enhance quality and reduce price. The producer who wishes to enlarge his profits must increase his sales. To do so, he must offer the consumer more goods for less money. As he adds to quality and subtracts from price, his rivals are compelled to do the same. The changes which he initiates soon spread throughout the trade. Consumers get more and pay less.

Competition is conducive to the continuous improvement of industrial efficiency. It leads some producers to eliminate wastes and cut costs so that they may undersell others. It compels others to adopt similar measures in order that they may survive. It weeds out those whose costs remain high and thus operates to concentrate production in the hands of those whose costs are low. As the former are superseded by the latter, the general level of industrial efficiency is accordingly enhanced.

Competition makes for material progress. It keeps the door open to new blood and new ideas. It is congenial to experimentation. It facilitates the introduction of new products, the utilization of new materials, and the development of new techniques. It speeds up innovation and communicates to all producers the improvements made by any one of them. Competition is cumulative in its effects. When competitors cut their prices, consumers buy more goods, output increases, and unit costs decline. The lower prices compel producers to seek still further means of cutting costs. The resulting gains in efficiency and in technology open the way to still lower prices.

Competition may operate slowly; but it tends ultimately to serve the common good. It induces the businessman to maximize total output, to achieve full utilization of productive capacity, and to provide full employment for labor. It obtains his services for society at the lowest profit for which he is willing to perform them and forces him to distribute to workers in higher wages and to consumers in lower prices a major part of the gains resulting from improvements in technology. It harnesses the profit motive and puts it to work, increasing the output of goods, distributing them more widely, and raising the plane of living toward the highest level which productive resources and technical skill can maintain.

The Disadvantages of Competition

Although competition operates, in general, to serve the consumer, it does not invariably do so. It calls forth a needless variety of models and sizes and places undue emphasis on style and fashion. It diverts a substantial share of the nation's resources from the production of goods to the elaboration of advertising and salesmanship. Competition in persuasion is not always competition in service. Competitors, like monopolists, may misrepresent the quality of their products and the consumer may not detect the deception. Under pressure to cut costs, they may be more likely than monopolists to give short measure and to adulterate their goods.

When labor is fully employed, competition to obtain workers operates to raise wages, shorten hours, and improve the conditions of work. But when there is a large reserve of idle labor, competition may have the opposite effect. Competitors may endeavor to cut costs by reducing wages, lengthening hours, and impairing the conditions of work. The employer who wishes to pursue a policy more favorable to labor may find it impossible to meet the prices charged by his rivals if he attempts to do so. Under such circumstances, competition operates to depress the standards of labor. In fact, it is in certain of the most highly competitive trades that such standards have been notoriously low. Monopoly did not produce the sweatshop.

Competition causes inefficiency in the utilization of natural resources. Competition in the production of timber, bituminous coal, and petroleum hinders the application of improved technology and encourages the employment of wasteful methods of exploitation. It may provide present consumers with a large supply at a low price, but it does so at the expense of future generations. Competition is not conducive to conservation.

Where competition does contribute to efficiency, the gain is offset, in part, by the wastes which it entails. Competition involves an unnecessary duplication of plant, equipment, and personnel. It makes for secrecy and impedes the communication of new ideas. It multiplies the effort required to obtain information concerning conditions affecting a trade. It necessitates costly negotiation over matters which monopolists would handle by the issuance of orders. It compels managements to direct toward bargaining attention which they might otherwise devote to the improvement of internal efficiency. In certain fields, it prevents the coordination of services that might be better rendered by a single firm. It may even make it impossible for individual plants to attain the most efficient scale of operation.

Competition is not without its costs. It may require a high rate of business mortality; it may inflict serious losses on investors. Nor are the inefficient the only ones to suffer. The bankruptcy which eliminates a business entity does not destroy the productive equipment which it owns. Such equipment may be acquired at bargain prices by other concerns. With lower costs, they may proceed to undersell their rivals in the trade. Inability to meet their prices may bankrupt other firms, regardless of efficiency. A whole industry may thus be caught in a vicious circle of failure, loss, recapitalization, further failure, and repeated loss. Bankruptcy in small doses may prove healthful for a trade. But bankruptcy in too large a measure may impair its usefulness. At best, the process is a wasteful one.

The Advantages of Monopoly

There are but a few areas in which it is clear that the public interest can be better served by monopoly than by competition. In the natural resource industries, the need for conservation suggests the desirability of noncompetitive exploitation. In certain other fields, as in the telephone business, the nature of the function performed is such as to demand co-ordinated development under common control. In still others, the adequacy of the service rendered may be improved by unification. It is possible, too, that there are fields in which the technology of production is such that the most efficient scale of operation can be attained only if a single firm is permitted to produce the whole supply. But such fields cannot be numerous. Realization of the economies of large scale production seldom requires monopolistic control. The efficiency of size has to do with the scale of production, marketing, and financing operations, not with the extent of control over supply in a market. It is probable that the demand for the vast majority of products is sufficiently great to enable a large number of plants, each under separate ownership, to realize the economies of size.

The advantages of monopoly, in general, are the converse of the disadvantages of competition. Monopoly can avoid wasteful duplication of productive facilities. It can simplify and standardize its products. It can minimize expenditure on advertising and salesmanship. It can command essential information and cut the cost of bargaining and negotiation. It need not shroud its technology in secrecy; it can apply the discoveries resulting from research to the entire output of a trade. The monopolist is under no competitive pressure to give short measure or to adulterate his goods. He is not driven to depress the standards of labor. If he wishes, he can so conduct his business as to serve the common interest. But, in the absence of effective public regulation, he is under no compulsion to do so.

Monopoly may afford the investor greater security and a steadier return than he could obtain under competition. It is designed to prolong the life of the business unit. It is likely to sacrifice progress to stability. It need not go through a continuous cycle of bankruptcy induced by bankruptcy. But monopoly does not invariably serve the interest of the investor. Its formation and its preservation frequently involve the acquisition of extensive properties at an excessive price. Its prospective profits are often so highly capitalized as to yield the purchaser of its securities a small and uncertain return. Its price policy is likely to be one that obstructs adaptation to economic change and thus imperils investment both in monopolized and in competitive fields. Under monopoly, as under competition, the investor must run the risk of incompetent or dishonest management and loss of markets through shifts in consumer demand.

The Disadvantages of Monopoly

The counts in the indictment of monopoly are ten: First, it causes an uneconomic allocation of productive resources. The monopolist limits his output to the quantity that the market will take at the established price. Consumers who would be willing to purchase larger quantities of his product at lower prices are forced, instead, to buy goods that are wanted less. Capital and labor are thus diverted from those things which the community prefers to those which are, at best, a second choice. The resources that are excluded from the superior occupation compete with others for employment in inferior ones and their productivity declines.

Second, monopoly affords the consumer no protection against extortion. The monopolist may persist in offering inferior quality at a high price, since the purchasers of his product lack the alternative of turning to another source of supply. He may obtain his profit, not by serving the community, but by refusing to serve it.

Third, monopoly affords the worker no protection against low wages, long hours, and poor conditions of employment. The firm that possesses a monopoly in the sale of its products may also enjoy a monopsony in the purchase of the labor required for their production. It may control the only market for special types of skill, the only market for labor in a whole region. Such a situation deprives the worker of the alternative of turning to another employer for better terms. His only protection lies in organization for collective bargaining, enforced by the threat to strike.

Fourth, monopoly inflicts no penalty on inefficiency. The monopolist may achieve economies through combination and integration; he may eliminate wastes and cut costs; but he is under no competitive compulsion to do so. Through inertia, he may cling to traditional forms of organization and accustomed techniques. His hold upon the market is assured.

Fifth, monopoly is not conducive to economic progress. The monopolist may engage in research and invent new materials, methods, and machines, but he will be reluctant to make use of these inventions if they would compel him to scrap existing equipment or if he believes that their ultimate profitability is in doubt. He may introduce innovations and cut costs, but instead of moving goods by price reduction he is prone to spend large sums on alternative methods of promoting sales; his refusal to cut prices deprives the community of any gain. The monopolist may voluntarily improve the quality of his product and reduce its price, but no threat of competition compels him to do so.

Sixth, monopoly prevents the full utilization of productive capacity. Monopolistic agreements may, for a time, yield so large a profit that they attract new enterprises into the fields which they control. Capacity is increased but prices are maintained and output is not allowed to grow. A large part of the productive plant is condemned to idleness.

Seventh, monopoly obstructs adjustment to economic change and thus contributes to general instability. In the competitive sector of the economy prices are flexible; in the monopolized sector they are rigid. In the former area, price is cut to maintain output when demand declines. In the latter, output is cut to maintain price. By refusing to sell at figures which would move his goods, the monopolist leaves factories idle and labor unemployed. Consumer income falls and, with it, the demand for products of competitive industries. The prices of these products are further depressed. Their producers can no longer buy the goods whose prices are maintained. The resulting stalemate may persist for months or years. The necessary adjustments, when they occur, are violent instead of gradual. By stabilizing price, the monopolist unstabilizes the whole economy.

Eighth, because monopoly does not compel the reduction of prices, fails to penalize inefficiency, is not conducive to economic progress, prevents full utilization of productive capacity, and creates industrial instability, it makes the total output of goods and services smaller than it otherwise would be.

Ninth, monopoly contributes to inequality in the distribution of income. The monopolist is under no compulsion to pass on to labor in higher wages or to consumers in lower prices the gains resulting from improvements in technology. As a purchaser of labor and materials, he may be in a position to depress their prices and thus reduce his costs. As a seller of goods and services, he sets his own price to maximize profits. The monopolist's price will almost always be above the one that he would charge if he were under the necessity of meeting competition. His freedom from competitive or regulatory restraints enables him to obtain a profit much larger than that required to enlist his services in the administration of industrial activity. Monopoly thus makes for economic inequality. Laborers whose incomes may be limited by the monopolist's failure to pay wages equal to their productivity are numerous. Producers of materials, whose incomes are depressed by the low prices that the monopolist sometimes pays, may also be numerous. Consumers whose real incomes are reduced by the high prices that the monopolist charges are likewise numerous. Stockholders who share the unnecessarily high profits that the monopolist thus obtains are few in number. A more nearly perfect mechanism for making the poor poorer and the rich richer could scarcely be devised.

Tenth, and finally, monopoly threatens the existence of free private enterprise and representative government. In some fields monopolistic arrangements cannot be established or enforced without legal coercion. Here, competitors who do not wish to compete may call upon the State to impose restraints upon those who do. In an effort to escape the consequences of freedom, they may be willing to sacrifice freedom itself. The legislation which they seek, and frequently obtain, may fasten a straitjacket upon every firm in a trade. Monopoly in any field may so abuse its power that small producers, workers, and consumers will demand the enactment of regulatory laws. Private administration may then be subjected to public supervision; management may be compelled to submit essential decisions to the approval of governmental agencies; the area of business freedom will be accordingly curtailed. Concentration in economic power begets concentration in political power. The resulting order in business and in government must differ materially from that envisaged by the philosophers of liberalism. Indeed, it may be questioned whether democratic processes can survive the trend toward centralized economic control. Monopoly threatens democracy when its contribution to industrial paralysis, to unemployment, and to distributive inequality, induces those widespread attitudes of hopelessness and resentment that make ready converts for the propagandists of revolutionary change.

35

Innovation:

Another Side to Competitive Rivalry[*]

JOSEPH A. SCHUMPETER
Late Professor of Economics, Harvard University

Traditionally, economists have placed great stock in competition to stimulate efficient performance in business, meaning primarily low prices. Schumpeter contrasts this kind of competitive performance with the function (in his judgment more important) of giving newer and better products and services. Like Charles Darwin's concept of the survival of the fittest of biological organisms, Schumpeter's kind of competition engages all of the faculties. And, like Darwin, Schumpeter assumes the continual evolution of his combatants. Business performance, he contends, can only be realistically evaluated in terms of its dynamic process of "creative destruction."

Two Unrealistic Propositions

The theories of monopolistic and oligopolistic competition and their popular variants may in two ways be made to serve the view that capitalist reality is unfavorable to maximum performance in production. One may hold that it always has been so and that all along output has been expanding in spite of the secular sabotage perpetrated by the managing bourgeoisie. Advocates of this proposition would have to produce evidence to the effect that the observed rate of increase can be accounted for by a sequence of favorable circumstances unconnected with the mechanism of private enterprise and strong enough to overcome the latter's resistance. However, those who espouse this variant at least avoid the trouble about historical fact that the advocates of the alternative proposition have to face. This avers that capitalist reality once tended to favor maximum productive performance, or at all events productive performance so considerable as to constitute a major element in any serious appraisal of the system; but that the later spread of monopolist structures, killing competition, has by now reversed that tendency.

Capitalism is Evolutionary

First, this involves the creation of an entirely imaginary golden age of perfect competition whereas it is quite clear that perfect competition has at no time been more of a reality than it is at present. Most important, the modern standard of life of the masses evolved during the period of relatively unfettered "big business." If we list the items that enter the modern workman's budget and from 1899 on observe the course of their prices not in terms of money but in terms of the hours of labor that will buy them — *i.e.*, each year's money prices divided by each year's hourly wage rates — we cannot fail to be struck by the rate of the advance which, considering the spectacular improvement in qualities, seems to have been greater and not smaller than it ever was before. Nor is this all. As soon as we go into details and inquire into the individual items in which progress was most conspicuous, the trail leads not to the doors of those firms that work under conditions of comparatively free competition but precisely to the doors of the large concerns — and a shocking suspicion dawns upon us that big business may have had more to do with creating the standard of life than with keeping it down.

The essential point to grasp is that in dealing with capitalism we are dealing with an evolutionary process. It may seem strange that anyone can fail to see so obvious a fact which moreover was long ago emphasized by Karl Marx. Yet that fragmentary analysis which yields the bulk of our propositions about the functioning of modern capitalism persistently neglects it. Let us restate the point and see how it bears upon our problem.

Capitalism, then, is by nature a form or method of economic change and not only never is but never can be stationary. And this evolutionary character of the capitalist process is not merely due to the fact that economic life goes on in a social and natural environment which changes and by its change alters the data of economic action; this fact is important and these changes (wars, revolutions and so on) often condition industrial change, but they are not its prime movers. Nor is this evolutionary character due to a quasi-automatic increase in population and capital or to the vagaries of monetary systems of which exactly the same thing holds true. The fundamental impulse that sets and keeps the capitalist engine in motion comes from the new consumers' goods, the new methods of production or transportation, the new markets, the new forms of industrial organization that capitalist enterprise creates.

The history of the productive apparatus of a typical farm, from the beginnings of the rationalization of crop rotation, plowing and fattening to the mechanized thing of today — linking up with elevators and railroads — is a history of revolutions. So is the history of the productive apparatus of the iron and steel industry from the charcoal furnace to our own type of furnace, or the history of the apparatus of power production from the overshot water wheel to the modern power plant, or the history of transportation from the mailcoach to the airplane. The opening up of new markets, foreign or domestic, and the organizational development from the craft shop and factory to such concerns as U.S. Steel illustrate the same process of industrial mutation — if I may use that biological term — that incessantly revolutionizes the economic structure *from within,* incessantly destroying the old one, incessantly creating a new one. This process of Creative Destruction is the essential fact about capitalism. It is what capitalism consists in and what every capitalist concern has got to live in. This fact bears upon our problem in two ways.

First, since we are dealing with a process whose every element takes considerable time in revealing its true features and ultimate effects, we must judge its performance over time, as it unfolds through decades or centuries. A system — any system, economic or other — that at *every* given point of time fully utilizes its possibilities to the best advantage may yet in the long run be inferior to a system that does so at *no* given point of time, because the latter's failure to do so may be a condition for the level or speed of long-run performance.

Second, since we are dealing with an organic process, analysis of what happens in any particular part of it — say, in an individual concern or industry — may indeed clarify details of mechanism but is inconclusive beyond that. Every piece of business strategy acquires its true significance only against the background of that process and within the situation created by it. It must be seen in its role in the perennial gale of creative destruction. In other words, the problem that is usually being visualized is how capitalism administers existing structures, whereas the relevant problem is how it creates and destroys them.

The Totality of Competition

Economists are emerging from the stage in which price competition was all they saw. In capitalist reality, it is not that kind of competition which counts but the competition from the new commodity, the new technology, the new source of supply, the new type of organization (the largest-scale unit of control, for instance) — competition which commands a decisive cost or quality advantage and which strikes not at the margins of the profits and the outputs of the existing firms but at their foundations and their very lives. This kind of competition is as much more effective than the other as a bombardment is in comparison with forcing a door, and so much more important that it becomes a matter of comparative indifference whether competition in the ordinary sense functions more or less promptly; the powerful lever that in the long run expands output and brings down prices is in any case made of other stuff.

It is hardly necessary to point out that competition of the kind we now have in mind acts not only when in being but also when it is merely an ever-present threat. It disciplines before it attacks. The businessman feels himself to be in a competitive situation even if he is alone in his field or if, though not alone, he holds a position such that investigating government experts fail to see any effective competition between him and any other firms in the same or a neighboring field and in consequence conclude that his talk, under examination, about his competitive sorrows is all make-believe. In many cases, though not in all, this will in the long run enforce behavior very similar to the perfectly competitive pattern.

Many theorists take the opposite view which is best conveyed by an example. Let us assume that there is a certain number of retailers in a neighborhood who try to improve their relative position by service and "atmosphere" but avoid price competition and stick as to methods to the local tradition — a picture of stagnating routine. As others drift into the trade that quasi-equilibrium is indeed upset, but in a manner that does not benefit their customers. The economic space around each of the shops having been narrowed, their owners will no longer be able to make a living and they will try to mend the case by raising prices in tacit agreement. This will further reduce their sales and so, by successive pyramiding, a situation will evolve in which increasing potential supply will be attended by increasing instead of decreasing prices and by decreasing instead of increasing sales.

Such cases do occur, and it is right and proper to work them out. But as the practical instances usually given show, they are fringe-end cases to be found mainly in the sectors furthest removed from all that is most characteristic of capitalist activity. Moreover, they are transient by nature. In the case of retail trade the competition that matters arises not from additional shops of the same type, but from the department store, the chain store, the mail-order house and the supermarket which are bound to destroy those pyramids sooner or later. Now a theoretical construction which neglects this essential element of the case neglects all that is most typically capitalist about it; even if correct in logic as well as in fact, it is like *Hamlet* without the Danish prince.

36

Big Business, Monopoly, and Economic Growth*

Daniel Hamberg
University of Buffalo

Economics has not lost the art of controversy. The author of this piece draws upon recent empirical studies and general theoretical reasoning to contend that large-scale and/or monopoly power are neither necessary nor sufficient conditions for research and technological progress.

The Cost Argument

For a number of years we used to be treated to the defense of giant, plural-unit corporations with monopoly powers, on the grounds that these were needed to achieve the economies of mass production made possible by modern technology. This argument always suffered from a certain lack of conviction, though, if for no other reason than the fact that in numerous cases the giant firms represented amalgamations of other firms that by any measure had been large and efficient corporations unto themselves; witness, for example, the absorption of Carnegie Steel by United

---

* Taken and adapted from "Size of Firm, Monopoly, and Economic Growth," *Employment, Growth and Price Levels,* Hearings before the Joint Economic Committee, Part 7 (Washington, D.C.: U.S. Government Printing Office, 1959), pp. 2337–2353.

States Steel. Empirical support for this argument was also hard to obtain. Other reasons centered on the widespread belief that most of the economies of mass production were to be found in the large-scale plant, as opposed to the large firm. This belief seemed to gain support from the efforts of some of the largest firms to decentralize many of their operations to the point where individual plants or subdivisions were encouraged to compete with one another.

A Newer Argument for Business

Failing to carry the day on "cost" grounds, the defenders of giant corporations and monopoly power have more recently been treating us to another brand of argument as follows:

The independent inventor is now passé. In his place have come the giant corporations as the cradles of invention; only these great firms possess the resources to finance the skilled teams of scientists and engineers, working in splendidly equipped laboratories, that are now the providers of new production methods and new products.

Not only has the independent inventor been swept aside by the invention of new ways of inventing, the argument continues, but the small- and medium-size firms are also losing out in this process. Those who may be concerned about the monopoly powers of the giant corporations are assured that this is a small price to pay for the contributions to technology, and consequent improvements in our living standards and overall power, that the corporate giants are now making. Although there is undeniably a basic element of truth in this view, it is easily, and indeed has been, greatly exaggerated. It will be my task in the first half of this paper to seek the answer to four related questions:

1. Is it true, really, that technical development is now the exclusive preserve of the teams of scientists and engineers working in the research laboratories of the giant concerns?

2. Do the large corporations in fact finance the bulk of modern research activity?

3. Has large size *per se* been a guarantee of serious interest in research, so that we have reason to look to an important offset in the form of progress to the monopoly powers of the giant firms?

4. To what extent is large business size a necessary condition of modern research, and under what conditions?

The Sources of Inventions

As we have noted, the belief that large business size and economic progress go together rests considerably on the conviction that invention is now the exclusive domain of the giant corporation. How accurate is this view? A recent study of important inventions made since 1900 discloses that 40 inventions out of the group of 61 selected as a sample of important inventive activity since 1900 have been the product of research carried on by the independent inventor or in the research laboratories of relatively small firms. Among these were such diverse inventions as air conditioning, automatic transmissions, bakelite (the first commercial plastic), power steering, catalytic cracking of petroleum, the cotton-picker, cellophane, the gyrocompass, the helicopter, the jet engine, quick freezing, streptomycin, insulin, and the continuous casting of steel. Assuming the sample of 61 inventions is reasonably representative of major inventive activity in the current century, these figures certainly cast serious doubt on the thesis that technological progress is now the bailiwick of the large numbers of research workers employed in the great laboratories of the big firms.

All this is not meant to denigrate the contributions of the industrial laboratories of the large firms; the latter have been responsible for some very important inventions. Nylon, of course, was the product of the immense research facilities of the Du Pont laboratories, and if these did not discover cellophane — an individual did that — they were responsible for the development of its present moisture-proof qualities. The General Motors laboratories discovered Freon refrigerants and tetraethyl lead and were responsible for the final developments of the diesel-electric locomotive that made it commercially feasible — although the work had already been done by two small firms that were absorbed by General Motors, along with some of the most experienced workers in the field. The fabulous transistor was the product of the Bell Telephone laboratories, and so on. Altogether, about 11 of the 61 important inventions mentioned earlier may be traced to the work of teams working in the industrial laboratories of large firms.

All this evidence combined seems to tell us that those who believe that the great industrial research laboratories of the giant firms are now the primary leaders along the path of technical advance in our brave new world have a seriously distorted view of things. There is little doubt that the laboratories are much more important in this century than they were in the last one, but apparently they are a far cry from having become the chief source of (qualitatively important) inventions.

Large Size and Research

It seems clear that the prodigious increase in corporate research and development spending since 1940, about which so much has been heard, has been largely the result of government financing for defense reasons. Further, most of this spurt in research activity has been concentrated in relatively few industries, largely those with defense connections. That is to say, most manufacturing industries and firms have not shared in this spectacular growth in spending on research and development. In fact, other data show most manufacturing firms, large and small, carry on very little of this activity; they concentrate on manufacturing.

Even in the relatively few industries where corporate research is carried on in a big way, in view of the stimulus that they have received from Federal financing, what can we expect from them in the future? Some may assert that war preparations are here to stay, so that we can look forward to a continued strong interest in research.

Others will insist that even if the Federal government steps out of the financing picture the firms who are now spending on research in a big way will get in the habit of doing so, and will continue to do it in the future. Again, this may or may not be true. Certainly, there is room for some skepticism. Inviting caution on this point are the number of instances of firms that were quite aggressive in their research interest and spending at one time and lapsed into a state of semisomnolence at another. Once the government stops footing the bill, there is always the possibility that the comptrollers and accountants, with their everlasting myopic attitudes toward research, will find continued large-scale spending in this direction wasteful and expendable. This, too, has happened before, and it can happen again.

Among those who believe that large size and technical progress have become as one, there seems to be the implicit notion that all or most giant firms have become sponsors of industrial research. Our previous discussion of the comparatively small proportion of important inventions since 1900 emanating from the giant corporations should be enough to cause strong skepticism on this score. Beyond that, we need only to note a number of important industries dominated by very large firms where interest in research has traditionally been at a minimum. The steel industry is a notable case in point. Since the turn of the century, this industry — particularly the largest firms — has not been noted for its progressiveness. Virtually all the important recent advances in the methods of producing primary steel have come either from outside the industry or from small firms within the industry.

The cigarette industry is almost totally innocent of any serious interest in research. In the equally if not more concentrated auto industry, it is fair to say that most of the recent engineering improvements have come from without the large firms of this industry. Again, during the years when the aluminum industry was a virtual monopoly of Alcoa, two of the three most important advances in production methods originated outside the industry. In the basic metal industries generally, where firms tend to be quite big, relatively little is spent on research. The same is true of the food products and agricultural machinery industries, both dominated by large firms. And so on through such similar industries as linoleum, plumbing equipment, meat products, distilled liquors, and so forth.

Is Large Size a Necessary Condition for Research?

Large size is not a sufficient condition for interest and spending on research in the modern world. On the other hand, can it be said that large size is still a necessary condition? Would breaking up the large corporations, for example, be tantamount to depriving us of the major source of research into new techniques and products that will pave the way for future economic progress? In a sense, our earlier examination of the sources of inventions implies a negative answer to this question. But the persistence of unsubsidized research in certain industries, like the chemical and petroleum refining industries, both characterized by very large firms, suggests that in some cases there may indeed be some connection between expenditures on research and size of firm.

This connection seems to lie in fields of research or invention where the path to success is not a systematic one, but rather rests on a protracted and expensive series of experiments and tests. The element of chance assumes a large role, or often, a long series of tests may be performed in the mere hope of discovering unknown properties of certain compounds that will yield useful applications.

The significance of research of this type for the problems at hand is not hard to discern. When inventions or discoveries involve innumerable observations from a long series of experiments, teams of research workers, with ample and sometimes elaborate research facilities at their disposal, may provide the fastest and most efficient way of achieving results. Here, then, the financial resources of the big firms may be required to provide both the facilities and the teams of workers. Moreover, where the element of chance is great, the large firm is in a better financial position to absorb the costs of the many failures involved before success is achieved.

However, we must not exaggerate the potential of the large firm in this respect. For one thing, the kind of expensive experimentation just described appears to apply mainly to chemical and related inventions. For another, this type of research is not new, and has been successfully conducted in the past by individuals or small teams of workers utilizing a bare minimum of equipment. This was true in connection with the discovery of the first aniline dye and the vulcanization of rubber in the previous century, for example, and of Freon refrigerants, tetraethyl lead, and nylon in the 20th century. In fact, some of the very large firms operate a number of small laboratories rather than one large one.

The foregoing discussion should be sufficient to raise serious doubts that the great industrial laboratories are now the repositories of research and invention in the Western World that they have been made out to be and to caution against the glib tendency to identify large firms with serious research interests. This discussion should also prompt us to guard against glib assumptions that large teams of organized scientists and technicians working under close administrative guidance, with their tasks and goals carefully preestablished, are indeed the best approach to invention. It certainly remains to be demonstrated that there is a definite correlation between size of research organization and quality as well as quantity of inventive achievement. On the contrary, it is disquieting to hear of the number of research administrators who remark on the amount of piddling that goes on in the great laboratories and the heavy spending on marginal improvements designed to maintain patent controls. And students of invention have often commented on the number of truly important inventions that have been the work of individuals unassociated with an industry and thereby able to approach its problems with a completely fresh and detached outlook.

Monopoly and Economic Progress

There are many who claim not only that the giant firm is needed to undertake research in the modern era, but that the substantial degree of monopoly power that large size usually confers is equally vital to economic progress. Starting with the pronouncements of the late Professor Schumpeter in the thirties and forties, we have been told that monopoly, far from being undesirable, is actually advantageous when economic progress is taken into consideration. In general, the case rested on the thesis that substantial monopoly power creates an environment propitious to both capacities and incentives for innovation. Far from being exorcised by the existence of significant monopoly power, these people see in it a definite advantage aiding our quest for technical progress and higher living standards. This advantage is felt to outweigh by a considerable margin the losses from oft-admitted monopolistic powers. So, without further ado, let us see of what fabric this argument is made.

As usual, there are at least two sides to every question, and this is no less true on the issue of the role of monopoly power in the innovation process. For one thing, it would be an egregious mistake to identify the growth of monopolistic power with superior entrepreneurial ability. The greatest source of impetus to these movements originated in the desire to curb competition and from the great profits for the promoters of these mergers. Today, such things as tax considerations, desires to assure sources of supply or market outlets, or product diversification seem to be fostering mergers, rather than any unusual entrepreneurial talents — at least of the type that necessarily bodes well for technical progress.

Moreover, quite the opposite from being a convenient vehicle for the exercise of the talents of the dynamic and imaginative entrepreneur, the large corporation can lead, and has led, to developments not conducive to the risk taking that is associated with innovation. Chief among these is the emergence of bureaucratic organizations of officials to carry out the multiple, complex functions inherent in modern large-scale enterprise. The bureaucrats of the large corporations, usually cloaked with substantial monopoly power, develop a strong sense of security about their jobs, a career attitude toward managerial positions, that make it imperative to be a good organization or team man, to follow the accepted rules of action and behavior. These are not the qualities of the prospective innovator. Risky ventures are avoided that might destabilize existing market situations and threaten the position of the entrenched managerial bureaucracies, which operate better in a stable, rather than a changing, environment. These bureaucracies tend to become instruments of resistance to, not promoters of, change.

Moreover, it must be remembered that innovations that are substitutes for existing products and processes involve losses from the scrapping of existing plant and equipment. Firms protected by monopoly power may be expected to try to avoid such losses by postponing innovation until the existing capital goods have considerably depreciated. Why render obsolete with a new innovation what may have been painfully built up in the past? And this is no less true of firms that spend large sums on research than of those who do not. In fact, for the former, much of their research may be aimed at the protection of existing monopolistic strength, as well as the avoidance of capital loss through obsolescence — by obtaining patents ahead of others threatening the firm's entrenched position. Scrutiny of the innovational behavior of the electric lamp, radio and television, railway locomotive, and telephone industries, among others, discloses that innovations of competitive products have occurred only after long periods of market exploitation of old products. The investigations of a number of writers have brought them to the conclusion that new firms are very often needed if radically new innovations are to take place.

This information should not be unexpected. Innovation is certainly expensive and risky. The intelligent entrepreneur is all too aware of this, particularly if he has recently experienced the trials and tribulations of innovation and market consolidation. Following this experience, a period of quiescence is apt to be the most attractive situation. With good profits, monopoly powers that may insulate well against potential competition, executives are more prone to refrain from innovation, to be content with protecting the fruits of past efforts. They are hardly likely to want to render obsolete soon afterward with a new innovation.

Competition and Innovation

These problems do not arise when there is active and intense competition, although not necessarily pure competition. The adoption of new techniques or products by some firms under competitive conditions literally forces the rest to follow suit, to abandon its existing equipment and write off the losses, or else run the risk of being undersold or losing customers to the new products being introduced by the competitors. In addition, a firm without significant monopoly power, whose share of the market is small, will find the adoption of the latest techniques and products especially attractive as a means of underselling competitive firms and invading their markets. For the losses from scrapping existing equipment will seem rather minor compared to the profits to be garnered from the enlargement of its markets. It is the monopolistic firm, with a sizable portion of the market, that finds losses on sunk capital large compared with prospective profits from further broadening of its market share.

Likewise, competition in contrast with strong monopoly situations, is ordinarily associated with freedom of entry, with the full freedom of new firms to enter an industry with new and cheaper techniques or new, substitute products. The new firm, too, is likely to be a more aggressive innovator. By definition, it has no vested interest in maintaining the capital values of existing plant and equipment, no vested interest in maintaining existing markets. It will want to take advantage of the latest techniques and equipment, and in doing so will force the existing firms to fall in line or be outsold.

Monopoly, on the other hand, obstructs the entry of new firms. Sometimes it does this by deliberate action, as by threatening destructive price competition, patent shelving, and expensive and drawn-out patent litigation, controls over supplies of important materials, etc. At other times, the mere strength of the monopolistic firm's hold on the market may act as a strong deterrent to the entry of new firms.

Perhaps the outstanding feature of active, intense competition in connection with the innovating process is the persistent pressure it exerts to search for and adopt innovations that would otherwise be delayed if introduced at all. It is sometimes said that strong monopoly power is not necessarily inconsistent with innovation. This is true; there are indeed firms with such managements.

But the advantage of active, intense competition lies in the fact that it does not leave innovative ability and behavior to pure chance. The persistent pressures from competition provide a compelling force to innovate or fall behind and perhaps eventually disappear altogether. Competition is also the proper stimulant to prevent firms from seeking "the quiet life," from being content to reap the fruits of past efforts and rest on their laurels.

In reply, it is often argued that even firms with apparent monopoly power are not immune to strong competitive pressures. There have been dramatic struggles in monopolistic markets; new firms have overcome obstacles in the past. In brief, competition is an ubiquitous and pervasive force from which no firm can ever completely cut itself off and enjoy peace and tranquility.

There may be a strong element of truth in this view, although there certainly have been protracted periods during which many large firms have been able to enjoy peace and quiet. Irrespective of the truth of these remarks, however, they can hardly be regarded as a defense of monopoly power. They merely show that despite its existence elements of competition may make their presence felt. This sounds like a very good case for enlarging the area in which competition is allowed to operate, that is, for weakening the forces of monopoly.

• *37*

Criteria for Anti-Monopoly Policy*

ALFRED E. KAHN
Cornell University

Economists have developed two major criteria or standards for evaluating American business and public policies toward business enterprise. One emphasizes the structure of markets and the market power of business. The other looks to business perform-ance and affirms "by their fruits ye shall know them." In the following article, Professor Kahn compares and appraises these two standards and comments briefly upon a third: business conduct.

Criticism of Antitrust

Academic economists have in the past frequently criticized the antitrust authorities for their inactivity and the laws themselves for their impotence in dealing with big business. Recently, however, increasing numbers of them have been attacking antitrust policy from the opposite direction, asserting that the application of the laws is too strict and the zeal of

* Taken and adapted from "Standards for Antitrust Policy," *Harvard Law Review*, November, 1953, pp. 28–54. Reproduced with permission.

enforcement agencies excessive and misdirected, in so far as the treatment of business size, integration, and competitive tactics is concerned.

The present essay seeks to evaluate these latter-day criticisms by appraising the alternative standards for public policy which they suggest.

The Market Structure Test of Monopoly

1. *Its nature.* Economists have developed two fairly distinct tests of monopoly. One looks to market structure for evidences of those characteristics from which, according to the theory of the firm, undesirable results follow. The other criterion applies the maxim "by their fruits ye shall know them." It may begin by identifying structural impurities, but its primary emphasis is on the economic record, that is, market performance; only if the results are "bad" is the monopoly power deemed excessive.

The two tests are not mutually exclusive; it is seldom suggested that either be applied without consideration of the other. Both assume that a radically imperfect market structure will sooner or later produce a defective performance. However, it is clearly one thing to apply judgments to a market situation *per se* and quite another to attempt to evaluate the results, judging the structure mainly in terms of those findings.

It is the author's thesis that the courts have not followed the lead of the critics (or friends) of recent decisions, that they have been wise not to do so, and that the antitrust laws will continue to play an effective role in preserving workable competition only if the courts resist some of the policy implications of the new economic criticism as well as they have resisted the old.

2. *Its difficulties.* The concept of workable competition strongly suggests the expediency of the traditional approach to antitrust problems in preference to applying a market structure test. If monopoly elements inevitably pervade the economy and are in some measure essential to a good performance, it would clearly be quixotic to attack monopoly power *per se.* If the courts were really prepared now to outlaw "the power to raise prices," as some enthusiastically read the 1946 *American Tobacco* decision, few sellers would be exempt; the economy would have to be "purified" right out of the twentieth century. Yet there exists no generally accepted economic yardstick appropriate for incorporation into law with which objectively to measure monopoly power or determine what degree is compatible with workable competition.

The scrutiny of the law might be directed at the sources of monopoly power, rather than toward the power itself. But these causal factors, similarly, are neither measurable nor, taken individually, unequivocal in their implications concerning the workability of competition. Whether their influence is, on balance, beneficent or harmful depends on a host of conditioning circumstances which defy incorporation into legal prohibitions: every market structure is in large measure *sui generis*.

Product differentiation, for example, is often a means of competition that serves the public, providing minimum assurances of quality and catering to a real consumer desire for product improvement or variation. Difficulty of entry, when not deliberately devised or imposed, or the concentration of patents scarcely provide a sufficient basis for antitrust action against firms whose monopoly power they may enhance. Similarly, there are serious dangers in setting upper limits to business size or market shares *ex ante*. They include: the difficulty of defining products and markets in a way that will be generally acceptable and will stay put; the risk of preventing unmeasurable economies of scale, including the economies of experience, technical skill, and research; the possible damping effect on business enterprise of such upper limits; the possible compatibility of oligopoly and forthright rivalry, particularly in innovation; the tendencies of giant business units constantly to change their product "mixes" and thereby to intensify inter-product and inter-industry competition.

It does not follow that the market structure concept of monopoly has nothing to contribute to effective antitrust policy. It may supply guidance for legal remedies when a business has habitually indulged in practices which violate the law, by suggesting for removal market elements which may have fostered the illicit conduct. And the avoidance or offsetting of industrial concentration may very well assume a central position in guiding other Government policies which bear on business performance. It suggests the need for measures beyond the antitrust laws to curb and counteract the forces which help to generate monopoly power: revising the tax laws, organizing technical research and assisting private, cooperative research organizations; providing credit facilities for new ventures, defining quality standards and enforcing grade labeling, underwriting full employment, ensuring sustained, adequate supplies and fair distribution of scarce raw materials, assisting private parties to resolve patent infringement controversies, and so on. Such measures are, of course, not at all incompatible with the traditional focus of antitrust policy. On the contrary, they would further implement the traditional conception of unfair competition by attacking positively what the law already attacks negatively — competitive disadvantages not attributable to inefficiency.

The Market Performance Test

1. *Its nature.* Should antitrust scrutiny, then, be focused mainly on market performance? In 1949, Professor Edward S. Mason suggested an appraisal of an industry's performance as one possible way of deciding, at

law, whether it was workably competitive. More recently, Professor Clare E. Griffin has provided a judicious expression and elaboration of this thesis. Both concepts, market performance and workable competition, are essentially pragmatic. How much competition, how many sellers, how standardized a product, how free an entry, how little collusion are required for workability? Enough, it is averred, to give the consumer a real range of choice, to ensure efficiency, to hold profits to reasonable levels, to yield technological progress and a passing on of its gains in lower prices while avoiding cut-throat competition. The law, these economists imply or openly suggest, should evaluate the economic results in the light of the available alternative market structure and attack the structure only when the foregoing tests warrant it. In legal terms, their suggestion is that the rule of reason be revivified, given an essentially economic content, and applied in all antitrust proceedings. The legality or illegality of all business structures and practices would then turn on their impact on the workability of competition, as judged in turn largely by economic results.

2. *Its difficulties.* Apart from devising judicial, administrative, or legislative remedies, the usefulness or validity of this criterion as the basic, self-sufficient guide to public policy is as much open to question as is that of market structure.

First, it must be recognized that market performance is not necessarily a sign either of competition or monopoly. It is a "way of looking at competition," in Mason's words, only in the sense that it looks for the results which idealized competition is supposed by static theory to achieve. And if the results are "good," the market which produced them becomes, *ipso facto,* "workably competitive." Such an approach has an obvious attraction. Ignoring the irrelevant forms, dismissing the complexities of traditional legal inquiries, it judges situations in terms of what really counts, their results. It recognizes the commonplace axiom that competition is, after all, not an end in itself. As for the axiom, while the general American bias in favor of competition is indeed rationalized largely by an expectation that in the long run it will produce the best economic results, it is also true that fair competition is an "end in itself." For it is indissolubly linked with the non-economic values of free enterprise — equality of opportunity, the channeling of the profit motive into socially constructive channels, and the diffusion of economic power.

To put the matter bluntly, the market performance test looks at the wrong end of the process. The essential task of public policy in a free enterprise system should be to preserve the framework of a fair field and no favors, letting the results take care of themselves. Obviously, if the results go too far astray the legislative process may have to be invoked to reexamine and reconstitute the institutional framework, either in particular phases or in its entirety. Obviously, too, where it appears that it is some antitrust proscription which is responsible for the poor performance, that proscription should be revised. But the most arresting aspect of much of the current criticism of antitrust policy is the paucity of concrete economic evidence adduced to demonstrate that the kinds of market structure and behavior consistent with the antitrust laws fall short in their performance in ways which only a relaxation of those statutes will remedy.

Yet on the basis of this sketchy evidence of public necessity, the proponents of a market performance test for antitrust would dilute if not eradicate the suspicion with which the law now regards the practices of collusion, coercion, and exclusion. They would permit business men to do these things provided they can at some future date, when and if called upon to do so, demonstrate in any of a great number of possible ways that the practices produced "good" economic results. In view of the weak punitive provisions of the antitrust laws, which most of these critics would further dilute by shutting the door to treble damage suits where the violations were not "wilful," it is difficult to doubt that the adoption of such a rule of reason would be regarded by the business world as an invitation to "reasonable cartelization" of the economy.

The insistence of economists on economic tests might be understandable if objective standards capable of commanding general acceptance had in fact been developed. Certainly the second deficiency of the market performance test as a substantive basis for antitrust is its vagueness and uncertainty. The grounds on which the courts have for over fifty years refused to evaluate the reasonableness of prices collusively fixed still command respect today. The adoption of vague tests of "public welfare" could only weaken the legal safeguards of the competitive system, by providing antitrust defendants with an unlimited supply of legal loopholes. Economic results are to be used as a basis for acquittal only: no critic has yet suggested that a poor performance provides a sufficient basis for prosecution. If "efficiency," "progressiveness," and "usefulness for national defense" are to acquit a company or industry, the Government should presumably condone most instances of cartelization or monopolizing in the fields of electronics, chemicals, petroleum, and chain store distribution, regardless of whether the specific restraints had anything to do with the good over-all performance. If it is to be left to the courts or administrative commissions to determine whether, in the absence of the restraints, progress might or might not have been even more rapid, prices and profits even more reasonable, grave difficulties will be encountered because of the elusiveness of this test. The burden surely rests on the critics of the antitrust laws to demonstrate that those predatory or collusive actions which the law attacks are indeed requisite to a good performance. This is something they have for the most part failed to do.

The Alternatives in a Free Enterprise System

Only two general methods of regulating private business appear practicable. One is to establish fairly definite standards in statutory law, leaving businessmen free within those limits to pursue their own interest. So far as this writer can see, such standards can only be standards of *conduct*. In this case, legal uncertainties will arise only at the boundaries, though these boundaries may admittedly be vexatiously elusive. It is difficult to envisage equally clear criteria of acceptable and unacceptable economic performance. Poor results may issue through no conscious actions or fault of the businessman concerned. A progressive and efficient company may yet violate the law in ways which contribute little or not at all to its good performance or which may have kept the record of its industry from being even better.

The only effective alternative is to leave the maintaining of competition to an administrative commission, vested with broad and pervasive powers of investigation, reorganization, and regulation, industry by industry. Such a commission would have to decide, in each case, whether particular prices or profits had been too high or too low, capacity too great or little, progress in reducing costs, improving quality, and introducing new products too rapid or too slow; and it would have to be empowered, on the basis of such decisions, to fashion such alterations in business structure as might appear appropriate. It is questionable whether any group is competent to make such decisions, whether such delegation of responsibility would be politically acceptable, and whether such a change would make for greater clarity and dependability of businessmen's expectations than the antitrust laws as they now stand.

• 38

Alternatives for Public Policy*

WALTER ADAMS
Michigan State University

Of all countries, the United States is rightfully recognized as most devoted to the ideals of competitive private enterprise. No other country has developed in such high degree laws for restricting monopoly in business. The goals and effectiveness of this anti-monopoly policy have given rise to debate as times and situations have changed. The following selection compares and appraises three major alternatives for public policy toward business enterprise in the American economy today.

Depending on their point of view, economists will recommend one of the following policy alternatives with respect to concentrated industries: 1) maintenance of the status quo which, by and large, is regarded as satisfactory; 2) imposition of public regulation or public ownership; or 3) rejection of both private and public monopoly, and the promotion of vigorous competition under the antitrust laws.

The Status Quo

The defenders of the status quo generally advocate a policy of non-interference with respect to our concentrated industries. They seem satisfied with the prevailing industrial structure, either because they believe that bigness and concentration are now controlled by the "right" people or because they refuse to regard concentration as indicative of pervasive monopolization.

Three distinct, though related, facets of this position are discernible. One is the belief that the business leader of today is a far cry from the robber baron of yesterday; the belief that industrial statesmanship, social responsibility, enlightened self-restraint, and progressive labor, customer, and supplier relations have replaced the exploitative behavior, the sharp-shooting competitive practices, and the "public-be-damned" attitude of a bygone age; in short, the belief that the present managers of giant corporate enterprise have demonstrated their capacity for exercising industrial stewardship.

The second facet of the status quo position is the "workable competition" thesis. Its supporters hold that bigness and concentration are no cause for alarm, because competition is present and *working* in an economy such as ours where constant technological progress is reflected in ever-increasing output, lower prices, and new and improved products. They urge that the effectiveness of competition be judged not in terms of market structure (*i.e.* the degree of concentration in particular industries) but rather by market results (*i.e.* performance in the public interest).

The believers in workable competition usually buttress their position with the suggestion that "old-fashioned" competition — *i.e.* competition among sellers and among buyers *within* an industry — be replaced with a more dynamic concept of *inter-industry* or technological competition. Their argument is this: classical, intra-industry competition tends to promote maximum output, minimum prices, and optimum utilization of capacity; in short, it stimulates efficiency. But this efficiency is static and unprogressive in character. It makes no allowance for economic growth. While it prevents concentration, it stifles progress. To have progress we need more, not less, concentration. Only bigness can provide the sizable funds necessary for technological experimentation and innovation in the industrial milieu of the twentieth century. Only monopoly earnings can provide the bait that lures capital to untried trails. The consumer need not rely, therefore, on the static competition between large numbers of small firms as protection against exploitation. In the long run, he can find greater safety — and better things for better living to boot — in the technological competition of a small number of large firms who, through research and innovation, eventually destroy any position of market control which may be established.

The third facet of the status quo position is the recently promulgated "countervailing power" thesis which concedes the pervasiveness of concentration and monopoly, but maintains that the dangers of exploitation are minimized by certain built-in safeguards in our economy. According to this thesis, the actual or real restraints on a firm's market power are vested not in its competitors, but in its customers and suppliers. These restraints are imposed not from the same side of the market (as under classical competition), but from the opposite side. A monopoly on one side of the market offers an inducement to both suppliers and customers to develop the power with which they can defend themselves against exploitation. The result will be, so the argument runs, a balance of power within the economy — the creation of almost automatic checks and balances requiring a minimum of interference or "tampering."

The foregoing arguments in defense of the status quo are subject to a number of criticisms. As to the beneficence of industrial stewardship and workable competition, what assurance do we have that the workable competition of today will not be transformed into the abusive monopoly or oppressive conspiracy of tomorrow? How, in the absence of competition or constant and detailed supervision, can we ever determine whether the performance of industrial giants does, in fact, serve the public interest and will continue to do so in the future? By what concrete yardsticks do we measure the workability of competition?

Secondly, with regard to the countervailing power thesis, it can be argued: 1) that countervailing power is often undermined by vertical integration and top level financial control which blend the opposing sides of the market into one; 2) that the bilateral monopolies created through the countervailance process often conclude bargains prejudicial to the consumer interest (for example, wage increases for the steelworkers followed by price increases for the steel industry); 3) that the countervailing influence of technological or inter-industry competition is often subverted by a combination of the potential competitors (for example, the merger between motion picture houses and television networks); 4) that any countervailance through government action is often undermined by unduly intimate affiliation between regulator and regulatee (for example, the I.C.C. which seems to have degenerated into a lobby on behalf of railroad interests); and finally 5) that the whole thesis rests on the dubious assumption that industrial giantism is inevitable under modern technological conditions — an assumption which still awaits scientific validation.

Public Regulation or Public Ownership

The advocates of public regulation or public ownership hope simultaneously to insure industrial efficiency and to avoid the abuses of private monopoly — not by the dissolution of monopoly but by its social control. Their argument runs along these lines: Competition in many basic industries is a thing of the past and has been replaced by trade agreements and price fixing, cartels and monopolies. While legislation to eliminate specific abuses of monopoly power can do some good, it cannot compel a return to competition in industries where it would be wasteful and undesirable. The facts of life are that efficient organization in mass production and mass distribution fields requires unification, coordination, and rationalization. Only monopoly can bring this about. But private monopoly is no guarantee of efficiency. By fixing prices, allocating production, imposing levies on the efficient to keep the inefficient in production, the general level of prices is kept high, and incentives to modernization may be lacking. Hence, if monopoly is inevitable, it is preferable that such monopoly be publicly supervised or publicly owned.

Basic to this argument is the assumption that monopoly, or at least cooperation on a comprehensive scale, is necessary in many industries — the assumption that monopoly is inevitable under modern industrial conditions.

Unfortunately, faith in independent regulatory commissions has, in the light of American experience, not proved justified. These commissions — the Interstate Commerce Commission, the Civil Aeronautics Board, the Federal Power Commission, the Federal Communications Commission — have at times failed to regulate their respective industries in the public interest. Often these commissions adopted regulatory techniques which did little to promote operational efficiency and innovative progress; which were ineffective, costly and debilitating; and which suffered from administrative incompetence, unimaginativeness, and dishonesty. Moreover, no satisfactory solution seems yet to have been found for the vexing problem of watching the watchers.

Dissatisfied with the past record of regulatory commissions, some groups have gone further and advocated the nationalization, *i.e.* outright government ownership, of concentrated industries.

According to the socialist, nationalization is preferable both to public regulation and to private monopoly. It is better than public regulation, because the latter has proved generally ineffective. It is better than private monopoly, because the power to control basic industries, and hence the economy, must be "democratized." Such power must, according to the socialist, be held by the many and not as hitherto concentrated — without corresponding responsibility — in the hands of a few. There must be assurance that monopoly — a system which can be used for good or evil — will be used in the public interest. According to the socialist, a nationalized industry affords such assurance, simply because its management will be motivated by considerations of public interest and not private profit.

The disadvantages of public ownership are fairly obvious: administrators in nationalized industries may easily succumb to the disease of security, conservatism, procrastination, and bureaucracy. Their enterprises, as a result of supercentralization and lack of competitive incentives, may come to suffer from inflexibility and inelasticity. Moreover, the public enterprise may develop a tendency of using its monopoly power as a cloak for inefficient operation by resorting to the ready device of raising prices to meet increased costs, and thus avoid showing a deficit.

In summary, public regulation and public ownership suffer from the same basic drawback as private monopoly, *viz.*, the concentration of power in the hands of a few. Such power may be used benignly or dangerously, depending on the men who possess and control it. They may be good men, benevolent men, and socially minded men; but society still confronts the danger of which Lord Acton so eloquently warned: power corrupts, and absolute power corrupts absolutely.

The Promotion of Effective Competition

The advocates of promoting greater competition through vigorous anti-trust enforcement reject both the Scylla of private monopoly and the Charybdis of public ownership. Believing that the preservation of competitive free enterprise is both desirable and possible, they point out that this does not mean a return to the horse-and-buggy age, nor a strict adherence to the textbook theories of "perfect" or "pure" competition. What they advocate is a structural arrangement in private industry characterized by decentralized decision-making and "effective" competition.

Among the ingredients necessary for effective competition, the following are considered of primary importance: 1) an appreciable number of sellers and buyers for substantially the same product, so that both sellers and buyers have meaningful alternatives of choice; 2) the economic, as well as legal, freedom to enter the market and gain access to essential raw materials; 3) the absence of tacit or open collusion between rivals in the market; 4) the absence of explicit or implicit coercion of rivals by a dominant firm or a group of dominant firms; 5) the absence of "substantial preferential status within the market for any important trader or group of traders on the basis of law, politics, or commercial alliances"; 6) the absence of diversification, subsidization, and political motivation to an extent where giant firms may escape the commercial discipline of a *particular* market or a *particular* operation.

Some economists feel that the maintenance of this type of competition may, under modern conditions, be difficult if not impossible. They contend that antitrusters are faced with the dilemma of choosing between monopoly and efficiency, on the one hand, and competition and relative inefficiency, on the other.

The supporters of vigorous antitrust enforcement deny that such a choice is necessary, at least in many of our highly concentrated industries. The following reasons are usually given for rejecting the ostensible conflict between competition and efficiency. *First,* large firms, while technologically imperative in many industries, need not assume the Brobdingnagian proportions of some present-day giants. The unit of technological efficiency is the plant and not the firm. This means that, while there are undisputed advantages in the large-scale integrated steel operations at Gary or Pittsburgh or Birmingham, there seems little technological justification for combining these functionally separate plant units into a single administrative giant. *Second,* it seems significant that many of our colossal firms were not formed to gain the technical advantages of scale, but organized instead to achieve monopolistic control over the market and to reap profits from the sale of inflated securities. Giantism in industry today is not unrelated to the investment banker's inclination of yesteryear to merge and combine competing companies for the sake of promoter's profits.

Finally, to the extent that profit figures are valid as measures of comparative efficiency, it seems that in a number of cases medium-sized and small firms outperform their giant rivals. Moreover, a breaking down of huge firms does not necessarily have fatal effects on efficiency *or* profitability. In the public utility field, for example, the comprehensive dissolution program carried out under the Public Utility Holding Company Act of 1935 has resulted in increased efficiency and profitability among the successor companies. This was demonstrated in the above average appreciation in the security values of the successor companies which occurred despite declining utility rates, higher costs, and the inevitably higher taxes.

If such an unmerging process were to be accomplished through antitrust action, a case-by-case approach seems preferable to any absolute prohibition on size *per se.* Moreover, to avoid any major conflicts with vested interests, enforcement might at first be confined to new industries where the problem of concentration is not yet extreme and where structural arrangements have not yet been solidified. This may have significant results, since ours is a dynamic economy in which new industries — if they remain competitive — can substantially curb the power of older and more entrenched interests. Finally, to forestall any possible interference with industrial efficiency, antitrust prosecution might be confined to cases where the goals of competition and efficiency are not in conflict. Toward that end, the antitrust laws can be amended to provide that "any corporation whose size and power are such as to substantially lessen competition and tend to create a monopoly in any line of commerce shall be dissolved into its component parts, *unless* such corporation can demonstrate that its present size is necessary for the maintenance of efficiency." Given a provision of this sort, the dilemma of antitrust may be resolved and our twin goals of competition and efficiency actively promoted.

• 39

Policies to Deal with Sellers' Inflation*

EMMETTE S. REDFORD
University of Texas

In Section 10 it was pointed out that there are two kinds of inflation. Policies to stop demand-pull inflation focus on decreasing the supply of money, raising taxes, reducing government spending. Cost-push or market-power inflation, on the other hand, necessitates other policies appropriate to its causes.

Inflationary Concentrations of Market Power

It can be assumed that there is a public interest in avoidance of inflation, and that inflation is manifested in the price level. There is also evidence now that inflation may be caused in two ways. One is through an increase in demand so as to put pressure upon the supply of goods which is commonly referred to as demand or demand-pull inflation. The other is through an independent increase in wages or prices and is called sellers' or cost-push inflation.

* Taken and adapted from Study Paper Number 10, "Potential Public Policies to Deal with Inflation Caused by Market Power," *Study of Employment, Growth, and Price Levels,* Materials Prepared for Consideration by the Joint Economic Committee, Congress of the United States (Washington, D.C.: United States Government Printing Office, 1959), pp. 1–10, 27–29.

Key economic decisions on wages and prices are now made for vital areas of the economy by organizations of great size and power. Wages are fixed by agreement between organizations; such wages are now often referred to as administered wages. Prices may be fixed by organizations in accord with objectives desired to be attained and such prices determine or influence the pricing levels for an industry or product; such prices are sometimes called administered prices. Whenever one or more organizations acting singly, concurrently, or jointly have the ability through the administration of wages or prices to exact more income for the amount and quality of labor, capital, commodity or service supplied than could be obtained in the absence of such organizational action they may be said to have market power.

The effective exercise of market power may contribute to inflation in several ways. The first is through the passing on of the particular item of cost which is controlled. For example, market power over producers' prices of steel will be reflected in succeeding stages of distribution and ultimately in consumer's costs. Because successive sellers often increase their dollars-and-cents markups more than the increase in their purchase costs the amount of the price increase will swell as the commodity moves through successive stages of production and distribution. This pyramiding of prices through the pricing practices of successive groups of sellers enlarges the inflationary effect of original cost increases in producer industries. Second, market power may contribute to inflation if exercised under such conditions as to create a pattern to be followed in other industries, thus creating movements of pyramiding prices which further enlarge the effect of the original exercise of market power. This kind of enlargement of the effects of cost increases is now familiar as a result of the pattern-setting wage negotiation and the pattern-setting price movement of firms in a leadership position. Third, exercises of market power may give rise to repetitive cycles of wage-price or price-wage increases.

There is, therefore, latent inflation in the existence of market power. When concentrations of power are sufficient to create market power these concentrations become inflationary concentrations of power; that is, they are capable of producing inflationary effects. This capability creates the threat of sellers' inflation. Whether such inflation actually develops will be dependent upon the exercise of market power in situations which create one or more of the types of chain reaction described above and upon the nonexistence of measures to counteract these effects.

Basic Approaches in Policy

The existence of market power is now widely recognized as a cause for deep concern. The business community is concerned over the existence of this power in labor organizations. Labor organizations are concerned over the existence of the power in industrial organizations. Others in a more independent position than either of these contending forces are concerned over the phenomena accounting for both statements, namely, the concentration of power in organizations.

The problem of concentrated private power is complicated, and it is probable that the responsible Government official will find only partial answers and that even these will be found in several complementary approaches. There are, in general, five lines of approach suggested for public policy.

Corrective Forces Within the Economy

One line of approach suggested is that Government depend upon the corrective forces operating within the economy. Three types of argument are currently advanced in favor of this approach.

One argument is that society will be best protected by the conscience and restraint of those who possess market power. The argument is not for a completely let-alone policy by Government, for it is assumed that the conscience of man can be buttressed by legal standards of trusteeship developed in courts or in legislatures.

It is likely that courts and legislatures will indeed develop additional standards of trusteeeship for organizations of capital and of labor; at the same time, it may be doubted whether management and labor will be able consistently to view specific questions of wages and prices in terms of public interests rather than that of the interests of the groups which they are under compulsion to represent.

Another argument is that of countervailing power, which is that private concentrations of power beget opposed concentrations. The argument is supported by the fact that concentrations of labor have arisen to meet concentrations of capital and that concentrations of buyers or sellers have often arisen to meet concentrations of the other. The wise course for Government to follow, it is suggested, is to support movements for rise of countervailing power, as it did for labor through the National Labor Relations Act, or to aid those areas of the economy where countervailing power has not arisen, as it has done for agriculture.

Although countervailing power may be protection for the public, both critics and proponents of the idea have noted that it may not always exist or may not be operative. Large organizations of buyers and sellers may collaborate with each other and pass the cost to the consumer or freeze out competitors. Many organizations are either not faced with opposing organizations of power or are faced with opposing organizations with too little strength to resist. The chief limitation on the protection of counter- vailing power is that in times when demand is high and relatively inflexible, buyers find little cause to resist the cost-push pressure of sellers. It be- comes easier to accept the increased cost and pass it along. Even the will of the managers of industry to resist the demands of labor is weakened. In other words, cost-push of labor, the market power of industry, and the demand pull of buyers all contribute to upward movement of prices. It is not likely, therefore, that policymakers will accept countervailing power as sufficient in itself to protect the public interest.

Still another argument is that of freedom of enterprise. This argument is often presented as a denial of the existence of effective market power. The argument for freedom of enterprise is also presented as a claim that, whatever may be the adverse effects of private market power, these cannot be as bad as the effects of public power exerted through legislatures and administrators. Presented in this way the issue appears to be between those who trust private power and those who trust public power. Many, however, will be interested in searching for ways by which public power may be exerted to avoid excessive uses of private power without leading into the main dangers in use of public power. This desire will lead to consideration of other approaches in policy.

Demand Controls

A second line of approach is through controls over demand, chiefly through monetary and fiscal measures.

The reason for support for this policy is that management of monetary and fiscal measures may dampen demand pressures and thus prevent sellers from obtaining price increases. But such measures are most effective for the highly competitive sectors of the economy and may "touch lightly, or even exempt," the markets where firms are large and prices are administered. To be effective in markets where there is concentrated market power, monetary and fiscal controls would probably have to be so drastic that they would create recession in the economy generally. It would be economically undesirable and politically infeasible to use monetary and fiscal controls on so drastic a scale. The cost-push element may require other types of controls.

Antitrust

A third approach is maintenance or restoration of competition through antitrust. Alertness in detection and vigor in enforcement may narrow the range of collusive and coercive practices. Adoption of some rather arbitrary legislative tests on legality of business conduct might simplify standards of enforcement and expand the role of antitrust. Selected industries of high concentration and chain-producing effects could be studied to see whether enlargement of competitive forces, either under existing or new laws, would be possible. Actions of a rather drastic type on the antitrust front could presumably prevent the development of situations which would lead to consideration later of much more drastic remedies, including price controls of some sort.

Nevertheless, the limitations of antitrust are of common knowledge. Periods of weak enforcement or of weakening judicial construction, limited funds for enforcement and prolonged litigation, loopholes — these and other difficulties are known. More significant perhaps are the issues presented by the proposals to solve the wage-push problem by expansion of antitrust prohibitions with respect to labor organizations. There is much argument for clarification and expansion of legal restriction on such exercises of labor power, but the practical problems in definition of types of action to be covered are difficult and this form of public action would in all probability not materially affect the potentialities for wage-push inflation. Congress has already given considerable attention to problems of this kind. The plain fact is, however, that legislation on labor practices may have little effect upon the bargaining power of most big unions. Moreover, insofar as such proposals encompass limitation of industrywide or multiple-unit bargaining there are many problems. Some think market-wide bargaining is desirable. Some think it is preferable to whipsaw tactics through which a union threatens each employer in turn with a strike; a ban on multiple-unit bargaining would probably not be effective without a limitation on multiple-unit union organization. So drastic a step is not likely, for it runs counter to traditional public policy with respect to unionization and would meet powerful political opposition.

Withdrawal of Government Support for Market Power

Another approach would be to retreat from governmental measures which have the effect of supporting or protecting private market power.

Many Government policies tend to establish a protective shield around market power. Among those which may have this effect are the following:

(*a*) Protective tariffs and quotas.

(*b*) Resale price maintenance laws.

(*c*) Production controls for oil.

(*d*) Patent grants.

(*e*) Government — especially defense — purchasing and disposal policies.

(*f*) Safeguards for rights of unionization and collective bargaining.

(*g*) Protections against competition and rate reductions in regulated industries.

The listing of these measures underscores certain basic realities with respect to public policy affecting price levels. Public policy encompasses many objectives which may conflict with that of preventing inflation, including such objectives as national security, conservation of resources, and support of the purchasing power of various groups. The public official will take account of varied economic and noneconomic objectives and make choices among policy objectives which are in conflict with each other. It is apparent that the motivations which have led to the various public policies will not disappear and hence that there will be no general retreat from these policies. It may be expected that a government that is responsive through representative institutions will yield to many group demands which have the effect of sustaining or increasing price levels.

Public Consideration of Wage and Price Increases

The inadequacies of internal corrective forces, the ineffectiveness of demand-limiting controls of monetary and fiscal types as restraints upon sellers' inflation, the imperfections of antitrust law and ineffectiveness of antitrust enforcement, and the unlikelihood of general retreat from price-prop and price-protective policies probably account for the recent suggestions for public consideration of wage and price increases. The proposals for public consideration all look to some type of executive or administrative consideration of specific price and/or wage increases. The proposals vary from mere surveillance and publicity to public determination for one or a few industries. They may be arranged to show an order of progression of increasing severity.

1. *Notice.* — Firms of great size and power would be required to give notice of intention to increase prices to some public authority. Such proposals for notice always include one or more of the following means of public followup action.

2. *Hearings.* — Hearings might accompany notice requirements or hearings might be held in the absence of notice requirements whenever economic stability was, in the opinion of the President or other authority, threatened by a prospective price and/or wage increase. Notice and hearing for a category of industries or products would require a standing agency to administer the hearing requirements; hearings on an intervention basis could be held by a standing agency or by ad hoc groups designated by the President or other authority.

3. *Factfinding.* — A finding of facts could be made on the basis of facts (*a*) gathered in a study, or (*b*) obtained in a hearing, or (*c*) adduced in both ways. Thus, factfinding is possible with or without hearings.

4. *Publication of findings.* — The mildest form of sanction for notice and hearing, hearing, or factfinding requirements would be the force of an informed public opinion. Publication of finding is, therefore, an essential feature of proposals for these forms of public participation.

5. *Advisory opinions.* — Publication of findings could be accompanied by an advisory opinion or recommended decision. This means of increasing the extent of public participation has been included in various proposals.

6. *Delay.* — Suspension of wage or price increases might be provided by law (*a*) for a period after notice, (*b*) until hearings were held or a

factfinding or other report issued, or (*c*) for a period after the date of issuance of a report or advisory opinion.

7. *Public decision.* — Utility-type control has been suggested for one or a few industries, particularly steel. This would mean refusal of permission to make proposed price increases. In addition, public decision might be substituted for collective bargaining in such industries where there was a threat of cost-push inflation. This would mean refusal of permission to make wage increases.

Conclusions

The administrative difficulties to be faced in public effort to prevent the use of market power to produce inflationary increases in prices and wages would be tremendous. Over what industries, companies, or products would surveillance be necessary? Could the public effort be successful without surveillance over a wide range of American industry? Could public effort be pinpointed at the strategic centers from which new inflationary pressures would arise? Could public attention be brought to these centers in time to prevent the beginning of new inflationary chain effects? What type of public action would be needed? Would notice of prospective price and wage increases be necessary? If so, would exceptions to the requirements for notice be required to meet special situations in industry? What follow-up action would be taken after receipt of notice? Could the consideration of filings and the making of fact studies or holding of hearings be completed in the brief period within which judgment would be required? Would factfinding, report on hearings, and advisory recommendations carry real weight with the companies or unions seeking increases? What standards could be used in determining whether to investigate or hold hearings, what to pinpoint in factfinding or hearing reports, what recommendations to make? How could public participation be organized so as to produce confidence in the reports but at the same time to produce enough support from the Government to carry weight with the parties affected? Could public authority be exercised with aggressive and continuing attention to public interests or would organs of administration become sluggish and weak in motivation? Would a continuing type of control, similar to utility control, be desirable for a few sectors of the economy? If so, for which sectors? Could agencies for administration of such controls maintain the independence and vigor needed for success?

Government surveillance of price and wage increases would have political effects. New issues in politics would be created and these would relate to matters of intense interest to parties. The pressures on Government from labor and investor interests would be increased, and the political struggle among groups might be intensified. The political resistance to adverse Government actions on wages and prices would be great, so great in fact that it could be expected that only the power and prestige of the Presidency could be expected to carry weight against the resistance. And allegations of Presidential partiality toward particular groups would be unavoidable.

The ultimate test of public surveillance would lie in the economic and social results. The surveillance would need to be exercised with consideration of multiple objectives, including not only that of price stability but the effects upon economic growth, employment, and purchasing power, national security, and justice to economic groups. To balance these objectives and give each its proper weight in a rapidly changing economy, and to conclude public consideration with the expedition required to avoid adverse effects on the economy, would constitute a large challenge to administrative and political authorities seeking to avoid inflationary wage and price increases.

40

Antitrust *Trends and New Constraints**

JESSE W. MARKHAM
Princeton University

An eminent attorney in the field has declared that "There are changing fashions in antitrust as there are in other areas of human experience." This selection, in effect, expresses the opinion that the styles recently pieced together in the nation's law courts and in the Federal Trade Commission do not leave big business with much room to move around.

United States antitrust policy will celebrate its seventy-fifth anniversary in 1965. Such birthday celebrations are convenient occasions for looking backward and seeing where antitrust policy has been, for taking stock of where it now is, and for advancing a few cautious predictions of where it seems to be going.

Heretofore, only the corporate elite had to give serious attention to the antitrust implications of a proposal to buy a supplier in Pittsburgh, a customer in Cleveland, a small competitor in Chicago, or a firm in an unrelated line of business in Boise. Antitrust professionals periodically reminded their audiences that the ghost of Senator Sherman sat at the board meetings of many large corporations in the United States, but it was — to paraphrase Chief Justice Marshall — invisible, intangible, and

* Taken and adapted from Jesse W. Markham "Antitrust Trends and New Constraints," *The Harvard Business Review*, May–June, 1963, pp. 84–92. Reproduced with permission.

existed only in contemplation of extraordinary and highly dubious corporate trade practices.

Rising Incidence of Actions

The increase in the volume of antitrust actions alone now makes it imperative that corporate managements rely on neither ghosts nor the infrequent case for protection from antitrust prosecution:

In the immediate postwar period (1945–1948), the Department of Justice initiated an average of about 36 cases annually. In the past four years (1959–1962), the annual rate has more than doubled, averaging about 78 cases per year.

The increase in activity by the Federal Trade Commission has been even more spectacular. Where only a decade ago the FTC averaged slightly over 100 cases per year, it now averages close to 600.

Harsh Prohibitions

The most important recent antitrust development from the viewpoint of managerial decision making is the tightening up of the prohibition against corporate mergers and acquisitions. Business firms typically have expanded into a new product line, reached into a new geographical market, and vertically integrated by acquiring existing companies. Merger has even been an important means for gaining access to a new technology and managerial and technical personnel.

One of the few quantitative inquiries into the role merger has played in company growth shows that about 80 large corporations owed between one-third and one-quarter of their 1948 size to past acquisitions and mergers, and one reviewer of the study offered persuasive reasons for believing that the fraction is significantly higher, enough higher to warrant the conclusion that "merger has been the basic method by which individual firms have acquired high shares in major industries in the United States."

Management's Underestimation

Growth by merger goes on apace, almost as though the constraints that public policy has imposed on growth by this means are no more severe than they traditionally have been. As a consequence, business management is now saddled with an unprecedented volume of lawsuits under Section 7 of the Clayton Act. While the "convenient vagueness" of most of our antitrust legislation makes it reasonably certain that the pipeline of cases will seldom if ever run completely dry, it is clear from the present volume of actions that a serious gap exists between what the antimerger statute in fact is and what business management thinks it is.

Of the top 500 U.S. corporations, 57 are now, or recently have been, defendants before the FTC or the courts for mergers consummated sometime within the past decade. A few of these may be chalked up to the law's vagueness; a few others may possibly be attributed to management's disregard of the law. But the 11% incidence among the top 500 of alleged or proven violations of Section 7 is attributable for the most part to the gap in management's understanding of the growing stringency in the application of the law.

Consulting antitrust economists — still a small but rapidly growing profession — have become accustomed to managerial proclamations of innocence. It may be true that the challenged merger today may be a much smaller one than the firm, or even a larger rival, successfully consummated ten years ago; that after the merger the defendant firm will still be significantly smaller than the industry's leader; and that when management decided on the merger, it honestly *thought* that the move would increase rather than decrease competition. These and similar protestations, however righteous the indignation that prompts them, reveal the failure of management to stay abreast of the legal status of merger, and go a long way toward explaining the more than 100 merger cases initiated by the government since 1952.

Congressional Intent

The dimensions of the specific constraints that recent antitrust developments impose on managerial decisions are to be found in individual cases rather than the over-all statistics on government wins and losses. A sequence of Section 7 decisions beginning with the *Pillsbury* case in 1953 and continuing through the *Bethlehem-Youngstown* case in 1958 had made it abundantly clear to business management that significant horizontal mergers were a hazardous road to expansion. In view of the prominent role played by market concentration studies in the Congressional hearings leading up to the 1950 Celler-Kefauver Section 7 Amendment, these decisions could scarcely have come as a surprise to the business community. The new law had explicitly prohibited mergers that may "substantially lessen competition or tend to create a monopoly."

New Standard

In more recent cases, however, the standard of injury to competition in the marketplace has given way to the standard of probable injury to smaller competitors.

In four recent decisions, the commission and the courts, in one case the Supreme Court, have gone a long way toward accepting the new standard.

The most far-reaching of the four decisions is the *Brown Shoe Company* case:

> The bare market statistics on which the government sought to have the case decided were relatively unimpressive, at least for the vertical aspects of the case. Brown, the fourth largest shoe manufacturer, accounted for only 4% of national shoe production. Kinney (the desired acquisition), although the largest independent family-style shoe chain in the country, sold only 1.6% of all shoes at the retail level.

The trial court decided against the merger almost entirely on the basis of its vertical aspects. The trial judge noted —

1. That Brown typically insisted that its retail subsidiaries handle Brown's shoes, and presumably would insist that Kinney stores also handle them.

2. That a trend in the industry toward vertical integration was drying up available outlets for small unintegrated shoe producers; and the Brown-Kinney merger, as a participant in this trend, would foreclose a substantial amount of business from such independent producers.

3. That this vertical integration would reduce the total costs of manufacturing and distributing Brown's shoes; and the price reductions made possible by such cost reductions would further disadvantage small independent and unintegrated shoe manufacturers and retailers.

The Supreme Court upheld the trial court's decision on the vertical aspects of the merger, and only Justice Harlan dissented from the additional finding of horizontal illegality. However, the Court did not accept the "quantitative substantiality" rule as the basis for its decision. As Professor Milton Handler has pointed out, the Court considered market shares to be the beginning but not the end of its inquiry. Thus:

1. In addition to the market statistics, "numerous independent retailers" would be disadvantaged because "strong, national chains of stores can insulate selected outlets from the vagaries of competition in particular locations and . . . can set and alter styles in footwear to an extent that the independents are unable to maintain competitive inventories."

2. Further, "retail outlets of integrated companies, by eliminating wholesalers and increasing the volume of purchases from the manufacturing division of the enterprise, can market their own brands at prices below those of competing independent retailers."

3. Finally, there was "the history of tendency toward concentration in the industry." The Court, while noting that this was attributable largely to vertical acquisitions, found this tendency to have brought "even greater numbers of retail outlets within fewer and fewer hands." The Kinney acquisition brought the largest remaining independent retail chain "into an already substantial aggregation of more or less controlled retail outlets."

On the basis of all these facts, the Court thought this was an appropriate place to call a halt.

Other Policy Developments

Public policy toward business practices other than merger has experienced less spectacular change, but it has consistently changed in the direction of imposing more stringent constraints on corporate decision making. The *Alcoa* and *United Shoe* decisions have made a high order of market occupancy illegal under the Sherman Act even though the means employed, in the court's language, are "honestly industrial." The Supreme Court's decision requiring Du Pont to divest itself of its stockholdings in General Motors 40 years after the event has put intercorporate stockholdings of long standing in legal jeopardy.

Constraint on Decisions

These recent developments in antitrust may be condemned or applauded, depending on one's antitrust philosophy. The stream of commentaries on them provides an abundance of both. But the point that deserves emphasis is that the nation's antitrust policy, once reserved for demonstrable enhancement of market power, has now been extended to those business transactions that corporate executives engage in all the time as ordinary events of industrial and commercial life. *It therefore imposes on the decision-making process of business a new and significant constraint.* Further, the mounting volume of antitrust actions against business each year is persuasive evidence that the magnitude and dimensions of this constraint have not yet been recognized by those who exercise important decision-making functions.

"Injury to Competitors"

This new constraint evolves principally from the recent shift in standards from "injury to competition" to "injury to competitors." While the annals of antitrust contain copious evidence that the previous standard was certainly not applicable to concrete situations with slide-rule accuracy, the business community after 60 years of experience had gradually acquired an understanding of what it meant. There was, to be sure, a "gray" area that separated the clearly legal from the clearly illegal, but business executives and their antitrust counsel generally knew within tolerable limits which transactions fell where.

Under the new standard the gray area has been expanded to include much of what the business community accepts as the essence of competitive enterprise. The natural, normal, and predictable consequence of a competitive strategy used successfully by one firm is a disadvantage

— momentary or enduring — to those firms with which it competes. It may not have been inevitable that Brown Shoe would seek to improve its competitive position by acquiring Kinney's retail outlets, that Foremost would acquire several dozen widely scattered dairies to obtain the advantages of geographical and product diversification, that Consolidated Foods would seek entry into the rapidly growing dehydrated onion and garlic business by acquiring the second largest of four competing firms, or that Reynolds would acquire a specialty aluminum foil customer.

But the central thread running through all four Section 7 cases is that in each of them a firm confronting larger rivals considered its actions as conventional means of competitive growth. The fact is that when one firm grows more, its competitors, unless they counter with equally effective measures, usually grow less; hence most mergers can be found to be contravention of Section 7 under the new standard.

Possible Future Extensions

If this standard is appropriate in merger adjudications, a logical case can be made for extending it to other areas of antitrust. If disadvantage to competitors is to be the test of illegality, there would seem to be no reason for distinguishing among disadvantages attributable to a rival's vertical acquisition and those attributable to its advertising campaigns, pricing policies, and a host of other competitive strategies.

There is evidence that extension of the new standard is already in progress.

The increased velocity, as evidenced by the rapidly mounting volume of antitrust cases, has caught the decision-making bodies of many corporate houses unprepared. In consequence, the antitrust laws, which all save a select few of the largest corporations could previously ignore, now impose significant constraints on those who conduct the affairs of corporate enterprise.

Conclusion

The important question confronting management is whether the new standards of illegality are temporary or enduring. Given the historical vagaries of antitrust, predictions in this area of public policy are obviously not without hazard. But the judicial trend is clear. When this trend is considered in the light of present proposals before Congress, of the grounds on which the large volume of pending cases were initiated, and of the over-all political climate that now conditions the affairs of corporate enterprise, the direction in which things are moving seems well established and not likely to change in the foreseeable future.

Many of the pending cases are not against big business that obviously wields substantial market power; they are against companies that simply have smaller — and larger — rivals. In the *Brown Shoe* case, the Supreme Court laid down the doctrine that corporate action potentially disadvantageous to smaller rivals, however "honestly industrial" and whatever the cost incentives, is contrary to public policy. Supreme Court decisions, especially those passed down by a unanimous court, are likely to withstand the historic vacillations of antitrust policy.

If the new constraints are in fact reasonably permanent, corporate conduct is in for substantial change. By definition, most business firms have smaller rivals. This fact, in and of itself, now limits freedom of entrepreneurial action. Heretofore business firms have grown through geographical expansion, vertical integration, and diversification — expanding into different or adjacent lines of commerce as the prospective returns there on additional capital investment loomed larger than those for lines in which the company was already engaged.

Frequently such growth has been accomplished through merger and acquisition, not altogether out of necessity but frequently out of convenience and always for what internally seemed to be sound business considerations: the assets could be acquired at a lower cost than comparable assets could be built, the location was good, the technical and managerial personnel of the acquired company were not available elsewhere, or entry into the new line could be effected in less time. The contemplated expansion needed only to avoid market arrangements that lessened competition. Similarly, companies could avoid contractions in established product lines by adopting competitive pricing strategies which could be squared with the meeting of an equally low price of a competitor in good faith.

These tests no longer suffice. Instead, the company must assess the probable impact of a contemplated acquisition on its smaller, less integrated, and less diversified rivals, in both its present product lines and those of the firm it plans to acquire.

While the new constraints are especially applicable to decisions concerning mergers and acquisitions, they are gradually encompassing other corporate activities. How business management will cope with them is not entirely clear. One possibility, of course, is to substitute internal expansion for merger. The former is governed by the Sherman Act, where illegality hangs on the possession of monopoly power. In view of the historical frequency of merger and acquisition, however, this course may purchase reasonable immunity from antitrust prosecutions at a very high price. Alternatively, business management may still expand by acquisition but carefully assess the possible impact of such acquisitions upon smaller single-product rivals. This will entail a much more careful analysis of potential acquisitions than has been given them in the past, and a much more thorough understanding of how Section 7 is currently administered. It will also probably call for more extensive use of legal and economic analysts in the making of acquisition decisions.

One thing is clear. Acquisition and merger decisions obviously can no longer be entrusted to the ghost of Senator Sherman. This board member, however revered his name in antitrust circles, is too inarticulate and very much out of date.

1. *What is the "farm problem"?*

2. *Are labor unions becoming increasingly conservative?*

3. *What has happened to America's "income revolution"?*

4. *Is poverty obsolete in the United States?*

PART THREE WAS CONCERNED WITH the price system and the operation of the business unit. There are elements of the economy other than business which also require special attention. The purpose of Part Four is to examine several of the most important of these: agriculture, labor, consumption, the distribution of income, and its corollary — the problem of poverty.

Agriculture

In every country farmers are affected by some of the forces existing in the United States, although most countries do not have our "problem of plenty." (In fact, many of the world's people do not, by minimum nutritional standards, get enough to eat.) An inherent disadvantage of farming, from the standpoint of the producer, is the extreme variability of the prices of his products compared to the prices that he pays to other types of producers for their goods and services.

Actually, farmers by no means suffer equally from the vagaries of weather and the market. Farming in the United States today covers a wide range of entrepreneurial situations, from large and highly mechanized businesses employing thousands of workers in veritable "factories in the field" to the much more numerous, but productively less important, family farms employing little hired labor and sustained mainly by the efforts of the owner and his family.

One essential of the "farm problem" in this country is that agricultural productivity has increased very rapidly with the result that there are many more farmers than are needed to produce the quantity of commodities that can concurrently be consumed. Indeed, it has even been proposed that agricultural output has been increasing at such a rate that we should hold in abeyance our programs which raise agricultural productivity. On the other hand, the point is repeatedly made that there are many poor people in farming who cannot be effectively aided by raising the prices for farm products. This viewpoint is bolstered by the observation that the real income of average farm families has continued to decline.

Labor

It has been asserted that unionism has changed, that the labor leader today is an organization man much like his business counterpart. According to this view labor's pioneering struggles for employer recognition are now past and the outlook of today's labor leader is a reflection of the resultant stability and security. However, we will note when we discuss specific union leaders, that they differ widely from one another in many respects (including ethics), just as businessmen do.

Irrespective of the accuracy of this picture, unionism is still by no means taken for granted or removed from controversy. There are those who are as ideologically opposed to unions as ever. Two areas of dispute that are almost certain to arise in any discussion of unions, at least by non-unionists, are their favored treatment over employers in being allowed to organize monopolies and also their ability, because of their bargaining power, to raise wages and, thereby, to raise prices. The fact is that unions do enjoy relative impunity under the anti-trust laws, and the question which must be answered is whether this has some rational explanation or is simply outrageous discrimination. Prices and wages, inquiry discloses, are party to a complicated process and it would be a glib man who would venture to suggest that prices are either (a) determined by, or (b) immune from, wage changes in all circumstances.

On the whole, however, the prospects for unionism and its influence in the next decade seem to lie somewhere between its era of low vitality in the 1920's and its robust expansion in the late '30's and early '40's. This opinion, however, is worth very little unless related to information about the potential sources of new union membership and judgments about the future state of the economy as a whole.

Consumption

"Consumption," said Adam Smith in 1776, "is the sole end and purpose of production." Despite the undeniable element of truth in this assertion and the fact that literally everyone (including business, farmers, and workers) consumes products and services, the consumer is often represented as the forgotten man in our society. For all actively employed people, the picture is, of course, at best only a half-truth — true only of the non-producer side of their economic behavior.

Yet it is probably true (and, after all, not very surprising) that most of us tend to identify our interests most strongly with our roles as producers — with the ways and conditions whereby we obtain our incomes rather than the ways in which we spend them. Businessmen, farmers, and workers are often associated collectively in powerful large-scale organizations (corporations, labor unions, farm organizations), and actively influence both economic activity and policies of governments. It is often noted that consumers are much less effectively organized than producers and, in an economic system in which important gains go to the highly organized, this can be a definite disadvantage. As consumers, we can only share with all others the advantages of general increases in production and productivity, whereas through our bargaining powers as producers we might be able to wrest for ourselves a disproportionately large part of the gain.

However, consumption and production are closely interwoven, and where the consumer interest touches the producer interest directly, the response can be significant. The Consumer Price Index, designed as a measure of consumer welfare, has become a device in producer bargaining. It has frequently provided the last word in an adjustment of wage rates in many industries and is an example of this intertwining.

Advertising washes over, almost envelops it would seem, the American consumer. It has been said that "you can tell a country's ideals by its advertising" which, under the circumstances, is possibly an uncomfortable reflection upon ourselves. What are the *general economic effects* of out-lays for advertising (which are of great consequence in many industries)? This is a question surprisingly seldom asked.

The rationality of money-making pervades producing, but money-saving does not to the same degree govern consuming. A long time ago Thorstein Veblen, and more recently Vance Packard, pointed out the influence of status-seeking. Without pausing either to praise or to con-demn it, we can observe that *style*, the impulsive, "non-engineering" changes in goods, does evidently have a good deal to do with making the economic wheels go round.

Income Distribution

Closely related to consumption are the issues of the distribution of income. There are a variety of ways of looking at the subject of how the product of the economy is allocated among the population. Income is distributed by occupational groups, by educational level, by so-called functional shares (wages and salaries, profits, interest, and rents), by quintile or decile or some other uniform division of the population. What is the point of all this analysis? Partly it is just curiosity, but it is also to seek explanations of how our economic society induces its members to per-form its work, to weigh issues of incentive versus equity, to evaluate the adequacy of personal income for sustaining total spending in the economy at a stable level at or near full employment.

Poverty

The facts of income distribution lead naturally enough to consideration of the problem of seriously deficient incomes, as a condition of poverty. A generation ago, President Franklin Roosevelt spoke of a third of the nation as ill-housed, ill-clothed, and ill-fed. The percentage is smaller now in our contemporary "affluent society," but there are those who argue that the plight of today's poor is more hopeless, something less amenable to the historic American process of economic mobility. Poverty is, after all, a relative thing. It is reported, for example, American teen-agers have spending money (from earnings and allowances) greater than the per capita incomes of the people of most of the world's countries. Still, the relative circumstances of *some* people in this affluent country are abject indeed. Poverty again has become a much-discussed problem in the 1960's, but it is always something of an issue because, as Pericles said, it is "no disgrace to acknowledge but a real degradation to make no effort to overcome."

A. AGRICULTURE

41

Is Agriculture "Different"?*

WALTER W. WILCOX
Library of Congress

Should public policy toward agriculture be any different from that toward any other sector of the economy? Should farmers be treated any differently from, say, automobile manufacturers? Your answer to these often-debated questions may depend, at least partly, upon your appraisal of whether or not the economic problems of farming are different from those of other parts of the economy. The following selection summarizes some of the prominent differences between farming and other occupations and relates these differences to various aspects of the "farm problem."

Farm leaders have always maintained that their problems are "different." Is this true? If so, what are the key differences which in recent years have caused farmers to turn to government to improve their posi-

* Taken and adapted from *Social Responsibility in Farm Leadership: An Analysis of Farm Problems and Farm Leadership in Action* (New York: Harper & Brothers, 1956), pp. 11–17. Reproduced with permission.

tion in the economy? Some farm leaders have maintained that farming is more important than other vocations because of the physiological requirements of the body for food in order to maintain life. Others have affirmed that farmers are the key economic group in the economy, causing the economy as a whole to prosper when they prosper and vice versa.

Certainly farmers are producers of one of the important groups of raw materials. Prices of raw materials usually fall first and farthest in a business decline and lead other prices up in a period of inflation. In this sense farm price movements often foreshadow other economic developments. But investigations have not uncovered any peculiar characteristics of farmers which make them more or less important than any other group in the economy which receives the same percentage of the national income.

Farming a Biological Industry

Farming does differ from most other industries because of the biological nature of its production processes. In many respects farming is as sensitive to price changes as is any other industry. There is much shifting from one product to another on this account, but the responses are delayed several weeks to several years. It takes about a year to increase the number of laying hens on hand, and from two to three years to bring dairy heifers into milk production. An increase in market demand, which sets economic forces in motion to increase the supply of farm products, may not continue until the increased production is ready for market.

Farm prices vary widely, with small changes in supply or demand. The physical basis of the demand for food changes slowly with the increase in domestic population and with trends in food consumption habits. Families, in the aggregate, tend to spend a constant percentage of their income for food. This gives rise to changes in the amount spent for food when either unemployment or inflation occurs.

A drop in the demand for food because of general unemployment causes farm prices to fall sharply, since farmers cannot quickly cut back their production. In fact, except in a few years when severe droughts have occurred, total farm output has always been stable or on an upward trend. Supply and demand are kept in balance when the market falls by selling approximately the same quantities in the retail markets at lower prices. Since marketing and processing charges are relatively stable, moderately lower retail prices cause severe declines in farm prices. Roughly speaking, the change in either direction in farm prices is from two to two and one-half times as great as the change in retail food prices.

In periods of inflation we have the opposite of periods of unemployment, and expenditures for food rise with increases in consumers' income.

Retail prices rise moderately, and farm prices rise sharply. After a period of time supplies of farm products may increase and prices decline.

There is considerable variation in individual crop yields from year to year because of the weather. While annual crops such as potatoes, cabbage, or individual grains may be increased or decreased in acreage in line with economic conditions, farmers seldom let productive land lie idle, and if one crop is reduced others are increased. It is partly because of this practice of fully utilizing the land each year that the total supply of farm products maintains a relatively stable upward trend regardless of price changes.

Agricultural and Industrial Prices Contrasted

One great difference between farmers and manufacturers is in their price and production policies in a depression. The classic example occurred in the years 1929–1932. During that period industrial prices dropped only 23 per cent, while manufacturers cut production 40 per cent. In contrast, farm production dropped only 3 per cent (due to weather), while farm prices declined 57 per cent.

There are several reasons for this vastly different economic behavior of farmers and manufacturers. It can be summed up by saying that farm families minimize their losses by keeping up or increasing production even though prices fall. On the other hand manufacturers' costs and markets are such that they minimize their losses by laying off workers and cutting production — measures that tend to maintain relatively stable prices.

Inflation and Farming

In earlier years farm leaders were often inflationists. Farmers had difficulty in paying their debts in periods of falling prices. As late as 1910, 83 per cent of the total capital invested in farming was represented by the value of farm lands and buildings. Farmers who went into debt to buy or improve farm land in prosperous years were often unable to pay off those debts because of a drop in the general price level. No other major industry except mining and petroleum production requires such a high investment in "permanent capital" in relation to the value of its annual production.

Moreover, farming is the only industry where most of the investment is on an individual or family basis. Well over half the families engaged in farming since colonial times have owned their own farms, in contrast with corporate ownership of most mines and oil wells. Miners and oil field workers work merely for wages and are but little affected by price-level declines so long as they continue to hold their jobs. With farm ownership widespread, it is no wonder that farm leaders have been the largest group of inflationists in periods of falling and depressed prices.

The Race Between Output and Markets

Farm output has been increasing at a surprisingly steady rate of 2 to 3 per cent a year for several decades. In the 1930's the rate of increase dropped off because of the Great Depression and a series of drought years. Farm production took an unusual spurt, however, in the early 1940's, resulting in a level of production in 1950 as high as if the normal rate of increase had occurred throughout the 1930's.

Except for years of widespread drought farmers have never decreased their total production from one year to another. A series of good crop years, such as in the early 1950's at a time when foreign market outlets were declining, resulted in excessive supplies and sharp declines in market prices. Many people looking beyond the immediate future, however, expect population increases within a period of twenty to twenty-five years to be so great that farmers may find it difficult to feed the urban dwellers.

On the other hand, the increase in farm output from year to year is now equal to or in excess of our rate of increase in population. If the rate of increase in farm output continues to exceed the rate of population increase, as now seems probable, farmers are indeed in for a period of relatively low prices and incomes. We now export around 10 per cent of our farm production, largely cotton, wheat, tobacco, fats and oils, and dried fruits. The possibilities of expanding our exports at profitable prices are limited. The possibilities of increasing per capita consumption in the domestic market except at the expense of sharply lower prices are no more encouraging.

If, on the other hand, the rate of population increase should exceed the rate of increase in farm output, farm prices will strengthen. Under such conditions we would export less and probably draw on other parts of the world for a larger share of our food supplies.

Agriculture is different from most industries in that in many ways these two vital trends are independent of each other. This is readily seen in the case of the trend in population. The factors which will determine our future birth and death rates are numerous, and the level of output of United States farms is only one of the minor factors.

The relative independence of the upward trend in farm output requires a little more explanation. Since 1920 increases in farm output have been due almost entirely to increased yields per acre and increased production per animal. We have not increased the acreage of land cropped, yet we increased output 50 per cent, while workers on farms dropped 25 per cent. Improved technology, including improved varieties of crops and breeding stock, the substitution of tractor for horse power, and much heavier use of fertilizers, is the basis of our uptrend in the output of United States farms. Favorable farm prices cause farmers to accelerate their rate of adoption of improved technology. But, as was seen in the 1929–1932 period, unfavorable prices do not cause production to decline; they merely slow down the rate of increase.

How fast will farm production increase in the future? Probably between 2 and 3 per cent per year. It will increase faster if prices are favorable, but it may continue to increase faster than our population increases, even though prices are unfavorable. Continued economic advantages in the adoption of improved production practices in periods of a cost-price squeeze lead to increased output even though net returns from farming are unsatisfactory.

Too Many Farms Too Small

In spite of all our farm programs of recent years, many of our farms remain too small or too poor to provide full-time employment and sufficient income for a farm family. For the most part small unproductive farms, in communities lacking nonfarm employment opportunities, are found in the Southeast. They also are found in the cut-over and hilly areas of the lake states and, in limited numbers, in every state of the Union.

Key Differences

There are many other ways in which farming differs from other occupations; length of hours worked per day and the relative isolation of the farm family, to name but two. We wish, however, to focus attention on those differences which have given rise to farmers' demands for government action to improve their economic conditions. From this point of view the key differences between agriculture and other industries are the widespread ownership of land and tools of production in agriculture, creating unusually difficult credit problems in periods of falling prices; the biological nature of the production processes which makes production adjustments slow and difficult to control; the fact that most labor cannot be dismissed in periods of falling prices, making it uneconomic to contract total output in business recessions even though sharp price declines occur; the tendency for the rate of technological improvement to exceed the rate of population increase, resulting in "burdensome" market supplies in periods of normal or favorable weather; and well over a million farms which are too small to be economic family units. These are the aspects of the agricultural industry which people have in mind particularly when they say that agriculture is "different."

42

Getting People Out of Agriculture[*]

JAMES G. MADDOX
North Carolina State College

America's biggest farm surplus, it is sometimes said, is too many farmers. If this is true, one way to reduce the surplus and to raise national efficiency would be to encourage a movement of labor resources from farm into non-farm occupations. Alternative means to accomplish this objective are explored and evaluated in the following selection.

Approximately 21.2 million people were living on farms in the United States in the spring of 1959. This was the smallest farm population reported since data first became available in 1910. It was 15.5 per cent below the 25.1 million people who lived on farms in 1950. Since 1940 there has been a net decline of 9.3 million farm people, which must have been the sharpest decrease in any twenty-year period in the history of the country.

Nevertheless, there is evidence that American agriculture is still overstaffed. The federal government is spending large sums to support the prices of several farm products. It also maintains complex programs of acreage control. Yet, surpluses continue to mount; the purchasing power of farm commodity prices declines; and much of the labor employed in farming earns less than many nonfarm workers in fairly comparable types

[*] Taken and adapted from "Toward Better Use of Human Resources in Agriculture," *The Annals of the American Academy of Political and Social Science,* September, 1960, pp. 85–91. Reproduced with permission.

of employment. These considerations alone point to the conclusion that too many people are trying to make a living by farming.

But this is only a part of the picture. The natural rate of population increase in rural America is much higher than is necessary to maintain a stable farm population. At the same time, a technological and organizational revolution is sweeping through agriculture and rapidly decreasing the labor required to produce a given output. Fewer farm people would be employed in the future than in the past, even if there were no price and surplus problems. Clearly, if equal returns to comparable kinds of farm and nonfarm labor are to be achieved — a condition which would both increase the efficiency of the national economy and improve the income position of agriculture — many people now employed in farming, as well as those who are coming into the farm labor force each year from the natural rate of population growth, must shift to other occupations.

Oversupply of Labor

How great is the oversupply of labor in agriculture? How many people would have to leave farming during the next decade in order to bring the earnings of labor in agriculture to a level comparable to those in nonfarm occupations? On the basis of existing knowledge about the way in which the total supply of agricultural products responds to changes in prices and costs and the extent to which capital can economically be substituted for labor, an accurate answer to these questions is virtually impossible. An annual net migration of one to one and one-quarter million people out of agriculture, for the next ten years, could probably take place with relatively little effect on total farm output. A shift of this magnitude would drain off the net natural increase in farm population as well as an additional 900,000 to 1,000,000 farm people per year. Though such a rate of change might have little effect on total farm output, it would result in a significant rise in per capita farm income.

There are wide variations in the incomes of farm people. About 62 per cent of all farms in the United States in 1954 produced approximately 91 per cent of the total value of agricultural products, while the remaining 38 per cent produced only about 9 per cent of the value of farm output. The former group, which we call "high production farms," had gross sales of $2,500 or more per farm in 1954. The latter group, designated as "low production farms," had gross sales of less than $2,500 per farm.

The major problem of low returns to agricultural labor is certainly centered on the low production units — which numbered approximately 1,800,000 farms, not including residential and institutional units, in the United States in 1954. The number has probably decreased since that time, and the migration of young people from such farms has been heavy. However, it is likely to be in the range of 5 to 7 million.

Approximately 48 per cent of the low production farms in 1954 were in the ten southeast states. The South is the center of the most serious low-income problem in American agriculture. In this region, farms are small, capital is scarce, the natural rate of population increase is high, there are relatively few nonfarm jobs, and those which are available are most commonly in low-wage occupations. If equality of returns among farm and nonfarm workers of comparable abilities is to be achieved, occupational shifts must be far greater in the South than in any other major region of the country.

Possible Public Action

Public action will be needed in the years ahead to stimulate the growth of nonfarm jobs and to assist farm people to shift into nonfarm occupations. A rapidly growing economy requires a high degree of geographic and occupational mobility among members of the labor force. Public policy may need to give attention to this problem in several sectors of the economy, but agriculture is the major sector, at the present time, in which greater occupational mobility would increase national efficiency significantly. The following types of public action are in order:

First, the rate of economic growth in the total economy should be raised.

Second, the abilities of farm people to become productive workers in nonfarm occupations should be enhanced.

Third, farm people should be given more assistance than they now receive in analyzing and evaluating their future prospects in various types of employment.

Fourth, farm people should be supplied with more adequate information respecting nonfarm employment opportunities than they now receive.

Fifth, a specialized loan program to aid selected farmers and maturing farm youths to shift out of agriculture should be inaugurated in those states where low incomes, high rates of population increase, and limited opportunities in agriculture are prevalent.

Sixth, there are numerous "special areas" in which a complex of integrated activities aimed at developing nonfarm jobs and reorganizing existing farm units should be undertaken.

Enlarged Educational Opportunities

Programs to enhance the abilities of farm people to become productive workers in nonfarm occupations would involve enlarging the educational opportunities of the rural population.

In most southern states, where the need for education is greatest and where educational expenditures per pupil are lowest, a higher percentage of personal income is devoted to education than in other regions. If rural education is to be improved significantly in the states where the need is greatest, federal aid will be essential.

Some changes in rural education, however, are not wholly dependent on a new program of federal aid. There are opportunities to make adjustments in the uses for which present funds have been allocated. For instance, there appears to be little justification for a continuation, at the present scale, of vocational agricultural training in rural high schools. Most future graduates of agricultural high school courses will not enter directly into modern, commercialized farming. The aims and methods of the present system of vocational agricultural training should be shifted to give greater emphasis to training youngsters for nonfarm jobs.

Career Counseling

The third suggested area of public action is greater assistance to farm people in analyzing and evaluating alternative employment opportunities. The important aim would be to teach farm people, particularly young people, how to think through the problem of choosing a career. The need is for a continuing program, in which the focus of emphasis is on teaching farm people how to analyze their future prospects in various types of occupations.

Nonfarm Employment

The fourth area of needed public action — providing to farm people more adequate information with respect to nonfarm employment opportunities — appears to call for a revitalization of the United States Employment Service and its affiliated state agencies. This organization does not appear to be serving farm people in an adequate manner. In many areas of the South, where farm incomes are low and farming opportunities are scant, there is a noticeable paucity of information about job opportunities in the urban areas of the North and East. For the Employment Service to serve the best interests of farm people in low-income areas, a specialized program may be necessary.

Loan Programs

The South and a few other scattered areas have such a high ratio of rural population to capital and land resources, such a high natural rate of population increase, such a deficiency of nonfarm job opportunities, and such a plethora of low-income farm people that a special loan program to enable maturing farm boys and girls to obtain apprenticeship training or to attend specialized vocational schools or colleges should be inaugurated.

Such features as the eligibility requirements of borrowers, the maximum size of loan, the length of the repayment period, the type of security, and the interest rate should be established by the lending agency. Loans of this type would probably range from $200 to $2,500 and would be repayable in monthly installments after the borrower had finished his or her period of training. They would be analogous to loans which many colleges now make to selected students. In most cases, however, they would be made to rural youths who are interested in taking a specialized vocational course which would range from only a few months to perhaps as long as two years. Ten million dollars per year for loans of this type, over a ten-year period, would be of inestimable value to thousands of farm boys and girls.

Redevelopment Programs

In various regions of the country, but particularly in the South, there are numerous areas of chronic rural poverty, which are in need of specialized redevelopment programs. Many of these areas are heavily populated, lacking in natural resources, culturally isolated from the main stream of economic development, and poorly supplied with roads, schools, and other community facilities. Within recent years many young people have migrated out of such areas, but farm enlargement is taking place slowly and industrial growth appears to be centered mainly around the larger cities. As a result, many of the areas of chronic rural poverty are in great need of new capital and new entrepreneurship.

Integrated programs of redevelopment which provide liberal amounts of credit and farm planning assistance to those who remain in agriculture so that they can enlarge and improve their farms, which provide vocational training for those whose only opportunities are in nonfarm occupations, and which encourage the growth of industry and service trades in these areas are sorely needed.

The areas of public action which have been suggested in the preceding paragraphs involve a combination of federal and state action. Those which are educational or informational in content should be national in scope and should become continuing functions of government. The educational loan program and the special-area redevelopment activities should be limited mainly to the South and a few other relatively small areas where the low production farm problem is most serious. If this combination of programs were pursued with vigor and imagination for the decade ahead, it would greatly increase the efficiency of the national economy and improve the incomes of the people who leave agriculture, as well as those who remain in farming.

• 43

The Farm Problem Is Not Hopeless*

HENDRIK S. HOUTHAKKER
Harvard University

Agricultural policy presents a distressing prospect of great governmental expenditure (second only to defense-related expenditure in the Federal budget) and slight discernible achievement. In adding one more prospectus to those already proposed for reform of the farm program, Professor Houthakker points out how we judge the agricultural sector of the economy by the standards of performance of free markets, but ironically proceed to frustrate the opportunity for these forces to work their therapeutic effects in agriculture.

The Policy Stalemate

After more than 30 years of active government intervention in agriculture, a durable solution to the farm problem has yet to be found. The two most influential sources of ideas on farm policy — the U.S. Department of Agriculture and the American Farm Bureau Federation — agree on one thing: that the government should take more dramatic steps to cut back production. They only disagree on methods of curtailment.

But reduction of agricultural output by government intervention can hardly be called an answer to the farm problem. If such a policy is to

* Reprinted from CHALLENGE, The Magazine of Economic Affairs, a publication of the Institute of Economic Affairs, New York University.

work at all, the cutbacks would have to be increasingly severe because farm technology is constantly improving. More seriously, it is clearly inconsistent for the government to curtail activity in this important sector while pursuing the universally accepted goal of general economic expansion elsewhere. To say that a more rational approach is politically impossible does not say much for the American system of government.

The persistence of this stalemate clearly suggests that some fundamental rethinking is needed. The deadlock is not merely a standoff between conflicting pressure groups; it is also due to a failure of analysis. To reconcile opposing interests, after all, is the daily work of politicians. But before this can be done, the nature of these interests has to be clearly recognized. In agriculture, however, a number of widely held but fallacious convictions becloud the main issues and complicate the search for a lasting solution. Before we can consider a solution, then, we must refute seven basic fallacies about farm problems and policies.

Seven Fallacies

First of all, there is the *farm income fallacy* — the belief that the aggregate income derived from farming should rise at least proportionately to nonfarm income, and any falling behind of farm income is an inequity which the government should correct. But the fact is that in a growing economy the shares earned by different sectors inevitably vary over time. Since farm products are mostly "necessities," consumers do *not* increase their purchases from farmers proportionately as their incomes rise. Thus, a rise in agricultural productivity will not benefit farmers as long as they fail to adjust their production plans. For, if this increased farm output is to be sold, prices will have to fall, and this offsets the gain in volume.

By improving their techniques, then, farmers work themselves (or other farmers) out of a job. The less efficient farmers must find more useful work — which, of course, enables those who do stay on farms to keep their income on a par with the rest of the economy. The resulting gradual reduction of the farm labor force has now gone on for hundreds of years, and it will no doubt continue in the future. If there is anything unfair about it, the blame must be laid on Engel's law, which says that people spend proportionately (but not absolutely) less on food as their incomes rise. This is perhaps the best-established proposition of economics.

Any attempt to obscure the necessity of reducing the farm labor force by establishing high price supports merely perpetuates the problem and creates a spiral of ever-higher surpluses and ever-higher expenditures. The recent history of farm policy amply demonstrates this process. This does not mean that the government should be indifferent to the income of farmers (or the income of any other group); it does mean that farm supports have to be administered in such a way as to facilitate rather than counteract the needed adjustments in the labor force. To keep up farm income by keeping up farm prices is impossibly expensive in the long run. As we shall see, there is a better way.

Second, there is the *family farm fallacy*. Many people feel that the government should preserve the family type of farm production — even though it has lost its economic viability — because of its alleged noneconomic benefits. Whatever moral virtue there is in independent country living, however, will be eroded if it can be achieved only by government handouts, no matter how disguised. Rural politicians are fond of arguing that agriculture is the nation's backbone, but this is hardly a reason for government intervention. Of what use is a backbone that needs to be supported?

Moreover, a large share of the benefits of programs purporting to help the family farm now go to large-scale operators (often corporations). According to the 1954 *Census of Agriculture* (still the most recent source available), three per cent of the country's cotton farms were receiving, at that time at least, 30 per cent of the support benefits. (This pattern is even more pronounced in wheat.) Several cotton-growing corporations receive more than $1 million a year each from the Commodity Credit Corporation.

It should not be thought that the benefits could be spread more evenly by limiting the "loans" that any farm can receive: as long as prices are kept high, it makes little or no difference whether a large grower sells his crop in the open market or receives a "loan" on it from the government. Even if there are reasons for favoring the family farm, price supports are too blunt a tool for the purpose.

A third misconception is the *acreage fallacy* — the belief that production can be controlled by restricting acreage. Although there can be no doubt that farmers will abandon the least productive acreage, the Agriculture Department still chooses to ignore this fact in such schemes as the Emergency Feed Grain Plan.

In fact, this scheme, which allows farmers to wait until crops are grown before deciding which acreage to abandon, puts a positive premium on harvesting only the most productive acres. To take an extreme case, a field that yielded no crop at all because of flooding can still serve to meet the farmer's commitment to reduce acreage in return for an incentive payment. It is not surprising, therefore, that the very costly Emergency Feed Grain Plan of 1961 had only a very slight effect on feed grain output.

Fourth, we must consider the *research fallacy*. This amounts to a belief that agricultural research will improve the relative position of farmers in the economy. As was argued above, improved productivity (the principal result of research) will not help farmers as long as all of them stay on farms. Such research may, of course, benefit the economy as a whole, but it only intensifies the need for adjustments in the farm sector. The government should promote research only if it is prepared for its economic consequences. This principle also applies to other productivity-raising government programs such as irrigation and conservation.

The fifth mistaken conviction about farm problems — the *free market fallacy* — is that farmers are too numerous and too weak to bargain effectively and, thus, in a free market they will always come out on the bottom. But bargaining between various sectors of the economy has little influence on the distribution of national income. Far more important is the willingness of producers to supply even at low prices. Farmers are willing to do this because their purchased inputs are small in relation to their output, largely because most of the land and labor they use is their own.

Because the supply elasticity of farm products is low (at least in the short run), farm prices in a free market are likely to fluctuate considerably. From the farmers' point of view, this is a more serious defect of the free market than the alleged bargaining weakness. The fluctuations can be mitigated by greater foresight (including more use of the futures market by farmers) and, if necessary, losses can be compensated for by social security and welfare devices.

Sixth, we have the *middleman fallacy,* which is related to the free market fallacy. Because the farmer's share of the consumer's dollar is steadily declining, many feel that there must be a conspiracy on the part of middlemen. But the simple truth is that farm products are reaching the consumer in ever more highly processed form. Not only does the proportion of income spent on food decline as income goes up, but production on the farm accounts for a diminishing share of the proportion that continues to be devoted to food, while the share of processing, distribution and transportation increases. It is not a conspiracy, therefore, that causes the farmer to receive less and less of the total value of food sold in a growing economy. This is equally true in the clothing sector.

Indeed, if the "middlemen" were powerful enough to deprive the farmer of his just reward, they would be making a much bigger profit than they do. But meat packing, cotton textiles, transportation and food retailing are all low-return industries. The plight of the cotton textiles industry is probably due primarily to the high support price of raw cotton and not to imports, as the industry prefers to think.

Finally, the *idea that agriculture can be isolated from the rest of the economy is perhaps the most dangerous fallacy of all.* I refer to the belief that the purpose of agriculture is to provide an income to farmers rather than to supply the world with food and fibers. The corollary is that only the farmers themselves should decide what farm output and farm prices should be. "Supply management," which refers to the centralized control of output under government-sponsored cartels, is unlikely to improve the

farmers' bargaining position. Such a system would force the more efficient farmers to operate far below capacity and therefore discourage their
cooperation. Supply management is on a level with the medieval guilds
in terms of economic sophistication: it protects the inefficient at the
expense of the efficient. Supply management would make it legal, even
compulsory, for farmers to adopt the same practices for which the
executives of General Electric and Westinghouse were sent to jail.
"Supply management," in fact, is merely a euphemism for "monopoly."
Farm policy is judged by odd standards.

Ideas of this sort are wholly out of place in a democratic society devoted to the freedom and welfare of *all* its members. The frequency with
which they appear is all the more alarming. Congressional committees
on agriculture listen every year to literally hundreds of witnesses representing farm interests, but rarely, if ever, to a single witness with any
claim to speak for the consumer. This one-sided approach is hardly likely
to lead to balanced legislation — nor, as recent experience indicates, to
any permanent legislation at all.

Separating Prices and Incomes

So much for the basic fallacies underlying past, present and proposed
agricultural policies. The alternative I have in mind avoids all of these
pitfalls. It is, I believe, a rational policy which recognizes the needs of
farmers without putting unnecessary burdens on the rest of the economy.
Essentially, I believe an attempt should be made to restore agriculture to
a healthy and useful condition by separating the issue of farm *income*
from the issue of farm *prices*. Farm prices should be allowed to return to
levels at which supply and demand would reach equilibrium without an
accompanying build-up in surpluses or the necessity of ever-tighter
controls.

Obviously, sudden changes in farm income are undesirable. Thus, to
cushion the initial shock of a return to market prices, acreage payments
should be made, over a limited number of years, to the present holders
of acreage allotments for basic commodities. The acreage payment
should be set at a level equal to the value per acre of current price supports at current levels of output. Thus, if the price of cotton were to
drop by 10 cents per pound upon the restoration of free markets, and
the average yield per acre is 400 pounds, then the acreage payment
would start at $40 per acre and taper off gradually in subsequent years.
Each farmer would be free to produce more or less than he does now, or
to abandon production.

Unlike other schemes, this plan does not require farmers to continue
production in order to receive the benefits — a requirement which would
hinder the needed adjustments in output. On the other hand, the acre-

age payment is not a reward for not producing, as is the case under the Soil Bank and Emergency Feed Grain Plans; the incentive for output reduction (where needed) is provided by lower prices. New entrants to farming would not receive acreage payments, but otherwise they would not meet any restrictions. There would consequently be no problems of enforcement.

Another advantage of the acreage payment scheme is that the distribution of its benefits would correspond more closely to need than is the case under the present program, which gives large farms an inordinate share. This is so because, on the average, large farms have higher yields per acre and thus get more under bushel supports than they would under acreage payments.

The cost of acreage payments for cotton, corn and wheat, using Department of Agriculture estimates of free market prices, would be somewhat less than $3 billion in the first year (about a billion each for corn and wheat, and $750 million for cotton). In contrast, the current agriculture budget amounts to $7 billion; in fact, the Emergency Feed Grain Plan alone, ineffective as it is, last year cost the taxpayers about $800 million — and this leaves out the cost to consumers. In addition, lower U.S. farm prices would eliminate the need for export subsidies and the "equalization" tariff on cotton textiles.

From the point of view of implementation, the advantage of the plan is its flexibility. It could be put into effect, to begin with, on only one commodity. (Cotton is the logical candidate, but the problems in corn are perhaps even more pressing.) *If necessary,* the plan could be combined with some form of price stabilization — but with support prices set at much lower levels than they are at present. And if Congress should be unwilling to see the acreage payments taper off, there would be no problem as far as resource allocation is concerned, since the program, even at the beginning, would be far less expensive than the agricultural program currently in effect.

The most important advantage of the acreage payment plan is that it would restore agriculture to its proper role in the economy. When supply and demand are in equilibrium, farm produce will no longer be a burden on the economy but will contribute significantly to its steady and orderly growth.

The farm problem is not as hopeless as it seems.

• *44*

The Changing Character of American Unionism*

RICHARD A. LESTER
Princeton University

The 1930's was a period of social change, economic distress, more liberal labor laws, and the formation of many new unions and the extension of their power into previously non-union industries. Since this time unions have settled down. Despite some instances to the contrary, the process of maturation will probably continue in each of three important aspects of union behavior.

Since the mid-1930's, unions in this country have experienced certain internal changes. Many, especially the newly formed industrial unions, have been shedding youthful characteristics in the process of settling down.

* Taken and adapted from Richard A. Lester, *As Unions Mature: An Analysis of the Evolution of American Unionism* (Princeton, New Jersey: Princeton University Press, 1958), pp. 21–34. Reproduced with permission.

Some support exists for the theory that institutions tend to pass through stages of development, that organizations like unions, which aim at altering the balance of rights and privileges, experience a natural evolution of organizational life, particularly if they are successful. In their early stages such organizations will be militant and turbulent, with internal factionalism and vigorous external opposition. At first they must fight for existence as well as for goals that generally are considered radical. Under the circumstances membership participation is likely to be high and leadership positions in the organization are apt to be won by the agitator and the table-pounder.

Later on, as the organization gains acceptance and security and succeeds in establishing new rights and other aims, a transformation tends to occur not only in the organization's goals but also in the nature of its leadership, in its internal operations, and in the distribution of power and functions among different structural levels. Instead of being simply an opposition or anti-body, the new organization becomes more and more integrated into the life of the community. Instead of pursuing a crusade against the "enemy," it cooperates increasingly with other groups in industry, government, and society. As some of the organization's initial goals are achieved, its objectives tend to broaden and become more complex, so that they are increasingly difficult to define and delimit. As the organization grows in size and its activities and responsibilities enlarge, it faces new problems of administration, discipline, and public relations. The need for specialists becomes more pressing, a hierarchy and bureaucracy tend to develop, and the relationship of top officials to the rank-and-file grows more impersonal.

Internally, three significant changes have occurred in American unions in recent decades. In many unions, greater centralization has developed with the transfer of functions and decisions from the locals to national headquarters. Second, the status and outlook of top union leaders has been changing with increased size, stability, and responsibilities. Third, union militancy and demagoguery have tended to give way to carefully prepared presentations and disciplined representation.

Centralization of Functions and Control

A number of factors have been instrumental in shifting some functions, decisions, and power from the local level to the national headquarters of unions. In the first place, expansion of the size of the national union, by means of growth in the number of locals and perhaps by merger also, serves to reduce the importance and influence of a particular local within the union. Furthermore the larger the national union, the more patronage there is by which to build up a political machine with control from the top, and the more union communications (including publications) are likely to be centrally controlled. Also, large unions tend to have comparatively large staffs of specialists and experts, upon whom locals come to rely for guidance. Indeed, the assumption generally is made that, with unions, large size means more effectiveness, efficiency, and power.

Expansion in the area of collective bargaining and enlargement of the spread of bargaining patterns have also contributed to central determination of union policies. The national seeks a common program for the whole industry or area of competitive production. Bargaining strategy necessitates some central control of demands, along with headquarters' approval of settlements.

A change in the character and subject matter of negotiations has likewise added to the dependence of the locals on the top echelon of the union. Collective bargaining has tended to be increasingly factual, statistical, and full of economic reasoning, so that the amateur negotiator feels himself at a disadvantage. But it is particularly the technical nature of the new subjects in negotiations that has increased the role of the national headquarters and the staff. Subjects like job evaluation, time-and-motion study, pensions, medical and hospital care, and supplementary unemployment benefits, are generally beyond the training and know-how of persons at the local level. For guidance in such matters, the union may need to rely upon the advice of staff experts.

Alteration in Top Leadership

As unions expand and become accepted by the community, subtle changes tend to occur in their top leadership. The founding fathers and the early recruits with a missionary zeal die or retire with the passage of time. They are replaced by a second or third generation of leaders, who personally have not experienced the bitter struggles for existence in the union's early days and who are less likely to have had the influences of an immigrant background or socialist convictions in their youth. As already indicated, such successors tend to be, not the crusading agitator, but the skillful political operator and level-headed administrator able to manage a large organization and to perform the necessary desk duties. The president of a union has a variety of administrative responsibilities. Among other things, he is the employer of a staff, the head of a political machine, and the highest union authority in the enforcement of collective agreements.

As unions settle down, the path to top leadership tends to be a steady climb through the various levels of the hierarchy. Stratification in organizations generally increases with their size and age. In mature organizations, the selection and training of leaders at the lower levels are likely to be controlled from the top. High union officials are organization men, who are prone to stress unity and to frown on insurgency. The prospects for advancement may also discourage insurgency. Mobility within the labor movement is largely vertical in one national union; seldom do union leaders transfer from one union to another, which might imply some lack of loyalty to the union's administration. Yet as unions mature, their growth curve tends to flatten out, which means that advancement is largely confined to replacements in the hierarchy.

The promotional outlook is, however, but one aspect of the psychological change which is likely to occur. The gap between the members' wages and the salaries of the presidents of the larger unions has increased relatively during the 1940's and 1950's. The heads of the dozen largest unions have salaries ranging from $18,000 to $60,000 a year, plus ample expense accounts and frequently other perquisites. That union presidents sometimes urge conventions not to increase their salaries does not alter the fact that it is possible for them to live on a scale equivalent to that of business executives and that, in the newly-built union headquarters, the presidential offices are as impressive as those of high corporate officials.

Nowadays the presidency of a union carries a wide range of duties and responsibilities. The concept of the office has broadened as union presidents have increasingly held positions on community, industrial, educational, and governmental boards. The president of a sizeable union may be expected to make pronouncements on national economic policy, foreign policy, domestic politics, and all sorts of legislative proposals as well as the problems of his industry. Many of his activities might be considered extraunion, and in connection with them he associates with leaders in all walks of life.

Many union leaders in the past have been unconventionally motivated —men with a mission to alter the economic and social order, with little thought of personal gain. There are indications that the concept of the successful union president may have been changing somewhat in the 1940's and 1950's, even in the minds of many holding that office. As their interests and associations have broadened, they may place more stress on their reputations with the general public.

Factors have been at work which are influencing the evolution of union leadership. Unless new factors — such as a severe business depression, upsetting internal crises in particular unions, or perhap a war — arise to alter the direction of the drift, the differences between union executives and business executives in living standards, in daily activities, and in business interests, are likely to continue to diminish.

Decline in Militancy

Generally speaking, unions have lost some of the militancy and rambunctiousness that characterized them before World War II. During the 1940's and 1950's they became more disciplined and businesslike.

Doubtless the developments already discussed — centralization of control and changes in union leadership — have been contributing factors. But, equally if not more important have been developments outside the union, namely, greater employer acceptance and cooperation with labor organizations, the increase in workers' living standards under full employment, and the growth of moderation and middle-of-the-road attitudes in American society during the postwar years.

Union militancy is one reaction to employer hostility and threats to the union's existence. Unions also tend to be aggressive when their security is challenged by government, left wing competitors, or internal troubles and rebellion. Indeed, as the main channel for worker protest, they are agitated by any increase in employee discontent whether arising from unemployment, technological change, or arbitrary management decisions.

The adventurous and demanding quality of the American worker supplies a force for change. A people, stemming from immigrants who protested against authority in Europe and developed self-reliance in frontier communities, may be quick to take forceful action in pursuit of their demands. Of course, the longer they are accustomed to settled, suburban living the more conditioned they may be against resort to violent protests.

The passage of time and generations does seem to have strengthened various factors that tend to "calm down" our unions. The success of unions in establishing rights and in negotiating gains has served, in most industries, to reduce the "core of conflict" and to contract the uncharted areas where unions might present new challenges to management rights.

Collective bargaining institutionalizes conflict by building up orderly processes, joint machinery, and other administrative restraints against unruly or precipitate action. The United Mine Workers provides an example. In May 1956, John Lewis and the UMW executive board sent notice to all miners stating that unauthorized stoppages were in violation of union policy, that the machinery of the joint agreement must be used to settle disputes, and that fines would be levied on the treasuries of locals which engaged in unauthorized work stoppages. In October 1956, Mr. Lewis announced that such fines had been levied, that the union would act to protect men observing the contract, and that repeated violations of the UMW policy would bring stiffer fines and perhaps also charges by the national union against the leaders of such strikes.

One must, of course, recognize that in matters such as new organization, strikes, and left wing challenges, the development is uneven and individual unions may have experience at variance with the general drift. Within a union, there may be wide variation in attitudes and stage of development, with rather bitter skirmishes at union outposts in the South or in rural areas. And always the possibility exists that developments such as economic depression, automation, legislation, or large-scale organization, may stir things up sufficiently within the labor movement so as to cause an alteration or even some reversal in the main drift — at least temporarily. But union behavior has been changing; the challenges which face the union have been modified as left wing unionism and dual unionism have given way to a more unified labor movement.

45

The Monopolistic Power of Labor Unions*

DONALD DEWEY
Columbia University

"Nothing contained in the antitrust laws shall be construed to forbid the existence and operation of labor . . . organizations . . . or to forbid or restrain individual members of such organizations from lawfully carrying out the legitimate objects thereof . . ."

—38 Stat. 731, U.S. Code, Sec. 17
(*The Clayton Antitrust Act of 1914*)

Labor Unions and the Antitrust Laws

Over the years the attention devoted to the impact of the antitrust laws on labor unions has greatly exceeded the importance of the subject. This is not to say that the activities of labor unions are not an important part of the monopoly problem. One may plausibly argue, as did Henry Simons, that policywise they present the toughest issues. Neither the Attorney General nor the courts, however, have been disposed to probe the economics of labor monopoly in cases arising under the antitrust laws. Except for a brief period prior to World War II when Thurman Arnold headed the Antitrust Division, federal officials by their inaction have given labor unions a virtual immunity from governmental supervision. In private litigation, the courts have often affirmed that some

* Taken and adapted from *Monopoly in Economics and Law* (Chicago: Rand McNally & Company, 1959), pp. 264–269. Reproduced with permission.

activities of labor unions may violate the antitrust law, but they have long employed a double standard which accords far greater freedom of action to labor unions than to business firms.

In general, the "normal" activities of labor unions in no sense constitute unlawful combination regardless of their effect upon wages, employment, or the price of an industry's product. Under the antitrust laws, as under the common law, an organized worker demand for improved working conditions backed by a collective refusal to work — and nothing more — has hardly ever subjected labor unions to criminal penalties, damage suits, or equitable restraints.

The Case for Leniency toward Labor Monopoly

Probably only ardent social planners and authoritarians of various hues now believe that labor unions should be treated as conspiracies against the public interest when they try to improve the lot of their members by collective bargaining. Among moderate men, the wisdom of a double standard in antitrust policy is almost universally acknowledged. There is, however, some difference of opinion regarding the reasons why labor unions should be accorded immunities not granted to employer groups.

1. By one view, labor unions ought to enjoy immunity from the antitrust laws because the economic significance of their activities is negligible — they have no appreciable power over wages, hours, and working conditions. Doubtless the great majority of the 15 million-odd union members in the United States belong to unions so weak that collective bargaining does little, if anything, for their incomes, but unless most labor leaders are wasting their time, the presumption must be that unions can — and sometimes do — perceptibly influence labor costs and hence the distribution of manpower and materials in the economy.

2. Many authorities argue that labor unions should not be treated as combinations in restraint of trade because they intend no harm to consumers of final products. Indeed they are often criticized for precisely this oversight by economists who contend that the high wage policies of unions "cause" unemployment by raising prices to consumers and encouraging employers to change the factor combination. But absence of wrong intent is no adequate reason for exempting labor unions from the consequences of their acts.

3. One may fall back on the venerable argument that labor unions are good because they countervail the employer's monopsony power in the labor market; that by making it impossible for him to depress wage rates by reducing his demand for labor, they may cause more, not less, labor to be hired. This argument is valid in so far as employers who are subject to union pressure have monopsony power and the union strength does no more than countervail such power. It may command respect in a case

where skilled workers are pitted against their employer in an isolated community that offers them no comparable jobs, *e.g.*, in many a West Virginia mining community. But the argument clearly does not hold for the vastly greater number of situations where organized unskilled and semi-skilled workers confront employers in urban areas.

4. Similarly, an exemption of unions from the antitrust laws can be justified because employers and employees alike give hostages to one another in the form of quasi-rent — that portion of the joint product that can be taken by one party without causing any other to diminish his efforts and hence reduce the size of the joint product itself.[1] In the absence of collective bargaining, employers are doubtless well placed to appropriate the greater share of that part of the joint product whose division can be bargained over.

5. The best reason for not treating labor unions as suspect conspiracies is, of course, that most people would view such a policy as grossly unfair. The commonplace view assumes that most labor disputes are private contests between masters and hands, that masters are richer than hands, and government intervention against unions would serve the unacceptable purpose of making the rich richer. This view further assumes, in effect, that (a) workers can command a higher total wage bill from an employer if collective bargaining is possible and (b) the gains of collective bargaining will mainly be exacted from the employer rather than the public.

a. In the short run, the existence of quasi-rent ensures the "indeterminacy" of the wage rate and wage bill under collective bargaining. Nor is the validity of this assumption controverted by the probability that the wage bill of the employer will eventually decline as he becomes able to withdraw capital from the business or change his factor combination. Since some union members will also die, retire, or quit with the passing of time, thus relieving the employer of the necessity of firing anyone in the interest of profit maximization, workers understandably disregard the long-run effect of union policy upon the fortunes of their union and their employer.

b. The allocation of the burden of a wage increase between employer and public will depend upon (1) the elasticity of demand for the employer's product, (2) the technical possibilities of substitution for labor in the factor combination, and (3) the willingness of the union to accept a reduction in employment, *i.e.*, its willingness to allow the employer to avail himself of the opportunity to minimize the impact of the wage concession upon his costs. In the case of a regulated public utility company which, as a matter of right, is entitled to a "fair return on a fair valuation

---

[1] "Quasi-rent," in other words, means that part of an income which hypothetically could be taken away from a worker or an owner without causing him to work less hard or invest less money. Sometimes, quasi-rent is called *economic surplus*.

of investment," the whole of any wage increase could conceivably be passed on to the public. In the case of most firms, the presumption is that consumer demand is quite elastic and, hence, that in the short run a wage increase is likely to be borne mostly by the employer.

The Case Against Union Monopoly in the Long Run

When attention is limited to the more immediate economic consequences of collective bargaining, the usual labor dispute is a clash of wills and bargaining skill between private parties over the distribution of quasi-rent in which the government is not particularly concerned. The long-run economic consequences of collective bargaining are likely to be blunted by the difficulty that the union will face in "covering the market," *i.e.*, organizing all workers in the industry so that unionized firms paying higher wages do not lose ground to their unorganized competitors; and by the inability of the union to keep employers from cutting down on labor in response to the concession of higher wages. We may conclude, then, that the public benefits to be gained by having the State intervene in the usual labor dispute over wages and hours are highly nebulous — a truth which most judges have perceived ever since we have had reported decisions.

Nevertheless, in so far as a union does manage to cover the labor market, the private conflict between an employer and his workers over the division of quasi-rent is transformed into a contest in which the public interest lies on the side of the employer — hence, the hostility of many economists to the idea of industry-wide bargaining. Indeed, if the life of the law were logic, the libertarian would be obliged to support measures that would allow unions to countervail the employer's bargaining power — but nothing more. This limitation could most directly be secured by confining collective bargaining to the company level and treating the concerted action of the organized employees of different firms as unlawful conspiracy. But as the admirers of Justice Holmes will never let us forget, the life of the law is, in fact, experience. This country should have no more encouraged the spread of industry-wide bargaining than it should have permitted the wholesale mergers that produced the present level of corporate concentration in the economy; yet the error was made with a vengeance. The libertarian may properly seek to withdraw this power by installments, but it would be immoral — and unthinkable politics — to attempt a frontal assault.

46

Do Unions Cause Inflation? *

ALBERT E. REES
University of Chicago

It would seem that this question must be answered by "Yes," "No," or "Maybe." However, the author of this selection decides differently. His answer may have more meaning, though it may not be more persuasive, after reading Selection 48.

The most widely accepted position on the relation of wages to inflation is the view that there is a wage-price spiral. I do not agree with most of the implications of this view, and I shall try to show why.

The Union Impact on the Wages of Union Members

It is usually assumed that unions have the power to raise the wages of their members. This is, I think, a correct assumption, but not a very helpful one unless something is said about (a) the probable magnitude of the effect of strong unions on wages; (b) the length of time over which additional wage gains can be made; and (c) what part of the present American union movement can be said to exert such an influence. Unless it can be shown that unions substantially affect the wages of a large number of members, unions are not likely to be powerful enough to initiate general wage and price movements under any circumstances. We do

* From *Labor Problems–Cases and Readings*, 2nd edition, by George P. Schultz and John R. Coleman. Copyright © 1959. McGraw-Hill Book Company. Used by permission.

have some evidence of substantial union effects, though perhaps these effects are smaller than many people believe.

Let me attempt a rough guess, on the basis of our present sketchy knowledge, of the effects on wages of American unions during periods of relative prosperity and price stability. The membership of U.S. unions in 1956 was about 17½ million, about one-third of wage and salary employment excluding agriculture and domestic service. Of these members perhaps one-fourth are in unions that have raised wages 10 to 20 per cent. This group probably includes the skilled building trades and printing trades, the operating railroad brotherhoods, the coal miners, the maritime unions, some of the teamsters, and various smaller craft unions. Perhaps half the total number of union members are in unions that may have raised earnings 5 to 10 per cent. Included here are the unions in durable-goods manufacturing, some unions in nondurable manufacturing and communications, and the transportation workers and unskilled construction workers excluded from the first group. Finally, the remaining fourth are in unions with little or no influence, largely because they do not fully control their jurisdictions. Included in this group are the members of the retail and white-collar unions, of unions in the shoe and textile industries, and of unions in the apparel industry. This group also includes members of government workers' unions, which do not really engage in collective bargaining over wages.

The General Level of Wages and Prices

In the past decade we have become familiar with the reasoning summarized by the term "the wage-price spiral." Closely akin to the wage-price spiral is the belief that wage increases won by unions spread to non-union workers and thus set the general level of wages. If this argument can be broadly accepted, it is not relevant to measure the effect of unions in relative terms. Unions can then raise the wages of nonmembers as fast as the wages of members and can cause inflation even though the relative wage structure remains undisturbed.

The notions of the wage-price spiral and the general spread of union wage gains have descriptive, but not analytical, validity under special monetary and fiscal conditions. Failure to specify these conditions may lead to acceptance of the reasoning under circumstances in which it is not applicable.

Wage Price Relations

The spiral concept was born in the immediate postwar years when the financing of higher wage and price levels was assured by the existence of tremendous liquid-asset holdings by firms and individuals. The holders would have wanted to spend these holdings on goods in any case. But this is only to say that wage increases provided an avenue through which a disequilibrium situation could be brought to balance. At times, wage increases may offer producers a convenient excuse for revising prices that lie below the demand schedule for the products in question.

If there is no preexisting excess demand, wage increases can lead to inflation only in one of two ways. In the first, wage increases could automatically tend to expand the supply of money or increase its velocity of circulation. This would happen if businessmen drew down cash balances or turned to the banks and obtained additional credit to finance higher wage bills, increased values of inventories, and perhaps increased investment in labor-saving equipment. Similarly, higher incomes could lead workers to expand their purchases of durable goods and thus lead to an expansion of installment credit. These effects will operate only if the Federal Reserve System is unwilling or unable to control the volume of bank credit so as to stabilize prices. It is hard to imagine how it could be unable to do so except in some broad political sense.

The second way in which a wage increase can force the financing of its own survival and spread could arise if there were a firm commitment on the part of government to maintain full employment at all times. If higher wages threatened to produce any unemployment above an irreducible minimum, the government would have to create new demand through monetary or fiscal policy. But such a full-employment guarantee would probably be inflationary even without union pressures.

The price rise of 1955–1957, the sharpest peacetime price rise of recent years, has been widely blamed on the wage-price spiral. But this position loses most of its plausibility when the price rises are examined in detail. The sharpest rise in wholesale prices of finished goods was for finished producer goods, where a major investment boom caused a sharp rise in demand. At the consumer level, the largest price increases were for foods and services, both produced in weakly unionized sectors of the economy. Consumer durables, produced in highly unionized industries, had a lower retail price level in 1957 than in 1951–1953.

Unions "Spread" Inflation

Let us turn now to the second main form of the argument that unions can cause inflation, which involves the spread of wage increases from union to nonunion industries. In a union's immediate sphere of influence, there are some unorganized workers who will always benefit immediately from a union wage gain. These include the clerical and supervisory employees of employers whose production workers are organized. They also include the employees of the few nonunion employers in strongly organized industries or communities. Such employers follow union wage patterns as part of the price of keeping unions out.

In a broader sense, however, the transmission of wage patterns depends heavily on the strength of aggregate demand. If union employers can pay higher wages and still continue to expand their work forces, they tend to pull more and better workers away from other employers and thus lead these employers to raise wages in order to hold their labor. But if higher wages force the union employers to curtail employment, the effects will be very different.

If wages elsewhere are flexible downward, the workers released will soon be hired by other employers and the nonunion level of wages will tend to fall. There will be little movement in the general level of wages, and if there is any, its direction will depend on the precise shapes of the demand schedules of union and nonunion employers. If wages are inflexible downward in the nonunion sector, as is usually true, the general wage level must rise, but unemployment will be created that will tend to check any further rises. Certainly few nonunion employers will emulate union wage increases.

The choice between the alternative outcomes is not the unions', except that they can forego wage increases that seem likely to curtail employment. The choice is again basically that of the monetary and fiscal authorities.

Unemployment, Wages, and the Price Level

It is clear that there is some level of unemployment high enough to check price rises by curtailing the demand for goods and services and to check wage rises by curtailing the demand for labor. But much depends on how high this rate is and whether it is regarded as tolerable or excessive. More broadly, we may ask on what terms can decreases in unemployment be exchanged for increases in prices.

For example, we might find that a 4 per cent average unemployment rate over the whole business cycle implies an average annual price rise of 2 per cent but that a 5 per cent average unemployment rate is consistent with price stability. In this case, we might regard price stability as worth the cost. We might find, however, that increasing the average unemployment rate from 4 to 5 per cent reduces the average rate of price rise from 2 per cent to 1.5 per cent. In this case, we might prefer the lower rate of unemployment. The task of determining what terms of trade actually prevail is a very difficult one, for two reasons. First, movements of prices and unemployment that are causally related may not occur at the same time. Second, there may be an upward bias in our price indexes that makes the terms of trade seem less favorable than they really are.

Let us look first at the matter of timing. In 1950, we had a sharp rise in prices associated with the Korean War, and unemployment was high, though declining rapidly. The following three years, 1951 to 1953, were years of very low unemployment and relatively stable prices. It has been argued from this experience that price stability is consistent with a very low unemployment rate — perhaps 3 per cent. Unemployment, however, would undoubtedly have fallen less if there had not been a sharp price rise in 1950. The price rise was produced in large part by the building up of stocks in the hands of both consumers and businesses (including users' stocks of consumer durables). These stocks helped to moderate the demand for civilian goods in the following years. Without "scare buying," the rise in prices and the trough in unemployment would have coincided more closely than they did.

The second difficulty in assessing the relation between unemployment and price stability arises from the probable upward bias of the Consumer Price Index. Although this index is one of the best price indexes in the world, it is far from perfect. It is quite possible for the index to rise too much and for too long when the true price level is rising and to fall too little and for too short a time when the true price level is falling. Over a period of years, this bias can have a large cumulative effect.

Closely related to the problem of quality change is the problem of completely new products. Typically the price of new products falls rapidly relative to other prices when the product is first introduced. Later the price may stabilize or rise. The trend of price indexes will be influenced by the time when such new products are first included in the index. Typically such products have been introduced into the Consumer Price Index only after they have been in use for a considerable period, and this may contribute to an upward bias of the index. It is not clear that there has been any rise in the true level of consumer prices over the past decade except for the brief rise caused by the Korean War. If this is so, the problem of the wage-price spiral may be largely illusory.

47

The Future of American Labor Unions[*]

JOSEPH SHISTER
University of Buffalo

If we could foresee the future, we would be less concerned about the past. As it is, what has already happened is material for conjecture about the future. Labor unionists inevitably use their era of mushroom growth commencing about thirty years ago as their standard of comparison. There is reason to suppose that today's labor leader must feel some apprehension as he looks back on that epoch.

To say that many an American labor leader is unhappy about the poor rate of union growth in recent years is the height of understatement; this relative stagnation has caused deep concern. And yet, the concern has not been translated into action which has successfully come to grips with the problem. Is, then, the labor movement itself to blame for the stagnation? Or does the problem lie dominantly beyond the control of the unions? And, whatever the answers to these queries, is there likely to be an upsurge in union growth in the near future?

[*] Taken and adapted from "The Outlook for Union Growth," *The Annals* of the American Academy of Political and Social Science, November 1963, pp. 56–62. Reproduced with permission.

Environmental Factors

The historical record, buttressed by analysis, clearly shows that the great waves of organization have been associated with deep depression or war and very poor industrial personnel practices and policies. This is not to imply that these forces alone are sufficient to explain the waves of organization; "creative" union leadership and other elements have also been at play. But the point that needs stressing is that these forces generated the environment within which the other elements could operate successfully. Absent this environment, there would not have been anything like the relevant waves of union growth.

All the forces emphasized above are dominantly beyond the control of the labor movement. Whether we have war or peace is not something that will depend in any large measure on union activities. The state of the economy can be influenced to some degree by union collective-bargaining policies, but hardly enough to matter very much if one focuses not on what unions *should* do but rather on what they will do — given their objectives and the institutional realities. And, even if one argues that union policies can and will be shaped to influence significantly the course of the business cycle or the pattern of long-run economic growth, it is totally unrealistic to assume that unions will pursue policies designed to bring on deep depression so that they can be successful in organization. The same impotence prevails in regard to union influence on the character of personnel practices and policies in unorganized firms. If anything, union collective-bargaining policies have induced sound personnel management in many nonunion concerns, and it is heroically wide of the mark to predict that unions will purposely become passive in their economic pursuits — not press vigorously for wage gains, fringe benefits, security measures, and the like — in the hope that the unorganized firms will relax their viligance, slip into sloppy personnel habits, and thus deliver the unorganized workers into the waiting hands of the unions.

Granted, then, that there are various forces which are necessary — although by themselves insufficient — to generate a wave of union growth and that they lie beyond labor's control, what is the likelihood of these forces materializing in the near future?

No one knows with any meaningful degree of certainty whether we shall be involved in a nuclear conflict. Any predictions on that score are likely to be riddled with speculation. What is more, even if one predicts an all-out nuclear war, one can still say nothing about its impact on unionism — or other socioeconomic matters — with any significant degree of certainty; there is no historical trend to extrapolate or recent experience on which to draw. For purposes of analysis, therefore, one must logically assume the absence of nuclear conflict in the foreseeable future.

By contrast, we can predict with reasonable accuracy whether we shall have a deep depression in the near future. While periodic recessions, it would seem, will continue to be with us, deep depressions — say, like the one of the thirties — are now merely of historical interest. The instruments for preventing such an economic holocaust — fiscal policy, monetary policy, and related measures — are at hand and well known. And no administration, whether it be Democratic or Republican, will sit idly by in Washington while the economy falls into such a downswing; it would spell political suicide. Moreover, American loss of international prestige that would stem from a deep depression is still another deterrent to a repetition of any such disaster.

Personnel practices and policies in American industry have undergone nothing short of a revolution since the thirties. The changes in the organized firms are obvious. But the point that needs stressing here is the changes which have occurred in the unorganized firms. As already implied, the presence of unions has acted as an important — perhaps a vital — spur to this revolution in nonunion concerns. But there have been other factors, too, including scarcity of labor for considerable periods of time, the professionalization of management, and government influence. But, whatever the causes, personnel practices and policies have changed radically — and for the better. Many unorganized firms have developed very sound — and even highly sophisticated — personnel practices and policies which will match just about anything the union has to offer the prospective member.

The soundness of personnel practices and policies in the unorganized firms is not something that is likely to disappear in the near future. If these firms were to suffer dramatic economic setbacks, they might well slip back into unsound personnel pursuits that could conceivably jeopardize their hold on the unorganized status. But the point is precisely that such a situation is unlikely to obtain on any large scale short of a deep depression, and we have already ruled that out as a likely occurrence in the near future.

If one grants, then, that in the near future we experience no deep depression and that unorganized firms will continue with sound personnel management, how can unions realistically hope for a wave of organization even if they are ready to spend massive sums of money, develop innovating structures and techniques for organization, and count on favorable public policy. What powerful incentive is there for the unorganized to join unions on a large scale when they are experiencing steady employment, good wages or salaries, satisfactory fringe benefits, and fair treatment by their employers?

True, as already stated, we shall continue to experience periodic recessions. But a recession is one thing, deep depression quite another. A recession — notably an intense one — may well lead to employee dissatisfaction. And such dissatisfaction may well induce unionization in specific situations — that is, if labor capitalizes effectively on this dissatisfaction. But the record since the end of World War II clearly indicates that recessions alone are not enough to induce anything even remotely resembling a wave of organization. In fact, none of the four recessions has apparently been a powerful enough force to generate, directly or indirectly, even a significant rise in union membership, let alone a wave of organization. The only material rise in the postwar period was linked to the Korean conflict.

Factors within Union Control

As already implied, there are factors shaping union growth which would seem to be within the control of the unions. What, then, are these factors? And is there any validity to the thesis, often expressed, that if these factors were favorable, we would witness a significant upsurge in unionism in the near future?

Organization is a costly business — notably so in the present socio-economic climate. The first requirement, therefore, for successful organizing drives is the injection of massive funds into organizing efforts. At first blush, this seems like something unions can do if only they will it. But things are not so simple as all that. The American Federation of Labor and Congress of Industrial Organizations (AFL-CIO) and most of the national unions are not exactly flushed with money. The expulsion of some labor groups from the federation and the loss of membership in quite a number of unions because of "automation" and other influences have taken their toll. And anyone familiar with the political realities of union life knows what a difficult matter it is to raise dues for a truly crash organizing program — and dues are a *sine qua non* for any successful large-scale union organization effort.

But even if one grants the availability of massive financial resources, adequate leadership for successful organization becomes necessary. Unionization does not take place automatically, even where the environment is conducive to rapid union growth. A fortiori, when the general economic climate will be anything but that of a deep depression, when management will continue to pursue sound and sophisticated personnel practices and policies, and when legal obstacles to organization will continue to abound. What is called for is leadership that is not only driving and energetic but also able to devise new and creative techniques for organization which stand a chance of attracting the unorganized workers to unionism. But, at the present time, such leadership is conspicuous by its absence. To begin with, many of the most influential labor leaders are well along in years. They are, in the words of one of the younger men in the movement, tired; they have fought the great battles; their energy is sapped; they are quite content to live on their laurels and retire

— or pass away — gracefully. These older leaders purely and simply lack the physical energy and the drive to head a great new crusade. One should hasten to add that such weariness — both physical and psychological — is not limited solely to older leadership in the labor movement; it is characteristic of older leadership in most any institution, be it management, government, education.

This aging process among the influential is enough of an obstacle to successful large-scale organization. But there is more: The traditional organizing techniques — handing out leaflets at the gate, talking to workers, visiting their homes — are not enough in the present socioeconomic climate. The sixties are not the thirties. And even if one argues that these techniques, properly executed, can still be successful among blue-collar employees, the fact remains that the potentially great source of union membership is not the blue-collar area but the white-collar segment of the economy. Given the changing complexion of the work force, the unions must make serious inroads into the white-collar sector if they are to achieve a rapid growth rate in the foreseeable future. Yet it is precisely among the white-collar employees that the traditional organizing techniques are unlikely to "take."

And the higher the skill level of the groups being organized, the less successful are the traditional techniques likely to be. Thus far, no trail blazing has become even dimly visible in the techniques employed by unions. Furthermore, successful white-collar organizing efforts may well require basic structural changes in American unionism. The obstacles to such change are too obvious to require elaboration. And equally clear are the implications for jurisdictional warfare if, somehow, the changes suggested do materialize.

But, even if one disregards the relative lack of physical energy, psychological drive, and social inventiveness in organizing structure and techniques, there are other characteristics of present-day union leadership which act as an obstacle to large-scale unionization. There is, today, a cleavage between "business-union" and "social-union" leadership in the American labor movement. This distinction has customarily been used to explain union policies with respect to collective bargaining and the role of government in society: The business-union leader is concerned almost solely with clear and immediate gains for the particular group of workers he represents; the social-union leader, while protecting the interests of his group first and foremost, nevertheless has a broader outlook and presses for public policies designed to obtain socioeconomic changes which, in his view, are beneficial to society. This distinction spills over into the character of organizing activity. The social-union leader needs a very large labor movement because he is eager to use unionism as a vehicle for reorienting the direction of American society. He knows full well that it takes very considerable political power to achieve such change, and, therefore, the larger the labor movement, the greater its political strength — even if organized labor cannot always, or even dominantly, "deliver the vote." But the business-union leader takes a radically different view of the matter. Not particularly interested in reorienting American society, concerned almost exclusively with economic gains through collective bargaining his focus is almost solely on the bargaining power of his union. If that power is satisfactory, he cares relatively little what the size of the labor movement is. He shows real concern about unionizing the unorganized only to the extent that these adversely affect the bargaining power of his union.

This means that the business unionists have no strong incentive — as do the social unionists — to spend huge sums of money for the purpose of organizing large numbers of workers who do not significantly affect the bargaining power of their unions. There is more: Not only does the business-union leader lack a strong desire to organize on a large scale, but he has reason to believe that, if the organization efforts were successful, the balance of power in the labor movement — which now favors his "philosophy" — might well be tipped the other way. Why, then, engage in activities which strain the budget and might conceivably lead to a loss of personal and institutional power?

In sum, the factors shaping union growth that are within's labor's control do not currently present a picture particularly favorable to success in large-scale organizing activity. Even if they did, the crucial question would remain: Would such a favorable picture be enough to insure successful organization of very large numbers of white-collar employees?

Undoubtedly a crash organizing program with creative-leadership ingredients would make some penetration into the white-collar ranks, notably at the lower levels of this highly heterogeneous category. But the vast bulk of the white-collar sector would remain immune to these appeals — massive and creative though they might be. For, as already noted, one should not realistically expect another deep depression or the return to poor personnel practices and policies in unorganized firms. There is more: The white-collar sector of the economy is expanding rapidly enough so that, in many instances, the spread of automation among these occupations — say, data-processing machines — has not caused unemployment, as has automation in some blue-collar sectors, but has, instead, been accompanied by a growth in the relevant labor force. And it is precisely the increased demand for white-collar labor that has in large measure generated rising salaries and other economic benefits. When to all that is added the antipathy, or even outright antagonism, toward unionism by many white-collar employees — particularly those at the higher skill levels — because of family background, education, experience, and related factors, it is not difficult to visualize why even vastly improved organizing structures and techniques backed by adequate financing will not make any massive inroads into this sector of the work force.

Public Policy

Unquestionably, public policy is an important factor shaping the rate of union growth. But certain dimensions of public policy, in relation to the problem at hand, may not be quite so obvious and therefore call for brief comment.

Public policy, strictly speaking, is not an independent factor. Within limits, it reflects the climate of opinion. The Taft-Hartley Act could not have been born in 1935, nor the Wagner Act in 1947. What this clearly implies, of course, is that the ability of the labor movement to influence the direction of public policy is a rather limited one. It follows that labor's attempts to obtain more favorable legislation designed to facilitate union organizing activities have little chance of success so long as the climate of opinion continues to be what it is — a climate which is certainly not sympathetic to union goals, to put it mildly. And there seems to be nothing on the horizon to indicate that the climate will change in the near future. The conservatism of affluence, the relative decline of the blue-collar work force, the accelerated pervasiveness of middle-class aspirations, emergency strikes — these and other factors point to a continuation of the unsympathetic climate.

Doubtless, the labor movement can have *some* influence on public policy even in an unfavorable climate, for, while organized labor cannot "deliver the vote," it can, nonetheless, contribute significantly in some instances to the election or defeat of some important public officials. But this, while very much welcomed by unions, is hardly enough to tip the public-policy scales in a fashion that will lead to a wave of unionization. To begin with, the basic statutes are still the same and cannot long be ignored. Furthermore, public policy is merely a permissive force. It does not automatically bring workers into the union ranks; the workers must be desirous of joining. And, there is no indication that, at present, the great reservoir of the unorganized — the white-collar group — is very eager or even desirous of flocking to the unions.

Prospects

In brief, then, the probability of a wave of unionization in the near future is small indeed. The forces which are necessary, although not sufficient, to generate such a wave are largely beyond the control of the labor movement; there seems little likelihood that these forces will materialize in the foreseeable future. The forces that are within labor's own control cannot, by themselves, insure large-scale union growth. And what is more important perhaps: thus far, the labor movement has not shaped these forces to maximize their effectiveness.

All this is not to argue that there will be no growth in union membership in the near future. Quite the contrary. There will be absolute growth, and there may even be some small improvement in relative growth — percentage of the eligible labor force organized. But that is a far cry from a wave of unionization.

C. THE CONSUMER

• 48

Using the Consumer Price Index*

RICHARD RUGGLES
Yale University

Few pieces of economic information are taken as seriously in everyday affairs as the Consumer Price Index. In many industries, wages are adjusted automatically in response to its movements. Its changes have provided controversy for numerous political campaigns. Yet, as in the case of the physician's electrocardiogram, the total condition of the subject cannot be surmised from the ups and downs of one chart. Moreover, some of the movement is benign; in fact, to stretch the analogy a bit further, no movement at all may indicate to the economist, as to the physician, that the patient is dead!

What You Get for Your Money

To understand what has *really* been happening to prices, we must first examine the factors responsible for the rises in the index. For this purpose let us take a look at the 12 per cent increase in the Consumer Price Index

* Reprinted from CHALLENGE, The Magazine of Economic Affairs, a publication of the Institute of Economic Affairs, New York University.

that has occurred since the Korean war. There are major segments of consumer purchases for which prices have not risen at all since that time. The price index for consumer durables, for example, shows a decline of approximately three per cent. On the other hand, the index for medical care rose by more than 30 per cent. On the average, the prices of services rose a substantial 23 per cent, while those of commodities rose only six per cent.

This difference in behavior largely reflects the fact that the price of a service is generally the rate of compensation of those performing it. And these wages naturally rise as per capita income rises. In the last 50 years the prices of services relative to those of commodities have risen continually as a consequence of such general rises in living standards. Commodity prices, on the other hand, can sometimes reflect increased productivity. If the increase in output per man-hour is greater than the increase in the wage rate, the cost of production may actually fall, thus permitting lower commodity prices despite higher wages.

The identification of price indexes with rates of pay in the service industries involves the implicit assumption that the productivity of the service industries has remained unchanged. In some instances, this assumption may be correct, but in others quite wide of the mark.

In the case of medical care, for example, the apparent price increase must be qualified by considering the increase in medical knowledge, better drugs and the new preventive medicines. Certainly the Salk vaccine was a tremendous medical advance which, in addition to sparing many lives, will save consumer dollars that would have gone for the treatment of polio.

Basically, then, the measurement of price changes comes down to a question of whether one gets more or less for his money. In the field of medical care it can be argued that most people would rather pay today's prices for today's medical care than yesterday's prices for yesterday's medical care. The fact that diseases were treated more cheaply in yesterday's world is more than offset by the increased knowledge and new drugs available for curing disease today. Although it is difficult to measure improvement in the *quality* of medicine in quantitative terms, there is no justification for ignoring it — which is what our present method of computing price indexes does.

The problem of measuring changes in quality also arises in the commodity components of the Consumer Price Index. In the Congressional hearings on government price statistics conducted early this year, Prof. Zvi Griliches of the University of Chicago reported on the effect that changes in specifications had upon automobile prices. Dr. Griliches computed the value of specifications such as size, automatic transmission, horsepower, etc., by taking the price differences for a given year among cars with these varying specifications. Automobile prices were then adjusted to take into account the different features included as standard equipment in each year.

On this basis, using the value of specifications given by the 1954 price schedule, the prices of the "low-priced three" dropped 27 per cent from 1954 to 1960, although their unadjusted list price rose 34 per cent, and the Consumer Price Index for these automobiles reported a rise of 11 per cent. The significance of this study is not that the Consumer Price Index for automobiles needs some minor adjustment to reflect the true price situation, but rather that the overemphasis on price change is itself in question. Instead of an 11 per cent price increase over this period, there may have been a price reduction of as much as 27 per cent.

This same kind of analysis could, of course, be applied to other major kinds of consumer durables, such as home laundry equipment, refrigerators and freezers, portable radios, cameras and hi-fi equipment. Almost all of these have shown considerable change in recent years. If the change in *quality* were taken into account the price index for consumer durables would have fallen far more than the three per cent reported.

Ignoring Innovation

The index of consumer prices is purposely designed so that the introduction of new goods or the dropping of old ones will have no effect. Thus the introduction of such things as television, synthetic fibers and plastic products has had no effect upon the index.

But the introduction of new products obviously *does* have an influence upon consumers' standards of living, just as do quality improvements in existing products. It is quite possible to imagine an economic system which obtains its higher standard of living through the introduction of new products which are superior to the old ones they replace. In such a system, the consumer might continuously get more value for his dollar, even though the prices of the old products rose steadily due to rising wage and material costs. Yet conventional price indexes would show this situation as one in which prices are rising and consumers are getting less for their dollars. Although, of course, in our economy not all of the improvement in the standard of living comes about through the substitution of new products for old, it does seem clear that much of it has been achieved in this way, despite the systematic exclusion of this factor from price indexes.

Innovations and new products are not restricted to the durable goods field. They have, for instance, been highly significant in the food industry over the last decade. Meals are much easier to get and the choice available to the housewife is much greater. There will be those who claim that the additional packaging and processing now common is an undesirable element of cost, and that the personal contact between the individual proprietor and the customer has been lost. Conversely, it can be argued that increased attention to packaging not only standardizes the merchandise, but it raises the level of sanitation and grading. In addition, the freedom to examine goods allows the customer to make comparisons before buying in a way that would not have been possible before.

It is, of course, not possible to measure accurately the dimensions of quality and product change. Nevertheless, one can safely suggest that, given the size of the average yearly increase in the Consumer Price Index since Korea, quality and product improvements may well have been much greater, so that we may actually have had declining rather than rising prices.

This does not mean that price indexes are completely invalid. Price indexes are useful in that they can show the relative differences in price behavior over time or between countries. For example, the eight per cent increase in the price index at the beginning of the Korean war indicates that prices were rising more rapidly in this period than at any other time in the decade of the Fifties.

In periods of hyperinflation, such as have been experienced by some Latin American countries in recent years, where the price index may rise by as much as 80 per cent in a single year, the indexes give a good indication of what is happening since such large increases cannot be offset by quality change. It is only in periods when price changes are relatively small that it becomes a serious error to use the indexes as an exact measure of what is taking place in the economy. In such periods the systematic biases of the price index may well be greater than the reported price change.

Government and Producers' Goods

The defects of the Consumer Price Index are also inherent in the other price indexes which are used to deflate the gross national product to measure the change in real output. Two major categories of goods are produced by the economy besides consumer goods. These are goods and services purchased by the government, ranging from school teaching to missiles, and plant and equipment purchased by producers for use in later production. To measure the quantity of output in these categories, we need price indexes to calculate it in noninflationary terms.

In measuring the output of government, it is assumed — as it is throughout the service sector — that the productivity of civil servants never changes. The price indexes for this area are merely based on the changes in pay of government employees. While one may be tempted to agree with this evaluation of civil servants, the fact is that the introduction of computers, office machines and other automatic equipment has greatly increased the effectiveness of the individual worker. For example, the 1960 census data were processed by microfilming the original schedules and automatically producing magnetic tape for the electronic computers. Automatic equipment performed jobs which took thousands of clerks in previous censuses. Not only was the payroll reduced, but far more information was made available in a much shorter space of time. Output per census employee thus rose very considerably.

Similar examples of the increased output of government employees can be cited at the local level. For example, policemen have been provided with radio-equipped patrol cars and, more recently, transistorized walkie-talkies. Street cleaners have been given mechanized equipment. In some areas — education, for instance — progress is more difficult to measure. Yet most of us would be unwilling to have our children given the same education as we received, especially in the areas of sciences and mathematics.

In producers' durable equipment, once again, the price indexes leave out quality change and new products. But there are probably very few industries in which producers in 1960 would have been willing to buy 1950 models of machines even if they could get them at the 1950 prices. According to the Wholesale Price Index, the 1960 price of producers' durable equipment was 23 per cent above the 1950 price; if producers' durable equipment showed as much quality change as was shown in the study referred to above for automobiles, it seems probable that in fact prices actually fell.

For construction, both industrial and residential, the index is computed on the basis of wage rates and material costs. Thus again it is assumed that productivity does not change. While the construction industry is notorious for its lack of progressiveness, if we consider the new methods of off-the-site fabrication of components it is obvious that this assumption is not entirely valid. Once again, it seems that price indexes have greatly exaggerated the actual price rise.

Thus, we see that for almost every category of goods, whether purchased by consumers for household consumption, by government for public services or by producers for plant and equipment, the conventional price indexes do not reflect the effects of the introduction of new products and the improvement of existing products, or the increased productivity of those performing services. These omissions mean that the price indexes are higher than they should be. And since the indexes are used to deflate the value of current output and calculate its worth in noninflationary terms, our rate of growth is thus considerably understated.

A half-century ago many more industries were producing the kind of output that could be measured quite satisfactorily in quantity terms. Today new major industries such as electronics, chemicals, machinery and household appliances account for an increasingly important share of our output. In all these industries the changes in prices and output are very difficult to measure, since the nature of the products is continually changing. It may mean, therefore, that the national concern over a sagging economic growth rate is really not warranted. The problem may be our inability to measure growth represented by product changes and increased productivity in the service industries. The inadequacy of the price indexes will become even more glaring in the years ahead.

Implications

It is interesting to speculate on what will happen to our measurement of output when further growth does not take the form of additional consumption of identical items, but rather of the consumption of goods of improved quality, the substitution of new products for old and the consumption of higher quality services. In such a world, our conventional price indexes would fail to catch the quality improvement; they would not recognize that the substitution of new products for old was any increase in the standard of living; and they would report the continued increase in the use of services solely in terms of the rates of remuneration. Thus they might show an economy with constant output and rising prices, even though the standard of living was increasing rapidly. What is perhaps more serious, the conventional price and output indexes would fail completely to distinguish between a dynamic economy and one that was truly stagnant.

At the quiver of a decimal point in the Consumer Price Index, the government has instituted restrictive monetary and fiscal policies. Its objective has been to restrain demand so that producers would find themselves with excess capacity and thus would not raise prices; and labor unions would be deterred by the existence of unemployment from seeking wage increases. The economy has been either in a depressed state or under restraining monetary and fiscal policies throughout almost the entire period since Korea. It is small wonder that in such an environment the rate of investment is low. In an economy where a false fear of inflation continually holds demand in check, even a low level of investment creates capacity which cannot be fully utilized.

With this in mind, it is appropriate to inquire what a faster rate of growth and better utilization of our capacity would do to our price indexes. Historically, if we look at any period of upward change in the general level of activity, we find that the price indexes rise. Thus, for example, in the recovery from the depression of the 1930s, prices in certain sectors responded sharply to the increase in demand. Farm prices rose by about 85 per cent in the five years from 1932 to 1937. Even in the metals industry, prices went up about 30 per cent. At the same time, unemployment dropped from 25 per cent to about 14 per cent. It cannot very well be argued that these price rises were the result of excess demand pressing on fully employed resources.

In other words, growth and the increase in real income tend to produce price increases in certain sectors irrespective of the pressure on resources.

The Council of Economic Advisers has estimated that in early 1961 the economy was operating at a level some 10 per cent below full capacity. The figure seems far too conservative when one takes into account the additional man-hours available and their relation to potential output. If past performance is a guide, it would not seem unreasonable to suppose that the 10 or 12 per cent additional man-hours which were available in the spring of 1961 could have been utilized to produce 25 per cent more output. This seems all the more likely since, by late summer of 1961, output had risen by about five per cent and unemployment had not fallen at all.

It is true, of course, that an increase in real output of 25 per cent, even though it created no pressure on resources, would cause our price indexes to rise. Under present anti-inflation policy we would then move quickly to prevent such real output increases from occurring. In fact, that is exactly what we are doing, even though the increase in real output has been far less than this. The price indexes have quivered, and there is talk of putting the brakes on.

The loss in potential output may not seem to be very impressive when expressed in percentage of total output, but, in fact, we waste through underutilization an amount equal in size to two or three times what we now spend on defense, or 20 to 25 times as much as we now are giving in foreign aid. These wasted resources could rebuild our cities and automate our factories within a few short years; they could raise our rate of growth to equal or surpass that of any other nation.

This then is the cost of taking our price indexes too seriously. We inhibit real growth, because growth by its very nature must lead to increases in the price indexes. And because this inhibited growth in output does not keep up with the growth in our capacity to produce, we have ever-present excess capacity. The excess in machines is self-limiting; producers soon learn when investment is unprofitable. But the excess in manpower is harder to dispose of — the unemployed are there, and you can't really make the problem go away by saying that they don't exist.

Romantically Speaking*

LEONARD S. SILK
Business Week Magazine

Economics has its jargon, but so does bookkeeping, dramatics, auto mechanics, or baseball. A technical vocabulary is a necessary and precise short cut to convenient communication within the confines of a given area of subject matter. Usually, it has little utility outside its own professional backyard. In the following little spoof, though, economic terminology finds a new use.

He: Darling, the gross national product is still climbing and we are nearing the cyclical peak of the family-formation curve.
She: So what?
He: Well, I thought possibly we, too, ought to constitute a household unit.
She: And what'll we use for personal disposable income?
He: Well, I have been thinking of entering the labor force, because automation will probably create more jobs than it destroys.
She: That may be, but I must warn you that I have an awful marginal propensity to consume.
He: Angel! Another thing we hold in common! But my annual increases in productivity are bound to keep the rate of growth of our consumption sustainable.

* As told to Bennett Cerf, "Trade Winds," *Saturday Review,* December 3, 1955, p. 9. Reproduced with permission.

She: And reduce inflationary pressures, other conditions remaining the same.

He: Yes, you do see. There really are no significant disincentives.

She: But are you sure I am the one?

He: Well, I've tried a random sample and you were modal.

She: . . . Sweet.

He: You're all the future I ever extrapolated for. Say you will!

She: But I never made a long-run projection.

He: We could have the dearest little dwelling unit.

She: I don't know. . . . Do you think we should form a farm or a non-farm household?

He: Non-farm, definitely. At the same time I believe in outmigration from the high-density urban area.

She: So do I. I have my heart set on a single-family dwelling in a one-class neighborhood.

He: What sort of a fertility pattern do you think we should have?

She: Well, as you know, I've always thought of myself as an average sort of girl. I'd like 1.87 children — if I said yes, of course.

He: Then say it!

She: The Federal Reserve Index of production has topped 1.40, at that.

He: And it would make the Census Bureau so happy.

She: Well, I probably will.

• 50

The Dependence Effect*

John Kenneth Galbraith
Harvard University

It is customary to view economics in terms of the allocation of scarce resources to the production of goods to satisfy human wants. But what if these very wants are created by the process of production itself? What if our desires are not established independently, but are rather dependent upon the preferences of other consumers and the sales promotion activities of producers? Under these conditions, producing in order to satisfy consumer wants may be somewhat akin to the meaningless perambulations of a squirrel in a wheel.

Real and Contrived Wants

The notion that wants do not become less urgent the more amply the individual is supplied is broadly repugnant to common sense. Yet who can say for sure that the deprivation which afflicts him with hunger is more painful than the deprivation which afflicts him with envy of his neighbor's car? In the time that has passed since he was poor his soul may have become subject to a new and deeper searing. Thus the scholar

* Taken and adapted from *The Affluent Society* (Boston: Houghton Mifflin Company, 1958), pp. 152–156, 158. Reproduced with permission.

334

who wishes to believe that with increasing affluence there is no reduction in the urgency of desires and goods is not without points for debate.

However, there is a flaw in the case. If the individual's wants are to be urgent they must be original with himself. They cannot be urgent if they must be contrived for him. And above all they must not be contrived by the process of production by which they are satisfied. For this means that the whole case for the urgency of production, based on the urgency of wants, falls to the ground. One cannot defend production as satisfying wants if that production creates the wants.

Were it so that a man on arising each morning was assailed by demons which instilled in him a passion sometimes for silk shirts, sometimes for kitchenware, sometimes for chamber pots, and sometimes for orange squash, there would be every reason to applaud the effort to find the goods, however odd, that quenched this flame. But should it be that his passion was the result of his first having cultivated the demons, and should it also be that his effort to allay it stirred the demons to ever greater and greater effort, there would be question as to how rational was his solution. Unless restrained by conventional attitudes, he might wonder if the solution lay with more goods or fewer demons.

So it is that if production creates the wants it seeks to satisfy, or if the wants emerge *pari passu* with the production, then the urgency of the wants can no longer be used to defend the urgency of production. Production only fills a void that it has itself created.

The point is so central that it must be pressed. Consumer wants can have bizarre, frivolous, or even immoral origins, and an admirable case can still be made for a society that seeks to satisfy them. But the case cannot stand if it is the process of satisfying wants that creates the wants. For then the individual who urges the importance of production to satisfy these wants is precisely in the position of the onlooker who applauds the efforts of the squirrel to keep abreast of the wheel that is propelled by his own efforts. Among the many models of the good society no one has urged the squirrel wheel.

That wants are, in fact, the fruit of production will now be denied by few serious scholars. Emulation has always played a considerable role in the views of economists of want creation. One man's consumption becomes his neighbor's wish. The more wants that are satisfied the more new ones are born. The implications of this are impressive. The notion of independently established need now sinks into the background. Because the society sets great store by ability to produce a high living standard, it evaluates people by the products they possess. The urge to consume is fathered by the value system which emphasizes the ability of the society to produce. The more that is produced the more that must be owned in order to maintain the appropriate prestige.

Advertising and Want Creation

A direct link between production and wants is provided by the institutions of modern advertising and salesmanship. These cannot be reconciled with the notion of independently determined desires, for their central function is to create desires — to bring into being wants that previously did not exist. This is accomplished by the producer of the goods at his behest. A broad empirical relationship exists between what is spent on production of consumers' goods and what is spent in synthesizing the desires for that production. A new consumer product must be introduced with a suitable advertising campaign to arouse an interest in it. The path for an expansion of output must be paved by a suitable expansion in the advertising budget. Outlays for the manufacturing of a product are not more important in the strategy of modern business enterprise than outlays for the manufacturing of demand for the product. None of this is novel. All would be regarded as elementary by the most retarded student in the nation's most primitive school of business administration. The cost of this want formation is formidable. In 1956 total advertising expenditure — though not all of it may be assigned to the synthesis of wants — amounted to about ten billion dollars. For some years it has been increasing at a rate in excess of a billion dollars a year. Obviously, such outlays must be integrated with the theory of consumer demand. They are too big to be ignored.

But such integration means recognizing that wants are dependent on production. It accords to the producer the function both of making the goods and of making the desires for them. It recognizes that production, not only passively through emulation, but actively through advertising and related activities, creates the wants it seeks to satisfy.

The fact that wants can be synthesized by advertising, catalyzed by salesmanship, and shaped by the discreet manipulations of the persuaders shows that they are not very urgent. A man who is hungry need never be told of his need for food. If he is inspired by his appetite, he is immune to the influence of Mssrs. Batten, Barton, Durstine & Osborn. The latter are effective only with those who are so far removed from physical want that they do not already know what they want. In this state alone men are open to persuasion.

The Effect of Increasing Wealth

The general conclusion is that as a society becomes increasingly affluent, wants are increasingly created by the process by which they are satisfied. This may operate passively. Increases in consumption, the counterpart of increases in production, act by suggestion or emulation to create wants. Or producers may proceed actively to create wants through advertising and salesmanship. Wants thus come to depend on output. In technical terms it can no longer be assumed that welfare is greater at an all-round higher level of production than at a lower one. It may be the same. The higher level of production has, merely, a higher level of want creation necessitating a higher level of want satisfaction. This process may be called the Dependence Effect.

• *51*

Behind Market Demand: The Dynamics
of Style Change*

DWIGHT E. ROBINSON
University of Washington

*Prices, technological innovation, personal income, and savings
preferences are the variables most frequently mentioned by
economists in accounting for market demand. In this article, we
take an excursion off these well-trodden paths to explore the ways
that style and taste express their powerful and capricious influence upon ultimate consumer appeal in the marketplace.*

The Meaning of Fashion

The behavioral complex underlying all stylistic innovation — by this I
mean all changes in design which are not purely the results of engineering advances — can conveniently be summed up under the single word
fashion. And fashion, defined in its most general sense, is the pursuit of
novelty for its own sake. Every market into which the consumer's fashion
sense has insinuated itself is, by that very token, subject to this common,
compelling need for unceasing change in the styling of its goods.

The reason for this is that the stimuli of fashion derive solely from the
comparisons that consumers draw between new designs and the old

* Taken and adapted from Dwight E. Robinson "Fashion Theory and Product
Design," *Harvard Business Review*, December 1958, pp. 126–138. Reproduced with
permission.

designs they replace. No single style of design, no matter how brilliantly it is conceived, can claim any independent fashion significance at all, nor can it possess more than a fugitive lease on life.

Rule of Excess

Paul Poiret, the top Paris couturier of the 1920's, once summed up his credo by declaring, "All fashions end in excess" — a principle which is the beginning of wisdom for all who are concerned with style policy. He was aware that the overriding responsibility of the designer in a fashion market is the unending provision of novelty. Implicitly he recognized that one of the most exacting problems the stylist ever faces is that of deciding what to do when he has exhausted the possibilities of a current direction in styling emphasis.

Poiret knew that the appetite for novelty, arising from the twofold insistence of the lady of fashion on preserving her inimitability from the onslaught of the vulgar and on demonstrating her affluence through unrelenting expenditure on newly cut costumes, is never satisfied with any one mode of presenting the figure.

Whether, at a given time, the particular form of emphasis is toward padding out or constricting, toward concealment or exposure, once such a movement is launched it must be intensified each season, ensuring that the ultrafashionable will be able to disport themselves in more of a good thing than their less-favored contemporaries.

Corollary of Reversal

The most important corollary of Poiret's axiom is this: a fashion can never retreat gradually and in good order. Like a dictator it must always expand its aggressions — or collapse. Old fashions never just fade away; they die suddenly and arbitrarily.

The reason for this is simple and logically inescapable. The one thing fashion cannot stand is to repeat the recently outmoded style, the *passé*. Better for the lady of fashion to look like a freak than to be mistaken for her grocer's wife dolled up in a cheap version of something she herself sported a year or two ago.

Classic Compromise

What lies behind these swift and extreme changes? If functional criteria could be more precisely defined, the game of fashion change might be interpreted as a series of departures from, and returns to, the norm of function. Unfortunately, this is not the case.

The designer has learned that the usefulness of a garment — together with all the functional criteria surrounding utility — is a consideration of only incidental relevance to his purposes. Naturally, he is more than willing to play up the merits of a new design by claiming that it permits greater freedom of movement, better accentuates the feminine figure, or is more suitable to modern living. But he does this with tongue in cheek. He is only too aware that, judging by results, the aims of feminine coquetry have been as well served by the dress designs of one era as by those of another.

Fashion is concerned only with appearances, with decoration. While decoration must always to some extent adapt itself to the function of the article it embellishes, it is still very much an end in itself. It is in this respect that the problems involved in styling changes are essentially the same from industry to industry.

The American Home

A look at the home and its decoration will illustrate my thesis.

Fashion's Parallels

As far as the study of style changes is concerned, the differences between architectural trends and fashion trends should not be overestimated. Surprising as it may seem, the long-term, society-wide swings between the two extreme poles of elaboration and ornamentation, on the one hand, and simplicity and functionalism, on the other, dominate the exterior and interior decoration of the home just as powerfully and unfailingly as they do costume. Despite the pronounced differences in durability between the two media, the timing of these swings in each case is almost exactly parallel.

True, fashions in dress, which can be discarded so readily, do exhibit a much greater frequency of short-term excursions and alarms, but there the difference ends.

Perhaps this over-all parallelism is not so surprising after all. As psychologists have pointed out, the symbolism inherent in the house and its furnishings is only one degree less intimate and personal than that of dress itself. It is hard to imagine that when people's tastes in architecture are bent on either simplicity or elaboration, they should adhere to the opposite of one or the other in their clothing. But the most telling consideration of all is that it appears to be the workings of the human memory rather than comparative durabilities of goods which determine the major fashion rhythm. After two generations have passed, few people will remember a once-popular but long-outmoded style. By that time, basic design features reminiscent of the old style can be reintroduced as if they were fresh and novel.

Succeeding Styles

What is more, we find that the reactions in taste which follow the excesses of either extreme tend to be almost as sharp and drastic in architecture and furnishings as in dress. The only difference is that, naturally enough, it takes a longer time to translate these taste changes into action — which is to say production — where the household is concerned.

Only a century ago John Ruskin declared: "Ornamentation is the principal part of architecture." That dictum sounds well-nigh incredible to those of us brought up in the ascendancy of Frank Lloyd Wright, Gropius, Le Corbusier, and their functionalist followers. Yet thus did the acknowledged mentor of the most edified taste of his day herald the late-Victorian gingerbread.

However, it was only 40 years later, in 1892, that Louis Sullivan, the first American exponent of modernism, was writing that "ornament is mentally a luxury, not a necessary," and that "it would be greatly for our esthetic good, if we should refrain entirely from the use of ornament for a period of years, in order that our thought might concentrate acutely upon the production of buildings well formed and comely in the nude."

Yet the functional school is already meeting its Waterloo in the monotony it has imposed on urban building and even on interior decoration.

In his valuable book, *The Tastemakers*, Russell Lynes concludes with no hesitation that as far as domestic architecture is concerned, the flat-roofed, cubistic, and glass-walled house has been almost totally superseded by something quite different, which, for want of a better name, he calls the "ranch house." Indeed, it appears quite evident that Le Corbusier's modernistic concept, "the machine for living," though a few examples of it are still being built, is itself rapidly becoming outmoded.

The contemporary American house is the suburban house. What are the central tendencies of the contemporary suburban house? What have been its origins, and what is its future?

The fundamental feature appears to be "one-level living." This is accompanied by picture windows, a gently sloping, peaked roof, and rather muted reference to one or more of the styles of the architectural past — which the eclectic school of architects used to copy so literally in the 1920's.

Are fresh reactions against the simplified rambler in the making? Prediction, of course, does not follow automatically from analysis, largely because fashion may desert any particular variation for another. For example, the public and its architects may decide to leave the dimensions of the house as they are and concentrate rather on the introduction of new building materials, new colors, and the like. We can only suggest that after more than a half-century the trends toward architectural nudity and toward lowness have nearly reached the end of the road.

As early as 1954, in fact, home-building journals were beginning to report that in certain of the most populous areas of the country the "split-level" house (defined as a dwelling "with at least three separate levels, two of which are located one above the other, and all of which are one-half level apart in elevation") was actually outselling ranch types four to one. This halfway, yet decisive, return to verticality and a more "impressive" look is precisely what this analysis would lead us to expect.

About Face Detroit?

How does our theory of fashion leadership apply to automobile styling? The present turbulent state of affairs in the automobile market gives every indication that Poiret's nemesis of excess is once again in the process of making itself felt with decisive impact. This impact is portentous of great change for the shape and dimensions of the car body.

The Long, Low Look

Automotive stylists are thoroughly aware that the dynamics of styling in their industry correspond closely with the experience of other industries. William M. Schmidt, executive stylist of the Chrysler Corporation, states:

> "The low silhouette is the most important and universal key to contemporary design. Low, ranch-type houses are in demand. Low, modern furniture is handsome, comfortable, and popular. More and more household appliances are being designed with the low look in mind. Modern office buildings, hotels, shopping centers, and civic and cultural centers are designed for the eye appeal of low parallel lines. To fit into its surroundings gracefully, the automobile also must have a contemporary appearance."

What should Detroit do now? If it cannot go much farther forward, should it gradually retrace its footsteps? I think not. Having utilized gradual compression and lengthwise expansion of the body as a means of differentiating new-model cars from old for so many years, it would be entirely self-defeating for the industry to start building them a few inches shorter or higher. The reason? This would be tantamount to repeating the dimensional style characteristics of 1957 or 1958. The new cars would then be duplicates of silhouettes already cluttering up the used car lot, the last place Detroit wants to wind up.

Invasion From Europe

It is all too easy to misinterpret the significance that the soaring popularity of foreign cars holds as an index of shifts taking place in the tastes of the car-buying public. The unlikelihood that the representative American family will ever be satisfied with a really small car is not so much a question for the style analyst as a matter of cold reason.

If the popularity of the imported car is a meaningful symptom of where domestic fashions are tending we must recognize that the American motorist is looking for a change and is seeking it through the dual approaches of functional experiment and antiquarianism in much the same way he has been doing in residential architecture and in furniture.

Drastic Changes

Summing up, the force of fashion's fundamental reactions between the extremes of simplicity and elaboration or horizontality and verticality are suggestive of basic shifts in the design of the American car. The unsuitability of gradual reverses in fashion trends suggests that when these shifts set in, they are bound to be sharp and decisive. We are moving toward ornamentation and stateliness and probably veering toward the upright look once more. Finally, if the lessons of experience in the styling changes of other products are to be repeated, the transformation which lies ahead will be implemented both by a wave of functional innovation and by a revival movement.

Conclusion

I have sought to point out that fashion — the impulse underlying the dynamics of style — is both a less mystifying and a more profound force in social behavior than is commonly supposed.

Of course, I do not intend to put forward a formula or nostrum for the automatic prediction of style trends. History does not repeat itself any more neatly and prettily in styles than it does in any other sphere. My objective has been only to present a systematic exposition of a few of the insights that have long been the guideposts of fashion's most adept practitioners.

Nobody's crystal ball can show up the fashion future in complete detail. But this much is certain: Fashion is absolutely and callously indifferent to any monumental achievements in manufacturing proficiency. She, and not the so-called fashion dictator is the true autocrat; and only in a totalitarian state, where the consumer's taste is legislated by government edict, does she meet her match.

• *52*

The Distribution of Income: National Trends and International Comparisons*

ROBERT M. SOLOW
Massachusetts Institute of Technology

Given the size of the pie, Lucy can get more only if Charlie Brown gets less. Even if the size of the pie increases, Lucy can get a larger share only if Charlie's share diminishes. This selection identifies some of the broad trends, nationally and internationally, in "who gets what" that have taken place in recent decades. To our and the author's regret, the statistics cannot be pushed back much beyond the present generation. Even so, there have been some noteworthy changes both in the source of incomes (labor and property) and in the size of incomes (rich and poor).

* "The Distribution of Income: National Trends and International Comparisons" by Robert M. Solow, from POSTWAR ECONOMIC TRENDS IN THE UNITED STATES, edited by Ralph E. Freeman. Copyright © 1960 by the Massachusetts Institute of Technology. Reprinted with the permission of Harper & Row, Publishers, Incorporated.

Our categories of income do not correspond exactly to the distinction we would like to draw in theory. One thinks first of the large rent component in the earnings of highly skilled people. The profits of unincorporated businesses are also compounded of a mixture of property income and the services earnings of the owners, and we have little but conjecture to help us separate the two. No less inconvenient is the fact that our tax system has in recent years provided a powerful inducement to transform what is "really" one kind of income into what is nominally something else. Executive salaries are converted into capital gains on common stock shares and deferred pay. In closely held corporations it often pays to convert profits into salary and escape corporate income taxes. The reverse operation may also be profitable. And above all there is the inducement to convert large incomes of any kind into capital gains and thus escape both high marginal rates and, incidentally, the national accounts. Yet even if the outlines are fuzzy, it is worth surveying the facts of income distribution. The subject is too interesting to pass up.

Postwar Changes in Labor and Property Incomes

What do the figures show about postwar American society? Clearly the market has dispensed a larger share of the goods of the world to labor. The wage-salary share of disposable income has increased fairly steadily from 62 per cent in 1929 to 77 per cent in 1956.

Between 1929 and 1957 the relative share of income from unincorporated business fell by a third, from 17 per cent to 11 per cent. Almost two-thirds of this we have already attributed to labor, to be canceled off against the increase in employees' compensation. The small remainder represents a further decrease in the relative claims of property against the national product. But the sociological importance of this trend is better measured by the full labor-and-property decline, and it may exceed even that. The small independent proprietor who so caught the imagination of Alexis de Tocqueville in the early nineteenth century has dwindled still further in significance in the last thirty years, off the farm as well as on. Enterprise in this sense, it is plain to us all, is no longer an important highway of economic and social mobility. The data show this to have been happening since the turn of the century and perhaps since the Civil War.

Comparisons over long periods are most interesting but necessarily delicate. The Department of Commerce series begins in 1929, which is especially tantalizing since the very beginning of their span is dominated by the Great Depression. As one goes back in time, the basic data become poorer and the definitions are not quite the same. Thus minor fluctuations must not be taken too seriously. But some further conclusions can be drawn. In the first place, since the wage-salary share averaged about 60 per cent in the decade of the twenties, the appearance of increase, with due allowance for the depression, is not voided when the base is extended back beyond 1929. Secondly, since it appears that about 55 per cent of the national income was paid out to employees in the decade 1900–1909, the tendency for this share to increase — to 60 per cent in the twenties and closer to 70 per cent in the last five years — has endured for a full half century.

As against this, the figures do tend to overstate the extent of the swing in favor of labor income. There are three reasons for this. First, the full fifty-year span encompasses a substantial increase in the government's share of economic activity and brings into play a purely statistical bias. Second, account must be taken of the measurable decline in noncorporate entrepreneurial income, which was already substantial during the first quarter of the century. Since something over half of this income is imputable to labor, the effect is to raise the labor share all along the line, but noticeably to diminish the upward gradient. Third, the long-run decline of agricultural income introduces special problems of its own. Money returns in agriculture are and have been lower than those in industry. This is counter-balanced (and partly explained) by the higher purchasing power of agricultural money incomes.

Comparisons across countries are also dubious, but they are too interesting to omit. Table 1 gives some figures for western Europe and the United States.

The biggest danger in interpreting the table is to forget that the share of unincorporated enterprise — especially farms — differs widely from

Table 1. Compensation of Employees as Share in National Income
(In Percentages)

	1938	1949	1955
Austria	—	57.1	58.1
Belgium	45.7	54.6	53.9
Denmark	—	52.9	55.9
Finland	50.4	61.8	61.2
France	52.0	56.0	59.1
Western Germany	55.4	60.8	63.6
Ireland	51.6	49.0	51.6
Italy	40–42	—	48–50
Netherlands	50.7	53.3	54.1
Norway	50.2	54.7	55.4
Sweden	52.0	59.8	62.7
Switzerland	49.2	60.0	58.5
United Kingdom	62.7	71.5	71.1
United States	68.1	72.4	76.3

country to country. In 1955, for instance, it was 31 per cent in France, of which well over a third was agricultural, and 10 per cent in the United Kingdom, of which under a quarter was agricultural. Obviously this may have a substantial effect on the true labor shares. However, inter-temporal comparisons within countries are probably not much affected by this. Every country on the list, with the revealing exception of Ireland, shows wages and salaries taking a larger share of the national income in 1955 than they did before the war. This parallels the American development. There is a difference though. In over half the cases the change was substantially complete by 1949, and in most of the others it was well under way. In the United States, on the contrary, the share in 1937 was the same as in 1949, with the postwar increase coming later. It is possible that the depth of the depression of the thirties in this country muddies all such comparisons.

Fortunately, since unincorporated businesses are about equally unimportant in the United States and the United Kingdom, we may pursue this most interesting comparison. The wage share has moved in approximately the same way in the two countries. In 1938 the labor share was a bit higher in the United States; by 1949 it had increased sharply in the United Kingdom and, if anything, fallen slightly here; and by 1955 a solid increase in the United States had moved the two figures into approximate equality. I think it is the similarity rather than the residual differences that should be stressed. For my present purpose it is more important simply to note that the postwar shift in favor of wages and salaries is common to the two great Western industrial countries (and western Germany as well) and may well be largely independent of direct political action.

Occupational Earnings Differentials

There are two kinds of information which can be brought to bear on the problems of changes in the economic status of occupations and broader occupational groups. One is the extensive literature on occupational wage rates and wage differentials. Another source, which throws more direct light on our problem, is the census data on annual earnings by occupation. The basic fact is that between 1939 and 1951 wage and salary income became more equally distributed among recipients. It seems reasonable to attribute some of the change after 1939 to the reduction in unemployment. Lastly, there was a slight shift in the occupational composition of the labor force. The socially and economically lowest ranked occupations declined most in relative numbers, and the middle occupations gained more than the very top ones. These changes might be expected to contribute to both the over-all increase in the level of annual earnings and to their diminished dispersion.

The pattern of changes since 1950 has been slightly different. Data for 1956 showed a gain in relative numbers for the professional and clerical groups, largely at the expense of the skilled and unskilled manual laborers and occupations connected with sales and agriculture. This probably represents a net upgrading, and probably also a slight further decline in inequality. As between 1940 and 1956, the major changes are the decline in agricultural occupations, the increase in professional, managerial, and clerical employment, and the redistribution within the group of manual workers, with the skilled and semiskilled categories gaining at the expense of unskilled and domestic service workers.

Altogether, then, we have concluded that there has been in recent years a slight shift in favor of labor incomes and against incomes from property; at the same time, the distribution of people among occupations has changed in such a way as to promote equalization. Similar movements have occurred in the earnings of various broad occupational groups and in the distribution of earnings within even narrow occupational groups. To anticipate another conclusion, the distribution of income by size has also become a bit, but only a bit, more equal in the last decade as compared with earlier periods. In view of the close connection between economic status and social status, all this suggests that postwar full employment has brought with it a consistent but slight narrowing of social-class differences. There has been no revolutionary reversal of traditional differentials, but merely a small equalization, in the economic field at least.

Changes in the Size Distribution of Income

When all is said and done, one of the reasons we care about the distribution of income is that we care about the distinction between rich and poor. The sources of inequality — how much is personal ability, whether genetic or environmental; how much is inherited wealth; how much is chance; how much is the tendency of any initial advantage to increase itself; how much is inherent in the social or economic rules of the game — all this is too deep a question to be discussed here. But we can at least sketch the facts of the size distribution of income in the years since the war and compare them with the earlier period and with concurrent developments in Europe.

Table 2 gives the relative distribution of personal income before personal income tax for 1935–1936 and at intervals during and since the war. Certainly, the most striking impression the figures make is to confirm the belief that this is a facet of economic life which changes slowly when it changes at all. Between the beginning and end of the period represented, real GNP increased 2.5 times, prices doubled, the unemployment rate fell from 20 per cent to 2.5 per cent; and against this background the relative

Table 2.   Distribution of Pre-Tax Personal Income by Quintiles and Top 5 Per Cent of Consumer Units, Selected Years.

Quintile	1935–1936	1941	1944	1947	1950	1954	1956	% Change 1935–1936 to 1954
Lowest	4.1	4.1	4.9	5.0	4.8	4.9	5.0	20
Second	9.2	9.5	10.9	11.0	11.0	11.4	11.3	24
Third	14.1	15.3	16.2	16.0	16.2	16.6	16.5	18
Fourth	20.9	22.3	22.2	22.0	22.3	22.4	22.3	7
Highest	51.7	48.8	45.8	46.0	45.7	44.7	44.9	–14
Top 5%	26.5	24.0	20.7	20.9	20.4	20.5	20.1	–19

distribution of income changed by inches. But change it did, and pretty consistently.

This leads to the second conclusion one can draw from Table II — that over two decades there was a distinct movement toward equality. In 1935 the 20 per cent of families with the highest incomes earned more than half of all the income. By 1954 this fraction had fallen by a seventh, and the top 20 per cent of families had a bit less than 45 per cent of the total. For the top 5 per cent of families the decline was even sharper. Their share of the melon diminished by a fifth from 26 per cent to 20 per cent in 1956. Each of the four lower quintiles increased its share of personal income, with the second highest quintile making a relative gain substantially smaller than the others.

A third conclusion is of some importance because it fits in with some observations made earlier. Most of the movement toward equalization was complete by 1947, possibly even by 1944. Since 1947 there has been a slight further tendency for the three middle quintiles to gain at the expense of the top fifth. But this change is small as compared with that distinguishing the prewar period from the postwar period as a whole. The suggestion is that the source of the equalization was the full employment brought about in the first instance by the war and maintained with only minor interruptions since.

So far we have looked at the distribution of income as the market imputes it to individuals and families. The distribution of actual consuming power is of course further modified by taxation before it becomes available to families. It is worth taking a look at the distribution of after-tax disposable income by size, since it is perhaps a better measure of the extent to which the differential availability of goods and services has changed over the years. There are two conventional aspects to the data of Table 3 which require mention. First, capital gains and/or the undistributed net profits of corporations are excluded from the definition of income, with a corresponding apparent worsening of the position of top groups. Secondly, although the effects of personal and corporate income taxes and certain transfer payments are allowed for in the figures, there are other real-income-redistributing activities of governments (such as the provision of recreational facilities and schools) which are excluded.

The table shows about what one would expect. The progressive nature of the federal income tax is reflected by the greater equality of the distribution of post-tax income as against that of pre-tax income. But the difference is slight. And the trend toward equalization, at least over the period 1941–1954, goes at about the same rate whether or not one takes account of income tax.

Table 3.   Distribution of Family Personal Income After Federal Individual
Income Tax Liability, by Quintiles for Consumer Units Ranked by Size
of After-Tax Income, 1941, 1950, 1954, 1956.

Quintiles	1941	1950	1954	1956
Lowest	4.3	5.1	5.3	5.3
Second	9.9	11.4	12.0	11.9
Third	15.9	16.8	17.3	17.1
Fourth	23.0	22.7	22.7	22.7
Highest	46.8	44.0	42.7	43.0
Top 5%	21.7	19.2	18.4	18.0

Comparisons between developments in this country and in a few of the industrial countries of western Europe show that the movement over time has been toward equality; but the movement has been slight. One important difference shows up between European and American experience. In the United Kingdom, the Netherlands, and Sweden, there is some evidence that the process of equalization has continued past the end of the war. In this country, after 1947 only very small changes took place in the pre-tax distribution of income. But in the United Kingdom the share of the top quintile fell by more between 1949 and 1955 than it had between 1938 and 1949. In the Netherlands the whole process seems to have begun after 1946. Sweden started in 1935 with the most unequal distribution of any we have recorded and wound up in 1954 with one of the least unequal. One is tempted to connect this with the fact that, of all the countries represented, real personal income per head increased fastest (between 1938 and 1954) in Sweden.

Contrasting this country with Europe, we started off in the thirties with a slightly less equal distribution of personal income than the United Kingdom, about the same as the Netherlands, and a rather more equal distribution than in Germany or Sweden. By 1954 we had more equal distribution than the Netherlands and western Germany, about the same as the United Kingdom, and a trifle less than Sweden. It appears that in recent years the lowest quintile has had a noticeably smaller share of total income in the United States than in the United Kingdom or in Sweden. Whether this is a consequence of the extent of social security programs, or of demographic facts, or of still other economic and sociological factors would require detailed investigation.

I think it is fair to say that the similarities among the countries surveyed are considerably more striking than the differences. And this is so whether one looks at the picture statistically or in terms of changes over time.

No discussion of income inequality is complete without some mention of the demographic changes which play perhaps the most important role of all in the movement toward equalization. While the average number of persons per family declined over-all between 1935 and 1952, the decline was far larger in the lowest quintile of the income distribution than elsewhere, so that even a constant degree of inequality on a family basis would be converted into an equalization on the per capita basis that is most significant for economic welfare. The rich may be getting richer, but it is no longer so true that the poor have such disproportionately large families.

The Cash Value of Education*

HERMAN P. MILLER
Bureau of the Census

In the crassest terms, investment in education "pays off," personally as well as socially. The "persistent intrusion of brain power" into the upper income brackets, noted in the following selection, underscores the effects of education upon the distribution of income.

The Big Change in the American Rich

Work is the rule for the American rich. In 1960, only one family out of a hundred in the top 5 percent (those making $15,000 or more a year) lived entirely on unearned income — interest, dividends, rents, royalties, and the like. Only three out of every hundred families in the top 1 percent (those making $25,000 or more a year) lived entirely on unearned income. The great majority of families in the top 5 percent income group are there because they are headed by a man whose skills are much in demand and who therefore has high earning potential.

The most distinctive feature about the top 5 percent is the kind of work they do. The big change in this group is the persistent intrusion of brain power. The small businessman and the farmer have given way to the engineer, scientist, college professor, plant manager, and others who deal primarily with ideas, not things.

* *Rich Man, Poor Man* by Herman P. Miller. Copyright © 1964 by Thomas Y. Crowell Company, New York, publishers.

In 1950, the dominant group within the top 5 percent were the self-employed. They accounted for over two-fifths of the total. By 1960, the importance of this group was greatly reduced, to only one-fourth. In contrast, salaried managerial and professional workers, who essentially represent "brain power," rose considerably, from 28 percent in 1950 to nearly 50 percent in 1960. Small business has been taken over by the big corporation; but the change does not end there. The corporation executive today is often more than just an administrator. He must also be qualified to handle complex technical problems. Many of the people who are now called managers or officials are in reality scientists or engineers. Automation, computers, research — these all require skill and brains which are great in demand and short in supply. That is the simple explanation behind the rapid growth in brain power within the top income groups.

The Cash Value of Education

Every study of the relation between earnings and education shows that the more highly educated the man, the greater his earnings.

Perhaps it is regrettable to stress the value of education in such crass terms. The main reason for focusing on the economic advantages is a simple one. At present, they are the only ones that can be measured even approximately. But there is at least one more reason for stressing the pay-off from education — to convince our poor, whose children are badly in need of schooling, that it may be a way out of their present dilemma.

In every year for which data are shown the completion of an additional level of schooling was associated with higher average incomes. In 1959, elementary school graduates made $3,800, high school graduates made $5,600, and college graduates made $9,200. In that one year the difference between the incomes of the average high school and the average college graduate was considerably greater than the cost of a year of college. This finding parallels that obtained in numerous other studies dating back to the early part of this century.

Although the income levels have changed considerably during the past twenty years, the basic relationship between the extent of schooling and income appears to have remained much the same.

Schooling Pays—Even for a Bricklayer

Everyone knows that it pays to go to college. But does schooling pay off if you are only going to be a carpenter, a plumber, or a bus driver? Definitely. The figures show that in many occupations the high school diploma is worth about $1,000 a year — roughly $40,000 over a working lifetime.

Why the difference? There are many reasons. High school graduates have higher IQ's. This is partly due to their greater education. It may also reflect greater native intelligence and aptitude to learn. But there are other reasons.

Employers give preference to high school graduates. With a diploma you can drive a bus for a transcontinental bus company; without it, you're lucky to get a job with the Podunk Transit Company. Unions also prefer high school graduates. Increasingly, the diploma is becoming a prerequisite to qualify for apprentice training. The reasons are varied, but the facts are clear. Education pays off.

Lifetime Earnings

Estimates of lifetime earnings provide better measures of financial returns associated with education than annual earnings. On the basis of conditions in 1959, an elementary school graduate could expect to earn during his lifetime about $41,000 more, on the average, than the person who quit before completing the eighth grade. This large difference cannot be entirely due to the completion of several additional years of elementary school. You just don't learn that much in grade school. The chances are that failure to complete elementary school is, by and large, symptomatic of other traits that lead to low productivity and low income. Here again caution must be exercised lest the figures be misunderstood, for there are exceptions.

The difference between the expected lifetime earnings of the average elementary school and high school graduate is equally striking. In 1959, the average elementary school graduate could expect lifetime earnings of about $184,000 as compared with about $247,000 for the average high school graduate — a difference of $63,000.

The difference in average income between high school and college graduates in one year is more than enough to pay for the cost of a year in college. So you can well imagine that the difference in income over a lifetime will be enormous. A college degree is required for many, if not most, high-paying jobs. And the greatest gains associated with additional schooling appear at the college level. In 1959, a college graduate could expect to earn about $417,000 during his lifetime as compared with $247,000 for the average high school graduate. During his lifetime, the average college graduate earns about $38,000 *extra* for each year of college. Even if these earnings are matched against the high cost of college training — a cost generally borne by the parents rather than the children — the rate of return is obviously substantial.

• 54

Techniques for Promoting Equality
in a Capitalist Economy*

A. G. B. FISHER

International Monetary Fund

Throughout history, there have been rich people and poor people. The poor, and their supporters (including, at times, some of the rich), have studied and proposed all sorts of ways to reduce the gap and thus promote greater equality. The following selection compares and appraises two major alternative techniques, "direct" and "radical" respectively, for fostering equality in a private enterprise-capitalist economy.

The causes which have produced the current pattern of income distribution are complex. They may be grouped in two broad classes: those which explain the differences in earnings arising from different kinds of work and those which explain the differences in the amount of property owned by individuals.

The decision to support any particular measure for diminishing inequality cannot of course be made exclusively on one's judgment of its probable efficacy for that purpose alone. Other effects it is certain to have, for example, upon the efficiency of production, and these may be of over-

* Taken and adapted from "Alternative Techniques for Promoting Equality in a Capitalist Society," *American Economic Review, Papers and Proceedings,* May, 1950, pp. 356–368. Reproduced with permission.

whelming importance. In the first instance, however, we may ignore these effects, and concentrate our attention upon the distinction between the two divergent points of view which have in fact determined the character of most recent efforts to diminish inequality.

If our preference favors what I shall later call the "radical" approach, we should begin by examining the causes of inequality, and, having determined which of them can be most easily removed or weakened, we should look about for instruments for this purpose.

The effects produced in the pattern of income distribution by changes which weaken some of the causes of inequality are not likely to be seen at once. Those who are impatient for quick results have therefore often naturally enough preferred a more direct attack upon the income structure as it exists at the time; observing the inequalities which appear as the current "normal" processes of distribution allocate their shares to each unit in the economy, they then attempt to remedy inequality by compulsory direct transfers from those to whom the "normal" processes allocate more than the average to those who are receiving less.

The "Direct" Method

Direct transfers, by way of private charity, have long been practiced in economies at every stage of development and of every conceivable kind of structure and have found respectable support in appeals to both religious and ethical sentiment. Their economic significance has, however, usually been slight and is likely to remain so.

In recent years the redistribution of income through taxation and public expenditure has been much more important than private charity. Sometimes the redistribution has been fairly direct; money has been collected from one set of people and paid out to another; e.g., old age pensioners. Sometimes it has been more indirect, the obligation to pay and the right to benefits financed by the state being shared by everybody, but both being so arranged that, in proportion to their means, the rich pay more than the poor, while at the same time they are also likely to make less use of the facilities and enjoyments which are financed out of taxation.

Such methods accept, at least tacitly, the existing pattern of gross income distribution as a datum. The "normal" economic processes, from which emerges the real national income, are permitted to allocate a certain fraction of the whole to each individual. This original distribution is then corrected by lopping off part of the gross income allocated to certain individuals and handing it over to others. This direct redistribution will have some effects upon production, which in turn will produce some incidental effects upon the pattern of gross distribution. By its very nature, however, redistribution along these lines must be endlessly repeated.

Criticism of this Approach

This method of redistribution now has a lengthy and respectable history, and we are unlikely ever entirely to dispense with it. Redistribution by means of taxation and social services has become a commonplace, to which in principle few will seriously object. The controversies which still rage in this field are usually on questions of degree. There are still many countries where there is a strong case for pressing for more intensive use of this technique. Experience has shown that most economies can stand a great deal more of it than many supposed when the first modest experiments were made. There is always some risk that it may be pushed too far, and in some countries the view has been expressed — and not only by those who are lukewarm toward measures of this kind — that the limits of redistribution by taxation have already been reached. The discouraging effects of high taxation upon production and in particular its effects upon willingness to undertake the risks associated with the more novel types of investment and work may be so serious as to justify restraint.

Moderation in all things is usually a sound working principle. As the average level of taxation rises everywhere, the problem of maintaining incentives for economic activity may become acute, and the risk is increased that the limit may be passed beyond which it is unsafe to raise the level further. The limit is probably flexible, but it is not indefinitely extensible.

The "Radical" Method

It is in any event a little odd that so many people should have a marked preference for the continuous large-scale transfer of income from the relatively wealthy to the relatively poor — motions which can never produce permanent results — and should show little interest in other techniques the results of which would be much more permanent. The alternative approach to the problem which was briefly indicated above is genuinely "radical" in the true sense of that word: it seeks to go to the root of the matter. An anti-inequality policy based upon this approach would work simultaneously along two lines. It would seek to alter permanently the relative scarcities of different types of skill and service, which are the basis of many of the more striking inequalities in income derived from work, and it would also remodel inheritance.

When one kind of work is paid for at higher rates than another, it may usually be assumed that those who are competent to perform the better paid work are, relatively to the demand for their services, scarcer than those who are competent to perform work which is less remunerative.

So far from justifying the conclusion that the pattern of distribution is inexorably fixed, reflection upon the implications of this doctrine should direct our attention to the possibility of remolding the pattern by changing the basic structure of supply and demand upon which it rests. Particularly on the side of supply, the institutional factors which greatly influence the allocation of labor are capable of much more modification than in most countries they have received. There can be little doubt that the most important influence determining the disparities between the normal earnings of men and women are the various obstacles which impede the entry of women into certain occupations. The institutional factors of which this is an obvious illustration are usually closely connected with educational practices, and the most obvious modifications on the supply side are in the field of educational policy.

The Effects of Education

There are no doubt many factors which may be grouped under the heading of "natural forces" which limit the number of people with the intrinsic qualities needed for the more highly paid types of work, and thus create "natural" scarcities, from which in the ordinary course definite and important inequalities would emerge. But upon the effects of these "natural" scarcities there are superimposed the effects of other scarcities, which are not at all natural, arising from the expense and other difficulties involved in the acquisition of many types of skill. The removal of these difficulties might be expected to have far-reaching and permanent effects upon income distribution.

There are, of course, numerous individual exceptions, but the general rule is that the ranks of unskilled labor are recruited from the less educated members of the community and some educational foundations are usually necessary to acquire even an ordinary artisan's standard of skill, and much more any of the skills demanded in still more highly paid occupations. If a change in educational policy makes it easier to gain the qualifications which command higher pay and thus to avoid entry into the ranks of unskilled labor, we may expect the wages of unskilled labor relative to the remunerations paid for other types of work to rise, just as the wages of carpenters or the incomes of medical men would tend to rise if it were made more difficult to become a carpenter or to enter the medical profession.

The immediate effects upon income inequality or even drastic changes in educational practice will seldom be very substantial. For the most part they can affect only new entrants into the labor market; and the number of new entrants into any one occupation at any given time will usually be small in relation to the total supply. Changes in educational policy will increase or diminish their number only slowly. At least a generation must elapse before the full effects of any radical educational reform can be felt.

Even if we had no concern at all with inequality, and were interested exclusively in expanding the volume of production, the same reforms would necessarily occupy an important place in our program. In particular they would make available adequate supplies of key types of labor the scarcity of which often slows down economic progress, and this should be a point of special interest to those for whom employment policy is the dominating concern. The risk that a high general level of effective demand may produce inflationary pressures should be diminished by an educational policy which widens some of the bottlenecks in the customary labor supply. If our efforts to correct income inequality start from this point, it is unlikely, therefore, that at any time we shall feel it necessary to restrain them lest they should impair the progress of production. It is likely rather that the educational reforms most effective for expanding the volume of production will also be the most satisfactory from the standpoint of distribution.

The Problem of Inheritance

The inequalities of income which result from inequalities in the distribution of property are, however, often much more important. Here the institution of inheritance stands out most clearly as something immediately susceptible to treatment. By means of inheritance, old inequalities are perpetuated and new inequalities injected into the situation. In general, and neglecting individual cases, there is no tendency for inequalities based on these foundations to disintegrate with the passage of time, and inheritance taxes seem to have done little more than limit to some slight extent the cumulative general effects of inheritance.

This is not a convenient place in which to examine in detail the complicated and difficult practical problems which arise in any attempt to reform the institution of inheritance. The maintenance of an unlimited right of inheritance is indeed a comparatively modern phenomenon, and it has been subjected to much criticism upon a wide variety of grounds.

Summary

In principle the contrast between the two methods of reducing inequality is obvious enough. In practice the dividing line is less clear. A "radical" approach to inheritance will rely heavily upon taxation, and education is one of the most important of the social services to be financed by taxation. Nevertheless, the distinction between measures which modify the basic structure of income distribution and measures which attempt merely to modify its consequences remains valid.

• 55

The Emergence of an "Under-Class" in America*

GUNNAR MYRDAL

Institute for International Economic Studies, Stockholm University

Americans, it is sometimes said, resent criticism from foreigners, even though they indulge in much self-criticism. The studies of Dr. Gunnar Myrdal, a Swedish economist of world reknown who has spent so much time in the United States that he calls this country one of his two "spiritual fatherlands," seem to enjoy special status, however. His comments here, he has said, are made from the viewpoint of "American ideals of liberty and equality of opportunity."

The Emergence of an "Under-Class"

The facts about unemployment and its immediate causes are well known in America due to its excellent statistical reporting.

* Condensed from CHALLENGE TO AFFLUENCE, by Gunnar Myrdal. © Copyright 1962, 1963 by Gunnar Myrdal. Reprinted by permission of Pantheon Books, a Division of Random House, Inc.

Less often observed and commented upon is the tendency of the changes under way to trap an "under-class"[1] of unemployment and, gradually, unemployable and underemployed persons and families at the bottom of a society, while for the majority of people above that layer the increasingly democratic structure of the educational system creates ever more real liberty and equality of opportunity, at least over the course of two generations.

The American self-image was, and is, that of a free and open society where anyone who is of a sound body and soul and has the drive can find work, at least when business is on the upturn, and where he can climb to the highest and most rewarding positions. It was this image, and the considerable degree of reality that actually corresponded to it, that induced millions of poor people in Europe to seek their opportunity in America right up to the First World War.

Reality never agreed entirely with that image. And over the last few generations a process has been under way that, while it opened more opportunities to more people, also closed ever more opportunities to some. Now in the end it threatens to split off a true "under-class" that is not really an integrated part of the nation but a useless and miserable substratum.

To start at the heights, the "self-made man" with great wealth and a supreme command over men and productive resources has been disappearing in America ever since the time when college education became so common that a man without a degree could hardly advance in business. Business itself has tended to become increasingly large-scale and highly organized. This process was well under way over half a century ago.

But even if the highest economic and social positions were closed to those who started from the bottom, it was still possible to advance and advance far in many occupations, and in practically every field there was an expansion of opportunity for a long time. In addition, there was at least plenty of unskilled work to be done and, when business was good, there was always demand for it. After the end of the Great Depression this was still so in the war years and in the early postwar boom.

We have to remind ourselves, however, that to a considerable extent this American image was always something of a myth. Even leaving out the highest social and economic positions that have now been closed up to those starting without higher education, the opportunity to rise in society, or even to maintain a decent and respectable level of living and to participate in the nation's general culture and the solution of its problems, was not always that open in the old days. Great masses of people

---

[1] The word "under-class" does not seem to be used in English. In America where, as opinion polls over several decades show, the great majority reckon themselves as "middle class," this is particularly understandable on ideological grounds. Nevertheless, the term will be used in this book as the only one adequate to the social reality discussed.

had no possibility of sharing in the American image of liberty and opportunity of rising economically and socially. This applied to the cotton farming Negro tenants in the South, the white hillbillies not far south of Washington, D.C., and similar groups of poor whites elsewhere in the country, the migrant workers on the big California farms, and to the workers in the sweatshops in the cities. Moreover, there were the new immigrants in the city slums, handicapped in many ways, who often suffered miserable hardships before they came into their own.

Finally, in the periodic slowdowns in business activity a large number even of well integrated workers found themselves unemployed and without an income. The series of such reverses culminated in the Great Depression when up to 20 per cent or more of the labor force was unemployed.

Abject destitution for millions of people is thus nothing new in America. The trend has definitely been to decrease the number suffering from it or even running a major risk of it. Major causes of this have been the rising productivity of the American economy and also the facts that educational facilities have been vastly improved and that good schools and college education have been placed at the disposal of an ever increasing portion of the people, earlier and more generously than in any other Western country.

The New Threat

Nevertheless, there is something threatening in the very recent changes and in the trend for the foreseeable future. The displacement of unskilled and even of much skilled labor has a definiteness that must compel us to stop and think.

What is happening is similar to the disappearance more than half a century ago of the "self-made man" from the highest positions as a result of the widening of college education and training for leadership in business as it increasingly became large-scale, organized, and stratified. This process has continued steadily downwards, first to middle positions and then to ever lower strata of employees in industry and commerce, until it is now beginning to make unskilled and many skilled workers redundant.

This is a new threat. For when the process has proceeded that far, without a parallel change for educating and training the *whole* labor force to correspond to the new demands, there is no longer any vast space left beneath for economic advance and social mobility as when the self-made man at the top disappeared. Those not needed are true "outcasts." They simply become unemployed; and indeed largely unemployable, or underemployed. It is almost as difficult for them to get and hold a good job as it long ago became to start as a shoe-shine boy and end as the president of a big corporation.

This emergence of an American "under-class" of unemployed and largely unemployable and underemployed occurs at a time when those educated and trained to fit the new direction of labor demand are experiencing a brisk demand for their work, and when the general levels of living of the majority of well employed Americans — and thereby the general conception spread by the mass-communication industry of what the American way of life is like — have risen high above what a few generations ago were considered comfortable standards. In society at large there is more equality of opportunity today than there ever was. But for the bottom layer there is less or none.

The disappearance of the self-made man was a slight change in society compared to that now under way, closing all good jobs and soon almost all jobs worth having in affluent America to those who have happened to be born in regions, localities, or economic and social strata where education and training for life and work in this new America are not provided as a normal thing. For the larger part of America there is social and economic mobility through the educational system. Beneath that level a line is drawn to an "under-class." That class line becomes demarcated almost as a caste line, since the children in this class tend to become as poorly endowed as their parents.

The fact that the substratum is not very articulate in America and is, therefore, not much noticed by the ordinary, well educated Americans who are busily and happily enjoying both their work and their leisure, does not detract from the gravity of this development. On the contrary, it is fatal for democracy, and not only demoralizing for the individual members of this under-class, that they are so mute and without initiative and that they are not becoming organized to fight for their interests. For its own health and even preservation an effective, full-fledged democracy needs movements of protest on the part of the underprivileged.

A Vicious Circle

The essential question when probing into the social impact of the formation of this under-class is the character of the selective process which determines whether a man comes above or beneath the dividing line. The selection operates on the criterion of education and training. When old people have failed, and young people are now failing, to get an education up to levels which correspond to national standards and the direction of the demand for labor, the explanation is usually that they have been living in an environment of poverty and squalor.

It has become customary to describe the situation in underdeveloped countries as one of a vicious circle where "poverty perpetuates itself."

But the same vicious circle operates in an underprivileged class in the richest country. To begin with, unemployment means loss of income. Particularly for those who become permanently unemployed and for those whose employment is casual and in fields not covered by unemployment compensation, the lost income is total or very substantial.

They will become disheartened and apathetic. As parents they will not be able to pay toward such support of the education of their children that would be needed. Instead, they will have an incentive to take them out of school early if any employment, even at low wages and promising no secure future, offers itself. The home environment of the unemployed and poor will generally be less conducive for children and youth to become educated and trained for good jobs.

The unemployed will be forced to live in the slums or, more probably, they will always have lived in the slums. Whatever the regulations are, the schools will be bad in the slums as they will be in the districts where the backwoods farmer lives. And the whole way of life in the crowded slum quarters in the cities or the rural slum districts will be destructive for the will and ability to advance in life.

A remarkable tendency in America has been that parallel and prior to the rise in unemployment the efforts of slum clearance in the cities have mainly benefited the middle third of the nation who could afford to pay the rents in the new houses which only to a smaller extent have really been "low-cost housing." Those made homeless have been pressed into other already crowded slum districts or into districts which in this process of change became slum districts.

This perverted tendency in American housing policy has its parallel in almost all other social policies. Various social security schemes as well as to an extent the minimum wage regulations happen to stop just above the very neediest groups of people. In the same way agricultural policy has mainly aided the big and progressive farmers and has done little if anything for small farmers, small tenants, and agricultural workers.

There is a political factor in this vicious circle of circular causation leading to a cumulative process. The poor in America are unorganized and largely mute. They exert no pressure corresponding to their numbers and to the severity of their plight. They are the least revolutionary proletariat in the world.

As they represent the big unutilized reserve of potential voters, the platforms of both Democrats and Republicans worked out before every election will regularly seem to imply a radical departure from policies pursued up till then — though most often couched in general and noncommittal terms. When the elections are over, however, and many of the poor are seen to have still stayed away from the polls, actual policies return to the routine of not doing much for them.

Increased Inequality in the Midst of General Equality

It is perfectly possible for the majority of Americans to live, together with practically everybody they have primary contact with, in a situation of full and even overfull employment where there is brisk demand and competition for their labor, while they read in the newspapers that there is large and growing unemployment beneath them. That this can be so is the result of the nature of unemployment being to a large extent structural in character.

While this is happening at the bottom of American society it is perfectly possible that there is ever greater social mobility, liberty, and equality of opportunity and a generally rising economic and cultural level in majority America. More and more individuals and families may move further away from the neighborhood of the dividing line. And there might even be some successful passing of the poverty line by individuals coming from beneath it, which then gives a false assurance that America is still the free and open society of its cherished image and well established ideals.

But as less and less work is required of the type the people in the urban and rural slums can offer, they will be increasingly isolated and exposed to unemployment, to underemployment, and to plain exploitation. There is an ugly smell rising from the basement of the stately American mansion.

Defining *Poverty and Combating It**

PRESIDENT'S COUNCIL OF ECONOMIC ADVISERS

Poverty, like wealth, is a relative matter. Below some approxi-mate point on the income scale, however, human existence is just that. Below minimum income levels, it simply is not possible to experience the material well-being or the opportunities of the American economic way of life. Locating this point, identifying in dispassionate statistical terms the main categories of the American population to whom it applies, and outlining the leading elements in an "overall attack on poverty" is the scope of the following observations.

Measurement of poverty is not simple, either conceptually or in prac-tice. By the poor, we mean those who are not now maintaining a decent standard of living — those whose basic needs exceed their means to satisfy them.

There is no precise way to measure the number of families who do not have the resources to provide minimum satisfaction of their own particu-lar needs. But for our society today a consensus on an approximate standard can be found. Since needs differ from family to family, an at-tempt to quantify the problem must begin with some concept of average need for an average or representative family. On balance, recent studies provide support for using as a boundary a family whose annual money

* Taken and adapted from "The Problem of Poverty in America," *Economic Report of the President together with the Annual Report of the Council of Economic Advisers* (Washington: U.S. Government Printing Office, 1964), pp. 55–73.

income from all sources was $3,000 (before taxes and expressed in 1962 prices). This is a weekly income of less than $60.

A $3,000 annual budget supposes the expenditure of about one-third of the total on food, i.e., for a 4-person family about $5 per person for food per week. Of the remaining $2,000, a conservative estimate for housing (rent or mortgage payments, heat, and other utilities) would be another $800. This would leave only $1,200 — less than $25 a week — for clothing, transportation, school supplies, and books, home furnishings and supplies, medical care, personal care, recreation, insurance, and everything else. Obviously it does not exaggerate the problem of poverty to regard $3,000 as the boundary.

The Changing Extent of Poverty

There were 47 million families in the United States in 1962. Fully 9.3 million, or one-fifth of these families — comprising more than 30 million persons — had total money incomes below $3,000. Over 11 million of these family members were children, one-sixth of our youth. More than 1.1 million families are now raising four or more children on such an income. Moreover, 5.4 million families, containing more than 17 million persons, had total incomes below $2,000. More than a million children were being raised in very large families (six or more children) with incomes of less than $2,000.

Serious poverty also exists among persons living alone or living in nonfamily units such as boarding houses. In 1962, 45 percent of such "unrelated individuals" — 5 million persons — had incomes below $1,500, and 29 percent — or more than 3 million persons — had incomes below $1,000. Thus, by the measures used here, 33 to 35 million Americans were living at or below the boundaries of poverty in 1962 — nearly one-fifth of our Nation.

Substantial progress has been made since World War II in eliminating poverty.

The progress made since World War II has not involved any major change in the distribution of incomes. The one-fifth of families with the highest incomes received an estimated 43 percent of total income in 1947 and 42 percent in 1962. The one-fifth of families with the lowest incomes received 5 percent of the total in 1947 and 5 percent in 1963.

Even if poverty should hereafter decline at the relatively more rapid rate of the 1947–56 period, there would still be 10 percent of the Nation's families in poverty in 1980. And, if the decline in poverty proceeded at the slower rate achieved from 1957 on, 13 percent of our families would still have incomes under $3,000 in 1980. We cannot leave the further wearing away of poverty solely to the general progress of the economy.

The Composition of Today's Poor

Objective evidence indicates that poverty is pervasive. The poor are found among all major groups in the population and in all parts of the country. Yet there are substantial concentrations of poverty among certain groups. For example, families headed by persons 65 years of age and older represent 34 percent of poor families. Moreover, they appear among the poor 2½ times as frequently as they appear among all families. Other categories of families that appear among the poor also more than twice as often as among the total population are: non-white families, families headed by women, families headed by individuals not in the civilian labor force, families with no wage earners, and rural farm families. Of course, some of these groups overlap considerably, but the data help us identify the poor.

The Roots of Poverty

Poverty is the inability to satisfy minimum needs. The poor are those whose resources — their income from all sources, together with their asset holdings — are inadequate.

1. *Earned Income.* Why do some families have low earned incomes? Some are unemployed or partially unemployed. High overall employment is a remedy of first importance, yet it is clear that this is only a partial answer. Even for those able and willing to work, earnings are all too frequently inadequate, and a large number of the poor are unable to work. The incidence of poverty is 76 percent for families with no earners. The incidence rate is 49 percent for families headed by persons who work part time.

The problem of another group of families is the low rates of pay found most commonly in certain occupations. For example, the incidence of poverty among families headed by employed persons is 45 percent for farmers and 74 percent for domestic service workers.

The chief reason for low rates of pay is low productivity, which in turn can reflect lack of education or training, physical or mental disability, or poor motivation. Other reasons include discrimination, low bargaining power, exclusion from minimum wage coverage, or lack of mobility resulting from inadequate knowledge of other opportunities or unwillingness or inability to move away from familiar surroundings.

The importance of education as a factor in poverty is suggested by the fact that families headed by persons with no more than 8 years of education have an incidence rate of 37 percent. Nonwhite and rural families show an even higher incidence of poverty. The heads of these families are typically less well educated than average.

2. *Property Income and Use of Savings.* Some families with inade-

quate current earnings can avoid poverty thanks to past savings, but most families with low earnings are not so fortunate. If avoiding poverty required an income supplement of $1,500 a year for a retired man and his wife, they would need a capital sum at age 65 of about $19,000 to provide such an annuity. Few families have that sum. The median net worth of the fifth of all spending units having the lowest incomes was only $1,000. Most families — including the aged — whose incomes are low in any one year lack significant savings or property because their incomes have always been at poverty levels.

The persistence of poverty is reflected in the large number who have been unable to accumulate savings. The mean amount of savings used by poor families in 1959 was $120; and only 23 percent of the poor drew on savings at all.

3. *Transfer Payments and Private Pensions.* Poverty would be more prevalent and more serious if many families and individuals did not receive transfer payments. In 1960, these payments constituted only 7 percent of total family income, but they comprised 43 percent of the total income of low-income spending units. At the same time, however, only about half of the present poor receive any transfer payments at all. And, of course, many persons who receive transfers through social insurance programs are not poor — often as a result of these benefits.

It is important to distinguish between insurance-type programs and assistance programs, whether public or private. Assistance programs are ordinarily aimed specifically at the poor or the handicapped. Eligibility for their benefits may or may not be based upon current income; but neither eligibility nor the size of benefits typically bears any direct relationship to past income. Eligibility for insurance-type programs, on the other hand, is based on past employment, and benefits on past earnings.

The Federal-State unemployment insurance system covers only about 77 percent of all paid employment and is intended to protect workers with a regular attachment to the labor force against temporary loss of income. Benefits, of course, are related to previous earnings.

While the largest transfer-payment program, OASDI, now covers approximately 90 percent of all paid employment, there are still several million aged persons who retired or whose husbands retired or died before acquiring coverage. Benefits are related to previous earnings, and the average benefit for a retired worker under this program at the end of 1963 was only $77 a month, or $924 a year. The average benefit for a retired worker and his wife if she is eligible for a wife's benefit is $1,565 a year.

Public insurance-type transfer programs have made notable contributions to sustaining the incomes of those whose past earnings have been adequate but they are of least help to those whose earnings have never been adequate. Public assistance programs are an important support to low income and handicapped persons.

Private pensions, providing an annuity, are additional resources for some persons and families. In 1961, the beneficiaries of such plans numbered about 2 million (as against about 12 million receiving OASDI benefits), and total benefits paid were about $2 billion. While the combination of OASDI and private pensions serves to protect some from poverty, most persons receiving OASDI receive no private pension supplement. In any case, benefits under private pension plans range widely, and since they are typically related to the individual's previous earnings, they are low when earnings have been low.

Thus, although many families do indeed receive supplements to earnings in the form of pensions, social insurance benefits, and incomes from past saving, those families with a history of low earnings are also likely to have little of such supplementary income. And since most poor families have small amounts of property, they cannot long meet even minimum needs by depleting their assets.

The Vicious Circle

Poverty breeds poverty. A poor individual or family has a high probability of staying poor.

A Michigan study shows how inadequate education is perpetuated from generation to generation. Of the families identified as poor in that study, 64 percent were headed by a person who had had less than an eighth grade education. Of these, in turn, 67 percent had fathers who had also gone no further than eighth grade in school. Among the children of these poor families who had finished school, 34 percent had not gone beyond the eighth grade; this figure compares with 14 percent for all families. Fewer than 1 in 2 children of poor families had graduated from high school, compared with almost 2 out of 3 for all families.

A study of dropouts in New Haven, Connecticut, showed that 48 percent of children from lower class neighborhoods do not complete high school. The comparable figure for better neighborhoods was 22 percent.

Other studies indicate that unemployment rates are almost twice as high for dropouts as for high school graduates aged 16 to 24. Moreover, average incomes of male high school graduates are 25 percent higher than those of high school dropouts, and nearly 150 percent higher than those of men who completed less than 8 years of schooling.

Recent Changes in the Pattern of Poverty

In spite of tendencies for poverty to breed poverty, a smaller proportion of our adult population has been poor — and a smaller fraction of American children exposed to poverty — in each succeeding generation.

But, at least since World War II, the speed of progress has not been equal for all types of families.

The incidence of poverty has declined substantially. But there are some notable exceptions — families (1) with no earner, (2) with head not in the civilian labor force, (3) with head 65 years of age or older, (4) headed by a woman, and (5) on farms. It is also striking that in these classes, poverty is high as well as stubborn. Poverty continues high also among nonwhites, although there has been a large and welcome decline in this incidence. With the sole exception of the farm group, the total number of *all* families in each of these categories has remained roughly the same or has increased. Hence the high-incidence groups, including the nonwhites, have come to constitute a larger *proportion* of the poor.

Strategy Against Poverty

1. *Maintaining High Employment.* The maintenance of high employment — a labor market in which the demand for workers is strong relative to the supply — is a powerful force for the reduction of poverty. In a strong labor market, there are new and better opportunities for the unemployed, the partially employed, and the low paid. Employers have greater incentive to seek and train workers when their own markets are large and growing. For these reasons, tax reduction is the first requisite of a concerted attack on poverty.

2. *Accelerating Economic Growth.* In the longer run, the advance of standards of living depends on the rate of growth of productivity per capita, and this in turn depends on science and technology, capital accumulation, and investments in human resources. Growth also expands the resources available to governments and private organizations to finance specific programs against poverty.

3. *Fighting Discrimination.* A program to end racial discrimination in America will open additional exits from poverty, and for a group with an incidence of poverty at least twice that for the Nation as a whole. The economic costs of discrimination to the total society are large. By discrimination in employment, the Nation denies itself the output of which the talents and training of the nonwhite population are already capable. But the basic case against discrimination is not economic. It is that discrimination affronts human dignity.

4. *Improving regional economies.* In a dynamic economy, whole regions lose their economic base when their natural resources are depleted or changes in taste and technology pass them by. Appalachia and the cutover areas of the Northern Lakes States are contemporary examples. State and regional programs, assisted by the Federal Government through the Area Redevelopment Administration, seek to restore in such regions a viable economic base suitable to their physical and human resources.

5. *Rehabilitating urban and rural communities.* Overcrowded, unsanitary, and unsafe neighborhoods are a drag on the economic progress of a whole city. Eradication of slums can provide improved opportunities for their residents and enable them to contribute more to the community. Improved relocation programs are essential to avoid pushing the poor from an old slum to a new one. Improved community facilities and services, including day care centers for children of working mothers, are needed in low-income urban areas. Among facilities that are critically needed for slum families are adequate housing, hospitals, parks, libraries, schools, and community centers. Improvement of the physical environment, however, is not enough. Especially when newcomers to urban areas are involved, there need to be programs to facilitate adaptation to the new environments. The Administration's proposed National Service Corps could aid and supplement local efforts to provide these and other urgently needed services.

Parallel programs for rehabilitation are needed in depressed rural areas. In some rural communities, even in whole counties, almost every family is at the poverty level. In such situations local resources cannot possibly provide adequate schools, libraries, and health and community centers. A healthy farm economy is basic to the strength of farm communities. Particular attention must be paid to the special problems of depressed nonfarm rural areas — such as the Ozarks or the larger part of rural Appalachia; of Indians on reservations; and of migrant workers.

6. *Improving labor markets.* Improved employment information can help potential workers learn about and take advantage of new job opportunities, sometimes in different industries, occupations, and locations. A strengthened Federal-State Employment Service, better guidance and counseling services, development of a system for early warning of labor displacement resulting from technological change, assistance in worker relocation (as provided by the Trade Expansion Act and in the recent amendments to the Manpower Development and Training Act), increased amounts and duration of unemployment insurance benefits and extension of its coverage — all these will enable more persons to maintain or increase their earnings.

7. *Expanding educational opportunities.* If children of poor families can be given skills and motivation, they will not become poor adults. Too many young people are today condemned to grossly inadequate schools and instruction. Many communities lack resources for developing adequate schools or attracting teachers of high quality. Other communities concentrate their resources in the higher income areas, providing inadequate educational opportunities to those at the bottom of the economic ladder. Effective education for children of poor families must be tailored to their special needs; and such education is more costly and surely more difficult than for children from homes that are economically and socially

more secure. The school must play a larger role in the development of poor youngsters if they are to have, in fact, "equal opportunity." This often means that schooling must start on a pre-school basis and include a broad range of more intensive services.

8. *Enlarging job opportunities for youth.* Recent legislation for Vocational Education will help to improve the preparation of teen-agers for productive employment. Improved counseling and employment services are needed for those leaving school. The Administration's proposed Youth Employment Act will strengthen on-the-job training and public service employment programs, and will establish a Youth Conservation Corps.

9. *Improving the Nation's health.* The poor receive inadequate medical care, from before birth to old age. And poverty is perpetuated by poor health, malnutrition, and chronic disabilities. New and expanded school health and school lunch programs will improve both health and education.

Legislation has recently been enacted to increase the supply of physicians and dentists, and to expand mental health services. The poor have a special stake in our ongoing programs of medical research. Many aged persons are confronted by medical needs beyond their financial means. Passage of the program to provide hospital insurance for the aged under the social security system is an urgent immediate step.

10. *Promoting adult education and training.* In an economy characterized by continual technological advance, many adults will not be able to earn incomes above the poverty line without new skills and training. The Manpower Training and Development Act and the training programs under the Area Redevelopment Act represent public recognition of this need. These and other programs to train and retrain workers must be expanded and strengthened, placing more emphasis on those with the greatest educational deficiencies. In particular, our relatively modest efforts to provide basic literacy have proved the value of such training.

11. *Assisting the aged and disabled.* Continued long-run improvement of social insurance benefits, along with expanded programs to cover hospital-related costs for the aged, and augmented construction of housing to meet the particular needs of the aged, are necessary steps in a continuing campaign against poverty.

Conquest of poverty is well within our power. About $11 billion a year would bring all poor families up to the $3,000 income level we have taken to be the minimum for a decent life. The majority of the Nation could simply tax themselves enough to provide the necessary income supplements to their less fortunate citizens. The burden — one-fifth of the annual defense budget, less than 2 percent of GNP — would certainly not be intolerable. But this "solution" would leave untouched most of the roots of poverty. Americans want to *earn* the American standard of living by their own efforts and contributions. It will be far better, even if more difficult, to equip and to permit the poor of the Nation to produce and to earn the additional $11 billion, and more. We can surely afford greater generosity in relief of distress. But the major thrust of our campaign must be against causes rather than symptoms. We can afford the cost of that campaign, too.

• 57

The Economic Base and Limits of Social Welfare*

GERHARD COLM

National Planning Association

The problem of poverty occasions a serious look at the relation between the wealth of society and its distribution. Aesop's fable of the goose that laid the golden egg reminds us of the perils of not appreciating the dependence of well-being upon the productive process. The present selection provides a needed examination of our capacity to afford additional programs for social welfare.

The social security legislation of the 1930's was a response to the conditions of the depression, but in a more fundamental way it can be said that the depression broke down traditional resistance to the broad social security legislation which is an essential feature of a modern industrial society.

Since the end of World War II, there has been increasing trust that the Government, with its responsibility under the Employment Act of 1946, is determined and able to combat depressions of the duration and severity of that of the 1930's. However, the rapid technological advances of the last decade have created additional sources of insecurity. Furthermore, the individual needs of workers and their families for more adequate provision for education, health, recreation, employment security,

* Taken and adapted from *Monthly Labor Review*, June 1963, pp. 695-700.

375

and old age have become more widely recognized and more articulated.

Social security and welfare programs expanded in the postwar period on the Federal and on the State and local levels, both in number of beneficiaries and dollars disbursed. The increase remained small, however, in relation to the rise in total production of goods and services.

In the West European countries, a much larger share of total production is allocated to the beneficiaries of government social programs. For a comparison, presented in Table 1, we have selected Sweden, which is

Table 1. Social Security and Welfare Expenditures[1] of Central and Local Governments as Percent of Gross National Product, United States, Germany, and Sweden, Selected Years, 1935–62

Year	United States	Germany (Federal Republic)	Sweden
1935–40	6.5	6.0	. . . .
1950	6.1	12.0	. . . .
1956	5.3	. . . .	10.8
1958	6.7	14.1	11.9
1959	7.0	13.6	12.0
1960	6.9	. . . .	12.2
1961	7.6	12.6	. . . .
1962	7.6	12.7	. . . .

[1] Includes expenditures for social insurance, public aid, health and medical programs, veterans' programs, public housing, and other welfare services (e.g., vocational rehabilitation, school lunch program); excludes expenditures for education. Because of differences in concepts, the comparison is only of approximate validity.

often considered the country most advanced toward the "welfare state," and Germany, which is often considered the nearest approximation to a "free enterprise" country. Actually, the relative size of social security and welfare expenditures is nearly the same in both countries, and in both countries, far higher than in the United States.

The development of social insurance and welfare programs in the United States has certainly not come to an end. There is still a great deal of unfinished business in this respect. It is the purpose of this article to identify some of the considerations which should be taken into account in evaluating the Government's responsibility for workers' security and welfare.

The Economic Requisite

With respect to the past, it would be difficult to prove that the rise in the welfare programs has interfered with high employment and a larger rate of growth. It is more plausible to argue that the welfare programs have introduced an element of stability into our economic system and were one of the factors preventing postwar recessions from developing into depressions. For example, during the 1960–61 recession, personal incomes continued to rise although production declined. That personal incomes and consumer expenditures cushioned the impact of the recession was in part due to the fact that social insurance payments and Government welfare expenditures rose.

With respect to the future, an increase in welfare programs if properly dosed and timed may support economic growth and thereby help to strengthen its own economic basis. If improperly dosed and timed, however, such an increase in welfare programs could interfere with economic growth and thereby become self-defeating. Conversely, in connection with programs in support of economic growth, social security and welfare measures may become feasible which would be oppressive if associated with policies of economic restriction.

It is one question to ask what the economic burden of adequately providing for workers' security would be, assuming that the slow progress in the opening up of job opportunities be continued. It would be another question to ask what the result would be, assuming that through a combination of monetary, fiscal, and related policies a faster rate of growth and a more adequate creation of new job opportunities is achieved. The expansion in security and welfare measures which we can "afford" depends to a large extent on the answers to these questions, namely whether a slower or faster rate of economic growth can be expected for the foreseeable future.

A satisfactory rate of growth would make it possible to reduce unemployment, to open up job opportunities in compensation of laborsaving advances, and to increase social security benefits and welfare programs without a corresponding increase in tax rates. Labor demands for restrictive measures would have less persuasiveness and force.

If we could assume that approximately full use would be made of the potential production of our economy, we could hardly fail to conclude that we could "afford" more adequate provision for the aged, the unemployed (including those who have no skills or whose skills have become obsolete), the disabled, and the sick. In the last decade, we could have produced about $22 billion more each year, on the average, if we had succeeded in keeping unemployment to a reasonable minimum. Assuming that 50 percent of this potential increase in production would have been needed to supply the additional wage earners with more consumer goods (wages being higher than receipts of the unemployed) and to provide for additional expansion and maintenance of plant and equipment which would be needed to achieve the higher rate of growth, this would have made about $11 billion per year available for other public and private purposes. If future production of goods and services should increase each year by, say, 4–4½ percent, this would mean an additional increase of $20–$25 billion. Granting that again a part of this increase would be "preempted" for wages and the expansion and maintenance of productive facilities, welfare programs could nevertheless be expanded by very substantial amounts without any redistribution of incomes. This assumes, of course, that the increase in production is not fully absorbed by other claimants, as for example, a rapidly rising defense program.

The Economic Limits

In an economy growing at a satisfactory rate, a substantial but not unlimited increase in security and welfare expenditures is feasible. To explore some of the limits for such programs, the requirements of a growing economy must be examined.

There is first the age-old conflict between resources that can be made available for current personal consumption and those needed for additional capital outlays in the interest of growth and increased future consumption. This factor is of crucial importance for the so-called underdeveloped countries. It is of less significance in the United States because full utilization of currently underemployed resources would permit a substantial increase in security and welfare expenditures, and at the same time, an increase in capital outlays. Actually in the industrial nation, a slight relative decline in the share of investment in plant, equipment, and inventories tends to be compatible with economic growth because of simultaneous productivity increases for both labor and capital.

Furthermore, if the definition of capital outlays could be broadened to include all current outlays which contribute to economic growth, it would sharpen judgments on the desired balance between outlays for consumption and for capital in the broadened definition. Outlays for public health, education, training, research, are designed for the benefit of individuals whose life is enriched, but in some part, they can also be regarded as investments in the future which increase the productivity of labor. Similarly, some support for residential construction not only brings decent housing within the reach of low- and middle-income families but also adds to the mobility of labor and thereby contributes to economic growth. This line of reasoning should not, of course, lead to the conclusion that we need not be concerned with adequate investments in the conventional definition, particularly in the expansion and modernization of plant and equipment, nor that every increase in welfare outlays also contributes to economic growth. Increases in physical capital and improvements in health, skills, and knowledge should be complementary. Nevertheless, the fact that certain outlays at the same time serve human welfare and promote economic growth increases the limits within which an expansion of welfare services is not only desirable but also economically feasible.

A related question is whether expansion of welfare and security measures may interfere with the amount of savings needed in a growing economy. When social insurance programs were first adopted, fear was often expressed that provision for old age and other contingencies might reduce the individual's motivation to provide for private insurance and for savings. Actually, the opposite has happened.

Another question is whether the increase in progressive tax rates incident to the very large increase in Federal expenditures since the period before World War II has reduced the savings available for future expansion and modernization, especially whether individual income tax rates in the higher brackets have reduced the supply of risk capital. As already mentioned, it cannot be said of the American economy in general that development is handicapped by lack of savings. Most of the capital required for business expansion and modernization of corporations is provided by undistributed profits and accrual of depreciation allowances. Also the annual accrual in private and public social insurance and welfare funds is so large that it probably has offset, if not more than offset, the reduction in savings which could be attributed to the tax requirements for financing social security and welfare programs. In considering how much this reduction might be, we should estimate what part of the total increase in expenditures is attributable to social security and welfare programs and what part to other programs, particularly to national defense. Less than 10 percent of the increase in total expenditures financed by general revenue is due to the increase in welfare programs. Welfare expenditures, in the fiscal year 1963, amounted to about 12 percent of the total Federal expenditures of the administrative budget.

It is also relevant to estimate what part of the Federal general taxes (i.e., except employment taxes) is likely to be paid by the wealthy whose ability to save might thereby be reduced. In taxes paid by the wealthy, we include besides individual income taxes of people with gross incomes of $20,000 or more, all Federal estate taxes, one-half of corporate taxes (assuming that the other half is passed on to consumers), and 5 percent of excise taxes. The resulting estimate suggests that from total budget revenue of $85.5 billion in fiscal year 1963 about $24 billion, or 28 percent, were paid directly or indirectly by the wealthy. Assuming that 12 cents of every tax dollar is used for Federal welfare expenditures financed by general revenue it follows that $2.8 billion, or about one-fourth of these welfare expenditures were financed by taxes of the wealthy.

We assume that the employment taxes which finance social insurance are largely paid by employees, either by direct deductions from their wages or salaries or indirectly through lower wage and salary rates than they could command if employers did not have to pay employment taxes. Some part of these taxes also is passed on in higher prices and thus is paid by consumers in the lower and middle-income brackets. Only a small proportion, perhaps 20 percent, is assumed to be eventually borne by the wealthy through a squeeze on profits with the resulting effect on dividends and stock values.

Combining the welfare programs financed by general revenue and the social insurance programs financed by employment taxes, we reach the conclusion that of the whole $30.7 billion expenditures for social security and welfare in fiscal year 1963, possibly $5.6 billion, or less than one-fifth are directly or indirectly financed by the wealthy. The part of social security and welfare programs financed by the wealthy is even smaller if State and local finances are included, because the tax systems of these governments are less progressive than that of the Federal Government. Nor can we expect any substantial change in those relationships in the future. In our modern economy, the wealthy are only to a small extent "taxed for the benefit of the poor." Actually, the financing of security and welfare measures has become mainly a transfer of funds by employers and other members of the lower- and middle-income classes from the time they are earning a living, to the time they retire or find themselves in distress. Thus, it appears that only a minor part of any reduction in venture capital that has resulted from the increase in taxes on the high-income brackets can be attributed to the increase in welfare expenditures.

In Conclusion

For advances in the security and welfare of labor as a whole, the most effective, if not the only truly effective, measure is a policy promoting economic growth. And a successful policy of economic growth, in turn, will increase both workers' income and Government revenues — at existing or even lower tax rates. Increasing Government revenue directly increases the means available for financing additional Government welfare programs. However, more is needed than additional revenue to deal with the residual problems of poverty. For today, although wage and salary employees are distributed throughout the lower and middle brackets of the income pyramid and poverty is no longer a characteristic of labor per se, it has become increasingly a characteristic of specific conditions.

The conventional welfare programs will not solve the problems of the adolescents looking for jobs without adequate schooling; they will not solve the problems of workers of advanced age who have been replaced by technological developments; they will not solve the problems of those suffering from racial discrimination or those lacking opportunities because of physical or mental handicaps; they will not solve the problems of workers in depressed areas. Specific programs have been initiated or proposed to deal with each of these causes of poverty, such as policies combating discrimination in employment practices, educational and training programs, drives for employment opportunities for the handicapped, for depressed areas, the youth corps, and others. These programs require money which will become more easily available in an economy of satisfactory growth, but even more, they require tolerant and generous attitudes of management, labor, and the general public. With the technical knowledge of our age, we will have the material means available for eliminating poverty as a mass phenomenon. We can only hope that we also will develop the attitudes necessary to use these resources for the benefit of those who will not automatically benefit from economic growth and rising incomes and from the conventional security and welfare programs.

1. *What is the balance of payments?*

2. *How rapidly should the American economy grow?*

3. *How can world living standards be raised?*

4. *What are the main issues in the "battle of the isms"?*

5. *Are world economic systems diverging or converging?*

UP TO THIS POINT, our study of economics has been concerned mainly with the domestic economy of one country, the United States. Now we shift our attention to economic relations among national states, to the problem of world poverty, and to the different systems of economic organization in the world today. Judging from much of the popular discussion which surrounds the subject of world economic affairs, it may seem that the economics which we have studied so far does not apply beyond the water's edge. This is not so. Most economists would probably maintain that fundamentally the distinction between domestic and international economies is not nearly so sharp as the division between macro- and microeconomics.

Foreign Trade and Aid

In the field of economics, the complications we observe as we move from the national setting to the international arise partly from distance and more particularly from the division of political control in the world among numerous distinct and sovereign governments. Different govern-

PROBLEMS

ments give rise to different systems of currency and finance, of economic organization, of law and custom, and to obstacles deliberately intended to inhibit commercial relations with foreigners. These obstacles — tariffs, import quotas, currency controls, embargoes — are among the most important features distinguishing international economics from domestic economics. Recent American policy and practice suggests that, while the United States has professed to favor widening trading opportunities, we have actually introduced some practices which, in piecemeal fashion, restrict trade.

While very significant, these inhibiting institutional considerations, nonetheless, do not alter the basic economic principle of the scarcity of resources with which we attempt to satisfy virtually unlimited human wants. All economic systems face this fundamental economic problem and the trade relations among all countries, therefore, no matter how complicated by regulations, express the advantages of specialization.

The "real" problems of international trade are supplemented by and related to the "monetary" problems of international finance, summarized in the balance of payments and symbolized by balance of payments deficits, surpluses, and gold flows. Recent discussions have emphasized the need for making adjustments to balance of payments deficits or surpluses consistent with keeping restrictions upon international trade to a minimum and also with the maintenance of domestic full employment, price stability, and economic growth.

One great and significant fact in present-day international economic affairs is the enormous disparity in living standards among countries. This promises to become even more important as the awareness and power of the less privileged areas of the world increase. At first to sustain the fighting efforts of our Allies in World War II, and then to save them from imminent economic disaster and Communism after the War, and more recently to raise foreign living standards, we have become involved in programs of economic assistance to other countries. Scarcely anyone can now doubt that this involvement has become practically permanent, although the magnitude of our endeavor is not a significant part of our income. (Current expenditures by the United States for foreign economic assistance represent about one-half of one per cent of the Gross National Product.)

For a variety of reasons, our early postwar efforts succeeded remarkably well. In fact, the comparatively developed countries of Western Europe and Japan are now able to pay their own way in trade with the United States, and then some. This has been the basis for some alarm that our country may no longer be able to compete in trade with foreigners, although it has not prevented us from enacting more liberal foreign trade legislation.

Economic Growth and Development

No authority believes that foreign economic assistance alone is a sufficient solution to the problem of low living standards in many countries, nor is an immediate increase in existing standards of personal consumption in those countries an effective, long-run solution. Rather, the main concern, most experts agree, is to find ways and means whereby the economies of these countries can be made to expand and to expand at a rate faster than that of population increase.

Many economists appear to feel that there are growth stages in terms of which various national economies may be examined. If they are correct, and if we may generalize from past experiences of developed countries, then we may infer from this history what appropriate policies can now be applied to facilitate the expansion of underdeveloped economies. Without concluding whether or not future developments in the underdeveloped countries will show much resemblance to the past of the developed countries, it is noteworthy that this idea has attracted rather widespread attention among economists and non-economists alike.

Quite recently, American economists have become preoccupied not only with the problems of growth in other countries, but with our own rate of economic growth, which some regard as unduly modest considering the magnitude of our resources and our great wealth. It has been suggested that we must become increasingly concerned with our rate of growth, because only by means of greater growth can we meet our international responsibilities as well as make ample provision for economic and social well-being within our own country.

Comparative Economic Systems

There are some parallels to be made between the conduct of economic life even in countries so different as the United States and Soviet Russia. Basically, however, the United States and the Soviet Union are regarded as not only the world's two most powerful nations but as representative of two opposite extremes in methods of economic organization. No other country is more symbolic than Russia of the "success" of economic regimentation as a means to economic development. At the other end of the scale is the comparatively decentralized American economy where responsibility rests with many thousands of separate business and other decision-making units (though it should be recognized that the organization of the American economy has not remained static with the passage of time).

Between the extremes represented by the United States and the Soviet Union are a variety of mixed or hybrid economies, the fundamental organizing principle of which is the intermingling of elements traditionally associated with both capitalism and socialism. The question for these countries has become less one of kind than of degree, although for many of them, the co-joining of democratic political institutions with a mixed economy has produced a result quite different from that of Soviet Russia and much closer in spirit and substance to the United States. However, changes are taking place in the structure and behavior of the Soviet-type economies as well as the economic systems of the West, changes which have tempered somewhat the extent of divergence between them. The monolithic character of Stalinist Communism is breaking up and innovations are being tried or at least discussed within the Communist bloc which have modified western conceptions of how the Soviet economies work.

In underdeveloped countries there is a great deal of interest in the relative merit of the American, Soviet, and other economic systems, particularly in regard to fostering economic growth. It is held that these countries cannot afford the luxury of such a market-oriented system as that of the United States for fear that resources needed for future development will be siphoned off for higher personal consumption now. On the other hand, there are excessive sacrifices in terms of economic choices and personal freedom which the goals of Soviet totalitarianism require. In some underdeveloped countries, there is much interest in possible procedures whereby they will forego some degree of autonomous decision-making in accepting a system of state planning, although not at the price of as much sacrifice of personal freedom as in the Soviet Union, even if this means they must accept a significantly lower rate of growth. The notable, but by no means sole, example of this position is India which, like both Russia and Communist China, has set forth its economic goals in a succession of plans, but which, at the same time, plans for the indefinite continuance and expansion of both nationalized and privately owned business.

Thus we see that the subject of international economics is extremely broad. Our occupation with it includes the traditional one of facilitating the freer movement of resources. It encompasses the more recent necessity for advanced countries to give economic help to the less advanced, but the importance of this program is tempered by a recognition that such contributions can be of little avail except in an atmosphere of structural change. Finally, we see that international economic affairs involve the recognition and comparison of different systems of economic organization and that the differences among these systems have become much more than a matter of mere economics or even politics, but involve ethics and the choice of a "way of life."

• *58*

The Trade Expansion Act of 1962*

HARRY G. BRAINARD
Michigan State University

"Free trade, one of the greatest blessings which a government can confer on a people, is in almost every country unpopular."
— *Lord Macaulay, 1824*

Legislating in an old field, Congress has produced a new species and overcome time-honored prejudices about the purposes of the tariff.

On October 11, 1962 President Kennedy signed into law the Trade Expansion Act of 1962, which was hailed as a landmark in the foreign trade policy of this country. Whether or not this act ranks as a milestone in the history of United States international commercial policy depends upon the answers to three major questions.

First, does the Trade Expansion Act represent a new approach in philosophical terms to our tariff policy? In other words, is this nation

* Taken and adapted from *Business Topics*, Winter 1963, pp. 7–19. Reproduced with permission.

387

now going to embark upon a distinctly new and different approach to the protection of American products from competition abroad? Second, are the provisions of the new law designed to meet objectives which are new and different from those sought by the Reciprocal Trade Agreements program initiated in 1934? And finally, does the act provide new devices or techniques for implementing our commercial policies with other nations?

Foreign Trade Policy

The answer to the first question, namely, the basic philosophy of the Trade Expansion Act of 1962 in comparison with the Reciprocal Trade Agreements program, is neither yes nor no. It is, rather, that in certain important ways the new law represents a change in thinking on the part of the government; in other respects there is no change in the general approach to the foreign trade policy of this country. In order to give substance to this observation it is necessary to take a look at the tariff history of the United States during the past 30 years.

Hawley-Smoot Act

Congress in 1930 passed the Hawley-Smoot Act which established the highest tariff rates in the history of the nation. It was thought that the best way to save jobs for American labor and to provide orders for business was to drastically limit competition from foreign industry and agriculture. This was a philosophy of economic self-containment.

Under the guidance of Secretary of State Cordell Hull, the Roosevelt administration promoted a foreign trade program which differed sharply from that embodied in the Hawley-Smoot Act. The new approach could not be characterized as "free-trade" in the literal sense, but it was based on a belief that a policy of economic isolation could not contribute to the creation of greater business activity. Trade, it was argued, is a two-way street and a nation can export only if it also imports.

Reciprocal Trade Agreements Act

The Reciprocal Trade Agreements Act of 1934 implemented the basic philosophy of the Roosevelt administration and represented a milestone in United States tariff history. Henceforth tariff rates on selected commodities were to be reduced through bilateral negotiations with other nations in order to expand trade. This was a bold new program and a direct break with the philosophy expressed in the Hawley-Smoot Act. It is to be emphasized, however, that this was not a free trade program; instead it was a means to promote freer trade.

From 1934 to 1962 the Reciprocal Trade Agreements Act was renewed on 11 different occasions and typically for a period of three years. There were no significant changes in the legislation until 1948, although certain administrative procedures had been introduced to meet congressional criticism.

Peril-point and Escape Clauses. When the Reciprocal Trade Agreements Act was under consideration for renewal in 1948 the proponents of the no-injury philosophy of tariff negotiations were successful in including in the act of that year a peril-point provision and an escape clause. The law required a review by the Tariff Commission of each list of commodities proposed for tariff negotiation for the purpose of establishing the maximum concession that could be granted without inflicting injury on the industry concerned. Even though the no-injury provisions were withdrawn the following year, the protectionist philosophy was again expressed in 1951 when peril-point and escape clauses were written into the law, where they have remained ever since.

A Shift in Attitude. The no-injury philosophy of the Trade Expansion Act of 1962 represents a sharp break with the past. The peril-point clause was dropped. An escape clause was retained, but the remedy provided is not to be found in an upward adjustment of rates but rather in helping those concerned to meet the new competition. In other words, it is assumed that in the administration of the Trade Expansion Act industries, firms, and workers can expect to be injured by tariff concessions. This is a reversal of the philosophy of tariff negotiations which has prevailed since 1948.

Objectives of the Act

The language of the Trade Expansion Act of 1962 is clear and unequivocal in stating the purposes to be attained. There are two main objectives.

The first is to achieve certain specific ends by lowering trade barriers through tariff negotiations. The resulting agreements will afford mutual benefits to such basic interests as the general welfare, foreign policy, and national security. In more precise terms these specific ends are:

1. To benefit the economy of the United States;
2. to strengthen economic and political relations between the United States and the other countries of the free world and in particular with the European Economic Community;
3. to assist the economies of countries in the earlier stages of economic development;
4. to counter penetration by international Communism.

A second purpose of the act is to expand the total amount of trade of the United States even though various segments of the business world may be subjected to loss of markets, profits, and even jobs. This objective is based on a rejection of the no-injury philosophy which had prevailed for more than a decade.

When the objectives of the Trade Expansion Act of 1962 are put along-side those of the Reciprocal Trade Agreements Act of 1934 as amended, it becomes clear that the new law represents a significant departure from the past.

Expansion of Foreign Trade

Concerning the procedures by which the expansionist philosophy of the act is to be implemented, one finds here that improvements have been made on the former tariff negotiating procedures and new methods have been created.

Broadening of the Bargaining Unit

A feature of the Trade Expansion Act of 1962 relates to a broadening of the bargaining unit. Specifically, the new law recognizes the European Economic Community as an economic entity for trade negotiations as distinguished from its member nations (The Netherlands, Belgium, Luxembourg, West Germany, France, and Italy). When the Reciprocal Trade Agreements program was first established, trade negotiations were conducted on a bilateral basis. Thus the United States government entered into separate bargaining sessions on a nation-by-nation basis and worked out a trade agreement containing tariff reductions on commodities of most importance to the country concerned. The lower rates thus negotiated were then extended to all other nations with which the United States maintained friendly trading relations. This was done in conformance with the most-favored-nation policy. During the first 13 years of the program, 1934–1947, 29 reciprocal trade agreements were negotiated on a purely bilateral basis.

Beginning in 1947 the trade agreement negotiating process was modernized when the United States and 22 other nations met in Geneva, Switzerland, as a group to bargain collectively. There were altogether 123 sets of negotiations covering roughly 50,000 items. The end product of the conference was the adoption by the participating nations of the General Agreement on Tariffs and Trade (GATT). Since that first bargaining session additional negotiating conferences have been held. Only for individual nations that are not members of the GATT are bilateral sessions held.

What the new law does is to carry the trade negotiating process one step further by providing that tariff bargaining will henceforth be conducted between the United States and the European Economic Community instead of its member nations individually. This is a logical procedure because there will be coming into existence over a period of years a single uniform external tariff schedule applicable to all nations trading with Common Market countries. Hence it makes sense to deal with the European Economic Community as an entity in itself, and as the Common Market expands to include more nations, so will the importance of bargaining with it become more all-inclusive.

A Special Representative

As a corollary to the broadening of the bargaining unit Congress wrote into the Trade Expansion Act a section providing for the creation of a Special Representative for Trade Negotiations.

By establishing an agency for the expressed purpose of conducting trade negotiations, Congress departed sharply from previous procedures by removing responsibility for the bargaining process from executive departments of the government.

A new provision of the act relates to the role of Congress itself in trade negotiations. This clause stipulates that two members of the House Ways and Means Committee and two from the Senate Finance Committee shall participate in tariff bargaining sessions. This is the first time since the beginning of the Reciprocal Trade Agreements program that Congress has insisted upon taking part in trade negotiations. Previously it has been content to receive reports periodically on the conduct of trade negotiations. These reports will continue to be submitted and the Tariff Commission will provide the President and Congress with technical information and assistance as needed.

Greater Bargaining Authority

The heart of the Reciprocal Trade Agreements program has been the authority Congress has granted to the President to negotiate trade concessions and to enter into foreign trade agreements.

It is in the authority to grant additional concessions with the European Economic Community that the new law gains special significance. In the first place, the President is permitted to reduce *by more than 50 percent* or eliminate entirely duties on categories of articles instead of item by item when it can be established that the United States and Common Market countries together accounted for 80 percent or more of the free world trade in these groups of commodities in a representative base period. Secondly, similar duty reductions can be granted on certain agricultural goods when a determination is made that such reductions will tend to assure the maintenance or expansion of United States exports of similar articles. A final special negotiating authority is dependent upon similar action by the European Economic Community. Specifically, duties on tropical agricultural and forestry products may be reduced by more than 50 percent if it can be shown (1) that similar commodities are not produced in significant amounts domestically, and (2) that Common

Market countries have agreed to give these products access to their market on equally favorable terms.

Limitation on Use of Authority

In accordance with previous legislation, the new trade law places certain restrictions on the bargaining power of the President. These limitations are in all major respects the same as those of the Reciprocal Trade Agreements Act of 1958. First of all, duties on articles which have been the subject of escape-clause treatment cannot be changed for at least four years. The President is also restrained from negotiating reductions on certain commodities if a finding has been made by the Office of Emergency Planning that their importation may threaten the national security. And as a matter of fact, restrictions may be imposed to limit the flow of such products into the country to the point where they no longer constitute a national security risk.

A limitation in the administration of the bargaining provisions of the act thus requires in general that reductions in duties are to be made in five annual stages. The purpose of this provision, of course, is to allow domestic producers time to adjust to foreign competition. Another restriction concerns trade with any area or country controlled or dominated by Communism. Under this provision no concessions granted through trade agreements with other nations can be extended to the Soviet Union or its satellites.

Foreign Import Restrictions

A section of the present law which is a carry-over from preceding legislation allows the President to withhold tariff concessions from nations that impose import restrictions which discriminate against products from the United States. The purpose of this provision is to give greater bargaining power to the administration as it negotiates trade agreements.

A New Approach to Injury Cases

The new law contains special provisions for dealing with injury cases. This approach to hardship situations is a complete break with earlier legislation and, therefore, merits special attention.

Industry Adjustment. If it appears that an entire industry is adversely affected by a tariff concession, two kinds of relief are available. Under the terms of the escape clause carried over from the 1958 Act, the President may proclaim an increase in, or the imposition of a duty on, the article in question to the degree necessary to prevent serious injury to the industry.

Another kind of action that appears for the first time in the Trade Expansion Act is to negotiate agreements with foreign countries to permit the orderly marketing of certain commodities exported to this country. It is to be emphasized that industry relief will be given as a last resort and only after it is certain that the various adjustment measures designed to assist firms and their workers to meet the new conditions are inappropriate.

Company Adjustment. An increase in imports arising out of reduced trade barriers may not affect an entire industry but rather be felt by certain firms only. It is quite possible for a high-cost domestic producer to be forced out of the market while other more efficient firms are able to meet foreign competition. To provide relief for adversely affected firms and their workers, Congress has written into the present law special adjustment provisions for individual companies and employees. The relief made possible by the act is not intended to shield the firms or workers from foreign competition; instead, it is designed to enable them to shift to the production of other kinds of commodities and employment. This kind of relief is new in tariff legislation and constitutes a rejection of the no-injury philosophy.

Assistance may take the form of technical aid which will be provided by a governmental agency or in unusual cases by outside firms or individuals. Appropriate technical assistance may include market and other economic research, managerial advice and counseling, training, and help in research and product development. A second kind of aid may take the form of financial help including guarantees of loans, agreements for deferred participation in loans, or outright loans. The extent of financial assistance is limited to the amount that will contribute to the firm's economic adjustment. Finally, a firm may be granted tax relief.

The granting of assistance by any of the above methods is conditioned upon the acceptance by the government of a definite proposal of the firm applying for relief. A proposal will be approved if it can be expected (1) to contribute to the firm's economic adjustment, (2) to give adequate consideration to the interests of its workers, and (3) to require the company to make all reasonable efforts to use its own resources in the adjustment process.

Assistance to Workers. Just as firms may be eligible for assistance due to injury caused by tariff concessions granted in a trade agreement, so also may workers in industries thus affected be given aid. If the Tariff Commission finds an injury, workers may apply to the Secretary of Labor for assistance. Eligible workers who meet minimum qualifications may receive unemployment compensation up to 65 percent of their average weekly wage instead of the current national average of about 35 percent.

Of more importance are two other kinds of assistance. The first of these is the aid that can be given to train a worker for a different kind of employment. Governmental agencies can make available to these workers testing, counseling, training, and placement services to the greatest extent possible. Where the appropriate kind of training program is not available in his own community, the worker may be given financial aid to defray transportation costs and living expenses while away from home. For the worker who is totally separated from his job, who cannot find suitable employment locally, and who obtains a satisfactory position elsewhere, a relocation allowance may be granted. This allowance includes the reasonable and necessary expenses incurred by the worker in transporting his family and household effects to a new community. In addition, the worker is entitled to a lump sum payment equal to two and one-half times the average weekly manufacturing wage.

The training and relocation allowances are of special significance, since they are designed to do for labor what technical, financial, and tax relief programs do for injured firms, namely, to promote a shift of resources to more efficient uses.

Conclusions

Among the many virtues of the Trade Expansion Act three are deserving of special comment. The acceptance of the European Economic Community as an entity for bargaining purposes is important because it is a recognition of the trend throughout the world towards economic regionalism. Where a trading area with a common external tariff exists it makes sense to deal with it as a unit. Other trading areas are coming into existence, the most notable being the common market established by the nations of Central America.

The Interagency Trade Organization, as a replacement for the Interdepartmental Committee, will serve to strengthen considerably the administration of the act. The new organization is a creation of Congress with clearly specified duties and with responsibilities going well beyond tariff bargaining to include problems of injury adjustment. The administrative machinery is further strengthened by the establishment of the office of Special Representative for Trade Negotiations. This activity will constitute the Special Representative's sole responsibility where formerly it was but one of the many duties of first the Secretary of State and more recently the Secretary of Commerce.

The strongest feature of the Trade Expansion Act is its rejection of the no-injury concept of tariff bargaining. By assuming that an expansion of trade will cause hardship to industries, firms, and workers, and by providing intelligent adjustment procedures, Congress in passing this act clearly set our foreign trade policy on a new and forward-looking course. In this sense the new law constitutes a milestone in the international commercial policy of the United States and gives this nation added stature as a leader in world affairs.

59

Long-Run Prospects for United States Balance of Payments*

Edward M. Bernstein
Consulting Economist, Washington, D.C.

Can any country with a persistent deficit in its balance of international payments and sustaining continuing losses of gold from its reserves maintain its money as a "key currency" — a means of international payment freely exchanged and accepted in all trading countries — and contribute an undiminished burden in aid to other countries? What possibly encourages the author of this selection to reply, in effect, "Excelsior!"

U.S. Payments Problem

With the exception of 1957, the balance of payments of the United States has been in deficit since 1950, using the definitions of the Department of Commerce. The payments deficit was relatively moderate from 1950 to 1957, averaging about $1.3 billion a year. It was substantially larger from 1958 to 1960, ranging from $3.3 billion to $3.9 billion. In 1961, considerable progress was made in reducing the payments deficit

* Taken and adapted from *Factors Affecting the United States Balance of Payments*, Compilation of Studies Prepared for the Subcommittee on International Exchange and Payments of the Joint Economic Committee of the Congress of the United States (Washington: U.S. Govt. Printing Office, 1962), pp. 371–94.

and, despite some adverse factors, it declined to $2.5 billion. Further progress is being made and in the first three quarters of 1962, the payments deficit was down to $1.4 billion, partly because of extraordinary receipts from prepayments of debts to the U.S. Government by France and Italy.

While the improvement in the U.S. balance of payments in 1960–62 is encouraging, particularly as this occurred during a period of cyclical expansion in the United States, the payments deficit is still large and the pressure on U.S. reserves is increasing. From 1950 to 1957, net sales of gold by the U.S. Treasury averaged $260 million a year, and the increase in foreign short-term and liquid dollar assets, official and private, averaged just over $1 billion a year. From 1958 to 1961, however, net gold sales averaged $1.4 billion a year, and the increase in foreign short-term and liquid dollar assets averaged $1.9 billion a year.

For most countries, the measures necessary to solve a balance-of-payments problem, however difficult, are clear cut — that is, to restrain the demand for imports and to encourage an inflow of short-term funds. The United States must be careful in using such measures, because it is a prime mover in the world economy, and its own economy is lagging. A reduction in aggregate demand to restrain imports will depress the U.S. economy and cause difficulties for other countries dependent on exports to the United States to keep their balance of payments in order. Nor can the United States eliminate its payments deficit by attracting a large influx of funds from other financial centers through a sharp rise in interest rates. The high interest rates would hamper the growth of the U.S. economy, and the influx of funds would shift the payments problem to other countries. The solution to the U.S. payments problem must be found in an environment of expanding world trade supported by a high level of economic activity in this country.

The U.S. payments problem can be better understood only as part of a long postwar adjustment designed to restore a pattern of international payments under which the world economy can prosper and grow. This has involved the rebuilding of the productive capacity of Western Europe and Japan, the strengthening of their competitive position through the depreciation of their currencies in 1949, the resumption of their important role in world trade, and the establishment of convertibility of their currencies. The international economic policies of the United States have been directed to the attainment of these objectives since 1946. These policies have been remarkably successful as indicated by the high level of production and trade, the balance-of-payments surplus, and the greatly increased monetary reserves of Western Europe and Japan. It is not surprising that the adjustment that has been going on for so many years should have resulted in a great shift in the pattern of international payments.

The postwar adjustment is apparently coming to an end, although it may continue for a year or two more. In the meantime, the long-run strength of the U.S. international economic position is asserting itself. An analysis of three important sectors of the U.S. balance of payments shows that there are forces acting on U.S. trade, U.S. capital outflow, and U.S. Government expenditures which may be expected to eliminate the payments deficit in the next few years. It is still essential, however, for the United States and other countries to follow policies that will make possible the maintenance of a strong pattern of international payments and that will facilitate the solution to payments difficulties in the future.

U.S. Competitive Position in World Trade

U.S. Exports

The United States provides by far the largest amount of exports in world trade.

The payments difficulties of the United States are not caused by a lag in exports, although it is necessary to increase exports as part of a broad program to strengthen the U.S. balance of payments. As a share of total world trade, U.S. exports, excluding transfers under military grants, have been fairly stable since 1953. With the exception of 1956–57, when they were unusually large, and 1959, when they were unusually small, U.S. exports have tended to be about 17 percent of the world total throughout the 10 years from 1953 to 1962. United States exports have not increased as much, proportionately, as those of continental Western Europe and Japan; they have increased more than the exports of the United Kingdom and Canada. The United States no longer dominates world markets as it did from 1946 to 1951. As a practical matter, one purpose of the postwar adjustment in trade was to reduce the excessive dependence of the world on exports from the United States financed by U.S. aid.

The deterioration of the competitive position of the United States is said to be revealed by the sharp decline in its share of exports of manufactures. In 1950, the United States supplied about 27.3 percent of the exports of manufactures by the leading industrial countries. This share fell steadily to 21.3 percent in 1959. The principal cause of the decline was the recovery of production in continental Western Europe and Japan and the resumption of their traditional place in world markets. This adjustment is coming to an end.

Now that the reconstruction of their productive facilities has been completed, the growth in industrial production in Western Europe will tend to be slower. With its efficient economy, the United States should be able to match the increase in productivity in Western Europe in the future, as it has, in fact, since 1958. Furthermore, the high level of production and employment in Europe is being accompanied by a much greater rise in wage rates, so that costs of production in manufacturing are apparently rising more in European countries than in the United States. The appreciation of the mark and the guilder in 1961 has also facilitated the adjustment of relative costs. Inevitably, the greater rise in European costs will affect the prices of their exports of manufactured goods.

U.S. Imports

A deterioration in the competitive position of the United States in world trade should manifest itself in a rise in imports relative to the gross national product or to domestic expenditures on commodities. As the United States has relatively low tariffs and few quantitative restrictions, a tendency for prices to rise more in the United States than in other leading countries would be expected to lead to a considerable increase in the propensity to import. In fact, there are no indications that U.S. imports have risen relative to the gross national product. On the contrary, since 1951 the ratio of imports to the gross national product has had a downward trend and in 1961, when there was a recession, the ratio was the lowest of the postwar period.

The lower ratio of imports to the gross national product in recent years probably reflects two separate factors. One is the steady decline in the prices of basic commodities which constitute a large part of U.S. imports. The second is the continued rise in the proportion of the gross national product in the form of services whose import content is considerably less than that of commodities. As a proportion of gross expenditures on commodities, imports have tended to be fairly constant in recent years. It would have been expected that with the greater availability of manufactured goods from Western Europe, imports would have risen relative to expenditures on domestic goods. The behavior of U.S. imports in recent years does not support the view that the competitive position of the United States has deteriorated. Even where imports increased considerably, for example, of European automobiles, there is reason to believe that price was a minor factor.

In fact, the trade surplus of the United States has increased markedly in recent years. Provided European markets remain prosperous and are open to U.S. exports on liberal terms, the strong trade position of the United States in this region should be maintained.

U.S. Private Capital in the Balance of Payments

One of the major factors in the balance of payments deficit of recent years has been the very large outflow of U.S. private capital. From 1950 to 1955, the outflow of U.S. private long-term and short-term capital averaged about $1.1 billion a year. In 1960 and 1961, recorded U.S. private capital outflow was $3.9 billion a year.

Direct Investment

In the early postwar period, U.S. direct investment was held back by uncertainties regarding the strength and stability of the world economy. The rapid rise in direct investment since 1956 reflects the effort made by U.S. companies to restore their role in production and trade to a level better suited to economic prospects abroad. This has required an unusually large volume of investment in recent years to make good the deficient level of investment in the earlier postwar period. Once this deficiency has been made good, U.S. direct investment may be expected to fall to a lower level.

U.S. companies were slow in resuming direct investment on a large scale in Western Europe. Because of the remarkable growth of their production and trade, U.S. direct investment in the countries of Western Europe has increased enormously in the past 5 years. The establishment of the European Common Market has been another factor inducing U.S. direct investment in this area. If allowance is made for the bulge in 1960, resulting from the acquisition of outstanding stock in British Ford, U.S. direct investment in Western Europe has been increasing steadily since 1958.

New funds going into U.S. direct investment may be expected to decline slightly for 2 or 3 years. U.S. enterprises abroad will undoubtedly continue to grow at a relatively rapid rate, but a larger part of the capital for their expansion will be derived from reinvested earnings and from funds raised locally. When the rise in U.S. direct investment is resumed, after a few years, it may be expected to be at a much more moderate rate.

New Issues of Foreign Securities (Indirect Investment)

As in other types of U.S. private long-term investment abroad, the outflow of capital through new issues of foreign securities in the United States has become very much larger since 1956.

An important factor in the increase of new issues of foreign securities in recent years has been the borrowing of some European countries, several Commonwealth countries, Japan, and Israel. This reflects, of course, the greater confidence in the economic position of these countries and their stronger payments position.

The factors that make the issue of foreign securities in the United States attractive are the lower interest rates and the low issuing costs. Although many continental countries of Western Europe have a large balance of payments surplus and some of them were important capital exporting countries in the past, their interest rates on bonds, except in Switzerland, are generally higher than in the United States. It is necessary for the surplus countries of Western Europe to open their financial markets to foreign security issues. Closer cooperation among the monetary authorities on long-term interest rates and on new security issues could be helpful in directing a greater part of the need for foreign capital in this form to the surplus countries of Western Europe.

Income from Foreign Investment

U.S. private foreign investment is a source of large receipts in the current sector of the balance of payments. The large excess of U.S. receipts over payments on income from foreign investment is due to several factors. First, U.S. investments abroad, particularly private investments, are much larger than foreign investments in this country. Second, about 90 percent of U.S. private investments abroad are long-term and two-thirds of these are direct investments in U.S. enterprises abroad. Foreign assets and investments in this country, on the other hand, are predominantly liquid assets that yield a low return. Of long-term foreign assets in the United States, one-third is direct investment and about two-thirds marketable securities. Finally, U.S. direct investment abroad is concentrated in the high-risk industries that yield a high return while a considerable part of foreign direct investment in the United States is in finance, insurance, and trade, where risks and earnings are smaller.

Remittances from U.S. private foreign investments have been rising steadily. In 1950, U.S. payments on income from foreign investments were $345 million and they reached about $1 billion in the early 1960's. Because of the large net receipts from foreign investment, nearly $2.5 billion in 1962, the private capital sector, which has placed a great strain on the U.S. balance of payments in recent years is likely to be a source of great strength in the future. This will be particularly so as the capital outflow becomes more moderate, while earnings remitted to this country continue the rapid rise of recent years.

U.S. Aid and Military Expenditures

The U.S. balance of payments is unique in the very large transfers and payments of a political or quasi-political character. In one form or another, they have a direct or indirect effect on the U.S. balance of payments.

Effect on the Balance of Payments

The impact on the balance of payments is not the same for all types of U.S. Government transfers and payments, nor is the impact the same at different times. Military grants, for example, involve equipment made in the United States. Such grants have only an indirect effect on the U.S. balance of payments. Their production requires some imported raw materials, so that U.S. imports may be slightly higher than they would otherwise be. Furthermore, dollar sales of U.S. military equipment would probably be slightly larger if it were not made available under military grants. On the whole, military grants have a negligible effect on the U.S. balance of payments, particularly as a considerable part of such grants is in the form of surplus equipment no longer used by U.S. forces.

In contrast, expenditures in connection with U.S. forces stationed abroad involve payments of dollars to foreigners for goods and services provided to the Defense Department or U.S. personnel, which were nearly $2,947 million in 1961.

Economic grants and Government loans have an impact on the balance of payments between these extremes. Where the grants or loans are directly for the purpose of buying surplus agricultural commodities, there is no adverse effect unless such sales displace normal dollar sales that would otherwise have been made. Where grants or loans are used to purchase goods abroad, the balance of payments effect is the same as that of any capital outflow not directly or indirectly related to U.S. exports.

In the immediate postwar years, when the United States dominated the export markets of the world, it made little difference how and where the dollars paid for military expenditures abroad and U.S. aid were used. The need for U.S. export goods was so great, and alternative sources of supply so limited, that dollars made available to other countries through military expenditures and aid tended to be spent in this country or, if spent abroad, were used by the exporting country to pay for its purchases in the United States. The situation is far different now. If such funds are spent abroad, they may be retained by the exporting country to be added to its reserves. Or if the exporting country uses the dollars to pay for imports, they may be spent in surplus countries that add the dollars to their reserves. Because the indirect stimulus to U.S. exports is smaller than it was in the past, the balance of payments effect of U.S. military expenditures abroad and of U.S. aid will depend primarily on whether there is a commitment on the part of the recipient countries to spend such funds in the United States.

There is no way of projecting with assurance the possible changes in U.S. Government expenditures for military purposes abroad or for economic aid. Except in 1958, expenditures for economic aid have been rising steadily. This tendency is certain to continue for the next few years. Even wider participation by other high-income countries in the provision of economic aid to underdeveloped countries is unlikely to do more than hold back the rise in U.S. expenditures for this purpose.

Limiting the Balance-of-Payments Effect

As it is not possible to make balance-of-payments considerations a primary factor in determining U.S. military expenditures abroad or U.S. economic grants and Government loans, it has been necessary to take other measures to limit their adverse effect on the U.S. balance of payments. Apart from greater economy in procuring goods and services for military purposes abroad, by shifting more of the supply to U.S. sources, the United States has arranged with a number of countries in which U.S. forces are stationed to make offsetting purchases of U.S. military equipment.

Measures have also been taken to reduce the adverse impact on the U.S. balance of payments of economic grants and U.S. Government loans. Transfers under agricultural disposal programs and Export-Import Bank disbursements are by their nature tied to U.S. exports. Expenditures for other economic grants and Government loans are being directed in greater part to purchases in the United States. In the fiscal year 1962, about 63 percent of the commodity expenditures of the Agency for International Development were made in the United States. This proportion may be expected to rise as disbursements of new allocations of aid funds are guided by the rules requiring purchases in the United States. Such measures are reducing the adverse impact of economic grants and Government loans on the U.S. balance of payments. They have, unfortunately, also put pressure on the balance of payments of some countries, particularly Japan, that are themselves having payments difficulties.

Despite the measures that have been taken, the transfers and payments of the U.S. Government on account of military expenditures, military grants, economic grants, and Government loans will continue to place a heavy burden on the U.S. balance of payments in the next few years. The expenditures for our forces abroad and for military grants can be reduced only if other countries assume a larger share in the costs of the common defense. Economic aid for the underdeveloped countries cannot be decreased in the foreseeable future, although the pressure to increase U.S. aid would be lessened if other high-income countries participated more generously in the provision of such aid.

International Cooperation and Reserves

The international economic position of the United States is very strong. This strength is based on its large and productive economy, on the responsiveness of prices and costs to the competitive situation at home and abroad, on its enormous creditor position on private investment account, and on the substantial debts of some of the high-income countries of Western Europe to the U.S. Government. The difficulties incident to the postwar adjustment of the pattern of international payments since 1950 have temporarily offset these long-run favorable forces. When the postwar adjustment is completed, these forces will assert themselves, as is already apparent in some sectors of the balance of payments.

Need for Cooperative Measures

Despite this, it would be a serious mistake for the United States to neglect its payments difficulties on the grounds that natural corrective forces will ultimately restore the payments surplus which is essential to its position as a reserve center and as the leader of the free world. The strengthening of the U.S. balance of payments is a matter of concern, not only for the United States, but for other countries as well.

Further efforts must be made to increase U.S. exports. The United States will remain the principal source of capital for international investment and of aid for other countries. To meet these responsibilities, the balance of payments on current account must provide a surplus equivalent to the net capital outflow and the transfers and payments of the U.S. Government. Such a surplus on current account can be achieved only if U.S. exports are increased relative to imports. For this, the U.S. economy must hold down costs and improve its competitive position. At the same time, other countries must remove the restrictions applied against U.S. exports and, together with the United States, lower the barriers to world trade.

The United States is by far the largest source of international capital through new issues of foreign securities. While it is to be expected that a considerable part of such placements should be made in the United States, it is necessary for the surplus countries of Europe to provide a greater part of the capital raised in this form. Long-term interest rates must be brought down in the surplus countries to match their greater savings. Their capital markets should be encouraged to develop the necessary facilities for raising capital for domestic and foreign borrowers. The United States and other countries should cooperate on measures to induce foreign borrowers to raise more of the capital they need in the surplus countries.

It is also necessary to have a more equitable allocation of the common burdens of defense and aid. The arrangements already made with some countries to offset U.S. military expenditures with purchases of military equipment in this country are reasonably satisfactory for the time being. The United States will have to continue to provide a very large part of the funds for economic aid. This should be supplemented to a much greater extent with aid from other high-income countries. When more economic aid is made available by other countries, the United States should remove the restrictions that require the use of its aid funds in this country. The most constructive arrangement for providing economic aid for the underdeveloped countries would be to have international contributions to a multilateral agency whose allocations could be used by the recipient in any participating country.

The only way to end a balance-of-payments deficit is to increase foreign exchange receipts relative to foreign exchange payments. With the steady growth of world trade and the continued reduction of barriers to trade, any country should be able to put its balance of payments in order by following appropriate policies. For the United States, this must be done without generating a deflation in this country and in the world economy. Fortunately, both the United States and other great trading countries are aware of this. We may confidently hope that their policies will be directed toward establishing a strong pattern of international payments in a prosperous world economy.

60

Let's Get Rid of Our Cross of Gold*

ABBA P. LERNER
Michigan State University

Selection 21 is also by the author of this piece. It has become virtually an economic classic for its incisive logic on the proper use of government budgets, but when it first appeared it was almost daring in its brisk and matter-of-fact critique and re-formulation of fiscal orthodoxy. Time will tell whether the novel solution for the U.S. "gold crisis" which Professor Lerner here proposes will acquire a similar position in international finance.

Gold Outflows

The $9 billion decline in the U.S. gold stock since 1948 is the least damaging result of our balance of payments problem. Indeed, it is a good thing for us to get useful goods and services in exchange for an idle stock of yellow metal. The evil is that in our hysteria over the gold outflow, we have resorted to damaging restrictionist policies, giving the lie to our declared devotion to freedom of trade.

Tying our foreign aid to compulsory purchases of American goods, keeping the wives of servicemen from joining their husbands abroad, cutting tourists' custom-free imports, and imposing a tax on foreign lending may not seem so serious. But the fear that domestic prosperity will

---

* Reprinted from CHALLENGE, The Magazine of Economic Affairs, a publication of the Institute of Economic Affairs, New York University.

worsen our balance of payments (because prosperous citizens spend more on imports) is now a primary justification for policies permitting a high level of unemployment (costing about $50 billion a year) and for our puny rate of economic growth (threatening our position of leadership in the world).

We suffer the foregoing evils, fearing that a continued gold outflow will force us to devalue the dollar sooner or later in terms of gold. Such a development would not only be a great shock to world trade and international finance, but a breach of faith with foreign holders of dollars.

A devaluation of the dollar in terms of gold is the same thing as a rise in the dollar price of gold. But why is gold so valuable and threatening to become still more valuable? The answer is that we have pursued a long-term policy of supporting the price of gold — i.e., we have been ready in the past to buy any amount of gold at the fixed price of $35 an ounce. Thus we have established a system based on the worldwide confidence that an ounce of gold will always be worth at least $35, and possibly more.

We are thus in a fix of our own making, but, unlike Sinbad the Sailor, we can easily throw off our Old Man of the Sea. To develop a more rational international monetary system permitting reasonable solutions for our balance of payments problem, we have only to put an end to our support price for gold. Our payments problem is terrifying, dangerous and insoluble only as long as we are burdened with our cross of gold.

And Balance of Payments Deficits

The mechanics of our payments problem are essentially simple. We have been getting about $20 billion worth of foreign currency in payment for our exports, and using up only about $16 billion to pay for our imports (so that we have been running a $4 billion *balance of trade surplus*). But for reasons of international policy, we have been paying out an additional $7 billion on military account, for foreign aid and for capital investments. We have thus had in 1963 a $3 billion *balance of payments deficit*, and have covered part of it with our gold (while borrowing abroad to cover the rest).

Our balance of payments deficit is thus the same thing as an excess demand on our part for foreign currency. Our demand is for $23 billion worth (to pay for our imports, military expenses, foreign aid and capital investment), while only $20 billion worth is being supplied in payment for our exports. The natural cure, just as for any other excess demand, say for tin, is a rise in price. A rise in the exchange valuation of foreign currency would make our purchases from abroad more expensive in terms of dollars and we would buy less. Our exports would become cheaper for foreigners and they would step up their buying. The increase in our exports and decrease in our imports would provide the extra foreign currency needed.

Whether we call the increase in the dollar price of, say, West German marks an appreciation of the mark or a depreciation of the dollar is quite important psychologically. An "appreciation" of the mark makes the Germans feel proud. A "depreciation" of the dollar undermines American confidence in the dollar.

In the days of old, gold came to be the unquestioned standard of value for excellent reasons. Gold was not only the most convenient form for holding wealth, but currencies like the U.S. dollar owed their value to the guarantee of redemption in a fixed quantity of gold. But gold is no longer suitable as backing for the world's monetary supply because of two important developments.

In the first place, the U.S. economy has grown tremendously in magnitude and the dollar is used much more than gold in international payments transactions. Thus gold is valuable because it can be exchanged for dollars rather than the other way around.

In the second place, the world gold supply has not expanded sufficiently to satisfy the need for international money (usually called "international liquid reserves"). In spite of the enormous growth of gold substitutes (such as dollars and other "key currencies") to help meet the demand, gold has been and still remains in short supply.

As a result, a country losing gold frantically seeks to stem the outflow. But while the U.S. has resorted to damaging restrictive measures to cut its deficit, other countries which have acquired the gold lost by the U.S. have shown little inclination to implement *expansive* measures that might check the gold inflow. It has been argued that the world gold stock and gold substitutes are adequate to satisfy all rational international requirements, but as long as the central banks *behave as if* there is a shortage, *a shortage exists.*

Devaluation and Restrictionism

Given the scarcity of gold, the "natural" cure would be a depreciation of the dollar and an upward valuation of foreign currencies. As long as we continue to work with gold, the only way to raise the dollar price of foreign money is by raising the dollar price of gold — that is, by *devaluation.*

But for a variety of subjective and objective reasons, the U.S. is unwilling to devalue the dollar. Also, it is doubtful whether the devaluation would have the desired result. Other countries would probably nullify our move by raising the price of gold in their own currencies in a *competitive devaluation.* Furthermore, a devaluation would lead to a much greater outflow of our gold. The outflow would accelerate because foreigners would no longer be willing to hold dollars as a "gold substitute."

But if devaluation is impractical, it might seem that restrictionism offers the only way out of our current predicament. We can reduce imports and our capital investments abroad by *taxing* imports and foreign lending or by running our economy at still lower gear, with still more unemployment, so that our people will not be able to spend so much on imports (and, incidentally, on domestic products, too). But restrictionism can reduce the deficit only until other countries retaliate with *competitive restrictionism*. There's no way out as long as we continue to submit to the tyranny of gold.

Cutting the Gordian Knot

The Gordian knot can be cut only by going on the offensive. Instead of trying to *defend* the dollar, we can *attack* and depose gold. We possess the means to free ourselves from the tyranny of gold. We need simply announce that we will no longer buy gold, and plan to sell all the reserves we possess. We could dump our entire gold supply, $15 billion worth, on the market. We could sell our gold gradually, or we might simply stop trying to check our gold outflow and thank the buyers for giving us useful goods in exchange for our gold.

At the same time, we could increase the general acceptability of the dollar for international liquid reserves by combating inflation more energetically — i.e., by maintaining the purchasing power of the dollar and by extending a purchasing power guarantee (in additional dollars) to all foreign holders of dollars. In other words, the guarantee would assure foreigners that the purchasing power of their dollar holdings would not be eroded even if U.S. prices increased, despite the federal government's vigorous anti-inflation policy.

The plan could be much strengthened by the inclusion of sterling and the Canadian dollar. A large fund — say $10 billion — should then be set up in these currencies to cover any temporary imbalances between their accounts.

International confidence in gold would necessarily be shaken by the policy which I have outlined. Of course, the value of our own gold stock would also diminish. But the purely nominal markdown of the bookkeeping valuation of a stock of metal would constitute only a negligible consideration compared with the real economic loss we are currently enduring from our low level of employment and slow economic growth.

The decline in the dollar value of the international liquid reserves, insofar as these consist of gold stocks held by the monetary authorities of the world, would increase the need for other forms of international liquid reserves. Dollars (and sterling), fortified by the purchasing power guarantee, would be available to fill this gap. Countries wishing to replenish their reserves would try to increase their holdings of dollars (and sterling) by selling more to us and buying less from us. This would mean an increase in our deficit, but it would be covered by our supplying dollars to satisfy their need for international reserves.

The final result would be the establishment of an automatic dollar (or dollar-sterling) standard, working just like an ideal gold standard. An ideal gold standard is one in which the supply of gold is never too scarce or too plentiful, but increases sufficiently whenever a scarcity of gold tends to raise its value, and decreases sufficiently whenever an abundance of gold tends to lower its value, so as to keep its value stable.

The purchasing power guarantee would enable any country to obtain a stable unit of international reserves at any time by producing and selling a constant amount of goods as specified in the purchasing power guarantee. It would be just as if, under the gold standard, every country had gold mines and could always produce an ounce of gold by devoting a constant amount of effort toward digging and refining it.

There would, of course, be losers — South Africa and the Soviet Union, as gold-producing countries, and such speculators as had placed their trust in gold.

The European central banks could conceivably prevent a gold devaluation by buying up at $35 an ounce all the gold that was offered for sale. But to do this they would have to mobilize $15 billion or $16 billion, plus additional funds which might be needed to buy up the gold thrown on the market by other countries and by frightened gold hoarders.

Even if those who wanted to protect gold succeeded in preventing its price from declining, there would be no depreciation of the dollar, i.e., no *increase* in the price of gold, unless they tried to buy up *more* than the entire amount of gold dumped on the market; and they would not want to do that even if they could. Their success in protecting the value of gold would prevent us from setting up a better international monetary system. But by releasing our great stock of gold we would still have relieved the gold shortage, and by our purchasing power guarantees (making the dollar a better substitute for gold) we would have relieved the gold shortage still further, perhaps even completely curing the current shortage in international liquid reserves and therewith the U.S. balance of payments crisis.

False Optimism?

The difficulties and dangers of devaluation have led to a search for palliatives. If our deficit is temporary and will be followed by an equally large surplus, we need no policy. We need only *borrow* enough to tide us over till better days come.

Our false sense of optimism has been buttressed by a flood of authoritative pronouncements.

But only the talk is optimistic. We are actually following a makeshift policy of *borrowing* to reduce the gold outflow, and *restricting* employment, imports and capital outflows to reduce the deficit. The resulting economic slack may *increase* the deficit by driving capital abroad, and any relief from our restrictions may be negated by foreign retaliation. Meanwhile, we could gradually lose all our gold, exhaust all our borrowing possibilities and be forced to devalue the dollar after all. Our only hope lies in breaking the siege by mounting a daring attack.

Thus far the possibility of going to the attack has not been seriously considered, so thoroughly have we been brainwashed into unquestioning acceptance of gold's sovereignty. This contention is beautifully demonstrated by Under Secretary of the Treasury Robert V. Roosa who grouped reform proposals into three categories. The first is a return to a "full gold standard," with a doubling or tripling of the price of gold. This is rejected for the good reason that the gigantic devaluation with which it must begin would destroy the confidence on which it must rest. The second proposes "that each currency fluctuate in price against the others." It, too, is rejected since it is unpopular with monetary authorities and threatens competitive devaluations. The opposition of monetary authorities is an obstacle rather than an objection to the policy itself, and competitive devaluation is meaningful only *in terms of gold*.

Only the third category of reform, built on "gold supplemented by various forms of credit," Roosa concludes, constitutes "a promising avenue for constructive advance." Interestingly, *all three* approaches are considered only in the context of the continued sovereignty of gold. Our "fourth" approach, to begin by crashing the gold barrier, is not even considered in this authoritative survey!

Conclusions

Questions will, of course, be raised on aspects of the plan which need to be spelled out in greater detail than is possible in this article. One question concerns the nature of the purchasing power guarantees. Another concerns the short-term effects of the expected drop in the price of gold. And, of course, powerful resistance could prevent the proposed plan from being carried out.

But the plan I have suggested has important advantages: by revolting against the tyranny of gold and dethroning it by simply ceasing to support it, we can set up a dollar or dollar-sterling standard that would automatically provide all the international liquid reserves needed for world prosperity and economic stability, just like an ideal gold standard.

• *61*

Objectives and Criteria for
*Foreign Assistance**

HOLLIS B. CHENERY
Agency for International Development

To apply the economist's professional preoccupation with the efficient allocation of resources is to formulate criteria, "rules of the game," for achieving this objective. The author of this selection, a former economics professor, is the Assistant Administrator of our foreign aid program. His professional impatience shows in his criticism of the past history of foreign aid, its tendency to concentrate upon temporary crises and pay less attention to long-run programs, governed by rules. Appropriately, he proposes what he considers to be some economically sound rules for conducting long-run programs.

Discussions of the rationale of foreign aid are complicated by the fact that there are several accepted reasons for the United States to extend assistance to other countries. Each of these reasons leads to a different set of criteria for determining whether a country should receive aid and how much. Since these several criteria often lead to conflicting conclusions, it is necessary in each case to identify the nature of the United

* Taken and adapted from Robert A. Goldwin, editor, *Why Foreign Aid?* (Chicago: Rand McNally & Co., 1963), pp. 32–45. Reproduced with permission.

States interest in a particular country before trying to evaluate our aid program.

A second complication in judging aid programs arises from the fact that different types of assistance — loans, development grants, military assistance, and technical cooperation — typically affect more than one of the United States objectives in a country. This fact prevents the making of a clear-cut separation among types of aid according to both their nature and their function and has caused successive Administrations to vary the categories of aid over the years. This change in nomenclature and coverage has added to the confusion as to the fundamental objectives and mechanisms of foreign assistance.

In presenting the Act for International Development to Congress in the spring of 1961, the Kennedy Administration made an effort to relate the several categories of aid as clearly as possible to their primary objectives. At the same time, it attempted to shift the emphasis in aid programs from short-term political and military objectives to long-term economic and social objectives. In this context, the conflict among aid criteria frequently becomes even more acute.

The present paper attempts to define the functions of foreign aid as one of the instruments of American foreign policy and to clarify the several objectives and categories of aid. My principal objective is to provide an analytical framework for the discussion and evaluation of aid programs.

Aid Objectives and Instruments

The Objectives

In the most general sense, the main objective of foreign assistance, as of many other tools of foreign policy, is to produce a political and economic environment in which the United States can best pursue its own social goals. The long-term economic and social progress of other countries can be regarded either as a prerequisite for the kind of international community that we need for our own selfish interest or as an end in itself. In either case, we should be concerned to promote rising levels of income, modernization of economies, independent political systems, and other features of societies that satisfy their own citizens as well as the international community.

The second objective, which concerns the immediate future, is internal stability, which is sought by giving financial support in times of economic crisis, by preventing internal disorders, and by other measures that help existing governments to stay in power. The measures taken to preserve economic and political stability may or may not also promote long-term economic and social development. The conflict is acute when the existing government is not development-oriented and a change might be more conducive to growth.

The third major objective of foreign assistance is security of the United States and its allies from external aggression. This objective is sought directly by the provision of armaments, the securing of military bases, and where critically important, the preclusion of Soviet-bloc penetration. External security is both a short-term and a long-term objective. It is supported in the long run by the economic development of the United States and its allies and in the short run by the maintenance of political stability.

While recognizing the interrelationships among these three objectives, we should keep them separate because the measures taken to achieve them vary in their impact and sometimes one must be sacrificed to another.

The Instrumentalities of Foreign Aid

The categories of aid that are incorporated in present and past legislation represent a compromise among three types of classification:

(a) *By method of financing:* hard loans, loans under easier terms, sales for local currency, grants.

(b) *By objective:* long-term development, political and economic stability, maintenance of military forces.

(c) *By type of resource transferred:* agricultural commodities, machinery and equipment, other commodities, personnel.

The principal categories of aid now used may be summarily described in terms of these three principles of classification as:

1. *Development Grants.* The provision of (a) grants for (b) development purposes. The resources transferred are to a large extent personnel. The main focus is on education, broadly defined. Capital goods and commodities related to technical assistance projects are also included.

2. *Development Loans.* The provision of (a) loans repayable in dollars for (b) long-term development purposes. Any type of resource may be transferred, but the main components are machinery and equipment (for project loans) and other commodities (for non-project or program loans).

3. *Supporting Assistance.* The provision of (a) grants or loans for (b) immediate political and economic stability and to offset the effects of military expenditures. The resources transferred may be any sort of commodity.

4. *Military Assistance.* The provision of (a) grants, loans, or sales of (c) military supplies and equipment and training services. The principal objective (b) is external security, but internal stability is an aim of increasing importance in some countries.

5. *Food for Peace.* The provision of (a) grants, loans, or sales for local currency of (c) surplus agricultural commodities. The objectives may be in any of the three categories.

Relations of Objectives to Instruments

To gauge the effect of foreign aid, we must look at the changes that a country makes in its total use of resources rather than just at what it does with our assistance. For example, if country X receives a development loan of $50 million for a steel mill and at the same time shifts $50 million of its own resources to its defense budget, the net effect of the loan is to finance an increase in military expenditure. The opposite may equally well be true. By financing imports of military equipment, we may enable a country to devote a higher proportion of its own foreign exchange and budget resources to developmental purposes. Since we usually relate our assistance to projects which both the United States and the recipient regard as having high priority, the added resources are likely to free some existing funds for use elsewhere. Therefore, the marginal increment in resource use does not in general correspond very closely to the type of aid provided. It is only when the expenditure desired by the United States is one that the country itself will forgo entirely in the absence of aid that the direct use of aid can be equated to the net effect on the economy.

The logical conclusions of the preceding argument are that (*a*) the donor of aid will have little or no control of the net impact of aid on the recipient unless he examines and influences the total proposed use of resources; and (*b*) the form of aid is largely immaterial to the receiving country so long as the proposed uses are known in advance and are within its own priorities for total resource use.

Criteria for Aid

The use of foreign assistance as an instrument of United States policy requires judgment on the following questions:

1. The probable effect of aid on the economy, military strength, and social structure of each recipient country.

2. As among countries, the relative importance to the United States of achieving the predicted results in each.

3. Alternative ways of achieving the same objectives.

4. The value received from additional foreign aid as compared to the value placed on alternative uses of United States budgetary funds.

A better judgment on these questions can be reached by considering alternative means of reaching given objectives and by reducing comparisons to quantitative terms whenever this is feasible.

For each of the three objectives of aid — external security, internal stability, and economic and social development — we can specify either a given set of requirements (targets) or a given amount of available resources. By either device the total problem is divided into three parts.

Each of these suballocation problems may then be stated as either: (*a*) to achieve the given requirements with minimum cost to the United States or (*b*) to achieve maximum progress toward the given objective from the fixed resources tentatively assigned to this use.

To resolve the over-all allocation problem, we can combine these two alternatives in various ways. One combination which corresponds reasonably well to the present philosophy of United States assistance is to fix minimum acceptable expenditures for the military security and internal stability objectives and then to maximize long-term social development of the less developed countries subject to these short-term limitations.

Aid for Economic and Social Development

Among the three general objectives, the rationale of aid for economic and social development is perhaps the clearest. Assume that the problem is to allocate a given sum among a number of countries so as to produce a pattern of social development that is in the best interest of the United States.

We can distinguish three links between the input of United States aid and the outcome of desired social development:

1. The effectiveness of aid in producing economic growth, as measured by the increase in national income and desirable changes in the economic structure.

2. The social changes that are likely to accompany (and be permitted by) economic improvement.

3. The importance to the United States of economic and social progress in the given country.

The economist's approach to this problem is to divide it into two parts: a *productivity aspect,* describing the first relation between aid and economic growth, and a *valuation aspect,* expressing the relative importance attached to the kind of social change that is expected to accompany economic growth. If we could give a numerical value to the social change produced in each country, it would be possible (conceptually, at least) to allocate aid among countries so as to produce a maximum return for a given amount of United States resources. Even in the absence of such measurements, this approach permits us to separate *productivity criteria* and *valuation criteria* in a useful way.

The criteria that received most attention in the presentation of foreign assistance legislation to Congress in 1961 were the productivity criteria. The best single measure of the productivity of aid is the amount of increase in the national product that is achievable from a given amount of aid over a given period of time. The following elements affect this productivity ratio:

(a) The country's endowment of natural resources.

(b) The foreign exchange earnings of the country and its need for imported goods. (Aid may have a very high productivity when there is a structural deficit in the balance of payments that takes several years to eliminate.)

(c) The total increase in skilled manpower that will result from the capital and technical assistance provided.

(d) The increase in total investment resources, including tax collections, that will take place as a result of the increase in incomes.

(e) The over-all efficiency of resource use in the country. In countries in which most of these factors are favorable, such as Japan, Israel, or Yugoslavia, the increase in total output per dollar of aid given may be very high because of the complementary nature of the external resources and the domestic resources that can be mobilized. In less favorable cases, there may be little mobilization of local resources as a result of aid, and a very low productivity ratio.

The elements in the valuation criterion are more difficult to specify with any precision. In general terms, our long-term social objective is to produce independent societies that are capable of self-sustaining economic and political evolution. The value that should be given to democratic forms (with perhaps less political stability) as compared to more central authority (with perhaps greater stability and economic growth) is a question that can at best be answered only for particular countries in the light of all the circumstances.

Two aspects of the development process are important to the making of intercountry valuations. The first is that a significant minimum change must be made in the social and economic structure of most underdeveloped countries in order to secure continued progress. An even spreading of United States assistance will therefore be less effective than a concentration which provides at least this minimum change in the more promising countries. Second, there is a point beyond which the need for external aid diminishes, as countries become more able to provide their own resources for growth.

In the past ten years, several less developed countries which formerly received substantial amounts of United States assistance have reached the point where they no longer require our aid for their continued growth. Included in this group are Italy, Japan, and Yugoslavia. Several other countries, such as Greece, Israel, and Taiwan, would be in this category if they did not have such heavy defense burdens. At the other extreme are countries that receive relatively little aid for opposite reasons: a low productivity of aid, despite a high valuation of the desirability of economic and social progress. In this second category, it is low absorptive capacity that limits the aid extended.

Aid for Political Stability

Economic assistance is one of the instruments of foreign policy that are used to prevent political and economic conditions from deteriorating in countries where we wish to sustain the present government. As with development aid, the analysis of this assistance can be broken down into a productivity aspect and a valuation aspect. The productivity of aid for stabilization depends in part on the nature of the government's economic difficulties and the extent to which they can be relieved by additional imports. The extent to which a government's political difficulties stem from the economic situation is also an important element.

A central question concerning this use of aid is the perverse incentive effect which it may have on governments that do not use their resources efficiently. Frequently, the availability of foreign help merely removes the pressure on the government to undertake needed political and economic reforms. Unlike the case of development aid, for which there are some objective measures of success, it is not possible to compare with any accuracy what has happened with aid for political purposes to what would have happened without it. It is a matter of political speculation whether Haiti, Bolivia, Jordan, and Laos, for example, are significantly more stable and progressive for having had substantial American assistance than they would have been with less or none.

The number of countries receiving aid mainly for short-run political reasons is relatively small, and this type of aid constitutes only 10 to 15 per cent of our total economic assistance programs. It is probably the most controversial feature of aid policy, however, and the one on which it is most difficult to form a judgment. Since the valuation aspect tends to dominate the productivity aspect in the decision on political aid, there is a tendency to use economic assistance to meet crises in which it can have relatively little effect unless accompanied by other political and economic measures that may not be forthcoming. The threat of a Communist takeover is the strongest political argument for aid, and it sometimes leads to the use of aid whose productivity is very low indeed. Moreover, the problem is complicated by the fact that the process is not readily reversible; whether the aid helps meet the crisis or not, the argument is often made that any sharp reduction in the aid would in itself create a crisis.

We must, however, accept the greater risks of failure that are inherent in this type of enterprise and not judge the immediate outcome in predominantly economic terms. Above all, we should not allow the fact that the importance of political stability sometimes leads us to undertake risky ventures in low-productivity countries to weaken or obscure the productivity criteria that we seek to apply to the great bulk of our economic aid. We should also resist the temptation to use aid in situations where it can have little effect, no matter how important the objective.

Aid for External Security

The preservation of the external security of the United States and its allies is probably the least controversial of the objectives of foreign assistance. Aid for this purpose is provided in the form of military goods and services under the Military Assistance Program. Additionally, the economic impact of military expenditure is also offset to some extent by the provision of nonmilitary commodities under Supporting Assistance and Food for Peace. Since the European countries have become able to take over almost all of their own defense costs, this type of aid now goes mainly to countries in the Middle and Far East. Correspondingly, the share of MAP in total aid has declined since 1954 from over 90 per cent to less than 40 per cent of total assistance.

The criteria for allocating military aid by country are in principle quite similar to the criteria for allocating development aid. The productivity aspect is measured by the increased defense effort that the recipient country is prepared to make in return for a given amount of assistance. The value to the United States of additional military strength varies greatly from country to country, however. As in the case of other types of aid, the valuation placed on an additional military effort in a certain country may be so high as to offset the low efficiency with which aid is used. Here again, neither the productivity test nor the valuation test can be used by itself.

One of the main problems in allocating aid for external security is to adjust our policy to changes in military technology and in the strategy of the cold war. In some countries, the threat of internal aggression may now be greater while the external threat may be less than when aid programs were initiated. Furthermore, the maintenance of the economic status quo is not sufficient to prevent internal unrest when economic development is taking place in other countries. In the long run, economic and social development are likely to be as important to the preservation of military security as military aid itself.

The Balance Among Objectives

Up to now, I have followed the procedure of breaking down the general United States objective of strengthening the nations of the free world into three more specific objectives: long-term social and economic development, political stability, and external security. In the actual formulation and execution of aid programs, each of these must in turn be translated into sectors of the economy to be strengthened, types of technical assistance to be provided, military missions to be performed, etc. The further we get from the over-all objective, however, the greater the need for comparison of the advantages of each type of program and for periodic re-examination of their total impact on each country.

After twenty years of United States experience with foreign assistance programs, there is now a general feeling that too much attention has been paid to the crises of the moment and not enough emphasis given to long-term improvements in societies. The most serious criticism that can be made of our aid programs is not that there has been occasional inefficiency or corruption in executing them but that their conception has often been too narrow and short-sighted. Somewhat paradoxically, the attempts to improve the efficiency of execution by focusing on particular projects may have contributed to this short-sighted view of the problem by diverting attention from the total use of a country's resources to the small fraction that is arbitrarily chosen for United States financing.

An attempt is now being made to reverse this trend and to provide aid on the basis of long-term development programs rather than merely for isolated projects. India, Pakistan, and Nigeria are the first countries to receive aid on this basis. It is anticipated that over the next several years a number of other countries will develop sufficiently well organized plans so that commitments can be made for their continuing support and aid can be related to the country's total use of resources.

The recognition that long-term development should receive relatively greater emphasis than in the past has implications both for the allocation of aid among regions and countries and for the composition of country programs. Among regions, Latin America and Africa should receive a greater share over the next few years because of this change in emphasis and because a high proportion of aid to these areas goes for long-term development. The main problem is to raise the productivity of aid to countries in these regions by helping them to make better use of their own resources as well as of those that we provide. This is one of the basic objectives of the Alliance for Progress. At the present time, development loans and grants to most countries in Latin America and Africa are limited more by the ability of these countries to use external resources effectively (the productivity test) than by a shortage of funds from the United States and other sources.

In order to promote long-term development to a greater extent, it may be necessary to take some risks in regard to the maintenance of existing governments. In the long run, however, support for progressive governments is likely to be a better way of combatting Communism around the world than giving funds on the basis of immediate political and military threats.

62

Foreign Aid: Strategy or Stopgap?*

Barbara Ward Jackson
Author, Lecturer

The following selection by a widely-known English writer on international affairs uses economic and political arguments to support the assertion that foreign aid should be reformulated as part of a long-run strategy. Like Hollis Chenery, she is an advocate of more rationality, more program, and less "shooting from the hip" in foreign aid, but also notice her more explicit attention to political objectives.

Semi-Modernization

What are programs of economic assistance *for?*

In the large context of peace and war, the fundamental aim of economic assistance is to build up stability in unstable states. This cannot be done by piecemeal patching up, by casual subsidies and handouts. The most successful of all programs of economic aid so far — the Marshall Plan — clearly illustrates the need for change in depth.

The same vision and daring are needed in the infinitely more complex pursuit of stability among the new states emerging from the old tutelage and lacking inner coherence. Action, therefore, is needed at two levels

* Taken and adapted from *Foreign Affairs* (October, 1962), pp. 90–104. Copyrighted by the Council on Foreign Relations, Inc., New York. Reproduced with permission.

— to complete the modernization of the local economies and to devise a world system that fosters the necessary change.

One should be wary of generalizations.

Yet in the last 150 years, the modernized states of the North Atlantic have broken up the static stability of traditional society — in Asia, in Africa, in feudal South America. They came in to search for raw materials — minerals, rubber, coffee, tea — and established small modernized export sectors. To these they attached their "infrastructure" of roads, railways and great coastal cities through which the materials flowed out to the West — and Western manufactures flowed back. Western incursion, however, did not stimulate or provide much local saving. Mines and plantations were often foreign-owned. As a result, little capital flowed back into the local economy — and without capital there is no growth, save in the single category of population. Food production remained unimproved. Industry did not develop. Revenue did not rise. Governments therefore could not afford expensive yet crucial services such as wider education. Only a small élite received some modern instruction — through the missionaries or the private enterprise of wealthy parents. Yet even so small a breach in the old stability undermined it. With the new goods came new ideas — sovereignty, nationalism, above all, equality between nations, equality within the state.

Such, then, is the anatomy of semi-modernization. Developed export sectors, the infrastructure they require, the beginnings of modern education — all these set in motion a passionate ferment through the vision they give of a wider and more commodious life. But the stark daily realities are of poverty, illiteracy, stagnant agriculture, marginal industry and a world economic system which offers no way out of the impasse. There is enough change to excite the desire for more, not enough to create it.

Objectives of Modernization

The essential task of economic assistance is, therefore, to correct and complete the old lopsided structure. Within the developing countries, it is a question of extending the colonial infrastructure, expanding education beyond a small élite, raising savings and channeling them into dynamic farming and growing industry where more savings can be secured by higher productivity. Thus the cycle of sustained growth can be set in motion. At the international level, the task is above all to restore a world-wide economy which stimulates and does not depress the possibilities of local development.

These are statements of high generality. Fortunately, in the last ten years, governments have begun to learn to fill in some of the details. The starting point is a progressive attempt to increase the flow of domestic capital. By general agreement it must rise to at least 15 percent of national income if sustained growth is to be secured. Such an increase does not happen easily or naturally in post-colonial economies. Hence the new importance placed on the formulation of country plans. Ten years ago, most plans were no more than the shopping lists of government departments. Today, their aim is at the very least to give a full picture of the economy, to lay down the forms of investment most likely to accelerate growth and to devise a financial strategy for raising the necessary capital and channeling it into the right enterprises.

At the core of the plan is the government's strategy for saving. The aim, in every country, is to keep resources rising in balance with a more ambitious scale of spending. It is a tricky balance. While there are no general rules, governments can hardly be said to be seriously bent on development unless they are willing to raise the level of taxation to some 20 percent of national income.

Where should the new resources go? To infrastructure, clearly — to fill in the gaps of the old pattern geared only to exports; and it is perhaps relevant to note that most developing governments underestimate the need for power and transport once growth begins in earnest. India's bottlenecks in its Third Plan are largely due to this. Yet the "infrastructure" of trained minds is even more important than railways or transmission lines. And in this vital field of education, it is very easy to get the balance wrong. Western and Eastern Nigeria have learned what happens if primary education is made very nearly universal before rural life has been improved enough to attract the school-leavers, or urban employment expanded to absorb them as they stream into the cities. For this reason a new emphasis is appearing on the need to plan investment in manpower in such a way that it fits into the general pattern of investment in the economy.

The universal test for all enterprise, public or private, must be its ability to operate at a profit. Profits imply above all a managerial competence and it is at this point that government planners tend to be most interested in the possibilities of investment by foreign firms. Virtually all developing countries have balance-of-payments problems and not one can hope to finance out of its own export income the foreign-exchange element in its plans for development. Even more dire than the scarcity of capital is the lack of industrial skills at every level, especially at the crucial level of management. The period of extreme dependence on outside skills can, however, be drastically shortened if the foreign firms are prepared to undertake imaginative programs of training which undoubtedly increase the acceptability of foreign enterprise. Yet there is an unsolved dilemma here. Massive foreign investment may hasten development; equally, however, local nationalist resentment will grow if a large part of the new industrial sector emerges — as it did in Cuba and could in Nigeria — under foreign control of one kind or another.

There is no escaping the problem. Foreign capital is an essential element in all industrialization since under-industrialized countries lack, by definition, the tools and machines for growth.

The workings of the world economy do not at present naturally provide sufficient access to the currencies of the developed, industrialized West. Western investment has always tended to go to other developed lands. The trend has not changed. If investment in oil is subtracted, the flow of private capital remains quite inadequate. When government grants and loans of all kinds are added, the flow today may reach between $7.8 and $8.7 billion a year. Yet, according to United Nations estimates, if over a billion developing peoples are to stay ahead of their exploding population and increase their rate of growth from 2 or 3 percent to 5 or 6 percent a year, capital coming in from outside should amount annually to some $10 to $12 billion. These are only broad orders of magnitude. The real gaps can be measured only plan by plan. But no one denies the gap. Nor does anyone maintain that the developing nations themselves, by increasing their trade with developing countries, can fill in the gap themselves.

Here the current system works wholly against them. The golden days for development in the last decade have had little to do with aid. They were sparked by the boom in world commodity prices after the Korean war. Then such lands as India and Nigeria financed their entire developmental expenditure. Today no poor nation can do so. The reason is not simply that the plans are bigger. In country after country in the last five years, the effect of economic aid has been very largely nullified by the steady fall in what the nations could earn by their primary exports and as steady a rise in the price of manufactures they import.

Nor is it simply a matter of unfavorable price levels. There is hardly a facet of Western trading policy that does not entail some disadvantage to the developing nations. The relative share of Atlantic income spent on raw materials produced elsewhere is still declining. A developing nation's first alternatives to primary exports — cheap textiles and semi-processed goods — are limited by Western quotas and differential tariffs. The picture is one of universal discouragement.

What Can Be Done?

With this question of the will to bring about the needed changes, we reach the tough political core of the assistance effort. At least three-quarters of the processes of modernization can be accomplished only by the recipients themselves. Yet bitter experience in the last ten years has shown that some kinds of society can do nothing with aid but waste it. What is to be done?

In theory, the path is clear. No government is worth supporting unless it is prepared to undertake the two or three key policies needed to set growth in motion. But in practice such governments often do not appear or cannot be coaxed into activity. After a century of Western control or at least predominant influence, nearly all developing governments react strongly, even violently, against attempts at direct Western political guidance. It represents precisely the tutelage from which they are trying to escape. In some areas, the reaction goes further. It does not take much insight to see that some of the necessary steps toward modernization imply radical social change. Mass education, land reform, wider taxation — all these break up the traditional patterns of authority. Can leaders be persuaded to reform themselves out of power? Is it not more likely that they will simply resist all changes in the name, say, of anti-Communism?

These risks vary from continent to continent. The worst deadlocks seem to arise in Latin America. Many of the rulers remain profoundly conservative — no recent colonial upheaval has widened their ranks. They enjoy friendly links with local American business interests. Neither group is precisely passionate for reform. Moreover, opinion in the United States — especially in Congress — inclines much more to conservative orthodoxy than does opinion in Europe where virtually the entire gamut of political upheaval has been traversed in the last 30 years.

What can be done? It is at this point that Western governments have to remind themselves of what they are really trying to do — to build viable states capable of coöperating in a viable world order. They have to remember, too, that they are not operating solely in terms of immediate conflicts, failures and successes but are attempting, over time, to produce profound modifications in the social order. To prop up, on any terms, a régime which will neither analyze its economy nor take the crucial steps to set it in motion can do no more than stave off and finally aggravate revolutionary upheaval. The reason why Latin America is more unstable now than it was five years ago has something to do with Fidel Castro. But it has much more to do with five years of declining export prices, general economic stagnation and perhaps 15,000,000 extra mouths to feed.

Funds given as foreign aid have to be given within a framework that at least aims at a strategy for growth. Governments with no plans for popular and technical education, with no policy for raising taxes toward the needed 20 percent of national income, with no ardor for land reform, with no general strategy for fostering savings and channeling them into productive investment — such governments are simply incapable of becoming valid partners in a serious effort of economic aid. Generous assistance must wait upon a change of heart and plan. The judgment may seem harsh. But what other way is there of convincing hesitant leaders that the reforms needed for growth are the preconditions of assistance?

Yet the most persuasive pressure is likely to come not from the negative side of refusing aid where reform is lacking but from the positive side of aid generously given when conditions are favorable. So far, this "demonstration effect" is missing. If the West seriously intended to coax the laggards along by carrots as well as sticks, the scale of Western commitments to India's Third Plan would not have been allowed to seem certain in 1961 and dubious again in 1962. Nigeria would not be wondering, six months after the publication of a sensible six year plan, whether, in addition to the $250 million pledged by the United States, any more of the $950 million it needs from abroad will in fact be available.

Western Strategy?

Do the Western powers really intend to develop an imaginative long-term strategy? The evidence seems rather contradictory. True, one can point to a number of promising signs that the Western effort is becoming more accepted and institutionalized. The funds available to the International Monetary Fund and to the World Bank have been doubled and the International Development Authority has been set up to provide less bankable loans. The United States agency for aid has been reorganized to make it more capable of undertaking sustained programs and Congress has given the Administration some latitude in aid-giving on a longer basis. France and Germany have Ministries of Coöperation, Britain a Department of Technical Coöperation. There is also more coördination — with the Alliance for Progress, under the Treaty of Rome with its common European Fund for Development, through the Atlantic-wide Organization for Economic Cooperation and Development with its Development Assistance Committee, through the United Nations Decade of Development.

Why, then, should one hesitate? The chief reason for concern is the fact that behind a good deal of governmental rhetoric and some solid governmental spending, the shape of a genuine Western strategy for aid and development remains very hazy. In other words, the second great task of world modernization — to provide a viable international framework for the developing nations — still hangs fire. If one takes three key issues in assistance — manpower, capital and trade — it is still impossible to discern anything like a clear and interrelated structure of policies.

To begin with manpower, there are also few firm plans — apart from France's effort and that of the small but valuable Peace Corps — for providing the massive number of teachers needed to carry out modernization, especially in Africa. The capital contribution made by the West, even including all forms of capital, is still too small by between $2 and $3 billion a year. It is over the issue of trade that one has most completely the sense of a blank in Western strategy. Only in the last year or so has the realization become more general that almost every aspect of Western trade policy discriminates *against* the developing world.

Behind the delays and tepidities of Western governments lies the indifference or the ignorance of Western electorates. Few voters feel a natural passion for voting themselves into taxes in order to assist foreigners.

Given this political context, efforts to persuade and enlighten the electorates of the West have to be intensified. The passage of time has not lessened the force of any of the old arguments. Enlightened self-interest among the trading nations of the West is still involved in any policy which systematically expands the economies and purchasing power of millions who, today, do not enter the market at all. In fact, the argument may now be stronger since, in the Western world, there are signs on all sides that Atlantic demand is near to saturation and new markets and new needs have to be opened up to keep the vast industrial system in trim.

There is equally no change in the argument that the alternatives to assistance are all worse. Aid may not absolutely ensure progress. But there is no "may" and "might" about the unchecked regression of unaided, unreformed economies toward anarchy and collapse. Aid, therefore, in the most literal sense, remains an essential instrument in Western security.

Above all, nothing has modified the argument which should be decisive for peoples who still like to boast of their Christian and humane inheritance and contrast their performance with the evils of "godless Communism." In the last decade, the national income of the Atlantic powers has grown by at least 3 percent a year. In the next decade, it is their declared intention to add to it another $500 billion. During this same period, the people of the poorer countries are barely keeping pace. In some areas, there has been a sharp decline. Given this contrast, no Western nation can plead inability. The issue is quite simply an issue of moral will. One may be forgiven for doubting whether the rich man's professions of idealism or religion have the faintest validity so long as the world's homeless are not sheltered and the hungry are not fed.

63

The Arithmetic of Underdevelopment*

PAUL ROSENSTEIN-RODAN, MAX MILLIKAN,
and DONALD L. M. BLACKMER
Massachusetts Institute of Technology

The patient reader is by now no doubt aware that comparison is the stuff of economics. Even in the international realm, where statistics are harder to assemble, the comparisons are to a great extent quantitative. We are asked not to question the derivation of the following figures in scrupulous detail. Their point is rather to indicate the relative ordering of relationships.

The following summary tables are designed to give a rough estimate of the external capital required over the next fifteen years to produce rates of growth in the underdeveloped countries which are regarded as feasible in the light of the absorptive capacity of these countries. The tables are derived from a study by Professor P. N. Rosenstein-Rodan, entitled "International Aid for Underdeveloped Countries." No attempt will be made here to justify these figures or to indicate the procedures by which they have been calculated. Those interested in the detailed country-by-country figures on which the summary tables are based and in the sources and methodology utilized should consult Professor Rodan's study, which was published in the May 1961 issue of *The Review of Economics and Statistics*.

* From *The Emerging Nations: Their Growth and United States Policy,* edited by Max F. Millikan and Donald L. M. Blackmer, by permission of Little, Brown and Company, publishers. Copyright © 1961, Massachusetts Institute of Technology.

Table 1 groups the world's countries by income levels, in terms of U.S. prices. It is derived from estimates of world GNP and population for 1961.

Table 2 gives estimates for 1961, 1966, 1971, and 1976 of the GNP of the underdeveloped countries in each major world area. The table is based on estimates for each underdeveloped country of the rates of growth of GNP which might be realistically anticipated if foreign capital were supplied according to criteria explained in the detailed study. These criteria relate to estimates of the absorptive capacity of the recipient countries. One of the important criteria proposed for the supply of foreign capital is that the recipient country should be making the maximum effort which can reasonably be expected to mobilize its own resources for growth purposes. In general, the estimates of absorptive capacity are based, first, on the record of the country in increasing its rate of investment in the recent past; second, on its recent record in raising its rate of savings and notably in achieving a higher marginal rate of savings than the average; and third, on a judgment as to the country's capability to

Table 1.   Estimated Distribution of World Income, 1961

Countries with GNP per Capita	Per Cent of World Population	Per Cent of GNP
$100 or less	0.4	0.1
($150 or less)	(26.6)	(6.3)
$101–$300	59.9	16.6
($151–$300)	(33.7)	(10.4)
$301–$600	8.7	6.4
$601–$1,200	15.1	21.9
Above $1,200	15.9	55.0

Table 2.   Estimated Gross National Product of Underdeveloped Countries, 1961–1976

	1961	1966	1971	1976
Africa	21	24	28	33
Latin America	65	79	98	122
Asia	65	80	99	123
Europe	21	25	31	39
Middle East	20	24	30	38
TOTAL	192	232	286	355

organize and administer its development effort. In making the estimates some improvement in each of these respects is assumed.

Table 3 summarizes for each of the next three five-year periods the estimated total capital inflow required by regions of the world and the estimated division of these totals between capital aid and private investment. Some elements of what has come to be called "foreign aid" in the American aid program are omitted from these figures (e.g., technical assistance and the emergency fund) because they do not constitute capital inflow in the usual sense. Also excluded are those elements of defense support which do not contribute directly to capital formation; that portion of surplus agricultural products which cannot properly be regarded as providing capital; and expenditures for so-called social development, en-

Table 3.   Estimated Capital Inflow Required Per Annum
by Underdeveloped Countries, 1961–1976
(*million dollars*)
A. 1961–1966

Region	Total Capital Inflow	Capital Aid	Private Investment
Africa	430	275	155
Latin America*	1,550	840	710
Asia	2,695	2,395	300
Middle East	640	475	165
Europe	385	305	80
TOTAL I	5,700	4,290	1,410

B. 1966–1971

Region	Total Capital Inflow	Capital Aid	Private Investment
Africa	605	395	210
Latin America*	1,495	585	910
Asia	2,380	1,965	415
Middle East	750	525	225
Europe	455	305	150
TOTAL I	5,685	3,775	1,910

C. 1971–1976

Region	Total Capital Inflow	Capital Aid	Private Investment
Africa	740	415	325
Latin America*	1,010	180	830
Asia	1,250	910	340
Middle East	400	180	220
Europe	360	185	175
TOTAL I	3,760	1,870	1,890

* Excluding Puerto Rico and the Virgin Islands.

compassing such items as education, health, and administration, which are not normally included in economists' statistical estimates of new productive capital.

The first column in this table estimates the capital inflow which would be required to produce the rates of growth assumed as reasonable in Table 2.

As a principle for dividing equitably among the developed countries the burden of supplying capital aid to the underdeveloped countries, we propose that relative shares be determined by applying to the per family GNP (in dollars) of the developed countries a rate of taxation which progresses with increasing income on the same basis as the present U.S. income tax. Table 4 applies this principle in "real" terms, that is, by valuing all elements of GNP at U.S. prices.

Table 4.   A Proposal for Sharing the Burden of Capital Aid*

	Weight Used (1)	GNP per Family (dollars) (2)	Tax per Family (dollars) (3)	Contribution (Per Cent)	
				With Soviet Union (4)	Without Soviet Union (5)
Belgium	1.23	6,632	729	1.2	1.4
Canada	1.00	7,954	1,002	3.4	3.7
Denmark	1.33	6,349	676	0.6	0.6
Finland	1.44	5,145	449	0.4	0.4
France	1.20	5,778	568	4.8	5.3
West Germany	1.43	6,366	679	7.0	7.7
Italy	1.44	3,587	164	1.5	1.6
Luxembourg	1.23	7,483	900	0.05	0.06
Netherlands	1.55	5,913	594	1.3	1.4
Norway	1.29	6,315	670	0.4	0.5
Oceania	1.33	5,877	585	1.7	1.9
Soviet Union	1.20	3,928	227	9.0	—
Sweden	1.30	8,096	1,033	1.4	1.6
Switzerland	1.25	7,778	944	0.9	1.0
United Kingdom	1.30	6,998	799	7.7	8.4
United States	1.00	11,161	1,728	58.6	64.4

* Based on the current U.S. progressive income tax schedule. Also, assuming GNP per family as a measure of income, with family consisting of four members.

B. ECONOMIC GROWTH AND DEVELOPMENT

• 64

The Stages of Economic Growth[*]

WALT WHITMAN ROSTOW
Massachusetts Institute of Technology

Historically-minded economists have long been interested in the idea of classifying the "stages" of a country's economic development. Contemporary economics places great emphasis upon the issues and problems of economic growth. Walt Whitman Rostow has constructed a modernized "stage theory" and has applied it to an historical interpretation of the growth process in a recent book, The Stages of Economic Growth: a Non-Communist Manifesto, *which, in London,* The Economist *has called "the most stimulating contribution to political and economic discussion made by any academic economist since the war."*

It is possible to identify all societies, in their economic dimensions, as lying within one of five categories: the traditional society, the precondi-

[*] Taken and adapted from *The Stages of Economic Growth: A Non-Communist Manifesto* (Cambridge: Cambridge University Press, 1960), pp. 4–8, 9–12, 17–18, 37–38. Reproduced with permission.

431

tions for take-off, the take-off, the drive to maturity, and the age of high mass-consumption.

The Traditional Society

First, the traditional society. A traditional society is one whose structure is developed within limited production functions, based on pre-Newtonian science and attitudes towards the physical world. Newton is here used as a symbol for that watershed in history when men came widely to believe that the external world was subject to a few knowable laws, and was systematically capable of productive manipulation.

The central fact about the traditional society was that a ceiling existed on the level of attainable output per head. This ceiling resulted from the fact that the potentialities which flow from modern science and technology were either not available or not regularly and systematically applied.

In terms of history then, with the phrase "traditional society" we are grouping the whole pre-Newtonian world: the dynasties in China; the civilization of the Middle East and the Mediterranean; the world of medieval Europe. And to them we add the societies which, for a time, remained untouched or unmoved by man's new capability for regularly manipulating his environment to his economic advantage.

To place these infinitely various, changing societies in a single category, we are merely clearing the way in order to get at the post-traditional societies, in which each of the major characteristics of the traditional society was altered in such ways as to permit regular growth.

The Preconditions for Take-Off

The second stage of growth embraces societies in the process of transition; that is, the period when the preconditions for take-off are developed; for it takes time to transform a traditional society in the ways necessary for it to exploit the fruits of modern science, to fend off diminishing returns, and thus to enjoy the blessings and choices opened up by the march of compound interest.

The preconditions for take-off were initially developed, in a clearly marked way, in Western Europe of the late seventeenth and early eighteenth centuries as the insights of modern science began to be translated into new production functions in both agriculture and industry, in a setting given dynamism by the lateral expansion of world markets and the international competition for them. Among the Western European states, Britain, favoured by geography, natural resources, trading possibilities, social and political structure, was the first to develop fully the preconditions for take-off.

The more general case in modern history, saw the preconditions arise from some external intrusion by more advanced societies. These shocked the traditional society and began or hastened its undoing.

This case fits not merely the evolution of most of Europe but also the greater part of Asia, the Middle East, and Africa.

Then there is the second case. This case covers the small group of nations that were, in a sense, 'born free': the United States, Australia, New Zealand, Canada, and, perhaps, a few others. These nations were created mainly out of a Britain already far along in the transitional process. Moreover, they were founded by social groups — usually one type of non-conformist or another — who were at the margin of the dynamic transitional process slowly going forward within Britain. Finally their physical settings — of wild but abundant land and other natural resources — discouraged the maintenance of such elements in the traditional structure as were transplanted, and they accelerated the transitional process by offering extremely attractive incentives to get on with economic growth. Thus the nations within the second case never became so deeply caught up in the structures, politics and values of the traditional society; and, therefore, the process of their transition to modern growth was mainly economic and technical. The creation of the preconditions for take-off was largely a matter of building social overhead capital — railways, ports and roads — and of finding an economic setting in which a shift from agriculture and trade to manufacture was profitable.

The Take-Off

We come now to the great watershed in the life of modern societies: the third stage in this sequence, the take-off. The take-off is the interval when the old blocks and resistances to steady growth are finally overcome. The forces making for economic progress, which yielded limited bursts and enclaves of modern activity, expand and come to dominate the society. Growth becomes its normal condition.

In Britain and the well-endowed parts of the world populated substantially from Britain (the United States, Canada, etc.) the proximate stimulus for take-off was mainly (but not wholly) technology. In the more general case, the take-off awaited not only the build-up of social overhead capital and a surge of technological development in industry and agriculture, but also the emergence to political power of a group prepared to regard the modernization of the economy as serious, high-order political business.

The beginning of take-off can usually be traced to a particular sharp stimulus. The stimulus may take the form of a political revolution which affects directly the balance of social power and effective values, the character of economic institutions, the distribution of income, the pattern of investment outlays and the proportion of potential innovations actually applied. Such was the case, for example, with the German revolution of 1848, the Meiji restoration in Japan of 1868, and the more recent achievement of Indian independence and the Communist victory in China. It may come about through a technological (including transport) innovation, which sets in motion a chain of secondary expansion in modern sectors and has powerful potential external economy effects which the society exploits. It may take the form of a newly favourable international environment, such as the opening of British and French markets to Swedish timber in the 1860's or a sharp relative rise in export prices and/or large new capital imports, as in the case of the United States from the late 1840's, but it may also come as a challenge posed by an unfavorable shift in the international environment, such as a sharp fall in the terms of trade (or a war-time blockage of foreign trade) requiring the rapid development of manufactured import substitutes, as with the Argentine and Australia from 1930 to 1945.

What is essential here is not the form of stimulus but the fact that the prior development of the society and its economy result in a positive, sustained, and self-reinforcing response to it.

The use of aggregative national-income terms evidently reveals little of the process which is occurring. It is nevertheless useful to regard as a necessary but not sufficient condition for the take-off the fact that the proportion of net investment to national income (or net national product) rises from, say, 5% to over 10%, definitely outstripping the likely population pressure and yielding a distinct rise in real output *per capita.*

During the take-off new industries expand rapidly, yielding profits a large proportion of which are reinvested in new plant; and these new industries, in turn, stimulate, through their rapidly expanding requirement for factory workers, the services to support them, and for other manufactured goods, a further expansion in urban areas and in other modern industrial plants. The whole process of expansion in the modern sector yields an increase of income in the hands of those who not only save at high rates but place their savings at the disposal of those engaged in modern sector activities. The new class of entrepreneurs expands; and it directs the enlarging flows of investment in the private sector. The economy exploits hitherto unused natural resources and methods of production.

One can approximately allocate the take-off of Britain to the two decades after 1783; France and the United States to the several decades preceding 1860; Germany, the third quarter of the nineteenth century; Japan, the fourth quarter of the nineteenth century; Russia and Canada the quarter-century or so preceding 1914; while during the 1950's India and China have, in quite different ways, launched their respective take-offs.

The Drive to Maturity

After take-off there follows a long interval of sustained if fluctuating progress, as the new regularly growing economy drives to extend modern technology over the whole front of its economic activity. Some 10–20% of the national income is steadily invested, permitting output regularly to outstrip the increase in population. The make-up of the economy changes unceasingly as technique improves, new industries accelerate, older industries level off. The economy finds its place in the international economy: goods formerly imported are produced at home; new import requirements develop, and new export commodities to match them. The society makes such terms as it will with the requirements of modern efficient production, balancing off the new against the older values and institutions, or revising the latter in such ways as to support rather than to retard the growth process.

Some sixty years after take-off begins (say, forty years after the end of take-off) what may be called maturity is generally attained. The economy, focused during the take-off around a relatively narrow complex of industry and technology, has extended its range into more refined and technologically often more complex processes; for example, there may be a shift in focus from the coal, iron, and heavy engineering industries of the railway phase to machine-tools, chemicals, and electrical equipment. This, for example, was the transition through which Germany, Britain, France, and the United States had passed by the end of the nineteenth century or shortly thereafter. Formally, we can define maturity as the stage in which an economy demonstrates the capacity to move beyond the original industries which powered its take-off and to absorb and to apply efficiently over a very wide range of its resources — if not the whole range — the most advanced fruits of (then) modern technology.

We offer the following sample as rough dates for technological maturity:

Great Britain	1850	Sweden	1930
United States	1900	Japan	1940
Germany	1910	Russia	1950
France	1910	Canada	1950

The Age of High Mass-Consumption

We come now to the age of high mass-consumption, where, in time, the leading sectors shift toward durable consumers' goods and services: a phase from which Americans are beginning to emerge; whose not unequivocal joys Western Europe and Japan are beginning energetically to probe; and with which Soviet society is engaged in an uneasy flirtation.

As societies achieved maturity in the twentieth century two things happened: real income per head rose to a point where a large number of persons gained a command over consumption which transcended basic food, shelter, and clothing; and the structure of the working force changed in ways which increased not only the proportion of urban to total population, but also the proportion of the population working in offices or in skilled factory jobs — aware of and anxious to acquire the consumption fruits of a mature economy.

In addition to these economic changes, the society ceased to accept the further extension of modern technology as an overriding objective. It is in this post-maturity stage, for example, that, through the political process, Western societies have chosen to allocate increased resources to social welfare and security. The emergence of the welfare state is one manifestation of a society's moving beyond technical maturity; but it is also at this stage that resources tend increasingly to be directed to the production of consumers' durables and to the diffusion of services on a mass basis, if consumers' sovereignty reigns. The sewing-machine, the bicycle, and then the various electric-powered household gadgets were gradually diffused. Historically, however, the decisive element has been the cheap mass automobile with its quite revolutionary effects — social as well as economic — on the life and expectations of society.

For the United States, the turning point was, perhaps, Henry Ford's moving assembly line of 1913–14; but it was in the 1920's, and again in the post-war decade, 1946–56, that this stage of growth was pressed to, virtually, its logical conclusion. In the 1950's Western Europe and Japan appear to have fully entered this phase, accounting substantially for a momentum in their economies quite unexpected in the immediate post-war years. The Soviet Union is technically ready for this stage, and, by every sign, its citizens hunger for it; but Communist leaders face difficult political and social problems of adjustment if this stage is launched.

Here then, in an impressionistic rather than an analytic way, are the stages-of-growth which can be distinguished once a traditional society begins its modernization: the transitional period when the preconditions for take-off are created generally in response to the intrusion of a foreign power, converging with certain domestic forces making for modernization; the take-off itself; the sweep into maturity generally taking up the life of about two further generations; and then, finally, if the rise of income has matched the spread of technological virtuosity, the diversion of the fully mature economy to the provision of durable consumers' goods and services (as well as the welfare state) for its increasingly urban — and then suburban — population.

• 65

The Economic Distance between Nations*

SURENDRA J. PATEL
United Nations Economic Commission for Africa

*The income gap between rich men and poor men has been de-
creasing in recent decades in the economically developed nations
of the West, largely through the process of general economic
growth. The same process, however, has increased the "economic
distance" between rich and poor economies. When did this gap
commence? "How long did the process take? What were the
dimensions of time and pace that brought it about? Can it be
bridged in the foreseeable future?"*

Throughout the ages most of mankind has spent most of its energy
making a living — finding food, clothing and shelter. The economic
problem was the nucleus of all its activities. Poverty and squalor were
the lot of most people. Economic inequality was an issue that always ex-
cited the most sensitive minds. Over the last century, however, the *per
capita* real income in the countries now called industrially advanced, has
risen seven- to ten-fold. In the process the age-old affliction of poverty
was swept away from the centre to the fringe. Domestic inequality
could no longer remain the battle-cry of social change in these countries.
A different type of inequality has now slowly impressed itself upon the

* Taken and adapted from "The Economic Distance between Nations: Its Origin,
Measurement and Outlook," *The Economic Journal*, March 1964, pp. 119–30, published by the Royal Economic Society. Reproduced with permission.

conscience of advanced thinkers — the vast gap in levels of living that divides rich and poor countries of the world. It has been characterised by Adlai Stevenson as "the most important and fateful fact in the world today." Now, on the second centenary of Adam Smith's advocacy of *laissez-faire,* nearly every country is planning to chart consciously the course of its development. And yet, the economic distance between the rich and the poor countries has continued to lengthen.

Some of the simplest, but obviously the most crucial questions concerning this economic distance still remain to be answered: When did it evolve? How long did the process take? How large is it? What were the dimensions of time and pace that brought it about? Can it be bridged in the foreseeable future?

The World Economic Landscape in 1850

The Industrial Revolution is dated to have begun nearly two centuries ago. But various indicators suggest that it could not have raised the average income much even in north-western Europe till about 1850. It would seem that in the economic landscape of the world in 1850 the industrial countries of to-day could not really have been the sunny mountain-tops and the pre-industrial ones the dark crevasses. As late as 1850, the average income in most countries was subsistence income — a rock-bottom level below which human existence would be impossible.

Evolution of the World Economy since 1850

How has the world economic landscape altered since 1850? How big and how rapid were these changes? What were the dimensions of time and pace? Rough data suggest a number of observations:

(1) The distribution of world population between the industrial and the pre-industrial countries has not altered significantly over these years. The population in the former increased slightly faster than in the latter.

(2) World population rose more than two and a half times. But world output multiplied by more than nine-fold, so that *per capita* income expanded nearly four times.

(3) Of much greater significance than these world averages are the marked disparate trends in the industrial and the pre-industrial countries. In the latter "the power of population" marched almost in line with the "power of production."

(4) In the industrial countries, population nearly trebled, but output increased by over twenty times. *Per capita* output rose more than seven times.

(5) In the industrial countries over these decades the share of agriculture fell from 40–50% of the total output to about 10%. On this basis,

agricultural output would appear to have increased about four- to five-fold, and its *per capita* availability by about 70%. The rise in industrial output, on the other hand, was spectacular — about forty-fold for total and fifteen-fold for *per capita* output.

(6) These trends have profoundly altered the distribution of world income. Half-way in the nineteenth century, the countries industrialised now accounted for about one-fourth of the population and one-third of the output in the world. By 1960, however, with only a slightly higher share of world population, they produced nearly 80% of world income.

(7) The average *per capita* income in the industrial countries by about 1850, was, as shown earlier, around 70% higher than in the pre-industrial ones. By 1960, however, it had grown to a level nine times as high as in the pre-industrial ones. It is thus only during the last century that in the long race for the conquest of poverty, the former have by far outdistanced the latter.

The analysis so far may be summarized thus: in terms of economic dynamics, the dimensions of time and pace for the evolution of international economic inequalities were: an annual growth of 1·8% in *per capita* output for 110 years in industrial countries against near stagnation in the pre-industrial ones.

Measurement of the Real Economic Distance

The outlook for economic growth in the industrial and pre-industrial countries over the years to come can hardly be assessed adequately without a working idea of the real economic distance between them. So far, the economic distance has been usually measured by the conventional yardstick of *per capita* income. Economists and statisticians have now produced such estimates for nearly every country. Take, for example, India and the United States.

(1) *Agricultural Output.* India is known as a land of agricultural scarcity. The United States, on the other hand, has faced an altogether different problem — agricultural surpluses. One might expect the difference in the output per head of total population between these two countries to be very wide. But if it is expressed in U.S. relative prices, as it should be for the purpose of comparison, the ratio is only 2·2:1.[1] *Per capita* income in the United States is nearly 30 times higher than in India, but agricultural output per head of population is only 2·2 times higher. The distance that separates agricultural surplus from scarcity is thus much narrower than has often been assumed.

---

[1] This is not as incredible as it may sound at first. The average U.S. stomach is little, if at all, larger than the average Indian stomach. The difference in *per capita* availability of food products in the two countries follows from the extent to which many stomachs remain empty and from the composition of diet in the two countries.

Once the gap is measured in this way, it can be suggested that at an annual *per capita* rate of growth of agricultural output of 2%, India would need about 40 years only to reach the present level of *per capita* output in the United States.

(2) *Industrial Output.* At current exchange rates the net value of industrial output per head of the total population in the United States is over 40 times higher than in India; but measured at comparable prices the ratio would seem to be in the range of 25–30. India would require roughly 70 years at a *per capita* rate of growth of 5% per year, 60 years at 6%, 50 years at 7%, 40 years at 9% and about 35 years at 10% to reach the present level in the United States. Although the gap is very wide, the time needed to overcome it would thus not be very long at a high rate (between 7 and 10%) — preferably much higher in the earlier and somewhat lower in the later period. These rates of growth are not very unusual. In recent decades many countries have attained and maintained them over considerable periods.

(3) *Total Commodity Output.* The adjusted total for *per capita* commodity output in India is about one-tenth of that in the United States. This is a gap which could be overcome in 80 years at an annual increase of 3% in *per capita* output; in 60 years at 4% and in 50 years at 5%. Thus, the dimensions of time and pace for the transition from abject poverty to relative affluence are five decades at a *per capita* growth rate of commodity output of about 5% per annum. Are these really forbidding magnitudes?

(4) The economic distance between India and the United States is wider than almost anywhere else in the world. For countries in the intermediate range the dimensions of time and pace for bridging the gap would be obviously smaller. Measured in this manner, the task of narrowing the gap — even at its widest — needs no more than half a century, or just an adult lifetime, and not endless and hopeless centuries. There is thus little ground for pathetic patience with postponing the possible — a very rapid elimination of want and poverty.

Outlook for the Decades to Come

At the centre of postwar growth analysis has remained the notion of the vicious circle of poverty, suggesting that a country is poor simply because it is poor. In the pre-industrial countries *per capita* income is low, consumption high and savings (and therefore investment) necessarily low. Under the circumstances it would be idle to expect a high rate of economic growth. The ascent from such a deep crevasse of poverty is thus bound to be a long, arduous and often a hopeless undertaking.

And yet, the countries industrialised now were not, around half-way in the nineteenth century, much richer (or even more enlightened) than most of the pre-industrial countries now or then. Only a century ago the economic landscape of the world was pretty flat — some countries slightly better than others, but not really very much. From then on the engine of economic expansion in the industrialising countries moved at a moderate speed — by 1·8% *per capita* per year. But continuous creeping for over a hundred years even at this slow pace has brought about massive economic expansion — a seven-to-ten-fold rise in average *per capita* income.

A number of factors could help towards the attainment of even a higher rate of growth in the pre-industrial countries. Assistance from the already industrialised countries can be expected to rise significantly, particularly with some success towards disarmament. Public pressure for accelerating the tempo of economic growth is acting as the most powerful solvent of the rigidities of an out-moded social set-up. Planning Commissions and Agencies are being established to steer the economies towards set goals. Even when their performance falls far short of expectations the wide acceptance of forward-looking goals is acting as a catalyst in the process of overcoming the obstacles — almost in the same manner as the goal of political independence swept away in less than a decade and a half those handicaps which were the hobby-horses of the professors of political science. The revolution of rising expectations is creating its own social forces — on a national as well as on an international scale — to fulfil itself.

The main task before a growth-economist to-day is to elaborate the concrete technical details for attaining a high rate of economic growth — say, 5% *per capita* per year for half a century. The final solution of the economic problem then would need no more than an adult's life-time.

66

Are There Primrose Paths to Economic Development?*

BENJAMIN HIGGINS
University of Texas

"Go the primrose way to the everlasting bonfire."
—*Shakespeare*

Can countries that are both poor and nationalistic raise living standards without sacrificing current consumption or relying upon foreign aid or investment? This selection analyzes and evaluates four nostrums for doing just this.

In countries which are both poor and nationalistic neither sacrifices from current consumption nor heavy reliance on foreign aid and investment is popular with the electorate. Hence, governments might be expected to cast about for nostrums that will raise standards of living without following either of these painful paths to development. Four kinds of primrose path for financing development have been seriously discussed: up by the bootstraps, controlled inflation, pump-priming, and expropriation of foreign investments.

* Reprinted from *Economic Development* by Benjamin Higgins. By permission of W. W. Norton & Company, Inc. Copyright © 1959 by W. W. Norton & Company, Inc.

Up by the Bootstraps?

Some recent writings suggest that economic development of under-developed areas may be possible, without substantial sacrifice of current consumption and without foreign capital, by effective use of the disguised unemployment that exists in most such countries. The argument is two-fold. First, it should be possible to devise means of increasing productivity per man-hour which do not require heavy investment of the kind prevalent in advanced countries. Mere transfer of the techniques employed in advanced countries, where labor is more scarce than capital, is inappropriate in countries where capital is more scarce than labor. Secondly, the disguised unemployment in agriculture could be attracted into industrial projects, permitting an increase in industrial output with no offsetting decline in agricultural production.

Moreover, the argument continues, governments should not be misled by the "financial illusion"; such projects may cost money, but they entail no real social cost, since no alternative production is sacrificed by using on these projects labor that would otherwise be effectively employed. Food supply will not be diminished, and farmers who previously provided food to the former disguised unemployed can sell their surplus to the same people, now employed as wage earners. The farmers will therefore be able to pay higher taxes, and these taxes can be used to finance the development project. The completion of the projects will result in increases in agricultural production. The increased income of farmers in turn can then be recaptured in higher taxes, leaving farmers little better off than before, it is true, but permitting the increased output of agricultural goods to be exported, in order to pay for capital imports for further development. The taxing away of the increased yields may also be necessary, to prevent any increased productivity from being dissipated in increased leisure or in higher rates of population growth. Thus, a process of economic development is generated without foreign capital and with only modest and temporary sacrifices of present consumption.

Development of something like this kind has taken place at least once, and possibly twice. England, as the first country to industrialize, was not in a position to finance much of its early economic development by borrowing from abroad. However, it is worth remembering the conditions under which English economic development took place. For one thing, English workers shared very little in the fruits of economic development during its first decades. Men, women, and even children worked ten to fourteen hours per day for extremely low wages. The condition of the English urban worker in the eighteenth century was probably worse than that of the English peasant, or even of the peasant in some under-developed areas today. Former peasants, *forced* off the land into the factories through the enclosure movement, lived in the cities under conditions of appalling poverty, misery, and squalor. Moreover, up to the mid-nineteenth century the fiscal structure was highly regressive. With revenues derived mainly from commodity taxes and much of the government expenditures going to servicing the national debt, subsidies to new enterprises, and the like, the fiscal system redistributed income from poor to rich, making possible high levels of saving. Meanwhile, the Reformation had created a puritanical attitude toward consumption and saving, so that the rich reinvested their earnings rather than engaging in conspicuous consumption. Trade-unions were illegal up to 1825 and even then were very weak. There was no "social security" for workers during this period. Public assistance was limited to the dole and the poorhouse. It might also be said that England at the beginning of its period of rapid industrial expansion had a very small population (about four million) and still had undiscovered resources.

Finally, the industrialization of England was neither rapid nor spontaneous. A series of external events spread over centuries contributed to the Industrial Revolution in England: the expansion of European trade following the Crusades; the new trading possibilities opened up by the geographic discoveries of the late fifteenth and sixteenth centuries; the "price revolution" of the sixteenth century, through which a flow of gold and silver from the New World through Spain to Northern Europe provided the base for "easy money" policies; the development of the Dutch and German trading and financial empires. Even in Britain industrialization was not entirely a bootstrap operation.

The second case, although superficially very different, shows fundamental similarities. Under a strong totalitarian government, Russia has been able to industrialize rapidly during the past thirty-five years. However, this industrialization was achieved, at least in its early stages, largely at the expense of the kulaks and peasants. The former were liquidated and the latter seem at times to have been literally starved, to provide a surplus of foodstuffs for the support of workers in the factories and on development projects.

In other words, the "up by the bootstraps" approach has succeeded only where severe sacrifices have been forced on the masses of the people, to provide a basis for capital accumulation. As proposed for underdeveloped areas today, the up by the bootstraps method does not necessarily require reductions in the standard of living to start the development process, but it does mean that the initial increases in output must be denied to the people, in order to provide an export surplus to finance further expansion. An integral part of the scheme is heavier taxation of farmers, first to compel them to produce as much as before although they have fewer mouths to feed, and secondly, to drain off the increase in output and income as the development projects have their effect. This rise in taxa-

tion, and consequent prevention of initial improvements in living standards, is necessary, not only to provide an export surplus, but also to
prevent the increased productivity from being converted into increased
leisure or a more rapid rate of population growth rather than into increased output. The proposed up by the bootstraps route to higher living
standards will prove, at best, only somewhat less uncomfortable than the
one actually followed in England and in Russia.

Moreover, it is misleading to suggest that this sort of project will produce sustained development with *no* capital. Even road construction or
irrigation requires some simple tools. Thus some increased saving will be
necessary at the beginning, even though the volume required may be less
than for a development program consisting mainly of capital-intensive
projects.

There is also a serious question as to how much this sort of project
alone can raise productivity. Some improvement can certainly be
achieved in this manner, but it is doubtful whether the rate of expansion
would be sufficient to overcome the inertia of an economy that has been
stagnant for centuries and to launch a process of cumulative economic
growth.

Finally, the amount of disguised unemployment in agriculture can
easily be exaggerated. With present techniques the entire labor force in
the rural sector is needed at planting and harvesting time. Substantial
numbers cannot be released from agriculture for full-time industrial jobs
without a drop in agricultural production unless the average size of holdings is increased and some degree of mechanization introduced.

Finance by Inflation?

Some writers have suggested that the simplest way to finance development for underdeveloped areas is to print money or borrow from the
banking system — in short, by inflation. In this fashion, it is maintained,
the population will be "forced" to save since the rise in prices will necessi-
tate a reduction in the volume of physical consumption.

Of course, in recommending inflation as a financing device, no one is
suggesting that underdeveloped countries should subject themselves to
the kind of hyperinflation that took place in advanced countries between
the wars. It is universally recognized that such cumulative inflations not
only disrupt the economy but pave the way for social and political
upheavals as well.

Even the "controlled" inflations which are advocated, however, may
have great disadvantages for underdeveloped countries. Most of these
suffer from a tendency for investment to be directed toward speculative
holding of inventories, rather than to the establishment or expansion of

productive enterprises. A constantly rising price level tends to aggravate this tendency by making speculation all the more profitable.

A development program which is financed in an inflationary fashion to begin with — say, by borrowing from the central bank — will not lead to a serious rise in prices, because any initial rise will result in absorption of the unemployed and increased output of goods and services. This argument, valid enough in advanced countries, does not hold in underdeveloped ones, because there is little excess capacity in farms or factories to match unemployment. Moreover, the tax system of many underdeveloped countries is so inelastic, that their governments could not count on the yield of taxes rising substantially with prices, so as to impose an "automatic stabilizer" effect. Further, many of the investment projects needed in underdeveloped areas are of a long-term nature which will bring increases in output only after a considerable lag and, once the "demonstration effect" begins to operate, people may spend an increasing share of their incomes on new consumers' goods.

Pump-priming

Under the combined pressures of continuing depression and "the New Economics," old-fashioned canons of "sound public finance" gave way in the late 1930's to ideas of "compensatory fiscal policy." To a few economists and to larger numbers of businessmen and politicians, however, the concept of increased government intervention in economic life, even for so worthy a purpose as stabilizing the economy, was abhorrent. Yet these people recognized the danger to democratic society of continued mass unemployment. There was a brief phase when persons of this political faith sought an escape from this dilemma in "pump-priming." The basic idea was that the Depression might be overcome by modest and temporary increases in public spending, designed to "prime the pump" and start the "normal" process of steady economic growth flowing again.

As understanding of the expansionary process increased, optimism about the efficacy of pump-priming dissolved. It was demonstrated that the nature of the expansion path depended upon interactions and relative magnitudes of the "multiplier" (increases in consumer spending resulting from an initial increase in investment) and the "accelerator" (increases in investment resulting from initial increases in consumer spending). If the accelerator were relatively low, the expansion path would have roughly the same shape as if the multiplier were operating alone: after a short period of increasing income, income would return again to its original level — assuming, of course, that the values of the multiplier and the accelerator coefficients did not change in the process.

The general effect of this closer study of pump-priming was to show the extremely small possibility that a short period of increased government spending followed by withdrawal would result in resumption of growth. The forlorn hope of finding in pump-priming an escape from the dilemma of continued depression on the one hand or increased government intervention on the other has its psychological counterpart today. In both developed and in underdeveloped countries, some people today, alarmed by the requirements for sustained economic growth, hope to find a means of producing a take-off without either increased taxes and savings at home or increased foreign aid and investment. Will not a large *initial* effort permit a return to "normal" and sustained economic growth as well?

Although it may be true that a big push is needed to launch economic growth, and although it may also be true that *percentage increases* in investment can be allowed to drop once the process of growth is under way, this does not mean that having once started economic growth it will be possible to reduce total investment, or even to reduce the proportion of national income devoted to investment purposes. Steady growth requires that both the amount of investment and the ratio of investment to income should continue to rise for some decades until a level equal to 15 or 20 per cent of national income is reached. This level must then be sustained if growth is to continue unabated.

Thus the concept of pump-priming as an escape from the hard facts of economic life is no more applicable to problems of development of underdeveloped areas than it was to the problem of steady growth in highly industrialized economies. There is no escape from the need to increase the rate of capital formation.

Confiscation of Foreign Enterprises

Most people in the Western world would probably reject confiscation of foreign enterprises an unworthy serious consideration, but the device has been seriously proposed. It has also been carried through by some governments of underdeveloped countries — notably Mexico, Iran, Egypt, and (on a very small scale) Indonesia — with varying degrees of success. It seems to have worked well in Mexico. In Indonesia, it seems to have delayed a take-off.

Obviously, unilateral action by the government of an underdeveloped area to confiscate foreign properties would undermine that country's relations with the outside world and would probably destroy temporarily any hopes of obtaining new capital assistance.

This approach has some serious limitations. First, there are relatively few underdeveloped countries where the additional financial resources that could be made available for economic development through confiscation would be sufficient to do the job. There would of course be substantial differences in this respect from one country to another; in countries where foreign enterprises comprise a large share of the economy and plough back little of their earnings within the country this limitation would not apply.

Secondly, the necessary technical and managerial personnel for operating such enterprises is often not available among nationals of underdeveloped countries. Obtaining them on a salary basis may not be easy if combined with confiscation, even when the confiscation takes place through international agreement.

Thirdly, the confiscation approach is essentially "isolationist" in character. From many points of view, an approach involving elements of "partnership" between the underdeveloped countries and the advanced ones is more attractive; it seems better designed to produce an integrated international economy.

Conclusions

Unpalatable though it may be to governments of underdeveloped countries, our main conclusion is clear: there *are* no "primrose paths" to economic development. Without a certain amount of national sacrifice, economic development will not occur. The sacrifice may take one or all of the following forms:

1. Working harder and better.

2. Saving voluntarily to finance development investment, public or private.

3. Paying higher taxes to finance development investment.

4. Encouraging foreign investment, with whatever temporary sacrifices of opportunities for national businessmen may be involved.

5. Accepting foreign aid, with whatever commitment is required as a condition for receipt of such aid. It is to be hoped that in future the only conditions imposed by grantor countries will be submission by the beneficiary country of a well-constructed development plan, as a basis for aid; but even a good development plan requires some commitment and some sacrifice.

67

Trends *in Economic Thought on*
*Underdevelopment**

Hans W. Singer
United Nations

The preceding selection emphasized the fact that there are no "primrose paths" to economic development, that development involves important sacrifices. The author of this selection was himself a contributor to earlier pessimism regarding prospects for development in underdeveloped economies with his concept of "a system not only of vicious circles, but of vicious circles within vicious circles, and of interlocking vicious circles."[1] Here he tempers that pessimism by a review of recent trends in the literature of economic underdevelopment, trends that are characterized by at least qualified optimism.

U Optimism, D Pessimism

In the great sweep of economic thinking from Smith and Ricardo to Keynes there were of course enormous doctrinal differences and a great diversity of interest, background, and experience. But despite all this

* Taken and adapted from *Social Research* (Winter, 1961) pp. 387–400, 413–14. Reproduced with permission.

[1] Cf. "Economic Progress in Underdeveloped Countries," *Social Research*, March 1949, pp. 1–11.

there was a surprising agreement that in already developed countries economic growth would sooner or later succumb to some kind of obstacle or come up against some kind of ceiling, while in countries where development had not yet begun, conditions were propitious to its initiation. With a convenient abbreviation of growth prospects in developed and underdeveloped countries, this long line of illustrious thinkers can be described as D pessimistic and U optimistic.[2]

It is true that Adam Smith, writing at the dawn of the industrial revolution, did not give much thought to where it might all end. He was too impressed by the beginnings of the process. But from Ricardo on there can be no doubt. To him the gravedigger of progress was, of course, the law of diminishing returns in agriculture. To Malthus it was population growth. Karl Marx's gravedigger was collapse of markets and insufficiency of purchasing power. Schumpeter's was the undermining of the entrepreneurial spirit. In Keynes' view, the villain of the piece was the "falling marginal efficiency of capital": new investment opportunities would be gradually used up and progress would come to a stop.

The U optimism of the great economists from Ricardo to Keynes was mainly a direct consequence of their belief that economic progress was self-limiting or gravedigging in character. Since the self-limiting factors were created by economic progress itself, it was clear that they could not operate in the early stages of progress. In underdeveloped countries the marginal-efficiency schedule, to take Keynes as an example, would not have had time to fall very much; splendid investment opportunities would abound, since they had not yet been used up by previous capital accumulation; rates of interest could still be brought down in many ways, by improved financial institutions or otherwise, before they would strike rock bottom.

This U optimism was also a reflection of the historical evidence of their day. They saw one country after another joining in the march of progress: first Belgium and Holland and France, then the United States and Germany, then Japan, then Russia, then Canada, Australia, New Zealand. Economic beliefs and policies (Japan, Russia) might differ from those of the pioneers. The march of progress seemed a little selective, seemed hesitant in tropical countries and non-white countries, but this could generally be explained on non-economic grounds, such as the effect of tropical climates on peoples' willingness or ability to exert themselves, the influence of fatalistic religions or philosophies. In economic principle the U optimism was general, even though in sociological application it tended to be limited to the white or European-style world. (The Japanese

---

[2] Editors' Note: Where do you stand after reading this article? Are you optimistic or pessimistic about U? Your opinion about these prospects should be given a consistent expression in what and how much you think should be done to facilitate economic development by the D countries.

always gave trouble in this scheme, but did they not live in a temperate climate?)

D Pessimism to D Optimism

In the decade after World War II this attitude of D pessimism and U optimism turned into its exact reverse. It now came to be the widely prevailing belief that the developed countries could continue in indefinite self-sustaining growth, and this was combined with a rather gloomy view of the formidable obstacles and vicious circles standing in the way of underdeveloped countries. Why this reversal?

Let us begin with D. In the first place, the depression of the 1930s was over. War had shown the great powers of industrial countries to expand their production even under conditions of great labor and raw-material shortages. The widely predicted postwar slump in their economies failed to materialize. The effectiveness of Keynesian policies in avoiding depression, stagnation, and inflation (at least of the galloping kind) was impressively demonstrated. A great speeding up of technical progress had occurred, partly under the pressure of war necessities but by no means limited to wartime applications. The development of synthetic materials had removed part of the Ricardian nightmare of diminishing returns. Perhaps even more important, the immediate postwar period most impressively demonstrated the capacity of industrial countries to overcome with unexpected ease the effects of even widespread war destruction and war dislocation.

All this served to direct attention, as regarded the developed countries, away from such factors as physical capital and dependence on natural commodities — in both of which lurked the dangerous traps of falling marginal efficiency or diminishing returns — and toward the human factor in development: skills, training, attitudes, institutions, research genius, methods for applying new research in production. Once this shift had taken place, the idea of self-sustaining growth became much more plausible. The human mind and its products are not subject to diminishing returns in the sense in which physical capital, labor, or natural materials alone may be assumed to be. On the contrary, there is good reason to assume something like a law of increasing returns in research and human development. As research proceeds, each new discovery has increasingly widespread and diversified potentialities for other lines of discovery. Investment in education not only is highly productive, but yields increasing returns in so far as cooperating teams of skilled and educated people are worth more than the sums of the individuals of which they are composed.

Yet another reflection, and perhaps also cause, of this change in thought was the notion of the "take-off into self-sustained growth," most popular in the form put forward by Walt Rostow in his *Stages of Economic Growth*. The metaphors of this school are drawn from aeronautics and space research: it is much easier for an airplane to continue in serene flight than it was to take off and gain altitude.

From U Optimism to U Pessimism

Now let us look at the other side of the coin, the changeover from U optimism to U pessimism. In some ways this follows directly from the opposite reversal in views concerning the more developed countries.

1. "The Take-Off"

This is particularly clear in the "take-off" theory proposed by Rostow. The underdeveloped countries, according to this theory, stand at the beginning of the runway, or are not even on it yet, and an enormous concentration of effort will be required to take them down the runway in exactly the right combination of circumstances and at very high speed, so that they may become airborne. They must first create a number of diverse preconditions, which include such tasks as changes in institutions and attitudes, the provision of social and economic overhead capital, the raising of agricultural productivity, a solution to land-tenure problems. Even the successful handling of these tricky matters will only place an underdeveloped country on the runway, and before take-off is achieved it must double, roughly, its rate of net investment within a comparatively short time — from 5 to 10 percent — must develop a leading manufacturing sector strategically placed and able to have strong linkage effects on the whole economic system, and must simultaneously create the capacity to transfer this impetus to other leading sectors as soon as the first leading sector begins to slacken. These are very formidable requirements indeed. In fact, one begins to wonder how any country has ever managed to achieve a take-off. At any rate, this view of the matter must certainly be classified as an expression of innate pessimism about the prospects of take-offs by the present underdeveloped countries.

2. Barriers and Obstacles — The Big Push

The general belief in this postwar U pessimism was that some kind of obstacle or barrier makes modest initial growth self-canceling rather than cumulative, and can be overcome only by some kind of "big push." The most obvious illustration is population. Small advances will simply be eaten up by a fall in the death rate, possibly accompanied by an initial rise in the birth rate. It would require an extraordinary advance in living standards, of such a kind as to change fundamentally the attitudes toward large families, in order to overcome the population hurdle; yet the achievement of this fundamental improvement is made well-nigh impossible by the self-limiting nature of the growth rates that are feasible. If only the "big push" could be achieved, it would then be downhill coasting — but how to get to the top of the hill?

The theory of the "big push" as a necessary condition for progress had many other implications, quite apart from population. The most important relates, as has been emphasized especially by Paul Rosenstein-Rodan, to the provision of overhead capital — transport and communications, housing, urban utilities, schools and educational systems, hospital and health systems. Such overhead capital is notoriously expensive to provide, for it has a high capital/output rate and a very long gestation period. If it is an essential precondition of growth, most or all underdeveloped countries may very well fail to achieve progress, for they may never be able to assemble first the required volume of overhead capital.

3. *Balanced Growth*

Another variation of the "big push" theory is the theory of "balanced growth," proposed particularly by the late Professor Nurkse that unless an underdeveloped economy has sufficient slack in it, and a sufficient volume of unutilized resources, to enable it to engage in simultaneous expansion along a broad front, the road to growth may be barred.

4. *Backwash Effects*

One of the clearest connections between the postwar trend toward D optimism and that toward U pessimism is evident in the so-called "backwash" theories, associated with the name of Gunnar Myrdal. According to these theories the growth of D, apart from any beneficial or "spreading" effects on U, also exerts there certain harmful or "backwash" effects — for example by leading to imitation and thus promoting a premature desire for high-level consumption or premature ideas about such goals as the welfare state, social insurance, minimum-wage legislation.

5. *The Vicious Circles*

In this turn toward pessimism the situation in underdeveloped countries was increasingly described as a system of "vicious circles." In the course of time, more and more were discovered, so many that one author said that "The road to economic development is paved with vicious circles": various factors are so interlocked that they mutually tend to produce a stagnant or stationary situation from which it is extremely difficult to move away. Perhaps the prototype of all vicious circles is the one that runs as follows: low incomes, low savings capacity, low investment, low output, back to low incomes.

From U Pessimism to U Qualified Optimism

But as the 1950s rolled toward their close, it became more and more apparent that economic thinking may have swung too far toward U pessimism. It began to be realized that despite the talk of an "increasing gap" between D and U, the actual data are not very clear on this point. During the postwar decade the national income of underdeveloped countries as a group increased at about the same rate as that of more developed countries as a group. A number of underdeveloped countries progressed quite rapidly during the postwar decade; for instance, the growth of the Latin American region as a whole compared rather favorably with that of the more developed countries. The impression of an "increasing gap" was perhaps due mainly to the fact that some underdeveloped countries or regions conspicuously failed to join in the march of progress, and also to an understandable concern about the continued existence of world mass poverty.

As regards the terms of trade of underdeveloped countries, the more pessimistic assumptions that they would undergo a steady long-term deterioration were not borne out during the postwar period; actually they were more favorable then than during the 1930s.

Another, and more clearcut, aspect of the factual situation has been the development of public foreign aid. It has become increasingly clear that a far-reaching and probably long-term change has occurred in the attitude of D toward the question of aiding U. The concept of a single world economy has risen on the horizon, and to a remarkable degree the developed countries have recognized a responsibility to assist the underdeveloped countries, by means that only a few years ago might have been rejected as too heterodox. Simultaneously, there has developed a great new international movement under the banner of "technical assistance," for transferring and adapting mankind's enormous stock of technical knowledge and expertise.

On the operational level, too, new orientations are emerging. It has been found that by using planning techniques, such as guided the war economies of the more developed countries, it is possible to make progress even with limited resources, concentrating them at strategic points with a maximum of linkage effect. Doubts have come to be felt whether the complete assembling of economic and social overhead capital is really a necessary precondition for progress in increasing actual production: the question has risen whether it is not possible, by judicious and strategic use of resources, to promote production even where there are shortages of such overhead facilities as transport and power, ultimately increasing their supply by means of the increased pressure. Countries like England, the United States, France, or even czarist Russia did not have to go through the kind of tremendous concentrated effort and uprise in investment ratio required by the idea of the "take-off." In fact, economic growth there was quite steady, gradual, and organic. And there now seems to be no compelling reason why this could not be the case also in the underdeveloped countries.

The readjustment that is now taking place in thinking about economic development is not a return to the somewhat romantic optimism, more implicit than argued, of the earlier economists. There is enough in the general picture to contradict that view: much evidence of stagnation, weakness of primary commodities, increasingly capital-intensive technology. The difficulties pointed out by the pessimistic theorists of the postwar decade are by no means absent; on the contrary, the spadework of those theorists has made us much more aware of the problems to be faced. But there is now seen to be much to relieve the gloom: evidence of progress, development of international aid and technical assistance, advances in development planning techniques. The difficulties are now felt to be in the nature of a challenge that is not beyond the capacities of human wisdom and human effort, rather than immutable and probably insurmountable obstacles.

The new trend is a pragmatic one, reflecting an effort to build on the more hopeful elements in the picture and to strengthen them, while reducing the effects of the unfavorable elements. More emphasis is placed now on the availability of unutilized potentials — in labor, human talent (including entrepreneurial abilities), resources of all kinds, savings capacity, fiscal capacity, directions of technological research — and on the possibilities of activating them.

We have seen that the postwar decade tended toward a pessimistic view regarding the underdeveloped countries, looking on their heavy capital requirements, low savings capacities, bad savings habits (gold, real estate, and so on), bad entrepreneurial habits (speculation, hoarding of goods, capital flight) as tremendous obstacles to investment. Today, without denying the accuracy of that analysis, we can regard the obstacles as somewhat less formidable. It now appears that the great problem lies deeper, in inadequate inducement to invest and an inadequate efficiency of investment, and that both of these are susceptible of change. A great deal has been learned about rational approaches to the productive use of scarce resources, whereby capital requirements can be minimized through strategic timing, selective economies, and the dynamics of mutual stimulation. The provision of public aid by the industrial countries is increasing, in forms and under conditions in which it can really be helpful to the underdeveloped countries. World conscience is thoroughly aroused, and the concept of an "interdependent world economy" is beginning to be more than an abstraction of the textbooks.

It seems, therefore, that we can be moderately optimistic about the economic trends in underdeveloped countries as a whole over the generation or so to come — though on rather different grounds from the romantic or dogmatic or philosophical optimism of the economists before World War II. Ours must be an optimism of gradualism. Given sufficient time, we can help the potentially generative forces to work themselves out. There is hope in the picture but no certainty.

68

On the Adequacy of Postwar Economic Growth in the United States*

WALLACE C. PETERSON
University of Nebraska

This selection poses an interesting paradox: Although output per capita is only slightly higher than in 1944 (6 per cent in 1960), the postwar period has been characterized by a "real and sustained increase in the standard of living." It is on the basis of this seeming contradiction, rather than in an examination of the growth rates themselves, that the author reaches the conclusion that the postwar growth record of the American economy has been too low. To maintain postwar increases in living standards in future years, he concludes that we must raise our rate of growth in real gross national product to 4–5 per cent per year.

The problem which concerns this paper is the adequacy of the growth record of the American economy in recent years.

The Nature of the Problem

The central question in any discussion of the adequacy of the growth record of the economy is that of criteria. What are the criteria that we

* Taken and adapted from "The Recent Economic Growth Record of the American Economy," *The American Journal of Economics and Sociology*, January 1964, pp. 1–18. Reproduced with permission.

may employ to determine whether or not in fact the growth record of the economy is adequate?

One direct and relatively widely used approach involves making an estimate of the rate at which the economy's potential for production — *i.e.*, its capacity — is likely to expand; this rate is then viewed as the "necessary" or "desirable" rate at which the economy ought to grow. To the extent that the actual rate of growth of real output appears to be falling short of the calculated potential, it follows that the economy's performance is unsatisfactory.

The National Planning Association, in an analysis of the output potential of the American economy in 1970, estimates that the gross national product is capable of growing at an annual average rate of 4.2 per cent a year during the period 1957–1970. The Council of Economic Advisors, too, has sought to evaluate the economy's performance in terms of the difference between actual output and the output that could be achieved at reasonable full employment of the labor force. Assuming that a 4 per cent rate of unemployment is the equivalent of substantial full employment, the Council has attempted to show how much additional output would result from the reduction of the actual unemployment rate to this level.

A second way to approach the problem is simply to compare very recent growth rates for the economy with the latter's record over a much longer period of time. This, in effect, is the position taken in a *Staff Report* of the Joint Economic Committee. In this study it is asserted that the economy has slowed down primarily because the annual average rate of growth of real product of 2.5 per cent for the period 1953–1959 is below the economy's historic, long-term average of 3.66 per cent. A major difficulty with this approach lies in the fact that the growth rate and hence judgment as to its adequacy is largely dependent upon the particular year selected as a starting point for the analysis.

A third approach to the problem, and the one that is favored in this paper, relies primarily upon the use of *per capita* national income and product data for the period under review. In this approach absolute changes in the per capita gross national product and the major components of the latter are used in preference to annual average rates of growth as criteria of the economy's overall performance. It is contended in this paper that the record *has not* been satisfactory, but that this cannot be demonstrated adequately by an appeal to the evidence of growth rates alone.

The use of per capita data and absolute changes in these data enables us to demonstrate that the economy's per capita growth in overall output has not been sufficient to account for the actual per capita growth recorded for certain of the component parts of the gross national product. More specifically, we seek to show through analysis of the per capita data that the bulk of the gains experienced in real per capita consumption and investment since the end of World War II are not primarily a consequence of economic growth during this period, but a result of a shift in the internal composition and end-use of the output total. The latter was largely made possible by World War II coming to an end.

The growth which made possible the spectacular increase in living standards experienced by the economy in the postwar era came largely during World War II.

The Evidence of Growth Rates

Before we develop more fully the foregoing thesis, it is appropriate and necessary to examine a series of actual growth rates and see what light they may shed on the question of the adequacy of growth in the postwar economy. In general, it appears that the evidence offered by growth rates is inconclusive with respect to the economy's postwar performance, although the rates demonstrate without doubt that the American economy experienced a truly massive surge of growth during World War II.

Over the 120-year period from 1839 to 1959 the data show that the economy's real gross national product rose at an average annual rate of 3.66 per cent, a growth record unsurpassed by any other economy. Gross national product per capita in real terms grew throughout this period at an average annual rate of 1.64 per cent, which would allow an approximate doubling of real output per person every 40 to 45 years.

Of more interest and significance for the thesis of this paper are the data for the war years, 1940–1944. What these statistics show without question is that the American economy experienced a truly startling surge of real growth under the stimulus of wartime-created demand. For the five-year period real gross national product rose at the astonishingly high average rate of 10.96 per cent per year, and real per capita gross national product rose almost as rapidly, as the average annual rate of increase recorded for this measure was 9.75 per cent. In absolute amount the 10.96 per cent average annual rate recorded during the 1940–1944 period meant that by the latter year the nation's real gross product had increased by more than 50 per cent. This wartime record of growth attests to the enormous potential for expansion inherent in the American economy when confronted with a real and urgent need.

It is interesting and important to note, too, that the real growth experienced by the economy in this period was not simply the consequence of putting the unemployed of the late 1930's back to work in wartime production. The war, it is true, brought full employment to the economy, a condition that was not achieved at all during the 1930's, but even so the growth in employment during the war years cannot by itself account for the expansion in real output. For the period 1940–1944 employment expanded at an average annual rate of 3.28 per cent, a figure well below the rate of expansion for total output. A clue to what actually took place is provided by data on productivity. Output per employed person grew at a more rapid rate during the war years than is true for any of the other periods covered. Thus, an important share of the real gains experienced by the economy during World War II must be attributed to productivity improvements as well as the restoration of full employment conditions.

For the post-World War II years the data on growth rates lend themselves to conflicting points of view as to the adequacy of the economy's postwar performance. For a modified postwar period 1948–1960, growth in real gross national product averaged 3.54 per cent per year, which is only slightly below the long-term average, and the average annual rate of growth of real per capita gross national product was 1.76 per cent, a figure above the long-term average.

A much less favorable picture emerges, however, if we limit our analysis to the period 1953–1960. For these years the average annual rate of growth of real gross national product was 2.85 per cent, and for real per capita gross national product 1.06 per cent. Both of these figures are below the economy's historic record. At best at this point we can only assert that growth rates in and of themselves yield inconclusive results with respect to the basic question of whether or not the economy's recent performance has been satisfactory.

Growth and the Standard of Living

Another and related approach to the problem is through analysis of data pertaining to the standard of living. Aggregate real consumption expenditures and per capita real consumption will provide us with a reasonably good indication of living standards prevalent in a society.

Over the period 1929–1960 total real consumption expanded at an average annual rate of 2.85 per cent, and per capita real consumption grew at an average annual rate of 1.56 per cent. The latter figure is the more significant as it is the most indicative of changes in standards during this period. Continued growth at the latter rate would mean a doubling of living standards approximately every 46 years.

Turning to the postwar period, we find that the average annual rates of growth for total consumption outlays are significantly higher than the average for the longer period, 1929–1960. The growth rates for per capita consumption are also higher in the postwar years with the exception of the period 1948–1960, when the rate, for all practical purposes, was about equal to the average recorded for the longer period of 1929–1960. For the postwar era overall (1945–1960) total consumption grew at an average annual rate of 3.99 per cent, a rate of growth 83.9 per cent higher than the average rate of expansion characteristic of the gross national product in this period. Consumption per capita expanded at an average annual rate of 2.29 per cent during these years; such a rate of growth, if continued, implies a doubling of living standards approximately every 31 years.

The rates of growth for consumption suggest that a steady and reasonably rapid advance in living standard has occurred in the postwar years. Put in a slightly different context, we can say that the evidence of growth rates suggests that in the postwar era the economy has been able to expand living standards at a more rapid pace than it has been able to expand overall output. This conclusion may appear somewhat paradoxical, but as we shall seek to demonstrate subsequently, there is a fairly simple and rational explanation for it.

The Findings on Growth Rates Summarized

It may be useful at this point to summarize briefly the main findings suggested by the various growth rates examined thus far in this paper. These are primarily three: first, the economy's real gross national product and per capita gross national product grew at an exceedingly rapid rate during the years of World War II (1940–1944); second, the economy's rate of growth during the postwar period may be said to be unsatisfactory in the sense that for the three postwar periods selected for examination the rate of growth of both gross national product and gross national per capita has not compared very favorably with the historic long-term averages (1839–1959) for these measures; and, third, the record of the economy in the postwar period for improvement in living standards, insofar as the latter are reflected in total and per capita real consumption, is appreciably better on the whole than the record for total output and per capita output.

These findings are substantiated by comparison of both total and per capita output and consumption for selected years in the war and postwar periods with various earlier levels for these same measures. To illustrate, the very rapid growth of the economy during the war years is reflected in the fact that by 1944 real gross national product was 54.5 per cent above the 1940 level, and real per capita gross national product was 47.4 per cent greater than in 1940. Compare this, though, with the fact that in 1960 real gross national product was only 38.7 per cent higher than the 1944 output, and gross national product per capita was a mere 6.2 per cent above the 1944 level.

An Alternative Hypothesis

In this section we shall direct our attention to the hypothesis that the economy's performance in the postwar era *has not* been satisfactory, and that the per capita data yield a clear and relatively simple explanation of why this is true.

An interesting and paradoxical situation has characterized the American economy in the postwar period. This paradox provides us with the key to an understanding of our thesis that the economy's growth record has not been satisfactory. The situation arises from the statistically demonstrable fact that, on the one hand, there has been a real and sustained increase in the standard of living since the end of World War II and, on the other, that gross output per person has hardly advanced at all in the same period over the level which prevailed in 1944. Thus, if we accept real consumption per capita as a measure of the economy's performance, there can be no doubt that substantial progress and growth have taken place; as we saw earlier, real consumption per capita in 1960 was 42.6 per cent higher than in 1944.

If we look at the other side of the coin, so to speak, we find very little evidence of any economic progress during the years since World War II; the basis for this statement is the statistical fact that in 1960 real gross national product per person was only 6.2 per cent higher than the 1944 figure. Further, as the growth rates suggest, total output has, in general, barely succeeded in keeping ahead of population growth most of the time between 1944 and 1960.

The explanation for the foregoing paradox is deceptively simple. The real advances in living standards attained in the American economy during the foregoing period are to be explained primarily through a shift in the end-use of the gross national product rather than as a consequence of its growth through time. The most important surge of growth in the American economy since the Great Depression of the 1930's came during World War II. During the war the bulk of the increase in real output was absorbed for war purposes, but since the end of the war we have, in a sense, been able to use the extra output resulting from the wartime-inspired expansion for peaceful pursuits, the most important of which has been improvement in the consumption standards of the population. If the economy had depended upon *actual* increases in output per capita as a source of improved living standards, the 42.6 per cent increase in real consumption per capita experienced between 1944 and 1960 would clearly have been an impossibility. Thus it is clear that the greater than 50 per cent increase in the nation's total output which took place in the relatively short period of the war years is the most important single source of the postwar prosperity of the American consumer!

To summarize, then, we may say that evidence based upon per capita data rather than growth rates suggests that the economy's performance from 1944 through 1960 was relatively unsatisfactory. Real gains of sizable proportions (over 42 per cent) were recorded in living standards as reflected in per capita consumption outlays, but the primary source of such gains was not the sustained growth in the economy as a whole, but a large-scale shift in the end-use of the nation's total output. As the

1950's drew to a close, however, the possibilities of further progress in living standards from this particular source were becoming exhausted. The same holds for any future increases in the other major components of the output total, particularly investment outlays. In retrospect, therefore, the era 1945–1960 was primarily one in which the fruits of the economy's massive wartime surge of growth were adapted to peacetime uses. It was not an era of satisfactory growth.

If we want the economy in the years that lie ahead not only to experience a continued expansion in consumption standards but to demonstrate a capability for real growth in investment, government expenditures, and the net export component of the per capita gross national product, it is manifest not only that the system must grow at a more rapid rate than has been characteristic of the postwar era but also that such a growth rate must be sustained. In view of this and in view, too, of probable trends in population, a rate of growth of between 4 and 5 per cent per year in the real gross national product does not appear as an unrealistic target for the American economy.

69

Economic Growth in the United States:
Sources, Projections, Alternatives, and Costs*

EDWARD F. DENISON
Committee for Economic Development

If we deliberately wish to apply private and public policy to increase the rate of growth in the United States, says the author of this selection, we must identify the past sources of growth, make projections of the future growth rate and its sources, identify the leading alternative measures to stimulate an increase in growth, and appreciate the fact that growth is not a "free good" but has prospective costs as well as benefits.

Potential Production Distinguished from Actual Production

It is absolutely essential to distinguish between (1) the growth of the nation's "potential" production, its *ability or capacity* to produce marketable goods and services, and (2) changes in the ratio of actual production to "potential" production. The former depends on changes in the quantity and quality of available labor and capital, the advance of knowledge, and

* Taken and adapted from Edward F. Denison "Economic Growth in the United States: Sources, Projections, Alternatives, and Costs," *The Sources of Economic Growth in the United States and the Alternatives Before Us* (N.Y.: Committee for Economic Development, 1962), pp. 3–7, 266–69, 273, 275–80. Reproduced with permission.

similar factors, while the latter is governed mainly by the relationship between aggregate demand and potential production.

Changes in the national product between any two dates are, of course, governed by both. But the causes of change, the interpretation to be placed upon them, the policy measures that must be taken to affect them, and the implications of such policies for future growth all are entirely different.

The average annual percentage increase in gross national product from late 1956, or 1957, to the second quarter of 1960 (the most recent cyclical peak) was below our average rate over the past 30 or 50 years only because we used our available resources less fully in 1960 than in 1956 or 1957. More than 5 per cent of the labor force was unemployed, as compared with 4 per cent or less in 1956 and 1957, and involuntary part-time work was more prevalent. Recovery from the 1958 recession to that date was not complete, and recovery was interrupted before becoming complete. Subsequently, output declined and unemployment rose until expansion resumed in 1961. There is no doubt at all that our ability to produce has increased at least as fast since 1956 or 1957 as it did, on the average, in the past.

Thus, the fact that our performance in this period fell short of our average past record stems from the partial failure of United States policy in the field that has been customarily described by such terms as business cycle policy, economic stabilization policy, or high-employment policy, not in policies affecting the growth of our productive potential. Three main tools are readily available to federal authorities to bring the actual rate of production closer to the potential. Monetary policy can increase the money supply, make credit more readily available, and reduce interest rates in order to stimulate spending (mainly for capital goods) by private businesses, individuals, and state and local governments. Federal taxes can be reduced, or federal transfer payments increased, in order to increase private buying by augmenting private disposable income. Federal purchases can be increased, which would add directly to aggregate demand and indirectly stimulate private purchases by adding to private income.

We should now move vigorously to reduce unemployment and use our productive capacity more fully. The loss of income and other costs imposed upon those unemployed or working short hours, and their families, is ample reason to do so. But the direct effect upon the long-term growth rate of bringing actual production closer to the potential should not be overestimated.

If in the second quarter of 1960 the economy had been operating at as high a ratio to its potential as in 1957, the national product would have been perhaps 3 per cent above the actual $505 billion annual rate. If by the second quarter of 1961 the ratio of actual to potential output had returned to a more satisfactory (say, the 1957) ratio and if, in addition, potential output itself had grown by, say, 3 per cent, then the one-year increase in actual output would have been 6 per cent. But the gain from raising the ratio of actual to potential output is a one-time gain that cannot be repeated. If potential output continued to grow at 3 per cent a year, then the average annual growth rate of actual national product measured over a ten-year period would be 3.3 per cent (the average of one "6" and nine "3's"), over a 20-year period 3.15 per cent, and over a 30-year period 3.1 per cent.

How Big is Big in the Context of Growth Rates?

Is the difference between a growth rate of 3 per cent per annum and 4 per cent or 5 per cent moderate or very large? Is the difference between 3.3 per cent and 3.5 per cent important or trivial? Actually, differences measured in tenths of a percentage point in the long-term rate *are* significant in terms of results. For example, a 4 per cent growth rate, although it is indeed 1 *percentage point* larger than a 3 per cent rate, is not 1 *per cent* larger. It is one-third, or 33 per cent, larger.

Moreover, over the 20 years from 1960 to 1980 the population of the United States is expected to increase from 179.8 million to 260.0 million, or at an average rate of 1.9 per cent a year. Hence, a 3 per cent growth rate in *total* national product would mean a 1.1 per cent growth rate in per capita national product, a 4 per cent growth rate in total product would mean a 2.1 per cent growth rate in per capita national product, and a 5 per cent growth rate in total product would mean an annual increase in per capita output of 3.1 per cent — nearly three times as fast as the 1.1 per cent implied by a 3 per cent growth rate in total product.

Considered in this way, a difference of 1 or 2 percentage points in the growth rate appears big. We should not be surprised, or disappointed, to find that measures to alter the growth rate by 1 or 2 percentage points would have to be very big — if, indeed, they exist at all. Differences measured in tenths of a point in the long-term growth rate, or even less, are significant, not trivial. If we approach the matter with this perspective, we may expect to uncover alternatives realistically open to this country that will make a meaningful difference in the future rate of long-term growth.

The Sources of Economic Growth: Past and Future

The 1929–57 Period. From 1929 to 1957 the real national output increased at an average annual rate of 2.93 per cent. What were the sources of this past growth? In Table 1, I have tried to allocate the increase in real output during these decades among its various sources.

Table 1. Allocation of Growth Rate of Total Real National Income Among the Sources of Growth

	Percentage Points in Growth Rate		Per Cent of Growth Rate	
	1929–57	1960–80	1929–57	1960–80
Real National Income	2.93	3.33	100	100
Increase in total inputs	2.00	2.19	68	66
Labor, adjusted for quality change	1.57	1.70	54	51
Employment and hours	.80	.98	27	29
Employment	1.00	1.33	34	40
Effect of shorter hours on quality of a man-year's work	−.20	−.35	−7	−11
Annual hours	−.53	−.42	−18	−13
Effect of shorter hours on quality of a man-hour's work	.33	.07	11	2
Education	.67	.64	23	19
Increased experience and better utilization of women workers	.11	.09	4	3
Changes in age-sex composition of labor force	−.01	−.01	0	0
Land	.00	.00	0	0
Capital	.43	.49	15	15
Nonfarm residential structures	.05	NA	2	NA
Other structures and equipment	.28	NA	10	NA
Inventories	.08	NA	3	NA
U.S.-owned assets abroad	.02	NA	1	NA
Foreign assets in U.S.	.00	NA	0	NA
Increase in output per unit of input	.93	1.14	32	34
Restrictions against optimum use of resources	−.07	.00	−2	0
Reduced waste of labor in agriculture	.02	.02	1	1
Industry shift from agriculture	.05	.01	2	0
Advance of knowledge	.58	.75	20	23
Change in lag in application of knowledge	.01	.03	0	1
Economies of scale — independent growth of local markets	.07	.05	2	2
Economies of scale — growth of national market	.27	.28	9	8

The results are experimental and tentative, are based upon strong assumptions, and will hopefully be improved by further research.

The broadest statement that can be made is that the increase in the quantity and quality of inputs was responsible for 68 per cent of total growth and the increase in productivity for 32 per cent. In summary, five sources contributed to an amount equal to 101 per cent of the growth rate, out of a total of 109 per cent contributed by all sources making a positive contribution. These were increased employment (34 per cent); increased education (23); increased capital input (15); the advance of knowledge (20); and economies of scale associated with the growth of the national market (9). The reduction of working hours accounted for minus 7 of the total "contribution" of minus 9 per cent to the growth rate provided by sources adverse to growth, and increased restrictions against the optimum use of resources for the remainder.

The 1960–80 Growth Rate. My projection is for a 3.3 per cent growth rate for 1960 to 1980. This projection implies that only five sources will contribute to growth an amount that differs importantly from their contributions to the 1929–57 rate: (1) Changes in employment and hours will contribute .98 percentage points to the growth rate as against .80 from 1929 to 1957. Employment will grow much more rapidly. The projected rate at which hours will be shortened is much below the 1929–57 rate, but its impact on total output will be larger because much less of an offset can be expected in the form of increased work per hour. (2) The contribution of increased capital is foreseen as .49 percentage points as against .43 in 1929–57. (3) I assume that changes in restrictions against the optimum allocation and use of resources will be neutral in the future, whereas they substracted .07 percentage points from the 1929–57 growth rate. (4) The shift of utilized resources from agriculture that is foreseen will contribute only .01 percentage points to the growth rate as against .05 from 1929 to 1957. (5) The advance of knowledge is seen as contributing .75 percentage points as against .58 from 1929 to 1957.

Whatever period we examine, it is clear that economic growth, occurring within the general institutional setting of a democratic, largely free-enterprise society, has stemmed and will stem mainly from an increased labor force, more education, more capital, and the advance of knowledge, with economies of scale exercising an important, but essentially passive, re-enforcing influence. Since 1929 the shortening of working hours has exercised an increasingly restrictive influence on the growth of output.

It is reasonable to conclude that these are also the growth determinants that ought to be examined most carefully in projecting the national product; and that would have to be influenced to change the future growth rate very much over an extended period of time.

How to Raise the Rate of Growth: The Alternatives Before Us

Considering past and prospective sources of economic growth, how could we raise the growth rate by, say, 0.1 percentage point, enough to raise the GNP by about 2 per cent of $20 billion a year by 1980? Generally speaking, we would have to increase either quantity or quality of labor, land, or capital inputs or else increase productivity. Specific measures might be as follows (each of which is estimated to be able to raise the growth rate by 0.1 points): (1) By 1980 cut in half time lost from work because of sickness and accidents. (2) Draw into the labor force one-tenth of all able-bodied persons over 20 years of age who will not otherwise be working in 1980. (3) Operate with a standard work week about one hour longer than otherwise. (4) Reduce cyclical unemployment below what it would be otherwise by 2 per cent of the labor force. (5) Add one and one-half years to the time that would otherwise be spent in school by everyone completing school between now and 1980, or make an equivalent improvement in the quality of education. (6) Raise the amount of annual private net investment by 1.4 per cent of the national income. (7) Devote an additional 1.4 per cent of national income to net additions to government-owned productive assets. (8) Reduce by two and two-thirds years the lag of average production practices behind the best known that would otherwise exist in 1980. (9) Increase by 0.09 percentage points a year the rate at which knowledge relevant to production advanced. (10) Eliminate all misallocation of resources resulting from barriers to international commerce and from private monopoly in product markets. (11) Eliminate resale price maintenance laws and eliminate all formal obstacles imposed by labor organizations against use of the most efficient production practices.

The Costs of Growth

Policies to stimulate growth impose costs. Some, such as those leading to more investment in private or public capital, or to a faster rate of advance in knowledge through more research, require that the nation consume less than it otherwise could. Others, such as diversion of resources to provide more education or better medical care, which are classified as consumption in the national product, require that the nation consume less in other forms. Still others, such as longer hours of work or enlargement of the labor force, require that more work be done. Except for increasing immigration, all of the changes that would permanently raise the growth rate by any considerable amount impose costs of one of these types.

Costs of this kind are not imposed by changes that would make the economy operate more efficiently. Also, the means by which such changes could be brought about are frequently obvious, often simply requiring the repeal of existing laws. From a broad standpoint such changes consequently are particularly attractive, even though their possible stimulus to long-term growth is temporary and rather small. Even these, however, require some real or imagined sacrifice on the part of some members of society. Were it not so, these changes would already have been made.

Decisions on whether or not to try to affect the growth rate by any of the means I have listed cannot sensibly be made without full consideration of their costs. Otherwise, what I have provided would be a shopping list without price tags rather than a menu for making choices.

Almost any policy to affect growth also has other consequences. Some of these consequences, such as improvement of health, reduction in crime, or a better educated citizenry, will be widely accepted as desirable. Others, especially any appreciable sacrifice of individual freedoms, will be as widely regarded as undesirable. Still others, including notably changes in the distribution of income, will be regarded as desirable by some individuals and undesirable by others. Among all the policies that might be adopted that would affect growth, there are few indeed where the effect on growth is, or should be, the primary consideration in their appraisal.

A serious effort to stimulate growth significantly would not, in my opinion, concentrate on one or two approaches but would be broadly based. This view is re-enforced in the case of steps to increase factor inputs by the phenomenon of diminishing returns. Large increases in either labor or capital input, but especially the latter, without increases in the other, would yield a proportional increase in the growth rate smaller than is implied by calculations used in the list above.

70

◢ *Comparative Analysis of Economic Growth: Soviet Russia and the West**

STANLEY H. COHN
Research Analysis Corporation

The Cold War adds apprehension to an already important economic issue — the comparative analysis of economic growth in different kinds of economies. The following study, prepared for the Joint Economic Committee of the U.S. Congress, compares the economic growth of the U.S.S.R. and several "market-oriented" economies (including the U.S.A.) during the decade of the 1950's.

The purpose of this paper is to compare selectively the economic growth of the U.S.S.R. and six leading market-oriented economies — the United States, France, Western Germany, Italy, the United Kingdom, and Japan — during the decade 1950–60. Apart from the trend in overall national products, comparisons will also be made of changes in the structure and distribution of GNP. In addition, the influences which changes in the labor force and its distribution, as well as trends in productivity of labor and of capital have exerted on each economy's overall growth, will be examined.

* Taken and adapted from "The Gross National Product in the Soviet Union: Comparative Growth Rates," *Dimensions of Soviet Power,* Hearings before the Joint Economic Committee, December 10 and 11, 1962, Part II (Washington, D.C.: U.S. Government Printing Office, 1963), pp. 69–89.

Structure of National Product

1. National product by end use

Table 1 shows the distribution of gross national product for the seven major industrialized economies in 1960 in terms of the principal end-use or purpose categories: personal consumption, government-civil consumption, defense, and capital investment.

Table 1. Gross National Product by End Use for 7 Major Economies in 1960 (percentage of total in factor cost)

Country	Private Consumption	Government Consumption	Defense	Gross Capital Investment
France	58.3	10.7	6.6	20.7
Germany (FR)	50.4	11.9	3.9	28.0
Italy	58.7	13.7	—	25.2
United Kingdom	61.3	11.8	7.1	18.3
Japan	48.9	9.6	—	35.4
USSR	47.1	10.1	10.2	31.3
United States	60.4	9.8	10.1	17.9

The distinctive features of Soviet resource allocation, and therefore of the official scale of priorities, are the large share of resources devoted to growth, the substantial defense commitment, and the relatively minor emphasis on consumption, both in its private and communal manifestations. In terms of the proportion of total product allocated to growth, the U.S.S.R. stands a close second to Japan and, as for its relative defense burden, it ranks equally with the United States and considerably above the other five major economies. In 1960 the Soviet consumer received a smaller share of available resources than did his counterpart in the other leading economies.

It would appear that the U.S.S.R., unlike other rapidly growing nations, has been striving both to maintain rapid expansion and sustain a considerable defense establishment. Germany, France, Italy, and Japan have been more fortunate in being able to channel their nonconsumption efforts more heavily into growth, or have been able to match the Soviet ratio of investment with a larger share of the national product available to the consumer.

2. National product by sector of origin

Table 2 shows the distribution of gross national product by originating sectors for the seven leading economies in various representative years of

Table 2. Gross National Product by Sector of Origin for Major Economies (percentage of total at current factor cost)

Country	Year	Agriculture	Industry and Construction	Transport, Trade Services
France	1956	12.5	44.2	43.0
Germany (Federal	1950	11.4	47.0	41.6
Republic)	1959	8.0	50.8	41.2
Italy	1950	28.3	37.3	34.4
	1960	17.1	43.1	39.8
United Kingdom	1950	5.7	45.4	48.9
	1959	4.2	47.2	48.6
Japan	1950	26.0	31.7	42.2
	1960	15.4	37.0	47.5
U.S.S.R.	1955	30.7	41.4	27.8
United States	1950	7.2	39.5	53.2
	1960	4.0	38.2	57.8

the 1950–60 period. The sector breakdown is roughly in terms of the division between primary (agriculture), secondary (mining and manufacturing), and tertiary production (services). Economic development is sometimes defined as the progressive shift of economic activity through this sectoral spectrum.

In comparison with the other major economies the Soviet Union is still heavily agricultural in spite of the high priorities granted to industrialization for nearly 35 years. While industry in the U.S.S.R. generates a somewhat smaller share of national product than in the other six major powers, the proportion emanating from services is strikingly less, both as a proportion of GNP and of nonagricultural product. This latter phenomenon, of course, reflects the low priority that consumer welfare occupies in Soviet economic policy. Furthermore, the structural shift since 1950 has reduced the share of agriculture considerably less than in countries such as Italy and Japan, which also originate a considerable share of their national income in farming. The persistence of agriculture's large role in total economic activity illustrates the drag the sector imposes on Soviet growth.

Growth of National Product

Both during the entire decade of the 1950's and during its latter half, the U.S.S.R. was expanding its output at over double the rate of the United States, somewhat faster than Italy's, but about the same as that of Western Germany, and less than that of Japan.

If individual years are examined more closely, the recent deceleration in the U.S.S.R. growth rate becomes more apparent. Through 1958 the Soviet economy managed to maintain the better-than-seven-percent annual advancement which had prevailed since 1950. Since 1958 there has been no secular increase in Soviet farm output. The stagnation of a sector generating nearly a third of national income has meant a sharp drop in the over-all growth rate to well under five percent, considerably below that of Germany, Italy, and Japan, and about equal to that of France in these years.

Table 3. Average Annual Rates of Growth of GNP for 7 Major Economies

Country	*1950–55*	*1955–60*	*1950–60*
France	4.5	4.2	4.3
Germany, Federal Republic	9.0	6.0	7.5
Italy	6.0	5.9	5.9
United Kingdom	2.6	2.7	2.6
Japan	7.1	9.4	8.8
U.S.S.R.	7.0	6.5	6.8
United States	4.3	2.3	3.3

Comparative Size of National Product

The unchallenged No. 2 position of the U.S.S.R. as an economic power is clearly evident from the table. While approximately 46 percent of the size of the U.S. economy, it is more than double the size of any third power. Another prominent magnitude that emerges from the comparison is the approximate parity between the size of the three principal Common Market economies (France, Germany, and Italy) combined and that of the U.S.S.R. and the definite predominance this West European aggregation would have with the addition of the United Kingdom.

Table 4. Comparative Levels of GNP in 1960
(in billions of current dollars)

Country	(*Internal Purchasing Power Conversion*)
France	84.8
Germany, Federal Republic	92.2
Italy	43.8
United Kingdom	85.4
Japan	N.A.
U.S.S.R.	235.5
United States	504.4

Manpower and Productivity as Factors in Growth

One approach to understanding the growth of an economy is to determine the contribution made by increases in the size and productivity of the labor force, the basic ingredient in all economic activity. Statistically productivity is that portion of growth which explains any increase in output proportionately greater than labor input in man-years.

In our analysis of the comparative growth of the national products of the U.S.S.R. and the six leading market economies, the productivity concept can be used to determine the degree to which relative expansion has been the result of increased employment or of the efforts, largely in capital investment, which have brought about rising labor productivity.

Table 5. Roles of Increases in Employment and Labor Productivity in Comparative Growth of GNP, 1950–60 (average annual rates of growth)

Country	Productivity[1]	Productivity as Share of Total[2]
France	3.9	90
Germany (Federal Republic)	5.2	73
Italy	4.3	78
United Kingdom	2.0	77
Japan	6.7	80
U.S.S.R.	4.7	74
United States	2.1	66

[1] Computed from index of GNP divided by index of employment. Productivity per man-year.

[2] Productivity increase as percentage of combined productivity and employment increase.

As for productivity accomplishments, the Soviet economy has been above average, but somewhat below that of Germany and considerably less than that of Japan. In terms of relative contribution of increases in productivity, as compared with higher employment, in explaining growth of national product, the U.S.S.R. occupied a below average position. At one extreme stood France with a very small addition to its labor force and at the other the United States, which showed both a large increase in unemployment and, along with the United Kingdom, the lowest growth in labor productivity.

Structural manpower shifts have been of no small importance in augmenting the urban labor force in other major economies. Nearly a quarter of German, a third of Italian, and nearly half of French additions to the nonagricultural labor force were recruited from the farms in the decade under review, while only a twelfth of such additions were so provided in the U.S.S.R. The price to the Soviet economy of low productivity advance in agriculture has been a costly one in terms of retained manpower and continues to remain so. In 1960 about 43 percent of the labor force of the U.S.S.R. was still on the farm, compared with only 26 percent in France, 14 percent in Germany, 31 percent in Italy, 29 percent in Japan, and 7 percent in the United States.

Investment as a Factor in Economic Growth

The key to the explanation of productivity advances can be found in the role exerted by capital investment. If the average annual growth of GNP per man-year is compared with that of the proportion of GNP devoted to nonresidential investment for each of the seven economies over the 1950–60 period, a close fit emerges. The position of the U.S.S.R. in this respect is not dissimilar to that of the other major economies.

Table 6. Relation Between Growth in GNP per Man-Year
and Nonresidential Investment Ratios for 7 Economies, 1950–60

Country	Average Annual Rate of Growth of GNP per Man-Year	Investment as Proportion of GNP
France	4.0	15.9
Germany (Federal Republic)	5.9	19.6
Italy	3.9	17.2
United Kingdom	2.2	13.4
Japan	7.5	23.3
U.S.S.R.	4.7	17.7–19.2
United States	2.3	12.9

Characteristics of Rapid Economic Growth and Distinguishing Features of Soviet Growth

It is possible from the foregoing presentation to draw tentative conclusions regarding the behavior of the rapidly growing economies and that of the U.S.S.R. in particular. As noted above, there is a close correspondence between proportions of GNP allocated to investment and rates of expansion of national product. Matching high rates of investment have been rapid increases in labor forces, except in France. The composition of the respective labor forces have been improved qualitatively by large-scale transfers from farm to urban occupations. Both the high rates of investment and the structural changes in the labor force have led to rapid increases in labor productivity. The economies with the most rapid growth have also experienced the greatest increases in the productivity of investment, as measured by incremental capital output ratios.

The Soviet Union has differed in several important respects from the performance of other rapidly growing major economies. While sharing the heavy common emphasis on investment, the U.S.S.R. has assumed a relatively heavier defense burden than all other countries in the comparison, except the United States. The drain which military research, development, and production has imposed on Soviet scientific, engineering, and managerial resources may be a major factor in explaining why the productivity of Soviet investment has been lower (higher incremental capital-output ratio) than in other economies with similar rates of growth. Correspondingly, the U.S.S.R. has devoted less of its resources to enhancing the welfare of the consumer, as evidenced by the much smaller role played by the tertiary sectors which largely cater to the consumer.

A persistent feature of Soviet performance has been its chronic agricultural problem. The U.S.S.R. has been less successful in the postwar period than other rapidly growing economies in reducing the role of agriculture. It has benefited less in its ability to use agriculture as a manpower reservoir for industry and other urban sectors. At the same time it has channeled a significantly larger portion of its investment resources inefficiently into agriculture with deleterious effects on over-all investment productivity. In part the Soviet agricultural dilemma is a price paid for autarchy; the other major economies, except for the United States, rely to a considerably greater extent on foreign sources of supply for food and fibers. Lastly, along with Japan, the U.S.S.R. has enjoyed a longer period of sustained rapid growth, but this may be a function of its lesser degree of development.

• 71

Economic Systems in Historical Perspective*

ROBERT L. HEILBRONER
Economist, Author, and Lecturer

New and different forms of economic organization have presented themselves in the twentieth century in challenging and bewildering array. The comparison of our own with these alternative economic systems seldom fails to evoke controversial and emotional debate. The following selection provides a more dispassionate review of the various "isms" than is generally found and places their study in a broad historical perspective.

The Drift Away from Capitalism

Now we must turn to a basic change in the economic orientation of the world. It can be described as the collectivization of twentieth-century economic life. Over the larger part of our history, we have faced a future in which our own form of economic organization, capitalism, was the tri-

* From *The Future as History* by Robert L. Heilbroner, pp. 93–114. Copyright 1960 by Robert L. Heilbroner. Reprinted by permission of Harper & Brothers.

umphant and dominant form of economic and social organization in the world. This is no longer true. Today and over the foreseeable future, traditional capitalism throughout most of the world has been thrown on a defensive from which it is doubtful that it can ever recover.

The nineteenth and early twentieth centuries were the era of capitalist growth. Within a century of its first full bloom in the Industrial Revolution, capitalism had reached out to become the commanding economic structure of the Western world. Most of Europe and North America became market-oriented, profit-stimulated, industrially based economies. These countries in turn exerted their influence over a vast portion of the non-capitalist world — that is, over its unindustrialized areas.

By 1913 the conquest of capitalism appeared complete. It had either displaced, or was fast crowding out, the previous feudal economies. No other competitor of any degree of power even remotely appeared to challenge its pre-eminence. It is some testimony to the solidity of the capitalist system that until 1917 no major government in the world had ever been headed by a Labor Party, much less by a socialist regime of any description.

Yet this genuinely impressive accomplishment was now succeeded by a still more astonishing denouement. For the progressive success of capitalism over ten generations was to be undermined in less than two. In 1913 socialism was still the economic utopia of a dissident minority movement, without either the respectability of official government power, or the possession, however disreputable, of de facto power. Forty years later, in various guises, socialism as an economic reality had swept around the world. The Sino-Soviet enclave alone embraced a population twice as large as the whole capitalist world of 1913. Among the new nations emerging from the rapid break-up of the colonial portion of that world, virtually all bore the stamp of socialist orientation. More significant yet, within the erstwhile citadel of capitalism, nation after nation had defected from the ranks of orthodoxy. By 1959, in Australia, Belgium, Denmark, France, Germany, Iceland, Italy, Netherlands, New Zealand, Norway, Sweden, and the United Kingdom — all staunchly capitalist governments in 1913 — a so-called "Socialist" administration had at least once come into power; and in most of these nations it was either still in power or now headed the party of the Opposition. That this was a very different kind of "socialism" from the communist organization of society in the East was, of course, apparent. And yet even more than the spread of militant communism and of anti-colonial revolutions, it was symptomatic of a basic and fundamental swing in the world's economic orientation. For it made apparent that *within* the capitalist powers themselves, the unquestioned supremacy of the old capitalist ideologies had been challenged by a new set of guiding ideas.

The Historic Role of Communism

How are we to account for this world-wide phenomenon? Let us start by picturing the communist and the Western European nations as the opposite ends of a spectrum of "socialist" economic organization. When we then compare the salient characteristics of the infrared and the conservative blue ends of this spectrum, a very important contrast strikes us. This is the difference in the stage of economic development of the two groups.

The Western nations, at the conservative end of the economic line-up, all have their developmental days behind them; they build atop an already firmly established foundation. The communist nations are without exception in the process of industrialization. Some, like China, are barely out of the subsistence-agrarian level; others like Russia appear as half-finished skyscrapers whose enormous framework has not yet been made suitable for occupancy. But note that with the exception of Czechoslovakia, which was won by coup, and East Germany, which fell as a war prize, no nation has gone communist which was not then a peasant economy.

This contrast of stages of development now suggests an important point. It is that communism, as a major economic movement of today, is playing the same role as did capitalism in the seventeenth and eighteenth centuries. For the Western "socialist" nations have also gone through their periods of repression and severity in the course of their own transitions from agrarian to industrial societies. These periods were considerably milder than present-day communism because the transitions began at a higher level of well-being and because they were then the vanguard and not the rearguard of advance. But one who recoils at the rigors and suffering of the Chinese and Russian transformations would do well to compare these travails with those of the West in its early capitalist throes. He will then find striking — and perhaps discomfiting — similarities between the movement of the Western pre-industrial world into capitalism and that of the East into communism. Behind both lies the impulsion for material growth and the leverage of a newly unleashed industrial technique. In both systems large volumes of savings are brought into being, concentrated in a few hands, and redirected back into the further development of the industrial framework. More important in terms of social reorganization is the forcible transfer of masses of workers from farm to industry — a process which took place by the enclosure of the peasant's land under early capitalism and by the collectivization of his land under communism. Again, in both transitions we find the social agonies attendant upon the violent redirection of a traditional, earth-bound, static way of life into a future-oriented, organized, electric tempo of modern existence. And finally, under capitalist as well as communist industrialization the human cost has been very great. Every student of early capitalism is shocked at the inhumanity of its conditions of labor and at the heartlessness of its ruling classes. We see a similar grinding of the human personality in communism today.

Communism, in the present stage of world history, is not so much the successor to but the *substitute* for capitalism. It is the manner in which the backward nations seek to reproduce in a few decades the transformations which capitalism carried out over two centuries.

What will happen to the harsh disciplining forces of the communist system once the great transition has been made we do not know. But surely the hope of the future rests in the possibility that with communism, as with capitalism, the completion of the industrial transformation may soften and mellow the rigors of the transitional phase.

The Historic Role of Western "Socialism"

It is a very different aspect of the world's economic reorientation which we encounter when we now turn to its manifestations in Western Europe.

Certainly by the Marxian touchstone of economic identification — property ownership — what we find here is hardly a revolutionary change. Even under the most ambitious socialist programs, as for instance that of Great Britain after the war, the nationalization of industry has been limited to a few sick or strategic sectors, and has been accompanied by the most meticulous compensation of former owners. Meanwhile the market mechanism and the profit motive, those capitalist motors of progress, continue to provide the basic economic impetus. If a heavily predominant private ownership and a profit-making direction of business constitute the hallmarks of capitalism, then Europe is unquestionably still capitalist.

Yet, just as unquestionably, it is not the capitalism of old. For if Europe is not socialist by any of the traditional criteria, it is nonetheless characterized by a phenomenon commonly associated with socialism. This is the growth of public control over and intervention into private economic life — of *planning* as an integral part of the economic system. Whether we look to the British "managed economy" or the French *économie dirigée*, to the Swedish "middle way," or even to the German *soziale Marktwirtschaft*, this is the most noticeable change in the character of European capitalism. It is the metamorphosis of a system of *laissez faire* into one of mild national economic collectivism. What is the cause and the meaning of this drift toward planning? The implications of this change are in some respects more historically significant than the far bolder leap into communism. Here we see *capitalism itself* in the process of change.

We need not retrace the long and complex history of Europe's economic centralization. Many forces contributed to its growth, including not least the powerful economic demands of total war. But it was not alone the blows of war which pressed the European economy toward collectivism. More fundamental yet was a process which lay at the heart of the capitalist dynamic itself. This was the tendency of business enterprise to enlarge, ramify, agglomerate its scale of production.

The consequences of this agglutination of productive power was to magnify the dangers inherent in that endemic weakness of capitalism, its recurrent economic recessions. But these depressions, which might be shrugged off as useful economic winnowing mechanisms when they eliminated only small and isolated units of enterprise, could no longer be so stoically accepted when the threatened victims were giant enterprises whose fall could imperil a whole industry, even a whole economy.

The result was that when severe depression rocked the entire capitalist system in the late 1920's and 1930's, "it was the capitalists — the industrialists, farmers, and financiers — who begged the state to save them by laying the foundation of an ordered economy."

Thus the movement toward planning, far from being in its origins a radical evolution beyond capitalism, must be understood as constituting a protective device for capitalism. Government control and intervention have been the means by which capitalism was able to co-ordinate its production for the efficient prosecution of war and by which it sought to guard against its growing vulnerability to economic crisis.

And yet it is also perfectly clear that by no means all the European planning movement is merely such a protective device. Much of European planning has a different purpose. It concerns itself with social welfare — not so much with the production as with the redistribution of wealth. We find elaborate planning mechanisms for the distribution of aid and allowances to the unemployed and the aged, for the provision of subsidies to multi-child families, for public services such as Britain's National Health Service. We find a limited but by no means dormant planning movement toward nationalization of industry. We encounter an insistence on full employment as an overriding goal of economic policy.

These are aspects of planning which clearly fall outside the general description of planning as a conservative protective mechanism. Americans would tend to identify these uses of planning as evidences of "welfare capitalism." But our own identification of them directly emphasizes the critical element in the evolutionary picture of European capitalism. In Europe the historic movement toward reform and welfare has not been identified with a capitalist tag. On the contrary it has been universally identified with the political ideology of socialism.

Europe at the Halfway Station

The roots of socialism in Europe reflect an inadequacy of long standing in the political workings of capitalism. To be sure there was also an inadequacy of economic performance — low wage rates, highly unequal income distribution, recurrent unemployment — all of which have been powerful factors in the promotion of socialism. Yet beyond this was a deeper failure of the European capitalist system. It was an inability to include the ambitions and aspirations of its lower orders within its own ideological framework. From the beginning, capitalism in Europe has been a self-consciously bourgeois institution, frankly suspicious of, not to say hostile to, the aims of its laboring classes. Nothing of the social consensus which bound up the American class divisions ever characterized the European scene.

Thus the direction in which working class aspirations naturally gravitated was toward socialism. No capitalist power in Europe ever thought to rally its working classes with the slogans of the bourgeoisie.

The realities behind the idea of socialism were often vague and contradictory. Nevertheless, in the word was a symbol of something which capitalism never achieved in its own name: a drive for social justice, an often crudely formulated but passionately felt movement toward the dismantling of economic privilege, and an ideological concern for the needs of the least favored and most numerous members of society. To the European lower classes — and to their powerful representatives among the intellectuals — socialism was a movement freighted with great destinies for the future, while capitalism was a system weighted with the irreparable injustices of the past. It was this ideological orientation, combined with planning — neutral or even conservative in itself — which provided the anti-capitalist momentum of European economic evolution.

There are signs, however, that the socialist inspiration for reform is today somewhat on the wane. In most European countries the aims and purposes of the socialist parties are confused and unsure. The frightening totalitarianism of Russia, the disappointments of nationalization in Great Britain, have taken much of the wind out of socialist sails. And the revelation that nationalization is no cure for the grinding realities, the dull tasks, the necessary hierarchies of the industrial process has made it clear that if socialism is to offer nothing more than nationalization it is scarcely to be preferred to a well-managed capitalism.

Hence the socialist movement in Europe is conservative. For the moment it contents itself with pressing in the direction of "welfare" — toward greater income equality, the extension of social services, and the diminution of social privilege. None of this is in any sense "revolutionary." More important yet, the sponsorship of reform is more and more ceasing to be the exclusive property of the Left, with the result that even the intellectual core of the socialist movement has increasing difficulty in defining how its program differs from that of the more enlightened conservative parties.

But it is much too early to say that the socialist movement in Europe has spent its force. Its waning in recent years has corresponded with a period of unprecedented boom; given a serious recession, a reactivation of the socialist ideological drive is by no means unlikely. Totally unlike the situation in America, capitalism in Europe is *on trial.* There is no guarantee, however, that should it fail it would be replaced by the socialism of an earlier vintage. As Hitler's National Socialism has unforgettably shown, the forces of the extreme Right may also wear the brassards of the Left.

In sum, the Western European nations are at halfway stations along an historic road. If they are no longer identifiable as the capitalisms of twenty years ago, neither have they attained an organization of society which would correspond to the socialist aspirations of twenty years ago. Instead we find the "socialist" mechanisms of planning being used to buttress an essentially capitalist economic structure; and given a reasonable accommodation of erstwhile socialist aims, as in England, there is no reason why this halfway station should not endure for a considerable period.

Whatever may be its fate as an ideology, however, one aspect of socialism has become irreversibly fixed into place. This is the emergence of collective social and economic goals as an integral part of the European economic order. A subservience of individual enterprise to the state, very different from the pre-war *laissez faire,* has become a salient reality of economic life and an unquestioned axiom of economic philosophy.

The American Inquietude

Against this last sweep of history the United States stands in a peculiarly exposed position. Virtually alone among the great powers of the world we still profess an unequivocal rejection of "socialist" ideals. Thus what we half see, half divine, as the meaning of the European economic movement fills us with unease. It seems to us incomprehensible that at the very time when capitalism, as we know it, has demonstrated its greatest economic and social success it should be thrown on the defensive and forced to adopt an "alien" collectivism in order to survive.

Behind the ideological differences of European "socialism" and American "capitalism" there is an important convergence of realities. Most of the institutional welfare arrangements which bear the socialist label abroad can be duplicated here under the label of capitalism. Many of the goals of social equality which the European socialists seek we already evidence. Yet between the *ideals* of "socialism" abroad and "capitalism" at home there is a deep mutual distrust and antipathy.

We have failed to understand socialism as a movement of profound spiritual as well as material protest against the conditions of human life. We are quick to point up the inevitable failings of socialism, and never weary of calling to our attention the cruelties and repressions of communism. But such denunciations, far from arming us against or clarifying our understanding of socialism and communism, only serve to muddy our minds. They obscure the fact that the literature of socialist protest is one of the most moving and morally searching of all chronicles of human hope and despair. To dismiss that literature unread, to vilify it without the faintest conception of what it represents, is not only shocking but dangerously stupid.

72

Rethinking Socialism in Great Britain[*]

PAUL T. HOMAN
Southern Methodist University

*The addiction of intellectuals to socialist aspirations and thinking
is an allegation with which we are all familiar. The following
selection documents a quite different theme: Since 1951, English
Laborite and socialist intellectuals have been "rethinking socialism" and are advocating programs for social and economic reform which are much closer in spirit and content to the notion of
"mixed economy" than to earlier and more doctrinaire conceptions of "socialism."*

Whither English "Socialism"?

After the electoral defeat of the British Labour Party in 1951, the
socialist intellectuals of the party began a process of what they called "rethinking Socialism."

The occasion for this reassessment arose out of the very success of the
Labour Party program during the party's period in office. It had nationalized all the industries it had set out to nationalize (coal, electricity, gas,
the transport industries, steel and The Bank of England); it had reen-
forced the position of the trade unions and tied their activities into national political objectives; it had initiated a large housing program; it had

[*] Taken and adapted from "Socialist Thought in Great Britain," *American Economic Review*, June, 1957, pp. 350–365. Reproduced with permission.

established a system of social welfare service as comprehensive and costly as the British economy could reasonably support; it had initiated a full employment policy based on financial controls; and through tax measures it had scaled sharply downward the personal income derived from property and high salaries. The Welfare State, as it came to be called, was a monumental accomplishment for a five-year tenure of power.

The new question is whether the Welfare State and reformist measures, built on a private enterprise base, are all that is wanted; or whether socialism in the traditional sense is to be sought through progressive enlargement of the nationalized area. The intellectuals of the British left are deeply divided on the correct answer to this question. But there is little evidence that the Labour Party intends to move towards socialization of the means of production.

On the other hand, thinkers of the left are proposing rather far-reaching innovations in the way of social and economic change, and are still calling themselves socialists. In reviewing recent writing within this field, I am left with three strong impressions: first, that the persistence of ideological stereotypes of capitalism and socialism muddies the discussion of ends and means; second, that the older socialists are frustrated in the attempt to formulate programs which give any considerable scope to their traditional socialist principles; and third, that action programs are tending to take a reformist turn which can be called socialist in principle only if the term takes on a much diluted and extended meaning.

Directions for Economic Policy

The really impressive item in the programmatic literature is Crosland's *The Future of Socialism*. Mr. Crosland, a former member of the economics faculty at Oxford and former member of Parliament, engages in economic analysis marked by a high degree of competency. His critical thought is uncluttered by traditional socialist clichés, and his thought on policy by old political commitments. His purpose is at bottom to crystallize a working program for a party of the left comprising three qualities: expediency in the sense of promoting economic progress, morality in the sense of promoting social justice, and practicability in the sense of winning elections. In carrying out the task, he avoids three common defects of much socialist thinking; emotionally overwrought criticism of capitalism, the Utopian fallacy, and Marxist dogma. He takes a fresh new look at contemporary problems and possible solutions.

The broad pattern of his thinking may be stated somewhat as follows: the British reforms of the past two decades have been so far-reaching that the appellation "capitalism" is hardly applicable in the sense in which it was applicable for the preceding century. The resulting subordination of private industry to social purposes and social control has brought into effect much of what the older socialists sought: the end of primary poverty, full employment, stability of livelihood, and greater equality of both personal and real income distribution through the social services. On the economic front, further rise in the standard of living depends upon increasing productivity. There is no prima-facie case that this will be promoted by much extension of nationalization. In general, the proper role of the state can be defined by operating pragmatically without too much regard to older socialist doctrine. In the context of rising income, greater economic equality can be achieved by a variety of means — through higher wages, extension of social services, taxation, dividend limitation, death duties, capture of capital gains and so on. Where capital investment and technical innovation lag, government can intervene to force the pace, as it can also to minimize the effects of private monopoly.

Looking over this statement of directions for economic policy, an American Fair Dealer might find them on the whole both familiar and acceptable. This effect is, however, somewhat illusory, since Crosland is more of a "statist" than one would normally find in American policy-making circles. He finds more probable occasions for state intervention and a higher degree of necessary state control than would appear in any programmatic statement in the United States.

Social Equality and Criticism of Nationalization

In any case, these precepts of economic action, while essential, do not provide the central focus to Crosland's agenda. To him, "socialism is about equality," but the greatest barrier to the kind of equality which should exist is social inequality. The peculiar British class basis of educational opportunity greatly restricts the field of "careers open to talent," poisons all social relations and exacerbates social resentments. The breaking down of class barriers therefore appears to Crosland as the first priority of social policy, and this cannot be directly accomplished by economic reforms, but only by a thorough-going revision of the educational system.

From the economist's viewpoint, no doubt the most interesting point in Crosland's analysis is his treatment of the reasons for abjuring extensive nationalization. On this point he is detailed, pointed and persuasive. Part of the reason is the unsatisfactory performance of the industries already nationalized. The bill of particulars is extensive, including the administrative difficulties of monolithic monopolies, the failure to attract the best administrative talent, and so on. As an economist, Crosland lays special emphasis on their failure to contribute to the essential process of capital accumulation, comparing them unfavorably with private industry on this point. Their price policy has been a cost-covering one only.

He finds no reason to suppose that nationalization, as a general rule, will either improve economic performance or contribute materially to a scheme of social relations conforming to the ideals of socialism. Given the powers of the state backed by a proper attitude toward their use, he finds the specific matter of ownership highly irrelevant. In developing this theme he provides a cogent refutation of Marxist thinking, as well as a deadly account of the Russian outcome.

The Meaning of Socialism

Since social ownership of the means of production is usually considered the benchmark of socialism, one begins to wonder how Crosland, repudiating this approach, can call his book, *The Future of Socialism*. To him the heart of the matter is in the ideals and not in the means. The economic role of government is large, its responsibility for promoting stability and growth is overriding, and its concern for just relations fundamental. These conditions place no taboo upon using private enterprise to the extent of its useful economic function consistent with pursuit of those ideals. The lines of policy already firmly embedded in British practice are described by Crosland as follows:

> it constitutes a major victory for the Left that the majority of Conservatives today would probably concede the right, indeed the duty, of the state to hold itself responsible for (1) the level of employment, (2) the protection of the foreign balance by methods other than deflation, (3) the level of investment and the rate of growth, (4) the maintenance of a welfare minimum, and (5) the conditions under which monopolies should be allowed to operate.

Dissolution of the "Road to Socialism"

"The road to socialism" used to imply a destination. In the minds of many British socialists, the idea of such a destination appears to be dissolving.

The reasons, I think, are not hard to find. First of all, it has been demonstrated by experience how far social objectives can be achieved without expropriating private owners and without displacing the strong private motives which have beneficial economic effects. Second, the close view of what is involved in operating nationalized industries makes socialist politicians chary of undertaking much more of the same, and makes them skeptical of this route toward the attainment of their ideals. Finally, socialist thinking is under the shadow of Labour Party politics. Elections are won by votes; and voters have to be removed by appeal to some felt interest or incentive. There appear to be no British majorities to be won by promising an active program of subversion.

At least in the short run then, the only feasible programs in pursuit of economic well-being, and of economic justice too, appear to be reformist in character, to be carried out through an improved version of the present system and through other policies consistent with its continued existence. The more successful these improvements and policies, the less, one would think, anyone will want to practice subversion. What, then, is "the road to socialism"? Only, as far as one can see, through some unpredictable train of social disaster.

One is tempted to conclude that the paths of economic destiny of Great Britain and the United States are not so very different — being basically the building of a welfare state on a predominantly capitalistic economic foundation. This might indeed turn out to be the case. But even if it did, the parallelism would probably not be very close. The history of the two countries has been very different, their sociological structure is different, and there is a striking difference of popular attitudes rooted in these two facts. Moreover, within the economic structure the United States retains a much more vigorous constituent of competition. In any case socialism as a goal is waning in Great Britain; the British left is in process of reorienting its whole line of policy toward new combinations of public and private endeavor — not to be blueprinted in advance, but arrived at pragmatically as circumstances and popular attitudes warrant. This approach has, indeed, long been influential in the trade union segment of the Labour Party. It is now sweeping the field among the younger intellectual leaders. The day of the prophetic Utopian vision, equally with the day of the Marxist imperative, appears to be over.

73

Government Economic Planning:

*European-Style**

WALTER P. BLASS
American Telephone & Telegraph Company

*The purpose of postwar government economic planning, Euro-
pean-style, is the more efficient guidance of capitalism and is
definitely not "a Marxist invention designed to turn a capitalist
economic system into a socialist or communist one," suggests the
author of the following selection. Although the "United States
must work out for itself" its own solutions in these matters, we
are well advised to study carefully the possible benefits of recent
European innovations.*

Before going into the details of Western European economic planning,
we should make one very important distinction: what we are talking
about is *not* Soviet-style planning with its centralized control over every
sector of the economy, reaching down to the individual factory and
collective farm. In the countries we shall study, there is not a huge,
heavy-handed bureaucracy running the country, allowing no room for
private initiative, decision making, or adjustments through the market.

* Taken and adapted from Walter P. Blass "Economic Planning, European-Style,"
Harvard Business Review, September–October 1963, pp. 109–120. Reproduced with
permission.

On the contrary, without exception, each one of these planning systems rests firmly on a market economy in which the choice of consumption expenditures and, to a large extent, the choice of investment expenditures are left in the hands of nongovernmental persons and companies. Furthermore, the voice of the "private sector," the dominant form in each of the Western European countries, is heard and respected in the councils of those who draw up the figures.

Current Forms

What is the status of economic planning in Western Europe today?

1. *In France*

France is currently in the midst of her Fourth Plan, a four-year program that aims to raise gross national product by 5½% annually.

About 150 government economists, statisticians, and functional experts comprise the nucleus of the fourth planning operation, called the Commissariat du Plan. After drawing up a preliminary draft based on Harvard economics professor Wassily W. Leontief's technique called an "input-output" table — a chart (like the mileage table on a map) showing what in the national economy is needed to produce what — the Commissariat du Plan farms out the draft among 25 Committees of Modernization. These committees are composed of businessmen in the individual industries affected, supplemented by academic and government experts. The validity of the preliminary draft, and the underlying input-output assumptions are gone over by these groups. They are criticized and even revised, based upon the specialized knowledge of the members.

The awareness of the committee members that the plan, once formulated and approved, will serve as a basic framework for production and distribution for them and their customers serves to bring a sober reality to the proceedings. These are not mere academic exercises with numbers, but the flesh-and-blood destiny of entire industries.

The work of the modernization committees is then reassembled and revised estimates are worked out. The Commissariat passes this document on to the rest of the executive branch of the French government, and eventually it is approved by the Parliament.

The ability of so small a group to play so powerful a role in the French economy is explained by a variety of factors:

(1) France has a substantially greater public sector than Americans are used to. Coal, electricity, railroads, the merchant marine, aviation, the major banks, insurance companies, and a substantial part of automobile and aircraft production are in government hands.

(2) Inducements to cooperation may be found in a considerable

flexibility in applying taxes, "liberal interpretations of regulations regarding parent corporations and subsidiaries," subsidies, priority access to credit, use of special government or Common Market development funds, and so on.

(3) In the major industries and companies of France the personnel who staff the modernization commissions are from the same social groups or are products of the same few schools as those who hold managerial positions in the government. These ties have a great deal to do with the mutual understanding and willingness to cooperate between the technocrats of government and the technocrats of business.

2. *In The Netherlands*

The Central Planning Bureau of The Netherlands has cut out for itself a distinguished reputation in the field of central planning. This bureau, supported by government funds, has no executive powers, but maintains a degree of independence and stands above partisanship in a way that is a model for similar organizations. Each year it formulates a forecast for The Netherlands economy, which is submitted to a Central Planning Committee composed of 11 government civil servants, 16 representatives evenly split between central employers' organizations (super NAMs) and central workers' organizations (super AFL-CIOs), and 3 economic experts.

On this basis is developed a short-term yearly plan — as opposed to the French four-year plan. It goes back and forth between the bureau and the committee several times for revision, then is presented to the Cabinet of The Netherlands government. If specific governmental action with respect to fiscal policy is called for, or other legislation is needed, such action is debated actively in the Dutch Parliament before being passed into law.

The Netherlands method of planning differs in some important respects from the French version discussed earlier:

It is essentially an attempt at true forecasting, and only secondarily an action guide for government policies. Furthermore, The Netherlands planning mechanism operates in an economy which is tremendously dependent upon exports (50% of GNP), which therefore must be highly fluid and highly adaptable to the changing circumstances in the economies of its trading partners. For this reason the planning exercise has generally emphasized wage policy rather than the more specific investment policies for individual industries of the French or Scandinavian type. Because of this highly commercial and responsive atmosphere, it is felt that ordinary monetary and fiscal policies for the economy as a whole — similar to the U.S. approach — suffice for The Netherlands, when supplemented with an explicit guide to wage policies by employers and unions.

3. *In Scandinavia*

The Swedish, Norwegian, and Danish governments were among the first to work up formal economic plans — or national budgets, as they are frequently called — as a way of utilizing governmental policies more rationally. The Swedish system serves as an illustration, since the other two are rather similar in their workings and organization.

The National Institute of Economic Research, an independent organization, supported, however, by government funds concentrates on making a *forecast* of the Swedish economy for the budget period. The results of this forecast are submitted to the government, which then takes remedial steps — such as, for example, in the case of a threatened inflationary movement, making a change in the bank rediscount rate, tightening up on credit, increasing sales taxes, or stopping a number of government investments. At the same time, the institute calculates the effects of such changes on the national economy. In this way, the national budget in Sweden serves both meanings of the word *plan* — the sense of *forecasting* of events that cannot be changed, and the sense of *coordinating* a country's efforts to cope with external events.

The Swedish planning effort is based on a combination of powers vested in the government because of the organization of the Swedish economy:

> There is, to begin with, a substantial public sector, including telephone and telegraph, railways, electricity, gas, and water, as well as state monopolies in tobacco and liquor distribution.
> Secondly, there is a labor-management bargaining mechanism whereby the wage rise is determined annually in a big powwow between the central labor federation and the employers' organization.
> Finally, the Swedish government has pursued a policy of special inducements to investment through tax incentives, investment taxes during boom periods, and investment reserves which are tax-free business income.

All of these devices are used *selectively, industry by industry,* in order to channel investment where it is most needed and to contain it during periods of excessive boom or inflationary pressures.

4. *In West Germany*

The idea that West Germany has any planning program in the sense that we have already discussed seems quite contrary to the impressions of most people. Economics Minister and Vice Chancellor Ludwig Erhard only this past winter spoke out against the "French handwriting" in the Common Market's program of action for the second stage of unification. He criticized planning on the ground that every type of planned economy contains the danger that a certain amount of force will be applied or threatened.

Yet Ludwig Erhard's own role in West Germany's "economic miracle" points to a strong governmental role in the economy. Between 1948 and

1957 slightly over 40% of all net investment in West Germany was furnished by public authorities (compared with 10% in the United States). Beyond that, in West Germany an extensive and complicated system of tax exemptions has influenced the direction of investible funds. For example:

> Under the Investment Aid Law of 1952, business was forced to supply 1 billion deutsche marks (DM), roughly $250 million, which was channeled into bottleneck sectors, especially mining, iron, and steel.

Alleged Benefits

The benefits of government planning in West Europe fall into two general groups — active and concomitant. The active benefits occur when a plan is carried out. The concomitant benefits occur whether a plan is carried out or not, largely as a result of the process of drawing it up.

Active Benefits

1. *Coordination of economic policies.* One of the major virtues of setting up a planning office is stated to be the coordination of at least the public sector's role in the economy. The planning effort can bring together into one place the knowledge and integration of what the governments at all levels are doing.

In France, moreover, it serves to coordinate both the government and private sector well within the bounds of the French interpretation of "free enterprise." French businessmen appear to feel that it is a net advantage to be consulted and that they benefit from the increased knowledge which comes from having participated in the decision-making process between both sectors.

2. *Setting economic targets.* Sales managers in the highly mercantile United States would hardly deny the benefits of sales targets as a management tool. Similarly, planners in Europe have been attracted to the prospects of sparkplugging businessmen who are satisfied with established market positions.

3. *Allocation of scarce resources.* Most of the European countries which engage in planning have generally operated since World War I under the threat of balance of payments crises, shortages of raw materials, lack of transport, inadequate power, and so on — if for no other reason, because the two world wars took care of the scrapping of a substantial amount of plant and equipment. Thus, planning received its start at a time when the national resources in Germany, France, The Netherlands, and the Scandinavian countries were drained or gutted, and stringent measures were needed to reorganize the intricate web of modern economic life. Furthermore, the blunt warning of General

George C. Marshall that the Europeans would have to coordinate their own needs before obtaining limited U.S. assistance made some form of macroeconomic planning with specific attention to individual sectors vitally essential.

Concomitant Benefits

1. *Better economic knowledge.* One of the more obvious benefits of a planning exercise for those involved is an immense awareness of how much is unknown about economics and what degree of effort is required to learn more. The accounts of Sweden's 15-year history of national budgeting make sober reading for any planner who is foolish enough to dash in with great expectations. Yet the very efforts made there now are being rewarded with better fiscal and monetary policy, greater awareness of the crucial variables in the economy, and a respect for the strengths of business activity which planning has to take into account.

2. *Identifying the problem areas.* Making quantitative comparisons of national economies and their sectors also pinpoints the problem areas. With quantitative comparisons available for growth rates of regions or industries, unemployment, unused capacity, cost factors, population statistics, and production indexes, far more is understood about why a region or industry is either "sick" or "booming" than in the past. Planning as an effort to pull together relevant facts, analyze them, and disseminate the information for action — regardless of who does it, government, business, or individuals — has helped in focusing attention on these factors.

3. *Making explicit "social" or "external economic" costs.* Every economics textbook includes a discussion of external economies or "diseconomies" of production. The extra smoke created by greater steel production or the costs of educating a great many young children of workers who move into an area to produce the extra steel are examples of such diseconomies. Conversely, location of a power plant next to an oil refinery may make possible the use of cheaper grades of fuel, and the presence of one major industrial plant will give the surrounding economic region a market of sufficient size to warrant the entry of many other smaller businesses.

The French planning officials have been particularly conscious of these effects, and as a result of their planning recognize the benefits of developing certain underdeveloped areas of France and the need for assessing the true costs of the urban sprawl of Paris. What is really taking place in such an analysis is a serious attempt to identify the true costs of economic growth, whether they are reflected in a private company's own profit statement or only in the community's gains and losses.

4. *Central and reliable source of national projections.* In contrast to the proliferation of economic data in the United States (to the point

where GNP is a common word in the daily newspapers and every trade association has a consulting economist), many Europeans expect their government to do this sort of work. The planning organization of necessity collects economic statistics and (in all of the countries discussed before, with the exception of West Germany) then distributes the analysis and supporting data. This activity is frequently mentioned as an important aspect of planning, though it is actually independent of the act of coordination.

Dispelling Fears: Planning and the United States

What does this look at the European planning experience suggest for us? What does it mean in terms of the planning the United States should do? By way of summary, there are two sets of answers, one which may serve to dispel some of the usual fears of U.S. businessmen, the other which may serve to point out some unexpected potentials in planning.

Unjustified Fears

Planning as currently used in Europe is not *control;* it is not even regulation, as the term is understood in the United States. It runs the gamut from influence to outright incentives and disincentives to follow certain policies. As such it is not much different from accepted U.S. policies. It does differ in that it is applied industry by industry, and sometimes company by company, and uses the larger role of government in all sectors to make cooperation with the plan profitable.

Planning is not inevitably an aggregation by government of greater power. It may actually serve to keep power to make decisions within the private sector. In Britain the effort of the National Economic Development Council is to motivate management and labor to raise productivity, expand exports, and become better "businessmen"; such policies are quite the opposite of nationalization.

Planning does not restrict freedom from what it was: it only redefines where the freedom to make decisions does lie. In France the power to control credit was already in the private-government banking system in the 1930's; in Sweden cartelization during the interwar period was replaced by an elaborate three-way understanding with labor and government. Thus, a small manufacturer may have more freedom when the decision is in the public sector than he had when he was turned down in the private sector. This may still result in *no greater* freedom, but that is different from *less* freedom.

Unexpected Potentials

In any complex economic society, problem areas exist which are not explicitly solved by the free market. Yet these can be identified, investigated, and solutions proposed. An effort at planning, regardless of whether it is done under public auspices *à la française* or under private auspices (such as the U.S. National Planning Association, the Southern California Regional Council) takes explicit account of these problems and attempts to make recommendations.

A country's institutions, the way government and business are organized, and the relationships that prevail have a great deal to do with what constitutes "planning." The same word used in two European countries can mean quite different things, depending on how the *functions* (as described earlier) are articulated through these institutions. Thus, being for or against "planning" is meaningless without specific reference to a country's institutions.

Given the prevalence of very large companies in modern capitalist economies and their effects on production and employment, it is already clear that long-range planning has an important role to play within these large companies. It is not farfetched to speculate that the methods devised for European *national* plans might have considerable relevance for intracompany plans in the United States. The formulation of goals, targets, and the means to reach them are equally valid and useful to a privately owned company as they are to a national economy.

The question of where planning should take place — within government or within private institutions — may prove quite secondary after such plans are drawn up. The conclusions may turn out to be quite similar or agreeable to both groups. For instance, French management seems quite pleased with the conclusions of the government-sponsored planning process in which it plays a considerable role — something called "planning by the planned." A similar attitude is found in the new cooperation between local governments and railroads in some large U.S. cities for more rapid urban transit projects.

Conclusion

What does it take to make businessmen operate at their optimum potential? The United States must work out for itself the system that calls forth the best response. It cannot rely on mere borrowing, just as the Europeans bridle at accepting the American primacy of private consumption and "gadgets."

Competition (the "invisible hand" of Adam Smith), as it broadly covers U.S. enterprise, has served us well in the past, but now we are concerned whether free, or relatively free, competition will do the job in a world of big business, big labor, and big government. Actually, competition has more vitality than we sometimes credit it with, and for this reason perhaps we should strive for more competitive solutions — as in agriculture — rather than less. Yet, at the same time, planning on a regional or national scale may serve to point up those areas which are most in need of attention — competitive *or* regulatory.

But that remains for others to answer. In this article I have described the European practices of planning rather than prescribing for the future of the United States.

74

The New Deal in Retrospect*

DANIEL R. FUSFELD
Michigan State University

The "New Deal" of the 1930's was "an improvised, makeshift affair, with no underlying social philosophy," say many of its critics. "Not so," says Daniel R. Fusfeld. "The New Deal," he alleges, "brought to dominance in America a new social philosophy that remains the basis for most government action today." He points out what he believes to be the major elements in this philosophy, as well as the central ingredients in the altered role of government in the American economy.

The New Deal: A Shift in Social Philosophy

It has been fashionable to view the New Deal as a makeshift program improvised to meet emergencies and with no consistent social philosophy, moving as political exigencies forced it to move in efforts to gain and retain political favor. Improvisation, not a fundamental social philosophy, has been said to be its underlying dynamic.

Yet, viewed from the vantage point of a quarter of a century later, that evaluation is clearly untenable. The New Deal brought to dominance in America a new social philosophy that remains the basis for most government action today. Its foremost contribution to our time is the view that

* Taken and adapted from *Challenge*, June, 1959, pp. 65–69. Reproduced with permission.

a self-adjusting market economy does not adequately protect human values, resources and society itself, with the corollary that government action to achieve socioeconomic goals is necessary. Allied to this position was a new view of man and a new approach to the purposes and functions of business enterprise in society.

The most important aspect of the social philosophy of the New Deal was the belief that society as a whole, functioning through government, must protect itself against the impersonal and amoral forces of supply and demand. It represented a great shift away from the philosophy that the self-adjusting market should be given free sway, and that people, resources and wealth ought to be treated essentially as commodities.

It is true that the old ideas were changing before the Thirties: witness the welfare legislation of New York and Wisconsin, the conservation movement prior to World War I, and the gradual acceptance by government of the use of monetary policy to promote economic stability. Crusaders and critics from the Populists onward had been forging the social philosophy of the New Deal.

Types of Government Intervention in the Economy

Three main types of direct intervention in economic affairs were the New Deal's method of achieving its goals.

1. The first was the assumption by government of responsibility for something close to full employment prosperity, although unemployment was never conquered until the war. The most effective approach developed by the New Deal was use of the federal budget to assure an adequate level of total spending, and the deficits of the Thirties were an effort to supplement inadequate private spending with public. There is little disagreement with this sort of policy today. It has been embodied in the Employment Act of 1946 and institutionalized in the President's Council of Economic Advisers. Both major political parties agree that responsibility for economic stability and expansion — with or without inflation — belongs with the federal government.

2. Less successful was the National Recovery Administration (NRA) experiment, that great effort to promote economic stability through cooperation between businessmen and labor in individual industries. The experiment failed, and has been one of the most heavily criticized of the New Deal programs. The New Deal itself abandoned it and in the later Thirties turned full circle to the perhaps equally untenable position of promoting competition as advocated by the Temporary National Economic Committee. Whatever the merits of the case, in two natural resource industries — pertoleum and coal — the spirit of the NRA lives on. In oil, the states regulate production, while the federal government supervises imports and acts to constrain oligopoly and quasi-cartelization

abroad. The coal industry is characterized by labor-management cooperation and coordination today. The basic philosophy of the NRA is still with us, although it is no longer part of the liberal creed.

3. The third main type of government intervention in economic affairs was regional land-use planning based on water resources. Typified by the Tennessee Valley Authority, the principle was the outgrowth of a number of pre-New Deal policies: reclamation, waterway development, forest conservation, city planning and the controversy over electric power development. Today we take for granted the desirability of unified development of water resources and related land uses. The debates are limited to the respective roles of the federal and state governments and private enterprise.

The Individual, the Businessman, and Society

Supplementing the New Deal's economic interventionism was a new view of the place of the individual in society. The older philosophy — that the individual seeking his own best interests would contribute most to society as a whole, and the corollary that those who were unsuccessful ought to bear the cost — was no longer tenable in a modern industrial society, particularly one plagued by a depression that crushed everyone, including intelligent, hard-working, sober businessmen. In its place came the belief that society had a responsibility for the welfare of each person, partly because the individual contributed to society by his work, by raising a family, and by his participation generally in the activities of the social order, and partly because the problems of an industrial society were often too great to be solved individually.

This position was given support by the belief that the individual can function best, both in his own interest and as a contributor to society, in a secure rather than an insecure environment. One of the goals of New Deal policy was the creation of an environment of economic security that would release greater individual energies and in the long run would more than compensate for the costs involved. In practice this meant a range of welfare legislation — unemployment insurance, social security, workmen's compensation, and federal grants-in-aid in health and education — which also have achieved general acceptance.

Another major building block of the New Deal's social philosophy was a new position on the social responsibilities of the businessman. In the pre-New Deal era profit and success were their own justification. Wealth came to one not only because of hard work and ability, but also because the search for wealth resulted in meeting the needs of others, "as if by an invisible hand."

The New Deal changed all this. Embodied in its attitude that the market economy often ran rough-shod over human and social values was the belief that individual gain was not always synonymous with the social good. This meant that success and profit, wealth and ease, were not enough. Business had to justify itself on other grounds. Nowhere were these broader goals spelled out in detail, but the import of New Deal legislation indicated that they included reasonably stable operations, broadly effective labor-management relations, prices that were not excessive, and straightforward financial activities.

It has sometimes been said that the antagonism of business to the New Deal was the result of the lesser place in society that was given business by the rise of government intervention, compounded by the aid to labor unions as a challenge to the businessman within his own enterprise. There may be much truth in that argument, but perhaps even more significant was the challenge to business as an end in itself. In effect, the New Dealer was saying to the businessman, "You're a success, but look at the mess you made of the economy and how much it has cost in human suffering." Such a viewpoint, assuming that the businessman bore sole responsibility for the "mess," is hardly calculated to make friends.

Whatever its origin, a new element has been added to business thinking. We can observe a major steel company cooperating vigorously with the local government to establish park and recreation facilities, another firm filing its annual reports with the plea that profits after taxes must be improved to enable the company to meet the needs of a growing America, and a national science scholarship program financed by a large electrical equipment manufacturer. Emphasis on the social responsibility of the businessman is taught at our leading colleges of business administration.

Bits and Pieces

It is important to note that the New Deal leadership did not fight its political battles on the grounds of its social philosophy, but on legislation that embodied bits and pieces of an applied program of action. Too pragmatic for ideological battles, and much too shrewd a politician for abstract argument, Franklin D. Roosevelt led the New Deal toward specific goals and specific legislation. This emphasis on practical action rather than theoretical debate was politically sound, and it was thoroughly within the American tradition. More important, it minimized the inevitable dissension, class conflict and ideological warfare that the rise of a newer social philosophy to predominance inevitably brings.

Especially helpful in reducing the bitterness that did result was preservation of individual decision-making by consumers and business — one of the basic tenets of American individualism — even though the socio-economic framework was to be restructured. Detailed economic and social planning or controls were never part of the New Deal philosophy, and the individual was left free to spend or save, to choose his occupation and to make his own business decisions.

Whatever its limitations, the New Deal has left a social philosophy that remains to this day a major influence on American life. Just as the New Deal built upon the ideas of earlier reform movements, future movements for change and reform will build upon the heritage of the New Deal.

75

The *Expanding Economic Role of*
*Government in a Dynamic American Economy**

SUMNER H. SLICHTER

Late Professor of Economics, Harvard University

The American economy today is quite a different animal from what it was 100 or even 30 years ago. One of the most important structural changes in our economy has been the growth in the role of government, both in absolute and in relative terms. The following selection catalogs the major areas of expanding government activities and suggests reasons for their past (and expected future) growth.

Government's Positive Side

The thesis of my remarks is that the government is not merely an expense — it is a service-rendering organization that repays its costs manifold in the services that it gives. In a dynamic society the demand for services from the government is constantly growing — not only the demand for the services of the traditional sort, but the demand for new kinds of services. In such a society it is likely to be wise to spend more, not less on the government.

* Taken and adapted from "Government Expansion in a Dynamic Society," *The Commercial and Financial Chronicle*, April 25, 1957, pp. 1–6. Reproduced with permission.

The Forms of the Growing Activities of the Government and the Reasons for this Growth

Behind the expanding activities of the government are many influences. In an age of science and machine industry, the ancient governmental functions of enforcing law and order, promoting health and safety, and regulating trade find new applications and take on new forms. Many of the things that the government did not do in days gone by simply reflected the fact that people were too ignorant of the causes of disease to demand protection, or that science and technology were not sufficiently advanced to provide tests or standards for the law to apply. Nearly all of the important work of the government in the field of public health (its control of the quality of the water supply, its rules governing ventilation and the installation of plumbing, its requirements for vaccination, its pure food and drug legislation, its inspection of seeds and plants) simply means that the government is led by scientific knowledge to perform ancient functions more adequately. All of them, however, are simply performing the ancient governmental functions.

The disturbed state of international relations requires a far larger defense establishment than was necessary before the Second World War. Here again, the expansion of the activities of government involves no new principles. The government has simply enlarged its activities to do what it has always done — protect the nation from the danger of outside attack and to provide appropriate military support for the country's foreign policies.

The government has always been an administrator of our national domain and a developer of our resources. We have always relied on the government to provide roads and to improve navigation. The demand for roads is greater than ever. When the government provides airports, it is not doing anything fundamentally new — its ancient function of providing transportation facilities is simply taking a new form. As the population grows in density, the way in which our natural heritage is used becomes of increasing general concern. Flood control, smoke control, protection of streams from pollution and of forests from fire, protection of wild life, preservation of areas for recreation, all grow in importance as population increases and the country fills up.

Seven Expanding Areas

Particularly interesting and significant is the expansion of the government into new fields, that has been going on for a little more than a century and particularly during the last 20 or 30 years. Seven new areas of government activity are particularly significant: 1. The first of these is education. Government offers tuition-free education, or almost tuition-free education, not only at the elementary school level, but at the high school, college, and technical school level. Until a little more than a century ago, education was regarded as necessary for only a few professional and business people and was in the hands of private charitable or religious organizations. The idea that the government should make some education freely available to everyone (and even compel attendance) aroused a great battle. It was regarded as unfair to tax some people to pay the cost of educating other people's children. Today no one questions the principle of free education.

2. A second relatively new major activity of the government is financing the acquisition of knowledge — the support of research. For several generations the government has supported research, at least on a small scale. Research in the state universities and in the agricultural experiment stations furnishes examples. Under the influence of the Second World War and the cold war, government outlays on research expanded eightfold from 1941 to 1955.

3. A third new major activity of the government has been the providing of information and technical help to business in general and to enterprises in many special lines of business. The invaluable statistical services of the government are an example of aid to business in general. The Department of Commerce and the Department of Agriculture provide many specific services to business, but by far the most important aid is that given by the agricultural extension system which has had an immense influence on farming practices.

4. A fourth important recent development in the activities of the government has been the lending of money and the insurance and guaranteeing of loans. The government has recently withdrawn in considerable measure from some of its lending operations, but it continues to grow in importance as an insurer or guarantor of mortgages in the housing field. The reasons behind this expansion appear to be a mixture of political and economic. The influence of pressure groups has been important, but experience seems to indicate that the government can take risks and make a profit at rates that private underwriters find unattractive.

5. A fifth important new activity of the government is the support of markets — a development which is almost completely bad. The ridiculous support of the silver market goes back some years. Under pressure from western metal mines, the government buys various metals in excess of the needs of the strategic stockpile. The largest support operation of all is that represented by the government's support of the prices of farm products. The price-support program made some sense during the war when there was need to stimulate farm production. Today the price-market program is highly wasteful because it encourages an excessive number of people to remain in agriculture and it induces farmers to produce the wrong things. Americans do not want more cotton, rice,

wheat, or peanuts — they want more meat, especially steaks. Although America is the richest nation in the world, it is still on a hamburger standard of living.

6. A sixth major new activity of the government is the provision of economic security. The government has always operated poorhouses or poor farms and given at least meager aid to the destitute, but during the last several generations a revolution has occurred in thinking about the problems of the needy. The idea has become generally accepted that a certain minimum protection against important economic hazards should be the right of every one, regardless of his circumstances, and that it is the government's duty to provide this minimum of security. This protection takes the form of pensions for the old, unemployment compensation for the unemployed, and various special benefits for the blind, dependent children, widows, and the disabled.

The notion that virtually all members of the community are entitled to a minimum of economic security was a great step forward in social philosophy. Among other things, it meant that the thrifty and the foresighted were not to be penalized for their thrift and foresight. It also meant that economic security was not to be a special privilege accruing only to the employees of a few progressive enterprises that provided pensions and other insurance schemes for their workers. Most important, it meant a strengthening of the ancient principle that misfortunes that are beyond the control of the individual should be the concern of the community.

7. A seventh major new activity of government is the assumption of responsibility for economic growth and stability. Behind the assumption of this important responsibility was another great forward step in thinking. People began to ask whether it was really necessary that the economy be subjected every now and then to severe contractions or whether the rate of growth had to be left to chance. The country has taken the momentous step of deciding not to let economic events just happen — that the country was going to have an economy that was stable and that had a satisfactory rate of growth.

Much of the great contribution that the government is making to stability and growth, it must be confessed, has been the result of accident. For example, much of the government's important contribution to stability comes from the fact that its spending is far larger relative to private spending than before the Second World War. Since government expenditures are little affected by the cyclical movements of business, they tend to dampen the cyclical movements, and the larger the relative importance of government outlays, the greater is their dampening effect.

Likewise, some of the government's most important contributions to economic growth are accidental in the sense that their purpose has not been to encourage economic growth. Perhaps the greatest contribution of the government toward economic growth comes from its enormous expenditures on research, and its immense purchase of electronic equipment and airplanes, and other war materials. All of this has accelerated technological progress and has stimulated the development of many important civilian products, and has accelerated the growth of productivity in civilian industries. These welcome contributions to technological advance and economic growth must be regarded as small offsets to the tragedy of the Second World War and the cold war. Neither we nor any other people possess enough economic sophistication voluntarily to use government expenditures as a way of fostering technological progress as we have been forced to do by the Second World War and as we are being compelled to do by the cold war.

But not all of the important contributions of government to stability and growth have been the result of accident. The imperative demand for stability and growth led to the establishment of the Federal Reserve System and to the strengthening of the banking system. Later the demand for stability and growth led to the creation of the Council of Economic Advisers and in Congress to the Joint Economic Committee with the responsibility of reviewing and proposing policies intended to promote stability and growth. The contribution of the government to stability and growth will undoubtedly continue to increase — partly because the country will demand that more be done to promote stability and growth and partly because there are some instruments for promoting stability and growth that only the government can use.

The Reasons for Expecting Continued Growth in Government Activities

Nearly all of the activities of government will continue to expand, and the government will continue to play a steadily increasing role in American civilization. This is inevitable in a progressive country in which the education of the people is improving, science and technology are advancing, production is growing, per capita income is rising, and population is increasing. The principal government activity that may be abandoned or severely curtailed is the ill-conceived and wasteful support of markets for farm products. The city people have been extraordinarily gullible, but it is inconceivable that they will indefinitely submit to paying large taxes for the purpose of keeping up the price of their food and of encouraging farmers to produce the wrong things. Possibly some day cuts in another big area of government activity — the support of the huge military establishment — can occur.

All of the other activities of the government will continue to expand. The policing and regulating activities will grow partly because there are more and more kinds of activities and organizations that require policing and regulating, and partly because the growth of science and other technology is showing the need for more rules and providing the tests required in formulating and administering rules. As industry and population grow and per capita incomes rise, the task of administering our domain will become bigger. We can't add 2,000,000 or more cars and 300,000 to 500,000 more trucks and buses a year to the number already on our roads without steadily improving and extending our roads and providing much larger parking areas. And if Americans are going to continue to take to the air in rapidly increasing numbers, the government must provide more and better airfields, more extensive and better traffic controls, and better provision for safety in flying.

The work week will gradually become shorter, and the habit of taking vacations is bound to grow as per capita incomes rise. The recreation areas of the country, both those in or near cities and those in the mountains or forests or along the seashore, are severely overtaxed and are rapidly becoming less and less adequate. The growth of water traffic and the increase in the size of barges is making many locks on inland waterways inadequate. As per capita incomes rise, the demand for schooling, especially schooling beyond the elementary and high school level, will grow. Government-supported schools must be expected to meet a large part of this need.

The enormous productivity of technological research means that government research programs are bound to grow. One should bear in mind that many of the most useful expenditures on research can only be made by the government or by some non-profit seeking organization. The reason is that if the investigation is successful, the benefits of the discovery accrue to everyone, not merely to the sponsors of the research. Businessmen are steadily learning the use of information and statistics collected by the government, and the uses of these services are increasing. The acceptance of the principle that the government shall provide a minimum amount of economic security assures that, as per capita incomes rise, benefits and coverage will increase. Finally, the government's new responsibility of promoting stability and growth will gain in importance. People have abandoned forever the fatalistic notions that they must accept whatever ups and downs of business and whatever rate of growth the fates decree. No one pretends that these matters are completely within control, but spreading realization of the fact that much can be done about them will subject the policy-makers both in business and in government to stronger and stronger demands that they find ways of keeping the economy stable and of keeping the rate of growth adequate.

76

Contemporary American Economic Ideologies*

R. Joseph Monsen, Jr.

Economic ideology, as defined in this selection, can ignore or transcend the technical opinions of professional economists and can be highly selective in its utilization of facts for the purpose of persuasion. Also, in contrast to scientific analysis in economics which focuses on explanation and prediction, economic ideologies embrace value judgments about how the economy ought to be organized or conducted. This is not to deprecate ideology, but rather to stress that we cannot necessarily expect to learn much technical economic analysis from following ideological controversies, nor, on the other hand, to deduce sweeping opinions and value judgments from the study of economics. One of the more enlightening aspects of the following exposition is the emphasis upon the plurality of competing American economic ideologies.

Ideology will be most completely defined as any set of ideas characteristic of a group, class, or nation that relates certain of their supposed attributes to some more commonly esteemed values in such a way as to

* Taken and adapted from R. Joseph Monsen, Jr.: *Modern American Capitalism: Ideologies and Issues* (Boston: Houghton-Mifflin, 1963), pp. 8, 18–32, 35–36, 38–39, 41. Reproduced with permission.

bestow honorific status upon them and their institutions and provide the basis for invidious comparisons against their competitors.

The Classical Capitalist Ideology

The Classical Capitalist Ideology in the United States today is disseminated largely through the publications of the National Association of Manufacturers (N.A.M.), The Foundation for Economic Education, The Committee for Constitutional Government, The United States Chamber of Commerce, and The American Enterprise Association, to name only some of the better known organizations.

It centers around the concepts of individually owned private property in a decentralized market operated by the forces of supply and demand in the quest for profit. The stand of the N.A.M. as officially declared is that the solutions to the problems of what, how, for whom, and at what price goods should be produced must be left to the voluntary adjustments of a free market rather than to central authority. This view holds that prices in a free market are the most efficient and responsive mechanism for allocating supply and demand and thus for meeting the wants and changing conditions of the economy. It is recognized that regulation of individual enterprise is necessary to assure the greatest benefits to society. Regulation, however, should be largely by competition. Government's function under this view is to act as a regulator to strengthen and "make more effective the regulation by competition." This view does not, as some people claim, demand that there be no government regulation. However, because of the effectiveness of competition as a regulatory device, the position is that government regulation is needed in only a limited form or amount. This is the classical argument for free competition that has been stated since Adam Smith's *Wealth of Nations* in 1776.

Of the major capitalist ideologies in the United States today, the Classical Capitalist Ideology is undoubtedly the one with the oldest tradition and the one that is most developed theoretically. It is precisely because of its age and being able to draw upon the body of classical economic theory that from an ideological viewpoint it presents the most thoroughly developed position. Thus, in a sense, it is the ideological version of the classically competitive economic theory.

There has, however, been a change within the classical thinking. For instance, while the Classical Ideology of today is concerned most with the problem of government power and its extension, this has not always been so. In previous periods, the Classical Ideology of Capitalism was fearful of all large power groups — business, too. The present classical view has stressed mainly concern over government power, and to a lesser degree that of labor, but shows little fear of Big Business.

When the Classical Capitalist Ideology is looked at against a backdrop of present conditions, it is obvious that a wide disparity between the two exists. The strain is particularly great — as would be expected in a philosophy developed several hundred years ago. What permits the tension created by this fact to be small enough to keep the ideology still prominent? Cultural lag is hardly an adequate explanation. A more satisfactory suggestion is that there is a general blending of the descriptive and prescriptive characters of the creed in most literature. Most of those who hold to the Classical Ideology of Capitalism today regard it as useful largely for prescribing rather than for describing present conditions. This fact is not always admitted, however.

It is not usually in the area of microeconomics or on the industry level that conflict between the Classical and other capitalist ideologies occur. It is in relation to the proper policies for developing full employment, stable prices, and economic growth that the Classical Ideology is in disagreement with the Managerial Ideology, as espoused by the C.E.D. and most economists today. By and large, the Classical Ideology will not accept most of the National Income Theory or Keynesian Economic Theory.

It should be added that among respected professional economists one man stands out in this country, frequently almost alone, as a protagonist for Classical Economics in its purest sense. This man is Professor Milton Friedman of the University of Chicago. In a book published in 1962, *Capitalism and Freedom,* he advocates a radical remolding of the U.S. economy into a system of free enterprise or laissez-faire capitalism that would do away with almost all government controls. He advocates not only complete abolition of tariffs, but doing away with the Federal Reserve System, the National Park Service, the Federal Communication Commission, and the Selective Service, to name a few. The draft would be replaced by a volunteer army paid sufficiently well to maintain it to desired size. Friedman's arguments do offer some support to the Classical Ideology — particularly among professional economic circles.

The Managerial Ideology of Capitalism

The Managerial Ideology of Capitalism takes its name from the stress placed upon the role played by the professional managers of the large corporation. The central proposition from which the rest of the doctrine is derived is that today's businessman is no longer the money- and power-hungry entrepreneur, such as John D. Rockefeller or Commodore Vanderbilt, but is a professional manager who is a steward of private, public, and worker interests. The picture such magazines as *Fortune* attempts to paint is one in which the manager of the large corporation is a trustee for the consumer, worker, and owner. This change is the great transformation in American business. This new ideology of capitalism is an attempt to rationalize and justify the development and functions of the large corporation in terms of the repeated claims that it was inimitable to the public welfare.

The Managerial Ideology is disseminated particularly by the Committee for Economic Development (C.E.D.) organized in 1942. Unlike the older business organization, N.A.M., the C.E.D. "accepted the fact that government was big and was constantly growing bigger and that there was no returning to a simpler, happier past in this respect. It believed that the question was not *how much* government should do, but *what* it should do, and once this was determined, how it could be done most effectively."

The Managerial Ideology is not based upon abstract economic theories which attempt to reconcile private gain and social welfare. Obviously, if corporations act for the public good, there is less need to prove that each businessman, acting for his own gain, promotes the social welfare as a whole — as traditional competitive theory declares. Additionally, the focus of the managerial theme is upon the organization rather than upon the whole competitive system. The organization is a social system in itself; workers, customers, stockholders, suppliers are all part of the organization, a change from the classical version which places the emphasis upon the owner as risk-taker, manager, and creator of the productive forces within the economy as a whole. The managerial theme stresses that the manager is a professional man who has been trained to coordinate and mediate among the various interest groups. This view, of course, does not place the setting of prices inexorably upon the forces of supply and demand, but emphasizes responsibility and competition in terms of quality and service as well. Thus the Managerial Ideology places its emphasis directly upon the function of the manager and the nature of the business enterprise. Since the main exponents of this view are the managements of the large corporations, the symbol of small business is given only token mention.

The public's ambivalence over the question of bigness is attacked directly by the creed. The idea that big business is required in a big country is stated frequently. Likewise, the stigma of bigness is counteracted by pointing to the large numbers of owners of the big corporations — they are owned by the people.

The proper function of government is one of the principal differences between the Managerial and Classical Ideologies. The managerialists feel the role of government is considerably greater than the traditionalists will accept. The C.E.D. has taken the position that government action is essential in attempting to mitigate cyclical fluctuations — even if such a policy would include deficit spending (a position strongly condemned by the Classical Ideologists). If government action is necessary, it is due to a failure in the duties of individuals. Government action in such cases is not condemned, but the bias is, nevertheless, in favor of timely private action. Keynesian economics, however, is finding increasing acceptance within the managerial credo. This is largely due to the publications of both the C.E.D. and *Fortune*.

The picture that the Managerial Ideology portrays of capitalism in the United States is somewhat more realistic than that given by the Classical Ideology, for the Managerial Ideology focuses upon the growth of the large corporation and the separation of management from ownership.

Further, the Managerial Ideology's acceptance of the role of government is considerably more realistic than that of the Classical Ideology. To a large degree, the Managerial Ideology of Capitalism is successful in that it provides argument and defense dressed in current terms. The strain between reality and the Classical Capitalist Ideology had become great enough to produce an ideological step-child.

The Countervailing Power Ideology

J. K. Galbraith is one of the few economists who has had the experience of coining a concept (or at least a phrase) and seeing it become immensely popular in less than a decade.

What is the concept of countervailing power? Most succinctly it is "the neutralization of one position of power by another." It is the "answering bargaining power" to check the power of sellers or buyers by the organizing of those subject to such power. "Private economic power begets the countervailing power of those who are subject to it." The development of strong unions then, in this argument, was inevitable in America to neutralize or balance the power of the large firms. Galbraith summarizes his idea by saying that "private economic power is held in check by the countervailing power of those who are subject to it. The first begets the second. The long trend toward concentration of industrial enterprise in the hands of a few firms has brought into existence not only strong sellers . . . but also strong buyers. . . ."

Galbraith's argument is that the two develop together. As one group becomes more concentrated, another develops to counter this power. Thus the thesis is that, generally, the development of one large bloc is offset by the growth of another group in an effort to prevent its own exploitation. Galbraith seems to feel that usually the strongest unions will develop in those industries where the strongest corporations exist. The role of the government is, or should be, to assist in this development of checks and counterchecks to power exploitation by the growth of other groups.

Galbraith's contention then is that the concept of competition as the autonomous regulator of economic activity (and with the state the only regulator) has been superseded. He grants that Adam Smith's ideas may possibly apply to some markets. This can be due only to the fact that no concentration of power or exploitation has arisen in such a market. As soon as it does, the self-generating force of countervailing power will assert itself and develop a new type of competition, a competition only in the sense that one group balances another. This is Galbraith's concept of modern American Capitalism.

The countervailing power argument is a post-World War II creation. The fact of its recent publication gives it an air of timeliness that is not felt to the same extent in the Classical creed.

Mr. Galbraith has developed a concept which has become a very effective ideology in the defense of modern American Capitalism. Its very *post hoc, ergo propter hoc* (after this, therefore because of this) approach to the development of economic institutions gives it considerable appeal to many groups. In Galbraith's hands, such teleology becomes an argument buttressing existing institutions; in other words, because certain institutions now exist, they really had to exist. This is undoubtedly what helps give the ideology of countervailing power much of its "persuasive" appeal. Further, it may be argued that the countervailing power approach is far more effective than the traditional ideology of capitalism in explaining the present structure of industry in the United States.

People's Capitalism

The label of "People's Capitalism" is becoming increasingly fashionable as a new title to describe the current American economic system. The title is purported to have been developed by the American Advertising Council for the United States Information Agency in 1956. Since that time, the term has been widely used. The U.S.I.A. has at times used the concept frequently abroad, and General Electric and Standard Oil (N.J.) have used the slogan in their ads. The New York Stock Exchange also speaks about "America, the people's capitalism." While by 1962 figures, over 16 million Americans owned stock (about half again as many as the total of about 11 million factory workers in the country), the use of the word "people's" may seem a little overoptimistic from the view of stock ownership alone. Yet it focuses upon what is perhaps the key to the general meaning of the term. Diffused property ownership seems to be the central concept of most definitions given for People's Capitalism. Although there is considerable literature, there is generally little detailed analytical discussion of what this new brand of capitalism is or should be. A book by Professor Massimo Salvadori, *The Economics of Freedom,* is one of the most comprehensive studies now available on the topic.

The essential feature of *people's* capitalism, the wide diffusion of the ownership of property, rests upon the wide distribution of policy-sharing processes and economic legislation which embodies freely expressed public will. What this definition boils down to is simply wide diffusion of property ownership coupled with an active democratic political system. It is the functioning of the system, therefore, more than the structure that distinguishes people's capitalism. Thus the transformation from the old to the new form of capitalism is attributed to the influence of the widening field of opportunities, increasing mobility, and high consumption goals within the reach of most people.

Regarding the crucial problem of how to deal with big business and its corollary big government, Salvadori feels that America seems to have found the right road. The government has developed into a supervisor and checker of abuses. The large enterprise is here to stay in both capitalistic and noncapitalistic countries. But the evils of excessive concentration of power in the large private corporation can be corrected and largely eliminated in a people's capitalism through a variety of developments. This, it is asserted, is already happening in the United States. Such developments are: (a) the diffusion of individual ownership of property; (b) the replacement of the owners by managers whose concern is more in terms of long-term prosperity than for short-term profits; (c) enactment and rigid enforcement of regulatory legislation over the large corporations; (d) the growth of "countervailing power" which represents, in the economic field, what checks and balances are in the political field.

Salvadori goes further to advocate that at a certain point in its expansion the corporation is no longer private but acquires a public or semi-public character. The responsibility for major decisions for economic units of this large size must be shared with more than just its managers since their actions affect the entire economy. Walter Reuther's two now seemingly radical proposals for job-security and profit-sharing will within one or two generations be commonly accepted, Salvadori claims. Thus Salvadori sees continued diffusion of income occurring, not only through the greater productivity of industrialization and collective bargaining (not to mention progressive taxation), but hints that government intervention will continue to spread incomes even more equally. The continued policies of increased social security benefits, etc., will aid as well in furthering People's Capitalism. Job security and profit sharing will come, Salvadori hints, either through labor's collective bargaining or government action. This may not be accepted by many of those who now advocate People's Capitalism, but such action is, at least, logically in keeping with the basic concept of the greatest possible diffusion of income and capitalist ownership. Other writers on this topic, such as Kelso and Adler in the *Capitalist Manifesto*, employ only more complicated means to achieve this end. This is a point that to some may come as a shock — particularly those who have been using the term People's Capitalism in a rather loose sense. Perhaps the difference among those using

World Economic Problems

the term of People's Capitalism lies in the attitude as to whether the United States now approximates this goal or has only begun the transformation. To some social critics, "the widespread diffusion of the theory of People's Capitalism signifies the effectiveness of organized propaganda" rather than an attainment of its precepts in reality.

• *77*

Changes in the Soviet Economy*

FRANCIS SETON
Oxford University

Some commentators have been fond of pointing out that the post-Stalin regime made the Soviet economy more "capitalistic." The evidence of this is seen in the Soviet's greater concern with marginal adjustments and incentives and, fundamentally, in a more pervasive rationality. In historical perspective, however, far from Communism being the successor to capitalism, the gross and lumbering command economy of the Stalin era may have been an indication that the country was not yet advanced enough to benefit from anything resembling the subtle and refined decision process we associate with contemporary capitalism.

Concerning Economic History

Because the range of alternatives in national policies is effectively limited by economic conditions, a significant change in these conditions will often make old policies futile and new ones attractive. There is little doubt that such a change has occurred in the Soviet Union since the last war, and that it has leapt into the consciousness of the party, government and people with particular abruptness owing to the shift in leadership with which it was roughly coincident.

* Taken and adapted from *Changes in the Soviet Economy* by Francis Seton, *Problems of Communism*, January–February 1961, pp. 34–41. Reproduced with permission.

The change has been noted by many observers and has received a variety of names. This author would prefer to characterize it as a structural shift in the economy making the *efficiency* of productive effort more telling than its mere volume. But whatever the terms used, the change is a product of the discovery that improvements in method can be more important than the continued accumulation of factory buildings and machines. In economic terms, the virtues of technical progress and innovation have come to outshine those of capital investment.

This change in economic climate goes to the very foundations on which a country's economic system is built. It parallels in encapsuled form one of the basic transformations which most developed countries may have undergone at one time or another.

The academic economist has perhaps minimized these transformations by the professional habit of looking on economic systems mainly as institutional contrivances which absorb scarce resources (labor, land, and machines) and work them up into a flow of final goods for the satisfaction of consumers. He is not always explicit that this conception is only relevant to one corner of space and time: Northwestern Europe and North America since the middle of the 19th century. Previously and elsewhere the chief concern may not have been the best *utilization* of existing land, labor, and capital, but the best remedy for the crying *deficiencies* of any or all of them. How can capital be *created* where it is dolefully inadequate; how can one type of labor be turned into another, or one type of capital into another? It is this *transformation* of productive resources and not their optimum *combination* which has been the stuff of economic history.

The economic history of Stalin's Russia is the story of a transformation of peasant labor into industrial labor, and of both into capital. It was this, far more than any proximate conversion of productive resources into consumer satisfaction, which determined its course, and it would be idle, therefore, to expect it to have followed the precepts of modern allocative economics.

Industry vs. Agriculture

Normally the transfer of a peasant laborer to industry might be expected to result in the loss of food output which in the absence of foreign trade or aid can only be made good by the return from industry of sufficient equipment or fertilizer to replace the departed laborer on the land. In fact, industry must somehow bear the "replacement cost" of agricultural labor. Now, it is true that in conditions of rural over-population, such as had prevailed in Russia for several decades, the marginal productivity of agricultural labor, and therefore its "replacement cost," was very close to zero. But even the drafters of the First Five-Year Plan realized that this was not the *whole* story. It would not be enough to keep agricultural output *unchanged* while labor was shifted to the towns; the transfer of each peasant would also have to be accompanied by a well-defined increment in food production. This was so, firstly, because he could only be lured away from his traditional pursuits by the offer of a better living standard than he had previously enjoyed; secondly, because the remaining peasants could not be prevented from consuming more per head once an unproductive mouth had left their farms; and thirdly, because the "work-spreading" habits to which the peasants were inured would dissipate some of the productivity gains which the departure of surplus labor would otherwise have brought about.

For all these reasons it is clear that industry must not merely replace the departed worker on the land in a technical sense, but must, over and above this, bear an "institutional surcharge" in order to equip agriculture for the production of the incremental output which his departure has necessitated. It will be convenient to refer to the "replacement cost" and the "surcharge" together as the "release price" of agricultural labor, as this is evidently the sum total of the industrial output which each peasant recruit has to bring about in order to pay for his own release from agriculture. Depending on conditions, this output may take the form of agricultural machinery, fertilizer, or even industrial consumer goods (to increase peasant productivity through incentives); but in the absence of peasant coercion it is an inescapable charge of industry, and any economist or planner pursuing industrialization in a particular country might do well to start by gauging its level and gearing his program accordingly.

Normally, as industrialization proceeds, one would expect the release price of labor to be subject to conflicting pulls. A number of factors will tend to make for its *decline:* it is likely, for instance, that the general increase in economic discipline and efficiency will spill over into agriculture and raise the productivity of capital on the land. At the same time the monetization and commercialization of agriculture will probably increase its responsiveness to incentives in the form of industrial consumer goods. On the other hand, the gradual inroads made into the rural surplus population will bring about a situation where each additional peasant transferred to industry will have to be replaced, or partly replaced, by progressively greater capital investment in agriculture, and this makes for a countervailing *increase* in the release price as industrialization proceeds.

Eventually the labor-capital ratio in agriculture will no longer be any less than it is in industry. At that point the historic transformation of one type of resource into the other is completed, and the release price of labor ceases to be the main constraint on the progress of the economy along its chosen path. It is only then that the center of attention shifts to the classical problem: What are the marginal adjustments in the employment of land, labor, or capital throughout the economy which will best serve the community, given its tastes and preferences? This brings us into the mature economy of the Northwest European or North American type.

Exploitation of Agriculture

Is Soviet Russia now approaching this stage? With a total labor force little more than 25 per cent above that of the United States, the Soviet Union still has 4.5 times as many people employed in agriculture — about three times as many per acre of crop land, and nearly 20 times as many per tractor (though Soviet tractors are bigger). Obviously there is still a good deal of leeway to be made up. It does seem, however, that the stage may now have been reached when the "replacement" component of the release price is rising quite sharply. There are no really adequate statistics to prove this, but a rough impression of the trend may be obtained by comparing the four-year periods 1935–38 and 1949–52, both of which were characterized by a substitution of rural capital for labor, leaving agricultural output virtually unchanged. During the earlier period the government was able to recruit nearly 10 million land workers for (temporary or permanent) employment elsewhere, "replacing" them by tractors to the tune of 3.9 million horsepower units. During the later period only 3.1 million peasants could be recruited in this way, even though the corresponding "replacement" was of the order of 5.3 million horsepower units — and this in spite of the fact that the collective farms' own investments were running at over three times the level of the earlier period.

Normally, as we have seen, the process of industrialization produces countervailing forces which bring the release price down; but it seems abundantly clear that the Stalinist system prevented them from operating. The hallmark of that system was the attempt to express the last ounce of manpower which agriculture could be made to yield (short of a catastrophic fall in food output) and to "finance" its release price by ruthlessly enforced, and sometimes murderous, inroads into the consumption standards of the remaining peasants.

But starving geese lay fewer and fewer eggs. While the whiphand of Stalinism helped to spark the industrialization process and drove it forward at unprecedented speed, it prevented the extension of the new efficiency from industry to agriculture, and delayed the monetization and full integration of rural life into the exchange economy, which alone could have increased its responsiveness to capital investment and incentive goods from industry. By 1952–53 Soviet agriculture was sucked dry of the power to stimulate, or be stimulated by, the progress of other branches of the economy. If industrialization was to proceed at anything like its previous rate, the government had to choose between a further turn of the screw of peasant coercion and an entirely new policy of partial atonement for past sins, reorienting agriculture towards the stimuli which could help to bring the release price down.

Reforms in Agriculture

After Stalin's death, it became clear that his successors chose the second alternative. The comprehensive reforms from 1953 to the present day are obviously designed to raise the responsiveness of agriculture to both *capital investment* and *labor incentives,* and it is this that explains the apparent vacillation between measures for more *intensive* and more *extensive* working of the land which seems to have confused a number of observers.

The situation is made somewhat more complicated by the judicious mixing of stimuli in such a way as to help the long-term struggle against the collective farmer's private plot, without compromising those types of farm work in which the private plot still has an edge over the collective in terms of efficiency (mainly livestock and vegetable production). The abrupt raising of state delivery prices by anything from 200 to 500 per cent, coupled with the lowering of delivery norms and finally the total abolition of these virtual levies in favor of a system of planned state purchases, were all measures clearly designed to stimulate production on both collective farms and private plots.

On the other hand, the gradual monetization of collective farm labor dividends, their prompter payment in advance of the harvest, and the lowering of collective farm income taxes were evidently aimed at making collective farm production more attractive compared with the private plot. This policy was given teeth by special measures designed to bring the permitted size of an individual's plot into direct dependence on his labor contribution in the collectivized fields. Yet from the very outset of the reforms the state was careful to warn local authorities against infringing private interests in matters of livestock breeding, and it instructed its procurement organs to pay urban market prices for all fruit and berries purchased from private orchards — surely the only instance where the Soviet government bound itself voluntarily to the verdict of a free market in matters of internal price formation. But the regime is not merely backing the collective farms against the private plot. It also wants to promote state farming against the traditional collectives for a more extensive use of capital on the land.

Industry under Stalin

Many of the great policy changes of the recent years will impose a new and unaccustomed burden on industry. Indeed, the stepping-up of incentives in agriculture and on the labor front is merely the obverse of the fact that henceforth industry will have to pay at least a portion of the release price of labor, and can no longer be harnessed exclusively to the production of capital for its own use. This, however, was its be-all and end-all under Stalin, and the total repudiation of this concept, along with so much that followed from it, is the true measure of the break which has occurred.

The problem of providing a continued flow of manpower for industry is aggravated at the present time by the population deficit caused by war and its aftermath. The cataclysm of the 1940's may have deprived the Soviet economy of as many as 25 million people who could still be at work now, and of the normal reinforcement of another 7–10 millions who would be entering the labor force in the present decade if normal birth rates had prevailed between 1940 and 1947. Given high fertility rates and lowered mortality, however, the Soviet population can quickly make good these once-for-all losses, and the present slackening of manpower inflows may well be followed by a limited period of acceleration within the next ten or fifteen years.

In a very real sense the Stalinist economy was a single integrated factory, with agriculture supplying manpower as the raw material of industry, and industry producing capital goods as the final output. A process of this sort lends itself most easily to administrative control from the center, since the basic criteria of success are pre-established, simple, and unconditional. Planners were judged by the degree to which their targets favored "growth levers" (machines rather than ordinary goods, machine-making machines rather than ordinary machines, etc.), with scant regard to balance in assortment, space, or time. Factory managers were judged by the extent to which they fulfilled their output targets, with scant regard to the cost at which this was achieved. In terms of industrial output the system produced spectacular results — and this remains so even when the official claim of a 15-fold expansion between 1928 and 1952 is scaled down to the lower indices suggested by Western observers. But it was increasingly realized that this output was bought not merely at the cost of keeping agriculture virtually stagnant and isolated, but also at the price of reducing the serviceability and economic effectiveness of the industrial products which were being turned out by the factories in such relentless profusion.

The trouble with the total-command economy of the Stalinist type is that it invariably deprives itself of the economic knowledge and rationality on which its commands are supposed to be based. A price system artificially devised to favor investment and facilitate administrative control cannot at the same time be a true reflection of relative scarcities in the economy. If it is used by administrators as an aid in judging the performance of executives, it will generate incentives pulling in the wrong direction. If it is used by planners as an aid to target-setting, it will cause misallocation of resources even *by the standards of the planners' own objectives.* There is ample evidence that the Stalinist system suffered badly from both these disabilities, and that it still does so wherever it continues to exist.

The Problem of Incentives

The story of distorted incentives is a familiar one. We know that Soviet production managers by concentrating on material-intensive lines of production, because these helped to boost their output indices with minimum calls on their own labor and resources, produced inventories choking with indigestible hardware in constant need of "galvanizing" campaigns. We also know that the rigid target system drove managers to distort the rhythm of their output. They would often empty the pipelines of production in an effort to fulfill a *finished-output* target (if this was at a premium), or block them up with stocks of semi-finished goods if *gross*-production targets carried greater weight. The resulting "syncopation" in the flow of output aggravated the supply situation and led to frequent switches in the definition of performance criteria ("gross" output, "commodity" output, sales, and so on).

In all these ways, and in many more, the hard-pressed executives of the Stalin era dodged and evaded the relentless impositions of the target system and, while submitting to the letter of its laws, often frustrated its real aims. It sent subordinate organs on a desperate search for protection and self-sufficiency, and helped to dissect the economy into the notorious ministerial empires that reached everywhere from major factories to far-flung sources of fuel and raw materials, and that were able to offer ever subtler and more effective resistance to central policy.

The proliferation of targets produced a situation in which the number of instructions circulating through the system became too large to be effectively coordinated by a single authority. Production managers were often faced with orders issuing from different sources, which on closer examination turned out to be incompatible, or could be made out to be so in self-defence. This opened up a new and welcome area of choice, as managers were able to select from the instructions received those which it was worth their while to fulfill and those which they could safely disregard.

Inefficiency

Soviet leaders have recently made determined moves to remedy the outstanding failures in resource allocation inherited from the past. Most of these sprang from the longstanding obsession with the quantitative accumulation of capital which hamstrung the full exploitation of the qualitative improvements offered by the accelerated flow of innovations in the last 20 to 30 years. There was a frequent disregard of the capital-saving trends characterizing so much of recent development in the West. Among the important technological revolutions that were bypassed in this way was the shift from coal to petroleum and gas as sources of energy. In the early 1950's, when the world at large consumed over 40 per cent of its energy in the form of non-solid fuels, the corresponding Soviet proportion was barely 20 per cent, even though petroleum and gas absorb less labor and capital per calorie unit than any other major fuel. The Soviets' lag in the development of liquid-fuels production delayed the switch from steam to diesel propulsion and the associated reduction in the cost of transport per ton-mile carried.

In the field of power generation, over-concentration on hydroelectric schemes led to the habitual freezing of capital resources during long gestation periods, and curtailed the building of thermal power stations which would have yielded their smaller returns more quickly. This was part and parcel of the chronic disease of "gigantomania," and led to a rapid increase in the proportion of annual investment locked up in unfinished projects — no doubt an important factor in the diminishing effectiveness of investment (in terms of output) that could be observed in so many fields.

As we know, determined moves are now being made to remedy these defects. The effort under the present Seven-Year Plan is largely concentrated on the shift of emphasis from coal to gas and petroleum, from partial to complete mechanization, from ferrous metals to plastics, and so forth. In general there is a distinct and very conscious move from growth by accumulation to growth by technical progress, and capital-saving techniques.

Toward the Mature Economy

The industrial reorganization or "territorialization" of 1957 was only one of the measures designed to alert the top executive organs — traditionally preoccupied with physical output targets to the exclusion of all else — to the need for economic thinking. At the same time the economic incentives to the lower echelons are being overhauled with similar ends in view: Since 1959 managerial premia are beginning to be based on cost reduction rather than output in a number of important industries, and the system of bonus payments to engineers and technicians is undergoing a process of thorough rationalization.

There is also much stirring in the field of economic theory and planning practice. The present discussions on the price system are untrammelled by the dictates of Marxian orthodoxy and address themselves to long-neglected problems. There is talk of introducing interest changes on fixed capital, raising the importance of profits, using differential rent and obsolescence — in fact of readmitting a host of demons from the capitalist underworld. Mathematical methods in social accounting and programming are enjoying a new respectability and may soon produce a serious impact on resource allocation.

Should the Soviet Union succeed in removing the economic and administrative hurdles which the Stalinist system has put in its way, it could progress towards a mature economy at a very fast pace. The day could thus draw nearer when neither capital nor labor would appear to be in such relative scarcity as to encourage the leadership to continue the process of converting one into the other. Peasant labor would then cease to figure as an "intermediate good" in anybody's calculation, and the economy *could* settle down to the relatively civilized business of making marginal adjustments in response to consumer demand or social policy. All this, however, is still a long way off, but enough has been said to show that the *economic* reforms of the last few years are at least not incompatible with the long-term pursuit of economic rationality.

• *78*

New *Directions in the Communist*

*Economies**

WILLIAM D. GRAMPP
University of Illinois, Chicago

The ideological conflict between Soviet Russia and Mainland China has revealed to Americans the heresy that is rife in the Communist World. This commentary discusses what contemporary Communism is like in Tito's independent and frankly revisionist Yugoslavia and in the countries constituting the integral parts of the Soviet bloc itself. What are the "new directions" of this surprising present-day permissiveness?

Major changes have occurred in the economic policies of the Communist world in the last fifteen years. They have been in effect long enough to invite some serious speculation over the kind of economic system that will emerge from them. They could bring into being a novel and remarkably interesting economic order containing elements of communism and capitalism but not altogether like either of them. The policy changes have been of two sorts: a decrease in the total amount of government direction and a change in some of its forms — decentralization and rationalization, respectively.

* Taken and adapted from William D. Grampp "New Directions in the Communist Economies," *Business Horizons,* Fall 1963, pp. 29–36. Reproduced with permission.

Decentralization

Decentralization, the more important of the two, has been carried furthest by Yugoslavia, which began it after leaving the Russian bloc in 1948. The government fixes the principal magnitudes, such as rate of growth, amount of investment, and the allocation of resources and division of output among agriculture, industry, and services. It does not specify exact amounts, as traditional Communist policy did, nor does it use direct means to achieve the targets. Rather, it seeks them by indirection: by taxes, by control of some investment but not all, and by setting minimum prices on some goods, maximum prices on others, but specific prices on very few. The most distinctive feature of Yugoslav policy is the self-management of the firms. Most are state owned and may produce whatever they choose so long as they make a profit. They are supposed to compete with each other and to allow the market to set prices. The market is also supposed to determine wages, and workers are meant to have substantial freedom in the choice of jobs.

The firms in Yugoslavia are supposed to be directed by a freely chosen workers' council. It delegates some authority to an executive group and to the plant manager who is himself selected with the advice of the council. Most farms are privately owned, and the rest are operated as the industrial firms are. After taxes of 50 per cent are paid, profits of all enterprises are distributed among bonuses for employees (including the manager), welfare expenditures, and investment.

Efficient Decision Making

What Yugoslavia has tried to do is to improve the efficiency of economic decisions, an objective familiar to economists but not well understood by others. In every country, decisions must be made about how best to use resources and to distribute what they produce. In a capitalist country, individuals make most of the decisions about where they will work, how to use their property, and which goods to buy. They also make decisions as businessmen — about what is most profitable to produce, what kinds of labor and capital to employ, and in what proportions to combine them. In the traditional Communist view, the government should make these decisions and write them into its economic plan. In Yugoslavia today, some decisions are made by the people, some by government, and some by both.

It matters very much whether the decisions are efficient or not. Efficient decisions mean maximum production and usefulness; inefficient decisions mean waste. The Yugoslavian method is probably more efficient than the traditional Communist method, and a few examples will show why. Whatever is the share of total production available for consumption, it will be more valuable to the people if it is what they want than if it is what the government believes they want (or ought to want). The people of Yugoslavia make known their wants by buying some goods and not others until all prices are such that the amounts bought and produced are equal. At these prices, firms will produce the goods that are most profitable; they will either find a cheaper way to produce the others or not produce them at all. Finding a cheaper way means finding how to put capital and labor together so that they produce more. Just how they are combined is something the individual firm decides, and it has an inducement to do well because it shares in the profits.

Coordinating the Market

The Yugoslav method is superior in another way — in the coordination of the kinds and amounts of goods that each firm produces. To produce steel, sufficient ore must first be produced and transported to the mills, and to get adequate ore and transportation, there must be steel for the ore mines and railways. So it is with every commodity and with most services. The economy must inform producers what is needed and make certain they act on their information. The market does this in its way. Its way is often far from perfect, but the way of central planning is still farther (or so one would infer from changes in Communist policy). The Yugoslavs have employed the market for some purposes, particularly to collect information about what should be produced and how, and as an inducement to use the information effectively. Their policy has been called market socialism, a somewhat misleading term because many features of a market system are absent. Decentralization is a better word.

Worker Incentives

Some decentralization has occurred in the Soviet Union. Retail prices and wage rates are usually set at amounts that clear the market. If buyers want more of a good than is available, its price is increased, and vice versa. This does not mean that consumers direct the economy, but they usually can spend their income as they choose and hence get more satisfaction from it than they could by spending it on fixed amounts of goods at fixed prices. The new method of price determination may increase their industry as well as their satisfaction, and it certainly reduces the costs of distribution. In labor markets, the wage rate is set high in occupations and regions to which the government wants labor to move. The state no longer employs the worst of the coercive methods used under Stalin: labor permit books, compulsory assignment to jobs, and extensive forced labor. Instead it uses material incentives. This does not mean the Russian worker is free. It means that the state coaxes more and coerces less than in the past.

It coaxes in other ways too. An individual may own his house, may borrow from a state bank to buy it, and may even own a second house.

He may deposit his savings in a bank, buy government bonds, hold currency, or buy consumer goods with an asset value, for example, watches and cameras (which may explain why their prices are *above* the market). Some go further and do what they may not, such as buying foreign currency. In agriculture, the collective farms sell a part of their output on entirely unregulated markets. Beyond and beneath these changes is a restiveness over central planning, a dissatisfaction with its methods and what they have achieved, and a groping for new techniques for the making and execution of decisions. For several years there has been talk of using profit as a measure of efficiency, and in 1962 the ideas emerged in systematic form in the celebrated Liberman Plan. It can be interpreted as another stage in the movement of the soviet economy, not toward a "profit system" as those words are used in the West, but toward a system that is meant to have all of its efficiency.

In Poland, policy has been reexamined in a searching way since 1956. The consensus among its economists now seems to be that centralized planning should be replaced by a policy similar to that of Yugoslavia but more sophisticated in its pricing methods. The idea is called "price socialism," but the prices cover more costs than those of a capitalist system and have a greater allocational effect.

The decentralizing of policy in the Communist world is most noticeable in the new method of setting prices, especially at retail; in the greater authority of plant managers and employees; in the greater freedom of workers to select jobs; in the use of wage differentials to allocate labor and increase productivity; and in the greater power of individuals over the disposition of their incomes. The changes are apparent to some degree in most of the Communist countries of Europe. As usual, China is a kingdom to itself, and its economic policy has been unique from the start — not orthodox or doctrinaire Marxism by any means, but novel, experimental, pragmatic, and changeable.

Rationalization

In European Communist policy, decentralization is just one of the changes. The other is a change in the forms of centralized planning and can be called rationalization. Ever since it began to plan, the Soviet Union has been trying to make planning more efficient and lately has studied Western methods of doing so.

There is something about rationalization that in the West would be called paradoxical and in the Marxian world dialectical. It is that capitalism should supply communism with the means of making centralized planning effective. That might be accomplished by using the marginal principle in centralized decision making, which is more feasible than ever because of the newer quantitative methods and computers. The paradox is compounded by the methods of rationalization, which pull economic policy back toward centralization while the use of market methods pulls it toward decentralization.

Efficiencies

Both kinds of changes are meant to increase the efficiency of the economy. Have they succeeded? Yugoslavia in the first ten years of decentralization grew more rapidly than before and apparently faster than neighboring Communist states. (Czechoslovakia found that the labor required just for administering the central plan was retarding the country's growth.) When Yugoslavia's growth rate fell in 1962, it returned to a few of the methods of centralized planning. That change seems at present to be a modification of a trend rather than a reversal of it. The Soviet Union appears to be doing at least as well as it did under Stalin. Communist China, on the other hand, used some extreme methods of centralization in the late fifties and early sixties. Its development actually seems to have been reversed, with total output declining. Let us suppose that among the Communist countries of the West the efficiency of their economies increases. What then?

Consumption per person will increase (so long as population does not increase unduly) because labor and capital will be used more productively in the consumer goods sector and because market pricing maximizes their usefulness. Consumption may even increase as a percentage of total output as individuals acquire more influence over policy decisions. It might be supposed that the growth rate would then decrease. But that need not happen. Efficiency in the investment sector may increase enough to compensate for the decrease in its relative size. Even more important is the fact that the labor force will become more efficient because so much is invested in training programs and vocational education.

In addition, an increase in per capita consumption can itself increase the growth rate by its productivity and incentive effects. As workers are better fed, housed, and clothed, they are able to produce more, and the prospect of having more often makes them want to work harder to get it. These things are likely to happen as consumption increases from small to moderate amounts. They are not as likely, however, when consumption continues to increase because people find purchasing additional consumer goods less valuable than holding assets. The important problem for the Communists then will be an ideological one.

Incentives

Promising and delivering more and more consumer goods are not enough to keep people industrious. The capitalist way is to allow people to accumulate wealth in various forms: ownership of productive property, of securities, of currency, and so on. It seems as though the accumulation of wealth would be anathema in a Communist country, but it is not. Even now people can hold government bonds, savings accounts, currency, housing, and in some countries, agricultural land and small business firms. The distribution of private wealth in the Soviet Union is extremely unequal and may be as unequal as the distribution of income; the latter, it has been known for some time, is probably more unequal than in the United States. But almost all productive property outside agriculture still is owned by the state. As real income increases, the Communist states will have to decide whether or not to permit some form of private ownership of that wealth. The very mention of it seems absurd.

Yet the cooperatives may provide a way. Even now, in Yugoslavia, the employees of a firm have in theory all the powers of the stockholders of an American corporation except the power to transfer assets (the power that comes from ownership).

The Communists almost always have recognized the place of cooperatives in the economy, and they may find it expedient to make that place quite large. By so doing, they may solve the problem of allowing the people to hold increasing amounts of assets — in the form of shares in producers' cooperatives — without having to return to private property in its familiar form. The rationale would be fairly simple; one can imagine them arguing it: "In a workers' state, the means of production are their property, in the past managed for them by the state via central planning, in the future by themselves via the workers' councils; to make a state-owned firm a cooperative is simply to transfer it from the ownership of all workers to particular workers. An economy of self-managing (and competing) cooperatives accelerates the movement of the workers' state to the condition that Engels called government by things instead of by people and so brings the nation closer to the final stage of communism." What it would produce in fact is a very curious form of enterprise, one in which there is no distinction between those who bear the major uncertainties (the owners) and those who do not (the workers) or between those who stand to profit and lose a great deal and those whose incomes are less uncertain. No capitalist country has ever wanted to erase this distinction. Yugoslavia, on the other hand, may have erased it already.

The changes in economic policy could also have far-reaching effects outside the domestic economy. They could affect the forms of rivalry between communism and capitalism, which might compete over the rate of increase in per capita consumption, rather than the gross national product or industrial production. Many would welcome the change, especially in the Communist countries.

Power and Progress

The policy changes could lead to an important amount of trade between the capitalist and Communist worlds. Each has its own trading bloc, the Common Market and Comecon. The Common Market countries have been energized beyond the most optimistic expectation. The countries of Comecon will not be helped nearly so much because it provides for much less foreign trade. One may expect, however, that as the domestic economies of the Communist countries become freer, so will the trade between them. Beyond that is the prospect of trade with non-Communist countries, just as the next step in the development of the Common Market ought to be the lowering of its external tariffs and the enlargement of trade with nonparticipating nations, including the Communist.

Should this happen, the effect on nationalism will be destructive. It is said, and truly, that international trade brings the nations of the world together in a mutually beneficial comity. It also reduces their ability to sustain themselves and thereby reduces their power to make war or even to threaten it. It also gives the importers and exporters of each country a selfish and powerful interest in maintaining peace. It cannot be said that free trade would eliminate conflict between (as well as within) the Communist and non-Communist worlds, nor would it diminish the nuclear power of the giants. But free trade would diminish the danger of nonnuclear conflict while at the same time adding to the real income of most countries, possibly all of them.

The total amount of power that Communist governments employ will probably decrease. They will divest themselves of much economic power and exercise what they keep by more impersonal, predictable, and hence less dictatorial means. Of course it could happen that as they give with one hand they will take back with another. But that is unlikely. Nearly all Western observers believe there is more political freedom in the Communist states than when Stalin was alive. The changes in economic policy have been made since his death, except in Yugoslavia, which began them earlier because it freed itself of Stalinism earlier.

It is remarkable that the present holders of economic power should have allowed new forms of policy to be considered at all. That they have suggests that they may see a place for themselves in the new system. That place is plant management, and it could be a handsome place. At present, the plant manager in Russia executes many more decisions than he makes. Although his income and position are relatively high, he is a subordinate in the system of authority. In Yugoslavia, the plant manager has all his Russian counterpart has and more — authority. Moreover, the income of the Yugoslav manager depends very much upon the effectiveness of his authority. He receives a bonus, just as the Russian does, but has more freedom in deciding how to increase it. The Yugoslav is presumably responsible to the workers' council, but it is less prescriptive, glacial, and unbending than a central planning agency. In addition, there is a mutuality of interest between the council and manager as there is not between either of them and a central agency. That mutuality, in fact, can be a curse to the economy by leading to syndicalism.

Support for decentralization may come then from those who now hold the power of centralized planning. It is almost sure to come from those who are plant managers, and it is likely to be welcomed by the workers. The latter two groups constitute a vested interest that can push the Communist countries more and more toward decentralization, or, in Marxian categories, they constitute the economic basis for a new class structure. It is not the eventuality that was forecast by the Marxists, and it was not forecast by any other doctrine I know of. But then no doctrine forecast the changes in economic policy. They could be the most arresting event since the revolution of 1917.

79

Índia's Development Strategy and the Third Five-Year Plan*

JOHN P. LEWIS
President's Council of Economic Advisers

Happenings in India are noteworthy if only because of the vast population of that country. The Indian experiment proffers an intriguing combination of government ownership and development planning with private enterprise and representative government. (Curiously, a smaller share of the Indian GNP at present originates in government than in the United States.) Because of this, it is the most arresting alternative to the Communist program of economic development.

The Development Strategy

The Goals

The Indian program of course is not exclusively production oriented. It seeks to promote social equity for traditionally underprivileged groups, greater equality of economic opportunity and of incomes, a reduction in the country's massive unemployment and underemployment, and adherence to constitutional processes of social change. But, most directly,

* Taken and adapted from Everett E. Hagen, editor, *Planning Economic Development* (Homewood, Ill.: Richard D. Irwin, Inc., 1963), pp. 82–85, 87–94. Reproduced with permission.

the strategy that has been adopted for the period 1961–66 is aimed at the following three goals:

First, India proposes to achieve the rate of increase in real income (and output) per capita that its government believes to be the minimum consistent with the maintenance of political stability and the retention of constitutional development procedures. In the third plan the authorities put this minimum annual average at 3.4 per cent, slightly less than the second plan's target of 3.7 per cent but much more than its achievement of 1.6 per cent. Taking account of an expected population growth of 2.4 per cent a year, the third plan therefore sets a target of more than 5.5 per cent for the annual gain in gross output.

Second, the purpose is to make this growth process, once established, domestically self-sustaining by assuring the steady expansion of the net investment, technical skills, managerial, and other input flows continuing growth requires.

Third, it is proposed that the expanding economy shall become self-supporting — that exports plus a continuing net inflow of foreign private investment shall balance imports — within a limited period. The third plan stretches out the target date for this achievement until 1975.

The Dominant Theme: Surmounting Critical Scarcities

Given these purposes, the dominant development strategy may be thought of as essentially a scheme for breaking the bottlenecks, loosening the restraints, and overcoming the critical scarcities that have been obstructing productive expansion.

A great deal of Western commentary as well as some of the general pronouncements of the Indian planners themselves would suggest that overwhelmingly the worst shortage impeding economic expansion in India is that of domestic saving. The fact seems to be that such a "saving-centered" development theory misjudges the Indian situation on two counts.

First, in spite of the low level of income in India, there is considerable private capacity to save, probably even among the rural masses, if adequate inducements exist; but also, by raising taxes or widening the cost-price spreads in the commodities it markets, a strong government has a sizable opportunity to increase government savings in the longer term.

Second, there are scarcities other than the domestic saving constraint that *do* seriously obstruct Indian economic development. These other, more critical scarcities include, in the first place, shortages of decision-making capacity, of skilled manpower, and of scientific and organizational technique. India is encountering a shortage of relevant technology; and it is plagued by a scarcity of specialized professional and skilled personnel to press the transformation and man and administer the new processes. Moreover, it is troubled by public administration and other organizational deficiencies.

The Pivotal Foreign Exchange Scarcity and the Doctrine of Balanced Growth

For a long time to come India is going to find it extremely hard to sell enough exports to pay for the importing that it will be disposed to do at rising income levels. If the country were to keep relying on foreign suppliers for all the types of goods and services it has poured abroad in the past, imports would rise precipitously — much faster than total income — because of the changing composition of consumer, enterprise, and government demand associated with expanding incomes. There will be no corresponding easy growth of either India's present types of exports or new products. Thus a balance of payments problem will persist.

The feasibility of import substitution is increased by the fact, first, that the Indian economy is enormous, and so are the potential sizes of its markets. Second, India is blessed with a fairly good mix of natural resources for servicing the material and energy needs for her projectable end-use requirements. Third, India's human and institutional resources include administrative, technical, and scientific sophistication that, although thinly spread, is unmatched in amount in most newly developing economies. This effort to economize on the use of foreign exchange in the longer run is the very thing that gives the development design such a heavy net import requirement in the shorter run.

Agriculture and Heavy Industry

The most important — and the most misunderstood — application of the balanced development strategy is India's attempt simultaneously to promote agricultural and heavy industrial expansion. The second five-year plan underestimated the rate of population growth and probably also the intensity of the effort that would be needed to achieve stated food production targets. But there has been an effort to redress these errors in the third plan, and, so adjusted, the latter proposes to continue the strategy's twin emphases upon agriculture and the economy's industrial core. The twin emphases are essential; development of either sector, by raising incomes, creates increased demand for the products of the other.

The Third Five-Year Plan

Size

In its final published form, the *Third Five-Year Plan* proposes that between fiscal year 1960/61 and fiscal year 1965/66 India's real net national income be raised 31 per cent, from a level of about Rs. 145 billion

($1.00 = Rs. 476) to about Rs. 190 billion, both measured in 1960 prices. It projects a total net investment during the third plan years of Rs. 104 billion — Rs. 63 billion public and Rs. 41 billion private — and an additional development outlay by central, state, and local Indian governments for noninvestment purposes of Rs. 12 billion.

These over-all dimensions are ambitious; they mean that, in the debate over the size of the third plan that had persisted in Indian public policy circles during most of the two preceding years, the advocates of boldness had largely prevailed. Yet there seems to be nothing in the quantitative outlines of the third plan that condemns it out of hand as being unrealistically large.

In general the aspect of the plan that in the light of achievement to date comes closest to being unrealistically ambitious in the projection of an average annual growth rate of 4.5 per cent in real farm output. Yet, as we have seen, the nation's basic development strategy cannot be satisfied with less than this. The plan's most dangerously unambitious aspect, shortly to be noted, is its concrete proposals for the activation of idle rural manpower.

The Allocation of Investment among Industries

Table 1 shows the allocations of investment among major industrial sectors proposed in the second five-year plan, actually achieved during the second plan period, and proposed in the third five-year plan. During the course of the latter's formulation the key allocation question appeared to be agriculture and related activities versus the so-called core industrial complex — manufacturing, electric power, transport, and communications. However, the striking thing about the program in the final third plan document with respect to the industry-agriculture split is the degree to which it calls for having one's cake and eating it too. Agriculture, community development, and irrigation are allotted a significantly larger share of the investment total than they actually had in the preceding five years. The share for industry is also larger than the actual percent in the second plan and larger than that proposed earlier by the industrial core oriented planners.

The compensating squeezes, compared with the second plan and, more particularly, with some of the preliminary thinking that had been done about the third plan, have been upon the projected investments in social services and housing and in transport and communications. The planning authorities have pared their social services allocations in order to weight their investment design toward sectors that promise relatively direct, quick, and predictable payoffs in additional output. The reason for the rather low allocation to transport and communications is less clear, especially in view of current transportation bottlenecks.

Table 1. Investment Allocation in India's Second and Third
Five-Year Plans

| | Second Five-Year Plan | | Third Five-Year Plan |
| | Projected | Actual | Projected |
	Per Cent	Per Cent	Per Cent
Agriculture, community development			
Major and medium irrigation	} 21.9	} 18.6	} 20.3
Social services (including housing)	19.7	19.1	16.3
Miscellaneous	2.1		
Inventories		7.4	7.7
Subtotal	43.7	45.1	44.3
Village and small industries			
Organized industry and minerals	} 18.5	} 26.8	} 28.8
Electric power	8.9	7.2	10.2
Transport and communications	28.9	20.9	16.7
Subtotal	56.3	54.9	55.7
Total	100.0	100.0	100.0

Employment Policy and Idle Manpower Mobilization

The plan's limited austerity with respect to social services construction
looks a little less admirable when one considers its employment projections. As in the second plan, the planners had as a goal the creation of
enough jobs to match the increase in the labor force so that the numbers
unemployed, while not curtailed, would not be allowed to rise. (This
modest target had not been achieved during the second plan years.) But
the unexpectedly high decennial census returns of March 1961 forced an
upward revision in the estimate of the labor force growth; so, in all
candor, the planners projected a five-year expansion in employment (the
equivalent of 14 million additional jobs) that falls 3 million short of the
probable growth in the labor force.

The least that the third plan document could do is to say, as it does,
that the generation of 3 million more jobs than it now projects "is considered to be an essential objective in the Third Plan." Its discussion of

what the nature of such a residual employment policy should be exhibits changes from second plan thinking that are distinctly encouraging. The focus now is away from cottage industries and on a greatly expanded rural public works program which is envisaged as providing an average of 100 days of work a year for some 2.5 million persons by 1965/66. A distressing fact is that the plan makes only a slight financial provision for the residual employment it projects.

The Split of Investment between Public and Private Sectors

Despite all the rhetoric that the issue of private enterprise versus public enterprise has generated in India, the debate over the division of investment during the plan formulation period was conducted within fairly narrow limits, and the outcome in the third plan document has caused little evident commotion.

The outcome (60.5 per cent public, 39.5 per cent private) would be perfectly consistent with an early resurgence of the private investment ratio as the economy becomes more highly developed. It does not guarantee this possibility, but neither does it foreclose it. It leaves this issue to be resolved later.

Foreign Exchange Dimensions

The third five-year plan estimates imports during the period at Rs. 58.8 billion and foreign exchange availability at Rs. 57.5 billion, of which 45 per cent is assumed to come from private foreign investment and public foreign aid. The curious indication of Rs. 1.3 billion of foreign exchange for which no explicit source is shown results from the planners' refusal to raise their estimate of external assistance above the Rs. 26 billion figure that had been set down in the plan's *Draft Outline* of June 1960. Even when this Rs. 1.3 billion is added to the estimated need for external assistance, it is the impression of most foreign observers that the need may be somewhat understated.

The planning authorities have evolved a notably more realistic timetable for India's longer run attainment of economic self-support. The *Draft Outline* clearly assumed that the country's need for aid-financed net imports would peak during the third plan and phase out entirely by the end of the fourth five-year plan. This pattern has now been stretched out for an additional planning period.

Domestic Finance

While moderately optimistic, projections of investment funds are all quite reasonable if the proposed expansions of real income are achieved at approximately the intended pace. The projected additional taxation, which would raise taxes from 8.9 per cent of the national income in

1960/61 to 11.4 per cent by 1965/66, will take a good bit of political and administrative courage but should be feasible.

The total new money financing presently proposed for public outlays in the third plan — something in the neighborhood of Rs. 7–8 billion — is not even in absolute terms greatly in excess of that in the second plan. Taking account of the comparative scales of the national product in the two periods, the general inflationary threat that the new scheme poses is distinctly less than that of its predecessor. My own opinion, accordingly, is that in view of the urgency of India's output and employment objectives there is still room in the third plan for upward of, say, Rs. 2 billion more new money financing, which would be more than enough to cover the estimated costs of the full supplementary rural public works program to which the plan aspires but which it does not propose to finance. Given enough United States surplus food imports to check its near-term pressures on food prices, a vigorous mobilization of India's idle rural manpower would appear to be within her present financial capabilities.

Physical and Operational Feasibility

To the best of my limited ability to judge, the final version of the third plan reflects realistic adjustments in the programs for those nonagricultural industries like coal, electric power, steel, and fertilizer manufacture which were particular objects of concern during the plan formulation period. In some specific programs, moreover, there is evidence of close attention to the availability of skilled manpower. However, the document contains no real evidence of the construction of a detailed and comprehensive skilled manpower budget paralleling and cross-checking the development scheme's commodity and financial budgets.

One can be reasonably confident that there is a fair degree of inter-industry and intercommodity consistency among the various five-year output targets the third plan projects, but it provides no similar basis for confidence that it hangs together through time in year-by-year and half-year-by-year fashion. The phasing of the program has been laggardly in its development. Indeed, this weakness illustrates the principal criticism that can be made of the Indian planning process. It is not enough that the general development strategy emerging from that process, while inviting amendment, is on balance a worthy one. If the strategy is to be made good it must be connected to specific operational decisions by more detailed kinds of planning. In the Indian case it is precisely in the realm of such implementational planning that there is greatest room for improvement.

80

Alternate Paths to Economic Development: The Choice of an Economic System*

JOHN KENNETH GALBRAITH

Harvard University

J. K. Galbraith, Harvard professor, former U.S. Ambassador to India, and provocative and controversial contributor to contemporary economic thinking and language ("countervailing power," "the affluent society," "the conventional wisdom," etc. See Selections 26 and 50), here turns his wit and pen to the war on poverty in underdeveloped economies and to the question of choosing an economic system appropriate for this task. Characteristically, Galbraith's choices are not conventional and the wisdom of his remedies challenges accepted modes of thought.

The country entering currently on nationhood is faced, at least in principle, with the interesting problem of selecting an economic system. The choice, one from which the developing countries of the eighteenth and nineteenth centuries were conveniently exempt, is between the economic, political, and constitutional arrangements generally associated with the Western democracies, on the one hand, and the policy and economic organization which avows its debt to Marx and the Russian Revolution, on the other.

The goal of the developing country is to bring itself as rapidly as possible into the twentieth century, and with the apparatus of individual and group well-being — food, clothing, education, health services, housing, entertainment, and automobiles — which is associated in every mind, urban and rural, bourgeois and Bolshevist, with twentieth-century existence.

Major Differences

Differences between the two broad designs for development are not difficult to detect. The problem is to identify those that are decisive, that make the difference between change and stagnation, success and failure. Of these critical differences there are three. The first is in the diagnosis of the causes of poverty and the related remedy. The second is in the way development is organized. The third is in the political and constitutional environment of development. I now take up these differences.

1. *Causes of Poverty*

Each of the systems drastically simplifies the causes of poverty and then proceeds to act on the basis of this simplification. In the Marxian view, poverty is caused principally by institutions which chain the country to its past — which hold it in colonial subjection, allow the exploitation and subjugation of the masses, deny the people the reward of their labor, make government not the efficient servant of the many but the corrupt handmaiden of the few, and which, in the aggregate, make any important progress impossible.

The Western view is amorphous. But in what may be called the working view, the poor are considered the victims of their poverty. All societies have capacity for growth, but the poor society has nothing with which to buy growth. Having less than enough for its current needs for food, clothing, and shelter, it has nothing for investment in education, improved agriculture, transportation, public utilities, or industrial enterprise.

Each of these views leads naturally to a prescription. If institutions hold a country to its past, the answer is the destruction of those institutions. If the problem is the self-perpetuating character of privation, the answer is to provide the catalyzing resources — specifically, economic aid and assistance in its use — which the country cannot supply to itself.

Here is the first difference: The Marxian emphasis is on institutions which inhibit progress and the need to eliminate them; our emphasis is on the self-perpetuating character of poverty and the catalyzing role of aid. Each system, we should note, has a cause and an accompanying remedy that are not without convenience to itself. The Soviets have always been short of capital, but they have had a revolution which could be exported at moderate expense. Accordingly, they found it convenient to associate backwardness with colonialism, feudalism, and repressive capitalism, all of which could be eliminated by revolution. By contrast, capital for us had been comparatively abundant. We could export it with comparative ease. On the other hand, American advocates of social revolution — of land reform, the elimination of feudal privilege — especially if in public office, often risk a measure of political reproach.

2. Organization of Development

The second difference between the systems is in the way development is organized. Although there is room for some national preference, and heresy cannot be entirely eliminated, the Marxian commitment is to state ownership of the means of production — of land, capital plant, and natural resources. Private ownership of productive resources and their use for private gain is, in fact, considered one of the retarding institutions.

The non-Marxian design for organizing development is not so easily typed. However, the main, and indeed overwhelming, reliance in non-Marxian development, both in agriculture and industry, has been on private ownership of productive plant. This is even true of countries such as India which nevertheless prefer to describe themselves as socialist.

The choice is thus between a comparatively firm commitment to public ownership of productive plant and resources and a blurred commitment to some combination of public and private ownership in which practical considerations as well as ideology determine the precise result.

Two major advantages lie with the Western or non-Marxian alternative. There is, according to ancient physical law, a certain difficulty in extracting blood from a stone. This is, in all respects, comparable with the problem of getting savings out of a poor society. When people do not have enough to eat, they are loath to forego any part of their meal that they may eat better in the future. Accordingly, the Western pattern of development, with its prospect of assistance from outside the country, eases one of the most painful problems of development. This is why economic aid has become such an important feature of Western foreign policy. It is the process by which savings are transferred from countries where saving is comparatively unpainful to those where it is very painful. It exploits one of the major advantages of our system.

To be sure, the Communist countries are not without resources in this respect. Communist economic and political organization deals more effectively — or ruthlessly — with unproductive and excessively luxurious consumption. Such consumption by a small minority is, as I have noted, a common feature of the poor country. And Communist organization can, within limits, squeeze blood from its turnip.

The penalty is the pain, and this cannot be avoided. The rioting in Poland in 1956 which brought Gomulka to power was occasioned in large measure by the enforcement of a rate of saving that was too stern for the people to bear. The larger consequence is that the process of Marxian development risks, as non-Marxian development does not, the alienation of the people. By contrast, India, after a decade of development, gave an overwhelming vote to the government that led the task. Had that government found it necessary to subtract the $7.3 billion it received in loans and grants from Western sources (as of 1963) from the meager incomes — an average of about $70 per year — of its own people, its popularity would certainly have suffered. One sees in India, in remarkably clear relief, the importance in the Western design of help in providing capital.

The second and equally substantial advantage of Western development is in the matter of agriculture. The undeveloped country is, by definition, a pastoral or agrarian country. Its agricultural policy is, accordingly, vital. And it is still far from clear, as a practical matter, whether it is possible to socialize successfully a small-scale, densely populated, peasant agriculture.

In the Soviet Union, after nearly half a century, the agricultural problem has not been wholly solved. And in this area of economic activity at least, there is no serious talk by the Soviets of catching up with the United States. On the contrary, in agriculture each year we insouciantly extend our advantage in man-hour productivity without effort and rather to our regret. Outside the Soviet Union, agriculture has been even more of a problem. Poland and Yugoslavia have had to revert to private ownership. By all external evidence, the effort to socialize agriculture brought a drastic crisis and forced the Chinese to turn to the West for some of the largest food imports in history.

There are good reasons for this difficulty with agriculture. Farmers, when they are small and numerous, can, if they choose, defeat any system that is available for their control. The employees of a factory, like the men of an army, are subject to external discipline. Failure in performance can be detected, judged and penalized. The same rule holds for certain types of plantation agriculture. A scattered peasantry, carrying on the diverse tasks of crop and especially of livestock husbandry, cannot be so controlled and managed. Certainly it cannot be controlled if it disapproves of the system. The farmer has it within his power when working for others or for the state, to work at the minimum rather than the maximum, and the difference between the two is enormous. He can be made to work at his maximum by giving him land and rewarding him with the fruits of his labor or some substantial share to consume or ex-

change as he wishes. But this is to restore individual proprietorship —
private capitalism — which doctrine excludes.

One day the Marxian economies may succeed in socializing agriculture.
Certainly no effort is being spared. And the ability of the small man in
agriculture to sabotage a system he dislikes or which treats him badly is
not confined to Communism. It is the reason for the low productivity
and backwardness of the latifundia of Latin America and the feudal vil-
lages of the Middle East. But the fact that independent agricultural proprietorship is accepted is the second clear advantage of Western development.

I come to the principal disadvantage of Western development. The
Marxian alternative, I have noted, emphasizes the destruction of the
bonds that tie the economy to the past. Our emphasis is on capital,
education, technical assistance, and the other instruments that promote
change. Until recently, at least, we have been tempted to suppose that
any society is a platform on which, given these missing elements, development can be built.

In fact, institutions do chain economies to the past, and the breaking of
these chains is essential for progress. The promise of drastic reform is a
valid and an appealing part of the Marxian case. There is no chance of
agricultural development in the underdeveloped (and hence agricultural)
country under systems of absentee landlordism where the workers or
sharecroppers are confined by law and tradition to a minor share of a
meager product. Progress requires the radical elimination of retarding
institutions. If elimination can be had from no other source, the Marxian
alternative will sooner or later be tried.

3. *Political Environment*

There is one further and different point of comparison between the two
systems, one which, unfortunately, has been much damaged by bad
rhetoric. From the earliest days of their development, personal liberty,
equal justice under law, and constitutional government have been important to Englishmen and to Americans.

And so it is in the underdeveloped country today. A widespread yearn-
ing for the dignity of democratic and constitutional government is more
common than is usually imagined. And it is widely agreed that liberty
and constitutional process are safer with the Western than with the
Marxian alternative.

Conclusion

On first assessment, then, the advantages of the non-Marxian alternative
for the developing country are considerable. It promises at least a partial
avoidance of the pain that for the poor country is inherent in finding sav-

ings for investment and growth. It promises an acceptable and viable system of agriculture rather than a certainly unpalatable and possibly unworkable one. And it offers personal liberty and constitutional process. Against this, the Marxian alternative promises a rigorous and effective attack on the institutions — the unproductive claims on revenue, and especially the feudal control of land — which exclude change.

The Marxian promise can be decisive. That is because the things we offer are effective and attractive only after the retarding institutions are eliminated. In a country where land and other productive resources are held by and operated for the benefit of a slight minority, and where the apparatus of government serves principally to reinforce such privilege, aid is of no use. It will benefit not the many but the few. And the Western promise of independent proprietorship in agriculture is obviously nullified so long as land remains in the hands of the few. And personal liberty and constitutional government have little meaning in countries where government is of the privileged, by the corrupt, for the rich.

We have no alternative, in short, but to meet the Marxian promise to be rid of archaic and retarding institutions. I doubt that we can organize revolution. But we can place our influence solidly on the side of reform and movements toward reform. We can close our ears to the pleas of vested interest. If we do so, and reform follows, our cards give us a clear advantage. To be sure, we must play them all. We must make good on our promise of a less painful savings and investment process. We must give firm support to the small farmer. We must be clear in our commitment to constitutional process and personal liberty and we cannot suppose that these are wanted only by people of Anglo-Saxon origin of good income.

Given these advantages, we may reasonably assume that people will opt for them.

C D E F G H I J — R — 7 3 2 1 0 / 6 9 8 7 6 5